KEEPING
FINANCIAL
RECORDS FOR
BUSINESS

Robert A. Schultheis, Ph.D.
Southern Illinois University
Edwardsville, Illinois

Burton S. Kaliski, Ed.D.
New Hampshire College
Manchester, New Hampshire

Dan Passalacqua, M.A.
Oak Grove High School
San Jose, California

VISIT US ON THE INTERNET
www.swep.com
www.thomsonlearning.com

South-Western
EDUCATIONAL PUBLISHING
Thomson Learning™

Australia • Canada • Denmark • Japan • Mexico • New Zealand • Philippines
Puerto Rico • Singapore • South Africa • Spain • United Kingdom • United States

Executive Editor	Eve Lewis
Project Manager	Carol Sturzenberger
Marketing Manager	Nancy A. Long
Production Manager	Tricia Boies
Art and Design Coordinator	Bill Spencer
Marketing Coordinator	Christian L. McNamee
Manufacturing Coordinator	Kathy Hampton
Editorial Assistant	Linda Adams
Composition/Prepress	Better Graphics, Inc.

About the Authors:

Robert A. Schultheis, Ph.D., is Professor Emeritus, Department of Computer Management and Information Systems at Southern Illinois University, Edwardsville. Dr. Schultheis has taught for more than 40 years at the high school and university levels, including teaching both high school and collegiate level accounting. He is the author of texts in both business education and information systems.

Burton S. Kaliski, Ed.D., is Professor of Business Education in the Graduate School of Business at New Hampshire College. He has served as a high school and two-year college teacher in his 38-year teaching career.

Dan Passalacqua, M.A., has been teaching business education for over 26 years at the high school level. He is also an author, educational consultant, and district coordinator of occupational programs. Currently, he is teaching accounting and is actively involved in total school restructuring at Oak Grove High School in San Jose, California.

ISBN: 0-538-69151-4

3 4 5 6 7 8 WC 04 03

Printed in the United States of America

For permission to use material from this text or product, contact us by

Web: www.thomsonrights.com

Phone: 1-800-730-2214

Fax: 1-800-730-2215

Reviewers

Contents

Chapter 11
RECORD KEEPING FOR PURCHASE ORDER CLERKS, 414

Chapter 12
RECORD KEEPING FOR ACCOUNTS PAYABLE CLERKS, 448

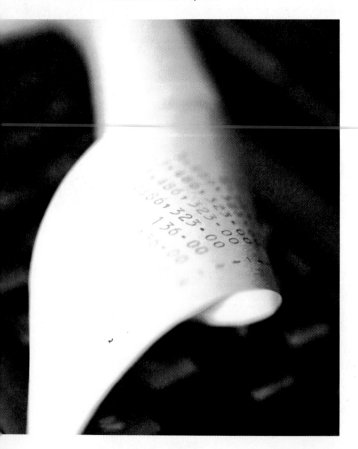

Chapter 13
RECORD KEEPING FOR SMALL BUSINESSES, 494

Chapter 14
FINANCIAL STATEMENTS FOR SMALL BUSINESSES, 544

Chapter 15
RECORD KEEPING FOR PAYROLL CLERKS: COMPUTING GROSS PAY, 582

Chapter 16
RECORD KEEPING FOR PAYROLL CLERKS: COMPUTING NET PAY, 628

To the Student

Keeping Financial Records for Business will give you a thorough background in the basic record keeping skills used in business. The skills presented will also serve as a sound background for employment in office jobs.

 HOW TO USE THIS TEXT

This textbook is carefully designed to function as a learning tool. It is organized into 16 chapters, with three to nine jobs per chapter. Each chapter begins with a brief introduction that describes the skills you will study in the chapter and why those skills are important to learn. Each skill is discussed in detail in its own job.

Each job begins with an **Applied Math Preview**, a set of problems that provides practice in the kinds of math you will need to use in the job. Printed at the start of most jobs is a **Key Terms Preview**, a list of new terms that are defined and used within the job. Next, there is a set of **Goals**, or learning objectives, that describe what you will learn in studying the job. Your work on each job should begin with solving the Applied Math Preview problems and reading the Key Terms Preview and Goals. Applied Math Preview answers are provided in Appendix E.

Each job is divided into three sections as follows:

• **Understanding the Job** provides definitions of terms and background information on the skill being presented.

• The **Sample Problem** (found in all except Job 1) gives step-by-step instructions for performing the skill.
• **Application Problems** provide the opportunity to practice using the skill demonstrated in the job.

In addition, many illustrations highlight concepts in the job. Note that each illustration is referred to within the job and has a caption that describes what is being illustrated. All new record keeping vocabulary terms are printed in bold type. The term and its definition also appear in the margin as a **Key Term** so that these definitions can easily be found for later reference.

The following features within the job enhance the learning experience:

- In the margins, **Tips** contain hints, reminders, or math information, while **FYI** notes add interest and background to the concepts you are studying.
- At the ends of jobs, **Building Your Business Vocabulary** sections require you to match definitions to Key Terms and provide you practice with important vocabulary words.
- **Steps Reviews** list all the steps demonstrated in the Sample Problem. For easy reference, the Steps Reviews appear just before the Application Problems.
- **Check Points** can be found in the margins of the Application Problems. They provide partial answers so that you can tell if you are working the problems correctly.

REINFORCEMENT ACTIVITIES

These special activities appear at the end of each chapter:

- **Check Your Reading** asks 3-4 questions covering basic concepts in the chapter.
- **Discussion** contains questions that help you review concepts presented in the chapter.
- **Ethics in the Workplace** and **Critical Thinking** are real-life business situations that require you to stretch your knowledge and apply reasoning skills. Each chapter contains one or the other of these features.
- **Communication in the Workplace** provides opportunities to write memos, directions, and letters related to record keeping.
- **Focus on Careers** covers job hunting and workplace skills.
- A **Focus on Global Business** feature is provided in five chapters. This

activity provides information you will need to work with co-workers, customers, and vendors in foreign countries.

- **Reviewing What You Have Learned** is a matching exercise to help you test your understanding of Key Terms used in the chapter.
- The **Mastery Problem** ties together two or more related concepts from the chapter.
- At the end of Chapters 3, 6, 9, 12, 14 and 16 are references to **Comprehensive Projects** that appear in the Working Papers that accompany *Keeping Financial Records for Business*. These projects are designed to reinforce major concepts of the chapters.

 ## SPECIAL FEATURES

Additional special features appear throughout the textbook:

- Each chapter opens with a **Focus on Technology** feature, introducing you to technological topics pertinent to business, such as computers, electronic equipment, and the Internet.
- **Cultural Notes** describe the contributions of a variety of cultures to record keeping and business. Some of these features focus on historical contributions while others describe a situation in the United States today. This feature will help strengthen your awareness of the value of diversity in the work force and in society.
- **Calculator Tips** show how to use calculator shortcuts and special keys to make work easier.

 ## TECHNOLOGY

Keeping Financial Records for Business provides opportunities for you to learn about technology and to practice applications. In addition to the Focus on Technology feature at the beginning of each chapter, template files are provided so you can use real-world software and get hands-on experience using the computer.

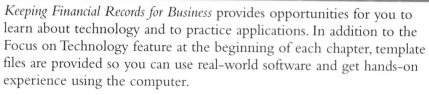

- The Automated Accounting icon identifies an Application or Mastery Problem that can be solved using the *Automated Accounting 7.0* (or higher) software. Data for these problems are available on the *Keeping Financial Records for Business* **template disk**.
- The Spreadsheet icon identifies end-of-Job Application Problems that appear on the *Keeping Financial Records for Business* **spreadsheet template disk**. This disk gives you the chance to use popular spreadsheet software to solve these problems.

 ## REFERENCE MATERIAL

Reference material at the end of the book includes five appendices, a glossary of terms, and an index:

- **Appendix A: Paying Your Income Taxes** provides instruction on filing a personal income tax return.
- **Appendix B: Applied Math Skills** provides a review of basic math skills.

- **Appendix C: Internet Basics** supplies information on networks, the Internet, the World Wide Web, browsers, and search tools. A Sample Problem is provided in which you search the Web for information.
- **Appendix D: Using Calculator Keyboards and Computer Keypads** discusses desktop calculators, hand-held calculators, and different kinds of computer keypad layouts. There is also a section on the ten-key touch system. Seven calculation drills are included.
- **Appendix E: Applied Math Preview Answers** lists the solutions to the Applied Math Previews that appear at the beginning of each job.
- The **Glossary** lists all the Key Terms, their definitions, and the page numbers on which the terms first appear.
- The **Index** shows the page location for each topic in the text. This can be useful if you need to look up a topic but do not know where to find it.

Chapter 1

Basic Record Keeping Skills

Almost every person keeps records—office workers, sales people, farmers, factory workers, and business owners. Schools, clubs, and organizations keep records, also. Keeping records plays an important role in both your personal life and in your business career. That is why it is important to learn the necessary skills.

In Chapter 1, you will learn how to enter record keeping information both manually and by using a computer. You will also learn how to file information numerically, chronologically, and alphabetically. Each job in the chapter begins with an Applied Math Preview. This preview will help improve your math skills, which you will need to be successful in record keeping.

The Internet and the Web

Many people today connect to the Internet so they can use the World Wide Web to find information, to buy products and services, and to distribute information to others. So, what is the Internet, anyway?

The *Internet* is a collection of computer systems that are connected together into a very large network. In fact, the computer systems are really connected by not one, but a collection of networks. For example, the computer in your computer lab may be connected to a network in that room. If your school has several computer labs, it may decide to connect each of those networks to form a small *network of networks*. Your school may then decide to connect its networks to an even larger network that connects other schools, libraries, universities, and private companies throughout the world. This very large network of networks is called the Internet.

The *World Wide Web*, Web for short, is made up of those computer systems connected to the Internet that let others view documents stored on them. These documents may be text documents, but they may also contain images, sound, and even video clips. The Web is useful to people because they can use their computer systems to connect to millions of other computer systems around the world and view and otherwise use information stored on those

other computer systems. The other computer systems may include:

● Airline computers that let you view plane schedules and order plane tickets

● Bank computers that let you view your account balance and write checks

● Museum computers that let you view photos and hear lectures about exhibits

● Book store computers that let you view descriptions of books and buy books

● Internal Revenue Service computers that let you view information about federal income taxes and obtain tax forms

For businesses and organizations, the Web provides a worldwide presence inexpensively. A small business located in a rural area can buy a computer, connect it to the Internet, and provide information about its products to everyone in the world who is also connected to the Internet.

To learn more about the Internet and the Web, have your teacher show you how to connect to the Web and go to this Web address:

● http://www.recordkeeping.swep.com

There you will find more information about the Web, the Internet, and the tools to use them both.

Job 1 RECORD KEEPING AND THE COMPUTER

Tips

Make sure that you align the decimal points when you copy the numbers in each problem.

key terms preview

- **Computer printout**
- **Electronically**
- **Enter**
- **Manually**
- **Merchandise**
- **Position**
- **Record**
- **Record keeping jobs**

goals

1. To learn about record keeping positons.
2. To learn why records are important.
3. To introduce you to careers in record keeping and computers.

UNDERSTANDING THE JOB

Key Terms

Position. Job.

Record. A form on which information is recorded.

Enter. To record information on a form or into a computer.

Manually. By hand.

Electronically. By computer.

No matter what kind of **position** or job you take when you graduate, you will probably have to keep some records as part of your work.

A **record** is a form on which information has been **entered**, or recorded. Many records are still completed and kept by hand, or **manually**. When records are kept manually, the information is usually recorded on paper.

Many records are also completed and kept by computers, or **electronically**. When records are kept electronically, the information is usually entered into a computer and stored on a disk.

A *sales clerk* in one store may fill out a sales slip for a customer manually. A sales clerk in another store may fill out a sales slip for a customer using a computer.

The sales slip prepared with the computer has the same types of information as the sales slip prepared manually. Knowing what a sales slip is and how to fill it out correctly is important to learn, whether you will use a computer or a pencil or pen to do it. You can also see that knowing about computers is very important in most jobs.

You might ask, "Why do we need to keep so many records?" The answer is that we need all kinds of information to run our stores, farms, factories, businesses, schools, and other organizations. For example, we need information to know:

  a. How much we have sold
  b. What our expenses are
  c. If we are making a profit

d. How much our customers owe us

e. How much we owe others

f. How much cash we have

g. How much tax we owe

h. If we have enough goods on hand to sell to our customers

Because of the large number of records we must keep, computers are often used to help complete and keep records. Computers have become common in homes, factories, farms, and offices because they help us keep records faster and more accurately. However, you should remember that we must keep the same information whether it is kept manually or on a computer.

Because computers are so common, nearly every job involves computers in some way. Some workers may use computers directly in their work. For example, an *order entry clerk* is a worker who prepares sales order forms for customers ordering **merchandise**, or goods that the business sells. Some order entry clerks may take an order over the phone from a customer and enter that order directly into the computer.

Other workers may use the computer indirectly. For example, a *stock clerk* may use a list of merchandise stored in the computer to find an item that a customer wants.

The list prepared by the computer is called a **computer printout**. Whatever the computer prints on a printer is called a printout. Knowing how to read and use computer printouts is very useful since they are used in many jobs today.

Key Terms

Merchandise. Goods that a business sells.

Computer printout. A document prepared by a computer.

Illustration 1A

A computer printout of some record keeping jobs

```
Employees who keep records about customers and what they buy:
        Accounts receivable clerk
        Billing clerk
        Invoice clerk
        Order clerk
        Telephone order clerk
Employees who keep records about employees:
        Benefits clerk
        Payroll clerk
        Personnel records clerk
        Timekeeper
Employees who keep records about the goods the firm buys:
        Accounts payable clerk
        Purchase order checker
        Receiving clerk
        Stock clerk
Employees who keep records about cash:
        Cash clerk
        Cashier
        Teller
        Ticket clerk
Employees who keep other kinds of records:
        Accounting clerk
        Data entry clerk
        Office clerk, routine
        Record clerk
        Voucher clerk
```

Record keeping jobs. Jobs where handling records is most of the work.

Nearly every job requires the use and handling of records. Those jobs in businesses, farms, factories, and offices in which workers spend most of their time handling records are called **record keeping jobs**. Look at the list of record keeping jobs shown in Illustration 1A.

To get and keep a record keeping job, you usually will need:

a. A high school diploma
b. Some training in record keeping principles and practices
c. Some knowledge of computer terms and equipment
d. The ability to operate office machines such as the telephone and calculator
e. The ability to keyboard
f. The ability to meet people, talk to them, and cooperate with others
g. The ability to read and follow directions
h. These work habits and attitudes:
   —accuracy in your math
   —accuracy in copying numbers and names
   —neatness in your writing, math, and record keeping
   —checking all your work all the time
   —completing all your work
   —promptness in getting to work
   —promptness in completing your work

The knowledge, skills, and work habits you will learn in this course will help you get and keep that first record keeping job. The same knowledge, skills, and work habits will also help you advance in your work to jobs with more responsibility and higher pay.

 ## BUILDING YOUR BUSINESS VOCABULARY

On a sheet of paper, write the headings **Statement Number** and **Words**. Next, choose the words that match the statements. Write each word you choose next to the statement number it matches. The first one is done for you to show you how. Be careful; not all the words listed should be used.

	Statement Number	Words
Sample Answer:	1	enter

Statements	Words
1. To record information on a form or into a computer	computer printout
	electronically
2. Forms on which information is recorded	enter
3. Goods that a business is selling	manually
4. A job	merchandise
5. By hand	position
6. Anything the computer has printed	record keeping jobs
7. By computer	records
8. Jobs in which workers spend most of their time handling records	sales clerk
	stock clerk

 ## APPLICATION PROBLEMS

Problem 1-1   Working papers are available for completing the problems in each job of this textbook. If the working papers are used, you do not have to copy headings or prepare forms on sheets of paper.

Directions

Write the numbers 1 through 10 on a sheet of paper. Next to each number place a *T* if the statement is true or an *F* if the statement is false.

CHECK POINT

1-1

Four answers are true.

1. Only a few jobs require you to use records.
2. A form prepared with a computer usually contains the same information as that same form would if it were prepared manually.
3. Any job in which records are kept is a record keeping job.
4. Knowing how to do math accurately is not important anymore, since computers do all the math in record keeping jobs.
5. One reason records are kept is to find out how much tax you owe.
6. Persons who do record keeping work alone. They do not need to be able to work with others.
7. A high school diploma is usually needed to get a record keeping job.
8. A promotion usually means more responsibility but not more pay.
9. Knowledge of computers is not important in record keeping jobs.
10. Knowing how to operate office machines is important in record keeping work.

Problem 1-2 Rita works in the stock room of a large business. One of her duties is to record the amount of each item that the business has in stock on a stock record. This is a form which lists the item number, the item description, and the amount of the item on the shelves.

When Rita is finished recording the amount of each item that the business has on the stock records, she gives the forms to another employee who records when the business buys or sells the item.

CHECK POINT

1-2 (4)

Promptness is an example of a work habit.

Directions

Write the numbers 1 through 4 on a sheet of paper. Write your answer to each of the following questions next to the correct number.

1. Look at the list of job titles in Illustration 1A, page 5. What might the title of Rita's job be?
2. What is the name of one record that Rita must keep?
3. What might happen if Rita makes a mistake in counting and recording the amount of any stock item?
4. What are three work habits a person working in Rita's position should have?

Problem 1-3 Tom works in the marketing department of a small business. One of his duties is to take customer orders over the phone. Tom completes a sales order form for every customer who orders merchandise.

When Tom receives a telephone call from a customer, he records the information on the sales order form.

CHECK POINT

1-3 (2)

A computer is an office machine.

Directions

Write the numbers 1 through 5 on a sheet of paper. Write your answer to each of the following questions next to the correct number.

1. Look at the job titles listed in Illustration 1A, page 5. What might the title of Tom's job be?
2. What are three types of office machines that Tom might use?
3. What are three work habits which would be important for anyone in Tom's position?
4. What is the name of one record that Tom must use?
5. What might happen if Tom makes a mistake entering the information?

Job 2 ENTERING RECORD KEEPING DATA

applied math preview

Copy and answer each problem. Do your work neatly.

1.	523	2.	36.92	3.	2007.198	4.	$87,106.54
	− 85		− 27.34		− 502.64		− 23,900.48

key terms preview

- Data
- Data entry clerks
- Double ruling
- Footing
- MICR
- Money column
- OCR
- Optical mark recognition
- UPC

goals

1 To learn how to enter and correct data on business forms.

2 To learn to read special data processing symbols.

UNDERSTANDING THE JOB

Key Terms

Data. Information.

Data entry clerks. Workers who enter data using a computer.

A frequent task of record keepers is to enter information, or **data**, into forms or records. Sometimes data are entered manually. For example, a store clerk may enter data about a sale onto a sales slip with a pen. Sometimes data are entered using a computer. For example, school office workers may enter data from student enrollment forms using a computer so that printouts of class schedules and class lists can be made. Workers who enter data using a computer terminal are called **data entry clerks**.

The important thing about entering data is that it must be done accurately and neatly. Entering accurate data in a computer is especially important. If you enter incorrect data into a computer, all printouts using that data will be incorrect.

In this job you will first learn how to enter data onto forms manually. Then you will learn about special symbols used to enter data with computers.

SAMPLE PROBLEM

Chris Severa is a record keeper for the Peoria Blades, a basketball team. Chris was asked to make a list of the bills that the team owes at the end of the month for the team treasurer. On November 30, Chris prepared the list shown in Illustration 2A.

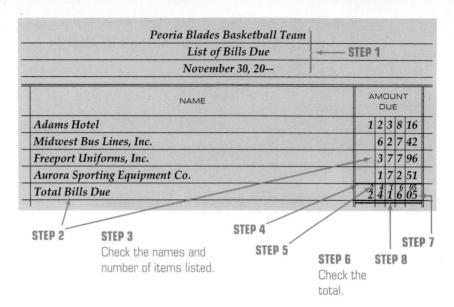

Peoria Blades Basketball Team					
List of Bills Due ← STEP 1					
November 30, 20--					

NAME			AMOUNT DUE		
Adams Hotel	1	2	3	8	16
Midwest Bus Lines, Inc.		6	2	7	42
Freeport Uniforms, Inc.		3	7	7	96
Aurora Sporting Equipment Co.		1	7	2	51
Total Bills Due	2	4	1	6	05

STEP 2   STEP 3   STEP 4
          Check the names and   STEP 5   STEP 7
          number of items listed.   STEP 6   STEP 8
                                         Check the
                                         total.

Now let's see how Chris did this job:

STEP 1 Enter the heading.

On most business forms there is a heading which tells WHO, WHAT, and WHEN about the form. The first line answers WHO. The second line answers WHAT. The third line answers WHEN. The heading that Chris entered was:

WHO the form is for: Peoria Blades Basketball Team
WHAT the form contains: List of Bills Due
WHEN the form was completed: November 30, 20--

STEP 2 Enter the names and amounts.

Chris took each bill and entered the name of the company to whom the bill was owed in the Name column. Then she entered the amount owed to each company in the column headed Amount Due.

A column on a form used for recording amounts of money is called a **money column**. A money column has vertical lines which help you keep the amounts of money you enter aligned. Look at Illustration 2B.

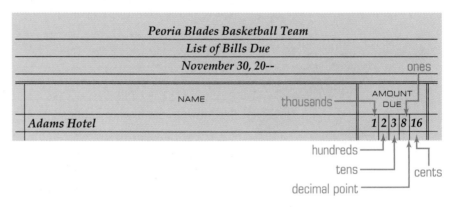

Peoria Blades Basketball Team					
List of Bills Due					
November 30, 20-- ones					

NAME	thousands		AMOUNT DUE		
Adams Hotel	1	2	3	8	16

hundreds
tens   cents
decimal point

Money column. A column on a form used for recording amounts of money.

To enter the amount of the first bill, $1,238.16, Chris went to the thousands space and wrote "1," for $1,000. She then entered the rest of the amount. Chris found the place to enter the 1 quickly because she knew that the thousands place is the first space to the left of the four vertical lines. Notice that these lines separate the hundreds, tens, and ones.

There are no special lines to separate thousands, ten thousands, or more. There is also no line separating ten cents from one cent.

STEP 3 Check the names and number of items listed.

Chris checked to see that she had spelled the name of each company correctly. She also counted the bills she had and compared that count with the number of bills she listed on the form. She counted four bills and found that she had listed four names on the form. She did this to make sure that she did not skip a bill or list a bill twice.

STEP 4 Rule the money column.

When Chris had entered all the bills due, she drew a line under the last amount. The line shows that the amounts are to be added. Chris used a ruler to make the ruling neat and straight.

STEP 5 Foot the column.

Chris added the amounts in the column and put the total in small figures just below the line. These figures are called **footings**. Record keepers use a sharp pencil to make their footings in small, neat figures.

STEP 6 Check the total.

To check the total, Chris added the amounts again. This time she added *from the bottom up* and got the same total.

STEP 7 Write in the final total.

Since Chris got the same answer as before, she wrote the words "Total Bills Due" in the Name column and then wrote the final total below the footings.

Sometimes a total or an amount is negative. This can happen when you return goods to the seller. For example, the Peoria Blades may have returned $200.00 in goods bought from Aurora Sporting Equipment Co. at an earlier date. This means that they really owe Aurora Sporting Equipment nothing. In fact, Aurora Sporting Equipment owes them $27.49, or the difference between the $200.00 of goods returned and the $172.51 bill owed.

When amounts are negative, record keepers often show them in parentheses. (See Illustration 2C.)

Key Terms

Footing. Total of money column written in small, neat figures.

Double ruling. Double line drawn under a total.

Illustration 2C
Entering negative amounts

| Aurora Sporting Equipment Co. | | (2|7|49) |

STEP 8 Double rule the money column.

Chris used a ruler to draw a double line under the final total. The double line shows that the record keeper is finished. Record keepers call this double line a **double ruling**.

You should notice some other things about the way the form was completed. Notice that

1. No dollar signs were entered. When using a lined money column, it is understood that the amounts shown are money.
2. No commas or decimal points were entered. When using lined money columns, the vertical lines replace the commas and decimal points.

Making Corrections

When record keepers make corrections in amounts on forms, they usually do not erase the old amount. Instead, they cross out the old amount and write the correct amount above or beside it. For example, after completing the List of Bills Due, Chris found that the amount owed to Freeport Uniforms, Inc. should have been $377.69 instead of $377.96. To correct the error, she did not erase the amount. Instead, the old amount was crossed out and the correct amount was written above it. Then the columns were re-added, the old total was crossed out, and the correct total was written beside it. Look at Illustration 2D.

Illustration 2D

Making corrections on a form

Peoria Blades Basketball Team		
List of Bills Due		
November 30, 20--		
NAME		AMOUNT DUE
Adams Hotel		1 2 3 8 16
Midwest Bus Lines, Inc.		6 2 7 42
Freeport Uniforms, Inc.		3̶7̶7̶ 9̶6̶ (377 69)
Aurora Sporting Equipment Co.		1 7 2 51
Total Bills Due	2415.78	2̶4̶1̶6̶ 0̶5̶

By making corrections this way, anyone can see exactly what happened. Another record keeper can quickly see that the old amount was changed, and so was the total. Anyone examining Chris's work could check the old bill for the Peoria Blades and see why the change was made.

USING THE COMPUTER TO ENTER DATA

Record keepers working with computer forms often have to read and write using a different set of numbers than those we normally use.

For example, the letter O looks much like the number 0. To avoid having a zero entered into a computer incorrectly as a letter O, record keepers may put a slash through the zero. In this way, a person entering data into a computer will know that a Ø is a zero, not an O. Other numbers may also be confused with letters of the alphabet, and so they may be written differently. For example, look at these numbers:

$$\varnothing \qquad 1 \qquad 7$$
zero   one   seven

Notice that the number one has been drawn with a base and a top to it. This may be done to make sure that the lower-case letter l is not entered instead of the number one. Also notice that a slash has been drawn through the seven. This is done so that it is not mistaken for a poorly written nine or a poorly written one.

Numbers may also be printed in a special way so that they can be read directly by the computer. Thus, they will not have to be entered by a person at a computer. One way to print numbers so they can be read directly by the computer is to use Magnetic Ink Character Recognition **(MICR)** numbers. Here is how the numbers 0 through 9 look in MICR:

0 1 2 3 4 5 6 7 8 9

Key Terms

MICR. Magnetic Ink Character Recognition.

OCR. Optical Character Recognition.

Banks print checking account numbers and their bank number on the bottom of checks in MICR. (See Illustration 2E.) This speeds their processing of all the checks that are brought into the banks.

Another way to print numbers so that they can be read directly by a computer is to use Optical Character Recognition **(OCR)** numbers. There are many styles of OCR numbers. Here is how one style of OCR numbers from 0 through 9 looks:

0 1 2 3 4 5 6 7 8 9

Ying Shih
6093 Hunt Street, N.
Portland, OR 97203-1893

No. **3889**

Date _May 15,_ 20 _--_

12-332
1260

Pay to the order of _O'Brien's Department Store_ $ _81.68_

Eighty-one 68/100 _____ **Dollars**

For Classroom Use Only

WESTERN NATIONAL BANK
Portland, OR 97223-8912

Ying Shih

⑈012600635⑈ 208⑈145

⏝ Bank Number   ⏝ Checking Account Number

Illustration 2E

A check printed with MICR numbers

Credit card account numbers are often embossed, or pressed into the card, in OCR form. The style of OCR numbers used on credit cards is shown in Illustration 2F.

Illustration 2F

A credit card embossed with the account number in OCR

When a customer pays by using a credit card, salespersons in stores usually check the credit card account number by using a computer or a book. The book lists those credit cards that have been lost or stolen. Many office and sales workers must know how to read OCR numbers as part of their jobs.

There are a number of other ways in which numbers and letters may be printed so that they can be read directly by a computer. These include

Key Terms

Optical mark recognition.
Allows pencil marks to be read by special machines.

UPC. Bar code read by special cash registers.

Illustration 2G
Optical mark recognition and the Universal Product Code

optical mark recognition and the Universal Product Code as shown in Illustration 2G.

Optical mark recognition is often used by water and gas meter readers and by persons who take tests. Pencils are used to mark numbers or letters on forms which can be read by special machines. The Universal Product Code, or **UPC**, is a bar code marked on store products which can be read by special cash registers. It is also used to mark railroad cars so that they can be tracked by computer.

Optical marks

Bar codes

71009   00595

BUILDING YOUR BUSINESS VOCABULARY

On a sheet of paper, write the headings **Statement Number** and **Words**. Next, choose the words that match the statements. Write each word you choose next to the statement number it matches. Be careful; not all the words listed should be used.

Statements	Words
1. Columns on a form used for recording amounts of money	data
2. The total of a money column written in small figures	data entry clerk
3. A set of lines used to show that the math on a form has been completed	double ruling
	electronically
4. Information	enter
5. To record something on a form	footing
6. By computer	MICR
7. Magnetic Ink Character Recognition	money columns
8. Optical Character Recognition	OCR
9. A worker who enters data into a computer system	optical mark recognition
10. A bar code placed on products which can be read by special cash registers	output
	printer
11. Allows pencil marks to be read by special machines	UPC

STEP 1 Enter the heading.

STEP 2 Enter the names and amounts.

STEP 3 Check the names and number of items listed.

STEP 4 Rule the money column.

STEP 5 Foot the column.

STEP 6 Check the total.

STEP 7 Write in the final total.

STEP 8 Double rule the money column.

Tips

Use the Steps Review as a reminder when you are working on the Application Problems or studying for a test.

APPLICATION PROBLEMS

Problem 2-1

You are a clerk in the purchasing department of Calico Co. At the end of the month, the department must prepare a list of how much money was spent and what the money was spent for.

Directions

a. On a sheet of paper, make a form with the headings and columns shown below. The form should have 3 lines at the top for the heading and 10 lines for the other entries.

DESCRIPTION	AMOUNT SPENT

b. Enter this heading on the top three lines of the form:

Purchasing Department
List of Expenses
April 30, 20--

c. Copy the following names and amounts in the correct columns of the form.

Names of Expenses	Amounts
Employee Wages	$34,208.42
Postage	2,977.29
Travel Expenses	808.65
Service Contracts	4,008.13
Telephone	2,569.01
Supplies	3,819.96
Delivery Service	1,003.08
Other Expenses	30.48

d. Check your work by comparing the names and amounts above to the names and amounts you listed on the form. Then count the number of expenses above and the number of expenses on the form.

e. Draw a line under the last amount in the Amount Spent column. Add the amounts and write the total as a footing just under the line.

f. Check the total by re-adding the amounts in the Amount Spent column starting from the bottom of the column and adding up. If you get the same answer as you did the first time, write "Total" in the Description column and write the final total below the footing, but on the same line.

g. Draw a double ruling below the final total.

Problem	2-2

You are an accounting clerk for Nome Porcelain Company. One of your duties is to make a List of Amounts Owed at the end of the week, September 15, 20--. Below is a list of companies and the amounts Nome Porcelain owes to them.

Directions

a. On a sheet of paper, make a form with the headings and columns shown below. The form should have 3 lines at the top for the heading and 10 lines for the other entries.

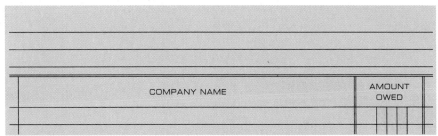

COMPANY NAME	AMOUNT OWED

b. Enter the heading on the top three lines of the form. The heading should include the name of the company, the name of the form, and the date.

c. Copy the names of and amounts owed to the following companies in the correct columns of the form.

Companies	Amounts Owed
Astoria Craft Shops, Inc.	$ 2,316.18
Portland Clay Company	12,015.92
Frisco Shipping Corporation	2,245.61
Tetons, Inc.	416.29
Phoenix Designs, Limited	207.85
Desert Colors, Inc.	11.75
Western Outlet Store Corporation	4,304.57

d. Check your work by comparing the names and amounts above to the names and amounts on the form. Then count the number of companies above and the number of companies on the form.

e. Draw a line under the last amount in the Amount Owed column. Add the amounts and write the total as a footing just under the line.

f. Check the total by re-adding the amounts in the Amount Owed column starting from the bottom of the column and adding up. If you get

the same answer as you did the first time, write "Total" in the Company Name column and write the final total below the footing, but on the same line.

g. Draw a double ruling below the final total.

Problem 2-3 You are a sales clerk for a department store. When customers pay with credit cards instead of cash, you must check to see if the credit card numbers are on a special list. This is a list of lost or stolen credit cards.

Directions

a. On a sheet of paper, write the headings "Credit Cards," "Lost or Stolen," and "OK." Then write the numbers 1 through 10 under the Credit Cards heading.

b. On the left below are ten credit card account numbers written in OCR. On the right is a list of lost or stolen credit cards. Compare each credit card number on the left to the list on the right. If you find the card number on the list, place a check mark under the Lost or Stolen heading. If you don't find the credit card number on the list, place a check mark under the OK heading.

CHECK POINT

2-3

One card is lost or stolen.

Credit Cards

1.	467	388	309	82
2.	478	388	398	28
3.	447	287	375	28
4.	498	403	128	01
5.	445	103	323	54
6.	508	791	898	31
7.	447	101	224	64
8.	476	343	311	90
9.	439	971	989	13
10.	433	101	422	46

List of Lost or Stolen Cards

431	374	183	49	467	382	021	98
432	375	287	31	467	388	309	82
432	377	301	28	471	343	410	88
433	101	603	82	476	343	311	99
434	402	101	11	477	101	224	12
444	403	128	01	477	997	351	63
445	488	323	19	478	103	322	54
446	791	898	31	478	383	398	54
447	101	224	46	498	101	422	64
449	103	323	33	508	971	898	13

Problems 2–4 and 2–5 may be found in the Working Papers.

Tips

When you multiply, your answer should have the same number of decimal places as the total number of decimal places in both numbers you multiplied. If you multiply 5.26 x 0.11, your answer should have four decimal places in it: 0.5786

applied math preview

Copy and complete each problem.

1. 26 x 58 =
2. 103 x 650 =
3. 50 x 200 =
4. 40 x $1.20 =
5. 10 x $37.62 =
6. 100 x $5.87 =
7. 1,000 x $4.90 =
8. $360 x 0.01 =
9. $14.20 x 0.05 =
10. $308.50 x 0.20 =

key terms preview

- **Data processing**
- **Input**
- **Output**
- **Processing**
- **Source documents**
- **Transposition error**
- **Verify**

goals

1 To learn about the data processing cycle.

2 To improve your verifying skills.

UNDERSTANDING THE JOB

In business, information is usually called data. When a business does something to data to make them more useful, that is called **data processing**. For example, all these tasks are data processing activities:

1. Recording data on a business form.
2. Comparing data on one business form to data on another.
3. Copying data from one business form to another.

All data processing activities, whether they are done manually or electronically, are done in a series of steps. These steps are called the *data processing cycle*. The steps in the cycle are shown in Illustration 3A.

Illustration 3A

Steps in the data processing cycle

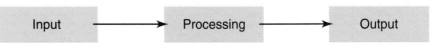

Input → Processing → Output

Key Terms

Data processing. Doing things to data to make them more useful.

Input. First step of the data processing cycle.

Source documents. Forms from which you get data.

For example, suppose that you go to your counselor to plan your class schedule for next year. After deciding what courses you should take, your counselor writes your name and the courses you are to take on an enrollment form like the one in Illustration 3B (page 18).

The counselor takes all the enrollment forms for the students to the school office. There, an office assistant enters the information from the enrollment forms into the computer. This is the **input** step, and it is the first step of the data processing cycle. The office assistant calls the enrollment forms **source documents** since these forms are the source of the information entered into the computer.

LANDON HIGH SCHOOL
STUDENT ENROLLMENT FORM

Student Name _Beverly White_   Student No. _1103_

Street Address _152 Lake Ave., E._

City _Tampa_   State _FL_   Zip Code _33603-0152_

Date of Enrollment _8 / 26 / 20--_

Course Choices:

1. _English II_   4. _Record Keeping_
2. _Social Studies II_   5. _Physical Education_
3. _Business Math_   6. _General Science_

Cultural Notes

Scribes, persons who could read and write, were very important people in the ancient civilizations of Asia Minor and northern Africa. Most scribes recorded transactions on a small lump of moist clay, which was then dried to create a somewhat permanent record. These scribes are an example of the earliest record keepers.

Key Terms

Processing. Second step of the data processing cycle.

Output. Third step of the data processing cycle.

Verify To check for accuracy.

Once all the student enrollment data have been entered into the computer, the computer assigns every student to a class. This is the **processing** step and the second step of the data processing cycle.

Finally, the computer prints out a class schedule for every student and class lists for the teachers. This is the **output** step and the third step of the cycle.

Notice that the computer started with the enrollment forms, or *source documents*, and finished with the class lists and student schedules, or *computer printouts*.

Workers who enter data into computers must check, or **verify**, their work very carefully. Errors made in entering data can cause many problems when the computer does its processing. You can see that just a few errors in entering student enrollment forms would throw the whole high school schedule off. In business, errors usually cost money. Look at Illustration 3C, below.

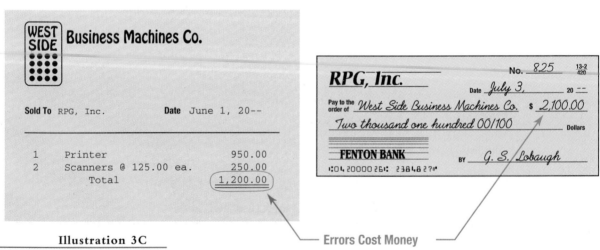

Verifying your work and the work of others is an important record keeping skill, whether you do your work manually or with a computer. There are several steps which record keepers take to verify their own and others' work. Some of these steps follow:

1. *Verify the accuracy of the math.* For example, add a column of figures the second time from the bottom up.

Transposition error. Switching order of numbers or letters.

2. *Check to see if there are omissions.* For example, check each item on a form to make sure that it is filled in. You can also count the number of source documents to make sure that one was not skipped.

3. *Check to see if there are duplications.* Count the number of source documents to make sure that one was not entered twice.

4. *Compare the information recorded* against the source document, number for number, letter for letter. Look out for a common data entry error in which the order of two numbers or letters is switched. For example, when the source document shows "1023 Clark St." and you enter "1032 Calrk St." These are known as **transposition errors**.

➡ **SAMPLE PROBLEM**

Illustration 3D shows a computer printout of a class list and an attendance list made by a teacher on the first day of class at Clark High School. Ted Yates, the school's office assistant, was asked to verify the information on the two lists. He did this by comparing the names on the class list with the names on the attendance list.

Let's look at the two steps Ted Yates used to complete this task.

STEP 1 **Prepare checklist.**

Ted prepared the checklist shown in Illustration 3D. He used the following column headings: Student No., Correct, Error, Not in Class.

STEP 2 **Compare data.**

Ted completed the checklist by comparing the names of the students on the class list to the attendance list.

Illustration 3D

A class list and an attendance list

STEP 2

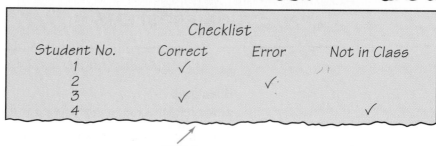

Clark High School Class List

Student No.	Student Name
1	Stacey Aaron
2	Fred Bernt
3	Lisa Chambers
4	Paul Demers

Clark High School Attendance List
8/31/20--

Stacey Aaron
Fred Brent
Lisa Chambers

Checklist

Student No.	Correct	Error	Not in Class
1	✓		
2		✓	
3	✓		
4			✓

STEP 1

When Ted compared the first name, Stacey Aaron, he found that the name was on both lists and compared exactly. So, he put a check mark in the Correct column on the line for Student No. 1 of the check-list.

When Ted compared the second name, he found Fred Bernt's name on both lists. However, the name was not spelled correctly on the attendance list. Therefore, he put a check mark in the Error column on the line for Student No. 2 of the checklist.

When Ted compared the third name, he found Lisa Chambers's name on both lists compared exactly. So, he put a check mark in the Correct column on the line for Student No. 3 of the checklist.

When Ted tried to compare Paul Demers's name, he found that it was on the class list but not on the attendance list. Ted put a check mark on the line for Student No. 4 under the Not in Class column.

 ## BUILDING YOUR BUSINESS VOCABULARY

On a sheet of paper, write the headings **Statement Number** and **Words**. Next, choose the words that match the statements. Write each word you choose next to the statement number it matches. Be careful; not all the words listed should be used.

Statements	Words
1. The first step in the data processing cycle	data
2. A job	data processing
3. A form on which information is kept	electronically
4. To check for accuracy	input
5. Doing something to data to make them more useful	manually
6. The forms from which you get the data you enter into the computer	merchandise
7. The third step in the data processing cycle	output
8. By computer	position
9. Information	processing
10. When numbers, letters, or other characters are switched in order	record
11. The second step in the data processing cycle	source documents
	transposition error
	verify

STEPS REVIEW: Verifying Data

STEP 1 Prepare checklist.

STEP 2 Compare data.

 ## APPLICATION PROBLEMS

Problem 3-1   You are a records clerk at Pekin High School. One of your duties is to verify the accuracy of the class lists on the first day of classes.

Directions

a. Make a checklist like the one in the Sample Problem using the same headings. Then write the numbers for 15 students under the Student No. heading.

Pekin High School
Class List

Student No.	Student Name
1	Trudy Anson
2	Carly Barr
3	Renee Calvin
4	Jeffrey Huang
5	Fred Kennedy
6	Susan Larmont
7	Victor Lyman
8	Madelin Frobel
9	Ira Norstein
10	Roberta Oliver
11	James Peloff
12	Robert Quigley
13	Terry Romano
14	Stuart Simons
15	Velma Tarrant

Pekin High School
Attendance List
9/1/20--

Trudey Anson
Carly Barr
Rene Calvin
Jeffrey Haung
Susan Lamont
Victro Lyman
Madelin Froble
Ira Norstein
James Peloff
Robert Quigley
Terry Romano
Velma Tarrant

CHECK POINT

3-1

If your work is correct, you should have 6 checks in the **Correct** column, 6 checks in the **Error** column, and 3 checks in the **Not in Class** column.

b. A class list prepared by a computer and a class attendance list made by the teacher on the first day of class appear above. Complete the checklist by comparing the names of the students on the class list to the attendance list. If the names are on both lists and are exactly the same, put a check mark in the Correct column. If the names are on both lists but are not exactly the same, put a check mark in the Error column. If a name on the class list is not on the attendance list, put a check mark in the Not in Class column.

Problem 3-2

You are an accounts payable clerk at Webster Company. One of your duties is to maintain a list of vendors, or businesses which sell merchandise to your company.

CHECK POINT

3-2

There are 4 errors.

New Vendor List

Vendor No.	Vendor Name and Address
105	Atwood, Inc. 215 Briar Lane
106	Award Design Co. 205 Seattle Drive
107	Awalt Products Co. 152 First St.
108	Axon Machinery, Inc. 2 South Waters St.
109	Aztec Vendors, Inc. 3402 Drury Avenue
110	Azure Plumbing Supplies 203 Freeman Boulevard
111	Bacloff Computer Center One Technology Drive
112	Baffin Color Displays 10678 Machine St.
113	Bagnel, Inc. 116 Lake Drive
114	Bagnelle Window Co. 1001 Yellow St.

New Vendor List

Atwood, Inc.
215 Briar Lane

Award Desing Co.
250 Seattle Drive

Awalt Products Co.
152 First Street

Avon Machinery, Inc.
2 South Waters Street

Aztec Vendors, Inc.
4302 Drury Avenue

Azure Plumbing Supplies
203 Freeman Boulevard

Backloff Computer Ctr.
One Technology Drive

Bagnel, Inc.
116 Lake Drive

Directions

a. Make a checklist like the one in the Sample Problem but with these headings: Vendor No., Correct, Error, and Not on List. Write the numbers for 10 vendors under the Vendor No. heading, starting with 105.

b. A new vendor list prepared by the computer and another prepared by the accounts payable department are shown on page 21. Complete the checklist by comparing the names and addresses of the vendors on the computer list to the department list. If the names and addresses are on both lists and are exactly the same, put a check mark in the Correct column. If the names and addresses are on both lists but are not exactly the same, put a check mark in the Error column. If a name on the computer list is not on the department list, put a check mark in the Not on List column.

Problems 3-3, 3-4, and 3-5 may be found in the Working Papers.

Job 4 FILING NUMERIC DATA

applied math preview

Copy and complete each problem.

1. $56 \div 8 =$
2. $744 \div 6 =$
3. $\$36.00 \div 6 =$
4. $\$78.00 \div 10 =$
5. $\$6,800 \div 100 =$

6. $\$3,140.00 \div 1,000 =$
7. $\$960 \div 40 =$
8. $\$72.60 \div 12 =$
9. $\$640 \div 160 =$
10. $\$1,890 \div 15 =$

key terms preview

- Alphabetically
- Central processing unit
- Chronologically
- Computer program

- Computer system
- Guides
- Input device
- Numerically

- Output device
- Printer
- Sort
- Tickler file

goals

1 To learn the names and uses of common computer equipment.

2 To learn how to file by numbers and by dates.

Tips

When dividing by 10, 100, or 1,000, move the decimal point in the number to be divided one, two, or three places to the left. The number of places to the left is determined by the number of zeros in the number you are dividing by. For example, $\$120.00 \div 10 = \$12.00$; $\$120.00 \div 100 = \$1.20$; $\$120.00 \div 1,000 = \$0.12$.

⇒ UNDERSTANDING THE JOB

Key Terms

Input devices. Used to enter data into a computer.

Central processing unit. Part of a computer that processes data.

Computer program. Set of instructions.

Printer. An output device.

Output device. Used to get data out of a computer.

Computer system. Input devices, central processing unit, and output devices.

You learned in the last job that all data processing follows a set of definite steps:

Input	→	Processing	→	Output

To do these data processing steps, you need tools. If you are doing manual data processing, you may use a pencil to record input data, a calculator to process the data, and a sheet of paper for the results or output.

In the same way, electronic data processing uses tools to complete the steps in the data processing cycle. For example, in the last job, the office assistant in the school office used a computer to enter the enrollment data. The computer's keyboard and mouse are called **input devices**.

The processing that is done, such as assigning students to the right classes, is performed by the **central processing unit** of the computer.

The central processing unit processes the data it is given according to a set of instructions. This set of instructions is called a **computer program**. For example, in order for the computer to process the enrollment data and print out the class lists and schedules, it has to be given a computer program which tells it how to do those tasks.

Another type of data processing tool is a **printer**. The printer is an **output device**. An output device is used to get information out of the computer.

The input devices, central processing unit, and output devices put together are called a **computer system**. The whole computer system

Key Terms

Sort. File data in some order.

Chronologically. By date.

Numerically. By number.

Alphabetically. By the alphabet.

Guides. Tabs to help find records.

is needed to complete the data processing cycle of input, processing, and output.

Large firms often use large computer systems. Smaller firms may use smaller computer systems known as minicomputers. Very small firms and many individuals use even smaller computer systems known as microcomputers.

One kind of processing which people and computers do is to **sort**, or file data in some kind of order. When the data are dates, they may be sorted in order of time, or **chronologically**. When the data are numbers, they may be sorted from the lowest number to the highest, or **numerically**. When the data are names, they may be sorted using the alphabet, or **alphabetically**.

You will learn about numerical and chronological sorting in this job. You will learn about alphabetic sorting in Job 5.

Numeric Filing

When people file records, they sort them in some way. Numeric filing means sorting records in numerical order. In this system, each record to be sorted must have a number. The records are first sorted in numerical order and then may be placed in a file with the *lowest number* at the *beginning* of the file.

Look at the numeric file in Illustration 4A (page 25). Notice that there are special tabs with numbers in the file. These are called **guides** and are used to help the record keeper find records faster.

Notice that the first guide reads 1–10; the second guide, 11–20; the third guide, 21–30; and so on. If you wanted to find a record numbered 9, you would find it behind the guide labeled 1–10. The record numbered 9 would be placed just after the record numbered 8.

If you were looking for a record numbered 27, you would look behind the guide labeled 21–30. There you would find the record numbered 27 right after the record numbered 26.

→ SAMPLE PROBLEM 1

You are a stock clerk for the Quebec Supply Company. One of your duties is to prepare and file records for new products at the end of each month. The records should be sorted numerically by stock number, with the stock item with the lowest number first and the highest number last.

STEP 1 Prepare the records.

At the bottom left on page 25 is an unsorted list of new stock items. On the right are the completed records for the new stock items.

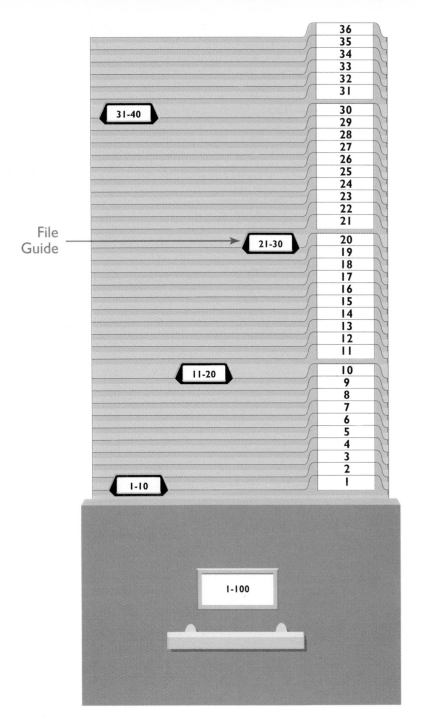

File Guide

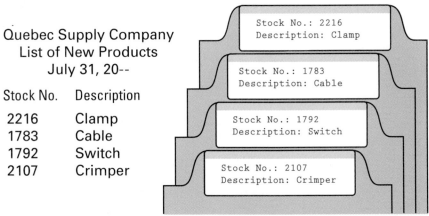

Quebec Supply Company
List of New Products
July 31, 20--

Stock No.	Description
2216	Clamp
1783	Cable
1792	Switch
2107	Crimper

STEP 2 Verify your work.

After completing the stock records, verify that you have copied the data correctly by

1. Comparing the numbers and descriptions on the records to the data on the list to see if you copied them correctly.
2. Counting the stock items on the list and comparing that count to the count of records you completed. This will let you know if you skipped an item or copied one twice.

STEP 3 File the stock records by stock number.

To file these stock items numerically, search through the records for the lowest stock number (1783). Put this record at the beginning of the other records. Then find the record with the next lowest stock number (1792), and place this record after the first one. File each of the remaining records in the same way.

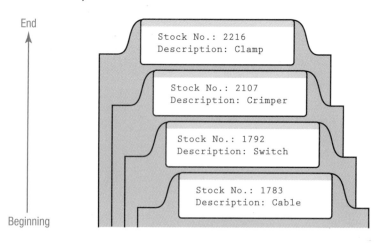

Chronological Filing

Filing records chronologically means sorting them according to the date that is on them. If you borrow books from a library, you are allowed to keep the books for a limited time, such as two weeks. Do you know how the librarian knows which books must be returned on any one day? Have you wondered how a record keeper remembers which bills must be paid by a certain date?

Look at the chronological file in Illustration 4B (page 27). This file is used by some librarians to help them remember what books are due on any date. It is called a chronological file, **tickler file**, or follow-up file.

Notice that there is a guide for each month. Behind the guide labeled January, there are guides for each day of the month. If you receive a bill on January 10 that has to be paid on January 20, you would place the bill behind the guide numbered 20. When January 20 comes, you will look behind the guide for that day and pay the bills you find there.

After paying the bills due on January 20, you would take the guide for that day and put it behind the guide for February. As each day goes by,

Tickler file. Chronological file used to remind workers of important dates.

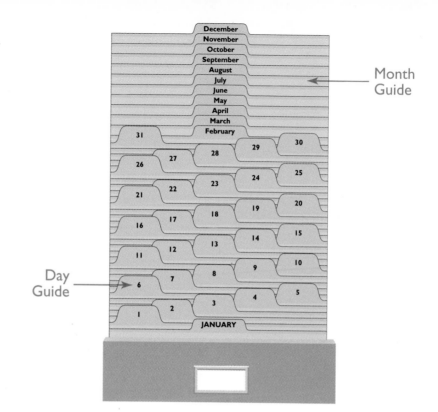

Month
Guide

Day
Guide

the numbered guide for that day would be shifted to the next month. By the end of January, all the numbered guides would have been shifted behind the guide for February. That is why there is only one set of guides numbered 1 through 31 in the file.

 SAMPLE PROBLEM 2

You are an office assistant for Information Systems Training, Inc. Information Systems Training provides training sessions, or seminars to people from government and business who want to learn about computer systems. One of your duties is to a make a schedule that shows which seminars are being held on what dates. The seminars should be listed *chronologically* by date.

STEP 1 Enter the heading.

On a sheet of paper, write the heading:

Information Systems Training, Inc.
Summer Seminar Schedule
March 15, 20—

STEP 2 File the seminars by date.

List the seminars, recording the seminar with the earliest date first and the seminar with the latest date last. The unsorted list of seminars on the left has been sorted in chronological order on the right.

Unsorted List of Seminars	Sorted List of Seminars
June 8, Database Seminar	May 10, Word Processing Seminar
May 25, Spreadsheet Seminar	May 25, Spreadsheet Seminar
May 10, Word Processing Seminar	June 8, Database Seminar
July 5, Local Area Network Seminar	July 5, Local Area Network Seminar

STEP 3 Verify your work.

After the seminars have been sorted by date, verify your work by:
1. Comparing the seminar dates and names on both lists to make sure that you have copied each date and seminar name correctly.
2. Counting the seminars on both lists to make sure that you have not copied one twice or failed to copy one at all.

BUILDING YOUR BUSINESS VOCABULARY

On a sheet of paper, write the headings **Statement Number** and **Words**. Next, choose the words that match the statements. Write each word you choose next to the statement number it matches. Be careful; not all the words listed should be used.

Statements	Words
1. By number	alphabetically
2. By date	central processing unit
3. To file in some order	chronologically
4. A group of input devices, output devices, and a central processing unit	computer program
	computer system
5. By the alphabet	data
6. The part of the computer system that does the processing of data	guides
	input devices
7. Used to get data out of a computer	manually
8. A set of instructions that the computer follows to process the data	numerically
	output device
9. Used to help find records in a file	printer
10. A chronological file which reminds workers of important dates	sort
	tickler file
11. Used to enter data into a computer	
12. An output device	

STEPS REVIEW: Filing Numeric Data

STEP 1 Prepare the records.

STEP 2 Verify your work.

STEP 3 File the records by number.

STEPS REVIEW: Filing Chronological Data

STEP 1 Enter the heading.

STEP 2 File the records by date.

STEP 3 Verify your work.

APPLICATION PROBLEMS

Problem 4-1

You are a records clerk in the payroll department of the Caseyville Public Works Department. The list of employees below is sorted alphabetically by employee name. Prepare another list sorted numerically by employee number.

CHECK POINT

4-1

If your work is correct, the first employee on your *numerically* arranged list should be Ramona Ramirez (102). The last employee should be Charles Clark (255).

Directions

a. On a sheet of paper, write the heading:

> Public Works Department
> Employees by Number
> December 31, 20--

b. Under the heading, write the column headings "Employee Number" and "Employee Name."

Employee Number	Employee Name
133	Ackerman, Rita
175	Brown, Laverne
255	Clark, Charles
228	Dierberg, Samantha
107	O'Brady, Timothy
102	Ramirez, Ramona
103	Steinberg, Ira
245	Tompkins, Donald
212	White, Devon
170	Yanos, Olga

c. Sort the employees numerically by employee number. Place the employee with the lowest number first.

d. Verify your work by comparing the numbers and names in the original list to your list and counting the names in both lists.

Problem 4-2

You are a clerk in the sales department of Colonial Furniture Company. You are given the lists of salespeople in each sales territory below. Rewrite each list so that it is sorted numerically by employee number.

Directions

CHECK POINT

4-2

The last employee in the West territory should be Meade (2616).

Employees by Sales Territories							
North		**South**		**East**		**West**	
1078	Justice	1108	Bates	2710	Chester	2061	Yancy
2716	Wu-ling	1008	Edison	1072	Rodriguez	1066	Quible
2218	Canata	1072	O'Hara	1027	Bernstein	1606	Powers
1087	Faraday	1801	Elmwood	1109	Davis	2606	Vasson
2128	Wellington	1782	Gales	1081	Wellen	2616	Meade

a. On a sheet of paper, write the heading:

> Colonial Furniture Company
> Salespeople by Territory
> March 31, 20--

b. Write the headings for each territory (North, South, East, West).

c. Sort the employees in each territory numerically by employee number. Record the employee with the lowest number in each territory first.

d. Verify your work by (1) comparing the original list of names to your list, and (2) counting the number of employees on both lists to be sure you did not copy a name twice or forget a name.

Problems 4-3, 4-4, and 4-5 may be found in the Working Papers.

Job 5 FILING ALPHABETIC DATA

Tips

To change a percent
to a decimal:
1. move the decimal
   point two places to
   the left
2. drop the percent
   sign.

applied math preview

Change each percent to a decimal.

1. 30%	6. 43%	11. 80%	16. 5%
2. 15%	7. 6%	12. 20%	17. 2%
3. 50%	8. 13%	13. 10%	18. 1%
4. 75%	9. 79%	14. 62%	19. 4.5%
5. 25%	10. 98%	15. 18%	20. 7.51%

key terms preview

- Documents
- Indexing
- Record clerks
- Retrieve
- Store
- Surname

goal

To learn basic rules for filing documents alphabetically in a manual filing system.

→ UNDERSTANDING THE JOB

Record clerks. Workers specially trained to store and retrieve documents.

Documents. Business papers.

Store File.

Retrieve. Find.

Almost everyone does some filing. Secretaries, managers, supervisors, stock clerks, salespersons, homeowners—all must file papers that are important to their job or personal life.

The job of filing is often done by special workers called **record clerks**. Record clerks are trained to keep data in an orderly way. They must be able to find information quickly and easily when it is needed.

Record control is important in any business. Organizations are responsible for maintaining and handling important records so they are not lost, misplaced, or accidentally destroyed. Any disorder in handling these records would be costly, if not disastrous—costly in terms of the time spent in search of a misplaced record, and perhaps disastrous if any records are lost or accidentally destroyed.

Companies maintain a wide variety of business records. Letters and memos, blueprints and maps, reports, inventory catalogs, sales and personnel records, and computer printouts are some of the types of office records. New office technologies and equipment have created new kinds of office records—*paperless* records.

Record clerks often use special terms in their work. They may call letters, bills, invoices, and other business papers **documents**. (See Illustration 5A on page 31.) When they file a document, they may say that they have **stored** it. When they get a document from the files, they may say that they have **retrieved** it.

Record clerks may store documents in many ways. They may store paper documents in file folders. They may store documents in *microfilm* form. They may also store documents using a computer system.

In this job you will learn how to file documents alphabetically. You will learn how filing is done with computer systems in the next job.

Business information is stored in many ways

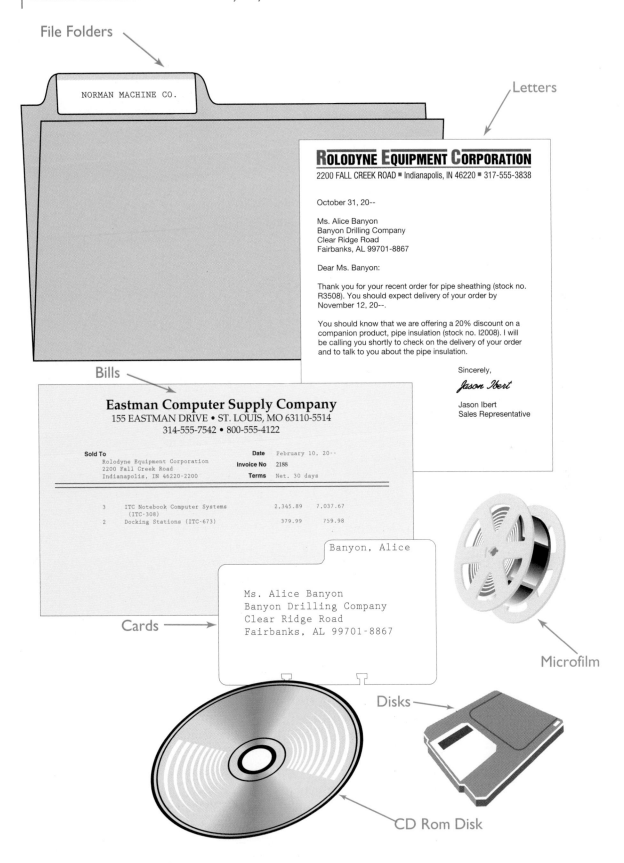

File Folders

NORMAN MACHINE CO.

Letters

Rolodyne Equipment Corporation

2200 FALL CREEK ROAD ■ Indianapolis, IN 46220 ■ 317-555-3838

October 31, 20--

Ms. Alice Banyon
Banyon Drilling Company
Clear Ridge Road
Fairbanks, AL 99701-8867

Dear Ms. Banyon:

Thank you for your recent order for pipe sheathing (stock no. R3508). You should expect delivery of your order by November 12, 20--.

You should know that we are offering a 20% discount on a companion product, pipe insulation (stock no. I2008). I will be calling you shortly to check on the delivery of your order and to talk to you about the pipe insulation.

Sincerely,

Jason Ibert

Jason Ibert
Sales Representative

Bills

Eastman Computer Supply Company
155 EASTMAN DRIVE • ST. LOUIS, MO 63110-5514
314-555-7542 • 800-555-4122

Sold To		Date	February 10, 20--
Rolodyne Equipment Corporation		Invoice No	2188
2200 Fall Creek Road		Terms	Net. 30 days
Indianapolis, IN 46220-2200			

| 3 | ITC Notebook Computer Systems (ITC-308) | 2,345.89 | 7,037.67 |
| 2 | Docking Stations (ITC-673) | 379.99 | 759.98 |

Banyon, Alice

Ms. Alice Banyon
Banyon Drilling Company
Clear Ridge Road
Fairbanks, AL 99701-8867

Cards

Microfilm

Disks

CD Rom Disk

SAMPLE PROBLEM

Filing documents alphabetically means sorting them according to the letters of the alphabet. Look at the alphabetic file in Illustration 5B. Notice that there is a guide for each letter of the alphabet and that each guide is arranged in alphabetical order: "B" is after "A"; "C" is after "B"; and so forth.

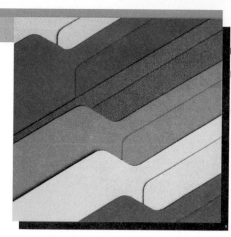

Illustration 5B

Alphabetic file with guides

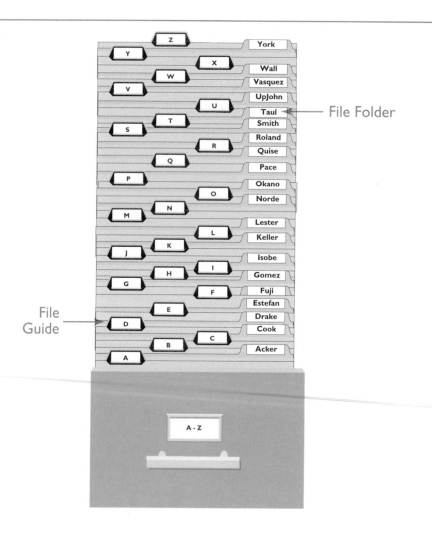

Now let's learn the rules to use this system.

RULE 1 File papers by the last name (surname).

If you need a document that was sent to your company by Anne Bailey, where in the files would you look for it? Behind guide "A" for Anne, or behind guide "B" for Bailey?

Key Terms

Surname. Last name.

Indexing. Putting in filing order.

Rule 1 tells you that you file documents according to the last name, or **surname**. So you would look behind the "B" guide for Anne Bailey's document.

Notice that on the tab of the file folder below, Anne Bailey's last name was put first. Arranging the parts of a name so that they are in filing order is called **indexing**. Anne Bailey's name has been put in indexing order on the file folder tab below.

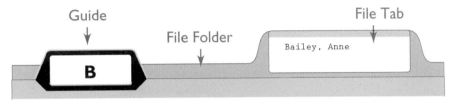

RULE 2 When the surnames of people begin with the same first letter, use the second letter in the name to decide which name is to be filed in front of the other. If both the first and second letters are the same, use the third letter, and so forth.

Suppose that you had to retrieve documents sent to your company from Tara Casey and Andrew Conner. Using Rule 1, you would look at the surnames. Since both begin with "C," you would use Rule 2 and look at the second letter in each last name. Since the second letter of C*a*sey is an "a" and the second letter of C*o*nner is an "o," you would find the document from Conner behind the document from Casey.

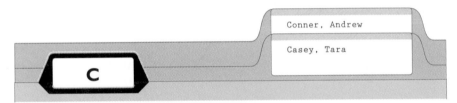

In the same way, you would find a document from Darcy Ri*v*era behind a document from Karl Ri*c*h. In this case, you had to go to the third letter in each name to find a difference.

RULE 3 File "nothing" before "something."

Suppose that you wanted to store documents from Larry Roberts and from Larry Robertson. Using Rule 3, you would file Larry Roberts before Larry Robertson since *nothing* follows the "s" in Roberts, but "on" follows the "s" in Robertson.

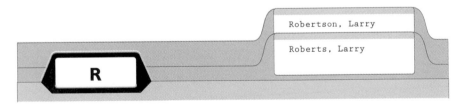

In the same way, a document from Ricardo Marti*n* would be stored before one from Ricardo Marti*nez*.

RULE 4 If the surnames of people are the same, compare the first letters of the first names to decide how to file them. If the first letter of the first names is the same, use the second letter, and so forth.

A document from *M*ica Thorpe would be filed before one from *T*yrone Thorpe. The last names are the same. So the first three rules do not apply. You must look at the first names of the persons. Since "M" in Mica comes before "T" in Tyrone, the document from Mica Thorpe would be found before the one from Tyrone Thorpe.

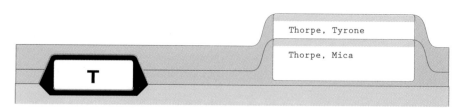

Do you know why a document from I. Stein would be found before a document from Ira Stein? Using Rule 3 (nothing comes before something), *I.* Stein would be stored before *Ira* Stein. This is because no letter follows the "I" in I. Stein while the letter "r"follows the "I" in Ira Stein.

RULE 5 A middle name or middle initial is used to decide alphabetic order only if the surnames and first names are both the same.

In the case of Dennis Victor Scott and Dennis John Scott, since both surnames and first names are alike, you would have to use the middle names to decide the order. You would find the document from Dennis John Scott before the one from Dennis *V*ictor Scott.

If a document from Dennis J. Scott was to be stored in the file, you would place it before the document from Dennis John Scott. Rule 3 tells you that nothing is filed before something. Since the surnames and first names are alike, you would use the middle names or initials to decide the order. The "J" in Dennis J. Scott had no letters after it, while the "J" in Dennis J. Scott had an "o" after it.

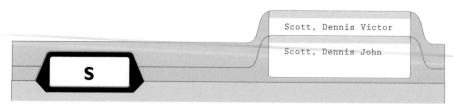

RULE 6 When a person's whole name appears in a business name, treat the name as if it were by itself.

Suppose you had to store documents from Keith Brewer Company and Keith Brewer in a file. Which one would you file first? Using Rule 6, you would first index the documents this way:

Brewer, Keith
Brewer, Keith, Company

Then, using Rule 3, you would file the document from Keith Brewer before the document from Keith Brewer Company, because you file nothing before something.

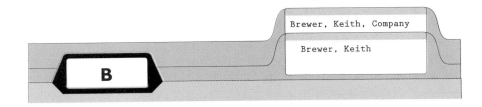

Brewer, Keith, Company

Brewer, Keith

B

RULE 7 Business names that do not contain the whole names of persons are filed according to their first words. If the first words are the same, the second words are compared, and so forth.

You store a document from the Allure Perfume Company behind the "A" guide because the first word of the company name begins with "A." A document from the A One Perfume Company would be filed behind the "A" guide also, since the first word of this company name begins with "A." The document from the A One Perfume Company would be filed before the document from the Allure Perfume Company. The first word in the A One Perfume Company is "A." The first word in the Allure Perfume Company is "Allure." Since Rule 3 shows that nothing comes before something, the document beginning with the word "A" comes before the document beginning with the word "Allure."

You would place a document from the Allure Perfume Company before a document from the Allure Travel Company. Since both company names have the same first word, you must compare the next word in both company names. Since "P" comes before "T," the perfume company document would be placed before the travel company document.

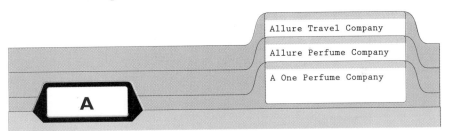

Allure Travel Company

Allure Perfume Company

A One Perfume Company

A

BUILDING YOUR BUSINESS VOCABULARY

On a sheet of paper, write the headings **Statement Number** and **Words**. Next, choose the words that match the statements. Write each word you choose next to the statement number it matches. Be careful; not all the words listed should be used.

Statements	Words
1. Workers trained to store and retrieve data	data entry clerks
2. Letters, bills, and business papers	documents
3. To file a document	double rulings
4. To find a document	footing
5. Metal tabs used to help record clerks find documents	guides
	indexing
6. A chronological file used to remind workers of important dates	money columns
	OCR
7. Workers who enter data in a computer system	record clerks
8. Used for recording amounts of money on a form	retrieve
9. The total of a column written in small figures	store
10. Arranging the parts of a name so that it can be filed	surname
11. Last name	tickler file

STEPS REVIEW: Filing Alphabetic Data

RULE 1 File papers by the last name (surname).

RULE 2 When the surnames of people begin with the same first letter, use the second letter in the name to decide which name is to be filed in front of the other. If both the first and second letters are the same, use the third letter, and so forth.

RULE 3 File "nothing" before "something."

RULE 4 If the surnames of people are the same, compare the first letters of the first names to decide how to file them. If the first letter of the first names is the same, use the second letter, and so forth.

RULE 5 A middle name or middle initial is used to decide alphabetic order only if the surnames and first names are both the same.

RULE 6 When a person's whole name appears in a business name, treat the name as if it were by itself.

RULE 7 Business names that do not contain the whole names of persons are filed according to their first words. If the first words are the same, the second words are compared, and so forth.

APPLICATION PROBLEMS

Problem 5-1

You are a records clerk for Talbot Community College. You store and retrieve documents about students. You have been asked by your supervisor to make a card file for the new students below.

CHECK POINT
5-1

The first name on the list should be Abert, Rhonda. The last name should be Wycham, Donald.

Directions

a. Copy on 3" x 5" cards, or separate pieces of paper, each name below. Write the names in indexing order (surname first, followed by a comma and the first name or initial); for example, Evans, Betty.

Lucinda Oliphant	Louise Meeker
Thomas Beeler	Thomas Bealer
Alice Merker	Elizabeth Sargeant
Rhonda Abert	Albert Merkel
Francine Kushner	Freida Sanders
Donald Wycham	LaDonna White

b. Arrange the cards or slips of paper in alphabetical order using Rules 1 and 2.

c. List each name in alphabetical order on another sheet of paper.

You work as an office assistant for a job placement office. Your supervisor gives you the following list of job applicants whose last names start with "C" and asks you to make a card file for them.

Directions

a. Copy on 3" x 5" cards, or separate pieces of paper, the name of each job applicant below. Write the names in indexing order (surname first, followed by a comma and the first name or initial).

Theodore Clarkson	Ronald Caster
Alicia Chevron	Bea Cramer
Rudolph Casper	Frank Cervais
Marla Clairborne	Carlotta Chester
Ruby Charon	Victor Clairet
Arnold Cruickshank	Beverly Cromer

b. Using Rules 1 and 2, arrange the cards or slips of paper in alphabetical order.

c. After sorting the names in alphabetical order, list each name in alphabetical order on another sheet of paper.

You still work as an office assistant for a job placement office. Today, your supervisor gives you the following list of job applicants whose last names start with "F" and asks you to make a card file for them.

Directions

a. Copy on 3" x 5" cards, or separate pieces of paper, the name of each player below. Write the names in indexing order (surname first, followed by a comma and the first name or initial).

Erica Fromme	Roberta Felstein
Rita Feller	Danice Farmer
Vincent Foglesby	Ramona Feldstein
Elicive Faber	Vernita Fogel
Veronica Fogelman	Denise Framer
Elizabeth Faberson	Edward Frampton

b. Using Rules 1, 2, and 3, arrange the cards or slips of paper in alphabetical order.

c. After sorting the names in alphabetical order, list each name in alphabetical order on another sheet of paper.

Problems 5-4, 5-5, and 5-6 may be found in the Working Papers.

Job 6 ENTERING AND FILING DATA ELECTRONICALLY

Tips

To change a decimal to a percent: 1. Move the decimal point two places to the right 2. Add a percent sign.

key terms preview

- Characters
- Cursor
- Database
- Field
- File
- Key
- Magnetic media
- Menu
- Record
- Update
- Vendor

goal

To learn how data are entered and stored in a data processing system.

UNDERSTANDING THE JOB

Key Terms

Magnetic media. What a computer stores data on.

In a manual filing system, you file documents in file folders. Then you file the folders in file cabinets.

A computer filing system is like a manual filing system in many ways. A document in a computer filing system looks a lot like a paper document. The difference is that the document in a computer filing system may be shown on the monitor of a computer instead of on a piece of paper, and is called a record instead of a form.

Look at the Student Enrollment Record on the screen in Illustration 6A on page 39. You can see that the data are arranged in about the same way as they were on the paper enrollment form in Illustration 3B in Job 3, page 18.

However, the computer does not store data in a filing cabinet. Instead, the computer stores data on **magnetic media** which are usually disks.

Data processing workers use special terms when they talk about documents in computer filing systems:

1. The blanks that have to be filled in on the enrollment form are called **fields**.
2. The enrollment form for any one student in the file is called a **record**.
3. A group of related records may be called a **file**.
4. If the disk contains many files, it may be called a **database**.

```
                    STUDENT ENROLLMENT RECORD


        STUDENT NUMBER      2 5 1 3
        STUDENT NAME        JUANITA RUIZ
        STREET ADDRESS      3275 CLARION STREET
        CITY                GLENDALE
        STATE               CA
        ZIP CODE            91207-0235
        ENROLLMENT DATE     08/23/20--
        FIRST COURSE        RECORD KEEPING
        SECOND COURSE       KEYBOARDING I
        THIRD COURSE        ENGLISH II
        FOURTH COURSE       SOCIAL STUDIES
        FIFTH COURSE        BUSINESS MATH
        SIXTH COURSE        PHYSICAL EDUCATION
        SEVENTH COURSE      MUSIC
```

Special Terms for Electronic Filing

Field = A group of numbers and letters
Examples: student number, student name

Record = A group of fields
Examples: student enrollment record, student grade sheet

File = A group of records
Examples: student enrollment records, student grade records

Database = A group of files
Example: A set of disks containing student files for enrollment, grades, absences, medical history, and test scores

Illustration 6B

Field, record, file, and database in a computer system

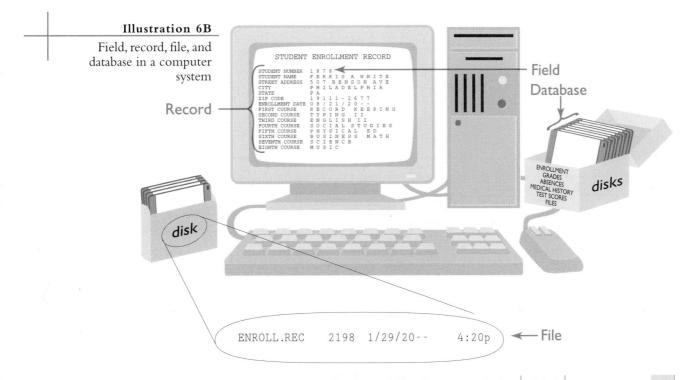

Record

Field

Database

disks

disk

ENROLL.REC   2198 1/29/20--   4:20p   ← File

One of the most important differences between a computer file and a manual file is that you do not have to sort the records in a computer file. The computer program will do that for you. If you enter many records into the file, the computer program will take care of placing them in proper order. After having to sort records in the last job, you can see that a computer filing system can save a lot of time.

You may enter data into a record in a computer file in a number of ways. One way is to type, or **key**, the data from the source document into the electronic form that is on the screen.

➡ SAMPLE PROBLEM

Benji Akita is a general office worker for the Peoria Blades, the basketball team you learned about in Job 2. One of his jobs is to key in data about new equipment that was purchased into the team equipment file. Here is how he does that job:

STEP 1 Choose the correct menu item.

Benji starts by turning on the computer. When he does, the screen looks like the one in Illustration 6C.

The information on Benji's screen is a list of tasks that can be done with the Equipment File. This list of choices is called a **menu**. The menu shown is the first menu in the program and is called the *main menu*.

The main menu shows that the program will let you add, update, and display equipment records, or print equipment records. **Update** means to replace old data in a record with new data.

At the bottom of the screen is a flashing marker called a **cursor**. The cursor shows Benji where he is on the screen. The cursor in Illustration 6C tells Benji that a choice must be made from the list. Since Benji is entering data about new equipment, he will have to add new equipment records. So he strikes the 1 key. When he does, the screen displays a blank equipment record like the one shown in Illustration 6D on the next page.

Menu. A list of choices on a computer screen.

Update. Replace old data with new data.

Cursor. Flashing marker on the display screen.

Illustration 6C

Equipment menu

```
        EQUIPMENT MENU
   1. ADD EQUIPMENT RECORD
   2. UPDATE EQUIPMENT RECORD
   3. DISPLAY EQUIPMENT RECORD
   4. PRINT EQUIPMENT RECORDS
   ENTER CHOICE■ ←——————— Cursor
```

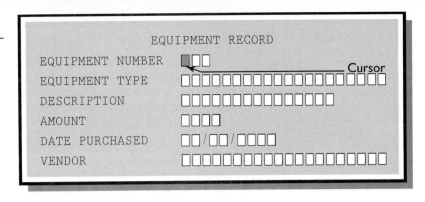

Illustration 6D — Blank equipment-record screen

EQUIPMENT RECORD

EQUIPMENT NUMBER

EQUIPMENT TYPE

DESCRIPTION

AMOUNT

DATE PURCHASED

VENDOR

Cursor

STEP 2 Key data into the first field.

Benji starts keying data into the blank record for the new equipment the team has just bought. His source documents are the bills that the team received from the sellers. The first bill shows that the team just purchased 30 professional basketballs, equipment number 16, from Abner Hoops, Inc. on September 17 of the current year.

Benji looks at the data on the first line of the bill from Abner Hoops, Inc., which is the equipment number. He keys that number into the first field on the screen. As he does so, the numbers that are entered appear on the screen.

EQUIPMENT NUMBER   *0 1 6*

Each box on the screen is a space for a number or letter. Numbers and letters are called **characters**. Benji cannot key more characters than the spaces provided for each field.

Notice that the first field contains space for only three numbers. When the computer program for the equipment file was written, the first field was given three spaces because the team had only 250 types of equipment. Only three spaces were needed to let Benji key any equipment number. In the same way, the Amount field was given only four spaces, since the team would never have more than 9,999 of any item of equipment on hand.

Benji keys the Equipment Number, 016, into the first field and presses the ENTER key on the keyboard. This tells the computer that the operator is finished entering data in that field.

Notice that he entered *016* instead of just *16*. Had Benji entered 16, these characters would have been placed in the first two spaces in the field. The computer would have read these characters as 160.

As soon as Benji presses ENTER, the screen looks like Illustration 6E below.

Key Terms

Characters. Numbers and letters.

Illustration 6E

Equipment number entered
into equipment record
screen

Illustration 6E — Equipment number entered into equipment record screen

EQUIPMENT RECORD

EQUIPMENT NUMBER   0 1 6

EQUIPMENT TYPE

DESCRIPTION

AMOUNT

DATE PURCHASED

VENDOR

Cursor

Notice that the cursor has moved to the next field, Equipment Type. As each field is filled in, the cursor moves down the form.

STEP 3 Key data into the remaining fields.

Key Terms

Vendor. Seller

Benji now keys data into the Equipment Type, Description, Amount, Date Purchased, and Vendor fields using the bills as the source documents. The **Vendor** field is used for the name of the company that sold the equipment to the team. The word vendor means seller.

Notice that the Equipment Type, Description, and Vendor fields have all been given different amounts of space. Notice also that the Date field has eight spaces. The eight spaces are divided into three groups of spaces. The first two spaces are for the month, the next two are for the day, and the last four are for the year.

The basketballs were purchased on September 5 of the current year. To make it easier and faster, numbers are used for each month instead of keying the whole name of the month. Here are the numbers that are used:

For Your Information

Older computer programs used only two digits to represent the year. The programs assumed that the first two digits were 19. If you entered 99 in the two year spaces, the program assumed you meant 1999. When the year 2000 was reached, these programs assumed you meant 1900 when you entered Ø Ø in the two spaces for the year. These programs suffered from the Y2K problem, or year 2000 problem, and had to be rewritten to use four spaces for the year. Companies and governments spent billions of dollars to rewrite their programs to correct for the Y2K problem.

01 January	07 July
02 February	08 August
03 March	09 September
04 April	10 October
05 May	11 November
06 June	12 December

Since September is the ninth month of the year, Benji keys 09 in the first two spaces for the date. The operator must key *09* instead of *9*. If just 9 was keyed in the first space, the computer would think that the number entered was 90.

Benji then keys 05 in the middle two spaces for the day. He then enters the four numbers of the current year in the last four spaces. When the date is entered completely, Benji strikes the ENTER key.

When the data are entered into the last field and Benji strikes the ENTER key, a blank equipment data screen will appear. Benji will then enter the data from the next bill. When all data from all the bills have been entered, the computer program will display the main menu like the one in Illustration 6C.

If Benji had made a mistake, Benji would key 2 from the main menu. If Benji needed to know how many basketballs the team had just bought, he would key 3. If Benji needed to print the record for a piece of equipment, he would key 4.

 BUILDING YOUR BUSINESS VOCABULARY

On a sheet of paper, write the headings **Statement Number** and **Words**. Next, choose the words that match the statements. Write each word you choose next to the statement number it matches. Be careful; not all the words listed should be used.

Statements	Words
1. A list of choices on a display screen	characters
2. Enter data using a keyboard	cursor
3. A group of files	database
4. A flashing marker on a display screen	field

Statements	Words
5. A group of fields	file
6. A group of numbers and letters	guides
7. Kinds of magnetic storage, such as disks	indexing
8. To replace old data with new data	key
9. Metal tabs used to help record clerks find something	magnetic media
	menu
10. Arranging the parts of a name so that it can be filed	record
	retrieve
11. A computer word for numbers and letters	tickler file
12. A seller	update
13. A group of records	vendor

STEPS REVIEW: Entering Data Electronically

STEP 1 Choose the correct menu item.

STEP 2 Key data into the first field.

STEP 3 Key data into the remaining fields.

APPLICATION PROBLEMS

Problem 6-1   You are a stock clerk for Blanco Athletic Supply Company. It is your job to key in data about new equipment items the company has bought, using a computer terminal.

CHECK POINT

6-1

Use 4 characters for amounts.

Directions

a. Make two blank equipment-record screens like the one shown in Illustration 6D (page 41).

b. Enter the data for the two new equipment items listed below into the screens. Use the current year. Print all the characters you enter. To avoid confusion, use these special symbols:

For the letter *O*   O
For the number *0*   Ø
For the number *1*   1
For the number *7*   7̶

New Equipment Items

Field	a.	b.
Equipment Number:	2Ø6	39
Equipment Type:	Soccer balls	Football tees
Description:	Professional	black
Amount:	23	25
Date Purchased:	Feb 15, 2Ø--	Feb 17̶, 2Ø--
Vendor:	Clay Co.	Teter, Inc.

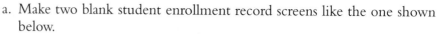

Problem 6-2

You are a clerk in the enrollment office of Edison College. Part of your job is to enter student enrollment data into a student enrollment file.

CHECK POINT

6-2

Use 8 characters for dates.

Directions

a. Make two blank student enrollment record screens like the one shown below.

b. Enter the data for two new students listed below into the screens. Use the current year. Print all the characters you enter. To avoid confusion, use these special symbols:

For the letter *O*	O
For the number *0*	Ø
For the number *1*	1
For the number *7*	7̶

New Students

Field	a.	b.
Student number:	341-Ø6-9116	349-17̶-2Ø7̶8
Last name:	Baer	Levin
First name:	Joshua	Marvin
Middle initial:	L.	S.
Home street address:	12 Holmes St.	3Ø2 Lang Ave.
Home city:	Newark	Wilmington
Home state:	DE	DE
Home zip code:	197̶11-4547̶	198Ø8-3627̶
Date admitted:	July 6, 2Ø--	July 8, 2Ø--
Dormitory assignment:	Beadle Hall	Randle Hall

```
        STUDENT  ENROLLMENT  RECORD


STUDENT  NUMBER        □□□-□□-□□□□
LAST  NAME             □□□□□□□□□□□□□□
FIRST  NAME            □□□□□□□□□□□□□□
MIDDLE  INITIAL        □
HOME  STREET  ADDRESS  □□□□□□□□□□□□□□□
HOME  CITY             □□□□□□□□□□□□
HOME  STATE            □□
HOME  ZIP  CODE        □□□□□ □□□□
DATE  ADMITTED         □□ / □□ / □□□□
DORMITORY  ASSIGNMENT  □□□□□□□□□□□□□□
```

Problem 6-3

You are a data entry clerk for the Unadilla Police Department. Part of your job is to enter data about arrests into an arrest incidence file. You use the arrest forms completed by police officers as your source documents.

Directions

Look at the partial screen on page 45, and answer the questions that follow.

1. The screen shows that you have entered part of the arrest number. What key should you press when you finish entering the number?

2. In what field is the cursor shown?
3. How many fields are shown on the partial screen?
4. How many spaces have been given for the Arresting Officer field?
5. How many spaces have been given for the Time Of Arrest field?
6. To enter May 9 of the current year, in the Date Of Arrest field, what would you key into these spaces: ☐☐ / ☐☐ / ☐☐☐☐?
7. When you finish keying in data in all the fields on the Arrest Incidence Record, what will appear on the screen?

CHECK POINT

6-3(6)

Be sure to use zeros when you enter the date.

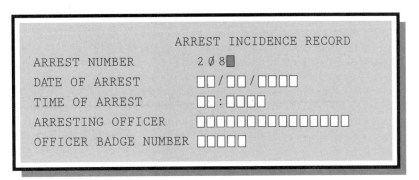

```
                          ARREST INCIDENCE RECORD
ARREST NUMBER            2 Ø 8■
DATE OF ARREST           ☐☐/☐☐/☐☐☐☐
TIME OF ARREST           ☐☐:☐☐☐☐
ARRESTING OFFICER        ☐☐☐☐☐☐☐☐☐☐☐☐☐☐
OFFICER BADGE NUMBER     ☐☐☐☐☐
```

Problems 6-4, 6-5, and 6-6 may be found in the Working Papers.

applied math preview

Copy and answer each problem.

1. $2,089.12
   790.62
   0.76
   45.35

2. $16,054.27
   − 9,263.14

3. 20 × $56.24 =
4. $186 ÷ 8 =
5. Change 0.954 to a percent.
6. Change 54.8% to a decimal.

key terms preview

- Cell
- Computer software
- Formula
- Run
- Spreadsheet software
- Template

goals

1 To learn about computer spreadsheet software.
2 To learn how to create spreadsheets.

UNDERSTANDING THE JOB

Computer programs are used often in business offices to complete business tasks quickly and accurately. A set of computer programs that perform related tasks is called **computer software**. For example, a computer game is a set of related programs that let you start a game on a computer, play the game, and keep score. **Spreadsheet software** is a set of programs that take the place of a pad of paper and calculator to find the answer to common business problems. Spreadsheet software lets you prepare tables, such as the lists of bills and amounts owed, easily and quickly.

SAMPLE PROBLEM

Key Terms

Computer software. A set of programs that perform related tasks.

Spreadsheet software. A program that takes the place of paper pad and calculator.

Cell. On a spreadsheet, where a row and column meet.

Carlota Fuentes is an office worker at a small office near her apartment house. As part of her job, she uses spreadsheet software to maintain the list of expenses shown on the computer screen in Illustration 7A on page 47.

The spreadsheet has both columns and rows. The columns are shown by letter, and the rows by number. Data are shown in **cells**, which are where columns and rows meet. For example, the word *Wages* is found in

List of expenses on a computer screen

Column

	A	B	C	D	E	F
1	Expenses					
2						
3	Type	Amount				
4						
5	Wages	3000.00				
6	Rent	1000.00				
7	Telephone	250.00				
8	Power	125.00				
9	Postage	100.00				
10	Other	450.00				
11						
12	Total	4925.00				
13						
14						
15						

Row

Cell

Cell A5, or where Column A and Row 5 meet. The number 3000.00 is found in B5, or where Column B and Row 5 meet.

Here is how Carlota created the list of expenses on her computer.

STEP 1 Run the spreadsheet software.

Each computer and each spreadsheet program is somewhat different. Your teacher will provide you with instructions for your computer and software. You should learn how to activate, or **run** your spreadsheet program on your computer. You should also learn to quit, or get out of, your spreadsheet program.

Carlota runs her spreadsheet program on her computer.

STEP 2 Move the cell pointer to the cell wanted.

Carlota's computer display screen looks similar to Illustration 7B on page 48.

Notice that cell A1 is highlighted with a black border. The highlighted cell is the cell pointer. It tells Carlota where she is in a spreadsheet. The cell pointer tells her that she is at Cell A1, and she may enter data into the cell. To move the cell pointer to other cells in the spreadsheet, Carlota uses the arrow keys on her computer keyboard.

Key Terms

Run. To activate a program on a computer system.

	A	B	C	D	E	F
1						
2						
3						
4						
5						
6						
7						
8						
9						
10						
11						
12						
13						
14						
15						

When you enter a word or name that is longer than a column is wide, the word spills over and hides the contents of the cell to the right.

Right edge

	A	B
1	B. Detweiler	
2		

To make the column wide enough to hold the word, move the mouse pointer, which looks like a cross, to the right edge of the heading of that column. The mouse pointer should change into:

Then, double click the left mouse button. This should size the column width to fit it contents.

STEP 3 Enter alphabetic data.

Carlota enters alphabetic characters into any cell by:

1. Moving the cell pointer to that cell.
2. Keying the characters.
3. Pressing the Enter key.

Since the cell pointer was already in cell A1, Carlota keyed in the title for the spreadsheet, Expenses. If she makes a mistake while entering the characters, she uses the Back Space key to erase the errors. Then, she reenters them correctly and presses the Enter key.

If Carlota spots an error in the cell after pressing the Enter key, she simply moves the cell pointer back to the cell and reenters the correct characters. When she presses the Enter key, the corrected characters are placed into the cell.

Carlota now moves the cell pointer to the next cell into which she wants to enter alphabetic data, Cell A3, and keys in the column heading, Type. Carlota continues by entering the second column heading into Cell B3, and then enters the names of all the expenses into Cells A5 through A10. She enters Total into Cell A12.

STEP 4 Enter numeric data.

Carlota enters numbers into cells the same way she enters alphabetic characters. She moves the cell pointer to each cell, enters a number, and presses the Enter key. She starts by moving the cell pointer to Cell B5, enters 3000.00, and presses the Enter key. She doesn't enter the comma or the dollar sign.

STEP 5 Enter formulas.

A **formula** is a set of math steps that are performed by the spreadsheet program. For example, a formula might instruct the spreadsheet program to add the amount in one cell to the amount in another cell and place the answer in a third cell.

Suppose that you had entered 100 in Cell C1 and 50 in Cell D1 and wanted to place the total of the two amounts in Cell E1. You could enter into Cell E1 this formula:

=C1+D1.

	A	B	C	D	E	F
1			100	50	=C1+D1	
2						

> You enter =C1+D1. But what you see on your computer screen is the total of C1 + D1, or 150.

You may wonder why you entered the equal sign before the C in the formula. The answer is that if you keyed in just C1+D1, the spreadsheet program would think that you were entering alphabetic characters and would not treat C1+D1 as a formula. Your spreadsheet would look like this:

To view the formulas in an Excel spreadsheet, press Ctrl and ~ (hold down the Control key and press the tilde key).

If you are using a spreadsheet by Lotus instead of Excel, formulas are handled a little differently. Lotus uses the @ sign instead of the = sign to indicate a formula. Lotus also shows a range of cells differently. Lotus uses periods instead of a colon. Thus, in Excel, a sum formula might be: =SUM(B5:B10). In Lotus you would enter: @SUM(B5..B10).

	A	B	C	D	E	F
1			100	50	C1+D1	
2						

Carlota could get a total of the expenses by using this formula in Cell B12:

=B5+B6+B7+B8+B9+B10

When you enter formulas, you tell spreadsheet programs to add, subtract, multiply, and divide by using these keys on your keyboard:

1. + for addition   Example: =C1+D1
2. – for subtraction   Example: =C1–D1
3. * for multiplication   Example: =C1*D1
4. / for division   Example: =C1/D1

Many spreadsheet programs let you enter formulas using special math functions, such as SUM, COUNT, and AVERAGE. These functions tell the spreadsheet program to perform the function on a range of cells. For example, to find the sum, or total, of the range of cells B5 through B10, Carlota might enter this formula into Cell B12:

=SUM(B5:B10)

The formula tells the spreadsheet to add the amounts found in the range of cells B5 through B10. This is a lot quicker and easier than entering =B5+B6+B7+B8+B9+B10.

Carlota moves the cell pointer to Cell B12 and enters a formula to find the total of the expenses. To save time, she uses the SUM function. After pressing the Enter key, the total, 4925.00, appears in the cell.

If Carlota wanted to count the number of expenses, she could move to Cell A13 and enter the words No. of Expenses. Then she could move to Cell B13 and enter this formula:

=COUNT(B5:B10)

Now the bottom of her spreadsheet would look like this:

9	Postage	100.00				
10	Other	450.00				
11						
12	Total	4925.00				
13	No. of Expenses	6				
14						
15						

If Carlota wanted to find the average of the expenses, she could move to Cell A14 and enter the words Average of Expenses. Then she could move to Cell B14 and enter this formula:

=AVERAGE(B5:B10)

Now the bottom of her spreadsheet would look like this:

9	Postage	100.00				
10	Other	450.00				
11						
12	Total	4925.00				
13	No. of Expenses	6				
14	Average of Expenses	820.83				
15						

Her spreadsheet now shows that the total expenses are $4,925.00, the number of expenses is 6, and the average expense is $820.83.

STEP 6 Save the spreadsheet.

Key Terms

Template. A spreadsheet that contains the headings, labels, and formulas that will not change.

Carlota saves her completed spreadsheet to her floppy diskette. Her spreadsheet software asked her to name the spreadsheet, and she named it Expenses. By saving her spreadsheet, she can use the same spreadsheet again to enter a new set of expense amounts. When she reuses the spreadsheet, she will not have to enter the heading or the names of the expenses. She will also not have to enter the formulas. When she enters the new expense amounts, the total and number of expenses will be recalculated automatically.

Many office workers create a spreadsheet **template** to use for repetitive tasks. A template is a spreadsheet that contains the headings, labels, and formulas that will not change. It does not contain those data that will change with each use. Carlota could create a template by deleting the expense amounts in the spreadsheet and leaving the headings, such as

Expenses, Type and Amount; labels, such as Wages, Rent, Total, etc.; and the formulas for finding the total and number of expenses. The next time she needs to create a list of expenses, all Carlota will have to do is to enter the expense amounts into the template.

The procedure that Carlota follows to save her spreadsheet will be similar but not exactly the same for different spreadsheet software. Your teacher will provide you with instructions that fit your computer and software.

STEP 7 Print the spreadsheet.

Carlota prints the finished spreadsheet for use in her office. She gives the printed spreadsheet to her supervisor.

The procedure that Carlota follows to print her spreadsheet will be similar but not exactly the same for different spreadsheet software. Your teacher will provide you with the instructions that fit your computer and software.

→ BUILDING YOUR BUSINESS VOCABULARY

On a sheet of paper, write the headings **Statement Number** and **Words.** Next, choose the words that match the statements. Write each word you choose next to the statement number it matches. Be careful; not all the words listed should be used.

Statements	Words
1. A set of programs that takes the place of paper pad and calculator	cell
	computer software
2. To activate a program on a computer system	cursor
3. On a spreadsheet, where a row and column meet	formula
4. A set of programs that perform related tasks	run
5. Math steps performed by a spreadsheet program	spreadsheet software
6. Contains the headings, labels, and formulas that will not change in a spreadsheet	template

STEPS REVIEW: Using Electronic Spreadsheets

STEP 1 Run the spreadsheet software.

STEP 2 Move the cell pointer to the cell wanted.

STEP 3 Enter alphabetic data.

STEP 4 Enter numeric data.

STEP 5 Enter formulas.

STEP 6 Save the spreadsheet.

STEP 7 Print the spreadsheet.

Problem 7-1

Kevin Andrews works in the office of the St. Louis Theater Guild. One of his tasks is to find the total donations received each day from members. The list for January 16 is shown below:

St. Louis Theater Guild
List of Donations
January 16, 2001

Name	Amount
R. Czernik	1500.00
A. Feldman	150.00
T. Smythe	230.00
S. Yakichi	325.00

CHECK POINT

7-1

Total, $2,205.00

Directions

a. Run your spreadsheet software.
b. Create a spreadsheet that contains the headings shown above in Cells A1, A2, and A3.
c. Enter the column headings Name and Amount in Cells A5 and B5.
d. Enter the names for each donor in Cells A7 through A10.
e. Enter the amounts given by each donor in Cells B7 through B10. Don't enter the dollar sign or enter commas for amounts of 1,000 or more.
f. Enter Total in Cell A12 and the formula for calculating the total donations in B12. Use the SUM function in your formula.
g. Save your spreadsheet on a floppy diskette. Name your spreadsheet Job7-1.
h. If your teacher instructs you to, print a copy of your spreadsheet.

Problem 7-2

It is now the next day and Kevin Andrews (see Problem 7-1) needs to find the total donations received on January 17, 2001, from members. The list for January 17 is shown below:

Name	Amount
B. Beliche	110.00
C. Diedic	450.00
Z. Reich	175.00
N. Watch	275.00

CHECK POINT

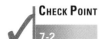

7-2

Total, $1,010.00

Directions

a. Run your spreadsheet software.
b. Start the spreadsheet that you created in Problem 7-1.
c. Change the date in Cell A3 to January 17, 2001.
d. Enter the names of the donors in cells A7 through A10 by placing the cell pointer in each cell and keying in the new donor names over the old names.
e. Enter the amounts given by each donor in Cells B7 through B10 by placing the cell pointer in each cell and keying in the new amounts over the old amounts.
f. Save your spreadsheet on a floppy diskette. Use the name Job7-2.
g. If your teacher instructs you to, print a copy of your spreadsheet.

Leslie Zimmer is an office worker at Vesco Insurance Company. One of her tasks is to find the total and number of payments received each day from customers. The list of payments received for October 6 is shown below:

Vesco Insurance Company
List of Customer Payments
October 6, 2003

Name	Amount
L. Benton	45.87
M. Drake	116.45
S. Euback	82.12
S. Franke	120.00
G. Gorsage	38.65

Directions
a. Run your spreadsheet software.
b. Create a spreadsheet that contains the headings shown above in Cells A1, A2, and A3.
c. Enter the column headings Name and Amount in Cells A5 and B5.
d. Enter the names for each customer in Cells A7 through A11.
e. Enter the amounts paid by each customer in Cells B7 through B11. Don't enter the dollar sign or enter commas for amounts of 1,000 or more.
f. Enter Total in Cell A13 and the formula for calculating the total amounts in Cell B13.
g. Enter No. of Payments in Cell A14 and the formula for counting the number of payments in Cell B14. The number of payments should be 5.
h. Save your spreadsheet on a floppy diskette. Use the name Job7-3.
i. If your teacher instructs you to, print a copy of your spreadsheet.

CHECK POINT

7-3

Total, $403.09

It is now the next day and Leslie (see Problem 7-3) needs to find the total payments received on October 7, 2003, from customers. The list for October 7 is shown below:

Name	Amount
A. Penn	21.17
F. Quaile	131.98
W. Roberts	52.81
B. Stein	66.35
F. Traechel	11.88

Directions
a. Run your spreadsheet software.
b. Start the spreadsheet that you created in Problem 7-3.
c. Change the date in Cell A3 to October 7, 2003.
d. Enter the names of the customers in cells A7 through A11 by placing the cell pointer in each cell and keying in the new names.
e. Enter the amounts paid by each customer in Cells B7 through B11 by placing the cell pointer in each cell and keying in the new amounts. The number of payments should be 5.
f. Save your spreadsheet on a floppy diskette. Use the name Job7-4.
g. If your teacher instructs you to, print a copy of your spreadsheet.

Problems 7-5 and 7-6 may be found in the Working Papers.

CHECK POINT

7-4

Total, $284.19

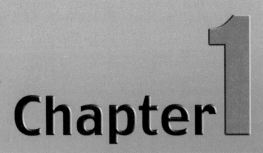

Chapter 1

CHECK YOUR READING

1. List five or more records that either you or your parents keep.
2. a. List five or more record keeping jobs in your community.
   b. List five or more skills required to obtain or keep a record keeping position.
   c. List five or more examples of source documents record keepers might handle or process.
3. List the three steps of the data processing cycle and provide an example for each step.

DISCUSSION

1. Entering data accurately into a manual or electronic data processing system is very important. What might happen if a clerk entered:
   a. A larger amount on a customer's bill than the customer owed?
   b. A smaller amount on a customer's bill than was owed and the salesperson was paid a commission on the amount of the sale?
2. Now that you have learned some of the jobs that record keepers do, think about what knowledge, skills, and attitudes you would look for in a record keeper if you were the one doing the hiring. List at least five of these. Then arrange them in their order of importance, with the most important being listed first.
3. You have begun to see how computers can save time in keeping records. Can you list other advantages of the computer to:
   a. The business owner?
   b. The record keeper?
   c. The customer?
4. What disadvantages might use of the computer have for:
   a. The business owner?
   b. The record keeper?
   c. The customer?

ETHICS IN THE WORKPLACE

Bill Workman has been a record keeper for Ellison Sales, Inc. for the last six months. Bill's job is to take customer orders over the phone and type them on a customer order form. He likes his work and his supervisor feels that he is very good at it.

The company is planning to install a computer system soon and wants Bill to use a computer to enter the customer orders. Bill has never used a computer before, and he is afraid to learn. In talking about his job with you, he is thinking of pretending to be sick so that he will miss the training sessions. Bill asks you what he should do. What might you tell him?

COMMUNICATION IN THE WORKPLACE

You were a beginning office worker for a manufacturing company for the last year. Your job was to enter data about customers into a computer system. You have now been promoted to the job of supervising other beginning office workers who do the same work.

One of your duties as supervisor is to teach new employees how to enter data into the computer system. This includes how to enter a date into a field like this: ☐☐ / ☐☐ / ☐☐☐☐. Write what you might say to a new worker to explain how to enter the date into this type of field. You should not use more than one page for your explanation.

FOCUS ON CAREERS

Record keepers who spend most of their time entering data into computer systems are called data entry clerks. There are many different types of data entry clerks. Most of these workers do not have the job title "Data Entry Clerk." Instead, the job titles they hold are usually related to the kind of data they enter.

For example, data entry clerks who enter sales orders are usually called *order clerks*. Some other examples are:

Entry-level jobs. Jobs in which first-time workers are placed.

Job Title	Type of Data Entered
Timekeeper	The hours employees work
Stock clerk	The merchandise bought for resale to customers
Premium clerk	The amounts people pay for insurance
Cashier	The goods bought by people and how much they paid for them

Young people who get their first jobs are often placed in data entry clerk positions. Jobs in which first-time workers are placed are called **entry-level jobs**.

Below is an advertisement for an order clerk position found in the Help Wanted section of a newspaper.

Order Clerk

Take customer orders over the phone. Computer keyboard skills. Ability to deal with people. Good math skills. High school diploma required. Call 555-3208, 8-12 and 1-5.

Answer these questions about the order clerk position:
1. What is the job title of the position?
2. What are three skills the position requires?
3. What education does the position require?
4. How do you apply for the position?

 REVIEWING WHAT YOU HAVE LEARNED

On a sheet of paper, write the headings **Statement Number** and **Words.** Next, choose the words that best complete the statements. Write each word you choose next to the statement number it completes. Be careful; not all the words listed should be used.

Statements	Words
1. Nearly everyone must keep some ____.	alphabetically
2. A worker who spends most of the time filing documents is called (a,an) ____.	cell
	central processing unit
3. In an electronic filing system, a group of files is called (a,an) ____.	chronologically
	computer software
4. A group of records is called (a,an) ____.	database
5. When you sort documents by the names of the persons on the documents, you are sorting the documents ____.	file
	menu
	numerically
6. A computer system is made up of input devices, (a,an) ____, and output devices.	printout
	program
7. A list of program choices on a display screen is called (a,an) ____.	records
	records clerk
8. A document prepared by a computer printer is called (a,an) ____.	terminal
9. A computer needs (a,an) ____ to process data.	
10. When you sort documents by the dates on the documents, you are sorting ____.	
11. A set of programs that perform related tasks is called ____.	
12. On a spreadsheet where a row and column meet is called (a, an) ____.	

 MASTERY PROBLEM

Torres Publications publishes and sells a magazine for do-it-yourself homeowners. Torres has not yet computerized its subscription system. You are a records clerk for the firm. Part of your job is to create cards for customers who subscribe to the magazine. The cards contain the customer's account number, name, and the date on which the magazine subscription runs out.

CHECK POINT

✓

(b)
There are 3 errors.

Directions

a. Make a checklist with these headings: No., Correct, Error. Write the numbers 1-10 under the No. heading.

b. Compare the handwritten customer data with the cards on the right. If both the handwritten data and cards are the same, put a check mark in the Correct column of your checklist. If they are not exactly the same, put a check mark in the Error column.

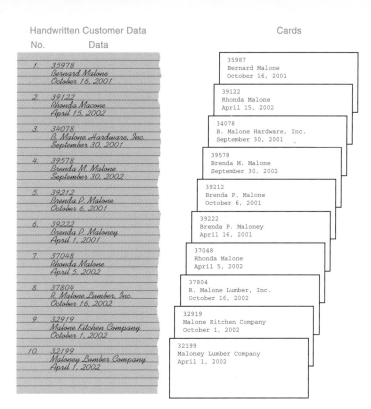

Handwritten Customer Data

No.	Data
1.	35978 Bernard Malone October 16, 2001
2.	39122 Rhonda Macone April 15, 2002
3.	34078 B. Malone Hardware, Inc. September 30, 2001
4.	39578 Brenda M. Malone September 30, 2002
5.	39212 Brenda P. Malone October 6, 2001
6.	39222 Brenda P. Maloney April 1, 2001
7.	37048 Rhonda Malone April 5, 2002
8.	37804 R. Malone Lumber, Inc. October 16, 2002
9.	32919 Malone Kitchen Company October 1, 2002
10.	32199 Maloney Lumber Company April 1, 2002

Cards

The company keeps three copies of every customer card. One copy is filed in numerical order using the customer account number. A second copy is filed in chronological order using the date the subscription ends. A third copy is filed in alphabetical order by customer name.

c. Using the handwritten customer data, print the data on blank cards so that the cards are filed in numerical order. The top card should be the customer with the lowest account number. The first line of each card should contain the account number; the second line, the customer name; the third line, the date.

d. Using the handwritten customer data, print the data on blank cards so that the cards are filed in chronological order. The top card should be the customer with the earliest cancellation date. The first line of each card should contain the date; the second line, the account number; and the third line, the customer name.

e. Using the handwritten customer data, print the customer names in indexing order.

f. Print the data about the customers on blank cards so that they are filed in alphabetical order. The first line should contain the customer name in *indexing* order; the second line, the account number; and the third line, the date.

CHECK POINT

(c)
Account number 39578 is last.

(d)
October 16, 2002, is the last date.

(f)
Maloney Lumber Company is the last customer.

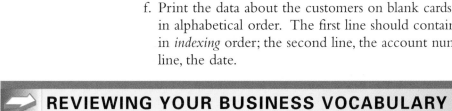

REVIEWING YOUR BUSINESS VOCABULARY

This activity may be found in the Working Papers.

Chapter 2

Budget Records

You may get an allowance each week. If you are careful and plan your spending, you will have enough money for the things you *need*. If you are not careful, you may spend too much money on things you *want*. That is why you need to learn how to complete a budget. A budget is a plan for spending your money. Many families use budgets to make sure that there is enough money on hand to pay the bills. Businesses also keep budgets for the same reason.

In Chapter 2, you will learn how to make budgets and to record receipts and payments. Budgets for an individual, for a family, and for a business will be covered. You will also learn how to use a calculator to save time and improve accuracy when you add up budget totals.

Voice Recognition Systems

In Chapter 1 you learned a few of the many ways in which data can be entered into a computer system. One additional way is *voice recognition*. Voice recognition systems let you speak to a computer and have it "understand" what you said. You may speak a command, such as "print" or "save document." You may also say data, such as the stock number of an item bought or a sentence in a document.

Voice recognition systems use microphones for input and special software to convert what is spoken so that the computer system can use it. Usually you must spend time talking to the system until it learns how you pronounce each word, command, or other data. In fact, if you get a bad cold, you may find that the system no longer understands you. Some systems make you pause between each word. Others let you speak normally, running your words together.

Today, voice recognition systems are at work in factories, offices, and even homes. For example, you can tell some telephones to "Dial 555-1397" or simply "Call Tim." Voice recognition systems let:

- Some office workers create documents faster than they might with a keyboard.

- Employees work with their hands while they enter data. For example, a sales worker can enter data into a sales slip while wrapping the customer's package.

- You call your bank to check your balance by saying simply, "I want to check the balance in my savings account."

- You access your e-mail while away from your office or home. You simply dial the system and tell it to read your e-mail. You can also compose and send replies to your e-mail over the phone.

- Physically handicapped workers hold jobs that require entering data into computers.

Tips

The total you get when you add down the numbers in the last column at the far right should be the same as the total you get when you add across the totals of the first four columns.

applied math preview

Copy and complete the problem below. Check your work by crossfooting.

1. $ 2.60 + $30.25 + $130.04 + $386.31 =
2. 12.30 + 58.71 + 308.19 + 64.10 =
3. 0.56 + 5.09 + 8.98 + 370.20 =
4. 8.34 + 27.18 + 877.78 + 801.33 =
5.

key terms preview

- **Budget**
- **Crossfooting**
- **Estimating**
- **Extend an amount**
- **Payments**
- **Receipts**

goals

1 To learn why you should keep a budget.

2 To learn how to keep a record of receipts and payments.

UNDERSTANDING THE JOB

Estimating. Making a careful guess.

Budget. A plan for receiving and spending money.

Receipts. Amounts received.

Payments. Amounts spent.

When you budget, you plan how to make your weekly allowance cover your weekly expenses. This means **estimating** how much money you will receive and how much you will spend. It also means deciding what you really need and making sure that your plan provides money for those needs. Money that is left over can be saved or spent on things that you want.

When people plan in advance how much money they will receive and how they will spend their money, they are making a **budget**. When people budget their income, they must keep careful records of their **receipts** (the amounts they receive) and **payments** (the amounts they spend). This way they can compare the amounts they spent with the amounts they planned to spend. They do this to see if they are really *living within their budget* and to see if their estimates were reasonable.

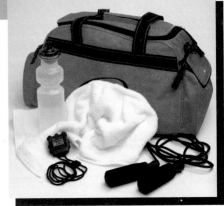

SAMPLE PROBLEM

Ramon Martinez, a high school student, gets an allowance each week. Ramon also earns money by working as a sales clerk at Sports Max. The money he receives must cover all his expenses except clothing. Ramon decides to budget his total receipts so that he does not overspend his money on his wants and then not have enough money left for his needs. Here is how he does it:

STEP 1 *Estimate receipts.*

Ramon knows that he will get an allowance of $15.00 a week from his parents. He also estimates that he can earn about $40.00 a week by working at Sports Max on Saturdays. Ramon feels that he can count on receipts of $55.00 a week.

Weekly allowance	$ 15.00
Estimated income from working	+ 40.00
Total estimated receipts for week	$ 55.00

STEP 2 *Estimate payments.*

Ramon lists the payments that he expects to make during the week. His list looks like this:

Lunches	$ 8.50
School supplies	7.50
Entertainment	14.00
College Savings Account	25.00
Total estimated payments	$55.00

STEP 3 *Record the headings.*

Ramon decides to keep a detailed record of his actual receipts and payments in a form like the one shown in Illustration 8A, below. Ramon used the top of the form for a heading containing:

WHO: Ramon Martinez
WHAT: Record of Receipts and Payments
WHEN: Week of September 4, 20--

Illustration 8A

Record of receipts and payments

STEP 1 Estimate receipts.
STEP 2 Estimate payments.
STEP 5   STEP 3   STEP 6   STEP 4

Ramon Martinez
Record of Receipts and Payments
Week of September 4, 20--

DATE		EXPLANATION (ESTIMATED)	TOTAL RECEIPTS ($55.00)	TOTAL PAYMENTS ($55.00)	TYPE OF PAYMENT			
					LUNCHES ($8.50)	SCHOOL SUPPLIES ($7.50)	ENTER-TAINMENT ($14.00)	COLLEGE SAVINGS ($25.00)
20--Sept.	4	Weekly allowance	15 00					
	5			1 75	1 75			
	6			3 75	1 75		2 00	
	7			7 25	1 75	5 50		
	7			6 00			6 00	
	8			6 25	1 75	4 50		
	9			1 75	1 75			
	10	Sports Max	40 00					
	10			20 00				20 00
	10			6 00	2 00		4 00	
	10	Totals for week	55 00 / 55 00	52 75 / 52 75	10 75 / 10 75	10 00 / 10 00	12 00 / 12 00	20 00 / 20 00
	11	Balance	2 25					

STEP 10   STEP 8   STEP 7   STEP 9

Notice that Ramon used separate columns for each type of estimated payment. At the end of the week, Ramon will be able to look at the total of each payment column to find out how much money he spent on each type of payment.

STEP 4 *Record the estimated budget amounts.*

To help him remember the amounts that he had estimated for receipts and payments, Ramon wrote them in parentheses under the column headings. For example, the $55.00 under the heading Total Receipts means that Ramon hopes to have $55.00 to spend for the week. If he receives less than $55.00, he will have to reduce his spending to *live within his budget*.

Ramon wrote $55.00 under the Total Payments heading because he plans to spend $55.00 during the week. If you add all the amounts under each of the headings in the Type of Payment columns, the total will be $55.00. This amount equals the $55.00 in the Total Payments column.

STEP 5 *Record each receipt.*

Ramon had these actual receipts and payments during the week beginning Monday, September 4, 20--:

Sept. 4 Received an allowance of $15.00 for the week.
       5 Paid $1.75 for lunch.
       6 Paid $1.75 for lunch and $2.00 for a ticket to a high school football game.
       7 Paid $1.75 for lunch and $5.50 for school supplies.
       7 Paid $6.00 for a ticket to a high school musical comedy.
       8 Paid $1.75 for lunch and $4.50 for school supplies.
       9 Paid $1.75 for lunch.
      10 Received $40.00 from Sports Max.
      10 Put $20.00 in his college savings account.
      10 Paid $2.00 for lunch and $4.00 for a movie.

Ramon entered these receipts and payments in the record shown in Illustration 8A.

The first money that Ramon received during the week was a $15.00 allowance from his parents. To record that amount, Ramon entered the date in the Date column. He recorded the year and the month at the beginning of the record. He will not enter the year and month again unless they change.

Ramon then wrote the words "Weekly allowance" in the Explanation column and entered the amount of money he received in the Total Receipts column. He followed the same steps on September 10 when he received money for working at Sports Max.

STEP 6 *Record each payment.*

Ramon recorded the payment he made on September 5 on the second line of the record. He entered the date, 5, in the Date column. He did not enter the year or month since they had not changed.

Since he spent only $1.75 on that day, he wrote $1.75 in the Total Payments column. Ramon also entered $1.75 again, or **extended** the payment for lunch into the Lunches column. Notice that every payment is recorded twice: once in the Total Payments column and once more in a

Type of Payment column. Ramon wrote nothing in the Explanation column since the heading of the Type of Payment column showed how the money was spent.

Often, Ramon makes several payments in one day. For example, on September 6, he spent $1.75 for a school lunch and $2.00 for a ticket to a football game. He recorded both payments on one line. He recorded the total amount he spent, $3.75, in the Total Payments column. He extended $1.75 into the Lunches column and $2.00 into the Entertainment column. Ramon wrote nothing in the Explanation column for September 6 since the column headings showed how the money was spent.

Ramon followed the same procedures for the other payments he made during the week. *Notice that the amount Ramon enters in the Total Payments column must equal the sum of all the payments he extends into the Type of Payment columns.* ($52.75 = $10.75 + $10.00 + $12.00 + $20.00)

STEP 7 *Total and foot each money column.*

At the end of the week, Ramon ruled a single line across the money columns to show that he was ready to total them. Then Ramon totaled each money column and wrote each total in small figures directly below the line.

STEP 8 *Verify the totals.*

Crossfooting. Adding across.

Ramon verified the column totals by **crossfooting**. The total of all amounts extended into the Type of Payment columns should have been recorded in the Total Payments column. Thus, the total of all the Type of Payment columns should be the same as the total of the Total Payments column:

Lunches	$10.75
School supplies	10.00
Entertainment	12.00
College savings	20.00
Total of Type of Payment columns	$52.75
Total of Total Payments column	$52.75

Sometimes people make errors when they record numbers or add them. You need to know how to find errors when they are made. Let's suppose that Ramon did not get $52.75 when he added the Type of Payment columns totals. What would he do to find the error or errors?

Ramon would first verify the addition in every column by re-adding them. If he had added down the first time, he would add the columns up to verify them.

If Ramon still did not find the error, he would verify that he had copied the amounts correctly to the Type of Payment columns. For example, he might have transposed numbers when he copied the amount spent on lunch on September 5. He might have entered $1.57 instead of $1.75 in the Lunches column.

Next, he would verify that he had added the amounts extended into the Type of Payment columns correctly and had written the correct total in the Total Payments column. For example, he might have added the amounts spent for a lunch ($1.75) and a football ticket ($2.00) incorrectly and entered that wrong total into the Total Payments column.

STEP 9 *Complete the record.*

After verifying the totals, Ramon entered them below the footings. To show that the math was done, Ramon ruled a double line across all the money columns.

STEP 10 *Record the balance of cash on hand.*

Ramon recorded the balance of money that he had left at the end of the week. To find out how much he had left, he subtracted the total payments ($52.75) from the total receipts ($55.00):

Total receipts	$ 55.00
Total payments	−52.75
Balance of cash	$ 2.25

He then entered the next date, 11, in the Date column, wrote "Balance" in the Explanation column, and put $1.25 in the Total Receipts column. Now Ramon is ready to record the receipts and payments for the next week.

Ramon compared his actual and estimated receipts and payments by using the totals of the Type of Payment columns. This is how they compared:

	Estimated	Actual
Total receipts	$55.00	$55.00
Payments:		
Lunches	$ 8.50	$10.75
School supplies	7.50	10.00
Entertainment	14.00	12.00
Savings	25.00	20.00
Totals	$55.00	$52.75

Ramon can now decide whether he is living within his budget. He can also decide whether he has to change any of the estimated budget amounts.

Each week Ramon puts money into a *savings account* at his bank. The bank pays him interest on the money he has in the savings account. He uses the savings account to set aside money for a college education and to help pay for unexpected expenses. By saving some of his earnings, Ramon will have money for the things he wants, as well as for the things he needs.

⇨ BUILDING YOUR BUSINESS VOCABULARY

On a sheet of paper, write the headings **Statement Number** and **Words**. Next, choose the words that match the statements. Write each word you choose next to the statement number it matches. Be careful; not all the words listed should be used.

Statements	Words
1. To check for accuracy	budget
2. The total of a money column written in small figures	crossfooting
	cursor
3. Making a careful guess	double ruling
4. A plan for receiving and spending money	estimating

Statements	Words
5. A column on a form used for recording amounts of money	extend an amount
	footing
6. A flashing marker on a display screen	money column
7. Amounts spent	payments
8. Adding across	receipts
9. To record an amount again in a second column	retrieve
	verify
10. A double line drawn under a total to show that the math on a form is done	

STEPS REVIEW: Keeping a Personal Budget

STEP 1 Estimate receipts.

STEP 2 Estimate payments.

STEP 3 Record the headings.

STEP 4 Record the estimate budget amounts.

STEP 5 Record each receipt.

STEP 6 Record each payment.

STEP 7 Total and foot each money column.

STEP 8 Verify the totals.

STEP 9 Complete the record.

STEP 10 Record the balance of cash on hand.

APPLICATION PROBLEMS

Problem 8-1   Stacey Patera is a high school student. She also works part-time at a music store and is saving money for a used car. Her estimated receipts and payments for the week of May 12, 20-- are:

Estimated Receipts		Estimated Payments	
From allowance	$20.00	Lunches	$10.00
From part-time job	48.00	School supplies	4.50
		Entertainment	17.50
		Savings	36.00
Total estimated receipts	$68.00	Total estimated payments	$68.00

Directions

a. Prepare a record of receipts and payments for Stacey like the one shown in Illustration 8A (page 61).

b. Enter the heading on the top three lines.

c. Record the estimated budget amounts under the column headings.

d. Record the actual receipts and payments shown on page 66:

May 12 Received an allowance of $20.00 for the week.
　　13 Paid $2.10 for lunch.
　　14 Paid $2.10 for lunch and $3.00 for notebook paper.
　　14 Received $50.00 in pay from part-time job.
　　15 Paid $2.10 for lunch and $8.50 for an compact disk.
　　16 Paid $2.10 for lunch and $.75 for a pen.
　　17 Paid $2.10 for lunch and put $42.50 in a savings account.
　　18 Paid $2.50 for a matinee movie.

CHECK POINT

8-1

Total Payments = $67.75

e. Rule and foot the money columns.
f. Verify the totals by crossfooting.
g. Write the totals below the footings and double rule the money columns.
h. Find the balance of cash on hand by subtracting the total of the Total Payments column from the total of the Total Receipts column.
i. Record the balance of cash on hand on the line below the double ruling. Use May 19 as the date and write "Balance" in the Explanation column.
j. Answer these questions:
　　1. What amount was spent for entertainment?
　　2. How much was spent for lunches?
　　3. On which item(s) did Stacey spend more than she had planned?
　　4. Did Stacey put more or less savings in the bank than planned?
　　5. Did Stacey receive more or less income than she had planned?

Problem　8-2

Rachel Raffio lives at home with her parents and commutes to Adams Dental College. To help pay for her education, Rachel works part-time at a restaurant. Her estimated receipts and payments for the week of October 20, 20-- are:

Estimated Receipts		Estimated Payments	
From allowance	$ 50.00	Auto expenses	$ 40.00
From part-time job	100.00	Lunches	15.50
		Books and supplies	33.25
		Entertainment	25.00
		Piano lessons	10.75
		Savings	25.50
Total estimated receipts	$150.00	Total estimated payments	$150.00

Directions

a. Prepare a record of receipts and payments with the following column headings:

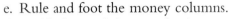

				TYPE OF PAYMENT					
DATE	EXPLANATION (ESTIMATED)	TOTAL RECEIPTS ( )	TOTAL PAYMENTS ( )	AUTO EXPENSES ( )	LUNCHES ( )	BOOKS AND SUPPLIES ( )	ENTER-TAINMENT ( )	PIANO LESSONS ( )	SAVINGS ( )

b. Enter the heading on the top three lines.
c. Record the estimated budget amounts under the column headings.
d. Record the actual receipts and payments:

Oct.	20	Received an allowance of $50.00 for the week.
	21	Paid $4.00 for lunch and $20.00 for a book.
	22	Paid $4.75 for lunch and $8.50 for a notebook and paper.
	22	Received $105.00 in pay from part-time job.
	23	Paid $3.25 for lunch and $15.00 for gasoline.
	24	Paid $3.80 for lunch.
	25	Paid $3.50 for lunch, $10.75 for piano lessons, and put $50.00 in savings account.
	26	Paid $10.00 for a football ticket and $10.00 for a parking sticker.

e. Rule and foot the money columns.

f. Verify the totals by crossfooting.

g. Write the totals below the footings and double rule the money columns.

h. Find the balance of cash on hand by subtracting the total of the Total Payments column from the total of the Total Receipts column.

i. Record the balance of cash on hand on the line below the double ruling. Use October 27 as the date and write "Balance" in the Explanation column.

j. Answer these questions:
1. What amount was spent for auto expenses?
2. How much was spent for books and supplies?
3. On which items did Rachel spend less than planned?
4. Did Rachel put more or less savings in the bank than planned?
5. Did Rachel receive more or less income than planned?

Problems 8–3 and 8–4 may be found in the Working Papers.

CHECK POINT

8-2(h)

Balance = $11.45

Check your work by crossfooting. The answer you get when you add the last column on the right should be the same as the answer you get when you add the bottom row of totals.

applied math preview

Copy and complete the problem below.

1. $142.00 + $116.02 + $120.58 + $138.05 =
2.   10.88 +   40.70 +   91.47 + 110.64 =
3.   7.56 + 310.10 + 275.20 + 614.87 =
4. 259.10 +   50.81 + 582.08 +   7.34 =
5.

key terms preview

- Classified
- Personal computer
- Scrolling
- Spreadsheet

goal

To learn how to keep budget records for a family.

→ UNDERSTANDING THE JOB

Classified. Grouped together.

Personal computer Microcomputer.

Keeping a record of receipts and payments for a family is a lot like keeping one for a person. However, the headings used in the Type of Payment columns may be different. A family record of receipts and payments will usually have Type of Payment headings such as household expenses, clothing, savings, health and personal expenses, education, entertainment, transportation, and gifts.

The types of payments usually **classified**, or grouped together, under these headings are shown on page 69.

Many families keep records to help them live within their budgets. Some families keep these records manually. Others use a microcomputer, or **personal computer**. In this job, you will learn about keeping family budgets in both ways.

→ SAMPLE PROBLEM

In addition to preparing a monthly budget, some families also prepare a yearly budget.

Elisa and Nathan Gruden are married and have one child. Elisa manages a clothing store and receives $3,100.00 in pay each month. Nathan Gruden is a supervisor at a computer manufacturing plant and receives $700.00 in pay a week. They have decided to keep a budget to see if they can spend their money more wisely.

Household Expenses:	**Education:**
Energy (electricity, gas)	School lunches
Furniture and appliances	School supplies
Groceries	Textbooks
Home repair and maintenance	Tuition and fees for college
Homeowner's insurance	
Kitchen utensils (dishes, pots, pans)	**Clothing:**
Property taxes	Clothes for all family members
Rent or mortgage payments	Clothing repairs and dry cleaning
Telephone service	
Utilities (water, sewer)	**Transportation:**
	Car and bus fare
Gifts:	Car insurance
	Car payments
Contributions	Car repairs, cleaning
Personal gifts	Oil and gasoline
Health and Personal:	**Entertainment:**
	Audio and video tapes, disks
Beauty salon and barber shop expenses	Computer games
Doctor and dentist bills	Dining out
Glasses, contact lenses	Hobbies
Health and accident insurance	Magazines, newspapers
Hospital expenses	Movies
Medicines	Vacation trips
	Savings:
	Stocks and bonds
	Savings accounts

Here are the steps they follow to keep their budget:

STEP 1 *Prepare an estimate of receipts and payments.*

Based on past experience, Elisa and Nathan estimated how their income would be spent. A budget that they felt they could live within for the month of September is shown in Illustration 9A.

Elisa and Nathan know that some payments, like household expenses, will be almost the same each month. Other payments, like entertainment, will change from month to month. Successful budgeting means looking ahead and planning for these varying payments.

Illustration 9A

Elisa's and Nathan's budget for September

Budget for September

Estimated Receipts		Estimated Payments	
Elisa Gruden, wages	$3,100.00	Household expenses	$3,200.00
Nathan Gruden, wages ($700 x 4)	2,800.00	Clothing	290.00
		Transportation	640.00
		Health and personal	210.00
		Entertainment	425.00
		Education	375.00
		Gifts	235.00
		Savings	525.00
Total estimated receipts	$5,900.00	Total estimated payments	$5,900.00

After the budget was prepared, Elisa and Nathan recorded their receipts and payments so they could compare their estimated and actual figures. To record the amounts, they used a Record of Receipts and Payments form.

Elisa and Nathan had to decide how they would record their receipts and payments. They could have recorded them each day, once each week, or once a month. They decided to:

1. Record all receipts on the day they are received.
2. Record all payments once each week on Saturday.
3. If the last day of a month isn't a Saturday, record payments made after Saturday at the end of the month.
4. Total and balance the record on the last day of the month.

Here are the receipts and payments made by Elisa and Nathan during the month of September, beginning with September 1, 20--:

Sept.
1 There was a balance of $440.70 left from last month.
2 Elisa received her monthly paycheck for $3,100.00.
3 Nathan received his weekly paycheck for $700.00.
6 The payments made since August 31 were:

Groceries	$ 161.00
Mortgage payment	1,549.41
Gas, electric	297.26
Sweaters, skirts	133.77
Gasoline for cars	51.00
Cough drops, cold medicine	12.67
Two video tapes	14.00
School lunches	10.00
Deposit in savings account	80.00

10 Nathan received his weekly paycheck for $700.00.
13 The payments made since last week were:

Groceries	$185.54
Blue jeans, shirts	84.58
Gasoline for cars	32.00
Beauty salon	25.00
Visit to doctor	25.00
Newspapers, magazines	35.00
Computer games	40.66
School lunches	10.00
School supplies	11.17
Contribution	40.00
Gift for Grandma	25.00
Deposit in savings account	90.00

17 Nathan received his weekly paycheck for $700.00.
20 The payments made since last week were:

Groceries	$126.48
Telephone, insurance bills	188.29
Work shoes, dress shoes	124.98
Gasoline for cars, car repair	107.92
Medicine, visit to doctor	29.00
Dinner out for family	55.00
School lunches, paper supplies	15.88
Gifts for mother's birthday	45.19
Deposit in savings account	70.00

24 Nathan received his weekly paycheck for $700.00.

27 The payments made since last week were:

Groceries	$167.08
New living room table	142.44
Jogging outfit, shoes	182.89
Gasoline for cars	33.90
Barber shop, beauty salon	48.00
Baseball game for family	34.00
School lunches	10.00
Contribution	25.00
Deposit in savings account	85.00

30 The payments made since the 27th were:

Groceries	$ 34.90
Gutter repairs on house	288.54
Gasoline for cars	26.50
Newspapers	7.80
School lunches	6.00

Illustration 9B

Completed record of receipts and payments

The completed record is shown in Illustration 9B:

STEP 1 Estimate receipts and payments.

STEP 2

Elisa and Nathan Gruden
Record of Receipts and Payments
For September, 20--

DATE		EXPLANATION (ESTIMATED)	TOTAL RECEIPTS ($5,900.00)		TOTAL PAYMENTS ($5,900.00)		HOUSE-HOLD EXPENSES ($3,200.00)		CLOTHING ($290.00)		TRANS-PORTATION ($840.00)		HEALTH & PERSONAL ($210.00)		ENTER-TAINMENT ($425.00)		EDUCA-TION ($375.00)		GIFTS ($235.00)		SAVINGS ($525.00)	
20--Sept.	1	Balance	440	70																		
	2	Elisa's pay	3100	00																		
	3	Nathan's pay	700	00																		
	6	Since 8/31			2309	11	2007	67	133	77	51	00	12	67	14	00	10	00			80	00
	10	Nathan's pay	700	00																		
	13	Since 9/6			603	95	185	54	84	58	32	00	50	00	75	66	21	17	65	00	90	00
	17	Nathan's pay	700	00																		
	20	Since 9/13			762	74	314	77	124	98	107	92	29	00	55	00	15	88	45	19	70	00
	24	Nathan's pay	700	00																		
	27	Since 9/20			728	31	309	52	182	89	33	90	48	00	34	00	10	00	25	00	85	00
	30	Since 9/27			363	74	323	44			26	50			7	80	6	00				
	30	Totals	6340	70	4767	85	3140	94	526	22	251	32	139	67	186	46	63	05	135	19	325	00
			6340	70	4767	85	3140	94	526	22	251	32	139	67	186	46	63	05	135	19	325	00
Oct.	1	Balance	1572	85																		

STEP 3 Compare estimates with actual figures.

Let's look at the Record of Receipts and Payments shown in Illustration 9B so that you can keep one like it. Take a close look at:

1. **The heading.** Notice that the heading on the top three lines answers the questions: Who? What? When?
2. **The beginning balance.** Notice that Elisa and Nathan entered a balance of $440.70 in the Total Receipts column on September 1. This amount is the difference between the total receipts and total payments for the month of August. Since Elisa and Nathan did not spend the money in August, it is available to spend in September.
3. **How receipts are entered.** Notice that Elisa and Nathan entered a

Tips

Enter receipts on separate lines.

receipt every time they received money. For example, Elisa received her monthly paycheck for $3,100.00 on September 2. Nathan received four weekly paychecks of $700.00 each. Each was recorded on the day it was received.

4. **The Total Payments column.** Notice that each amount in the Total Payments column is equal to all of the amounts in the Type of Payment columns on the same line. For example, the amount, $2,309.11, shown in the Total Payments column for September 6 was found by adding these amounts:

Groceries	$ 161.00
Mortgage payment	1,549.41
Gas, electric	297.26
Sweaters, skirts	133.77
Gasoline for cars	51.00
Cough drops, cold medicine	12.67
Two video tapes	14.00
School lunches	10.00
Deposit in savings account	80.00
Total payments for week	$2,309.11

5. **How the amounts were classified and entered.** Each payment for a week was classified and entered in the proper column. When two or more amounts were classified as the same type, only the total was entered. For example, the amounts spent for groceries, mortgage payment, and gas and electric were grouped together as household expenses. These amounts were then added and entered into the Household Expenses column.

Groceries	$ 161.00
Mortgage payment	1,549.41
Gas, electric	297.26
Household expenses	$2,007.67

Tips

Before entering any amount in a type of payment column, group together and add all payments for that payment type.

6. **The rulings and totals.** On the last day of the month, the Grudens:

    a. Totaled each money column.
    b. Footed each money column.
    c. Verified the totals by crossfooting.
    d. Wrote the totals below the footings.
    e. Double ruled the money columns.
    f. Entered the balance for the next month.

7. **The ending balance.** The balance on October 1 ($1,572.85) was found by subtracting the total monthly payments from the total monthly receipts.

STEP 3 *Compare the budget estimates with the actual figures.*

At the end of each month, Elisa and Nathan compare their actual receipts and payments with their budget estimates. This helps them to decide if they need to adjust their spending or their budget estimates.

Calculator Tips

Adding and crossfooting the totals in a record of receipts and payments takes time. Many record keepers use calculators to make this task easier.

You probably have used calculators before and can add a column of numbers using a calculator. If you can, you know that a calculator helps you add faster and more accurately. But did you know that you could use a calculator to find the totals of the Type of Payment columns and crossfoot those totals at the same time? If your calculator has *memory keys*, you can do this.

Many calculators have memory keys. Some have three memory keys and others have four:

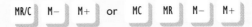

Here is how you can use the memory keys to crossfoot the Type of Payment totals.

STEP 1 ▶ Add the first Type of Payment column.

Add the first Type of Payment column in Illustration 9B (page 71), Household Expenses, by pressing these keys in order:

a. 2 0 0 7 . 6 7 +

b. 1 8 5 . 5 4 +

c. 3 1 4 . 7 7 +

d. 3 0 9 . 5 2 +

e. 3 2 3 . 4 4 +

The total, 3140.94, will appear in the calculator's window or display.

STEP 2 ▶ Add the total to the calculator's memory.

Press the M+ key. This adds the column total, 3140.94, to the calculator's memory.

STEP 3 ▶ Add the other column totals to memory.

Now add each of the other Type of Payment columns. When you get each column total, press the M+ key. This adds each column total to memory.

STEP 4 ▶ Display the total of memory.

When you have added every column total to memory, press the MR (memory recall) key or the MR/C (memory recall/clear) key once. When you do, your calculator display will show 4767.85. This is the total of all the Type of Payment columns. This amount should be the same as the total of the Total Payments column.

STEP 5 ▶ Clear memory.

To clear the calculator's memory, press the MC (memory clear) key. If your calculator has an MR/C key, press that key twice. When you press the MR/C key once, the display shows the contents of memory. When you press the MR/C key twice, you clear, or erase, the amount in memory.

Key Terms

Spreadsheet. A computer program which lets you create and enter data into forms.

Scrolling. Moving a record around on a computer screen.

Many people, families, and businesses keep budgets on computers using a computer program called a **spreadsheet**. A spreadsheet program lets you create forms like budgets and enter information into the rows and columns of the forms. If Elisa and Nathan used a spreadsheet to keep their budget, their Record of Receipts and Payments might look like the computer screen in Illustration 9C below.

The entire record does not show up on the screen since the record is too big. Elisa and Nathan would move the record shown on the screen from left to right and up and down to display the part of the record they want. Moving a record on the computer this way is called **scrolling**.

The nice part of using the spreadsheet program is that Elisa and Nathan only have to enter the amounts they receive or spend. All the math is done for them by the program. The totals for each column are added by the computer program and shown on the screen automatically.

Illustration 9C

A record of receipts and payments on a personal computer

	A	B	C	D	E	F
1:	Elisa and Nathan Gruden					
2:	Record of Receipts and Payments					
3:	For September, 20--					
4:						
5:			Total	Total	Household	
6:	Date	Explanation	Receipts	Payments	Expenses	Clothing
7:		(Estimated)	(5900.00)	(5900.00)	(3200.00)	(290.00)
8:	Sept. 1	Balance	440.70			
9:	2	Elisa's pay	3100.00			
10:	3	Nathan's pay	700.00			
11:	6	Since 8/31		2309.11	2007.67	133.77
12:	10	Nathan's pay	700.00			
13:	13	Since 9/6		603.95	185.54	84.58
14:	17	Nathan's pay	700.00			
15:	20	Since 9/13		762.74	314.77	124.98
16:	24	Nathan's pay	700.00			
17:	27	Since 9/20		728.31	309.52	182.89
18:	30	Since 9/27		363.74	323.44	
19:		Totals	6340.70	4767.85	3140.94	526.22
20:	Oct. 1	Balance	1572.85			

BUILDING YOUR BUSINESS VOCABULARY

On a sheet of paper, write the headings **Statement Number** and **Words.** Next, choose the words that match the statements. Write each word you choose next to the statement number it matches. Be careful; not all the words listed should be used.

Statements	Words
1. Making a careful guess	budget
2. When items which are alike are grouped together	classified
3. Amounts of money received	crossfooting
4. The total of a column of numbers written in small figures	estimating
5. To record an amount again in a second column	extend an amount
6. Adding a row of figures across a business form	field
7. A careful plan, made in advance, of cash receipts and cash payments	footing
8. To check	money columns
9. Columns on a form used to record amounts of money	personal computer
10. A microcomputer	printout
11. A computer program which lets you create and enter data into forms	receipts
12. Moving a record around on a computer screen	scrolling
	spreadsheet
	verify

STEPS REVIEW: Keeping a Family Budget

STEP 1	Prepare an estimate of receipts and payments.
STEP 2	Record receipts and payments.
STEP 3	Compare the budget estimates with the actual figures.

➡ APPLICATION PROBLEMS

Problem 9-1 Robert and Carla Reed have agreed to keep a record of receipts and payments like the one in Illustration 9B (page 71). Robert Reed is attending college and Carla Reed manages a local swim and racquet club.

Directions

a. Prepare a record of receipts and payments. Use a ruled sheet of paper with ten money columns.

b. Use as the heading for your record:

Robert and Carla Reed
Record of Receipts and Payments
For June, 20--

c. Enter the column headings and estimated totals below using Illustration 9B (page 71) as a guide.

1. Date
2. Explanation
3. Total Receipts ($4,400.00)
4. Total Payments ($4,400.00)
5. Household expenses ($1,600.00)
6. Clothing ($400.00)
7. Transportation ($650.00)
8. Health/personal ($350.00)
9. Entertainment ($320.00)
10. Education ($250.00)
11. Gifts ($90.00)
12. Savings ($740.00)

d. Record the following receipts and payments for June, 20--:

June	1 Balance of cash, $128.56.	
	4 Carla Reed received her paycheck for $1083.85.	
	8 The payments made since May 31 were:	
	Groceries	$ 205.88
	Mortgage payment	1100.00
	Toaster	49.95
	Gasoline, oil for car	25.10
	Barber shop	18.00
	Newspapers	10.23
	Textbook	45.00
	City museum donation	30.00
	11 Carla Reed received her paycheck for $1083.85.	
	15 The payments made since last week were:	
	Groceries	$112.72
	Gas, electric	127.17
	Dry cleaning	45.00
	Gasoline for car	28.00
	Automobile insurance	260.00
	Car repairs	175.48
	Cosmetics	22.00
	Magazine subscription	18.00

Movie	12.00
Notebook paper	5.25
Charitable contribution	10.00

18 Carla Reed received her paycheck for $1083.85.

22 The payments made since last week were:

Groceries	$125.13
Water bill	24.68
Gasoline for car, car wash	35.91
Dentist visit	125.00
Toothpaste, toothbrushes	17.36
Newspaper subscription	10.46
Video tape rental	12.00
Charitable contribution	50.00
Savings account deposit	400.00

25 Carla Reed received her paycheck for $1083.85.

29 The payments made since last week were:

Groceries	$121.08
Telephone bill	82.13
Shoe repair	15.25
Gasoline for car	24.88
Life insurance	150.00
Visit to doctor, medicine	133.67
Beauty salon	45.00
Newspapers, magazines	14.18
Charitable contribution	20.00

30 The payments made since the 29th were:

Food	$40.31
Gasoline, oil for car	18.29
Newspapers	5.23
Movie	16.00
Dinner out	65.00

CHECK POINT

9-1

New balance = $612.62

e. Rule and foot the columns. Verify the totals by crossfooting.

f. Write in the totals below the footings and double rule the columns.

g. Record the new balance for July 1.

Problem 9-2 Ella and Joey DiCicco decide to keep a record of receipts and payments like the one in Illustration 9B (page 71). Ella DiCicco is a sales and marketing representative and Joey is a computer operator for the same manufacturing company. Joey is studying for a degree in information technology at a nearby college.

Directions

a. Prepare a record of receipts and payments. Use a ruled sheet of paper with ten money columns.

b. Use as the heading for your record:

Ella and Joey DiCicco
Record of Receipts and Payments
For March, 20--

c. Enter the following column headings and estimated totals using Illustration 9B (page 71) as a guide.

1. Date
2. Explanation
3. Total Receipts ($3,000.00)
4. Total Payments ($3,000.00)
5. Household expenses ($1,500.00)
6. Clothing ($235.00)
7. Transportation ($450.00)
8. Health/personal ($150.00)
9. Entertainment ($175.00)
10. Education ($150.00)
11. Gifts ($40.00)
12. Savings ($300.00)

d. Record the following receipts and payments for March, 20--.

Mar.		
1	Balance of cash, $358.74.	
4	The DiCiccos received their paychecks (Ella, $317.31; Joey, $394.23). Use one line for each paycheck.	
7	The payments made since Feb. 28 were:	
	Groceries	$ 88.18
	Rent	780.00
	Electric knife	28.36
	Gasoline, oil for car	24.67
	Barber shop	14.00
	Newspapers	5.50
	Movie	17.00
	Textbooks	56.00
	Laboratory fees	25.00
	Charitable contribution	5.00
11	The DiCiccos received their paychecks (Ella, $317.31; Joey, $394.23). Use one line for each paycheck.	
14	The payments made since last week were:	
	Groceries	$131.74
	Utility bill	143.91
	Skirt	86.95
	Gasoline for car	62.21
	Automobile insurance	250.00
	Aerobics session at fitness center	10.00
	Dinner out	24.65
	Notebooks, paper	12.72
	Charitable contribution	5.00
18	The DiCiccos received their paychecks (Ella, $317.31; Joey, $394.23). Use one line for each paycheck.	
21	The payments made since last week were:	
	Groceries	$107.99
	TV repair	70.40
	Gasoline for car, car wash	64.51
	Doctor visit	46.00
	Medicine	45.75
	Magazines	17.00
	Newspapers	5.50
	Rock concert	88.00
	Charitable contribution	60.00
25	The DiCiccos received their paychecks (Ella, $317.31; Joey, $394.23). Use one line for each paycheck.	
28	The payments made since last week were:	
	Groceries	$102.37
	Telephone bill	61.88
	Dry cleaning	43.00
	Gasoline for car	63.01
	Car payment	253.33

Cosmetics	25.77
Newspapers	5.50
Charitable contribution	10.00
Savings account deposit	140.00

31 The payments made since the 28th were:

Groceries	$41.82
Gasoline, oil for car	24.71
Video tape rental	12.00
Anniversary gift for Ella's parents	50.28

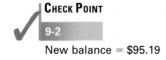

CHECK POINT

9-2

New balance = $95.19

e. Rule and foot the columns. Verify the totals by crossfooting.

f. Write the totals below the footings and double rule the columns.

g. Record the new balance for April 1.

Problems 9–3 and 9–4 may be found in the Working Papers.

Tips

Combine numbers that equal ten when possible to make your adding easier. For example, when cross-footing the first row of numbers ($2,078.44 + $3,451.15 + $16,063.46), combine the 4 cents with the 6 cents to make 10 cents. Then add the 5 cents to make 15 cents.

applied math preview

Copy and complete the problem below.

1. $ 2,078.44 + $3,451.15 + $16,063.46 =
2. 12,008.07 + 1,680.91 + 27,182.42 =
3. 14,321.82 + 848.25 + 10,340.84 =
4. 2,549.31 + 1,101.48 + 12,214.32 =
5.

key terms preview

- **Cash budget**
- **Cash flow**
- **Crossfooting**
- **Fixed payments**
- **Negative cash flow**
- **Positive cash flow**
- **Quarter**
- **Variable payments**

goals

1. **To learn how businesses use budgets.**
2. **To learn how to complete a business budget.**

UNDERSTANDING THE JOB

Persons and families usually keep budgets for two major reasons:

1. They wish to make sure that there is enough money on hand to pay the bills.
2. They want help in spending their money wisely.

Businesses keep budgets for these same reasons. To help prepare a budget, businesses may estimate their cash receipts and cash payments for a period of time, such as three months, six months, or one year.

SAMPLE PROBLEM

Most businesses change their budgets several times before they are finalized. Using an electronic spreadsheet to prepare a budget allows one to easily make changes.

Anita Mendoza owns Mendoza Plumbing Services. Mendoza Plumbing Services installs faucets and disposals, repairs broken pipes, cleans drains, and replaces water heaters. The company usually has these types of cash receipts:

Residential Sales: Sales of plumbing services to local homeowners

Commercial Sales: Sales of plumbing services to commercial businesses

The company usually has these types of cash payments:

Wages:	Payments to regular and part-time workers
Rent:	Payments for the office and the supply room
Utilities:	Payments for heat and electricity
Supplies:	Payments for replacement pipe, tools, plumbing uniforms, and other plumbing supplies
Office Expenses:	Payments for telephone service, printer paper, ink cartridges, paper clips, file folders, and other supplies
Repairs:	Payments for repairing plumbing equipment
Insurance:	Payments for insurance on equipment
Taxes:	Payments for local, state, and federal taxes
Equipment:	Payments for the purchase of equipment, such as trucks, ladders, and hydro-flushing units

Key Terms

Quarter. Three months.

In December, Anita wanted to plan how the company would operate for the first three months, or first **quarter**, of next year. Anita needed to know if the company would have enough money *at the right time* to pay the bills that would come due. To find out, Anita began a budget for the three-month period from January through March. The partially prepared budget is shown in Illustration 10A below.

Anita estimated what the cash receipts and cash payments for the company would be, month by month, for the quarter. Anita entered the estimated amounts for each type of cash receipt and cash payment in the correct monthly column.

You might wonder how Anita came up with these figures. Anita first looked at what the business had received and spent in previous first quarters. Anita then estimated how much more or less the cash receipts and cash payments would be during the upcoming quarter.

Illustration 10A

Partially prepared budget for Mendoza Plumbing Services

For Your Information

Business managers and owners make many business decisions each day. Budgeting is one tool managers and owners use to improve a company's profits.

DESCRIPTION	JANUARY	FEBRUARY	MARCH	TOTAL
Receipts:				
Residential Sales	14 4 0 0 00	1 5 0 0 00	8 8 0 0 00	
Commercial Sales	4 8 0 0 00	5 4 0 0 00	13 6 0 0 00	
Total Receipts				
Payments:				
Wages	11 6 0 0 00	11 6 0 0 00	13 0 0 0 00	
Rent	2 4 0 0 00	2 4 0 0 00	2 4 0 0 00	
Utilities	4 2 0 00	4 2 0 00	3 0 0 00	
Supplies	6 0 0 00	6 0 0 00	1 0 0 0 00	
Office Expenses	1 8 0 00	1 8 0 00	2 0 0 00	
Repairs	4 0 0 00	4 0 0 00	1 1 0 0 00	
Insurance	7 5 0 00	7 5 0 00	7 5 0 00	
Taxes	2 3 2 0 00	2 3 2 0 00	2 6 0 0 00	
Equipment			1 5 0 0 00	
Total Payments				
Balance				

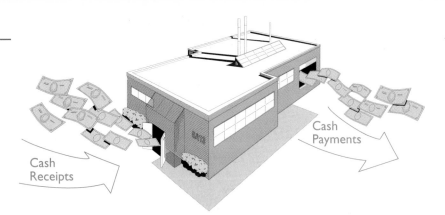

Cash Receipts

Cash Payments

Key Terms

Variable payments. Payments which change from month to month.

Fixed payments. Payments which do not change.

Cash flow. How money is received and spent over time.

Cash budget. A report of the cash flow.

Anita estimated that the cash receipts from commercial sales would be lower in some months than in others. For example, the cash receipts for commercial sales in January and February are estimated to be lower than in March. From past experience, Anita knows that many business customers delay plumbing repairs the first two months of a new year.

Anita also estimated that the business would spend $11,600.00 during January and February for wages, which would increase in March to $13,000.00. From past experience, Anita knows that her business will increase then and that she will have to hire more people in March to handle that business. Payments, like wages, which change from month to month are called **variable payments**.

Some cash payments are the same each month. For example, the amounts spent on rent and insurance are estimated to be the same for each month. These types of payments are known as **fixed payments** because they do not change.

When business persons estimate cash receipts and cash payments as Anita did, they are estimating the **cash flow** of their businesses. (See Illustration 10B above.) The report they prepare that shows the cash flow is called a **cash budget**. Anita will use the cash budget to find out whether there will be enough cash flowing into the business each month (cash receipts) to cover the cash flowing out of the business each month (cash payments). This will let Anita know in which months there may be more cash receipts than are needed to pay the bills. It will also let Anita know in which months there may not be enough cash receipts to pay the bills.

Anita estimated the cash receipts and payments for each month. She gave the cash budget to Willie Brown, her record keeper, to fill in the heading and find the totals and balances. The completed cash budget is shown in Illustration 10C on page 82.

Let's see what steps Willie took to complete the cash budget.

STEP 1 Complete the heading.

Willie entered the name of the business, Mendoza Plumbing Services, on the first line at the top of the form. He entered the name of the form, Cash Budget, on the next line.

Notice that the form is not called a record of receipts and payments. The reason is that the form is not used to record *actual* receipts and payments. It is used to record *estimated* receipts and payments.

Willie entered "For First Quarter, 20--" on the bottom line of the heading since the form includes the estimated cash receipts and cash payments for the first three months of the year.

Mendoza Plumbing Services
Cash Budget
For First Quarter, 20--

DESCRIPTION	JANUARY	FEBRUARY	MARCH	TOTAL	
Receipts:					STEP 1
Residential Sales	14 400 00	15 000 00	8 800 00	38 200 00	STEP 3
Commercial Sales	4 800 00	5 400 00	13 600 00	23 800 00	
Total Receipts	19 200 00	20 400 00	22 400 00	62 000 00	STEP 4
					STEP 5
Payments:					STEP 2
Wages	11 600 00	11 600 00	13 000 00	36 200 00	
Rent	2 400 00	2 400 00	2 400 00	7 200 00	
Utilities	4 20 00	4 20 00	3 00 00	1 140 00	
Supplies	6 00 00	6 00 00	1 000 00	2 200 00	
Office Expenses	1 80 00	1 80 00	2 00 00	5 60 00	STEP 7
Repairs	4 00 00	4 00 00	1 100 00	1 900 00	
Insurance	7 50 00	7 50 00	7 50 00	2 250 00	
Taxes	2 320 00	2 320 00	2 600 00	7 240 00	STEP 6
Equipment			1 500 00	1 500 00	
Total Payments	18 670 00	18 670 00	22 850 00	60 190 00	STEP 8 / STEP 9
Balance	5 30 00	1 730 00	(4 50 00)	1 810 00	STEP 11

STEP 10 ————— STEP 12 —————

STEP 2 Total the estimated cash receipts for each month.

Willie ruled and totaled the cash receipts columns. For example, Willie added the two cash receipts amounts for January, $14,400.00 + $4,800.00, and entered the total, $19,200.00, on the Total Receipts line in the column for January. In the same way, he entered the totals for the other months in the proper columns.

STEP 3 Total each type of estimated cash receipt.

Willie crossfooted the amounts of cash receipts for residential sales and entered the total, $38,200.00, in the Total column at the right. He then crossfooted the amounts for commercial sales and entered the total, $23,800.00, in the Total column.

STEP 4 Total the estimated cash receipts for the period.

Willie ruled the Total column and added the two amounts he had just entered, $38,200.00 + $23,800.00. The total, $62,000.00, is the total cash receipts Anita expects for the first quarter.

STEP 5 Verify the estimated cash receipts.

Willie verified the total receipts for the first quarter, $62,000.00, by cross-footing the total cash receipts amounts for each month:

Total estimated cash receipts, January	$19,200.00
Total estimated cash receipts, February	20,400.00
Total estimated cash receipts, March	22,400.00
Total	$62,000.00

Since the two totals agreed, Willie was reasonably confident that he had made no mistakes. Willie then double ruled the receipts columns to show that he was done with those amounts.

STEP 6 **Total the estimated cash payments for each month.**

Willie ruled the payments columns and added the payments for each month. He entered these totals on the Total Payments line of the form. For example, the total estimated payments for January were $18,670.00. Willie entered this amount on the Total Payments line in the column for January.

STEP 7 **Total each type of estimated cash payment.**

Willie crossfooted the amounts for each type of cash payment and entered the totals on the proper line of the Total column at the right. For example, he crossfooted the cash payments amounts for wages and entered the total, $36,200.00, in the Total column on the Wages line.

STEP 8 **Total the estimated cash payments for the period.**

Willie ruled the Total column and added the cash payment amounts. He entered the total, $60,190.00, on the Total Payments line in the Total column at the right.

STEP 9 **Verify the estimated cash payments.**

Willie crossfooted the total payments for each month as shown below:

Total estimated cash payments, January	$18,670.00
Total estimated cash payments, February	18,670.00
Total estimated cash payments, March	22,850.00
Total	$60,190.00
	$60,190.00

The total, $60,190.00, was compared to the total cash payments he found in Step 8. Since the two amounts agreed, he was reasonably confident that he had made no errors. He then double ruled the payments columns.

STEP 10 **Find the estimated balance for each month.**

Key Terms

Positive cash flow. More receipts than payments.

Willie saw that the estimated receipts were greater than the estimated payments for every month except March. When there are more receipts than payments in a period, it is called a **positive cash flow**. For months with a positive cash flow, Willie subtracted the total payments from the total receipts. He then entered the balance on the Balance line of the form. For example, in January, the receipts were $19,200.00, and the payments were $18,670.00. Willie subtracted the payments from the receipts and entered the difference on the Balance line in the January column.

Total estimated cash receipts in January	=	$ 19,200.00
Total estimated cash payments in January	=	− 18,670.00
Estimated balance for January	=	$ 530.00

In March, the payments were greater than the receipts. When there are more payments than receipts in a period, it is called a **negative cash flow**. Willie subtracted the total receipts from the total payments.

Total estimated cash payments in March	=	$ 22,850.00
Total estimated cash receipts in March	=	− 22,400.00
Estimated balance for March	=	$ (450.00)

Willie entered $450.00 on the Balance line in the March column. Because the balance was negative, Willie put parentheses around the balance.

STEP 11 Find the estimated balance for the period.

Willie subtracted the total cash payments for the three months, $60,190.00, from the total cash receipts for the three months, $62,000.00. He entered the difference, $1,810.00, on the Balance line in the Total column. This balance is the estimated amount of cash that Anita should have left at the end of the three months.

STEP 12 Verify the balances.

Willie added the positive monthly balances together. Then Willie subtracted the negative monthly balance from the total of the positive monthly balances. The difference should equal the balance for the three months which Willie found in Step 11.

Positive balances		
January	$ 530.00	
February	+1,730.00	
Total of positive balances		$ 2,260.00
Negative balance		− 450.00
Balance for three months		$1,810.00

Since the balances agreed, Willie was confident that he had made no mistakes on the form.

Anita can now look at the cash budget for the three-month period which Willie has completed. She can quickly see in which months she will probably have a positive cash flow and in which months she will probably have a negative cash flow. Anita must plan to save enough money from the positive months to cover the difference in the negative months.

BUILDING YOUR BUSINESS VOCABULARY

On a sheet of paper, write the headings **Statement Number** and **Words**. Next, choose the words that match the statements. Write each word you choose next to the statement number it matches. Be careful; not all the words listed should be used.

Statements	Words
1. Amounts of money received	cash budget
2. Cash payments that change from period to period	cash flow
3. When cash receipts are greater than cash payments	crossfooting
	extend an amount
4. A report showing the estimated cash flow of a business	estimating
	fixed payments
5. When cash payments are greater than cash receipts	money columns
	negative cash flow
6. To record an amount again in a second column	positive cash flow
7. Adding a row of figures across a business form	quarter
8. Cash payments that are the same from period to period	receipts
	variable payments
9. A three-month period	
10. How money is received and spent over time	

STEPS REVIEW: Keeping a Business Budget

STEP 1 Complete the heading.

STEP 2 Total the estimated cash receipts for each month.

STEP 3 Total each type of estimated cash receipt.

STEP 4 Total the estimated cash receipts for the period.

STEP 5 Verify the estimated cash receipts.

STEP 6 Total the estimated cash payments for each month.

STEP 7 Total each type of estimated cash payment.

STEP 8 Total the estimated cash payments for the period.

STEP 9 Verify the estimated cash payments.

STEP 10 Find the estimated balance for each month.

STEP 11 Find the estimated balance for the period.

STEP 12 Verify the balances.

APPLICATION PROBLEMS

Problem 10-1   It is March, and you are the record keeper for Mendoza Plumbing Services. Anita Mendoza wants to plan for the second quarter of the year. She has estimated the cash receipts and payments for Mendoza Plumbing Services for April through June. She has asked you to complete the cash budget.

Directions

a. Copy and complete the cash budget below. Follow Steps 1–12 in the Sample Problem. Use Illustration 10C (on page 82) as a guide.

b. Answer these questions about the completed cash budget:
1. Which cash payments are fixed cash payments?
2. Which cash payments are variable cash payments?
3. What are the total estimated cash receipts from residential sales for the quarter?
4. What are the total estimated cash payments for repairs for the quarter?
5. In what month(s) is there a positive cash flow?
6. In what month(s) is there a negative cash flow?
7. Is the cash flow for the entire quarter positive or negative?

CHECK POINT

10-1

Total estimated balance = $5,510.00

DESCRIPTION	APRIL	MAY	JUNE	TOTAL
Receipts:				
Residential Sales	7 2 0 0 00	7 0 0 0 00	9 0 0 0 00	
Commercial Sales	14 0 0 0 00	14 8 0 0 00	18 6 0 0 00	
Total Receipts				
Payments:				
Wages	13 0 0 0 00	13 0 0 0 00	14 0 0 0 00	
Rent	2 4 0 0 00	2 4 0 0 00	2 4 0 0 00	
Utilities	2 0 0 00	2 0 0 00	2 0 0 00	
Supplies	1 0 0 0 00	1 0 0 0 00	1 1 0 0 00	
Office Expenses	1 8 0 00	1 8 0 00	1 8 0 00	
Repairs	4 0 0 00	3 0 0 00	3 0 0 00	
Insurance	7 5 0 00	7 5 0 00	7 5 0 00	
Taxes	2 6 0 0 00	2 6 0 0 00	3 0 0 0 00	
Equipment		2 2 0 0 00		
Total Payments				
Balance				

Problem 10-2 You are a staff accountant for Saratoga Medical Supplies, a business that sells a variety of medical equipment including walkers, diabetes monitors, crutches, neck supports, bath rails, blood pressure kits, and other related products. The owner, Alex Coburn, has estimated the cash receipts and cash payments for the company for the first quarter of next year. He has asked you to complete the cash budget.

Directions

a. Copy and complete the cash budget below. Follow Steps 1–12 in the Sample Problem. Use Illustration 10C (page 82) as a guide.

b. Answer these questions about the completed cash budget:
1. Which cash payments are fixed cash payments?
2. Which cash payments are variable cash payments?
3. What are the total estimated cash receipts from hospital sales for the quarter?
4. What are the total estimated cash payments for taxes for the quarter?
5. In what month(s) is there a positive cash flow?
6. In what month(s) is there a negative cash flow?
7. Is the cash flow for the entire quarter positive or negative?

DESCRIPTION	JANUARY	FEBRUARY	MARCH	TOTAL
Receipts:				
Hospital Sales	13 0 0 0 00	13 0 0 0 00	13 4 0 0 00	
Medical Office Sales	7 8 0 0 00	8 4 0 0 00	7 6 0 0 00	
Total Receipts				
Payments:				
Wages	12 4 0 0 00	12 4 0 0 00	12 4 0 0 00	
Rent	2 0 0 0 00	2 0 0 0 00	2 0 0 0 00	
Insurance	8 0 0 00	8 0 0 00	8 0 0 00	
Telephone	5 0 0 00	5 0 0 00	5 0 0 00	
Utilities	3 4 0 00	3 4 0 00	2 6 0 00	
Taxes	2 2 0 0 00	2 2 0 0 00	2 7 0 0 00	
Equipment	2 0 0 00	6 0 0 00	6 0 0 00	
Supplies	1 2 0 0 00	1 2 0 0 00	1 2 0 0 00	
Other		2 2 0 0 00		
Total Payments				
Balance				

Problem 10-3   You continue to work as the staff accountant for Saratoga Medical Supplies. (See Problem 10-2.) It is now March, and Alex Coburn has estimated the cash receipts and cash payments for the company for the next three months. He has asked you to complete the cash budget.

Directions

a. Copy and complete the cash budget below. Follow Steps 1-12 in the Sample Problem. Use Illustration 10C (page 82) as a guide.

Check Point

10-3(b.7)

Cash flow for the quarter is positive.

b. Answer these questions about the completed cash budget:
1. Which cash payments are fixed cash payments?
2. Which cash payments are variable cash payments?
3. What are the total estimated cash receipts from medical office sales for the quarter?
4. What are the total estimated cash payments for taxes for the quarter?

5. In what month(s) is there a positive cash flow?
6. In what month(s) is there a negative cash flow?
7. Is the cash flow for the entire quarter positive or negative?

DESCRIPTION	APRIL	MAY	JUNE	TOTAL
Receipts:				
Hospital Sales	1 4 0 0 0 00	14 4 0 0 00	15 0 0 0 00	
Medical Office Sales	7 6 0 0 00	7 6 0 0 00	7 6 0 0 00	
Total Receipts				
Payments:				
Wages	12 4 0 0 00	12 4 0 0 00	12 4 0 0 00	
Rent	2 0 0 0 00	2 0 0 0 00	2 0 0 0 00	
Insurance	8 0 0 00	8 0 0 00	8 0 0 00	
Telephone	5 0 0 00	5 0 0 00	5 0 0 00	
Utilities	2 0 0 00	1 4 0 00	1 0 0 00	
Taxes	2 2 0 0 00	2 2 0 0 00	2 7 0 0 00	
Equipment	2 0 0 00	2 0 0 00	1 0 0 0 00	
Supplies	1 2 0 0 00	1 2 0 0 00	1 2 0 0 00	
Other	4 2 0 0 00			
Total Payments				
Balance				

Problem 10-4 may be found in the Working Papers.

Job 11 ANALYZING BUDGETS

Add all positive numbers. Then add all negative numbers. Then subtract the smaller total from the larger total. If the larger total is positive, the answer will be positive. If the larger total is negative, the answer will be negative.

applied math preview

Find the totals of each column. The amounts in parentheses are negative amounts. If an answer is negative, put it in parentheses.

1.	$220.00	2.	$192.50	3.	$ 29.25	4.	$ 35.15
	6.00		(63.40)		(41.30)		(52.12)
	(30.00)		4.75		(58.10)		(408.20)
	140.00		920.61		(167.11)		(62.40)
	(12.00)		(53.22)		44.63		(5.70)

key terms preview

- **Budget variance report**
- **Variance**

goal

To learn how to compare budgeted amounts with actual amounts.

UNDERSTANDING THE JOB

Budget variance report.
Compares budgeted amounts to actual amounts.

Many companies compare their actual cash receipts and payments with amounts on their cash budget to see if they have received or spent more than they had planned. In this way, they can make their budgets more realistic. They may also find that they must adjust their spending to bring future payments into line with their budget.

A form that compares budgeted amounts with actual amounts is called a **budget variance report**. This report shows how actual receipts and payments *vary*, or are different, from budgeted receipts and payments. A budget variance report for Mendoza Plumbing Services is shown in Illustration 11A on page 90.

STEP 1 **STEP 2** **STEP 3**

Mendoza Plumbing Services
Budget Variance Report
For January, 20--

	BUDGETED	ACTUAL	VARIANCE
Receipts:			
Residential Sales	14 4 0 0 00	14 6 4 0 00	2 4 0 00
Commercial Sales	4 8 0 0 00	4 7 4 0 00	(6 0 00)
Total Receipts	19 2 0 0 00	19 3 8 0 00	1 8 0 00
Payments:			
Wages	11 6 0 0 00	11 6 0 0 00	0 00
Rent	2 4 0 0 00	2 4 0 0 00	0 00
Utilities	4 2 0 00	3 8 0 00	(4 0 00)
Supplies	6 0 0 00	2 8 0 00	(3 2 0 00)
Office Expenses	1 8 0 00	2 4 0 00	6 0 00
Repairs	4 0 0 00	2 4 0 00	(1 6 0 00)
Insurance	7 5 0 00	7 5 0 00	0 00
Taxes	2 3 2 0 00	2 3 6 0 00	4 0 00
Equipment	0 00	0 00	0 00
Total Payments	18 6 7 0 00	18 2 5 0 00	(4 2 0 00)
Balance	5 3 0 00	1 1 3 0 00	6 0 0 00

STEP 5 (Residential Sales / Commercial Sales)
STEP 7 (Payments)
STEP 6 — STEP 4 — STEP 8 — STEP 9

SAMPLE PROBLEM

Anita Mendoza asks her record keeper, Willie Brown, to prepare a budget variance report for January. Here is how Willie completed the job:

STEP 1 Complete the heading.

Willie entered the name of the business, Mendoza Plumbing Services, on the first line of the report. He entered the name of the report, Budget Variance Report, on the next line. Willie entered "For January, 20--" on the last line of the heading. The budget variance report compares the differences between budgeted and actual amounts for the whole month of January.

STEP 2 Enter the budgeted amounts.

Willie entered the budgeted amounts for January receipts in the Budgeted column. He got these amounts from the cash budget form. (See Illustration 10C on page 82.) For example, he entered $14,400.00 on the Residential Sales line of the Receipts section in the Budgeted column.

Willie then entered the budgeted amounts for January payments. For example, he entered $11,600.00 on the Wages line of the Payments section in the Budgeted column.

Finally, Willie entered the planned balance for January, $530.00, on the Balance line in the Budgeted column.

STEP 3 Enter and total the actual cash receipts and payments.

Willie copied the actual cash receipts and payments for January from the company records. He entered each amount in the Actual column on the correct budget line. Then he ruled and totaled the cash receipts and cash payments amounts.

STEP 4 Find the actual cash balance.

Willie subtracted the actual cash payments from the actual cash receipts to find the actual cash balance. He entered this amount, $1,130.00, on the Balance line in the Actual column.

Actual Cash Receipts	$ 19,380.00
Actual Cash Payments	− 18,250.00
Actual Cash Balance	$ 1,130.00

STEP 5 Find the variance for each cash receipt.

Key Terms

Variance. Difference.

For each cash receipt, Willie found the **variance**, or difference; between the budgeted amount and the actual amount. Willie follows these rules to find variances:

1. Always subtract the smaller amount from the larger amount.

   For example, Willie subtracted the smaller amount for residential sales, $14,400.00, from the larger amount, $14,640.00. The difference, or variance, was $240.00. Willie entered $240.00 in the Variance column on the Residential Sales line.

2. If the actual amount is larger than the budgeted amount, the variance is positive.

   Willie knew that the variance was positive because the actual amount, $14,640.00, was more than the budgeted amount, $14,400.00.

3. If the actual amount is smaller than the budgeted amount, the variance is negative. Negative variances are placed in parentheses.

   Willie found the variance for commercial sales by subtracting the smaller amount, $4,740.00, from the larger amount, $4,800.00. The variance was $60.00. Since the actual amount was less than the budgeted amount, the variance was negative. Willie put parentheses around it.

STEP 6 Find and verify the total variance for cash receipts.

Willie found the total variance for cash receipts by subtracting the negative amount, $60.00, from the positive amount, $240.00. The difference was $180.00. This means that the company received $180.00 more in cash receipts than it had planned.

To verify his work, Willie subtracted the total budgeted cash receipts from the total actual cash receipts.

Total actual cash receipts	$ 19,380.00
Total budgeted cash receipts	−19,200.00
Total variance for cash receipts	$ 180.00

Since this amount was also $180.00, Willie was confident that he had done his work correctly. So, he entered the $180.00 in the Variance column on the Total Receipts line.

STEP 7 Find the variance for each cash payment.

Next, Willie found the variance for each cash payment. When there is *no difference* between the budgeted and actual amounts, there is no variance. Willie put 0.00 in the Variance columns for wages, rent, insurance, and equipment, since there were no differences between the budgeted amounts and the actual amounts spent on these items.

Willie found the variances for the other cash payments using the rules explained earlier. For example, Willie found the variance for office expenses by subtracting the smaller amount, $180.00, from the larger amount, $240.00. The difference was $60.00. He entered the difference in the Variance column on the Office Expenses line. Willie knew that this variance was positive because the actual cash payment, $240.00, was larger than the budgeted cash payment, $180.00.

Willie found the variance for utilities by subtracting the smaller amount, $380.00, from the larger amount, $420.00. He entered the variance, $40.00, on the Utilities line in the Variance column. Willie knew this variance was negative because the actual cash payment, $380.00, was less than the budgeted cash payment, $420.00. Willie put the variance in parentheses.

STEP 8 Find and verify the total variance for cash payments.

Willie added every positive amount in the Variance column for cash payments: $60.00 + $40.00. These are the items on which the company spent more than it had planned. The total was $100.00.

Willie then added the negative amounts (the amounts in parentheses): $40.00 + $320.00 + $160.00. These are the items on which the company spent less than it had planned. The total was $520.00.

Willie subtracted the smaller total, $100.00, from the larger total, $520.00. The difference, $420.00, is the total variance for cash payments. Because the larger amount was negative, Willie knew that the difference must be negative. This means that the company spent $420.00 less cash than it had planned in January.

To verify his work, Willie subtracted the total actual cash payments from the total budgeted cash payments.

Total budgeted cash payments	$ 18,670.00
Total actual cash payments	− 18,250.00
Total variance for cash payments	$ 420.00

Since this amount was also $420.00, Willie was reasonably confident that he had done his work correctly. So, he entered the $420.00 in the Variance column on the Total Payments line. Because the actual total cash payments were less than the budgeted total cash payments, the variance was negative. Willie put parentheses around it.

The budgeted cash balance was $530.00. The actual cash balance was $1,130.00. Willie subtracted the smaller amount from the larger amount.

Actual cash balance	$1,130.00
Budgeted cash balance	− 530.00
Cash balance variance	$ 600.00

Tips

When the actual cash balance exceeds the budgeted cash balance, the variance is positive.

Since the actual cash balance was larger than the budgeted cash balance, Willie knew that the variance was positive. The variance means that there was more cash on hand than had been budgeted. The company had $600.00 more cash on hand in January than they had expected. Willie entered the cash balance variance, $600.00, on the Balance line in the Variance column.

If the actual cash balance had been less than the budgeted cash balance, the variance would have been negative. For example, if the actual cash balance had been $240.00, Willie would have subtracted the actual cash balance from the budgeted cash balance:

Budgeted cash balance	$ 530.00
Actual cash balance	− 240.00
Cash balance variance	$ 290.00

Tips

When the actual cash balance is less than the budgeted cash balance, the variance is negative.

In this case, the company has less cash than it had expected. The amount of the shortage is $290.00. Willie would have entered the cash balance in the Variance column and placed parentheses around it.

BUILDING YOUR BUSINESS VOCABULARY

On a sheet of paper, write the headings **Statement Number** and **Words**. Next, choose the words that match the statements. Write each word you choose next to the statement number it matches. Be careful; not all the words listed should be used.

Statements	Words
1. A form that compares budgeted amounts with actual amounts	budget
2. Cash payments that change from period to period	budget variance report
	crossfooting
3. To record an amount again in a second column	extend an amount
4. Adding a row of figures across a business form	fixed payments
	negative cash flow
5. A plan for receiving and spending money	positive cash flow
6. When cash payments are greater than cash receipts for a period	quarter
	receipts
7. Amounts of money received	variable payments
8. A three-month period	variance
9. Difference	

STEPS REVIEW: Analyzing Budgets

STEP 1 Complete the heading.

STEP 2 Enter the budgeted amounts.

STEP 3 Enter and total the actual cash receipts and payments.

STEP 4 Find the actual cash balance.

STEP 5 Find the variance for each cash receipt.

STEP 6 Find and verify the toal variance for cash receipts.

STEP 7 Find the variance for each cash payment.

STEP 8 Find and verify the total variance for cash payments.

STEP 9 Find the variance in the cash balance

APPLICATION PROBLEMS

Problem 11-1

You are the record keeper for Ascar Computer Enterprises, a business that manufactures high-speed Internet equipment. You have been asked to complete the company budget variance report for April.

CHECK POINT
11-1

Total cash balance variance = $4,200.00

Directions

a. Complete the budget variance report below. Follow the steps in the Sample Problem, and use Illustration 11A (page 90) as a guide.

	BUDGETED	ACTUAL	VARIANCE
Receipts:			
Corporate Sales	133 6 0 0 00	132 5 6 0 00	
Government Sales	44 0 0 0 00	47 0 8 0 00	
Total Receipts	177 6 0 0 00		
Payments:			
Wages	109 0 0 0 00	109 0 0 0 00	
Mortgage Payment	4 7 8 0 00	4 7 8 0 00	
Gas and Electric	1 5 0 0 00	1 3 6 0 00	
Supplies	25 0 0 0 00	23 8 0 0 00	
Office Expenses	1 5 8 0 00	1 7 2 0 00	
Equipment	3 0 0 0 00	2 0 4 0 00	
Insurance	4 6 0 0 00	4 6 0 0 00	
Taxes	25 5 0 0 00	25 5 0 0 00	
Telephone	7 0 0 00	7 0 0 00	
Total Payments	175 6 6 0 00		
Balance	1 9 4 0 00		

b. Answer these questions about your completed budget variance report:
   1. Which cash receipts had a positive variance?
   2. Which cash payments had no variance?
   3. Which cash payments had a negative variance?
   4. Which cash payment had the largest positive variance?
   5. Was the actual cash balance greater or less than the budgeted cash balance?

Problem 11-2 You work in the finance department of Pacific Heating and Air Conditioning. Your supervisor has asked you to complete the company budget variance report for June.

Directions

a. Complete the budget variance report below. Follow the steps in the Sample Problem, and use Illustration 11A (page 90) as a guide.
b. Answer these questions about your completed budget variance report:
   1. Which cash receipts had no variance?
   2. Which cash payments had no variance?
   3. Which cash payments had a negative variance?
   4. Which cash payment had the largest negative variance?
   5. Was the actual cash balance greater or less than the budgeted cash balance?

CHECK POINT

11-2(b.5)

The actual cash balance was less than the budgeted cash balance.

	BUDGETED	ACTUAL	VARIANCE
Receipts:			
Heating Sales	74 175 00	74 175 00	
Air Conditioning Sales	34 600 00	36 125 00	
Total Receipts	108 775 00		
Payments:			
Wages	55 000 00	57 500 00	
Rent	7 900 00	7 900 00	
Gas and Electric	1 625 00	1 690 00	
Mechanical Parts	22 850 00	23 200 00	
Office Expenses	2 425 00	2 275 00	
Equipment Repair	1 250 00	1 072 50	
Insurance	2 880 00	2 880 00	
Taxes	11 875 00	11 240 00	
Telephone	745 00	780 00	
Total Payments	106 550 00		
Balance	2 225 00		

Problems 11-3 and 11-4 may be found in the Working Papers.

Chapter 2

CHECK YOUR READING

1. Why is it a good idea for an individual to prepare a budget?
2. If you were to move out of your home after completing high school, what type of expenses or payments would you face?
3. Why it is recommended to compare actual budget figures with planned receipts and payments?

DISCUSSION

Key Terms

Division of labor. Dividing a job among several workers.

In each problem in Job 10, the owner or manager worked with the record keeper to prepare the cash budget for the business. The owner provided the estimated amounts for cash receipts and cash payments. The record keeper completed the cash budget by filling in the heading and totaling and verifying the amounts. Dividing a job up like this is called **division of labor**. Can you think of any advantages of having division of labor in preparing a cash budget?

CRITICAL THINKING

Sometimes when we are faced with making a decision, we react emotionally and do not look for other possibilities or choices. The obvious answer to a situation is not necessarily the best. One critical thinking strategy in an emotional situation is to determine alternative actions, possibilities, and choices. At times, there may appear to be no alternatives. If you have difficulty determining other options, ask people for help. Keep looking until you find an alternative strategy that will help you the most. The obvious solution to a problem may not be the best until you have examined other possibilities.

Allen Palomo has just been hired as a record keeper for Zylar Digital Imaging Corporation. You have been asked to train Allen to complete cash budget reports. While you are teaching Allen how to verify the totals in the cash budget by crossfooting, Allen suggests that this step is not needed. He says that since you are using a calculator to find the totals, you cannot make any mistakes. He feels that it is a waste of time to verify the work by crossfooting the totals.

1. Is Allen right?
2. If Allen is not right, what errors could you make in finding the totals of the cash budget even if you are using a calculator?

REINFORCEMENT ACTIVITIES

3. If Allen is uncomfortable crossfooting his work, what alternative involving computer technology is available to Allen?

COMMUNICATION IN THE WORKPLACE

Marvin Williams and you are record keepers for the Palo Alto Medical Center. Marvin was given the job of completing the cash budget form by the manager, Kathy Krouse. When Kathy looked at Marvin's work, she found a number of math errors. Kathy was upset about these errors and let Marvin know that there was no excuse for making them.

Later, Marvin complained to you that Kathy was not very fair to have scolded him for the errors. Marvin felt that he had worked very hard to do a good job and had not made the errors on purpose. "After all," he said, "everybody makes errors once in a while."

What would you say to Marvin about

1. How he could have avoided making math errors on the cash budget report?
2. How important accuracy is on the cash budget report?

FOCUS ON CAREERS

Imagine that you work as a record keeper for Currie Ergonomic Work Stations. You are paid $1,400 per month. You are also given a number of *fringe benefits*. For example, you are given free parking, free hospital insurance, free life insurance, and a free pension plan. The fringe benefits amount to 25% of your monthly salary.

You are offered a job at Furniture West at $1,500 per month. The fringe benefits of this job include free hospital insurance and a free pension plan. These fringe benefits amount to 15% of the salary offered.

1. What is your real monthly pay in each job?
2. Which job offers the greatest total yearly income, and how much more is it per year?
3. Which job do you think is best, and why?

REVIEWING WHAT YOU HAVE LEARNED

On a sheet of paper, write the headings **Statement Number** and **Words**. Next, choose the words that best complete the statements. Write each word you choose next to the statement number it completes. Be careful; not all the words listed should be used.

Statements	Words
1. A form used to keep track of actual cash receipts and cash payments is called a ____.	budget variance report
2. A report which compares actual cash receipts and payments to budgeted cash receipts and payments is called a ____.	cash budget cash flow division of labor
3. Cash payments which change from month to month are called ____.	fixed payments negative cash flow
4. Cash payments which stay the same from month to month are called ____.	positive cash flow receipts
5. A form which shows the cash flows for a period of time is called a ____.	record of receipts and payments
6. Dividing a job up so that each part is done by a different person is called ____.	variable payments
7. When estimated cash receipts are greater than estimated cash payments, a business is said to have a ____.	
8. When estimated cash payments are greater than estimated cash receipts, a business is said to have a ____.	

 MASTERY PROBLEM

Phase 1: Budgeting for a Family

Judy and Steve Kaplan decide to keep a record of receipts and payments to help them spend their money more wisely. Judy is an account receivable supervisor, and Steve owns and operates a video service. Judy is also studying for a business degree at a DeAnza Community College.

Directions

a. Prepare a record of receipts and payments. Use a ruled sheet of paper with ten money columns.

b. Complete the headings for their record. Enter these estimated totals:

1. Date
2. Explanation
3. Total Receipts ($5,200.00)
4. Total Payments ($5,200.00)
5. Household Expenses ($2,200.00)
6. Clothing ($300.00)
7. Transportation ($800.00)
8. Health and Personal ($300.00)
9. Entertainment ($300.00)
10. Education ($400.00)
11. Gifts ($100.00)
12. Savings ($800.00)

c. Record the following receipts and payments for July of the current year.

July	1	The balance of cash was $408.18.	
	6	The Kaplans received their weekly paychecks which together totaled $1250.00.	
	7	The payments made since June 30 were	
		Contributions	$ 50.00
		Haircut	18.00
		Groceries	210.64
		College textbooks	95.33
		Rent	750.00
		Gasoline, oil for cars	48.16
		Newspapers, magazines	16.57
		Notebooks, paper	32.55
		Savings account deposit	100.00

13 The Kaplans received their weekly paychecks which together totaled $1250.00.

14 The payments made since last week were

Savings account deposit	$100.00
Electric bill	193.59
Groceries	127.16
Jacket	130.89
Gasoline for cars	51.61
Automobile insurance	160.23
Dentist visit	62.00
Beauty salon	50.00
Baseball game	20.75
College laboratory fees	85.00

20 The Kaplans received their weekly paychecks which together totaled $1250.00.

21 The payments made since last week were

Groceries	$133.77
Car repair	212.15
Doctor visit, medicine	82.91
Telephone bill	68.15
Magazines, newspapers	20.78
Gasoline for cars	49.71
Dinner out	40.95
Savings account deposit	100.00

27 The Kaplans received their weekly paychecks which together totaled $1250.00.

28 The payments made since last week were

Groceries	$159.81
Gasoline for cars	42.09
Movie	15.00
Hat, shoes	91.77
VCR	326.18
Magazine subscription	36.00
Savings account deposit	500.00

31 The payments made since the 28th were

Groceries	$ 46.48
Gasoline for cars	22.18
College textbooks	100.99

d. Rule and foot the columns. Verify the totals by crossfooting.

e. Write the totals below the footings and double rule the columns.

f. Record the new balance for August 1.

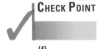

CHECK POINT

(f)
August 1
Balance = $1,056.78

Phase 2: Budgeting for a Business

Steve Kaplan also wants to plan the budget for his business, Kaplan Video, for the third quarter of the current year. The firm provides a full range of video services, including production, editing, digital graphics, and duplication, as well as the taping of special events, such as weddings, reunions, graduations, sports events, auditions, and banquets. He has estimated the firm's receipts and payments for July, August, and September. Copy and complete the cash budget.

71

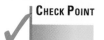

Total estimated balance = $6,900.00

DESCRIPTION	JULY	AUGUST	SEPTEMBER	TOTAL
Receipts:				
Production Services	9 0 0 0 00	10 0 0 0 00	10 0 0 0 00	
Special Events	11 0 0 0 00	12 0 0 0 00	13 0 0 0 00	
Total Receipts				
Payments:				
Wages	11 4 0 0 00	11 4 0 0 00	11 4 0 0 00	
Rent	2 4 0 0 00	2 4 0 0 00	2 4 0 0 00	
Loans	8 0 0 00	8 0 0 00	8 0 0 00	
Insurance	6 0 0 00	6 0 0 00	6 0 0 00	
Utilities	4 2 0 00	4 5 0 00	3 5 0 00	
Telephone	8 3 0 00	8 5 0 00	9 0 0 00	
Repairs	1 0 0 00	1 0 0 00	1 0 0 00	
Supplies	3 0 0 00	3 0 0 00	3 0 0 00	
Taxes	2 5 0 0 00	2 5 0 0 00	2 5 0 0 00	
Total Payments				
Balance				

Phase 3: Analyzing a Budget

Steve Kaplan has entered the budgeted and actual receipts and payments for July. Copy and complete the report.

Total cash balance
variance = $80.00

	BUDGETED	ACTUAL	VARIANCE
Receipts:			
Production Services	9 0 0 0 00	8 4 6 0 00	
Special Events	11 0 0 0 00	11 6 8 0 00	
Total Receipts			
Payments:			
Wages	11 4 0 0 00	11 4 0 0 00	
Rent	2 4 0 0 00	2 4 0 0 00	
Loans	8 0 0 00	8 0 0 00	
Insurance	6 0 0 00	6 0 0 00	
Utilities	4 2 0 00	5 1 0 00	
Telephone	8 3 0 00	8 7 0 00	
Repairs	1 0 0 00	1 5 0 00	
Supplies	3 0 0 00	1 8 0 00	
Taxes	2 5 0 0 00	2 5 0 0 00	
Total Payments			
Balance			

REVIEWING YOUR BUSINESS VOCABULARY

This activity may be found in the Working Papers.

Chapter 3

Credit Records

If you buy a camera on credit, you get the camera now but pay for it at some later date. Credit is common in today's world and is used by individuals, families, businesses, and governments. One way for individuals to buy on credit is to use a credit card. Another way is to buy on the installment plan. A third way is to borrow money from a bank.

In Chapter 3, you will learn about the advantages and disadvantages of using a credit card, how to apply for credit, and the way that stores and banks decide who gets credit. You will learn how to read and check credit card statements. Calculator Tips will also be given for figuring your payments when you borrow money.

FOCUS ON TECHNOLOGY

Computer Displays

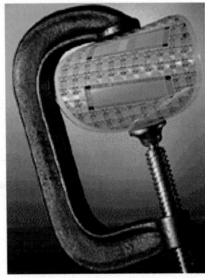

For output, most computer systems have a large, bulky, TV-like display screen that may be as much as 18 inches thick. Called a monitor, display screen, or simply a screen, it usually takes up a lot of space on a desk or table. A number of technologies have come along that are likely to change how we view computer output.

One technology is the *flat panel display*. This display is called flat because it may be less than 4 inches thick. Some are so thin that they can be hung on the wall like a painting. Right now, these displays are much more expensive than the old bulky ones. But, their prices will come down over time and make them available to many businesses.

Another technology that will reduce screen bulk even more is *plastic screen technology*. This technology uses a special plastic that "glows" when given an electric charge. It is expected that plastic screens will be first used in laptop or notebook computers and in the screens of consumer electronics, such as cellular telephones and TVs. Later, this technology may be used in desktop computer systems. Some screens are less than 1/8 inches thick, and what's more, the screens are flexible—they can be bent.

Still more fantastic is a technology that uses the back of the eye, or retina, as the actual display screen. This technology is called *virtual retinal display*. You wear what looks like a pair of eyeglasses that are connected to a computer system. The "eyeglasses" project the computer images to the back of your eyes, or your retina. The images seem to hang a few feet in front of you but you can look through them to objects in the distance. Imagine a salesperson reading a file about a customer while waiting on the customer. Imagine a computer repair person reading a page from a computer manual while working on a computer system.

Job 12   APPLYING FOR BANK CREDIT CARDS

Tips

To round a number to the nearest cent, use the Rule of 5. When the number to the right of the cents place is 5 or more, drop that number and add a penny to the answer. For example, to round $1.465 to the nearest cent, drop the 5 and add one cent to the answer. The answer becomes $1.47. When the number to the right of the cents place is 4 or less, drop that number and leave the answer as it is. For example, $1.784 is rounded to $1.78.

applied math preview

Copy and complete the problems below. When necessary, round your answers to the nearest cent.

1. $600.00 × 52 =
2. $450.00 × 52 =
3. $375.00 × 52 =
4. $428.65 × 52 =
5. $471.17 × 52 =

6. $36,000.00 ÷ 12 =
7. $15,756.00 ÷ 12 =
8. $18,540.00 ÷ 12 =
9. $14,258.86 ÷ 12 =
10. $22,524.12 ÷ 12 =

key terms preview

- Annual
- Authorize
- Charge account

- Credit
- Credit application
- Credit card

- Creditor
- Good credit risk
- Joint account

goals

1 To learn what factors are used in granting credit.
2 To learn how to apply for credit.
3 To learn the advantages and disadvantages of using a credit card.

Key Terms

Credit. Buy now, pay later.
Annual. Yearly.

➡ UNDERSTANDING THE JOB

When you buy something now and pay for it later, you are using **credit**. You use credit when you borrow money and pay it back later. For example, you may borrow money to buy a car. You use the money to get the car right away, but you pay back the money to the lender later.

Buying on credit must be done carefully. If you are not careful, you can buy too much and get very deeply in debt. You must be sure that you can pay for the item later.

Another disadvantage of buying on credit is that it may be more expensive. The stores that accept your credit cards have to pay the credit card companies a service fee of 3% to 5% of the purchase amount. Some stores will offer you a discount if you pay for your purchases with cash. Most credit card companies usually charge each user an **annual**, or yearly, fee. The fee charged is often between $25.00 and $65.00. Finally, credit card companies charge interest on any balance that is not paid when it is due. The interest rates that credit card companies charge may range from 7% to 21% a year.

On the other hand, buying on credit has many advantages. You do not need to carry cash for a credit purchase. If you plan to buy something that is very expensive, you do not have to shop with a large amount of cash. Buying on credit also allows you to spread out your payments. You may not have saved enough money to buy a $1,000 kitchen appliance with cash. You may, however, be able to afford to pay $100 a month for the appliance. Buying the appliance on credit allows you to get the appli-

Creditor. Lender.

Charge account. A form of credit offered by stores.

Credit card. Identifies the person buying on credit.

Credit application. Provides information about your ability to pay debts.

ance right away but pay for it over time. Also, buying on credit provides you with detailed records of your purchases.

There are many sources of credit available. You may borrow money from banks, insurance companies, credit unions, or personal finance companies. You can also borrow money from stores and credit card companies. When you buy an article on credit, you are really borrowing the money from the store. You get the article right away, but the store does not get its money until later. Sources of credit are called lenders or **creditors**.

Charge or Credit Cards

A common form of credit offered by department and chain stores is a charge account. A **charge account** allows you to purchase items now and pay for them later. When people buy using a charge account from stores, they may say they have bought an item "on account." This means that they have used the store charge account to make the purchase. Sometimes the store issues a charge card or **credit card** to the customer, like the one shown in Illustration 12A. This card contains the customer's name and account number, which are often printed in special raised characters on the card. Credit cards are used to identify the person who is making the credit purchase. Store credit cards can typically be used only in the store that issues them. For example, a chain department store may issue credit cards to customers for use in any of their stores.

Two other types of credit cards commonly used are gasoline credit cards and bank credit cards. Gasoline credit cards can usually be used only to purchase gas, oil, or other items from service stations. Bank credit cards are credit cards issued by banks. These cards are designed to be accepted at many stores and businesses for many different types of services and products. However, not all stores accept every bank credit card.

Applying for Credit

When you open an account with a creditor, such as a store, you usually complete a **credit application** form. The credit application form provides the lender or creditor with information about your ability to pay the money you owe. A completed credit application form is shown in Illustration 12B on page 107.

Illustration 12A

A store credit or charge card

BEST Department Store

16 021 515

Ann Welch

Good credit risk. Person likely to pay debts.

An employee in the credit department of the store will use the information from the credit application to decide whether or not you are a **good credit risk**. A good credit risk is a person who is very likely to pay the money owed. A bad credit risk is not likely to pay the money owed.

Lenders usually look at many factors before they grant you credit, including your income, the value of the things you own, the amount you already owe, and your past credit history. Successful businesses and people who own a lot, owe others little, and have steady incomes are likely to pay off their debts. They are good credit risks. Those who have paid off their debts in the past promptly and fully are likely to do the same in the future. They are also good credit risks.

SAMPLE PROBLEM

Selma Ramirez is applying for a ValuCard from the Flagstone National Bank. To get the ValuCard, Selma completed the credit card application form shown in Illustration 12B on page 107. Here is how she did it:

STEP 1 **Complete the Applicant section of the form.**

Selma entered her name, date of birth, social security number, address, and telephone number (questions 1–5) on the form. Selma has rented her apartment for the last 3 years and 4 months. Her rent is $625.00 a month. She entered these data into questions 6–8 on the form. She did not enter data about her previous address (questions 9 and 10). Data about her previous address would be entered only if she had lived at her present address less than 2 years.

Selma then entered the data about her current full-time job: the name, address, and telephone number of her employer, how long she had been employed, her job title, and her income (questions 11–16). The amount of pay that Selma receives each week after deductions is $445.00. This is her weekly net pay. The form asks for her monthly net pay. So, Selma had to calculate her monthly net pay.

To calculate monthly net pay, some people multiply the weekly net pay by 4 because there are 4 whole weeks in each month. For example, $445.00 \times 4 = \$1,780.00$. However, this amount is really less than their true monthly net pay. The reason is that most months have more than four weeks in them. To be accurate, you must

1. Multiply your weekly net pay by 52 (the number of weeks in a year) to find your yearly net pay.

$$\$445.00 \times 52 = \$23,140.00 \text{ yearly net pay}$$

2. Divide your yearly net pay by 12 (the number of months in a year) to get your monthly net pay.

$$\$23,140.00 \div 12 = \$1,928.33 \text{ monthly net pay}$$

Flagstone National Bank
VALUCARD

APPLICANT:

1. Name (Last)	(First)	(Initial)	2. Birthdate	3. Social Security No.
Ramirez	Selma	N.	3/5/72	264-87-1533

4. Address (Street)	(City)	(State)	(Zip)
1915 W. Mariposa Drive	San Antonio	TX	78201-3121

5. Area Code/Tel. Number	6. Lived At Present Address	7. __ Own ✓ Rent __ Other	8. Monthly Payment
512-555-8934	3 Years 4 Months		$625.00

9. Previous Street Address (if less than 2 years at present address)	10. Lived At Previous Address
	Years Months

STEP 1

11. Present Employer	12. How Long Employed	13. Job Title	14. Monthly Net Income
Superior Furnishings, Inc.	2 Years 1 Months	Supervisor	$1,928.33

15. Employer's Address (Street)	(City)	(State)	(Zip)	16. Area Code/Tel. Number
4163 Navajo St.	San Antonio	TX	78211-6511	512-555-3074

17. Previous Employer	18. How Long Employed	19. Job Title	20. Monthly Net Income
Red Rock Distributors, Inc.	3 Years 0 Months	Record Keeper	$1,207.00

21. Employer's Address (Street)	(City)	(State)	(Zip)	22. Area Code/Tel. Number
3410 Guadalupe St.	San Antonio	TX	78207-3341	512-555-5078

23. Other Sources Of Income	24. Net Income Per Month
Brevet's Department Store	$208.00

CO-APPLICANT: Complete this section only if a joint account is requested. (Spouse can be a co-applicant.)

25. Name (Last)	(First)	(Initial)	26. Birthdate	27. Social Security No.

28. Address (Street)	(City)	(State)	(Zip)

STEP 2

CREDIT REFERENCES:

48. Savings Account (Institution Name)	(Account No.)	(Balance)
Helena Savings and Loan Co.	20781	$813.21

49. Checking Account (Institution Name)	(Account No.)	(Balance)
Merona National Bank	342-787	$515.03

STEP 3

LOANS AND OUTSTANDING DEBTS: List all debts owing. Attach additional sheet if necessary.

50. Auto Make, Model, & Year	51. Financed By	52. Account No.	53. Balance	54. Monthly Payment
Ford Taurus, 20--	Halperin City Bank	3461-89	$6,859.00	$350.00

55. Name of Creditor/Lender	56. Account No.	57. Balance	58. Monthly Payment
Farmington's Department Store	23078	$128.50	$50.00

STEP 4

The above information is given to obtain credit privileges. I (we) hereby authorize the obtaining of information about any statements made herein, and I (we) agree to be bound by the terms of the National Credit Card agreement. Signers shall be jointly and severally liable.

Selma N. Ramirez	8/19/--	1
Applicant's Signature	Date	Authorized User(s)

STEP 5

Co-Applicant's Signature	Date	Relationship to Applicant	No. of Cards Requested

---

Illustration 12B

A completed credit card application form

Joint account. An account for two people.

Selma previously worked for 3 years for Red Rock Distributors, Inc. as a record keeper. She entered the company name, address, and telephone number, her job title, length of time employed, and monthly pay into questions 17–22 of the form.

Selma also earns $48.00 a week in net pay working part-time at Brevet's Department Store. Selma found the monthly net pay for her part-time job and entered these data into questions 23 and 24 of the form. Here are her calculations:

$$\$48.00 \times 52 = \$2,496.00 \text{ yearly net part-time pay}$$
$$\$2,496.00 \div 12 = \$208.00 \text{ monthly net part-time pay}$$

STEP 2 Complete the Co-Applicant section of the form.

If two people are applying for the same credit card, information about the other person, or co-applicant, is entered into this section. If Selma were married, she might have applied for a **joint account** with her husband. Information about her husband would then be entered into the

Co-Applicant section. This section has almost the same questions as the Applicant section. Since Selma is applying for a credit card for herself only, she left the Co-Applicant section blank. Because the Co-Applicant section was not used, it is not fully shown in Illustration 12B (page 107).

STEP 3 **Complete the Credit References section of the form.**

Selma listed the bank names, account numbers, and balances of her savings and checking accounts in questions 48 and 49.

STEP 4 **Complete the Loans and Outstanding Debts section of the form.**

Selma pays $350.00 a month on her Ford Taurus. She has $6,859.00 left to pay on her car loan which is financed by the Halperin City Bank. Selma entered the data about her car and her car loan in questions 50–54 of the form.

Selma also has a $128.50 balance in her charge account with Farmington's Department Store. She makes payments of $50.00 a month on the balance. She entered the data about the charge account in questions 55–58.

STEP 5 **Sign the form and return it to the credit firm.**

When Selma had finished entering the data, she checked the form over to make sure that she had completed it correctly. Then, she signed and dated the form. She also showed that she was the only person approved, or **authorized**, to use the credit card and asked that only one card be sent to her. She then mailed the application form to the Flagstone National Bank.

Authorize. To approve.

BUILDING YOUR BUSINESS VOCABULARY

On a sheet of paper, write the headings **Statement Number** and **Words**. Next, choose the words that match the statements. Write each word you choose next to the statement number it matches. Be careful; not all the words listed should be used.

Statements	Words
1. Buy now and pay later	annual
2. A source of credit; lender	authorize
3. A form of credit offered by stores	bank credit cards
4. Credit cards issued by banks	budget
5. Used to identify the person buying on credit	cash flow
6. People likely to pay off their debts	charge account
7. Provides information about your ability to pay your debts	credit
8. An account for two people	credit application
9. To approve	credit card
10. Yearly	creditor
	good credit risks
	joint account

STEPS REVIEW: Applying for Bank Credit Cards

STEP 1 Complete the Applicant section of the form.

STEP 2 Complete the Co-Applicant section of the form.

STEP 3 Complete the Credit References section of the form.

STEP 4 Complete the Loans and Outstanding Debts section of the form.

STEP 5 Sign the form and return it to the credit firm.

APPLICATION PROBLEMS

Problem 12-1

The weekly pay for 5 people is listed below.

CHECK POINT
12-1

(A. Berle) Yearly pay = $28,600.00; monthly pay = $2,383.33

Directions

Find the yearly and monthly pay for each person. Round to the nearest cent when necessary.

Name	Weekly Pay	Yearly Pay	Monthly Pay
A. Berle	$550.00		
B. Coster	$452.00		
C. Dazai	$286.90		
D. Espino	$340.60		
E. Frisch	$490.80		

Problem 12-2

Fred Bronner is applying for a ValuCard from the Flagstone National Bank.

Directions

Complete a credit application form for Fred Bronner using the data provided. Be sure to compute his monthly net pay accurately and to sign and date the form 7/18/--. Fred wants only one card and is the only authorized user.

Applicant Section Data:

Name: Fred L. Bronner
Birthdate: 3/22/70
Social Security Number: 304-45-9846
Address: 1913 Dogwood Road
City: Charleston
State: West Virginia
Zip Code: 25320-9087
Telephone Number: 304-555-1225
Other Data: Has rented his present apartment for 4 years and 6 months at
    $626.00 a month
Present Employer: R. B. Crouse, Inc., 5910 Kanawha Boulevard E.,
    Charleston, WV 25306-7839, telephone 304-555-2601
Present Job: Credit Clerk II for 1 year and 2 months with a weekly net pay of $382.32
Previous Employer: Tallworks, Inc., 7194 Young Street, Charleston,
    WV 25309-9922, telephone 304-555-6133
Previous Job: General Office Clerk for 3 years and 1 month with a weekly
    net pay of $212.43

CHECK POINT
12-2

Present Monthly Net Income = $1,656.72

Other Sources of Income: Part-time delivery person for Danville Delivery Service with a weekly net pay of $64.00

Credit References Section Data:

Savings Account: Account No. 32108 with a balance of $629.08 at Torrence Savings and Loan

Checking Account: Account No. 12-8907 with a balance of $339.03 at Edgemont Bank and Trust Co.

Loans and Outstanding Debts Section Data:

Auto Loan: A balance of $3,508.91, with monthly payments of $276.25, in loan account No. 12078 for a 20-- Buick LeSabre with Edgemont Bank and Trust Co.

Other Lender: A $227.00 balance, with monthly payments of $35.00, in account No. 44729 with Valley Electronics

---

Problem 12-3   Amy Weinstein is applying for a TotalCard from Fredonia City Bank.

Directions
Complete a credit application form for Amy Weinstein using the data provided. Be sure to compute her monthly net pay accurately and to sign and date the form 1/31/--. Amy wants only one card and is the only authorized user.

Applicant Section Data:

Name: Amy V. Weinstein
Birthdate: 9/16/72
Social Security Number: 342-12-5611
Address: 15 Azalea Lane
City: Madison
State: Wisconsin
Zip Code: 53711-3414
Telephone Number: 608-555-3978
Other Data: Has rented her present apartment for 2 years and 1 month at $495.00 a month
Present Employer: Telos Company, 1503 Oro Drive, Madison, WI 53714-2531, telephone 608-555-8898
Present Job: Solderer for 1 year and 2 months with a weekly net pay of $284.88
Previous Employer: Borkin Bros., Inc., 437 Merton Avenue, Madison, WI 53716-4077, telephone 608-555-8787

CHECK POINT

12-3

Previous Monthly Net Income = $1,004.77

Previous Job: Line worker for 3 years and 1 month with a weekly net pay of $231.87
Other Sources of Income: Part-time airport limousine driver for Reo Limousine Service with a weekly net pay of $102.64

Credit References Section Data:

Savings Account: Account No. 12-899 with a balance of $271.73 at Churchill State Bank

Checking Account: Account No. 22-3075 with a balance of $301.33 at Churchill State Bank

Loans and Outstanding Debts Section Data:

Auto Loan: A balance of $4,078.24, with monthly payments of $285.95, in loan account No. 6051 for a 20-- Olds Intrigue with Churchill State Bank

Other Lender: A $147.35 balance, with monthly payments of $25.00, in account No. 2158 with Ferrel Furniture Co.

Problem 12-4 may be found in the Working Papers.

applied math preview

Copy and complete the problems below.

1. $ 40.76	2. $ 104.75	3. $ 277.28	4. $ 1.43	5. $ 331.98
− 40.67	− 104.57	− 272.78	− 1.34	− 313.98

key terms preview

- **Chronological**
- **Credit card statement**
- **Embossed**
- **Imprinter**
- **Overcharged**

- **Sales slip**
- **Transaction**
- **Unauthorized charges**
- **Undercharged**

goals

1 To learn how to find the common errors on credit card statements.

2 To learn how to find the correct credit card balance.

→ UNDERSTANDING THE JOB

Key Terms

Sales slip. Written record of a sale.

Each time you use your credit card, a sales clerk completes a written record of the sale called a **sales slip**. For example, Vincent Aiello has a bank credit card from the Crestwood Bank. On April 2, 20--, he used the card to buy a book from Belden's Book Store. The store clerk at Belden's completed the bank credit card sales slip shown in Illustration 13A. Notice that the total amount of the sale, $15.73, is shown at the bottom and the top of the sales slip.

Illustration 13A

A bank credit card sales slip

ACCOUNT NUMBER 5489 784 022	SALE AMOUNT 00015.73			INVOICE NUMBER 507907	
4/X1 4/X3	DATE 4/2/--	AUTHORIZATION NO. --	SALES CLERK 72	DEPT. 6	
VINCENT AIELLO	QUAN.	DESCRIPTION	PRICE	AMOUNT	
	1	Book	14.98	14 98	
0037971 BELDEN'S BOOK STORE 14 CASSEN STREET MOBILE, AL 36617-2239					
	SIGN HERE X Vincent Aiello		SUBTOTAL	14 98	
			SALES TAX	75	
	SALES SLIP		TOTAL	15 73	

VISA OR MasterCard

MERCHANT: RETAIN THIS COPY FOR YOUR RECORDS

MERCHANT COPY / BANK COPY / CUSTOMER COPY

Embossed. Printed in raised characters.

Imprinter. A device which prints data from a charge card onto a sales slip.

Credit card statement. Shows the transactions and balances of a credit card account.

Transaction. Something that happens in a business that is recorded.

The customer's account number, name, and other data may be **embossed**, or printed in raised characters, on a charge card. This allows the clerk to print some of the data on the sales slip automatically, using an **imprinter**. This device prints customer data from the charge card onto the sales slip. The imprinter also prints the store's name, address, and account number, and the sale amount on the sales slip. You will learn in Chapter 7 that many businesses now use special electronic devices to read credit card information.

The store clerk gave Vincent a copy of the sales slip, kept one copy for store records, and sent a third copy to the credit card company. After the month was over, the credit card company sent Vincent a **credit card statement** listing each sales slip, the sales slip amount, any payments Vincent made, and the total amount that Vincent owes. The statement Vincent received for the month of April is shown in Illustration 13B.

Each purchase and payment that Vincent made was called a **transaction**. A transaction is something that happens in a business that a record keeper records, like sales, purchases, and payments of bills. The first transaction for Vincent in April was the purchase of the book from Belden's Book Store. The total amount of the purchase, $15.73, was recorded in the New Loans, Fees, & Purchases column.

On April 7, Vincent paid the credit card company $103.44. This amount was the previous balance due from the March statement. The payment was recorded in the Payments & Credits column.

On April 27, Vincent was charged his annual credit card fee. This

Illustration 13B

Credit card statement

Crestwood Bank
VISA · MasterCard

Transaction Date	Reference	Transaction Description		New Loans, Fees, & Purchases	Payments & Credits
04/02/--	03078912	Belden's Book Store	Mobile, AL	15.73	
04/06/--	07989721	Ventnor Car Repairs	Mobile, AL	157.45	
04/07/--	207078T2	Payment -- Thank You			103.44
04/18/--	10798372	T & R Electronics	Mobile, AL	88.98	
04/21/--	00391782	Shipley's Sporting Goods	Houston, TX	25.56	
04/27/--	91074392	Reppenour Restaurant	Mobile, AL	35.56	
04/27/--		Annual Fee		25.00	

How We Arrived At Your Finance Charge	Monthly Rate	Annual Percentage Rate	Balance to Which Monthly Rate Applied	Finance Charge

Previous Balance	Payments & Credits	New Loans, Fees, & Purchases	Finance Charge	New Balance	Minimum Payment Due
103.44	103.44	348.28	0.00	348.28	35.00

Billing Date	Date Payment Due	Credit Line	Account Number	In case of billing error, write to this address: P.O. Box 10787, Mobile, AL 36616-2978
04/30/--	05/25/--	2000	5489 784 022	Direct telephone inquiries to 1-800-555-1987

transaction, for $25.00, was recorded in the New Loans, Fees, & Purchases column.

SAMPLE PROBLEM

Key Terms

Chronological. By date.

Before Vincent paid the new balance due for the month of April, he examined the statement to make certain that the balance owed was correct. He used a credit card statement work sheet, like the one shown in Illustration 13C, to help him. Here is how he did this job:

STEP 1 Complete the heading.

Vincent entered the heading at the top of the work sheet. He wrote "For April, 20--" because the work sheet included transactions for the whole month of April.

STEP 2 Verify the sales slips.

Vincent saves the copies of the sales slips for every purchase he makes. When he receives his statement, he sorts the sales slips in **chronological** order. He then verifies that each sales slip is listed on the statement.

Vincent's first sales slip was for the book he bought. He checked the statement to see that the sales slip was recorded. Since it was, he placed a check mark next to the date in the Transaction Date column.

Illustration 13C

Vincent Aiello's credit card statement work sheet

Vincent Aiello
Credit Card Statement Work Sheet
For April, 20--

a. Unauthorized charges listed on statement:

Date	Store		Amount
4/21/--	*Shipley's Sporting Goods*	$	*25.56*
		$	

b. Corrections to amounts on statement:

For an overcharge:			For an undercharge:		
Charge on statement	$	*35.56*	Charge on sales slip	$	
Charge on sales slip	$	*35.16*	Charge on statement	$	
Amount overcharged	$	*.40*	Amount undercharged	$	

c. Calculating the correct new balance:

New balance from statement		$ *348.28*
Less: Unauthorized charges	$ *25.56*	
Overcharge on statement	$ *.40*	
		$ *25.96*
		$ *322.32*
Add: Undercharge on statement		$
Correct new balance		$ *322.32*

ACCOUNT NUMBER 5489 784 022		SALE AMOUNT 00035.16			INVOICE NUMBER 917039		
4/X1 4/X3		DATE 4/27/--	AUTHORIZATION NO. 307198		SALES CLERK --	DEPT. --	
VINCENT AIELLO		QUAN.	DESCRIPTION		PRICE	AMOUNT	
0048369		--	Dinner		33.49	33 49	
REPPENOUR RESTAURANT 2079 PORTER AVENUE MOBILE, AL 36606-2971							
		SIGN HERE X Vincent Aiello			SUBTOTAL	33 49	
					SALES TAX	1 67	
SALES SLIP					TOTAL	35 16	

MERCHANT COPY

MERCHANT: RETAIN THIS COPY FOR YOUR RECORDS   VISA   OR   MasterCard

Key Terms

Unauthorized charges.
Transactions not approved.

Overcharged. When you are charged more than you should be.

Undercharged. When you are charged less than you should be.

Vincent put aside those sales slips which are dated after the billing date shown on the statement, April 30, 20--. These sales slips will be shown on the next credit card statement that Vincent receives.

From time to time, Vincent has found that sales slips for other people have been recorded on his statement. Because Vincent did not approve these transactions, they are called **unauthorized charges**. For April, he found that the transaction dated April 21, 20--, should not have been listed on his statement. He found no sales slip for this transaction and did not make the purchase. Vincent listed the date, store, and amount of the sales slip on the line "Unauthorized charges listed on statement." He also listed the amount, $25.56, on the line "Less: Unauthorized charges" in the section "Calculating the correct new balance."

STEP 3   Verify the amount of each transaction on the statement.

Vincent has also found that occasionally the amount on the statement does not agree with the amount on the sales slip. For example, Vincent found that the transaction dated April 27 was incorrectly listed as $35.56. The actual sales slip shown in Illustration 13D shows a correct total of only $35.16. Vincent was charged more than he should have been, or **overcharged**. Vincent entered $35.56 on the "Charge on statement" line under the heading "For an overcharge." He then entered the correct amount, $35.16, under the incorrect amount and subtracted to find the amount overcharged, $.40. He entered the overcharge on the line "Overcharge on statement" in the section "Calculating the correct new balance."

If the amount on the statement had been less than the amount on the sales slip, there would have been an **undercharge**. Vincent would then have subtracted the amount on the statement from the amount on the sales slip, entering the data under the heading "For an undercharge."

STEP 4   Verify other charges.

Vincent examined the statement for other charges. He found that he was charged $25.00 for his annual fee. He knew that this was the correct amount, and he also knew that he should be charged the fee in April. His card membership is renewed every April.

STEP 5   Verify the payments.

Vincent looked at his checkbook to make certain that the payment listed for April 7 was correct. He also checked to make certain that $103.44 was the only payment he made during that month.

Calculate the correct new balance.

Vincent then calculated the amount he owed, or the correct new balance, in the section "Calculating the correct new balance." He entered the new balance from the statement, $348.28. He added the unauthorized charge and the overcharge and put the sum, $25.96, below the $348.28 and subtracted. Since there was no undercharge on the statement, the result, $322.32, is the correct new balance. He entered the correct new balance on the bottom line of the work sheet.

If there had been an undercharge, Vincent would have entered it on the line "Add: Undercharge on sales slip" and added it to get the correct new balance.

Vincent wrote a letter to the credit card company explaining why the new balance was incorrect. He included a copy of the sales slip for the restaurant meal as proof that he was charged too much.

Vincent could have called the credit card company using the telephone number provided on the statement. A representative of the company would have then advised him on how to handle the errors he found on his statement. However, by telephoning he may not have been able to protect all of his legal rights.

You have learned how to check credit card statements in this job. In a later job you will learn how to complete credit card sales slips as a store clerk.

 ## BUILDING YOUR BUSINESS VOCABULARY

On a sheet of paper, write the headings **Statement Number** and **Words**. Next, choose the words that match the statements. Write each word you choose next to the statement number it matches. Be careful; not all the words listed should be used.

Statements	Words
1. A written record of a sale	annual
2. A form showing the transactions and balances for a credit card account	authorize
	bank credit card
3. To check for accuracy	chronological
4. Something that happens in a business that is recorded	credit
	credit card statement
5. When you are charged more than you should be	creditor
	embossed
6. When you are charged less than you should be	imprinter
	joint account
7. A credit card issued by a bank	overcharged
8. When you buy now and pay later	sales slip
9. Yearly	transaction
10. A lender	unauthorized charges
11. A device for recording a credit card sale	undercharged
12. By date	verify
13. Printed in raised characters	
14. Transactions not approved	

STEPS REVIEW: Checking Your Credit Card Statement

STEP 1 Complete the heading.

STEP 2 Verify the sales slips.

STEP 3 Verify the amount of each transaction on the statement.

STEP 4 Verify other charges.

STEP 5 Verify the payments.

STEP 6 Calculate the correct new balance.

 APPLICATION PROBLEMS

Problem 13-1 **Directions**

Complete the following table by putting the amount overcharged or undercharged in the correct column.

CHECK POINT

13-1(1)

Undercharge = $0.09

	Total of Sales Slip	Amount Charged on Statement	Overcharge	Undercharge
1	$223.87	$223.78		
2	$409.18	$409.81		
3	$19.59	$119.59		
4	$72.08	$72.00		
5	$8.93	$8.99		

Problem 13-2

Jean Watson has saved each of her credit card sales slips for the month of June. Jean renews her card membership every June for a fee of $35.00. Her checkbook shows that she made a payment of $237.20 on June 15. She wants to verify her credit card statement for June.

Directions

 CHECK POINT

13-2

Correct new balance = $234.13

a. On pages 117 and 118, you are given Jean's credit card statement and the top sections of her sales slips for June. Use a work sheet like the one in Illustration 13C (page 113) to verify the statement.

b. List the date, store, and amount of every transaction which should not appear on the statement.

c. Compare the "sale amounts" on the sales slips to the amounts on the statement. If an amount is incorrect, find the overcharge or undercharge. Do not compare the "Amount" on the slips with the statement. The "Amount" and "Sale Amount" may differ because the bottom sections of the slips, showing sales taxes and totals, are not provided.

d. Find the correct new balance for the statement.

Spreadsheet

Slip 1

ACCOUNT NUMBER	SALE AMOUNT				INVOICE NUMBER	
4810 078 172	00015.20				186271	

DATE	AUTHORIZATION NO.		SALES CLERK		DEPT.	
6/3/--	--		12		55	

QUAN.	DESCRIPTION	PRICE	AMOUNT	
1	Book	12.48	12	48
1	Calendar	2.00	2	00

6/X1 6/X3
JEAN WATSON
0079182
TOLL'S BOOKSTORE

MERCHANT COPY

Slip 2

ACCOUNT NUMBER	SALE AMOUNT	INVOICE NUMBER
4810 078 172	00012.52	279183

DATE	AUTHORIZATION NO.	SALES CLERK	DEPT.
6/4/--	--	3	2

QUAN.	DESCRIPTION	PRICE	AMOUNT	
--	Gasoline	12.52	12	52

6/X1 6/X3
JEAN WATSON
0019728
RON'S 77 GAS

MERCHANT COPY

Slip 3

ACCOUNT NUMBER	SALE AMOUNT	INVOICE NUMBER
4810 078 172	00021.20	280188

DATE	AUTHORIZATION NO.	SALES CLERK	DEPT.
6/8/--	--	--	--

QUAN.	DESCRIPTION	PRICE	AMOUNT	
--	Dinner	20.19	20	19

6/X1 6/X3
JEAN WATSON
0020189
TRES BON RESTAURANT

MERCHANT COPY

Slip 4

ACCOUNT NUMBER	SALE AMOUNT	INVOICE NUMBER
4810 078 172	00112.16	700893

DATE	AUTHORIZATION NO.	SALES CLERK	DEPT.
6/18/--	2017983	4	6

QUAN.	DESCRIPTION	PRICE	AMOUNT	
1	Portable TV	106.82	106	82

6/X1 6/X3
JEAN WATSON
0088493
TOWN TV AND RADIO

MERCHANT COPY

Slip 5

ACCOUNT NUMBER	SALE AMOUNT	INVOICE NUMBER
4810 078 172	00010.16	280343

DATE	AUTHORIZATION NO.	SALES CLERK	DEPT.
6/22/--	--	3	2

QUAN.	DESCRIPTION	PRICE	AMOUNT	
--	Gasoline	10.16	10	16

6/X1 6/X3
JEAN WATSON
0019728
RON'S 77 GAS

MERCHANT COPY

Slip 6

ACCOUNT NUMBER	SALE AMOUNT	INVOICE NUMBER
4810 078 172	00027.89	330911

DATE	AUTHORIZATION NO.	SALES CLERK	DEPT.
6/29/--	--	10	1

QUAN.	DESCRIPTION	PRICE	AMOUNT	
1	FRAME	26.56	26	56

6/X1 6/X3
JEAN WATSON
0044909
HILL ART STUDIO

MERCHANT COPY

BANK of the MOUNTAIN

Transaction Date	Reference	Transaction Description		New Loans, Fees, & Purchases	Payments & Credits
06/03/--	20719834	Toll's Bookstore	Atlanta, GA	15.20	
06/04/--	91702930	Ron's 77 Gas	Atlanta, GA	12.52	
06/08/--	33307922	Tres Bon Restaurant	Atlanta, GA	22.10	
06/15/--	51072983	Payment -- Thank You			237.20
06/16/--		Annual Membership Fee		35.00	
06/18/--	20179833	Town TV and Radio	Atlanta, GA	112.16	
06/20/--	00982719	Range Riding Stables	Yuma, AR	55.00	
06/22/--	31057434	Ron's 77 Gas	Atlanta, GA	10.16	
06/29/--	15324150	Hill Art Studio	Atlanta, GA	27.89	

How We Arrived At Your Finance Charge	Monthly Rate	Annual Percentage Rate	Balance to Which Monthly Rate Applied	Finance Charge

Previous Balance	Payments & Credits	New Loans, Fees, & Purchases	Finance Charge	New Balance	Minimum Payment Due
237.20	237.20	290.03	0.00	290.03	30.00

Billing Date	Date Payment Due	Credit Line	Account Number	In case of billing error, write to this address: P.O. Box 3011A, Atlanta, GA 30307-1421
06/30/--	07/25/--	1500	4810 078 172	Direct telephone inquiries to 1-800-555-9811

Problem 13-3   Marvin Freeman has saved each of his credit card sales slips for the month of May. Marvin renews his card membership every May for a fee of $30.00. His checkbook shows that he made a payment of $312.77 on May 12. He wants to verify his credit card statement for May.

Directions

a. On pages 119 and 120, you are given Marvin's credit card statement and the top sections of his sales slips for May. Use a work sheet like the one in Illustration 13C (page 113) to verify the statement.

b. List the date, store, and amount of every transaction which should not appear on the statement.

c. Compare the "sale amounts" on the sales slips to the amounts on the statement. If an amount is incorrect, find the overcharge or undercharge. Do not compare the "Amount" on the slips with the statement. The "Amount" and "sale amount" may differ because the bottom sections of the slips, showing sales taxes and totals, are not provided.

d. Find the correct new balance for the statement.

Correct new balance =
$541.19

ACCOUNT NUMBER 3308 102 448	SALE AMOUNT 00167.98			INVOICE NUMBER 220325		
5/X1 5/X3	DATE 5/5/--	AUTHORIZATION NO. 339134		SALES CLERK 23		DEPT. 12
MARVIN FREEMAN	QUAN.	DESCRIPTION		PRICE	AMOUNT	
0408855	1	Jacket		159.98	159	98
EMORY CLOTHING						

MANT COPY

ACCOUNT NUMBER 3308 102 448	SALE AMOUNT 00017.33			INVOICE NUMBER 797985		
5/X1 5/X3	DATE 5/7/--	AUTHORIZATION NO. --		SALES CLERK 2		DEPT. 2
MARVIN FREEMAN	QUAN.	DESCRIPTION		PRICE	AMOUNT	
8839001	--	Gasoline		17.33	17	33
7TH ST. STATION						

MANT COPY

ACCOUNT NUMBER 3308 102 448	SALE AMOUNT 00247.23			INVOICE NUMBER 079313		
5/X1 5/X3	DATE 5/9/--	AUTHORIZATION NO. 107988		SALES CLERK 3		DEPT. 5
MARVIN FREEMAN	QUAN.	DESCRIPTION		PRICE	AMOUNT	
3930119	--	Car Repairs		235.46	235	46
V & R REPAIRS						

ANT COPY

ACCOUNT NUMBER 3308 102 448	SALE AMOUNT 00019.98			INVOICE NUMBER 635726		
5/X1 5/X3	DATE 5/15/--	AUTHORIZATION NO. --		SALES CLERK 8		DEPT. 10
MARVIN FREEMAN	QUAN.	DESCRIPTION		PRICE	AMOUNT	
8839979	1	Box Computer Disks		19.03	19	03
SUNDAY COMPUTERS						

ANT COPY

ACCOUNT NUMBER 3308 102 448	SALE AMOUNT 00033.60			INVOICE NUMBER 879116		
5/X1 5/X3	DATE 5/25/--	AUTHORIZATION NO. --		SALES CLERK 7		DEPT. --
MARVIN FREEMAN	QUAN.	DESCRIPTION		PRICE	AMOUNT	
4351569	4	Baseball Tickets		8.40	33	60
TICKET-O-RAMA						

ANT COPY

ACCOUNT NUMBER 3308 102 448	SALE AMOUNT 00025.07			INVOICE NUMBER 761001		
5/X1 5/X3	DATE 5/29/--	AUTHORIZATION NO. 841928		SALES CLERK 14		DEPT. 9
MARVIN FREEMAN	QUAN.	DESCRIPTION		PRICE	AMOUNT	
6179763	6	Video Tapes		3.98	23	88
MORE-MART STORES						

ANT COPY

CRESTVIEW BANK & TRUST COMPANY

Transaction Date	Reference	Transaction Description		New Loans, Fees, & Purchases	Payments & Credits
05/05/--	78121991	Emory Clothing	Detroit, MI	167.98	
05/07/--	44158742	7th St. Station	Detroit, MI	13.77	
05/09/--	99785127	V & R Repairs	Detroit, MI	247.23	
05/12/--	84571128	Payment -- Thank You			312.77
05/14/--	81672661	Staten's Body Shop	Boston, MA	213.98	
05/15/--	51641554	Sunday Computers	Detroit, MI	19.98	
05/20/--		Annual Fee		30.00	
05/25/--	61265993	Ticket-O-Rama	Detroit, MI	33.60	
05/29/--	37114987	More-Mart Stores	Lansing, MI	25.07	

How We Arrived At Your Finance Charge	Monthly Rate	Annual Percentage Rate	Balance to Which Monthly Rate Applied	Finance Charge

Previous Balance	Payments & Credits	New Loans, Fees, & Purchases	Finance Charge	New Balance	Minimum Payment Due
312.77	312.77	751.61	0.00	751.61	75.00

Billing Date	Date Payment Due	Credit Line	Account Number	In case of billing error, write to this address: P.O. Box 3872A, Detroit, MI 48223-6152
05/30/--	06/25/--	3000	3308 102 448	Direct telephone inquiries to 1-800-555-1987

Problem 13-4 may be found in the Working Papers.

Job 14   BUYING ON THE INSTALLMENT PLAN

→ UNDERSTANDING THE JOB

Key Terms

Installment plan. When you pay for an item by the month.

Cash price. The amount an item would cost if you paid cash for it.

Finance charge. The difference between cash and installment prices.

Installment contract. A form describing the time, place, and amounts of an installment purchase.

One way to buy on credit is to buy on the **installment plan**. When you buy on the installment plan, you pay for an item in monthly payments or installments. For example, you or a business may want to buy a car that costs $8,500.00. You may not have $8,500.00 in the bank to pay cash for the car, but you can afford monthly payments of $350.00. Buying the car on credit in this way allows you to have the car right away but pay for it over many months.

When you buy on the installment plan, you are really borrowing the seller's money and paying it back over time. For that reason, the installment price is usually more than the **cash price**, or the amount the item would cost if you paid cash for it. The difference between the cash price and installment price of an item is called the **finance charge**.

An installment buyer is usually asked to sign an **installment contract** like the one shown in Illustration 14A on page 122. You need to know how the amounts on an installment contract are found so that you can check them before you sign it.

In Tune Music Store, Inc.
2100 Lincoln Plaza
Philadelphia, PA 19118-5671

RETAIL
INSTALLMENT
CONTRACT

Contract No.: 197822   Item: Compact Disc Player, Model No. 56A34
Buyer's Name: Felicia Peters
Buyer's Address: 4512 Ferndoan Street
City: Philadelphia   State: PA   Zip: 19148-4478

STEP 1 →	1. Cash Price	$ 537.50
STEP 2 →	2. Down Payment	107.50
STEP 3 →	3. Amount Financed	430.00
STEP 4 →	4. Installment Price	647.02
	5. Finance Charge	109.52
	6. Annual Percentage Rate	18%

Buyer agrees to pay In Tune Music Store, Inc., at their offices, the installment price shown above in __24__ monthly installments of $ 22.48 . The first installment is payable on __June 6__ , 20-- , and all subsequent payments are to be made on the same day of each consecutive month until the installment price is paid in full, subject to the conditions on the reverse side of this contract.

Signed __Felicia Peters__

SAMPLE PROBLEM

Key Terms

Down payment. Part of purchase price paid at sale.

Amount financed. Amount borrowed.

Felicia Peters bought a compact disc player priced at $537.50 from the In Tune Music Store. The store asked her to pay 20% down and the rest in monthly payments of $22.48 for two years. The store also asked her to sign the installment contract shown in Illustration 14A.

Here is how Felicia checked the amounts on the contract before she signed it:

STEP 1 Find the amount of the down payment.

The **down payment** is part of the purchase price that you must pay right away. The down payment for the compact disc player is 20% of the cash price, which is $537.50. To find the down payment, Felicia multiplied the cash price by the down payment percent.

$$\$537.50 \times 0.20 = \$107.50 \quad \text{down payment}$$

Felicia then compared the down payment amount she calculated with the down payment amount shown on the contract.

STEP 2 Find the amount financed.

The amount that you borrow from the seller is called the **amount financed**. This is the amount Felicia must repay over time. Felicia found the amount financed by subtracting the down payment from the cash price.

$$\$537.50 - \$107.50 = \$430.00 \quad \text{amount financed}$$

Felicia then compared her calculation of the amount financed with the amount shown on the contract.

STEP 3 Find the installment price.

The **installment price** is the down payment plus the total of all the monthly payments. Felicia found the installment price by multiplying the monthly payment, $22.48, by 24 months (2 years). She then added that amount and the down payment.

$$\$22.48 \times 24 = \begin{array}{r} \$\,539.52 \\ +107.50 \\ \hline \$\,647.02 \end{array} \quad \begin{array}{l} \text{total of the monthly payments} \\ \text{down payment} \\ \text{installment price} \end{array}$$

Felicia then compared her calculation of the installment price with the amount shown on the contract.

STEP 4 Find the finance charge.

Finance charge = install-ment price − cash price

Key Terms

Installment price. Down payment plus total monthly payments.

Subsequent. After or following.

Annual percentage rate. Rate of finance charge.

The finance charge is the difference between the installment price, $647.02, and the cash price, $537.50. Felicia subtracted the cash price from the installment price to find the finance charge.

$$\$647.02 - \$537.50 = \$109.52 \quad \text{finance charge}$$

Felicia then compared her calculation of the finance charge with the amount shown on the contract. Since all of the amounts that Felicia calculated agreed with the amounts on the contract, she signed the contract.

If Felicia had found an error in one of the amounts, she would have crossed out that amount and written the correct amount to the right of the incorrect amount. She would then have corrected any amounts after, or **subsequent** to, the incorrect amount on lines 1–5 of the contract. For example, if the installment price had been incorrectly shown on the contract as $640.72 and the finance charge as $110.22, Felicia would have made these corrections:

3.	Amount Financed	430.00
4.	Installment Price	~~640.72~~ 647.02
5.	Finance Charge	~~110.22~~ 109.52
6.	Annual Percentage Rate	18%

The store would then have had to prepare a new, corrected contract for Felicia to sign.

Felicia will pay $109.52 more for the compact disc player on the installment plan than she would if she paid cash. If Felicia saved her money and waited until she could buy the player for cash, she would save $109.52. However, she would not get the use of the compact disk player until the needed cash was saved.

The finance charge is the cost you pay to borrow money from the seller. The finance charge is also shown as a percent on the contract and is called the **annual percentage rate** or APR. The annual percentage rate listed on the contract shown in Illustration 14A (page 122) is 18%. To find the APR on an installment contract, you must use a formula and a

Verifying the calculations of down payment, amount financed, installment price, and finance charge is easier when you use a calculator. The calculations in the Sample Problem could have been completed this way:

STEP 1 ▶ *Find the amount of the down payment.*

Press these keys in order:

$$5 \quad 3 \quad 7 \quad . \quad 5 \quad \times \quad . \quad 2 \quad =$$

The answer that appears in the display is $107.50, the down payment amount. Notice that it was not necessary to enter the ending zeros after .5 and .2.

STEP 2 ▶ *Find the amount financed.*

Press these keys in order:

$$5 \quad 3 \quad 7 \quad . \quad 5 \quad - \quad 1 \quad 0 \quad 7 \quad . \quad 5 \quad =$$

The display now shows $430.00, the amount financed.

STEP 3 ▶ *Find the installment price.*

Press these keys in order:

$$2 \quad 2 \quad . \quad 4 \quad 8 \quad \times \quad 2 \quad 4 \quad =$$

The display now shows $539.52, the total of the monthly payments. Leave the display as it is and press these keys in order:

$$+ \quad 1 \quad 0 \quad 7 \quad . \quad 5 \quad =$$

The display now shows $647.02, the installment price.

STEP 4 ▶ *Find the finance charge.*

Leave the installment price in the display and press these keys:

$$- \quad 5 \quad 3 \quad 7 \quad . \quad 5 \quad =$$

The display now shows $109.52, the finance charge.

table. You will not be expected to find the APR for installment contracts in this job.

BUILDING YOUR BUSINESS VOCABULARY

On a sheet of paper, write the headings **Statement Number** and **Words**. Next, choose the words that match the statements. Write each word you choose next to the statement number it matches. Be careful; not all the words listed should be used.

Statements	Words
1. A form of credit in which you pay for an item in monthly payments	amount financed
2. The amount an item costs if bought for cash	annual percentage rate
	bank credit card
3. The difference between the cash and installment prices of an item	cash price
	credit
4. A form which describes the time, place, and amounts for an installment purchase	creditor
	down payment
5. The part of the installment price paid at the time an item is bought	finance charge
	installment contract
6. After or following	installment plan
7. The amount borrowed from the seller in an installment purchase	installment price
	subsequent
8. The down payment plus the total of all monthly payments	
9. When you buy now and pay later	
10. The annual finance charge shown as a rate or percent	

STEPS REVIEW: Buying on the Installment Plan

STEP 1 Find the amount of the down payment.

STEP 2 Find the amount financed.

STEP 3 Find the installment price.

STEP 4 Find the finance charge.

APPLICATION PROBLEMS

Problem 14-1

Ellen Berman bought an electronic keyboard priced at $312.50 from Searles Equipment Company. The store asked her to pay 20% down and the rest in monthly payments of $22.58 for one year. The store also asked her to sign the installment contract shown at the top of page 126.

CHECK POINT

14-1

Finance charge = $20.96

Directions

a. Verify the down payment, the amount financed, the installment price, and the finance charge on the contract. If you find an error, cross out the incorrect amount and write the correct amount to the right of it. Correct any subsequent amounts on lines 1–5 of the contract in the same way.

b. If you find no errors in the amounts, sign Ellen's name to the contract.

Problem 14-2

Barry Young bought a copy machine for his business priced at $3,000.00 from Ortiz Office Equipment Company. The store asked him to pay 10% down and the rest in monthly payments of $133.50 for two years. The store also asked him to sign the installment contract shown on page 126.

Spreadsheet

Directions

a. Verify the down payment, the amount financed, the installment price, and the finance charge on the contract. If you find an error, cross out the incorrect amount and write the correct amount to the right of it. Correct any subsequent amounts on lines 1–5 of the contract in the same way.

SEARLES
241 Gardenia Street • Warwick, RI 02888-2978

RETAIL INSTALLMENT CONTRACT

Contract No.: 34078   Item: Electronic Keyboard, Model TR-3411
Buyer's Name: Ellen Berman
Buyer's Address: 23 Cordell Avenue
City: Warwick   State: RI   Zip: 02886-6598

1.	Cash Price	$ 312.50
2.	Down Payment	62.50
3.	Amount Financed	250.00
4.	Installment Price	333.46
5.	Finance Charge	29.60
6.	Annual Percentage Rate	15%

Buyer agrees to pay Searles Equipment Company, at their offices, the installment price shown above in 12 monthly installments of $ 22.58. The first installment is payable on August 12, 20--, and all subsequent payments are to be made on the same day of each consecutive month until the installment price is paid in full, subject to the conditions on the reverse side of this contract.

Signed _____

b. If you find no errors in the amounts, sign Barry's name to the contract.

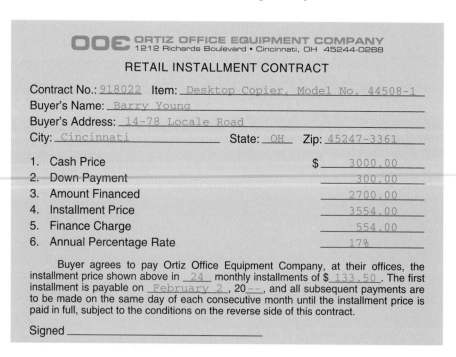

OOE ORTIZ OFFICE EQUIPMENT COMPANY
1212 Richards Boulevard • Cincinnati, OH 45244-0288

RETAIL INSTALLMENT CONTRACT

Contract No.: 918022   Item: Desktop Copier, Model No. 44508-1
Buyer's Name: Barry Young
Buyer's Address: 14-78 Locale Road
City: Cincinnati   State: OH   Zip: 45247-3361

1.	Cash Price	$ 3000.00
2.	Down Payment	300.00
3.	Amount Financed	2700.00
4.	Installment Price	3554.00
5.	Finance Charge	554.00
6.	Annual Percentage Rate	17%

Buyer agrees to pay Ortiz Office Equipment Company, at their offices, the installment price shown above in 24 monthly installments of $ 133.50. The first installment is payable on February 2, 20--, and all subsequent payments are to be made on the same day of each consecutive month until the installment price is paid in full, subject to the conditions on the reverse side of this contract.

Signed _____

Problems 14-3 and 14-4 may be found in the Working Papers.

key terms preview

- Amount due
- Date of note
- Due date
- Interest
- Principal
- Promissory note
- Time of note

goals

1 To learn about promissory notes.

2 To learn how to find the interest on a promissory note.

3 To learn how to find the amount due on a promissory note.

UNDERSTANDING THE JOB

Key Terms

Promissory note. A written promise to pay.

Businesses and people sometimes need to borrow money. A chain of clothing stores may need the money to buy merchandise in order to open a new store. A restaurant may need to buy equipment for a new kitchen so that it can serve more customers. In your personal life, you may need money to improve your home or cover large medical expenses.

When you borrow money from a bank for personal or business reasons, you usually sign a **promissory note** like the one shown in Illustration 15A. A promissory note is your written promise to pay back the loan.

Illustration 15A

A promissory note

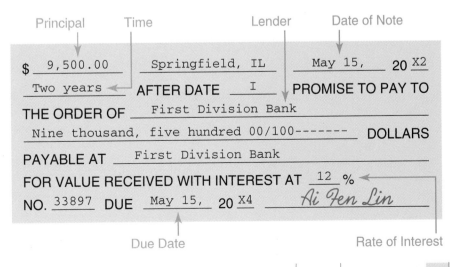

You usually have to pay for the use of the money you borrow. The amount you pay is called **interest**. The rate of interest that banks charge varies with changes in the economy. When interest rates go up, businesses and individuals may borrow less. When interest rates go down, businesses and individuals may borrow more.

SAMPLE PROBLEM

Key Terms

Interest. Money paid for the use of money.

Principal. Amount borrowed.

Date of note. Day the note was signed.

Time of note. Time for which money was borrowed.

Due date. Date note must be paid.

Ai Fen Lin wants to borrow $9,500.00 to expand her business. Her bank, the First Division Bank of Springfield, Illinois, will lend her the money using the promissory note shown in Illustration 15A.

Let's look at the promissory note. The amount borrowed, $9,500.00, is called the **principal**. The day the note was signed, May 15, 20X2, is called the **date of the note**. The time for which the money is borrowed, two years, is called the **time of the note** or just the *time*. The date the note must be paid, May 15, 20X4, is called the **due date**.

How much will Ai Fen have to pay in interest? How much will she have to pay the bank when the note comes due? To find the answers to these questions, Ai Fen followed these steps:

STEP 1 Calculate the interest.

Ai Fen found the amount of interest by using the formula

$$I = P \times R \times T$$
$$\text{Interest} = \text{Principal} \times \text{Rate} \times \text{Time}$$

The rate of interest shown on a note is always an annual rate, unless it is clearly stated that it is not. So, if you borrow $1,000.00 for one year at 10% interest, the interest is found this way:

$$I = P \times R \times T$$
$$I = \$1,000.00 \times 0.10 \times 1$$
$$I = \$100.00$$

Tips

To multiply by fractions, first convert the fractions to their decimal equivalents. The following are examples:
$1\frac{1}{2} = 1.5$
$\frac{1}{2} = 0.5$
$\frac{1}{4} = 0.25$

The amount of interest you pay depends on how long you borrow the money. If you borrow the $1,000.00 for $1\frac{1}{2}$ years at 10% interest, you must pay $1\frac{1}{2}$ (1.5) times the interest for one year:

$$I = P \times R \times T$$
$$I = \$1,000.00 \times 0.10 \times 1.5$$
$$I = \$150.00$$

If you borrow the money for six months, you must pay $\frac{6}{12}$, or $\frac{1}{2}$ (0.5), of the interest for one year:

$$I = P \times R \times T$$
$$I = \$1,000.00 \times 0.10 \times 0.5$$
$$I = \$50.00$$

Calculator Tips

Using a calculator to find the amount of interest and the amount due on the due date makes the job easier. Here's how you would find Ai Fen's interest and amount due with a calculator:

STEP 1 ▶ Calculate the interest for one year.

Press these keys in order:

The answer that appears in the display is $1,140.00. This is the amount of interest on $9,500.00 for one year.

STEP 2 ▶ Calculate the interest for two years.

Leave the amount in the display, and press these keys in order:

The amount that appears in the display is $2,280.00. This is the amount of interest on $9,500.00 for two years.

Notice that the interest calculation was two steps—not just one as shown in the Sample Problem.

STEP 3 ▶ Find the amount due on the due date.

Leave the amount in the display, and press these keys in order:

The amount that appears in the display is $11,780.00, which is the amount that Ai Fen must pay the bank when the note comes due.

If the time of the note was six months, you would multiply the annual interest by ½ year, or 0.5, instead of two years.

If your calculator has a *percent key*, you can find interest even faster by using it. Here is how to use the percent key on most calculators to find the interest for one year as you did in Step 1.

Press these keys in order:

The answer that appears in the display is $1,140.00. Notice that you did not need to convert 12% into the decimal 0.12. You only had to enter the interest rate and press the percent key.

Notice also that you did not have to press the equals key. Pressing the percent key displayed the answer automatically.

If you borrow the money for three months, you must pay $^3/_{12}$, or ¼ (0.25), of the interest for one year:

$$I = P \times R \times T$$
$$I = \$1,000.00 \times 0.10 \times 0.25$$
$$I = \$25.00$$

Since Ai Fen borrowed $9,500.00 at 12% interest for two years, she found the interest this way:

$$I = P \times R \times T$$
$$I = \$9,500.00 \times 0.12 \times 2$$
$$I = \$2,280.00$$

STEP 2 Find the amount due on the due date.

Ai Fen must pay the First Division Bank the principal plus the interest owed on the due date, May 15, 20X4. The amount she pays on the due date is called the **amount due**. To find the amount due on the due date, Ai Fen added the interest for the two years to the principal.

$$\$9,500.00 + \$2,280.00 = \$11,780.00$$

So, Ai Fen will have to pay the First Division Bank $11,780.00 on May 15, 20X4 to pay off the promissory note.

Amount due. Principal + interest owed on due date.

BUILDING YOUR BUSINESS VOCABULARY

On a sheet of paper, write the headings **Statement Number** and **Words**. Next, choose the words that match the statements. Write each word you choose next to the statement number it matches. Be careful; not all the words listed should be used.

Statements	Words
1. A written promise to pay	amount due
2. Money paid for the use of money	annual
3. The amount borrowed on a note	annual percentage rate
4. The day a note is signed	date of note
5. The amount of time for which money is borrowed on a note	down payment
6. The date a note must be paid	due date
7. Principal plus interest owed on the due date	interest
8. Yearly	principal
	promissory note
	time of note

STEPS REVIEW: Paying Back a Loan

STEP 1 Calculate the interest.

STEP 2 Find the amount due on the due date.

APPLICATION PROBLEMS

Problem 15-1 Robert Clark wants to borrow money to improve his home using the promissory note shown on page 131.

Directions
Answer these questions:

1. What is the principal of the note?
2. What is the time of the note?
3. What is the due date of the note?
4. How much interest must be paid when the note is due?

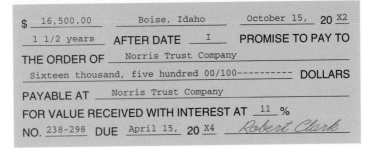

$ 16,500.00   Boise, Idaho   October 15, 20 X2

1 1/2 years   AFTER DATE   I   PROMISE TO PAY TO

THE ORDER OF   Norris Trust Company

Sixteen thousand, five hundred 00/100---------- DOLLARS

PAYABLE AT   Norris Trust Company

FOR VALUE RECEIVED WITH INTEREST AT   11 %

NO. 238-298 DUE April 15, 20 X4   Robert Clark

5. What is the amount due on the due date?

Problem 15-2   Eunice Hamilos wants to borrow money to start a gift shop using the promissory note shown below.

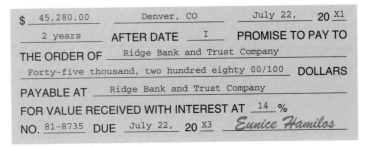

$ 45,280.00   Denver, CO   July 22, 20 X1

2 years   AFTER DATE   I   PROMISE TO PAY TO

THE ORDER OF   Ridge Bank and Trust Company

Forty-five thousand, two hundred eighty 00/100   DOLLARS

PAYABLE AT   Ridge Bank and Trust Company

FOR VALUE RECEIVED WITH INTEREST AT   14 %

NO. 81-8735 DUE July 22, 20 X3   Eunice Hamilos

Directions

Answer these questions:

1. What is the principal of the note?
2. What is the annual rate of interest?
3. What is the date of the note?
4. How much interest must be paid when the note is due?
5. What is the amount due on the due date?

Problem 15-3   Tyrone Wilson wants to borrow money to modernize his office using the promissory note shown below.

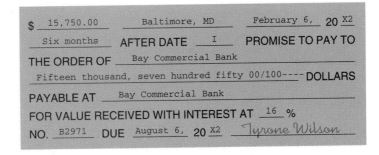

$ 15,750.00   Baltimore, MD   February 6, 20 X2

Six months   AFTER DATE   I   PROMISE TO PAY TO

THE ORDER OF   Bay Commercial Bank

Fifteen thousand, seven hundred fifty 00/100---- DOLLARS

PAYABLE AT   Bay Commercial Bank

FOR VALUE RECEIVED WITH INTEREST AT   16 %

NO. B2971 DUE August 6, 20 X2   Tyrone Wilson

Directions

Answer these questions:

1. What is the annual rate of interest?
2. What is the due date of the note?
3. What is the time of the note?
4. How much interest must be paid when the note is due?
5. What is the amount due on the due date?

Problems 15-4 and 15-5 may be found in the Working Papers.

Chapter 3

 CHECK YOUR READING

1. a. What does it mean to buy something using credit?
   b. List three or more advantages of using credit.
   c. List two or more disadvantages of using credit.
2. List four or more sources of credit available in your community.
3. List three or more reasons you or your family would take a loan from a bank.
4. Explain the term "interest."

 DISCUSSION

When you do not pay the balance on your credit card statement, the company will charge you interest. After all, you are borrowing their money.

Suppose that on your March statement, you had a balance of $100.00. Suppose also that you did not pay this balance during March. This is what part of your April statement would look like when you receive it:

How We Arrived At Your Finance Charge	Monthly Rate	Annual Percentage Rate	Balance to Which Monthly Rate Applied	Finance Charge
Previous Balance	1.5%	18%	$100.00	$1.50

Notice that the credit card company charged you 1.5% *per month* on the previous, unpaid balance you have in your account ($100.00 × 0.015 = $1.50). The monthly rate of 1.5% is equal to 18% *per year* (1.5% × 12 = 18%). Answer these questions:

1. If your previous balance had been $400.00, how much interest would your April statement show that you owe?
2. If your previous balance had been $600.00 and the credit card interest rate was 2% *per month*, how much interest would your April statement show that you owe?
3. If the credit card interest rate was 2% per month, what would be the *annual* percentage rate shown on the statement?

 ETHICS IN THE WORKPLACE

You work for a business that has a very large credit department. The manager of the department, Maria Quijano, supervises a large number of employees from many different cultural backgrounds. Maria thinks that it would be fun to have a cultural potluck luncheon next Friday. She wants to ask each employee in the department to bring a food dish from her or his culture to share. Maria discusses her idea with you and asks you to do the following:

1. Take a sheet of paper and draw a line down the middle from the top to the bottom.
2. On the left side of the paper, write the word *Advantages* at the top.
3. On the right side of the paper, write the word *Disadvantages* at the top.
4. On the left side of the paper, list all the advantages and positive outcomes of the luncheon.
5. On the right side of the paper, list all the disadvantages and any problems that you can think of.
6. Look at the advantages and disadvantages and write a brief recommendation either for or against the luncheon.

Loan clerks. Clerks who handle bank loans.

COMMUNICATION IN THE WORKPLACE

Suppose you were Vincent Aiello and received the incorrect credit card statement shown in Illustration 13B on page 112 of Job 13. Write a letter to your credit card company, Crestwood Bank, describing the two errors that were found on the statement. In your letter, show what the correct amount of the new balance should be.

FOCUS ON CAREERS

Banks and other lending institutions hire clerks who handle bank loans. Often these clerks are called **loan clerks**. Loan clerks calculate interest on loans, handle loan payments from customers, and answer questions about loan balances. The two want ads that follow describe two such positions:

Answer these questions about these two want ads:

1. Are either of the jobs entry-level jobs?
2. What does the commercial loan clerk job require that the loan service clerk job does not?

Commercial Loan Clerk

Local bank is seeking a qualified person to work in our Commercial Loan Department. This position is clerical in nature but is above the beginning level. 1-2 years experience in loan operations required. Good math skills, ability to deal with loan customers, experience in using a computer. Excellent salary and benefits.
Write: Human Resources,
    P.O. Box 3407, Topeka, KS 66605
    Equal Opportunity Employer

Loan Service Clerk

Lending institution is seeking personable individual with experience who is good with figures. Must have experience with personal computers. We offer complete benefits package. Call Human Resources for appointment at 555-3389 between 1 and 4 pm.
Equal Opportunity Employer

3. What do both jobs require?
4. How do you apply for the commercial loan clerk job?
5. How do you apply for the loan service clerk job?

GLOBAL BUSINESS: INTERNATIONAL TELEPHONE CALLS

You work for a large corporation that has many sales offices in Canada and Mexico. From time to time, you must call or send a fax to one of the sales offices to verify information. You can call offices in these countries by dialing directly, without the assistance of an operator.

For the offices in Canada, dial 1 + a three-digit area code + a seven-digit telephone number. To call Toronto, for example, dial 1-416-555-1234. This procedure is the same as placing a long-distance call within the United States.

When calling Mexico, or other foreign countries, the procedure is a bit more complicated. To make an international call, you must dial (1) 011, the International Access Code, (2) the country code, (3) the city code, (4) the local telephone number. To call Mexico City, for example, dial 011-52-5-555-1234.

The following chart shows selected country codes and city codes:

City	Country Code	City Code
Bangkok, Thailand	66	2
Berlin, Germany	49	30
Calcutta, India	91	33
Helsinki, Finland	358	9
Moscow, Russia	7	095
Rio de Janiero, Brazil	55	21

An International Telephone Calling Activity can be found in the Working Papers.

REVIEWING WHAT YOU HAVE LEARNED

On a sheet of paper, write the headings **Statement Number** and **Words**. Next, choose the words that best complete the statements. Write each word you choose next to the statement number it completes. Be careful; not all the words listed should be used.

Statements	Words
1. When you borrow money, the lender will usually charge you ____ for using the money.	annual percentage rate
2. A written promise to pay back the money you borrowed is called (a, an) ____.	date of note
	down payment
	due date
3. People who pay off their debts promptly and fully are considered ____.	finance charge
	good credit risks
4. The interest rate for a year is often called the ____.	interest
	promissory note
5. The date on which a promissory note must be paid is called the ____.	sales slip
	undercharged
6. The cost of borrowing money on an installment plan is called the ____.	
7. A written record of a sale is called (a, an) ____.	

Rose Stroud has a ShoppersCard from Heron Farmer's Bank that she uses to make personal purchases. She also owns Stroud's Trucking Company, a moving company specializing in household furniture and business equipment.

Phase 1: Checking a Credit Card Statement

Rose Stroud has saved each of her credit card sales slips for the month of June. Rose renews her card membership every June for a fee of $40.00. Her checkbook shows that she made a payment of $308.33 on June 6. She wants to verify her credit card statement for June.

Directions

a. Below and on page 136, you are given Rose's credit card statement and the top sections of her sales slips for June. Use a credit card statement work sheet to verify the statement.
b. List the date, store, and amount of every transaction which should not appear on the statement.
c. Compare the "sale amounts" on the sales slips to the amounts on the statement. If an amount is incorrect, find the overcharge or undercharge. Do not compare the "Amount" on the slips with the statement. The "Amount" and "sale amount" may differ because the bottoms of the slips, showing sales taxes and totals, are not provided.
d. Find the correct new balance for the statement.

CHECK POINT

(d)
Correct new balance = $554.79

ACCOUNT NUMBER 3375 885 322	SALE AMOUNT 00200.81		INVOICE NUMBER 641877		
6/X1 6/X4	DATE 6/2/--	AUTHORIZATION NO. 337802	SALES CLERK 32	DEPT. 13	
ROSE STROUD	QUAN.	DESCRIPTION	PRICE	AMOUNT	
1780928	1	Mantle Clock	139.89	139 89	
NORTHSIDE FURNITURE	2	Candle Holders	25.68	51 36	

ACCOUNT NUMBER 3375 885 322	SALE AMOUNT 00014.88		INVOICE NUMBER 999812		
6/X1 6/X4	DATE 6/5/--	AUTHORIZATION NO. --	SALES CLERK --	DEPT. --	
ROSE STROUD	QUAN.	DESCRIPTION	PRICE	AMOUNT	
0871116	--	Gasoline	14.88	14 88	
RT. 45 SERVICE					

ACCOUNT NUMBER 3375 885 322	SALE AMOUNT 00185.73		INVOICE NUMBER 641093		
6/X1 6/X4	DATE 6/9/--	AUTHORIZATION NO. 718372	SALES CLERK 12	DEPT. 21	
ROSE STROUD	QUAN.	DESCRIPTION	PRICE	AMOUNT	
0798902	1	Coat	176.89	176 89	
BARNEFF'S					

ACCOUNT NUMBER 3375 885 322	SALE AMOUNT 00018.78		INVOICE NUMBER 226179		
6/X1 6/X4	DATE 6/20/--	AUTHORIZATION NO. --	SALES CLERK 8	DEPT. 1	
ROSE STROUD	QUAN.	DESCRIPTION	PRICE	AMOUNT	
0756641	--	Dinner	17.89	17 89	
CASTLE INN					

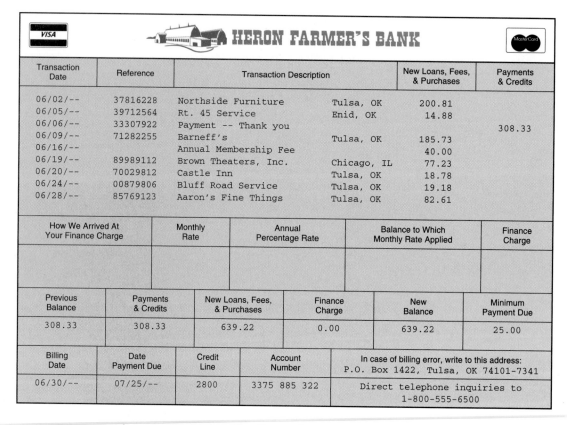

ACCOUNT NUMBER 3375 885 322		SALE AMOUNT 00011.98			INVOICE NUMBER 336419		
6/X1 6/X4		DATE 6/24/--	AUTHORIZATION NO. --		SALES CLERK 8		DEPT. 1
ROSE STROUD		QUAN. --	DESCRIPTION Gasoline		PRICE 11.98	AMOUNT 11 98	
0046007 BLUFF ROAD SERVICE							

MERCHANT COPY

ACCOUNT NUMBER 3375 885 322		SALE AMOUNT 00082.61			INVOICE NUMBER 711209		
6/X1 6/X4		DATE 6/28/--	AUTHORIZATION NO. --		SALES CLERK 14		DEPT. 21
ROSE STROUD		QUAN. 1	DESCRIPTION Mirror		PRICE 78.68	AMOUNT 78 68	
0023617 AARON'S FINE THINGS							

MERCHANT COPY

HERON FARMER'S BANK

VISA   MasterCard

Transaction Date	Reference	Transaction Description		New Loans, Fees, & Purchases	Payments & Credits
06/02/--	37816228	Northside Furniture	Tulsa, OK	200.81	
06/05/--	39712564	Rt. 45 Service	Enid, OK	14.88	
06/06/--	33307922	Payment -- Thank you			308.33
06/09/--	71282255	Barneff's	Tulsa, OK	185.73	
06/16/--		Annual Membership Fee		40.00	
06/19/--	89989112	Brown Theaters, Inc.	Chicago, IL	77.23	
06/20/--	70029812	Castle Inn	Tulsa, OK	18.78	
06/24/--	00879806	Bluff Road Service	Tulsa, OK	19.18	
06/28/--	85769123	Aaron's Fine Things	Tulsa, OK	82.61	

How We Arrived At Your Finance Charge	Monthly Rate	Annual Percentage Rate	Balance to Which Monthly Rate Applied	Finance Charge

Previous Balance	Payments & Credits	New Loans, Fees, & Purchases	Finance Charge	New Balance	Minimum Payment Due
308.33	308.33	639.22	0.00	639.22	25.00

Billing Date	Date Payment Due	Credit Line	Account Number	In case of billing error, write to this address: P.O. Box 1422, Tulsa, OK 74101-7341
06/30/--	07/25/--	2800	3375 885 322	Direct telephone inquiries to 1-800-555-6500

Phase 2: Checking an Installment Contract

Rose bought a big screen TV priced at $4,250.00 from Lockhart Electronics. The store asked her to pay 20% down and the rest in monthly payments of $212.92 for one and one-half years. The store also asked her to sign the installment contract shown in this problem.

Directions

a. Verify the down payment, the amount financed, the installment price, and the finance charge on the contract. If you find an error, cross out the incorrect amount and write the correct amount to the right. Correct any subsequent amounts on lines 1–5 of the contract in the same way.

b. If you find no errors in the amounts, sign Rose's name to the contract.

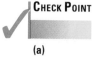

CHECK POINT

(a)
Finance charge = $432.56

LOCKHART Electronics, Inc.
1388 Borden Street
Tulsa, OK 74103-8278

RETAIL
INSTALLMENT
CONTRACT

Contract No.: __13933__ Item: __Ballow TV, Model LS-1200__
Buyer's Name: __Rose Stroud__
Buyer's Address: __245 West Bostonian Boulevard__
City: __Tulsa__   State: __OK__   Zip: __74107-3617__

1.	Cash Price	$ 4250.00
2.	Down Payment	850.00
3.	Amount Financed	3400.00
4.	Installment Price	4682.56
5.	Finance Charge	1282.56
6.	Annual Percentage Rate	15 1/2%

Buyer agrees to pay Lockhart Electronics, Inc., at their offices, the installment price shown above in __18__ monthly installments of $ __212.92__ . The first installment is payable on __July 24__ , 20 __--__, and all subsequent payments are to be made on the same day of each consecutive month until the installment price is paid in full, subject to the conditions on the reverse side of this contract.

Signed _____

Phase 3: Borrowing on a Promissory Note

Rose wants to borrow money to improve her business office using the promissory note shown below.

$ __17,200.00__   __Tulsa, OK__   __June 22,__ 20 __X1__

__6 months__ **AFTER DATE** __I__ **PROMISE TO PAY TO**

THE ORDER OF __Western Mining Bank and Trust Co.__

__Seventeen thousand, two hundred and no/100-----__ **DOLLARS**

PAYABLE AT __Western Mining Bank and Trust Co.__

FOR VALUE RECEIVED WITH INTEREST AT __12__ %

NO. __44718__ **DUE** December 22, 20 __X1__   *Rose Stroud*

CHECK POINT

(5)
Amount due = $18,232.00

Answer these questions:
1. What is the principal of the note?
2. What is the time of the note?
3. What is the due date of the note?
4. How much interest must be paid when the note is due?
5. What is the amount due on the due date?

REVIEWING YOUR BUSINESS VOCABULARY

This activity may be found in the Working Papers.

COMPREHENSIVE PROJECT 1

Comprehensive Project 1 has been designed to reinforce major concepts of this and previous chapters. The Comprehensive Project is found in the Working Papers.

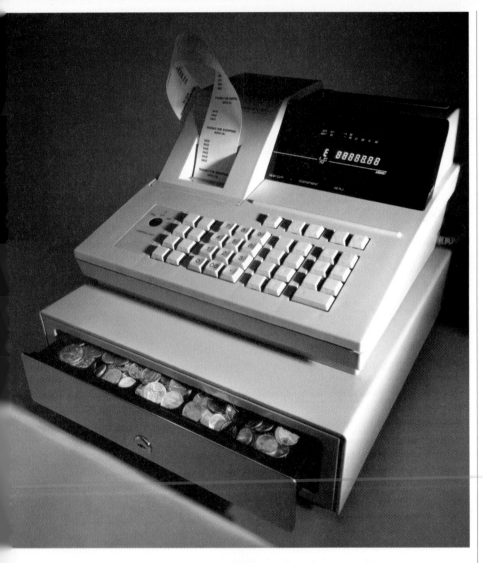

Cash Receipts Records

Many record keeping students are qualified to become cashiers. The main tasks of a cashier are to receive and pay out money. In a large business, one person may receive money while another person may pay out money. If the cashier works in a small business, both tasks may be done by the same person.

In Chapter 4, you will learn about the forms, machines, and procedures that cashiers use on the job. Various cashier positions in businesses will also be described. Calculator Tips will be given for completing a record of cashier's collections, proving cash, and completing a tally sheet.

FOCUS ON TECHNOLOGY

Point of Sale Systems

When customers pay for merchandise with cash, record keepers must keep track of the money they receive from the sale. It is at this point—the *point of sale*—that computers can be of great help to businesses. One of the most common point of sale computer systems is the electronic cash register, like the ones that are used in many stores today.

You will learn in this unit how to handle cash when customers buy merchandise. For example, you will learn how electronic cash registers are used to make sure that the cash received from and the change given to customers is recorded accurately. But cash registers, when they are also computer systems, can keep track of a lot more than just cash. And, *electronic cash registers* are just that—a computer system.

When an item is sold using an electronic cash register, the date, time of day, quantity sold, type of item sold, and sometimes the customer's identification are among the data recorded. This allows the business to:

● keep track of the amount of any item sold so that it can make sure it has enough stock left after the sale to handle other customers

● learn when certain items are most often sold, for example morning versus afternoon, on Mondays versus weekend days, or in spring versus fall, so it knows when it must have stock on hand

● learn when most sales are made so that it can make sure enough employees are on hand to handle the number of customers in the store

● learn what type of customer buys what type of merchandise so that it can plan advertising and sales campaigns

Some businesses even sell the information they collect with cash registers to other businesses. For example, a store may sell the information about <u>who</u> buys <u>what</u> merchandise <u>when</u> to a manufacturer. The manufacturer may then use that information to redesign merchandise for certain types of customers.

Some people feel that selling information about what they buy and when they buy it is an invasion of their privacy. Some states have created laws to protect buyers from having information about them sold to others.

Cash Receipts Records | Chapter 4 | 139

Tips

The sum of all the columns added across must equal the sum of all the rows added down. For example:

3 + 4 = 7

2 + 5 = 7

5 + 9 = 14

applied math preview

Copy and complete the following problems.

1. Add:

$$\begin{array}{r} \$ \quad 15.60 \\ 206.91 \\ 3{,}158.39 \\ 417.28 \\ + \, 1{,}200.09 \\ \hline \end{array}$$

2. Add across and then down:

a. 6 + 2 + 10 + 40 =

b. 20 + 40 + 50 + 60 =

c. 86 + 16 + 36 + 76 =

d. 97 + 27 + 57 + 67 =

e. 19 + 99 + 29 + 89 =

f. ___ ___ ___ ___

key terms preview

- Cash box
- Cashier
- Duplicate
- Grand total
- Receipt
- Stub

goals

1. To learn how to prepare receipts when you receive money.
2. To learn how to record receipts.

UNDERSTANDING THE JOB

Key Terms

Cashier. Employee who receives and pays out money.

The main tasks of a **cashier** are to receive and to pay out money. Some employees do both tasks because of their job responsibilities. For example, salespeople in retail stores usually collect money from customers and give back change when merchandise is sold.

There are many jobs in business in which cashiers receive money from other employees who also collect money. For example, cashiers may receive cash from news carriers who collect it from customers on their routes. Other cashiers may receive cash from employees who collect it from food vending machines, newspaper vending machines, subway turnstiles, and parking meters.

Most cashiers must meet and talk with customers and other employees as part of their jobs. The job of the cashier is important because cash must be handled accurately and carefully. It is also important because the cashier represents the business to customers.

Successful cashiers must know how to

a. Make change rapidly and accurately

b. Write numbers and words legibly

c. Recognize counterfeit money

d. Verify checks

e. Check their work

f. Listen to others

g. Greet people

h. Dress for the job

You are the cashier for the Gorbea Vending Company, which maintains food vending machines in a large city. The company hires employees to refill vending machines and collect the money deposited in them. Your job is to receive money from these employees when they return to the office after servicing the machines on their routes. The work is divided among a number of cashiers. You handle all the money received from routes on the east side of town.

On Monday, August 16, 20--, cash is brought to you by these route employees:

Key Terms

Receipt. A form issued for cash received.

Route	Amount	Carrier
205	$1,271.00	Amanda Carr
206	866.50	Robert Tieg
208	1,102.75	Lu Shen
210	567.25	Ben Rutman
211	954.50	LaDonna Wilson
214	495.75	James Dugan

Here is how you would do your job:

STEP 1 Count the money.

When you are handed the money by the employee for Route 205, count the money to make certain that it adds up to $1,271.00, as the employee claims.

STEP 2 Make out a receipt.

Illustration 16A

A receipt and stub

After you make sure that you have received the correct amount, make out a **receipt**, using a *receipt book*. Office supply stores sell many kinds of receipt books. Illustration 16A shows the form used by the Gorbea Vending Company.

No. **1078**

Date: _August 16_, 20 _--_

Received from: _Amanda Carr_

Route: _205_

Amount: $ _1,271.00_

Gorbea Vending Company   No. **1078**

Date: _August 16,_ 20 _--_

Received from: _Amanda Carr_ $ _1,271.00_

One thousand, two hundred seventy-one 00/100 —— Dollars

Route: _205_   For: _Route collections_

_____
(Your Name)
Cashier

STEP 1 Count the money.

STEP 2

Notice how you complete the receipt:

1. The amount is written both in figures and in words. This spelling list might help you to complete receipts in this job:

one	eleven	ten
two	twelve	twenty
three	thirteen	thirty
four	fourteen	forty
five	fifteen	fifty
six	sixteen	sixty
seven	seventeen	seventy
eight	eighteen	eighty
nine	nineteen	ninety

2. In the written amount, only the first word, "One," is capitalized.
3. A comma is used after the word "thousand" in the written amount. Commas are used in written amounts in the same places as they are used in figures.
4. A hyphen is used in "seventy-one." Hyphens are used when you write out the numbers twenty-one through ninety-nine.
5. The cents are written as a fraction, 00/100, even if there are no cents.
6. A line is drawn from the cents to the word "Dollars."

Hand the receipt to Amanda Carr, the employee for Route 205, leaving the **stub** in the receipt book.

Another commonly used form of receipt does not use a stub. Instead, a duplicate receipt is made using carbon or carbonless paper. The original receipt is torn out while the **duplicate** remains in the book. The duplicate receipt takes the place of the stub. The important thing to remember is that the cashier must have a record of every receipt issued.

Key Terms

Stub. Part of receipt which stays in book.

Duplicate. An exact copy.

Cash box. A box in which cash is kept.

For Your Information

Some people write no/100 instead of 00/100 to indicate that there are no cents.

STEP 3 Put the money in a cash box.

After you issue the receipt to Amanda Carr, put the $1,271.00 in a **cash box**. Cash boxes have compartments so that you can keep the different types of coins and bills arranged neatly. This reduces the chance of giving out the wrong change. Always make certain the money you receive is put in the cash box before you take care of the next route employee.

STEP 4 Record the amounts shown on the stubs in a record of cashier's collections.

At the end of each day, record the information found on the stubs in a record of cashier's collections. For example, you would record the route numbers, employee names, and amounts received on Monday, August 16, in the first three columns of the form. The completed record of cashier's collections for the week of August 16 is shown in Illustration 16B on page 143.

STEP 5 Total and verify each column total.

Total the amounts in the column for Monday by adding them from the top down. Record the total, $5,257.75, as a footing on the Totals line of the form. Then, verify the total by adding the amounts again from the

Gorbea Vending Company
RECORD OF CASHIER'S COLLECTIONS

Cashier _(Your Name)_   Week of _August 16,_   20 _--_

Route	Employee	Monday	Tuesday	Wednesday	Thursday	Friday	TOTALS
205	Amanda Carr	1271 00		856 25			2127 25
206	Robert Tieg	866 50			997 50		1864 00
207	Alice Renoir		524 75			846 25	1371 00
208	Lu Shen	1102 75		10028 75		12037 75	23169 25
209	Rita Ruiz		709 50		915 75		1625 25
210	Ben Rutman	567 25		594 25		684 25	1845 75
211	LaDonna Wilson	954 50		840 25		867 75	2662 50
212	Stan Wohl			512 75		648 50	1161 25
213	Mary O'Neal		335 75		691 50		1027 25
214	James Dugan	495 75		511 75		679 75	1687 25
	TOTALS	5257 75	1570 00	13344 00	2604 75	15764 25	38540 75
		5257 75	1570 00	13344 00	2604 75	15764 25	38540 75

Post money in cash box.

Illustration 16B
Completed record of cashier's collections

For Your Information

The *Occupational Outlook Handbook* estimates that cashier jobs will increase as fast as the average for all occupations through 2006. Part-time cashier job opportunities are also expected to be excellent.

Key Terms

Grand total. Total of totals.

bottom up. When you are sure that the total is correct, write it again below the footing. This means that you, the cashier, must have $5,257.75 in your cash box at the end of Monday, August 16.

You will repeat this procedure at the end of each day.

STEP 6   Find the weekly total for each route.

At the end of the week, find the total received from each route employee for the week. For example, you would crossfoot the amounts received during Monday through Friday for Route 205 and place the total, $2,127.25, in the Totals column at the right side of the form.

STEP 7   Find and verify the grand total and double rule the form.

Add the route totals that are in the Totals column and enter that amount as a footing at the bottom of the column. To prove your work, crossfoot the daily totals and compare that amount to the total of the Totals column. This amount is called a **grand total** because it is the total of other totals. In this case, the total of the route totals and the total of the daily totals must be equal.

Total of Route Totals	$38,540.75
Total of Daily Totals	$38,540.75

Since they are equal, write the grand total below the footing and double rule the money columns.

You can use the memory keys on your calculator, as you have before, to find the total receipts from each route and the grand total.

This is how you can do it:

STEP 1 ▶ Add the receipts for the first route.

Add the amounts in the row for Route 205 by pressing these keys in order:

The total, 2,127.25, will appear in the calculator's display. Record this amount in the Totals column for Route 205.

STEP 2 ▶ Add the total to the calculator's memory.

Press the M+ key. This adds the column total, $2,127.25, to the memory.

STEP 3 ▶ Record and add the other row totals to memory.

Now add each row for the other routes. When you get each row total, record it in the Totals column and press the M+ key. This adds each route total to memory.

STEP 4 ▶ Display the total of memory.

When you have added every route total to memory, press the MR (memory recall) or the MR/C (memory recall/clear) key once. When you do, your calculator display will show 38,540.75. This is the grand total. This amount should equal all the column totals for the days of the week.

STEP 5 ▶ Clear memory.

To clear the calculator's memory, press the MC (memory clear) key. If your calculator has a MR/C key, press that key twice. When you press the MR/C key once, the display shows the contents of memory. When you press the MR/C key twice, you clear or erase the amount in memory.

BUILDING YOUR BUSINESS VOCABULARY

On a sheet of paper, write the headings **Statement Number** and **Words**. Next, choose the words that match the statements. Write each word you choose next to the statement number it matches. Be careful; not all the words listed should be used.

Statements	Words
1. The part of the receipt which stays in the book	amount due
2. A form issued for cash received	budget
3. The total of a column of numbers written in small figures	cash box
4. To add a row of figures across a business form	cashier
5. A box in which cash is kept	crossfoot
6. A person who receives and pays out money	duplicate
7. An exact copy	footing
8. To check for accuracy	grand total
9. A total of other totals	receipt
	stub
	verify

STEPS REVIEW: Preparing and Recording Receipts

STEP 1 Count the money.

STEP 2 Make out a receipt.

STEP 3 Put the money in a cash box.

STEP 4 Record the amounts shown on the stubs in a record of cashier's collections.

STEP 5 Total and verify each column total.

STEP 6 Find the weekly total for each route.

STEP 7 Find and verify the grand total and double rule the form.

 APPLICATION PROBLEMS

Problem 16-1 You are a cashier collecting cash from route employees for the Gorbea Vending Company.

Directions

a. Use a record of cashier's collections form like the one in Illustration 16B (page 143). Complete the heading by using your name as cashier and October 12, as the week. Record the route numbers 205–214 in the Route column. Be sure to record the numbers in numerical order (205, 206, etc.).

b. You received money on Monday, October 12, as shown below.

Route No.	Employee	Amount
207	Alice Renoir	$ 762.50
210	Ben Rutman	631.75
211	LaDonna Wilson	925.00
214	James Dugan	1,563.75

Make a receipt for each employee. Be sure to fill out the stub first. The starting number for your receipts will be 101. Sign your own name as cashier.

c. Enter the information found on the stubs in the record of cashier's collections.

d. Foot, verify, and enter the total for the column headed Monday.

e. Fill in the record of cashier's collections for the rest of the week in the same way using the information given below. You are not required to make any more receipts.

Tuesday, October 13				Wednesday, October 14		
Route No.	Employee	Amount		Route No.	Employee	Amount
205	Amanda Carr	$ 976.25		207	Alice Renoir	$ 485.75
206	Robert Tieg	1,007.75		208	Lu Shen	1,002.50
211	LaDonna Wilson	251.75		210	Ben Rutman	644.25
212	Stan Wohl	1,125.25				
213	Mary O'Neal	741.50				

	Thursday, October 15			Friday, October 16	
Route No.	Employee	Amount	Route No.	Employee	Amount
205	Amanda Carr	$1,108.50	206	Robert Tieg	$ 700.25
209	Rita Ruiz	563.50	211	LaDonna Wilson	1,245.25
214	James Dugan	899.25	212	Stan Wohl	621.75

f. Find the total collected from each route for the week by crossfooting.

g. Foot the grand total for the week by adding the amounts in the Totals column.

h. Check your addition by crossfooting the totals for each day. The answer should agree with the grand total found in *g*. If the answer agrees, write the grand total below the footing. If the totals do not agree, find the error by re-adding all the columns.

i. Answer these questions about the completed record:
   1. On which route was the most money collected for the week?
   2. On which route was the least money collected for the week?
   3. On which day was the most money collected?
   4. On which day was the least money collected?

CHECK POINT

16-1

Grand total = $15,256.50

Problem 16-2 You have been hired as a cashier for the City of Glen Carbon. Parking meters throughout the city are maintained by Glen Carbon. Your job is to count the money collected daily from the route collectors and keep a weekly record of the collections.

Directions

a. Use a record of cashier's collections form like the one in Illustration 16B (page 143). Complete the heading by using your name as cashier and May 22, as the week. Head the second column Collector instead of Employee. Record the route numbers 612–621 in the Route column in numerical order.

b. You received money on Monday, May 22, as shown below.

Route No.	Collector	Amount
612	R. Ames	$125.15
614	L. Chen	88.05
620	E. Ibert	102.85
621	G. Jimenez	76.45

Make a receipt for each collector. Be sure to fill out the stub first. The starting number for your receipts will be 1201. Sign your own name as cashier.

c. Enter the information found on the stubs in the record of cashier's collections.

d. Foot, verify, and enter the total for the column headed Monday.

e. Fill in the record of cashier's collections for the rest of the week in the same way using the information given below and on the next page. You are not required to make any more receipts.

	Tuesday, May 23			Wednesday, May 24	
Route No.	Collector	Amount	Route No.	Collector	Amount
613	B. Banner	$31.65	612	R. Ames	$95.25
615	K. Diaz	70.95	614	L. Chen	76.65
616	Y. Epstein	21.55	617	N. Freitag	60.05
618	T. Grady	56.35	620	E. Ibert	39.95
619	D. Hiros	24.15	621	G. Jimenez	58.35

Thursday, May 25			Friday, May 26		
Route No.	**Collector**	**Amount**	**Route No.**	**Collector**	**Amount**
615	K. Diaz	$25.00	612	R. Ames	$38.85
616	Y. Epstein	87.75	613	B. Banner	76.45
619	D. Hiros	46.55	618	T. Grady	32.65
			620	E. Ibert	28.75
			621	G. Jimenez	65.10

f. Find the total collected from each route for the week by crossfooting.

g. Foot the grand total for the week by adding the amounts in the Totals column.

h. Check your addition by crossfooting the totals for each day. The answer should agree with the grand total found in *g*. If the answer agrees, write the grand total below the footing. If the totals do not agree, find the error by re-adding all the columns.

i. Answer these questions about the completed record:
1. On which route was the most money collected for the week?
2. On which route was the least money collected for the week?
3. On which day was the most money collected?
4. On which day was the least money collected?

Problems 16-3 and 16-4 may be found in the Working Papers.

CHECK POINT

16-2(i.1)

Route 612 collected the most money.

applied math preview

Copy and complete the following problems.

1. $ 1.89	2. $ 0.90	3. $ 7.35	4. $ 5.34	5. $ 1.94
28.00	0.77	2.06	3.98	0.34
2.78	2.08	4.30	1.48	2.67
5.29	5.19	0.49	1.65	0.88
0.48	0.18	0.37	4.55	0.15
1.98	4.12	0.84	6.87	1.33

key terms preview

- **Amount tendered**
- **Cash register**
- **Cash register receipt**
- **Subtotal**
- **Universal Product Code**

goals

1 To learn how a cash register is used to record sales.

2 To learn how to make change.

UNDERSTANDING THE JOB

Key Terms

Cash register: A machine used to handle money.

Cash register receipt: A printed record of transactions.

When cashiers must handle large amounts of money rapidly, they usually use a **cash register** instead of a cash box. A cash register helps to reduce errors and safeguard cash.

An electronic cash register used in a small business is really a microcomputer with a cash drawer, special keyboard, printer, and special displays. Cash registers used in large businesses are often terminals which are connected to minicomputers.

Cash registers provide printed receipts recording every transaction, called **cash register receipts** or cash register tapes. The cashier usually gives you the receipt, like the ones shown in Illustrations 17A and 17B on page 149. The receipt lists the amount charged for each item and shows the final total.

Many electronic cash registers print a very detailed receipt, like the one shown in Illustration 17B on page 149, listing the name of each item bought and its price. This allows customers to check their purchases easily.

Many cash registers have special keys for each department in a store, like the one shown in Illustration 17C on page 149. For example, supermarkets may have cash registers with special keys for sales of:

1. *Meat* (various fish and meat products)
2. *Dairy products* (butter, cheese, cream, eggs, milk, etc.)
3. *Produce* (fresh vegetables and fruits)
4. *Bakery products* (cakes, pies, donuts, etc.)
5. *Groceries* (canned foods, cereals, etc.)
6. *Health and beauty* (toothpaste, shampoo, bath soap, etc.)
7. *General merchandise* (items which are not included in the other depart-

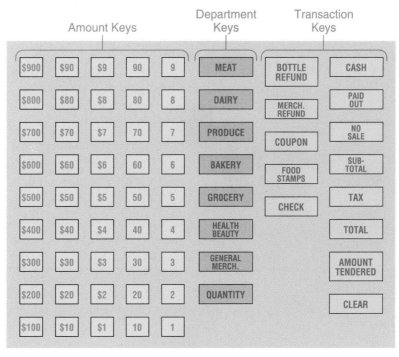

```
        YOUR RECEIPT

          THANK YOU

10/12/20-- 12:35PM  ← Date and Time
14 08972 REG 5      ← Cashier, sale, and
                        register number
   ME       $6.17   ← Meat
   DA       $2.15   ← Dairy
   DA       $1.75
   ME       $7.44
   PR       $1.79   ← Produce
   PR       $2.65
   BA       $2.29   ← Bakery
   GR       $2.15   ← Grocery
   GE       $1.89   ← General merchandise
   HB       $3.99   ← Health and beauty

   ST      $32.27   ← Subtotal
   TX       $1.61   ← Tax
   TL      $33.88   ← Total
   CA      $35.00   ← Cash received
   CG       $1.12   ←   from customer
                    └ Change given to customer
```

```
            BEST BUY
          FOOD STORES

MILK 1 GAL      2.83
LB CHEESE       2.09
ICE CREAM       3.79
LUNCH NAPKIN     .89
RC APPLE JCE    1.99
ALUMINUM WRAP   1.49
SHRED WHEAT     2.45
ORANGE JUICE
      3 a 1.67  5.01
CAKE MIX         .98
SWEET POTATOES
     3lb a .45  1.35
SUBTOTAL       22.87
TAX DUE         1.14
TOTAL          24.01
CASH TENDERED  25.00
CHANGE DUE       .99

12/10/20-- 10:58AM
STORE 7 REG 1 OPR 8
COMPARE OUR PRICES
```

ments, such as dishwashing soaps, laundry detergents, paper napkins, brushes, and soda)

The cashier must depress not only the keys for the selling price of each item, but also a key for the name of the department in which the item is found. For example, to record the sale of a gallon of milk for $2.83, the cashier would depress

If you watch the register display, you will see the selling price of the milk appear with the word "DAIRY."

Amount Keys   Department Keys   Transaction Keys

$900	$90	$9	90	9	MEAT	BOTTLE REFUND	CASH
$800	$80	$8	80	8	DAIRY	MERCH. REFUND	PAID OUT
$700	$70	$7	70	7	PRODUCE	COUPON	NO SALE
$600	$60	$6	60	6	BAKERY	FOOD STAMPS	SUB-TOTAL
$500	$50	$5	50	5	GROCERY	CHECK	TAX
$400	$40	$4	40	4	HEALTH BEAUTY		TOTAL
$300	$30	$3	30	3	GENERAL MERCH.		AMOUNT TENDERED
$200	$20	$2	20	2	QUANTITY		CLEAR
$100	$10	$1	10	1			

SAMPLE PROBLEM

You are a checkout cashier at RiteBuy Supermarket. A customer just bought cream cheese for $1.19, a package of meat for $4.89, and a can of apple sauce for $0.99.

Here is how you handled the customer's sale:

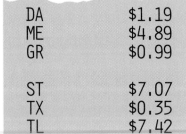

STEP 1   Enter each sale item.

You entered each sale item in the register by pressing the correct amount and department keys. For example, you entered the first item, cream cheese, by pressing these keys:

$1	10	9	DAIRY

As you entered each item, the amount and type for each item were shown in the cash register display. They were also printed out on the cash register receipt.

STEP 2   Find the total of the sale.

After entering all the items, you pressed the Subtotal, Tax, and Total keys in that order. The register calculated the subtotal ($7.07), the sales tax ($0.35), and the total ($7.42), and showed these amounts in the register display. These amounts were also printed out on the cash register receipt, as shown below.

Subtotal. Total on which other calculations will be made.

Amount tendered. Amount given to pay for a sale.

DA	$1.19
ME	$4.89
GR	$0.99
ST	$7.07
TX	$0.35
TL	$7.42

A **subtotal** is a total on which other calculations will be made. You will learn more about sales taxes in Chapter 7.

STEP 3   Accept the amount tendered by the customer and give the correct change.

The customer gave you a ten-dollar bill. This amount is called the **amount tendered**, or the amount that is given in payment of a sale. You placed the bill on the cash register but did not put it in the cash drawer of the register. You then pressed these keys:

$10	AMOUNT TENDERED

As you entered the amount tendered, $10, it was shown on the register display. It was also printed out on the cash register receipt.

GR	$0.99
ST	$7.07
TX	$0.35
TL	$7.42
CA	$10.00

The register calculated the amount of change the customer should receive ($2.58) and displayed this amount. It also printed the amount out on the receipt.

TL	$7.42
CA	$10.00
CG	$2.58

You handed the customer the receipt and the $2.58, using two one-dollar bills, a half-dollar, a nickel, and three pennies. As you handed the customer the change, you said, "Two dollars, fifty, fifty-five, and fifty-eight."

Older cash registers, which are not electronic, do not figure the correct change. If you use an older cash register, you must figure the change yourself. Cashiers usually figure the change mentally by adding coins and dollars to the total sale until they have reached the amount tendered. In the Sample Problem, you would have given the customer three pennies, a nickel, a half-dollar, and two one-dollar bills, saying, "$7.42 (the amount of sale), $7.45 ($7.42 plus the pennies), $7.50 ($7.45 plus the nickel), $8.00 ($7.50 plus the half-dollar), $10.00 ($8.00 plus the two one-dollar bills)."

Cashiers should never put paper money in the cash register until after they have given the change to the customer. In the Sample Problem, if the customer claims to have given you more than $10, you can show the customer the actual $10 bill.

Cashiers also should try to give the customer change with the least number of coins and bills possible. The customer does not usually want to receive a lot of small coins and bills as change.

Many items sold today have a special code printed on them. This code, called the **Universal Product Code** *(UPC)*, can be read and recorded by a special cash register system (see Illustration 17D).

In this system, an electronic cash register and a scanner are connected to a minicomputer. As each item is scanned, the code tells the computer the department, the brand, and the size of the product being bought. The computer finds the price of each item and figures the total amount owed. These amounts are shown in lighted numbers on the cash register display so that the cashier and the customer can see them.

Cashiers who use electronic cash registers must still know how to operate the register keyboard and to classify sales into departments. After all, some items sold may not have a UPC label on them (for example, fresh vegetables and fruit). Also, the bar code on some items may be damaged and cannot be read by the scanner.

In chain store systems, such as fast food chain stores, the data from each electronic cash register is sent to a central computer located in a central office. (See Illustration 17E on page 152) There the data are used by managers to keep track of each store's sales, items which are selling

Key Terms

Universal Product Code. A bar code.

Illustration 17D
UPC Code

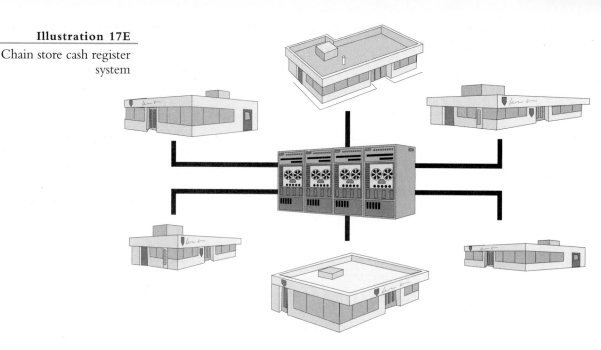

quickly, and items which are selling slowly. This information allows managers to improve the sales of the chain.

 ## BUILDING YOUR BUSINESS VOCABULARY

On a sheet of paper, write the headings **Statement Number** and **Words**. Next, choose the words that match the statements. Write each word you choose next to the statement number it matches. Be careful; not all the words listed should be used.

Statements	Words
1. The amount given to pay a bill	amount tendered
2. A machine used to handle money	cash register
3. An exact copy	cash register receipt
4. A special bar code read by electronic cash registers	cashier
	crossfoot
5. A written record of transactions printed by a cash register	duplicate
	grand total
6. A total of other totals	receipt
7. A form issued for cash received	stub
8. The part of the receipt which stays in the book	subtotal
9. A total on which other calculations will be made	transaction
10. Something that happens in a business that should be recorded	Universal Product Code

STEPS REVIEW: Using a Cash Register

STEP 1 Enter each sale item.

STEP 2 Find the total of the sale.

STEP 3 Accept the amount tendered by the customer and give the correct change.

APPLICATION PROBLEMS

You are the cashier at the Karbel Superfood Store. You use a cash register with the keys shown in Illustration 17C on page 149.

Directions

a. A customer buys the items shown below. Copy the items and prices, and next to each item, write the name of the department key you would use to enter the item into your cash register.

CHECK POINT

17-1(a)

Use the **General Merch.** key for batteries

Items Bought		Department Keys Used
$2.99	AA Batteries	
$4.71	Meat	
$1.69	Shredded cheese	
$2.98	Apples	
$3.49	Cold tablets	

b. After entering each item, your register shows a total sale of $15.86. The amount tendered by the customer is $20.00. List the types and numbers of the bills or coins you should give the customer for change.

Problem 17-2 You are the cashier at the Southside Store. You use a cash register with the keys shown in Illustration 17C on page 149.

Directions

a. A customer buys the items shown below. Copy the items and prices, and next to each item, write the name of the department key you would use to enter the item into your cash register.

Items Bought		Department Keys Used
$ .95	Sweet potatoes	
$2.89	Pumpkin pie	
$ .29	Canned corn	
$2.39	Dish detergent	
$5.89	Whole turkey	

CHECK POINT

17-2(b)

The change should include 1 half-dollar.

b. After entering each item, your register shows a total sale of $12.41. The amount tendered by the customer is $15.00. List the types and numbers of the bills or coins you should give the customer for change.

Problems 17-3, 17-4, and 17-5 may be found in the Working Papers.

applied math preview

Copy and complete the following problems.

1. $ 1.06	2. $ 0.65	3. $ 6.48	4. $75.00	5. $100.00
0.45	7.82	1.86	− 49.15	+ 50.04
4.78	1.91	0.08		
9.89	0.95	4.59		
+ 2.03	+ 2.14	+ 0.84	6. $50.00	7. $ 25.00
			− 38.98	+ 24.65

key terms preview

- Check-cashing privilege card
- Debit cards
- Policies
- Refund
- Third-party checks

goals

1 To practice making change.
2 To learn how to verify checks.
3 To learn how cashiers handle coupons and refunds.

➡ UNDERSTANDING THE JOB

Key Terms

Debit cards. Allow immediate payment from checking account.

Stores may allow customers to pay for their purchases in many ways. For example, food stores may allow customers to pay for part of their purchases with coupons, food stamps, bottle refunds, refunds of merchandise, checks, and even credit cards.

Some stores also accept **debit cards**. Debit cards are issued by banks and allow you to make payments from your checking account without checks or cash. Debit cards are similar to credit cards except that the amount of your purchase is subtracted from your checking account immediately instead of being added to a bill sent to you at the end of the month.

In some stores, you can pay for your purchase simply by inserting your debit card into a special terminal connected to your bank's computer system. The bank's computer system subtracts the amount of your purchase immediately from your checking account and adds the same amount to the store's bank account.

In this job you will learn how to handle refunds, coupons, and checks. You will learn more about credit card sales in Chapter 7.

Key Terms

Refund. Money given back.

Check-cashing privilege card. Allows you to cash checks at a store.

Policies. Rules or procedures.

Suppose that you are still working as a checkout cashier at RiteBuy Supermarket as you did in Job 17. You are using a register with the keyboard shown in Illustration 18A.

RiteBuy allows customers to return bottles and get a **refund**, or money back. You may give the customer cash for the bottles, or if the customer is buying other items, you can deduct the refund from the total amount due.

RiteBuy also accepts vendor coupons for items bought in the store. For example, a customer might buy a box of cereal for $1.25 and give you $1.00 plus a coupon. The coupon gives the customer 25¢ off the purchase price of the cereal.

Customers can cash checks at RiteBuy only if they have a special **check-cashing privilege card**, like the one shown in Illustration 18B on page 156. Customers must apply for the card in advance of their purchases. RiteBuy checks the credit histories of the customers. If they are found to be good credit risks, they are issued the card.

Other businesses may have other check-cashing **policies**, or sets of rules for accepting checks. For example, some may accept personal checks from customers if they provide some identification and the checks are from local banks. The identification required may be a driver's license or employee identification card from a local employer.

RiteBuy accepts personal checks from customers as long as the checks are completed properly, are made out to RiteBuy Supermarket, are from

Illustration 18A

Cash register keyboard

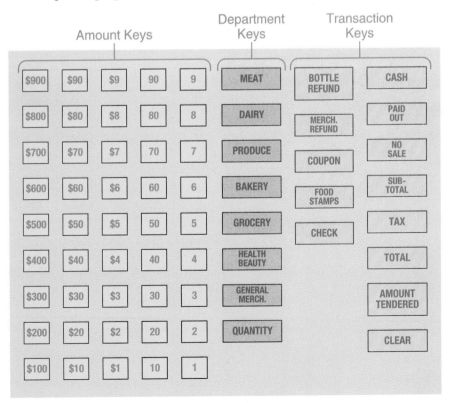

No. 1235
**Check-Cashing
Privilege Card**

This card allows: Drew Lansing
1645 Abel St.
Allentown, PA 18104-0423

**To cash checks for purchases according to the
restrictions printed on the back of this card.**

Customer
Signature *Drew Lansing* Date *May 5,* 20 __

Third-party checks. Checks
from persons other than customers.

local banks, are not dated for some future date, and are for no more than
$25.00 over the sale amount. Local banks are banks in the same town as
RiteBuy: Allentown, Pennsylvania. In addition, only customers who have
been given a check-cashing privilege card are allowed to cash checks in
the store.

RiteBuy does not accept checks which are made out to other people.
They only accept the checks of their customers which are made out to
RiteBuy. For example, they do not accept employment checks or government checks. Checks from people other than their customers are called
third-party checks.

Checks which do not meet the store's check-cashing policies must be
given to your supervisor. The supervisor then decides whether the check
can be authorized, or approved for cashing.

On July 19, Drew Lansing bought these items: a loaf of bread for
$1.49, a bunch of celery for $0.79, and a half-gallon of milk for $1.45.
He gave you a coupon, a bottle refund, and a $10.00 check. Here is how
you handled the sale:

STEP 1 Enter each sale item.

You entered each sale item by pressing these keys:

| $1 | 40 | 9 | BAKERY |

| 70 | 9 | PRODUCE |

| $1 | 40 | 5 | DAIRY |

STEP 2 Enter each coupon and refund slip.

Drew Lansing gave you a coupon for 15¢ off the loaf of bread. He also
gave you a bottle refund slip for 28¢. You pressed these keys in order:

| 10 | 5 | COUPON |

| 20 | 8 | BOTTLE REFUND |

You then placed the coupon and bottle refund slip in the back of the cash drawer of the cash register.

STEP 3 Find the total for the customer.

You pressed the subtotal, tax, and total keys in that order. The results, printed out on the cash register receipt, looked like this:

BA	$1.49
PR	$0.79
DA	$1.45
CO	-$0.15 ← Coupon
BR	-$0.28 ← Bottle Refund
ST	$3.30
TX	$0.17
TL	$3.47

STEP 4 Verify the check tendered by the customer.

Drew Lansing showed you his check-cashing privilege card (Illustration 18B, page 156) and gave you the following check.

DREW LANSING
1645 Abel Street
Allentown, PA 18104-0423

No. **1063**

Date *July 19,* 20 __

3-332 / 2784

PAY TO THE ORDER OF *RiteBuy Supermarket* $ *10.00*

Ten 00/100 _____ Dollars

For Classroom Use Only

HB HILLSTON BANK
Allentown, PA 18103-8890

Drew Lansing

⑆027840745⑆ 308⑈455⑈

You wrote the check-cashing privilege card number on the back of the check. You then verified the check using the checklist which was posted on your cash register:

RiteBuy Supermarket **CHECK VERIFICATION CHECKLIST**

If any of the items below are true, call your supervisor:

1. The customer's name or address is not printed on the check.
2. The name, address, or customer signature on the card does not match the name, address, or signature on the check.
3. The amount of the check in writing is not the same as the amount in figures.
4. The date on the check is a future date.
5. The check is not from a local bank.
6. The check is for more than $25 over the total sale.
7. The check is not made out to RiteBuy Supermarket.

Since none of the items on the checklist were true, you accepted it for payment. Had one or more of these items been true, you would have called your supervisor. The supervisor may have authorized the check after talking with the customer. The supervisor may also have asked the customer to make out a new check or refused to accept the check at all.

STEP 5 **Enter the amount of the check and give the correct change.**

You then entered the amount of the check in the register and pressed the Check key. The correct change to give the customer was shown on the display. The cash register receipt looked like this:

ST	$3.30
TX	$0.17
TL	$3.47
CK	$10.00 ◄——— The amount of the check tendered
CG	$6.53 ◄——— The correct amount of change to give the customer

You gave the customer the cash register receipt and the correct change in these amounts: a $5 bill, a $1 bill, a half-dollar, and three pennies. You then placed the check in the cash drawer.

→ BUILDING YOUR BUSINESS VOCABULARY

On a sheet of paper, write the headings **Statement Number** and **Words.** Next, choose the words that match the statements. Write each word you choose next to the statement number it matches. Be careful; not all the words listed should be used.

Statements	Words
1. Allow payments to be made from checking accounts immediately	amount tendered
	authorize
2. Money given back to a customer for returned bottles or merchandise	check-cashing privilege card
	debit cards
3. A total on which other calculations will be made	grand total
4. Rules or procedures	policies
5. Approve	refund
6. Amount given to pay a bill	stub
7. Allows you to cash checks at a store	subtotal
8. Checks from people other than customers	third-party checks

STEPS REVIEW: Handling Refunds, Coupons, and Checks

STEP 1 Enter each sale item.

STEP 2 Enter each coupon and refund slip.

STEP 3 Find the total for the customer.

STEP 4 Verify the check tendered by the customer.

STEP 5 Enter the amount of the check and give the correct change.

Problem 18-1

On May 17, you were a cashier at RiteBuy Supermarket and handled the five customers in this problem.

Customer 1:

After entering each item bought by Reba Hahn, your register displayed a total sale of $63.76. Reba gave you the check-cashing privilege card and check that appear below.

Directions

a. On a separate sheet of paper, write the heading "Check-Cashing Policies." Under the heading, write the numbers 1–7 for the seven check-cashing policies of RiteBuy Supermarket shown in the checklist in Step 4 (page 157) of the Sample Problem. Verify the check against these seven policies by placing a check mark next to any policy found to be true.

b. On the same sheet of paper, write the headings "Bills and Coins" and "Number Used." Then list the type and number of each bill or coin you should give the customer for change if you accept the check or if it is authorized by your supervisor.

CHECK POINT

18-1(a)

For Customer 1, check policies 2 and 5.

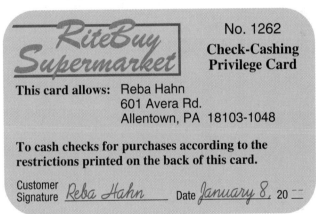

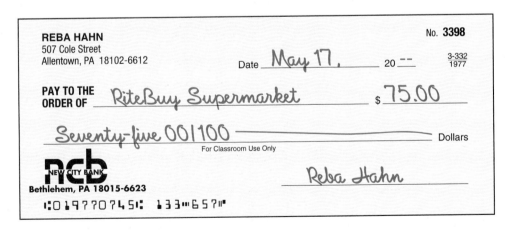

Customer 2:

After entering each item bought by Anthony Canata, your register displayed a total sale of $36.12. Anthony gave you the check-cashing privilege card and check that appear on the next page.

Directions

a. On a separate sheet of paper, write the heading "Check-Cashing Policies." Under the heading, write the numbers 1–7 for the seven check-cashing policies of RiteBuy Supermarket shown in the checklist in Step 4 (page 157) of the Sample Problem. Verify the check against these seven policies by placing a check mark next to any policy found to be true.

b. On the same sheet of paper, write the headings "Bills and Coins" and "Number Used." Then list the type and number of each bill or coin you should give the customer for change if you accept the check or if it is authorized by your supervisor.

RiteBuy Supermarket

No. 927
Check-Cashing Privilege Card

This card allows: Anthony Canata
107 Taylor Lane
Allentown, PA 18103-2298

To cash checks for purchases according to the restrictions printed on the back of this card.

Customer Signature *Anthony Canata*   Date *April 1,* 20 __

ANTHONY CANATA   No. **124**

Date *May 17,* 20 __   3-332
                                     2075

Pay to the
Order of *RiteBuy Supermarket* $ *50.00*

Fifty 00/100 _____ Dollars

For Classroom Use Only

Riverbend Bank
Allentown, PA 18105-3108

Anthony Canata

⑈0 2075074 5⑈ 9 12⑈008⑈

The problem material for Customers 3, 4, and 5 may be found in the Working Papers.

Job 19 PREPARING PROOFS OF CASH

applied math preview

Copy and complete the following problems.

1. 10 × $20.00 =
2. 11 × $10.00 =
3. 18 × $5.00 =
4. 87 × $1.00 =
5. 48 × $0.50 =

6. 17 × $0.25 =
7. 174 × $0.10 =
8. 177 × $0.05 =
9. 637 × $0.01 =

key terms preview

- **Cash count report**
- **Cash overage**
- **Cash shortage**
- **Change fund**
- **Denomination**
- **Detailed audit tape**
- **Proof of cash**

goal

To learn how a cashier proves that the amount of money in a cash register at the end of the day is correct.

⇨ **UNDERSTANDING THE JOB**

Detailed audit tape. Record of all cash register transactions.

In addition to being recorded on the cash register receipts that are given to customers, each transaction is also recorded on a **detailed audit tape** inside the cash register. What is recorded on this tape varies with each store. However, usually every item sold, its department, its price, the total amount of each sale, and the cashier's number are recorded.

The detailed audit tape is used to help the cashier prove that the amount of money in the cash register at the end of the day is correct. The detailed audit tape can also be used as a source document for keeping records of the business' total cash received and total sales of each kind of item. Being able to verify the money in the cash register and record total items sold are two more advantages of using a cash register. Businesses such as gas stations and convenience stores handle many cash transactions every day. Keeping cash records by hand would take a great deal of time. There would also be a greater chance of errors. Keeping records with a machine, such as a cash register, makes it much easier to keep track of totals and prepare proofs of cash.

Key Terms

Change fund. Amount cashier starts with.

Denomination. Value.

Yvonne White is cashier number 22 and operates register no. 11 for Upland Stores. Each morning Yvonne is given $100.00 in different coins and bills by the manager of the store. She will use this $100.00 as a **change fund**, or a source of money, from which she can give customers change. Here are the steps Yvonne will follow each day to check her work:

STEP 1 Verify the change fund at the beginning of the day.

Yvonne verifies that she has been given $100.00 in her change fund before she puts the money into the register. After counting the change fund, she puts the money in the cash drawer in the correct compartments.

STEP 2 Find the total sales for the day.

At the end of the day, Yvonne finds the total sales from the detailed audit tape in her register. It shows that she sold $2,716.30 during the day.

STEP 3 Find the cash paid out for the day.

Customers who return merchandise may have the amounts returned subtracted from their purchases. However, customers who are not buying anything may be paid cash for their returns.

At the end of the day, Yvonne finds the total amount of money that she has paid out to customers for returns from the detailed audit tape. The tape shows that she paid $42.60 in refunds to customers.

STEP 4 Find the total cash to be accounted for.

Although Yvonne's total sales were $2,716.30, she must account for $2,773.70 because

Sales for the day	$2,716.30
Plus: Change fund in register, start of day	+ 100.00
	$2,816.30
Less: Cash paid out during day	− 42.60
Equals: Total cash to be accounted for	$2,773.70

STEP 5 Count the actual cash in the register at the end of the day.

Since Yvonne knows how much cash she is supposed to have, she empties all the compartments in the cash register and sorts the bills and coins into their **denominations**, or values. She also sorts and counts the checks. This is what she finds:

UPLAND STORES, INC.
Cash Count Report

Date: _July 20,_ _____ 20 _--_

Cashier No.: _22_ _____ Register No.: _11_ _____

Quantity	Denomination	Amount	
58	$20.00 Bills	1,160	00
36	$10.00 Bills	360	00
21	$5.00 Bills	105	00
35	$1.00 Bills	35	00
7	$0.50 Coins	3	50
21	$0.25 Coins	5	25
25	$0.10 Coins	2	50
33	$0.05 Coins	1	65
80	$0.01 Coins		80
	Checks	1,100	00
Total Cash in Cash Drawer		2,773	70

Signature: _Yvonne White_ _____

Cash count report. Shows
how much cash is in register.

Proof of cash. Compares
amount of cash you should
have with actual cash.

Bills and Coins:

Quantity	Denomination
58	$20.00 bills
36	$10.00 bills
21	$ 5.00 bills
35	$ 1.00 bills
7	$ 0.50 coins
21	$ 0.25 coins
25	$ 0.10 coins
33	$ 0.05 coins
80	$ 0.01 coins

Total Checks: $1,100.00

She enters the quantity of each denomination of the bills and coins on the **cash count report** shown in Illustration 19A and multiplies the denomination by the quantity to get the amount. Then she enters the total amount of the checks.

STEP 6 Prepare the proof of cash.

Yvonne now compares the amount of cash she should have (Step 4) with the amount of cash she actually has (Step 5). She does this by preparing the **proof of cash** shown in Illustration 19B on page 164. She will turn in the cash proof form with her actual cash.

Since the cash in Yvonne's register agrees with the amount she is supposed to have, the cash is neither short nor over.

Sometimes the cashier will find that the actual cash in the register does not agree with the cash that should be in the register. Suppose the

UPLAND STORES, INC.
Cash Proof Form

Date: _July 20,_ _____ 20 _--_

Change fund	100	00
Add total cash sales from audit tape	2,716	30
Total	2,816	30
Less cash paid out from audit tape	42	60
Cash that should be in register	2,773	70
Cash actually in register	2,773	70
Cash short	0	00
Cash over	0	00

Cash Register No.: _11_   Cashier No.: _22_

Signature: _Yvonne White_

Key Terms

Cash shortage. Less cash on hand than there should be.

Cash overage. More cash on hand than there should be.

For Your Information

Even if you have a computerized (electronic) cash register, you will still have to count the cash you have in the register drawer and prove your cash using the detailed audit tape. There are some things that computers still are not used for in most stores!

cash in the register at the end of the day had been $2,773.20. The cashier would have completed the last part of the proof of cash form this way:

Cash that should be in register	2,773	70
Cash actually in register	2,773	20
Cash short	0	50

Since Yvonne would not have enough money, she would enter $0.50 on the Cash Short line of the form. This is called a **cash shortage**.

If the actual cash in the register had been $2,773.75, Yvonne would have completed the proof of cash form this way:

Cash that should be in register	2,773	70
Cash actually in register	2,773	75
Cash short	0	00
Cash over	0	05

Since Yvonne would have too much money, she would enter $0.05 on the Cash Over line of the report. This is called a **cash overage**.

Calculator Tips

You can use a calculator to make the job of preparing the proof of cash form easier. The calculator will let you add and subtract amounts the way you need to on a proof of cash form. For example, use the data from the Sample Problem, except let the actual amount found in the cash drawer at the end of the day be $2,773.75. Here is how you can use a calculator to find the amounts on the proof of cash form.

STEP 1 ▶ Add the amounts for the change fund and total cash received.

Press these keys in order:

The answer that appears in the display is 2,816.30. Enter this amount on the Total line of the cash proof form.

STEP 2 ▶ *Subtract the cash paid out.*

Without clearing the calculator, press these keys in order:

The answer that appears in the display is 2,773.70. Enter this amount on the Cash That Should Be In Register line of the form.

STEP 3 ▶ *Subtract the cash actually in the drawer.*

Without clearing the calculator, press these keys in order:

The answer that appears in the display is -0.05. This is really a minus five cents. This means that you have five cents more than you should in the drawer. Whenever the number is negative, you will know that there is a cash overage. Enter 0.05 in the Cash Over line of the form.

If the answer had no minus sign, you would have a cash shortage. You would then enter the amount on the Cash Short line of the form.

➡ BUILDING YOUR BUSINESS VOCABULARY

On a sheet of paper, write the headings **Statement Number** and **Words**. Next, choose the words that match the statements. Write each word you choose next to the statement number it matches. Be careful; not all the words listed should be used.

Statements	Words
1. The value of a coin or bill	cash count report
2. A record of all cash register transactions	cash overage
3. A form on which you compare how much cash you are supposed to have with what you actually have in the register	cash register
	cash shortage
4. A machine used to reduce errors and safeguard money	cashier
	change fund
5. A form issued for cash received	denomination
6. An amount given to a cashier at the beginning of the day for making change	detailed audit tape
	proof of cash
7. Something that happens in a business that should be recorded	receipt
	transaction
8. When there is less cash in the register at the end of the day than there should be	
9. Used to find the amount of cash in the drawer	

STEPS REVIEW: Preparing Proofs of Cash

STEP 1 Verify the change fund at the beginning of the day.

STEP 2 Find the total sales for the day.

STEP 3 Find the cash paid out for the day.

STEP 4 Find the total cash to be accounted for.

STEP 5 Count the actual cash in the register at the end of the day.

STEP 6 Prepare the proof of cash.

APPLICATION PROBLEMS

Problem 19-1

You are cashier no. 32 at register no. 3 at Allied Food Stores, Inc. At the end of the day on May 16, your cash drawer contained these items:

Quantity	Denomination	Quantity	Denomination
22	$20.00 bills	43	$ 0.25 coins
16	$10.00 bills	24	$ 0.10 coins
24	$ 5.00 bills	78	$ 0.05 coins
48	$ 1.00 bills	122	$ 0.01 coins
12	$ 0.50 coins		Total checks: $416.00

CHECK POINT

19-1

Total cash = $1,208.27

Directions

Prepare a cash count report like the one shown in Illustration 19A on page 163.

Problem 19-2

You are the cashier in Problem 1. On May 16, you started the day with a change fund of $150.00. At the end of the day, your register's detailed audit tape showed total cash sales of $1,079.87 and total cash paid out of $21.47. At the end of the day, your cash drawer contained the amount shown in the cash count report you completed in Problem 1.

CHECK POINT

19-2

Cash short = $0.13

Directions

Prepare a proof of cash like the one shown in Illustration 19B on page 164.

Problem 19-3

You are cashier no. 10 at cash register no. 10 for Buy-Wise Discount Store. On April 6, you started the day with a change fund of $100.00. At the end of the day, your register's detailed audit tape showed total cash sales of $2,222.78 and total cash paid out of $76.40. Your cash drawer contained these items: 28 $20.00 bills; 27 $10.00 bills; 16 $5.00 bills; 75 $1.00 bills; 56 $0.50 coins; 22 $0.25 coins; 57 $0.10 coins; 81 $0.05 coins; 233 $0.01 coins; and checks totalling $1,216.00.

Directions

a. Prepare a cash count report like the one shown in Illustration 19A on page 163.

b. Prepare a proof of cash like the one shown in Illustration 19B on page 164.

CHECK POINT

19-3

Cash over = $0.20

Problems 19-4, 19-5, and 19-6 may be found in the Working Papers.

goal

To learn how to prepare daily cashier reports for a store with many departments.

UNDERSTANDING THE JOB

Cashiers complete a number of reports about their work each day. These include the *cash count report* and the *proof of cash*, which you have already studied. These reports help cashiers verify the amounts in their cash registers.

Businesses use reports such as the cash count report and the proof of cash to provide control of their cash. It is very important for businesses not to waste or lose any of their cash. Cash registers, checking accounts (discussed in Chapter 5), petty cash funds (discussed in Chapter 6), and sales slips (discussed in Chapter 7) are other examples of ways to control cash.

There are four basic requirements in a good cash control system. First, there should be more than one person responsible for cash. The person who handles cash should not also be the person responsible for all the cash record keeping. Second, all cash received should be deposited in a bank that day. Third, no cash should be paid out unless approved by a supervisor

or other authorized person. Fourth, cash records should be checked from time to time. Ways of checking cash include surprise counts of cash on hand, verification of cash-related source documents, and comparison of bank records with business records.

Cashiers also complete reports that are helpful to managers. For example, cashiers may complete *departmental sales reports* for their registers. These reports may, in turn, be used to complete a *summary of departmental sales* for the entire store. These two reports show the total sales made during the day for each department. They help managers spot departments that are selling more or less than expected.

Tom Hanes is the manager of Main Street Sporting Goods. At the end of each day, each cashier completes a departmental sales report for each cash register. The cashiers complete their reports by copying the total sales for each department from their detailed audit tapes. A departmental sales report for register no. 1 is shown in Illustration 20A on page 169.

On March 5, the cashiers gave Tom their departmental sales reports, their detailed audit tapes, and the cash from their cash registers. Tom completed the summary of departmental sales report shown in Illustration 20B on page 169.

To complete the report, Tom followed these steps:

STEP 1 Verify the amounts and totals on each departmental sales report.

When electronic cash registers are connected to a central computer system, reports such as the departmental sales report and the summary of department sales report are completed automatically by the computer system.

Tom compared the amounts shown on each departmental sales report to the amounts on the detailed audit tape for the same register. For example, he compared the detailed audit tape shown in Illustration 20C (page 170) from register no. 1 with the departmental sales report completed by the cashier for register no. 1 (Illustration 20A on page 169).

Tom found that the cashier had copied the total sales for tennis incorrectly from the tape to the report. The cashier had copied the total sales amount correctly, however. Tom corrected the departmental sales report for register no. 1 by crossing out the amount for tennis and writing the correct amount next to it.

Department	Total
Cycling	$ 920.00
Running	1,380.00
Tennis	~~980.00~~ 890.00
Swimming	570.00
General	490.00
Total	$4,250.00

STEP 2 Copy the amounts to the summary of departmental sales report.

Tom copied the amounts from the departmental sales reports to the summary of departmental sales report. For example, Tom copied the total sales for cycling, $920.00, from the departmental sales report for register no. 1 to the line for cycling in the column for register no. 1 in the summary report.

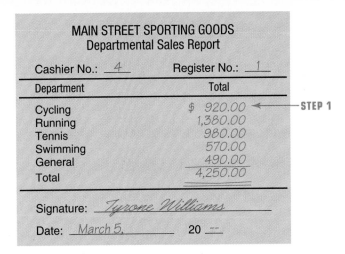

STEP 2

STEP 4

MAIN STREET SPORTING GOODS
Summary of Departmental Sales
MARCH 5, 20--

| Department | Registers | | | | | | | | Department Total | |
	1		2		3		4			
Cycling		920	00	345	89	651	98	201	90	2	119	77
Running	1	380	00	448	99	812	43	209	34	2	850	76
Tennis		890	00	2	009	58	312	45	2	298	33	5	510	36
Swimming		570	00	128	12	498	53	509	63	1	706	28
General		490	00	798	39	408	66	976	42	2	673	47
Total	4	250	00	3	730	97	2	684	05	4	195	62	14	860	64
	4	250	00	3	730	97	2	684	05	4	195	62	14	860	64

STEP 3

STEP 5

STEP 3 Find and verify the daily total for each register.

Tom added the columns for each register in the summary report and compared them to the totals shown on the departmental sales reports. He did this to insure that he had copied the amounts correctly. For example, Tom added the column for register no. 1 and entered the total, $4,250.00, as a footing. He then compared that total to the total on the departmental sales report for register no. 1. Since they were equal, he wrote the total below the footing on the summary of departmental sales report.

STEP 4 Find the daily total for each department.

Tom found the total sales for each department by adding across. For example, he added the cycling department sales from each register. The total sales for cycling for the day were $2,119.77. He entered this amount in the Department Totals column on the line for cycling.

STEP 5 Find and verify the grand total and double rule the form.

Tom added the amounts in the Department Totals column and entered that total, $14,860.64, as a footing at the bottom of the column. This amount is a grand total since it is the total of the Department Totals column and the total of the register column totals. To prove his work, Tom

Illustration 20C
Detailed audit tape showing
departmental sales totals

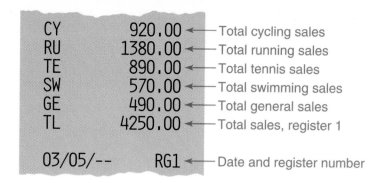

CY	920.00	← Total cycling sales
RU	1380.00	← Total running sales
TE	890.00	← Total tennis sales
SW	570.00	← Total swimming sales
GE	490.00	← Total general sales
TL	4250.00	← Total sales, register 1
03/05/--	RG1	← Date and register number

crossfooted the totals of the register columns and compared that amount to the total of the Department Totals column. Since these amounts were equal, Tom entered the grand total below the footing and double ruled the form.

BUILDING YOUR BUSINESS VOCABULARY

On a sheet of paper, write the headings **Statement Number** and **Words.** Next, choose the words that match the statements. Write each word you choose next to the statement number it matches. Be careful; not all the words listed should be used.

Statements	Words
1. Money given back to a customer for returned bottles or merchandise	amount tendered
2. A total of other totals	cashier
3. A special bar code read by electronic cash registers	change fund
4. The amount of cash given to the cashier by the customer	crossfooting
5. A form on which you compare how much cash you are supposed to have with what you actually have in the register	detailed audit tape
6. A person who receives and pays out money	footing
7. Adding a row of figures across a business form	grand total
8. An amount given to a cashier at the beginning of the day for making change	proof of cash
9. A record of all cash register transactions	refund
	subtotal
	transaction
	Universal Product Code

STEPS REVIEW: Preparing Cashier Reports

STEP 1 Verify the amounts and totals on each departmental sales report.

STEP 2 Copy the amounts to the summary of departmental sales report.

STEP 3 Find and verify the daily total for each register.

STEP 4 Find the daily total for each department.

STEP 5 Find and verify the grand total and double rule the form.

Problem 20-1

You are an office assistant for Key Food Mart. The manager has asked you to prepare a summary of departmental sales report, like the one shown in Illustration 20B (page 169), for July 6.

Directions

a. Verify each of the following departmental sales reports by comparing it to the detailed audit tape shown below it. Correct any departmental sales reports that contain errors.

Cashier No.: 4   Register No.: 1

Department	Total
Meat	$ 879.23
Produce	407.21
Dairy	303.67
Grocery	449.21
General	217.82
Total	$ 2,256.96

Signature: Victor Bell

Date: July 6,   20 --

```
ME          879.23
PR          407.12
DA          303.67
GR          449.12
GE          217.82
TL         2256.96

07/06/--       RG1
```

Cashier No.: 2   Register No.: 2

Department	Total
Meat	$ 699.29
Produce	310.06
Dairy	607.88
Grocery	421.87
General	439.76
Total	$2,478.86

Signature: Ana Lopez

Date: July 6,   20 --

```
ME          699.29
PR          310.06
DA          607.88
GR          421.87
GE          439.76
TL         2478.86

07/06/--       RG2
```

Cashier No.: 1   Register No.: 3

Department	Total
Meat	$ 809.98
Produce	531.54
Dairy	688.12
Grocery	708.34
General	433.80
Total	$3,171.78

Signature: Ed Tieg

Date: July 6,   20 --

```
ME          809.98
PR          531.54
DA          688.12
GR          708.34
GE          433.80
TL         3171.78

07/06/--       RG3
```

Cashier No.: 3   Register No.: 4

Department	Total
Meat	$2,003.39
Produce	698.23
Dairy	823.19
Grocery	399.31
General	729.11
Total	$4,653.23

Signature: Louise Clark

Date: July 6,   20 --

```
ME         2003.39
PR          698.23
DA          823.19
GR          399.31
GE          729.11
TL         4653.23

07/06/--       RG4
```

CHECK POINT

20-1

Grand total = $12,560.83

b. Copy the amounts from the departmental sales report for each register to the summary of departmental sales report for the whole store.

c. Find the column, line, and grand totals. Verify them by crossfooting, and double rule the report.

You are a clerk in the manager's office at Star Electronics, Inc. The manager has asked you to prepare a summary of departmental sales report, like the one shown in Illustration 20B (page 169), for April 12.

Directions

a. Verify each departmental sales report that appears below by comparing it to the detailed audit tape shown below it. Correct any departmental sales reports that contain errors.

b. Copy the amounts from the departmental sales report for each register to the summary of departmental sales report for the whole store.

c. Find the column, line, and grand totals. Verify them by crossfooting, and double rule the report.

CHECK POINT

20-2

Video Department total
$20,702.88

Cashier No.: 2	Register No.: 1
Department	**Total**
Video Systems	$ 2,801.34
Sound Systems	5,228.91
Computer Systems	11,010.99
Communications Systems	3,078.43
General	1,851.76
Total	$23,071.43

Signature: *Charles Turner*

Date: *April 12*   20 --

VS	2801.34
SS	5228.91
CO	11010.99
CS	3078.43
GE	1851.76
TL	23971.43

04/12/--   RG1

Cashier No.: 4	Register No.: 2
Department	**Total**
Video Systems	$ 3,211.31
Sound Systems	8,145.98
Computer Systems	10,208.23
Communications Systems	1,897.45
General	2,301.87
Total	$25,773.84

Signature: *Leslie Sykes*

Date: *April 12,*   20 --

VS	3211.31
SS	8154.98
CO	10208.23
CS	1897.45
GE	2301.87
TL	25773.84

04/12/--   RG2

Cashier No.: 3	Register No.: 3
Department	**Total**
Video Systems	$ 6,389.01
Sound Systems	3,207.98
Computer Systems	8,114.41
Communication Systems	3,781.31
General	1,506.82
Total	$22,999.53

Signature: *John Kriege*

Date: *April 12,*   20 --

VS	6389.01
SS	3207.98
CO	8114.41
CS	3781.31
GE	1506.82
TL	22999.53

04/12/--   RG3

Cashier No.: 1	Register No.: 4
Department	**Total**
Video Systems	$ 8,301.22
Sound Systems	4,109.99
Computer Systems	7,981.98
Communication Systems	2,113.01
General	1,556.65
Total	$24,062.85

Signature: *Eva O'Brien*

Date: *April 12*   20 --

VS	8301.22
SS	4109.99
CO	7981.98
CS	2113.01
GE	1556.65
TL	24062.85

04/12/--   RG4

Problem 20-3 may be found in the Working Papers.

Job 21 · PREPARING BANK DEPOSITS

Tips

When you multiply by 10 or 100, move the decimal point in the number multiplied to the right as many places as there are zeros in the number you multiply by. For example, 54 × 10 = 540. When you multiply by 0.01, move the decimal point in the number being multiplied to the left as many decimal places as there are in the number you multiply by. For example, 123 × 0.01 = 1.23.

applied math preview

Copy and complete the following problems.

1. 16 × $100.00 =
2. 42 × $50.00 =
3. 206 × $0.50 =
4. 724 × $0.25 =
5. 318 × $10.00 =
6. 130 × $5.00 =
7. 645 × $0.10 =
8. 981 × $0.01 =

key terms preview

- **Bank deposit**
- **Deposit slip**
- **Loose bills and coins**
- **Tally sheet**

goals

1 To learn how to prepare a tally sheet.

2 To learn how to prepare a bank deposit slip.

Key Terms

Bank deposit. Money placed in a bank account.

For Your Information

A night deposit box is also called a night depository, a night deposit slot, and a night deposit safe.

→ UNDERSTANDING THE JOB

The cash you collect using a cash drawer, cash register, or other means should be deposited, or placed, in the bank at the end of each day. It is not good business practice to keep large amounts of cash on hand after business hours. After proving cash and preparing the daily cash reports, you must prepare a **bank deposit** so that the cash collected can be deposited in the bank.

Many banks offer the use of a night deposit box. A night deposit box is usually located outside the bank. The bank supplies the customer with a deposit bag that can be locked. After the deposit bag has been placed in the night deposit box, the bag moves to a vault within the bank. A bank employee will remove the bag from the vault during the next day's banking hours. A night deposit box is especially useful for businesses that do not have their own safes and that collect large sums of cash that cannot be deposited during banking hours. Examples of such businesses are restaurants, gas stations, and movie theaters.

Kay Eads is the cashier for Riko's Cash and Carry Store. One of her jobs is to prepare a bank deposit of the money she receives daily. Here are the steps she follows on June 3:

STEP 1 Separate and wrap the bills.

Kay removes from the cash register all the bills that are to be deposited. She arranges them according to denominations so that $20 bills, $10 bills, $5 bills, and $1 bills are all in separate stacks. The bills are placed face up and counted in stacks of a hundred bills to a package. (Some banks prefer fifty bills to a package.) Kay uses wrappers supplied by the bank to wrap the money.

Kay usually finds that there are not enough bills of one denomination to make one complete package. For example, she may have 124 $1 bills. Only 100 of these bills are needed to make a full package. That means that 24 $1 bills are left over. Kay wraps the first 100 $1 bills in a wrapper. She places the 24 $1 bills left in a $1 wrapper also, but marks the wrapper "$24.00 only", as shown in Illustration 21A.

Illustration 21A
Wrapped bills

Mark packages that do not have the full number of bills

STEP 2 Separate and wrap the coins.

Kay removes from the cash register all the coins that are to be deposited. She uses the table below to help her sort out the coins and put them in the wrappers correctly.

Coin	Color of Wrapper	Number of Coins in Full Wrapper	Value of Coins in Full Wrapper
Half-Dollars	Tan	20	$10.00
Quarters	Orange	40	10.00
Dimes	Green	50	5.00
Nickels	Blue	40	2.00
Pennies	Red	50	0.50

Usually there will not be enough coins of one denomination to make a full roll. For example, if there are 31 quarters, Kay cannot prepare a full roll of quarters because 40 quarters are needed to make one roll. Kay puts the 31 quarters in a quarter wrapper and writes "$7.75 only" on the wrapper to show how much money is inside, as shown in Illustration 21B.

STEP 3 Tally the money to be deposited.

Kay sorts and wraps the money this way:

Bills	Coins
4 packages of $10 bills	8 rolls of half-dollars
6 loose $10 bills	7 loose half-dollars
2 packages of $5 bills	6 rolls of quarters
3 loose $5 bills	31 loose quarters
2 packages of $1 bills	14 rolls of dimes
24 loose $1 bills	8 loose dimes
	10 rolls of nickels
	16 loose nickels
	15 rolls of pennies
	11 loose pennies

Key Terms

Tally sheet. Checklist of money to be deposited.

Loose bills and coins. Do not fill a wrapper.

Deposit slip. Lists money to be deposited.

For Your Information

The largest bill ever printed was a $100,000 gold certificate in 1934. In 1969, the Treasury Department stopped distributing bills of $500, $1,000, $5,000, and $10,000. Every day the Bureau of Engraving and Printing prints more than 22,000,000 bills in denominations from $1 to $100.

Kay lists the sorted bills and coins on a **tally sheet**, or checklist of money (Illustration 21C on page 176). She enters the bills first. For example, she enters 4 in the Number column on the line for full packages of $10 bills. She multiplies the number of full packages (4) by the amount of a full package ($1,000.00) and enters the total ($4,000.00) in the first money column.

Then Kay enters the data for the loose $10 bills. She enters 6 in the Number column on the line for loose $10 bills. She multiplies the number of loose $10 bills (6) by their value ($10.00) and enters the total ($60.00) in the first money column.

Kay enters the data for the rest of the bills and coins in the same way. Notice that Kay finds the totals for both the bills and coins separately and enters these totals in the second money column.

Notice also that Kay lists the wrappers that were not full as **"loose" bills and coins** on her tally sheet. Of course, the bills and coins are not really loose. They are wrapped and specially marked. However, this is what bills and coins that do not fill their wrappers are called.

STEP 4 Prepare the deposit slip.

Once Kay completes the tally sheet, she prepares a **deposit slip** (Illustration 21D on page 176). A deposit slip is a form used to list all money placed in a bank account. The bank used by Riko's Cash and Carry Store supplies Kay with the deposit slips.

Illustration 21B

Wrapped coins

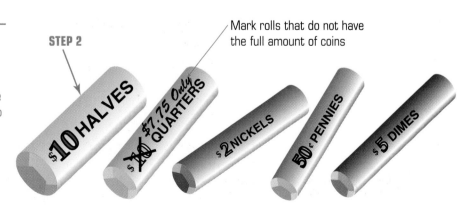

STEP 2

Mark rolls that do not have the full amount of coins

STEP 1
Separate and wrap bills.

NO.	BILLS							
	Packages of $100 bills x $10,000.00							
	Loose $100 bills							
	Packages of $50 bills x $5,000.00							
	Loose $50 bills							
	Packages of $20 bills x $2,000.00							
	Loose $20 bills							
4	Packages of $10 bills x $1,000.00	4	000	00				
6	Loose $10 bills		60	00				
2	Packages of $5 bills x $500.00	1	000	00				
3	Loose $5 bills		15	00				
2	Packages of $1 bills x $100.00		200	00				
24	Loose $1 bills		24	00				
	Total bills to be deposited					5	299	00
NO.	**COINS**							
8	Rolls of half-dollars x $10.00		80	00				
7	Loose half-dollars		3	50				
6	Rolls of quarters x $10.00		60	00				
31	Loose quarters		7	75				
14	Rolls of dimes x $5.00		70	00				
8	Loose dimes			80				
10	Rolls of nickels x $2.00		20	00				
16	Loose nickels			80				
15	Rolls of pennies x $0.50		7	50				
11	Loose pennies			11				
	Total coins to be deposited						250	46
	Total cash to be deposited					5	549	46

TALLY SHEET   Date: June 3,   20 --

STEP 3

To complete the deposit slip, Kay enters the date, the totals for the bills and coins, and the total deposit. Everything else is preprinted on the slip.

Notice that the totals for bills and coins are shown separately on the deposit slip. Kay gets these totals from the tally sheet. There is also a special place to list checks to be deposited. You will learn how to deposit checks in the next chapter.

Notice also that the deposit slip Kay completes has the bank account number of the business printed in Magnetic Ink Character Recognition

For DEPOSIT to the Account of

RIKO'S CASH
AND CARRY STORE

DATE June 3,   20 --

ALBRY STATE BANK
New York, New York

Subject to the Terms and Conditions of this Bank's
Collection Agreement

⑈0210 0625⑈   2418⑈639⑈

	Dollars	Cents
BILLS	5,299	00
COINS	250	46
Checks as Follows Properly Endorsed		
TOTAL DEPOSIT	5,549	46

1-5
210

179, 21-2
166

(MICR) on the bottom left side. The bank provides the business with deposit slips preprinted with its account number in MICR. When Kay takes the money and deposit slip to the bank teller, the bank will enter the total deposit in MICR on the slip. The bank's computer system can then read the account number and total deposit directly from the deposit slip.

The calculator can be used to make the job of completing a tally sheet much easier. Here is how you can use a calculator to complete the tally sheet used in the Sample Problem.

STEP 1 ▶ *For each line of bills, multiply the number of bills by the value and store the total in memory.*

For each denomination of bills, there is a line for a full package and a line for loose bills. For the full package, multiply the number of packages by the total value of the package. For example, multiply 4 by $1,000 to find the total for 4 packages of $10 bills. Do this by pressing these keys in order:

The answer that appears in the display is 4000, or $4,000.00. Enter this on the line for full packages of $10 bills. Then add the total to memory by pressing the M+ key:

For loose bills, multiply the number of bills by the denomination. For example, multiply 6 x $10 to find the total for 6 $10 bills. Do this by pressing these keys in order:

The answer that appears in the display is 60, or $60.00. Enter this on the line for loose $10 bills. Then add the total to memory by pressing the M+ key.
Follow these steps for each full package and loose dollar denomination.

STEP 2 ▶ *Find the total bills.*

Find the total bills by finding the total of the amounts you have been adding to memory. Do this by pressing the MR/C or MR key:

The answer that appears in the display is 5299, or $5,299.00. Enter this amount on the Total bills to be deposited line of the form.

STEP 3 ▶ *Clear memory.*

Now clear the memory by pressing the MC key once or by pressing the MR/C key twice.

Calculator Tips

STEP 4 ▶ *For each line of coins, multiply the number of coins by the value and store the total in memory.*

Calculate the totals for each full wrapper of coins and for the loose coins in the same way that you found the totals for bills. Enter each total in the form. After you find each total, press the M+ key to store the amount in memory.

STEP 5 ▶ *Find the total coins.*

Find the total coins by pressing the MR or MR/C key. The answer that appears in the display is 250.46. Enter this amount on the Total coins to be deposited line of the report.

STEP 6 ▶ *Clear memory.*

Clear memory by pressing the MC key once or the MR/C key twice.

STEP 7 ▶ *Add the total bills to total coins.*

Find the total amount of the deposit by pressing these keys in order:

5 2 9 9 + 2 5 0 . 4 6 =

The answer that appears in the display, 5549.46, is the total amount to be deposited. Enter this on the Total cash to be deposited line of the form.

⇨ BUILDING YOUR BUSINESS VOCABULARY

On a sheet of paper, write the headings **Statement Number** and **Words**. Next, choose the words that match the statements. Write each word you choose next to the statement number it matches. Be careful; not all the words listed should be used.

Statements	Words
1. Bills and coins that do not fill their wrappers	amount tendered
2. A form issued for cash received	bank deposit
3. A checklist of money to be deposited	cash overage
4. Money placed in a bank account	cash shortage
5. A form which lists all money deposited in a bank account	change fund
6. When there is more cash in the register at the end of the day than there should be	crossfooting
7. The amount of cash given to the cashier by the customer	deposit slip
8. Magnetic Ink Character Recognition	detailed audit tape
9. Adding a row of figures across a business form	loose bills and coins
10. A record of all cash register transactions	MICR
	receipt
	tally sheet

STEPS REVIEW: Preparing Bank Deposits

STEP 1 Separate and wrap the bills.

STEP 2 Separate and wrap the coins.

STEP 3 Tally the money to be deposited.

STEP 4 Prepare the deposit slips.

→ APPLICATION PROBLEMS

Problem 21-1
You are a cashier for 5th St. Quick Shop. The store has an account at Farmer's State Bank. At the close of each day, you must sort the cash in your cash register and prepare the money for deposit.

CHECK POINT
21-1

Total cash for
Oct. 5 = $2,498.33

Directions
The cash to be tallied and deposited for three days of the week is listed in this problem. For each day:
a. Prepare a tally sheet like the one in Illustration 21C (page 176).
b. Prepare a deposit slip like the one in Illustration 21D (page 176).

October 5:		October 6:		October 7:	
Quantity	**Denomination**	**Quantity**	**Denomination**	**Quantity**	**Denomination**
12	$50.00 bills	2	$100.00 bills	11	$100.00 bills
46	$20.00 bills	4	$ 50.00 bills	26	$ 50.00 bills
39	$10.00 bills	41	$ 20.00 bills	41	$ 20.00 bills
76	$ 5.00 bills	39	$ 10.00 bills	22	$ 10.00 bills
152	$ 1.00 bills	90	$ 5.00 bills	68	$ 5.00 bills
71	$ 0.50 coins	145	$ 1.00 bills	74	$ 1.00 bills
42	$ 0.25 coins	67	$ 0.50 coins	72	$ 0.50 coins
72	$ 0.10 coins	31	$ 0.25 coins	21	$ 0.25 coins
25	$ 0.05 coins	62	$ 0.10 coins	88	$ 0.10 coins
188	$ 0.01 coins	102	$ 0.05 coins	78	$ 0.05 coins
		301	$ 0.01 coins	221	$ 0.01 coins

Problem 21-2 may be found in the Working Papers.

Chapter 4

CHECK YOUR READING

1. List four or more businesses in your community that employ cashiers.
2. List six or more common business forms and three or more types of equipment cashiers work with.
3. List four or more forms of payment a cashier might handle when accepting payment for a purchase.

DISCUSSION

1. For five days last week, a new cashier had cash shortages of $4.25 and $3.12 and cash overages of $5.67, $3.14, and $4.45.
   a. What is one possible consequence of the cash overages?
   b. What is one possible consequence of the cash shortages?
   c. If you were the cashier's supervisor, what possible actions might you take if the shortages and overages continue?

2. Suppose that you are a cashier, and another employee gives you some cash and tells you that it amounts to $113.56. What might happen if you write a receipt for $113.56 and give it to the employee without counting the money first?

CRITICAL THINKING

In order to make a good choice or decision, it is very important to carefully study all the factors involved. By not doing so, a wrong choice might be made. This critical thinking strategy of *studying all the factors involved* before making a decision can be applied to many different types of situations. For example, what are the factors you would study before purchasing a new car? You might consider price, gas mileage, or color. Make a list of all the other items that you would consider before buying a car.

COMMUNICATION IN THE WORKPLACE

Suppose that you are a cashier at a store. A customer whose purchases total $7.14 gives you a $10 bill.
1. Write what you would say to the customer as you hand back the change if you were using a cash register that automatically figured the correct change.
2. Write what you would say to the customer as you hand back the change if you were using a cash register that did not figure change.

REINFORCEMENT ACTIVITIES

FOCUS ON CAREERS

Using the newspapers that are in your school library or at home, find the want ad section. Then:
1. Identify three titles of jobs that require the handling of cash.
2. List the requirements for each job on a sheet of paper. Then cross out those that are the same or very similar.
3. Be prepared to discuss the job titles and the job requirements in class.

REVIEWING WHAT YOU HAVE LEARNED

On a sheet of paper, write the headings **Statement Number** and **Words**. Next, choose the words that best complete the statements. Write each word you choose next to the statement number it completes. Be careful; not all the words listed should be used.

Statements	Words
1. When a cashier receives bills from a customer, the cashier should put the bills _____.	amount tendered
2. When the cashier receives money, it should be _____ before a receipt is given.	authorized
3. When a receipt is given for cash, the _____ is made out first and left in the receipt book.	cash register
4. The money that a cashier is given at the start of the day is called the _____.	change fund
5. When a store uses a cash register with a scanner and products with the _____, the cashier does not have to enter the data about each item sold.	counted
6. The cashier can find out the total sales by reading the _____.	detailed audit tape
7. The bank account number is usually printed on the deposit slip in _____.	loose bills and coins
8. Some stores will not cash _____.	MICR
9. The bills and coins left over after all others have been placed in full wrappers or rolls are called _____.	on the register
10. The amount of money the customer gives the cashier in payment of a bill is called the _____.	stub
	third-party checks
	Universal Product Code

Additional words listed: amount tendered, authorized, cash register, change fund, counted, detailed audit tape, loose bills and coins, MICR, on the register, stub, third-party checks, Universal Product Code

MASTERY PROBLEM

Elsa Stern is cashier no. 5 at Korte Super Markets. Elsa uses cash register no. 1 with the keys shown in Illustration 17C on page 149. On July 9, Elsa serves customers, makes change, and proves cash.

Phase 1: Making Change

Directions

a. A customer buys the items shown below. Copy the items and prices; next to each item, write the name of the department key Elsa should use to enter the item into her cash register.

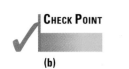
Items Bought		Department Keys Used
$8.19	Roast turkey	
$3.98	Oranges	
$1.09	Cake frosting	
$2.89	Light bulbs	
$2.88	Milk	

b. After entering the items, Elsa's register shows a total sale of $19.03. The amount tendered by the customer is $20.00. List the types and numbers of bills or coins Elsa should give the customer for change.

Phase 2: Proving Cash

Elsa started the day with a change fund of $150.00. At the end of the day, her register's detailed audit tape showed total cash sales of $2,078.83 and total cash paid out for bottle refunds of $63.25. She found the cash listed as follows in the drawer. There were no checks.

Quantity	Denomination	Quantity	Denomination
4	$50.00 bills	60	$ 0.50 coins
31	$20.00 bills	81	$ 0.25 coins
76	$10.00 bills	58	$ 0.10 coins
41	$ 5.00 bills	111	$ 0.05 coins
315	$ 1.00 bills	298	$ 0.01 coins

Directions

a. Prepare a cash count report.
b. Prepare a proof of cash.

Phase 3: Preparing a Summary of Departmental Sales Report

Directions

a. Verify each departmental sales report by comparing it to the detailed audit tape shown following it. Correct any reports that contain errors.

Cashier No.: 5	Register No.: 1
Department	**Total**
Meat	$ 512.89
Dairy	307.14
Produce	222.76
Bakery	202.18
Grocery	217.89
Health and beauty	310.69
General merchandise	305.28
Total	$2,078.83

Signature: Elsa Stern

Date: July 9,   20 --

Cashier No.: 8	Register No.: 2
Department	**Total**
Meat	$ 721.25
Dairy	417.12
Produce	388.98
Bakery	315.22
Grocery	289.99
Health and beauty	448.12
General merchandise	376.98
Total	$2,957.66

Signature: Alan Dempsey

Date: July 9,   20 --

ME	512.89
DA	307.14
PR	222.76
BA	202.18
GR	217.89
HE	310.69
GE	305.28
TL	2078.83

07/09/--   RG1

ME	721.25
DA	417.12
PR	388.98
BA	315.22
GR	289.99
HE	448.12
GE	376.98
TL	2957.66

07/09/--   RG2

Cashier No.: 2		Register No.: 3
Department		**Total**
Meat		$ 641.41
Dairy		315.11
Produce		387.01
Bakery		130.66
Grocery		333.51
Health and beauty		278.87
General merchandise		448.91
Total		$2,535.48

Signature: *Eve Lucco*

Date: *July 9,*   20 --

Cashier No.: 4		Register No.: 4
Department		**Total**
Meat		$ 801.68
Dairy		390.09
Produce		412.81
Bakery		200.18
Grocery		339.98
Health and beauty		100.98
General merchandise		414.54
Total		$2,668.27

Signature: *Lisa Bolger*

Date: *July 9,*   20 --

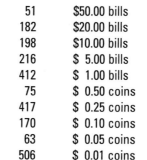

ME	641.41
DA	315.11
PR	387.01
BA	130.66
GR	333.51
HE	278.87
GE	448.91
TL	2535.48

07/09/--   RG3

ME	801.68
DA	390.09
PR	412.81
BA	200.18
GR	339.98
HE	108.99
GE	414.54
TL	2668.27

07/09/--   RG4

CHECK POINT

(c)
Grand total = $10,240.24

CHECK POINT

(a)
Total cash = $9,828.96

b. Copy the amounts from the departmental sales report for each register to the summary of departmental sales report for the whole store.
c. Find the column, line, and grand totals. Verify them by crossfooting, and double rule the report.

Phase 4: Tallying and Depositing the Cash

Korte Super Markets has an account at Marine Bank and Trust Co. At the close of July 9, manager Art Liebman must sort the cash in the registers and prepare the money for deposit. The sorted cash is listed below.

Directions
a. Prepare a tally sheet.
b. Prepare a deposit slip.

Quantity	Denomination
51	$50.00 bills
182	$20.00 bills
198	$10.00 bills
216	$ 5.00 bills
412	$ 1.00 bills
75	$ 0.50 coins
417	$ 0.25 coins
170	$ 0.10 coins
63	$ 0.05 coins
506	$ 0.01 coins

REVIEWING YOUR BUSINESS VOCABULARY

This activity may be found in the Working Papers.

Chapter 5

Checking Account Records

In today's world, it is not always convenient or safe to use cash when paying for items. Imagine for a moment that you just purchased a new automobile and that your payments will be $451.78 a month. Would you feel comfortable putting that much cash in an envelope and mailing it? Fortunately, there is an easier way.

The safest and most convenient way for you to pay your bills is to write checks and mail them directly to the companies. By using checks, you can avoid the expense and trouble of visiting each company's office to pay cash. Checks also provide you with a record of your expenses. And since your money in the bank, it is well protected.

In Chapter 5, you will learn how to open a checking account, prepare deposit slips, write checks and make sure your checking account is accurate. Learning how to properly handle a checking account is a skill that you will use the rest of your life. A Calculator Tip will be given for doing the math on check stubs.

FOCUS ON TECHNOLOGY

Banking on the Web

Many banks let customers complete some banking tasks from a Web site. Banking on the Web is sometimes called Web banking or e-banking. Banks that offer Web banking usually let you:

- View your current account balance and recent transactions.

- Pay bills from your checking account.

- Transfer funds between one account to another—for example, transfer money from your checking account to your savings account at the bank.

- Download your transactions for use with software on your PC.

MADISON BANK Always at Your Service	ACCOUNTS			
Account Name/Number	**Account Type**	**As of**	**Balance**	
Checking/01352	Checking	02/01/2000	$1,492.50	
Savings/02168	Savings	02/01/2000	$3,000.00	
Credit Card/7213X9	Credit Card	02/01/2000	$488.08	
Money Market/03221	Money Market	02/01/2000	$10,000.00	

Navigation menu: ACCOUNTS, TRANSFERS, PAYMENTS, MAIL, EXIT, MY SETTINGS, HELP

Illustration 5A   A page from a banking Web site

Job 22 OPENING A BANK CHECKING ACCOUNT

Tips

When writing dollar and cent amounts for addition or subtraction, be sure to line up the decimal points.

applied math preview

Copy and complete these problems.

1.	$4,200.00	2.	$342.20	3.	$ 0.83	4.	$162.58	5.	$3,148.56
	+ 620.00		+ 0.85		+ 0.78		16.90		841.50
							+ 0.63		+ 100.02

key terms preview

- ABA number
- Forged signature
- Individual checking account
- Joint checking account
- Personalized deposit slip
- Signature card

goals

1 To learn how to open a bank checking account.

2 To learn how to complete a signature card.

3 To learn how to complete a deposit slip for a personal checking account.

→ UNDERSTANDING THE JOB

Key Terms

Individual checking account. Used by only one person.

Joint checking account. Used by two or more persons.

Marty Werner is a full-time computer technician. On March 1, Marty decides to open his own computer and fax repair service. He plans to provide repair services out of his home. To start his business, Marty must pay these bills:

$4,750.00 for computerized diagnostic equipment
$820.00 to DTS Computer Supply for specialty tools
$122.45 for general office supplies

The safest and most convenient way for Marty to pay these bills is to write checks and mail them directly to the companies. In this way, Marty will not have the expense and trouble of visiting each company's office. Also, Marty's money will be protected since it is in a bank.

To be able to pay bills by check, Marty must open a bank checking account. Marty can open either an individual checking account or a joint checking account. An **individual checking account** lets only Marty write checks on the account. A **joint checking account** lets Marty share the account with another person or persons.

The first step in opening a checking account is to select a bank that will meet your needs. In choosing a bank, ask such questions as

—Is the bank convenient to your home or business?
—Does the bank provide the services you need?
—Does the bank charge for a checking account?

Marty considered the questions above and decided to open his checking account at the Monterey Bank of Commerce. After work on Wednesday, Marty went to the Monterey Bank of Commerce to open his account under the name of Marty's Computer and Fax Repair Service. Marty asked the bank's receptionist about opening an account, and she took him to see Ms. Jamie Gleed. Ms. Gleed is a bank employee who handles all new accounts. Ms. Gleed told Marty he needed to do two things to open a checking account:

1. Fill out a **signature card**.
2. Make an opening deposit of money.

Signature card. A form used to indicate to the bank which signatures to accept on signed checks.

Forged signature. A name falsely signed by someone else.

Filling Out a Signature Card

Ms. Gleed asked Marty to fill out and sign a signature card like the one shown in Illustration 22A. Marty learned that a signature card is a very important document because it allows the bank to make sure that signatures on Marty's checks are actually his. The bank would be held responsible if payment was made on a check with a **forged signature**.

Illustration 22A

A signature card

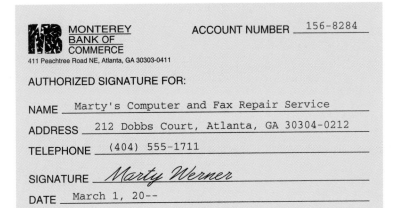

MONTEREY BANK OF COMMERCE 411 Peachtree Road NE, Atlanta, GA 30303-0411	ACCOUNT NUMBER	156-8284

AUTHORIZED SIGNATURE FOR:

NAME   Marty's Computer and Fax Repair Service

ADDRESS   212 Dobbs Court, Atlanta, GA 30304-0212

TELEPHONE   (404) 555-1711

SIGNATURE   *Marty Werner*

DATE   March 1, 20--

Ms. Gleed typed in all information except for the signature itself. She entered the business name, address, phone number, and the date. She also gave Marty an account number. The signature card was signed only by Marty. This means that no one other than Marty can write checks on the account. So, Marty has opened an individual checking account with his bank.

The Federal Deposit Insurance Corporation (FDIC) protects depositors from banks that fail. Bank deposits are generally covered up to $100,000 per depositor. Ask your bank if they are FDIC insured.

Making Deposits

Marty is now ready to make his first deposit. He decided to take $6,000.00 in cash from his savings. He also has a $200.00 check written

Key Terms

Personalized deposit slip. A deposit slip on which the depositor's name and address are preprinted.

ABA number. A number assigned to banks.

out to him for repairing two computers last month. Marty decided to deposit the $6,000.00 from his savings and also his $200.00 check. Thus, Marty's opening deposit will be for $6,200.00 ($6,000.00 + $200.00).

When money is deposited in a checking account, a deposit slip must be completed. Most banks today use personalized deposit slips. A **personalized deposit slip** is one on which the depositor's name, address, and account number are printed. This makes it easier for banks to process deposits and helps ensure that deposits will be processed correctly.

Marty completed a personalized deposit slip like the one shown in Illustration 22B. Since different types of money can be deposited (bills, coins, and checks), each type is listed separately on the deposit slip.

Illustration 22B

A personalized deposit slip

STEP 1		STEP 3	STEP 2
For DEPOSIT to the Account of			37-502 / 0810
Marty's Computer and Fax Repair Service		Dollars	Cents
212 Dobbs Ct. Atlanta, GA 30304-0212	BILLS	6000	00
	COINS		
DATE _March 1,_ 20 __	Checks as Follows Properly Endorsed		
	Stan Klor	200	00
MONTEREY BANK OF COMMERCE			
Atlanta, GA			
Subject to the Terms and Conditions of this Bank's Collection Agreement			
⑆08100135⑆ 1568284⑈	**TOTAL DEPOSIT**	6200	00
		STEP 4	STEP 5

Marty followed these steps in completing the deposit slip:

STEP 1 Enter the date.

Marty recorded March 1, 20--, in the Date space.

STEP 2 Enter bills deposited.

Marty recorded $6,000.00 on the Bills line.

STEP 3 Enter coins deposited.

You learned how to record coins deposited in Job 21. Marty had no coins to deposit, so he left the Coins line blank.

STEP 4 Enter checks deposited.

Marty is depositing a check for $200.00, so he entered this amount on the first line for checks. For future reference, Marty wrote the name of the person who gave him the check, Stan Klor, in the space provided. Some banks require that you enter instead a number assigned to the bank of the person who wrote the check. The number is called the **ABA number**. Monterey Bank of Commerce's ABA number, listed at the top of the deposit slip, is 37-502/0810. If Stan Klor's bank had an ABA number of 2-146/3624, Marty would enter 2-146 (leaving out 3624 to save space) on the line with the $200.00. (See Illustration 22C.)

Many deposits include more than just a few checks. If this occurs, the back of the deposit slip is used. The back is usually filled with 15 to 20

	Dollars	Cents
BILLS		
COINS		
Checks as Follows Properly Endorsed		
2-146	200	00	← STEP 4
TOTAL DEPOSIT		

additional lines for checks. The total of the back is then recorded on the front side.

STEP 5 Calculate and enter the total.

Marty then added the bills, coins, and checks, and entered the total, $6,200.00, on the Total Deposit line. After making his deposit, Marty received a receipt for the deposit from the bank. Most banks today use a machine that prints out a receipt like the one shown in Illustration 22D.

The number 156-8284 is Marty's account number which appears on both his signature card (Illustration 22A on page 187) and on his personalized deposit slip (Illustration 22B on page 188).

Illustration 22D

Marty's deposit receipt

MONTEREY BANK OF COMMERCE

The receipt of deposit should be held until verified with your next statement of account. Checks and other items are received for deposit subject to the terms and conditions of this bank's collection agreement.

March 01, 20-- #156-8284 $6,200.00

This is a Receipt for Your Deposit

→ BUILDING YOUR BUSINESS VOCABULARY

On a sheet of paper, write the headings **Statement Number** and **Words**. Next, choose the words that match the statements. Write each word you choose next to the statement number it matches. Be careful; not all the words listed should be used.

Statements	Words
1. A name falsely signed by someone else	ABA number
2. A number assigned to banks	coins
3. An account used by two or more people	deposit
4. An account used by only one person	deposit slip
5. A form completed when a deposit is made	forged signature
	individual checking account

Statements	Words
6. A form used to indicate to the bank which signatures to accept on signed checks	joint checking account
	personalized deposit slip
7. A deposit slip on which the depositor's name and address are preprinted	signature card

STEPS REVIEW: Completing a Deposit Slip

STEP 1 Enter the date.

STEP 2 Enter bills deposited.

STEP 3 Enter coins deposited.

STEP 4 Enter checks deposited.

STEP 5 Calculate and enter the total.

 APPLICATION PROBLEMS

Problem 22-1   You are opening your own checking account.

 CHECK POINT

22-1

Make sure to fill in every line and use the current year for the date.

Directions

Prepare a signature card as in Illustration 22A on page 187.

a. Enter your account number, 643-9214, on the Account Number line.
b. Print your name on the Name line.
c. Print your complete address on the Address line.
d. Enter your complete telephone number on the Telephone line.
e. Sign your name on the Signature line.
f. Enter the date, October 1, 20--, on the Date line.

Problem 22-2   On June 1, your employer, Rick Shires, asks you to prepare the opening deposit for Eastern Floral.

 CHECK POINT

22-2

If your work is correct, the total deposit should equal $177.71.

Directions

Prepare a deposit slip for the following items:

Bills:	$68.00	Checks:	$60.41 from Pat Reis
Coins:	$ 7.30		$42.00 from Paul Vane

Problem 22-3   On January 12, Caroline Bolaris started her own locksmith shop. In order to pay bills by check, Caroline opened a checking account under the name Bolaris Lock and Key. You have been hired as her record keeper.

Directions

Prepare a deposit slip for Caroline. She is depositing the following items on January 12:

 CHECK POINT

22-3

If your work is correct, the total deposit should equal $649.82.

Bills:	2	$50 bills	Coins:	$ 20.00 in quarters
	4	$20 bills		
	3	$10 bills	Checks:	$317.82 from Mary Nguyen
	4	$ 5 bills		$ 75.00 from Blake Hanson
	7	$ 1 bills		

Problems 22-4 and 22-5 may be found in the Working Papers.

Copy and complete these problems.

1. $6,258.89	2. $2,338.70	3. $1,494.58	4. $4,811.52
235.49	− 529.58	− 618.48	− 508.00
1,234.87			
414.68	+ 226.92	+ 351.60	+1,945.39
396.34			
+ 117.50			

key terms preview

- Check
- Check protector
- Check stub
- Checkbook
- Drawee
- Drawer
- Issue
- Legible
- Payee
- Postdated
- Void

goals

1 To learn how to complete check stubs.

2 To learn how to write checks.

➡ ## UNDERSTANDING THE JOB

Key Terms

Checkbook. A book of checks.

Check stub. Part of check kept by depositor.

Check. A written order by the depositor to his or her bank to pay a company or person.

In Job 22, you learned that a bank checking account is a safe and convenient way to pay bills. You also learned that to open a checking account you must fill out a signature card and make a deposit of money. In Job 23, you will learn how to write checks and keep a record of checks in a checkbook.

On March 1, Marty Werner opened a checking account at the Monterey Bank of Commerce. He was asked to fill out the signature card shown in Illustration 22A on page 187 in Job 22. Marty was asked to fill out a deposit slip and make an opening deposit. (See Illustration 22B on page 188, Job 22.) The bank then gave Marty a supply of deposit slips and a **checkbook** with pages of checks like the one shown in Illustration 23A on page 192.

The example in this job is a checking account for a business. However, checking accounts can be useful in your personal life, too. Paying your bills with checks is safer and more convenient than sending cash in the mail.

The steps for opening an account that were presented in Job 22 and the steps for writing checks that are presented in this job apply to personal checking accounts as well as business checking accounts.

Notice that there are two parts to each check in Marty's checkbook:

1. The **check stub** which remains in the checkbook as a permanent record of checks written.
2. The **check** which will be detached from the stub and sent to the company or person to whom Marty owes the money.

The stub gives Marty a record of the important facts about any check that he writes. Careful people always fill out the stub before writing the check. If they did not do this, they might mail the check and then find they have no record of the details about it.

Marty is now ready to use his checking account to pay his bills. Study the completed check shown in Illustration 23B.

Illustration 23B

Three parties to a check

Notice there are three parties involved in the check:

1. The **drawer**. The drawer is the person who writes the check. Marty has ordered the Monterey Bank of Commerce to *draw* $820.00 out of his account and pay it to DTS Computer Supply.

2. The **drawee**. The drawee is the bank that is ordered to pay a check from an account. The Monterey Bank of Commerce has been ordered by Marty to pay $820.00 out of his account.

3. The **payee**. The payee is the one who will be paid. DTS Computer Supply will receive $820.00 when this check is presented for payment.

Key Terms

Drawer. Writes the check.

Drawee. Bank that pays the check.

Payee. Receives check and is paid.

Issue. To send out.

SAMPLE PROBLEM

On March 6, Marty **issued** Check No. 1 for $820.00 to DTS Computer Supply. The completed check and check stub are shown in Illustration 23C. Here are the steps Marty used to complete the stub and check.

STEP 5
STEP 6
STEP 7

NO. 1 $ *820.00*

DATE *March 6, 20--*

TO *DTS Computer Supply*

FOR *specialty tools*

	DOLLARS	CENTS
BAL. BRO'T. FOR'D.	3/1	
AMT. DEPOSITED	6,200	00
TOTAL	6,200	00
AMT. THIS CHECK	820	00
BAL. CAR'D. FOR'D.	5,380	00

Marty's Computer and Fax Repair Service
212 Dobbs Ct.
Atlanta, GA 30304-0212

No. **1**

Date *March 6,* 20 __

37-502
0810

PAY TO THE ORDER OF *DTS Computer Supply* $ *820.00*

Eight hundred twenty and 00/100   Dollars

For Classroom Use Only

MB MONTEREY BANK OF COMMERCE
Atlanta, GA

Marty Werner

⑆08100135⑆ 1568284⑈

NO. 2 $ _____

DATE _____

TO _____

FOR _____

	DOLLARS	CENTS
BAL. BRO'T. FOR'D.	5,380	00
AMT. DEPOSITED		
TOTAL		
AMT. THIS CHECK		
BAL. CAR'D. FOR'D.		

Marty's Computer and Fax Repair Service
212 Dobbs Ct.
Atlanta, GA 30304-0212

No. **2**

Date _____ 20 ___

37-502
0810

PAY TO THE ORDER OF _____ $ _____

_____ Dollars

For Classroom Use Only

MB MONTEREY BANK OF COMMERCE
Atlanta, GA

⑆08100135⑆ 1568284⑈

STEP 8
STEP 9

STEP 3
Always use ink

STEP 4
Write Legibly

Illustration 23C

A portion of Marty's checkbook

STEP 1   Complete the top half of the stub.

Notice that the top half of the stub contains the following facts:

1. *Check number:* No. 1
2. *Amount:* $820.00
3. *Date:* March 6, 20--
4. *Payee's name:* DTS Computer Supply
5. *The reason the check is issued:* specialty tools

Fill in the required information on the top half of the stub.

STEP 2   Complete the bottom half of the stub.

After filling in the top half of the stub, complete the bottom half of the stub. Notice that the bottom half of the stub contains

1. *Balance Brought Forward (Bal. Bro't. For'd.).* Usually this space shows the amount of money left in the checking account after the last check was written. Since this was a new account, there was no previous balance to be brought forward. So, no amount was written in this space.
2. *Amount Deposited (Amt. Deposited).* The $6,200.00 recorded in this space

is the amount Marty deposited on March 1. Although no space is provided for the date of the deposit, some record keepers like to show the date on the stub. The number 3 in "3/1" stands for March because March is the third month of the year. It is a good idea to memorize the number for each month. You can use this shortcut for writing dates when the lack of space makes it necessary.

3. *Total.* Marty found the total by adding the balance brought forward to the deposit of $6,200.00. Since there was no amount to be brought forward, the total is $6,200.00.

4. *Amount of This Check (Amt. This Check).* Marty wrote the amount of the check, $820.00, in this space.

5. *Balance Carried Forward (Bal. Car'd. For'd.).* Marty found this amount by subtracting the amount of the check from the total:

Total	$6,200.00
Amt. This Check	− 820.00
Bal. Car'd. For'd.	$5,380.00

Since checks are always subtracted from the total, a minus sign is not used on the check stub. Notice that this amount, $5,380.00, is shown as the balance brought forward on the stub of Check No. 2. After each check stub is completed, the new balance is always carried forward to the next check stub. Before Marty issues Check No. 2, he will be able to look at this amount and see if there is enough money left in the account to pay the check.

Once Marty completed the stub, he then filled in the check using the following steps. His completed check is shown in Illustration 23C on page 193.

Key Terms

Legible. Clear and easy to read.

Postdate. To record a future date on a document.

STEP 3 Always use ink.

Checks should always be written in permanent ink. Names, dates, or amounts written in pencil or erasable ink can be easily changed. Avoid using broad felt-tipped pens as their broad tip makes it easier to forge a signature.

STEP 4 Write legibly.

Write **legibly**. Checks that cannot be read will not be accepted or paid by the bank.

STEP 5 Use the current date.

Write the current date on all checks. Checks with old dates may not be accepted by businesses. Checks that are **postdated**, that is, marked with a future date, often cause problems when they are cashed early. For example, if the checkholder cashes the check before the written date, there may not be enough money in the account to pay it. This can result in serious legal problems for the owner of the checking account.

STEP 6 Write the name of the payee.

After the words "Pay to the Order of," write the name of the payee. Remember, the payee is the person or business to whom a check is issued.

STEP 7   Write the amount of the check in figures.

Write the amount of dollars in figures close to the printed dollar sign, so that no other number can be added. Write the amount of cents after the decimal point.

STEP 8   Write the amount of the check in words.

Start writing the amount of the check in words at the left margin of the check. Write the number of cents as a fraction. Fill the unused space with a line all the way to the printed word "Dollars":

Eight hundred twenty 00/100————————Dollars

Only the first letter of the entire amount is capitalized. When you write the amount in words, remember to write the numbers twenty-one through ninety-nine with a hyphen.

Write numbers distinctly so they can be easily read. Avoid leaving spaces between numbers so that someone else cannot change the amount.

STEP 9   Sign your name.

Sign your name to the check in exactly the way that it appears on the signature card.

If you make an error in writing a check, make the check unusable by writing **VOID** in large letters on both the stub and check. A check with an erasure or correction will be questioned by the bank. Most people destroy voided personal checks, but businesses usually keep all voided checks for their records.

Void. Unusable.

Look at the number, 37-502/0810, shown in the upper right corner of the check in Illustration 23D below. This is called the ABA number. ABA numbers are assigned to banks by the American Bankers Association. They are used to help sort checks so that they can be sent to the right bank for collection. As you learned in Job 22, the top two parts of the ABA number may be used to list checks for deposit.

Illustration 23D

Rules of check writing

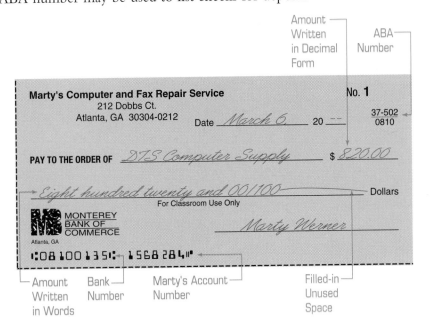

The numbers in the lower left corner of the check, 0810 0135 and 1568 284, are the bank number and Marty's account number, respectively.

NO. 1 $ *820.00*
DATE *March 6, 20--*
TO *DTS Computer*
Supply
FOR *specialty tools*

	DOLLARS	CENTS
BAL. BRO'T. FOR'D.		
AMT. DEPOSITED	*6,200*	*00*
TOTAL	*6,200*	*00*
AMT. THIS CHECK	*820*	*00*
BAL. CAR'D. FOR'D.	*5,380*	*00*

311

NO. 2 $ *122.45*
DATE *March 12, 20--*
TO *Pacific Stationery*
and Supply Co.
FOR *general office*
supplies

	DOLLARS	CENTS
BAL. BRO'T. FOR'D.	*5,380*	*00*
AMT. DEPOSITED		
TOTAL	*5,380*	*00*
AMT. THIS CHECK	*122*	*45*
BAL. CAR'D. FOR'D.	*5,257*	*55*

Marty's Computer and Fax Repair Service   No. **2**
212 Dobbs Ct.
Atlanta, GA 30304-0212   Date *March 12* 20 *--*   37-502
                                                        0810

PAY TO THE ORDER OF *Pacific Stationery and Supply Co.* $ *122.45*

One hundred twenty-two and 45/100 ———————— Dollars

For Classroom Use Only

MB MONTEREY
BANK OF
COMMERCE
Atlanta, GA   *Marty Werner*

⑈081001351⑈ 1568284⑈

NO. 3 $ ————
DATE ————
TO ————
————
FOR ————
————

	DOLLARS	CENTS
BAL. BRO'T. FOR'D.	*5,257*	*55*
AMT. DEPOSITED		
TOTAL		
AMT. THIS CHECK		
BAL. CAR'D. FOR'D.		

Marty's Computer and Fax Repair Service   No. **3**
212 Dobbs Ct.
Atlanta, GA 30304-0212   Date ———— 20 ——   37-502
                                                 0810

PAY TO THE ORDER OF ———————— $ ————

———————— Dollars

For Classroom Use Only

MB MONTEREY
BANK OF
COMMERCE
Atlanta, GA

⑈081001351⑈ 1568284⑈

Illustration 23E

Marty's checkbook on
March 12

Check protector. Machine
used to write checks.

These numbers are printed in MICR so that they can be read by the bank's computer. The ABA number, bank number, and Marty's account number are also printed on all his deposit slips.

On March 12, Marty issued Check No. 2 for $122.45 to the Pacific Stationery and Supply Company for general office supplies. The check and stub for Check No. 2 are shown in Illustration 23E. (Notice that the check stub for Check No. 1 is still in the checkbook even though Marty has already mailed the check.) Marty carried forward the balance of $5,257.55 to the stub of Check No. 3.

Businesses that issue many checks may use a machine known as a check writer or **check protector**. This machine prints the amount on the check in a way that makes changes impossible.

Other businesses may prepare their checks using a computer. Printers are used in a computerized system to print paychecks and checks to those companies to whom the business owes money.

On a sheet of paper, write the headings **Statement Number** and **Words**. Next, choose the words that match the statements. Write each word you choose next to the statement number it matches. Be careful; not all the words listed should be used.

Statements	Words
1. The person who writes the check	ABA number
2. The part which remains in the checkbook when a check is issued	check
	check protector
3. The person to whom a check is made out and who will receive the money	check stub
	checkbook
4. The word you print across the check and the check stub when you make an error	deposit
	drawee
5. The party who is ordered to pay the amount on the check	drawer
	issue
6. A special number assigned to a bank by the American Bankers Association	legible
	MICR
7. Clear and easy to read	payee
8. To send out	postdate
9. A machine used to write checks	void
10. A written order by the drawer to the drawee to pay the payee	
11. To record a future date on a document	

STEPS REVIEW: Completing Check Stubs and Checks

STEP 1 Complete the top half of the stub.

STEP 2 Complete the bottom half of the stub.

STEP 3 Always use ink.

STEP 4 Write legibly.

STEP 5 Use the current date.

STEP 6 Write the name of the payee.

STEP 7 Write the amount of the check in figures.

STEP 8 Write the amount of the check in words.

STEP 9 Sign your name.

 APPLICATION PROBLEMS

Problem 23-1   A list of amounts, in figures, is written in Column 1 of the following table. Copy each amount on a sheet of paper. Then, in Column 2, write each amount in words as it would appear on a check.

Column 1	Column 2
1. $ 8.00	_____ Dollars
2. $ 20.00	_____ Dollars
3. $ 210.00	_____ Dollars
4. $ 17.50	_____ Dollars
5. $ 350.35	_____ Dollars
6. $ 68.47	_____ Dollars
7. $ 51.12	_____ Dollars
8. $ 39.20	_____ Dollars
9. $ 86.30	_____ Dollars
10. $1,360.41	_____ Dollars

Problem 23-2

You are a record keeper for Julie Westmont, who owns a skateboard park. On July 1, Julie opens a checking account at the Midwest State Bank with a deposit of $2,000.00. She puts you in charge of keeping the checkbook. You are authorized to sign the checks with your own name.

Directions

a. On July 1, enter the opening deposit of $2,000.00 in the space for "Amt. Deposited" on the stub of Check No. 1. Fill in the total.

b. On July 5, write Check No. 1 for $325.00 to Jake's Refinishing for concrete repairs. Bring the new balance forward to the stub of Check No. 2.

c. On July 8, write Check No. 2 for $450.00 to Whitewater Insurance Company for liability insurance. Bring the new balance forward to Check No. 3.

d. On July 10, write Check No. 3 for $37.00 to the *Star Journal* for a newspaper advertisement.

CHECK POINT

23-2

If your work is correct, the **Bal. Car'd. For'd.** on Check Stub No. 3 should equal $1,188.00.

Problem 23-3

You are a record keeper for Robert Wedemeyer, who owns and operates an automobile parts and accessories business. On May 1, Robert opens a checking account at the Sedona National Bank with a deposit of $1,650.00. He puts you in charge of keeping the checkbook. You are authorized to sign the checks with your own name.

Directions

a. On May 1, enter the opening deposit of $1,650.00 in the space for "Amt. Deposited" on the stub of Check No. 1. Fill in the total.

b. On May 2, write Check No. 1 for $201.36 to Mustang Express for auto parts.

c. On May 5, write Check No. 2 for $63.20 to AutoCare Accessories for wood dash trims.

d. On May 6, write Check No. 3 for $371.00 to Auto Performance, Inc. for rear lip spoilers.

CHECK POINT

23-3

If your work is correct, the **Bal. Car'd. For'd.** on Check Stub No. 3 should equal $1,014.44.

Problems 23-4 and 23-5 may be found in the Working Papers.

Job 24 KEEPING A CHECKBOOK

→ UNDERSTANDING THE JOB

Insufficient funds. When there is not enough money in the checking account to pay a check.

You need to know the exact amount of money in a checking account before issuing a check. A business owner needs to make decisions about buying supplies or paying for personal expenses. If the balance recorded in the checkbook is lower than the correct balance, the owner may unnecessarily put off buying items necessary for business success. If the balance recorded in the checkbook is higher than the correct balance, the owner may purchase items with money that is not really available.

The bank will not pay a check that you issue unless there is enough money in your account to cover the amount of the check. If you issue a check without enough money in your account, the bank will return the check to the payee marked **"insufficient funds."** The bank will then charge you an extra fee for every check marked "insufficient funds."

If you regularly write checks that are returned for having insufficient funds, vendors may become angry if they cannot cash your checks. You may hurt your chances of obtaining loans and buying on credit in the future. Also, it is illegal to intentionally write a check that cannot be covered.

For this reason, you must keep an up-to-date record of the balance of your checking account. In this job, you will practice keeping the checkbook balance up-to-date as you record additional deposits and write checks.

On March 12, there was a balance of $5,257.55 in the checking account of Marty's Computer and Fax Repair Service. On March 13, Marty deposited the following cash:

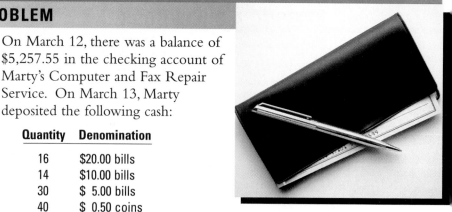

Quantity	Denomination
16	$20.00 bills
14	$10.00 bills
30	$ 5.00 bills
40	$ 0.50 coins
30	$ 0.25 coins

For Your Information

16 × $20 bills =	$320.00
14 × $10 bills =	$140.00
30 × $ 5 bills =	$150.00
Total Deposit of Bills =	$610.00
40 × $0.50 coins =	$ 20.00
30 × $0.25 coins =	$ 7.50
Total Deposit of Coins =	$ 27.50

Here are the steps Marty took to make the deposit and record it in his checkbook:

STEP 1 Prepare the deposit slip.

Marty counted the bills and coins to be deposited and filled out the deposit slip shown in Illustration 24A.

Illustration 24A

Deposit slip

STEP 1

For DEPOSIT to the Account of

Marty's Computer and Fax Repair Service
212 Dobbs Ct.
Atlanta, GA 30304-0212

DATE ___March 13,___ 20 __

MONTEREY
BANK OF
COMMERCE
Atlanta, GA

Subject to the Terms and Conditions of this Bank's Collection Agreement

⑈08⑈00135⑈   1568284⑈

37-502
0810

	Dollars	Cents
BILLS	610	00
COINS	27	50
Checks as Follows Properly Endorsed		
TOTAL DEPOSIT	637	50

STEP 2 Record the total deposit on the check stub.

The total amount of the deposit, $330.00, was recorded as one amount on the stub of Check No. 3 as shown in Illustration 24B.

Illustration 24B

Additional deposit on a check stub

NO. 3 $ _____

DATE _____

TO _____

FOR _____

STEP 2

	DOLLARS	CENTS
BAL. BRO'T. FOR'D.	5,257	55
AMT. DEPOSITED 3/13	637	50 ←
TOTAL	5,895	05
AMT. THIS CHECK		
BAL. CAR'D. FOR'D.		

STEP 3 Add the balance brought forward to the deposit.

Look at the Total line of the check stub in Illustration 24B on page 200. You can see that the total of $5,895.05 was found by adding the balance brought forward of $5,257.55 and the deposit of $637.50.

Bal. Bro't. Ford'd.	$5,257.55
Amt. Deposited	+ 637.50
Total	$5,895.05

Illustration 24C

A page of check stubs

NO. 3 $ 476.00

DATE March 15, 20--

TO PhotoMax

FOR Combination fax, printer, & copier machine

	DOLLARS	CENTS
BAL. BRO'T. FOR'D.	5,257	55
AMT. DEPOSITED 3/13	637	50
TOTAL	5,895	05
AMT. THIS CHECK	476	00
BAL. CAR'D. FOR'D.	5,419	05

NO. 4 $ 315.00

DATE March 17, 20--

TO Peninsula Supply House

FOR electronic parts & components

	DOLLARS	CENTS
BAL. BRO'T. FOR'D.	5,419	05
AMT. DEPOSITED		
TOTAL	5,419	05
AMT. THIS CHECK	315	00
BAL. CAR'D. FOR'D.	5,104	05

NO. 5 $ 750.00

DATE March 24, 20--

TO Cash

FOR personal use

	DOLLARS	CENTS
BAL. BRO'T. FOR'D.	5,104	05
AMT. DEPOSITED 3/21	900	00
TOTAL	6,004	05
AMT. THIS CHECK	750	00
BAL. CAR'D. FOR'D.	5,254	05

Study the check stubs in Illustration 24C. The check stubs show how Marty recorded the following checks and an additional deposit:

March 15 Issued Check No. 3 for $476.00 to PhotoMax for a combination fax, printer, and copier machine.

17 Issued Check No. 4 for $315.00 to Peninsula Supply House for electronic parts and components.

21 Deposited $900.00.

24 Issued Check No. 5 for $750.00 for personal use.

Look at the stub for Check No. 5 shown in Illustration 24C. The stub shows that the check was made payable to the order of "Cash" for $750.00. This is a common procedure when cashing a check for personal use.

All of Marty's business receipts are deposited in his checking account. One way he can withdraw funds from his checking account for his personal use is to cash a check at the bank. He does this by making the check payable to himself or by simply writing the word "Cash" after the words "Pay to the order of." Checks made payable to "Cash" must be handled with great care. If the check is lost, anyone finding the check may try to cash it.

Key Terms

Voucher check. A check with a special stub attached.

Voucher. Shows the purpose of the check and a description of the payment.

Voucher Checks

Some businesses use a special kind of check called a **voucher check**. A voucher check has a special stub, or **voucher**, attached to it. The voucher shows the purpose of the check and gives a description of the payment. A voucher check is shown in Illustration 24D on page 202.

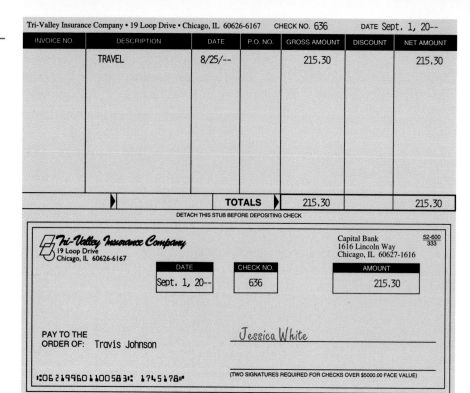

INVOICE NO.	DESCRIPTION	DATE	P.O. NO.	GROSS AMOUNT	DISCOUNT	NET AMOUNT
	TRAVEL	8/25/--		215.30		215.30
		TOTALS		215.30		215.30

Tri-Valley Insurance Company • 19 Loop Drive • Chicago, IL 60626-6167   CHECK NO. 636   DATE Sept. 1, 20--

DETACH THIS STUB BEFORE DEPOSITING CHECK

Tri-Valley Insurance Company
19 Loop Drive
Chicago, IL 60626-6167

Capital Bank
1616 Lincoln Way
Chicago, IL 60627-1616
52-600
333

DATE	CHECK NO.	AMOUNT
Sept. 1, 20--	636	215.30

PAY TO THE
ORDER OF: Travis Johnson

Jessica White

⑈06219960⑈100583⑈ 1745178⑈

(TWO SIGNATURES REQUIRED FOR CHECKS OVER $5000.00 FACE VALUE)

You can use your calculator to help you do the math on check stubs. Here is how you would fill out Stubs 3, 4, and 5 in Illustration 24C with the help of your calculator.

STEP 1 ▶ *Key in the Balance Brought Forward.*

Key in the Bal. Bro't. For'd. by pressing these keys in order:

$$\boxed{5}\ \boxed{2}\ \boxed{5}\ \boxed{7}\ \boxed{.}\ \boxed{5}\ \boxed{5}\ \boxed{+}$$

STEP 2 ▶ *Add the March 13 deposit.*

Add the March 13 deposit by pressing these keys in order:

$$\boxed{6}\ \boxed{3}\ \boxed{7}\ \boxed{.}\ \boxed{5}\ \boxed{0}\ \boxed{=}$$

The total, 5,895.05, will appear in the calculator's display. Record this amount in the Total space on Check Stub No. 3. *Do not clear your display.*

STEP 3 ▶ *Subtract the March 15 check.*

Subtract the March 15 check by pressing these keys in order:

$$\boxed{-}\ \boxed{4}\ \boxed{7}\ \boxed{6}\ \boxed{=}$$

The difference, 5,419.05, will appear in the calculator's display. Record this amount in the Bal. Car'd. For'd. space on Stub No. 3. Record it also in the Bal. Bro't. For'd. space on Stub No. 4. *Do not clear your display.*

Calculator Tips

STEP 4 ▶ *Subtract the March 17 check.*

Subtract the March 17 check by pressing these keys in order:

$$- \quad 3 \quad 1 \quad 5 \quad =$$

Record the difference, 5,104.05, in the proper spaces on Stubs 4 and 5. *Do not clear your display.*

STEP 5 ▶ *Add the March 21 deposit.*

Add the March 21 deposit by pressing these keys in order:

$$+ \quad 9 \quad 0 \quad 0 \quad =$$

Record the total, 6,004.05, on the Total line of Stub No. 5. *Do not clear your display.*

STEP 6 ▶ *Subtract the March 24 check.*

Subtract the March 24 check by pressing these keys in order:

$$- \quad 7 \quad 5 \quad 0 \quad =$$

Record the difference, 5,254.05, on Stub No. 5 in the proper space. Now that you are finished, clear your display by pressing the C key once or the CE/C key twice.

BUILDING YOUR BUSINESS VOCABULARY

On a sheet of paper, write the headings **Statement Number** and **Words**. Next, choose the words that match the statements. Write each word you choose next to the statement number it matches. Be careful; not all the words listed should be used.

Statements	Words
1. The person to whom the check is made out and who will receive the money	balance brought forward
2. The word you print across a check when you have made an error	drawee
3. The person who writes the check	drawer
4. To send out	insufficient funds
5. A check that has a special stub attached	issue
6. The new checkbook balance which is recorded on the next check stub	payee
7. The part of a voucher check that shows a description of the payment	verify
8. When there is not enough money in the checking account to pay a check	voucher
	voucher check
	void

STEPS REVIEW: Keeping a Checkbook

STEP 1 Prepare the deposit slip.

STEP 2 Record the total deposit on the check stub.

STEP 3 Add the balance brought forward to the deposit.

APPLICATION PROBLEMS

Problem 24-1

On Nov. 1, Serena O'Connell, who owns a financial consulting and income tax firm, had a balance of $6,320.00 in a checking account. She issued checks and made a deposit as follows:

CHECK POINT

24-1

If your work is correct, the **Bal. Car'd. For'd.** on Check Stub No. 85 should equal $2,442.50.

Nov. 4 Issued Check No. 83 for $760.00 to Office Mart for new conference table and chairs.
     7 Deposited $432.50.
   11 Issued Check No. 84 for $1,200.00 to Creekside Property Management for office rent.
   19 Issued Check No. 85 for $2,350.00 to Office Electronics, Inc. for a new computer.

Directions

Complete the check stubs for Check Nos. 83–85 as they would appear in Serena's checkbook.

Problem 24-2

On April 1, Gene Malekos, a nurse, had a balance of $2,310.55 in his checking account. He issued checks and made a deposit as follows:

CHECK POINT

24-2

If your work is correct, the **Bal. Car'd. For'd.** on Check Stub No. 214 should equal $1,786.75.

April 3 Issued Check No. 212 for $610.30 to Los Altos Uniform Service for new uniforms.
   11 Deposited $1,651.50.
   15 Issued Check No. 213 for $565.00 to Santa Cruz Medical Supply for an infant stethoscope.
   21 Issued Check No. 214 for $1,000.00 to cash for personal use.

Directions

Complete the check stubs for Check Nos. 212–214 as they would appear in Gene's checkbook.

Problem 24-3

You are a record keeper for Heritage Furniture Company. On May 1, Heritage Furniture Company opened a checking account at the Tennessee National Bank with a deposit of $6,000.00. You are placed in charge of keeping the checkbook. You are authorized to sign the checks with your own name.

CHECK POINT

24-3

If your work is correct, the **Bal. Car'd. For'd.** on Check Stub No. 103 should equal $5,008.60.

Directions

a. On May 1, enter the opening deposit on the stub of Check No. 101.
b. On May 5, write Check No. 101 for $500.00 to the *Tennessee Journal* for advertising.
c. On May 9, write Check No. 102 for $215.35 to Southern Bell Phone Company for phone installation.

d. On May 13, you deposit the following cash:

Quantity	Denomination
7	$20.00 bills
18	$10.00 bills
23	$ 5.00 bills
36	$ 1.00 bills
21	$ 0.50 coins
12	$ 0.25 coins
40	$ 0.10 coins
73	$ 0.05 coins

handwritten annotations: 140, 180, 115, 36, 21.5, 3, 4, 3.65

Prepare the deposit slip. Enter the total amount of the deposit on the stub of Check No. 103, and enter the new balance on the Total line.

e. On May 17, write Check No. 103 for $768.20 to Knoxville Sign and Lighting Company for new outdoor business sign.

Problem 24-4 may be found in the Working Papers.

Job 25 USING A CHECK REGISTER

applied math preview

Copy and complete these problems.

1. $ 326.82	2. $409.15	3. $2,008.46	4. $3,241.48
+ 294.30	−121.62	− 8.51	+ 630.00
− 91.40	− 109.43	− 84.32	+ 15.29
− 26.53	+ 624.30	− 263.34	− 975.25

key terms preview

- **Check register**

goals

1 To learn how to use a check register.

2 To learn how to write checks for less than one dollar.

UNDERSTANDING THE JOB

Check register. Book for recording checks and deposits when stubs are not used.

Some banks offer 24-hour automated phone services and online banking. This is especially helpful if you forget to record a check amount on a check stub or in your check register.

In Jobs 23 and 24, you learned that you can keep an up-to-date record of your checking account by completing a check stub each time you write a check. Another way to keep an up-to-date record is to keep a **check register**. Most people who open a personal checking account will use a check register instead of check stubs.

A check with a check stub is somewhat different from a check used with a check register. The check stub is attached to the check. The check is removed to make a payment. The check stub stays in the checkbook. A checkbook with stubs is usually more expensive than a checkbook with a check register. Also, a checkbook with stubs is often too big to fit in a purse or pocket.

A check used with a check register has no stub attached. The check register is a book that is separate from the pad of checks. The same information that is recorded on a stub is recorded in the check register. The check register, therefore, contains a record of each check that is written and each deposit that is made. A checkbook with a check register is usually less expensive than a checkbook with stubs. Also, a checkbook with a check register is small enough to fit in a purse or pocket.

In this job, you will practice keeping the check register up-to-date as you record additional deposits and write checks.

On January 1, Manuel Sousa has a balance of $756.42 in his personal checking account. Manuel uses a check register to keep an up-to-date balance of his checking account. The check register in Illustration 25A shows how Manuel recorded the following checks and additional deposit.

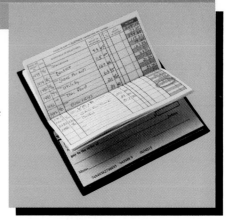

Illustration 25A

Completed check register

STEP 1 ── STEP 2 ──

RECORD ALL CHARGES OR CREDITS THAT AFFECT YOUR ACCOUNT

NUMBER	DATE	DESCRIPTION OF TRANSACTION	PAYMENT/DEBIT (−)	√ T	FEE (IF ANY) (−)	DEPOSIT/CREDIT (+)	BALANCE
					$	$	$ ►756 42
324	20-- 1/1	TO Snow World U.S.A	$ 120 00				− 120 00◄
		FOR snowboard boots					636 42
325	1/7	TO Sound World	43 00				− 43 00◄
		FOR compact disks					593 42
326	1/11	TO Metro Entertainment	84 00				− 84 00◄
		FOR concert tickets					509 42
—	1/14	TO Salary				870 00	+ 870 00◄
		FOR					1,379 42
		TO					
		FOR					

STEP 3 ──

January	1	Issued Check No. 324 for $120.00 to Snow World U.S.A. for the purchase of new snowboard boots.
	7	Issued Check No. 325 for $43.00 to Sound World for compact disks.
	11	Issued Check No. 326 for $84.00 to Metro Entertainment for concert tickets.
	14	Deposited salary check in the amount of $870.00.

Here are the steps Manuel followed in completing the check register:

STEP 1 Record the balance.

The first thing Manuel did was to record the balance of $756.42 on the first line of the check register in the space headed "Balance." Manuel copied the amount (brought forward) from the previous page of the check register.

STEP 2 Subtract the checks issued.

Before Manuel wrote each check, he recorded all the facts about the check in the check register. Manuel recorded the amount of the check in the Payment/Debit column and again on the top of the same line in the Balance column.

When the word "debit" is used by a bank, it means that your account balance is reduced. In the Balance column, Manuel found the new balance by subtracting the amount of the check from the previous balance.

This is why, on January 1, you see the following arithmetic for Check No. 324:

Balance	756.42
Check No. 324	− 120.00
Balance	636.42

On January 7, Manuel again found the new balance of $593.42 by subtracting $43.00, the amount of Check No. 325, from the old balance of $636.42.

Balance	636.42
Check No. 325	− 43.00
Balance	593.42

On January 11, Manuel found the balance of $509.42 by subtracting $84.00, the amount of Check No. 326, from the old balance of $593.42.

You should remember to record each check in the check register *before* you write the check, just as you completed check stubs before writing checks.

STEP 3 **Add the deposits.**

When Manuel deposited his salary of $870.00, he recorded the amount in the Deposit/Credit column. Since Manuel was recording a deposit and not a check issued, he put a dash in the Number column. He labeled the deposit "Salary" to show where the money came from. He also recorded the amount of the deposit on the top of the same line in the Balance column. He found the new balance by adding the amount of the deposit to the old balance.

When the word "credit" is used by a bank, it means that your account balance is increased. This is why, on January 14, you see the following arithmetic in the Balance column:

Balance	509.42
Deposit	+ 870.00
Balance	1,379.42

Some people use a home computer to keep their check register. Using a computer this way allows them to keep a record of their income and expenses. The computer records may then be used to help complete their income tax forms at the end of the year.

Writing a Check for Less than One Dollar

Most payments by check are for more than one dollar. Sometimes, however, you must write a check for less than one dollar. For example, on January 17, Manuel wanted a reprint of a newspaper article in *The North Valley Times* to be mailed to him. The cost of the reprint was 85 cents. He wrote the check shown in Illustration 25B for this amount since coins might be lost in the mail.

Notice that the number for 85 cents is shown as a fraction. It is written in words on the next line with the word "Only" before it, the word "cents" after it, and the printed word "Dollars" crossed out.

Manuel Sousa 1520 Heron Dr. Atlanta, GA 30301-0519	No. **327**

Date *January 17,* 20 -- 64-61 / 0715

PAY TO THE ORDER OF *The North Valley Times* $ *85/100*

Only eighty-five cents ~~Dollars~~

For Classroom Use Only

GREAT SOUTHERN
SAVINGS AND LOAN
519 Axel Road Atlanta, GA 30301-0519

Manuel Sousa

⑈071513612⑈ 411⑈2073⑈

BUILDING YOUR BUSINESS VOCABULARY

On a sheet of paper, write the headings **Statement Number** and **Words**. Next, choose the words that match the statements. Write each word you choose next to the statement number it matches. Be careful; not all the words listed should be used.

Statements	Words
1. To send out	balance brought
2. When there is not enough money in the checking account to pay a check	forward
	check
3. The new checkbook balance which is recorded on the Balance line	check register
	deposit slip
4. A book for recording checks when stubs are not used	drawee
	drawer
5. The part of a voucher check that shows a description of the payment	insufficient funds
	issue
6. The person who writes a check	payee
7. The word you print across a check when you have made an error	void
	voucher
8. A written order by the drawer to the drawee to pay the payee	

STEPS REVIEW: Using a Check Register

STEP 1 Record the balance.

STEP 2 Subtract the checks issued.

STEP 3 Add the deposits.

APPLICATION PROBLEMS

Problem 25-1

Write out the following amounts in words as you would when writing a check. Use Illustration 25B as an example. Remember to use a hyphen in numbers from twenty-one through ninety-nine.

1. _____ $\dfrac{\$45}{100}$ Dollars

2. _____ $\dfrac{\$82}{100}$ Dollars

3. _____ $\dfrac{\$63}{100}$ Dollars

4. _____ $\dfrac{\$51}{100}$ Dollars

5. _____ $\dfrac{\$20}{100}$ Dollars

6. _____ $\dfrac{\$97}{100}$ Dollars

7. _____ $\dfrac{\$19}{100}$ Dollars

8. _____ $\dfrac{\$55}{100}$ Dollars

9. _____ $\dfrac{\$78}{100}$ Dollars

10. _____ $\dfrac{\$09}{100}$ Dollars

Problem 25-2

You have a personal checking account at the Sierra Mountain National Bank. You use a check register to keep an up-to-date balance of your account. On October 1, you have a balance of $931.15 in your account.

CHECK POINT

25-2

If your work is correct, the balance in your check register on October 15 should equal $1,201.98.

Directions

a. Enter the October 1 balance on the first line of the check register in the column headed "Balance."

b. On October 3, issue Check No. 429 for $61.53 to Bay Electronics for an electronic personal organizer. Enter the check in the check register and find the new balance.

c. On October 8, issue Check No. 430 for $155.40 to the Pacific Insurance Company for monthly automobile insurance. Enter the check in the check register and find the new balance.

d. On October 12, issue Check No. 431 for $18.65 to Renalto Pizzeria for a vegetarian pizza. Enter the check in the check register and find the new balance.

e. On October 15, enter the deposit of your salary of $506.41 in the check register. Label the deposit "Salary." Find the new balance. Remember to put a dash in the Number column.

You have a personal checking account at the Tahoe National Bank. You use a check register to keep an up-to-date record of your account. On June 1, you have a balance of $615.34 in your account.

CHECK POINT

25-3

If your work is correct, the balance in your check register on June 14 should equal $475.44.

Directions

a. Enter the June 1 balance on the first line of the check register in the column headed "Balance."

b. On June 6, issue Check No. 112 for $206.00 to Almaden Automotive for car repairs and smog certificate. Enter the check in the check register and find the new balance.

c. On June 10, issue Check No. 113 for $45.00 to Oak Grove High School for lost textbook. Enter the check in the check register and find the new balance.

d. On June 12, enter the deposit of your salary of $396.20 in the check register. Label the deposit "Salary." Find the new balance. Remember to put a dash in the Number column.

e. On June 14, issue Check No. 114 for $285.10 to Western Stereo Works for DVD/CD player. Enter the check in the check register and find the new balance.

Problem 25-4 may be found in the Working Papers.

applied math preview

Copy and complete these problems.

1. $ 380.00	2. $ 8.91	3. $ 621.00	4. $3,202.13
420.00	100.06	106.86	163.77
16.50	53.09	41.53	22.21
121.62	228.42	88.18	408.44
3.83	36.68	293.41	6.09
+209.72	+72.54	+ 1.71	+ 326.43

key terms preview

- **Blank endorsement**
- **Canceled checks**
- **Clearinghouse**
- **Endorsement**
- **Full endorsement**
- **Leading edge**
- **Negotiable**
- **Restrictive endorsement**
- **Split deposit**
- **Trailing edge**

goals

1 To learn how to transfer checks from one party to another.

2 To learn how to cash or deposit a paycheck.

⇨ UNDERSTANDING THE JOB

Endorsement. Signature on the back of a check.

Negotiable. Transferable to another party.

Endorsements should be written in ink. Names signed in pencil or erasable ink might be erased or changed by another person. Always protect yourself!

What do you do with a check that you receive? For example, you receive your paycheck. You can cash the check for its full amount at the bank, deposit the full amount of the check, or deposit part of the amount and receive cash for the remainder. In order to do any of these three, you must transfer your ownership of the check to the bank. This transfer can be made by signing the back of the check. The signature on the back of a check that transfers ownership is called an **endorsement**.

A check can be endorsed (transferred) because of the words "Pay to the order of" that appear in front of the payee's name. Look at Manuel Sousa's paycheck in Illustration 26A (on page 213). The check reads "Pay to the order of Manuel Sousa." These words allow Manuel to "order" the transfer of his check ownership to another party (such as the bank). Because the ownership of a check is transferable to another party, it is said to be **negotiable**. The three ways Manuel can transfer the ownership of his check are shown in this job.

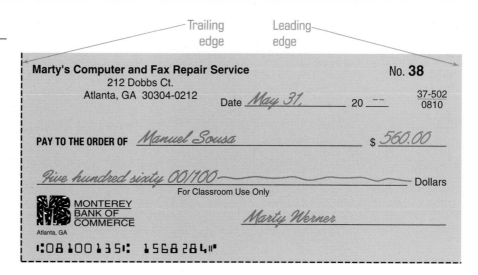

Trailing edge / Leading edge

Marty's Computer and Fax Repair Service
212 Dobbs Ct.
Atlanta, GA 30304-0212

No. **38**

Date *May 31,* 20 __

37-502
0810

PAY TO THE ORDER OF *Manuel Sousa* $ *560.00*

Five hundred sixty 00/100 ———— Dollars

For Classroom Use Only

 MONTEREY BANK OF COMMERCE
Atlanta, GA

Marty Werner

⑆08100135⑆ 1568284⑈

SAMPLE PROBLEM 1

Manuel decides to get cash for the full amount of the paycheck. He goes to his bank, Great Southern Savings and Loan, turns the check over, and signs his name at the top of the **trailing edge** of the check. (See Illustration 26A above.) He can use only the top 1½" of the check for his signature.

Illustration 26B on page 214 shows his **blank endorsement**. A blank endorsement means that he signs his name only. A blank endorsement does not state to whom the check is being transferred. If a check with a blank endorsement were lost, anyone who found it could use it. Manuel would use a blank endorsement only if he were endorsing the check right in the bank.

After showing proper identification, Manuel turns the check over to the bank and leaves with $560.00 in cash. Great Southern Savings and Loan must now collect the $560.00 from the drawer's bank. Marty Werner has ordered the Monterey Bank of Commerce to pay the money. Therefore, Great Southern Savings and Loan needs a way to get the money from the Monterey Bank of Commerce. Great Southern Savings and Loan will start by encoding the amount of the check in MICR so that a computer can be used in the collection process. (See Illustration 26D on page 215.)

Next, Great Southern Savings and Loan will endorse the back of the check in the section for Bank of First Deposit. The endorsement will be made by either computer or endorsement stamp. Illustration 26C on page 214 shows the endorsement stamp for the bank.

In a simpler world, a worker from Great Southern Savings and Loan would walk across town to the Monterey Bank of Commerce and collect the amount of the check. But, with billions of checks written daily, this personal touch is impossible. Instead, banks arrange a central place, called a **clearinghouse**, where they distribute and exchange checks every day. Computers read the bank numbers printed in MICR and sort the checks

Key Terms

Trailing edge. Left side of check.

Blank endorsement. Signature only.

Clearinghouse. Central place where banks exchange checks.

Tips

MICR stands for Magnetic Ink Character Recognition.

For Your Information

If more than one individual is named as payee, each payee must endorse the check before it can be cashed.

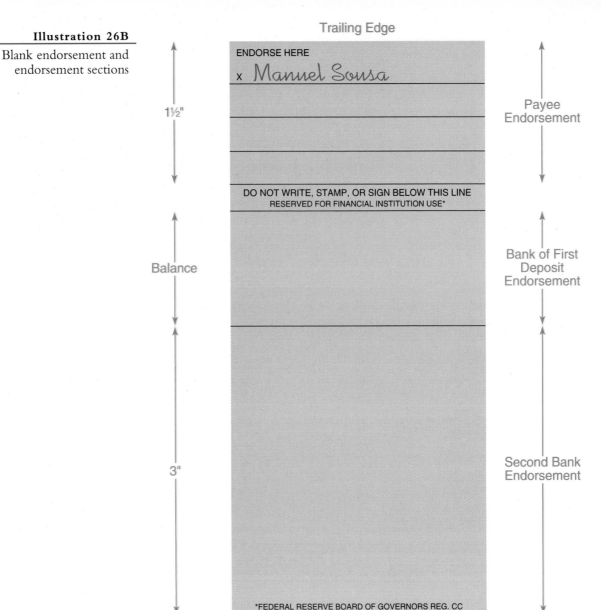

Illustration 26B
Blank endorsement and
endorsement sections

Trailing Edge

ENDORSE HERE

x *Manuel Sousa*

1½"

Payee
Endorsement

DO NOT WRITE, STAMP, OR SIGN BELOW THIS LINE
RESERVED FOR FINANCIAL INSTITUTION USE*

Balance

Bank of First
Deposit
Endorsement

3"

Second Bank
Endorsement

*FEDERAL RESERVE BOARD OF GOVERNORS REG. CC

Leading Edge

Illustration 26C
Endorsement stamp

Great Southern Savings and Loan
Atlanta, Georgia
0715 13612

Key
Terms

Leading edge. Right side of check.

rapidly according to the banks on which they were drawn. Funds are transferred from one bank to another on the central computer of the clearinghouse. Thus, money is transferred from the Monterey Bank of Commerce to the Great Southern Savings and Loan. The clearinghouse endorsement is then made in the Second Bank Endorsement section of the back of the check, near the **leading edge** of the check.

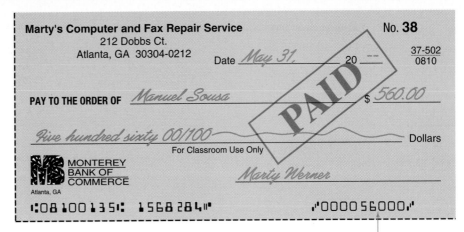

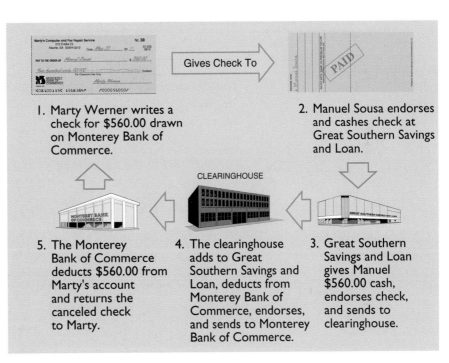

Illustration 26E

Diagram of check's route

1. Marty Werner writes a check for $560.00 drawn on Monterey Bank of Commerce.

2. Manuel Sousa endorses and cashes check at Great Southern Savings and Loan.

CLEARINGHOUSE

5. The Monterey Bank of Commerce deducts $560.00 from Marty's account and returns the canceled check to Marty.

4. The clearinghouse adds to Great Southern Savings and Loan, deducts from Monterey Bank of Commerce, endorses, and sends to Monterey Bank of Commerce.

3. Great Southern Savings and Loan gives Manuel $560.00 cash, endorses check, and sends to clearinghouse.

Over 7,000 years ago, the Babylonian civilization in Asia Minor had banks and a method for drafts to be drawn in one place and paid in another. The Babylonians required that most business transactions be put in writing and signed by the parties involved. This was the first verified use of source documents.

Canceled check. Checks that have been paid by the bank.

The check is sent from the clearinghouse to the Monterey Bank of Commerce, where it is deducted from Marty Werner's business checking account. The check is stamped "PAID" by Marty's bank, which makes the check a **canceled check**. Illustration 26D shows the canceled check. At the end of each month, all canceled checks are returned to Marty Werner. Illustration 26E shows the route of this check.

SAMPLE PROBLEM 2

Instead of cashing his paycheck, Manuel may decide to deposit the paycheck. If he does, he will follow three steps:

STEP 1 Endorse the check.

To deposit his check, Manuel must endorse it. As you see in Illustration

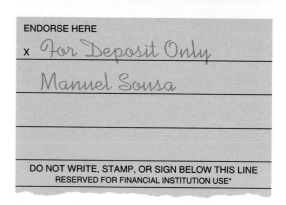

Restrictive endorsement. An endorsement which limits use of a check.

26F, Manuel writes "For Deposit Only" and then signs his name. He is using a **restrictive endorsement**. A restrictive endorsement limits the use of the check. In this case, it can only be used for deposit to his account. No one finding the check could cash it and keep the money.

STEP 2 Prepare a deposit slip.

Manuel prepares a deposit slip, as shown in Illustration 26G. Notice that he has listed the check by the ABA number, using the top part of that number.

Illustration 26G

Completed deposit slip

For DEPOSIT to the Account of

64-61 / 0715

Manuel Sousa
1520 Heron Dr.
Atlanta, GA 30301-0519

DATE May 31, 20 --

GREAT SOUTHERN
SAVINGS AND LOAN
519 Axel Road Atlanta, GA 30301-0519

Subject to the Terms and Conditions of this Bank's Collection Agreement

⑈071513612⑈ 411⑈2073⑈

	Dollars	Cents
BILLS		
COINS		
Checks as Follows Properly Endorsed		
37-502	560	00
TOTAL DEPOSIT	560	00

STEP 3 Record the deposit in the check register.

Manuel records the deposit in his check register. He adds the deposit to his previous balance, as shown in Illustration 26H.

Illustration 26H

Check register showing deposit

RECORD ALL CHARGES OR CREDITS THAT AFFECT YOUR ACCOUNT

NUMBER	DATE	DESCRIPTION OF TRANSACTION	PAYMENT/DEBIT (–)	√ T	FEE (IF ANY) (–)	DEPOSIT/CREDIT (+)	BALANCE
							$ 310 00
—	20-- 5/31	TO Salary	$		$	$560 00	+ 560 00
		FOR					870 00
		TO					
		FOR					

Split deposit. Part cash, part deposit.

Assume that this time, Manuel wants to deposit all of the paycheck except for $100.00, which he wants in cash. Manuel is making a **split deposit**. He will follow three steps again.

STEP 1 Endorse the check.

Manuel will use a blank endorsement since he wants some cash back and since he is at the bank.

STEP 2 Prepare a deposit slip.

Illustration 26I

Deposit slip for a split deposit

STEP 1 Endorse Check

BILLS		
COINS		
Checks as Follows Properly Endorsed		
37-502	560	00
Cash	(100	00)
TOTAL DEPOSIT	460	00

STEP 2

STEP 3 Record Deposit in Register

Illustration 26I shows the way a deposit slip is prepared for a split deposit. Notice that the full amount of the check is listed. Then the amount of cash to be received is deducted. The bottom line shows the amount to be deposited.

STEP 3 Record the deposit in the check register.

Illustration 26J

Full endorsement

ENDORSE HERE

x _Pay to the order of_

Barbara Pollard

Sue Pollard

DO NOT WRITE, STAMP, OR SIGN BELOW THIS LINE
RESERVED FOR FINANCIAL INSTITUTION USE*

Manuel will add $460.00 to the balance of the check register.

There are times when a bank will not allow you to receive any cash on the day of the deposit. In such cases, you must deposit your check and wait one or more days to receive cash. The purpose of this rule is to prevent your receiving cash for someone's check that may not be backed by sufficient funds. However, if you have an account in the bank with a balance equal to or greater than the cash you want, the check can be cashed.

There is another type of endorsement used when you want to transfer a check to a specific person. For example, suppose that you are Sue Pollard. You receive a check for your birthday, but you have no bank account. So, you decide to endorse the check to your mother, Barbara Pollard, and she will give you cash for it. You cannot use a restrictive endorsement ("For Deposit Only"), and you do not want to use a blank endorsement ("Sue

Pollard") in case the check is lost. So you use a **full endorsement**, writing "Pay to the order of" in front of your mother's name. Illustration 26J on page 217 shows a full endorsement.

BUILDING YOUR BUSINESS VOCABULARY

Full endorsement.
Endorsement which names person to whom check is transferred

On a sheet of paper, write the headings **Statement Number** and **Words**. Next, choose the words that match the statements. Write each word you choose next to the statement number it matches. Be careful; not all the words listed should be used.

Statements

1. The right side of a check
2. A central place where banks exchange checks
3. Checks that have been paid by the bank
4. A deposit that is part cash received, part deposit
5. An endorsement which limits use of a check
6. An endorsement by signature only
7. An endorsement which names the person to whom the check is transferred
8. The left side of a check
9. Signature on the back of a check
10. Transferable to another party

Words

blank endorsement
canceled checks
clearinghouse
endorsement
full endorsement
leading edge
legible
negotiable
restrictive endorsement
split deposit
trailing edge
voucher check

STEPS REVIEW: Endorsing Checks

STEP 1 Enter the check.

STEP 2 Prepare a deposit slip.

STEP 3 Record the deposit in the check register.

APPLICATION PROBLEMS

Problem 26-1

CHECK POINT

26-1

If your work is correct, the full endorsement for Check 3 should read:
Pay to the order of
Keith Damian
James Damian

James Damian has received three checks today. The first is his paycheck, which he will cash at the bank, so he will use a blank endorsement. The second is a check from a part-time job, which he will deposit; therefore, he will use a restrictive endorsement. The third is a check that he is giving to his brother, Keith Damian, for money he owes him, so he will use a full endorsement.

Directions
Prepare the endorsements that James will write on the back of each check.

Problem 26-2

Jennifer Thurman has received four checks today. The first is a check from a friend; she is going to deposit this check. The second is a check that she wants to transfer to her mother, Julia Thurman. The third is one of her paychecks that she wants to cash right at the bank. The fourth is another paycheck that she wants to transfer to Foothill Community College for a tuition payment.

Directions

Prepare the endorsements that Jennifer will write on the back of each check. Use the proper endorsement each time.

Problem 26-3 Khalid Meta is preparing a bank deposit on August 7, 20--. He is depositing cash and two checks.

Cash:	Quantity	Denomination
	3	$20.00 bills
	2	$10.00 bills
	7	$ 5.00 bills
	23	$ 1.00 bills
	12	$ 0.25 coins
	27	$ 0.10 coins
	5	$ 0.05 coins
	42	$ 0.01 coins

Checks:	ABA Number	Denomination
1	6-23	$ 82.00
2	8-46	$210.40

CHECK POINT

26-3

If your work is correct, the total deposit should equal $436.77.

Directions

a. Prepare the endorsements that Khalid will write on the back of each check to deposit them.
b. Complete the deposit slip.

Problems 26-4 and 26-5 may be found in the Working Papers.

applied math preview

Copy and complete these problems.

1. $ 73.00	2. $2,180.04	3. $ 214.92	4. $ 971.60
8.21	22.62	6.71	1,004.04
426.52	7.18	21.18	82.48
4.28	330.30	+ 200.00	+ 7.66
6.76	.81		
+ 172.80	+ 53.12	− 80.00	− 120.00

key terms preview

- ATM access card
- Automated teller machine (ATM)
- Cashier's check
- Electronic funds transfer
- Personal identification number (PIN)

- Savings account
- Service charge
- Stop-payment order
- Traveler's checks
- Withdrawal
- Withdrawal slip

goals

1. To learn how to select the proper type of savings account.
2. To learn how to open a savings account.
3. To learn how to prepare deposit and withdrawal slips.
4. To learn about other services that banks provide to their customers.

⇨ UNDERSTANDING THE JOB

Ryan Clabeaux is a sophomore at Morgan Hill High School. Last week he started a part-time job at the Uvas Cyclery. Ryan decided to find a job because he has two goals he wants to achieve by the time he graduates. His first goal is to earn money to purchase a used automobile. His second goal is to earn money to pay the expenses for his first year at the local community college.

Ryan's parents suggested that he open a **savings account** at Liberty National Savings, a bank near their home. A savings account at the bank would provide Ryan with the following benefits:

A safe place to keep his earnings.

An opportunity to earn interest.

A place where Ryan can deposit his work checks and withdraw cash.

Savings account. A bank account that earns interest.

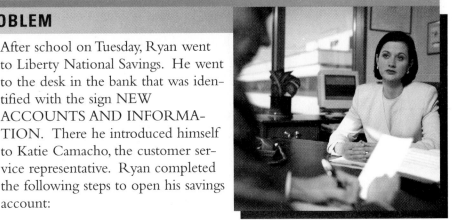

After school on Tuesday, Ryan went to Liberty National Savings. He went to the desk in the bank that was identified with the sign NEW ACCOUNTS AND INFORMATION. There he introduced himself to Katie Camacho, the customer service representative. Ryan completed the following steps to open his savings account:

STEP 1 Select a savings plan.

Ryan described his new job to Katie. He also discussed with her his savings goals. To help Ryan make a good decision, Katie explained the following four types of savings plans offered by Liberty National Savings:

Service charge. A fee for bank services.

Withdrawal. To take money out of an account.

1. **Regular Savings Account:** This interest-earning account at Liberty National Savings is opened with a minimum deposit of $300. Money may be added or taken out from a regular savings account at any time. However, the bank charges a fee, or **service charge**, of $1.00 per month unless a minimum of $300.00 is kept in the account.
2. **Money Market Account:** This account pays a higher interest rate than does a regular savings account. Liberty National Savings requires a minimum deposit of $750.00. An important advantage of the money market account is that the money in the account can be taken out by writing a check. **Withdrawals** by check, however, are limited. Money can be added to the money market account at any time. Liberty National Savings charges a service charge of $2.00 per month unless a minimum of $1,000.00 is kept in the account.
3. **Certificate of Deposit:** Currently, this account pays the highest interest rate at Liberty National Savings. A minimum deposit of $1,000.00 is required to open a certificate of deposit. Money cannot be added or withdrawn at anytime. The money in the certificate earns a fixed rate of interest. However, the money must be kept in the certificate for a fixed period of time. There is no monthly service charge for having a certificate of deposit.
4. **Special Savings Account:** Because Ryan is 16 years old and has only $91.75 to deposit, Katie recommended that he open a special student savings account. This special savings account, offered only to students, requires a minimum opening deposit of $50.00. There is no service charge until Ryan is 21 years of age. Money may be added or withdrawn from the account at any time.

Notice that interest rates, service charges, minimum deposits and minimum balances are different for each type of savings account. Furthermore, each bank has different rules for its savings plans. It is wise to compare these items before selecting a bank and an account. Select an account that best meets your savings goals. Bank employees can be very helpful to you in making a good decision.

STEP 2 Provide a form of identification.

Katie told Ryan that before he opened a student savings account, he must show some form of identification. Katie explained that Ryan could use a driver's license or student identification card.

STEP 3 Complete a signature card.

After showing Katie his driver's license, Ryan provided the information for the signature card like the one shown in Illustration 27A. Notice that it is very similar to a signature card for a checking account. Katie typed all the information except for the signature. She also gave Ryan an account number. The signature card was signed only by Ryan. The single signature means that Ryan opened an individual savings account and that only he can make withdrawals from the account.

STEP 4 Make an opening deposit.

After the signature card was completed, Ryan made his opening deposit of $91.75. He deposited $20.00 in bills, $4.22 in coin, and his first paycheck (ABA #12-210/4588) for $67.53. Just like checking deposits, savings deposits are recorded on a deposit slip. Ryan's completed deposit slip is shown in Illustration 27B. Whenever Ryan wants to receive money back from his paycheck, he will fill in the amount he wants next to "Less cash received" and sign the deposit slip in front of the teller.

Withdrawals

On December 20, Ryan made his first withdrawal of $25.00. To take money out of his savings account, Ryan first completed a **withdrawal slip**. A withdrawal slip is a bank form showing the date, your account number, the amount to be withdrawn, and your name and address. Ryan's

Key Terms

Withdrawal slip. A bank form used to withdraw money from an account.

Illustration 27A
Signature card

STEP 1
Select a Savings Plan

STEP 2

LIBERTY
National Savings
1600 Harbor Lane
Erie, PA 16502-1712

Account No.: 48-2706

AUTHORIZED SIGNATURE FOR:

Name Ryan M. Clabeaux

Address 1941 Blossom Hill Road, Erie, PA 16502-1710

Telephone (814) 555-3781

Account Type Student Savings   Mother's Maiden Name Albrecht

Soc. Sec. No. 822-33-6666   I.D. PO566821

Birthdate and Place 09/20/84 Madison, CT

Signature Ryan M. Clabeaux

Date November 5, 20--

STEP 3

STEP 4
Make an opening deposit

SAVINGS DEPOSIT			ACCOUNT NO.: 4 8 - 2 7 0 6		
			List checks by bank no.	Dollars	Cents
November 5, 20--			BILLS	20	00
DATE			COINS	4	22
Ryan M. Clabeaux			CHECKS 12-210	67	53
NAME (please print)					
1941 Blossom Hill Road					
ADDRESS					
Erie, PA 16502-1710					
CITY STATE ZIP CODE					
X			Subtotal	91	75
Please sign in teller's presence for cash received			Less cash received		
LIBERTY *National Savings*			TOTAL DEPOSIT	91	75

completed withdrawal slip is shown in Illustration 27C. Ryan signed the withdrawal slip to show that he received $25.00 in cash. If necessary, his signature could be compared to the one on his signature card.

SAVINGS WITHDRAWAL	ACCOUNT NO.: 4 8 - 2 7 0 6
	December 20, 20--
	DATE
Twenty-five 00/100 ———————— DOLLARS $ 25 00/100	
For Classroom Use Only	
X *Ryan M. Clabeaux*	Ryan M. Clabeaux
Please sign in teller's presence for cash received	NAME (please print)
	1941 Blossom Hill Road
	ADDRESS
LIBERTY *National Savings*	Erie, PA 16502-1710
	CITY STATE ZIP CODE

Key Terms

Automated teller machine (ATM). A machine that allows 24-hour banking.

ATM access card. A card that allows you to use an ATM to make deposits, withdraw cash, or transfer money.

Personal identification number (PIN). A secret number that allows you to use an ATM.

Electronic funds transfer. Use of a computer to transfer money from one party to another.

Bank Services

As you have learned, banks offer checking accounts and savings accounts for businesses and for individuals. However, there are some other common banking services with which you should be familiar.

Automated Teller Machines

As a convenience to customers, banks use **automated teller machines** or **ATMs** . These machines, found outside banks and in supermarkets, shopping malls, and restaurants, give you 24-hour banking. The depositor, using a special **ATM access card** and **personal identification number** or **PIN**, can make deposits, withdraw cash, or transfer money from one account to another.

Debit Cards

Some ATM access cards can also be used as a debit card. A debit card (as explained in Chapter 4, Job 18), when passed through a computer terminal, automatically subtracts the amount from your bank account. It is like writing a check without having actually written one.

A debit card is one example of **electronic funds transfer**, which means that a computer is used to transfer money from one party to another. In this case, money is going from your bank account to the bank account of the party whom you want to pay.

NO. 231	$ _____	
DATE _____		
TO _____		
_____		
FOR _____		
_____		

	DOLLARS	CENTS
BAL. BRO'T. FOR'D.	583	84
8/12 ATM ~~AMT. DEPOSITED~~	(60	00)
TOTAL	523	84
AMT. THIS CHECK		
BAL. CAR'D. FOR'D.		

Illustration 27D

Check stub with ATM withdrawal

Key Terms

Stop-payment order. A form instructing the bank not to pay a check.

Cashier's check. A check guaranteed by the bank.

Traveler's check. A safe form of cash for use when taking a trip.

For Your Information

Some banks offer discount brokerage services to their customers. Customers are allowed to buy stocks and bonds through the bank at special rates.

Remember, if you use electronic funds transfer, you must subtract these payments in your checkbook. An example of how to record an ATM withdrawal on a check stub is shown in Illustration 27D. Notice that the words "Amt. Deposited" were crossed out. The date of the withdrawal and the initials ATM were written in. The amount of the withdrawal, $60.00, was recorded in parentheses and subtracted from the Bal. Bro't. For'd.

Safe Deposit Boxes

For a fee, you may rent a safe deposit box. It is kept in the vault of the bank. You may put jewelry and valuable papers in the box. To get in the box two keys are required. You have one and the bank has one. When you want to access the box, you identify yourself by signature. Then, you and a bank employee go together to open it.

Stop-Payment Orders

What should you do if the person to whom you sent a check tells you that the check is lost? You should notify your bank at once, before someone finding the check can try to forge a signature and cash it. At the bank, you can fill out a **stop-payment order**. The bank will then refuse payment on the check. Banks usually charge a fee for stop-payment orders.

Cashier's Checks

What should you do if someone will not accept your personal check because she or he is not certain that you have enough money in your account to pay for it? You ask your bank for a **cashier's check**. A cashier's check is guaranteed by your bank for payment. The amount of the cashier's check is immediately deducted from your account and transferred to a special account at the bank. This guarantees that the money will be available when the cashier's check is presented for payment. You will pay a fee for this guarantee.

Traveler's Check

Finally, what should you do if you are planning a trip, do not want to deal with cashier's checks, and do not want to take a lot of cash? You can purchase **traveler's checks** from your bank. Traveler's checks are much like dollars. These checks are accepted most places as if they were cash. You will pay a small fee for the purchase of traveler's checks. Each traveler's check must be signed twice by you. When you buy one you sign it in front of the teller. Then, when you use one, you sign it again. Thus only you can use this safe form of cash. However, the best advantage of using traveler's checks is that if you lose them, they can be replaced.

⇨ BUILDING YOUR BUSINESS VOCABULARY

On a sheet of paper, write the headings **Statement Number** and **Words**. Next, choose the words that match the statements. Write each word you choose next to the statement number it matches. Be careful; not all the words listed will be used.

Many banks offer special checking accounts to students at low rates.

Statements	Words
1. A card that allows you to use an automated teller machine to make deposits, withdraw cash, or transfer money	ATM access card
	automated teller machine (ATM)
2. Use of a computer to transfer money from one party to another	cashier's check
	debit card
3. A bank account that earns interest	electronic funds
4. A form instructing the bank not to pay a check	transfer
5. Taking money out of an account	interest
6. A fee for bank services	personal identification
7. A secret code that allows you to use an automated teller machine	number (PIN)
	savings account
8. A machine that allows 24-hour banking	service charge
9. A check guaranteed by the bank	stop-payment order
10. A safe form of cash for use when taking a trip	traveler's check
11. A bank form used to withdraw money from an account	withdrawal
	withdrawal slip

STEPS REVIEW: Opening a Savings Account

STEP 1 Select a savings plan.

STEP 2 Provide a form of identification.

STEP 3 Complete a signature card.

STEP 4 Make an opening deposit.

 APPLICATION PROBLEMS

Problem 27-1

Kenneth Michetti has a savings account at Cupertino Federal Bank. His account number is 30-7423. His address is 404 Calaveras Avenue, Fairfield, CT 06430-5190.

Check Point

27-1

May 9 deposit = $267.56

Directions

Prepare savings deposit slips for the following deposits made by Kenneth:

May	9	Bills		$ 36.00
		Coins		9.12
		Checks (ABA# (6-421) 2709		149.60
		(ABA# 22-71) 3560		72.84
May	19	Bills		$ 10.00
		Coins		8.62
		Checks (ABA# 6-421) 2709		63.54
		(ABA# 36-28) 3780		206.88
May	23	Checks (ABA# 5-40) 4200		$311.40
		(ABA# 81-24) 3410		68.94
		Less cash received		50.00

(Sign Kenneth's name on the proper line for cash received.)

Audrey Pharr has a savings account at Glendale Bank of Wisconsin. Her account number is 00-7664. Her address is 1822 Landon Street, Dodgeville, WI 53595-1001.

Directions

Prepare savings withdrawal slips for the following withdrawals made by Audrey. Sign her name on the proper line for cash received.

January 12	$150.00
January 21	$ 93.41

Problem 27-3

You have a checking account and an ATM access card. You use your check stubs to record your checking account entries.

Directions
a. Enter a balance brought forward of $781.38 on Check Stub No. 603.
b. Record each of the following events on your check stubs:

CHECK POINT

27-3

Bal Car'd. For'd. from Stub
605 = $686.35

February 6 Issued Check No. 603 for $17.47 to Helium-Highs for a birthday balloon bouquet.
10 Deposited $236.04 (Record deposit on Stub No. 604)
14 Issued Check No. 604 for $173.60 to RoadRunner Rubber for two new tires.
20 Withdrew $80.00 using your ATM access card. (Record ATM withdrawal on Stub No. 605. Use Illustration 27D, page 224, as a guide.)
23 Issued Check No. 605 for $60.00 to your school for this year's yearbook.

Problem 27-4 may be found in the Working Papers.

key terms preview

- Bank reconciliation statement
- Bank statement
- Bank statement balance
- Checkbook balance
- Outstanding checks
- Reconciled

goals

1 To learn how to read a bank statement.

2 To learn how to find which checks are outstanding.

3 To learn how to prepare a bank reconciliation statement.

→ UNDERSTANDING THE JOB

Bank statement. Detailed record of the checking account from the bank.

Bank statement balance. Money left in account per bank's records.

Checkbook balance. Money left in account per depositor's records.

In Job 26, you learned that after a bank pays a check written by one of its depositors, it marks the check "Paid." The canceled check is then returned to the depositor. However, instead of returning canceled checks one at a time, most banks hold all of them for a period of about thirty days. At the end of that period, all of the canceled checks are returned at one time, along with a **bank statement**. A bank statement is shown in Illustration 28A on page 228.

All banks use computers to prepare bank statements. Data about all checks paid and all deposits received are entered into the computer in order to keep the depositor's account up-to-date. All of the data that are stored in the computer are printed out on the bank statement.

The bank statement shows the depositor's beginning balance, individual and total deposits, individual and total checks, and the ending balance. The ending balance, called the **bank statement balance**, is the amount of money left in the checking account according to the bank's records.

As you know, the depositor also has a record of deposits, checks, and balances. This record is kept either on check stubs or in a check register. The ending balance, called the **checkbook balance**, is the amount of money left in the checking account according to the depositor's records.

There will usually be differences between the checkbook balance and the bank statement balance. In this job, you will begin to learn how to

MONTEREY BANK OF COMMERCE

411 PEACHTREE ROAD ATLANTA, GA 30303-0411

| ACCOUNT OF: | | STATEMENT DATE: | 03/31/-- |

MARTY'S COMPUTER AND FAX REPAIR SERVICE
212 DOBBS COURT
ATLANTA, GA 30304-0212

ACCOUNT NO.: 156-8284

BEGINNING BALANCE:		0.00
TOTAL DEPOSITS/CREDITS:		7737.50
TOTAL CHECKS/DEBITS:		2168.45
ENDING BALANCE:		5569.05

Date	Checks/Debits	Deposits/Credits	Balance
03/01/--		6,200.00	6,200.00
03/08/--	820.00		5,380.00
03/13/--		637.50	6,017.50
03/14/--	122.45		5,895.05
03/17/--	476.00		5,419.05
03/21/--		900.00	6,319.05
03/28/--	750.00		5,569.05

Key Terms

Bank reconciliation statement. Statement that brings checkbook and bank statement balances into agreement.

Reconciled. Brought into agreement.

explain these differences by preparing a **bank reconciliation statement**. This statement is used to bring the checkbook and bank statement balances into agreement.

➡ SAMPLE PROBLEM

You have been hired by Marty Werner to help keep the business records for Marty's Computer and Fax Repair Service. Part of your job is to keep the checkbook and prepare the bank reconciliation statement. The stubs in the checkbook for checks written in March are shown in Illustration 28B on page 229.

The following canceled checks were returned to Marty in the same envelope with the bank statement:

Check No.	Payee	Amount
1	DTS Computer	$820.00
2	Pacific Stationery and Supply	122.45
3	Photo Max	476.00
5	Cash	750.00

You can see that the March 28 checkbook balance of $5,154.05 (from stub #6) does not agree with the March 31 bank statement balance of $5,569.05 (from Illustration 28A). You must find out why the balances do not agree. They must be brought into agreement, or **reconciled**. Here is how you proceed:

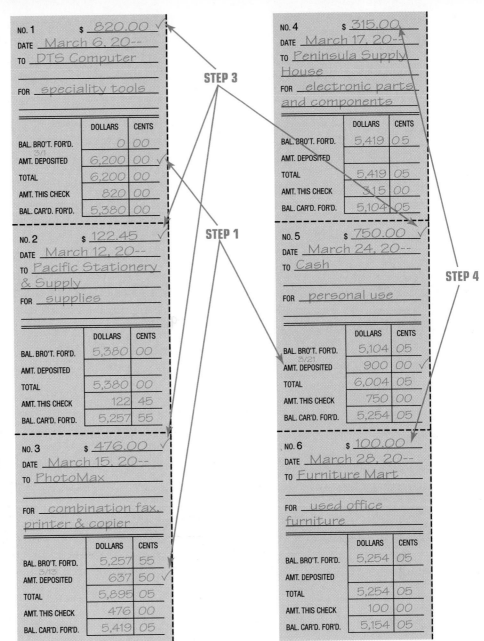

STEP 2
Arrange canceled checks in order.

STEP 5
Prepare Bank Reconciliation Statement

Check Stub No. 1

NO. 1 $ 820.00 ✓
DATE March 6, 20--
TO DTS Computer
FOR speciality tools

	DOLLARS	CENTS
BAL. BRO'T. FOR'D.	0	00
AMT. DEPOSITED 3/1	6,200	00 ✓
TOTAL	6,200	00
AMT. THIS CHECK	820	00
BAL. CAR'D. FOR'D.	5,380	00

Check Stub No. 2

NO. 2 $ 122.45 ✓
DATE March 12, 20--
TO Pacific Stationery & Supply
FOR supplies

	DOLLARS	CENTS
BAL. BRO'T. FOR'D.	5,380	00
AMT. DEPOSITED		
TOTAL	5,380	00
AMT. THIS CHECK	122	45
BAL. CAR'D. FOR'D.	5,257	55

Check Stub No. 3

NO. 3 $ 476.00 ✓
DATE March 15, 20--
TO PhotoMax
FOR combination fax, printer & copier

	DOLLARS	CENTS
BAL. BRO'T. FOR'D.	5,257	55
AMT. DEPOSITED 3/13	637	50 ✓
TOTAL	5,895	05
AMT. THIS CHECK	476	00
BAL. CAR'D. FOR'D.	5,419	05

Check Stub No. 4

NO. 4 $ 315.00
DATE March 17, 20--
TO Peninsula Supply House
FOR electronic parts and components

	DOLLARS	CENTS
BAL. BRO'T. FOR'D.	5,419	05
AMT. DEPOSITED		
TOTAL	5,419	05
AMT. THIS CHECK	315	00
BAL. CAR'D. FOR'D.	5,104	05

Check Stub No. 5

NO. 5 $ 750.00 ✓
DATE March 24, 20--
TO Cash
FOR personal use

	DOLLARS	CENTS
BAL. BRO'T. FOR'D.	5,104	05
AMT. DEPOSITED 3/21	900	00 ✓
TOTAL	6,004	05
AMT. THIS CHECK	750	00
BAL. CAR'D. FOR'D.	5,254	05

Check Stub No. 6

NO. 6 $ 100.00
DATE March 28, 20--
TO Furniture Mart
FOR used office furniture

	DOLLARS	CENTS
BAL. BRO'T. FOR'D.	5,254	05
AMT. DEPOSITED		
TOTAL	5,254	05
AMT. THIS CHECK	100	00
BAL. CAR'D. FOR'D.	5,154	05

STEP 3

STEP 1

STEP 4

Some banks now charge a small fee for returning canceled checks with the bank statement. If needed, copies of a canceled check can be obtained from the bank.

STEP 1   Compare the deposits.

Compare the deposits recorded on the check stubs with the deposits recorded on the bank statement. In this case, there are three deposits totaling $7,737.50. All three are recorded in both places. On Check Stub Nos. 1, 3, and 5, place a small check mark to the right of each deposit to show that each one is recorded by the bank. In Job 29, you will learn how to handle a deposit not recorded by the bank.

STEP 2   Arrange the canceled checks in order.

Look at the check numbers and arrange the canceled checks in numerical order. Notice that all of the canceled checks returned are listed on the bank statement. You may wonder why the dates of the checks on the bank statement do not agree with the dates listed on your check stubs.

This is because the dates on the bank statement show when the bank paid the checks, rather than when you wrote the checks.

STEP 3 Compare the canceled checks with the stubs.

Compare the canceled checks with the check stubs. Make a small check mark in the upper right corner of the stub if the canceled check has been returned and the amounts agree. In Job 30, you will learn how to handle a situation where the amounts do not agree.

STEP 4 Find the outstanding checks.

The check stubs without check marks indicate which checks have not been returned by the bank. These checks are called **outstanding checks**. They have been issued by the drawer and subtracted from the balance on the check stubs. However, the bank has not yet paid them nor subtracted them from your balance by the date of the bank statement. Check Nos. 4 and 6 are outstanding checks.

STEP 5 Prepare a bank reconciliation statement.

Check Nos. 4 and 6 have been subtracted from the checkbook balance, but not from the bank statement balance. Now, you must subtract them from the bank statement balance so that the two balances will be reconciled. The subtraction is done on the bank reconciliation statement. Illustration 28C shows a completed bank reconciliation statement.

The heading of the bank reconciliation statement answers these questions:

WHO?   Marty's Computer and Fax Repair Service
WHAT?   Bank Reconciliation Statement
WHEN?   March 31, 20--

STEP 5

Marty's Computer and Fax Repair Service						
Bank Reconciliation Statement						
March 31, 20--						
Checkbook balance	5 1 5 4 05	Bank statement balance			5 5 6 9 05
		Less outstanding checks:			
		#4	$315.00		
		#6	100.00		
		Total outstanding checks		4 1 5 00	
Adjusted checkbook balance	5 1 5 4 05	Adjusted bank statement balance			5 1 5 4 05

Illustration 28C

Bank reconciliation statement

The left side of the statement is used to show adjustments to the checkbook balance. None were needed on this statement. In Job 30, you will learn to make some adjustments to the checkbook balance.

The right side of the statement is used to show adjustments to the bank statement balance. Notice that the outstanding checks are listed separately and totaled. The total of the outstanding checks ($415.00) is subtracted from the bank statement balance ($5,569.05) to give an adjusted bank statement balance of $5,154.05. This amount is equal to the checkbook balance, so the balances are reconciled. Notice that the two equal adjusted balances are recorded, single ruled, and double ruled on the same line.

If the two balances could not be reconciled, you would have to find an error in either balance. If there is a bank error, notify the bank immediately. If there is a checkbook error, it should be corrected on the next check stub. Errors will be discussed in Job 30.

Although the bank statement shows that you have $5,569.05 in the bank, the outstanding checks will be deducted shortly. Therefore, you cannot write checks for more than the adjusted balance of $5,154.05, or you will be notified by the bank that you have insufficient funds.

BUILDING YOUR BUSINESS VOCABULARY

On a sheet of paper, write the headings **Statement Number** and **Words**. Next, choose the words that match the statements. Write each word you choose next to the statement number it matches. Be careful; not all the words listed should be used.

Statements	Words
1. Money left in an account per bank's records	bank reconciliation statement
2. Checks that have been paid by the bank	bank statement
3. A book for recording checks when stubs are not used	bank statement balance
	canceled checks
4. A statement that brings the checkbook and bank statement balances into agreement	check register
	check stub
5. Brought into agreement	checkbook balance
6. Detailed record of a checking account from the bank	negotiable
	outstanding checks
7. Checks issued by the drawer but not yet paid by the bank	reconciled
8. Money left in an account per depositor's records	

STEPS REVIEW: Reconciling Bank Statements

STEP 1 Compare the deposits.

STEP 2 Arrange the canceled checks in order.

STEP 3 Compare the canceled checks with the stubs.

STEP 4 Find the outstanding checks.

STEP 5 Prepare a bank reconciliation statement.

APPLICATION PROBLEMS

CHECK POINT

28-1

If your work is correct, the adjusted balances should both equal $2,100.00.

Problem 28-1

You are the record keeper for Willow Glen Travel Agency. Part of your job is to keep the checkbook and prepare the bank reconciliation statement. On July 31, the checkbook balance is $2,100.00. The bank statement shows a balance of $2,802.00. After comparing the canceled checks with the check stubs, you find that the following checks are outstanding:

#761	$62.00	#764	$410.00	#765	$230.00

Directions

Prepare a bank reconciliation statement as of July 31. Use Illustration 28C (page 230) as a model.

CHECK POINT

28-2

If your work is correct, the adjusted balances should both equal $3,170.52.

Problem 28-2

You are a staff accountant for United Pharmacy. Part of your job is to keep the checkbook and prepare the bank reconciliation statement. On June 30, the checkbook balance is $3,170.52. The bank statement shows a balance of $3,398.27. After comparing the canceled checks with the check stubs, you find that the following checks are outstanding:

#1108	$18.43	#1110	$6.12	#1113	$203.20

Directions

Prepare a bank reconciliation statement as of June 30.

Problem 28-3

You are the accounting clerk for Laser Telecommunications. Part of your job is to keep the checkbook and prepare the bank reconciliation statement. The check stubs show that the following checks were issued during October:

#428	$83.24	#431	$290.37	#434	$306.23
#429	61.08	#432	183.20	#435	62.11
#430	60.00	#433	75.30	#436	109.42

On October 31, the checkbook balance is $4,600.50. The bank statement shows a balance of $4,953.12. The following canceled checks were returned with the bank statement:

#428	$83.24	#431	$290.37	#434	$306.23
#429	61.08	#433	75.30	#435	62.11

CHECK POINT

28-3

If your work is correct, the adjusted balances should both equal $4,600.50.

Directions

Prepare a bank reconciliation statement as of October 31. (To find outstanding checks, compare the list of checks issued with the list of canceled checks.)

Problem 28-4 may be found in the Working Papers.

applied math preview

Copy and complete the following problems.

1. Balance	$3,230.50	2. Balance	$4,840.80	3. Balance	$3,722.65
Deposit	+ 728.06	Check #1	− 121.73	Check #1	− 200.00
Balance		Balance		Balance	
Check #1	− 683.12	Check #2	−1,302.91	Deposit	+ 878.41
Balance		Balance		Balance	
Check #2	− 58.37	Deposit	+ 640.00	Check #2	−653.27
Balance		Balance		Balance	

key terms preview

- **Outstanding deposit**

goals

1 To learn how to prepare a bank reconciliation statement when a deposit is outstanding.

2 To learn how to use a bank-supplied reconciliation form.

➡ UNDERSTANDING THE JOB

Key Terms

Outstanding deposit. Deposit not shown on bank statement.

In Job 28, you learned how to prepare a bank reconciliation statement when there are outstanding checks. There will also be times when a deposit that you have recorded in your checkbook is not yet recorded by the bank on your bank statement. This will happen when you make a deposit on the last day of a month or when you make a deposit after banking hours at the end of the month. Such a deposit is called an **outstanding deposit**. Outstanding deposits are another reason why the bank statement balance and the checkbook balance must be brought into agreement.

Outstanding deposits are included in the checkbook balance but not in the bank statement balance. An outstanding deposit must be added to the bank statement balance in order to reconcile it with the checkbook balance. The Sample Problem shows how a bank reconciliation statement with both outstanding checks and an outstanding deposit is handled.

For Your Information

Sometimes in a case where two parties disagree, a canceled check serves as proof of payment or purchase.

You are an accounting clerk for the Alpha Paging Service. Part of your job is to keep the checkbook and prepare the bank reconciliation statement.

On January 31, the checkbook balance is $4,630.00. The bank statement shows a balance of $4,887.00.

STEP 1 Compare the deposits.

After comparing deposits shown on the bank statement with deposits shown on the check stubs, you find that a deposit of $150.00 has not been recorded by the bank. This is an outstanding deposit of $150.00 that must be added to the bank statement balance.

STEP 2 Compare the canceled checks.

After recording the outstanding deposit, you compare your canceled checks with the check stubs and find these checks to be outstanding:

| #374 | $290.00 | #377 | $12.00 | #378 | $105.00 |

STEP 3 Complete the reconciliation.

Illustration 29A
Bank reconciliation statement

The checks are listed, totaled, and subtracted. The completed bank reconciliation statement is shown in Illustration 29A.

STEP 2

STEP 1

Alpha Paging Service
Bank Reconciliation Statement
January 31, 20--

Checkbook balance	4 6 3 0 00	Bank statement balance		4 8 8 7 00
		Add outstanding deposit		1 5 0 00
		Total		5 0 3 7 00
		Less outstanding checks:		
		#374	$ 290.00	
		#377	12.00	
		#378	105.00	
		Total outstanding checks		4 0 7 00
Adjusted checkbook balance	4 6 3 0 00	Adjusted bank statement balance		4 6 3 0 00

STEP 3

STEP 2

STEP 1

CHECKING ACCOUNT RECONCILIATION

CHECKS OUTSTANDING	
NUMBER	AMOUNT
374	290 00
377	12 00
378	105 00
TOTAL	407 00

ENTER BALANCE THIS STATEMENT $ 4,887.00

ADD DEPOSITS NOT CREDITED
ON THIS STATEMENT
1 _150.00_

2 _____

3 _____

TOTAL _5,037.00_

SUBTRACT CHECKS OUTSTANDING _407.00_

BALANCE $ _4,630.00_
SHOULD AGREE WITH YOUR
CHECKBOOK BALANCE

IF YOUR ACCOUNT DOES NOT BALANCE

• HAVE YOU CORRECTLY ENTERED THE AMOUNT OF EACH CHECK IN
YOUR CHECK REGISTER?

• DO THE AMOUNTS OF YOUR DEPOSITS ENTERED IN YOUR CHECK
REGISTER AGREE WITH YOUR STATEMENT?

• HAVE ALL CHECKS BEEN DEDUCTED FROM YOUR CHECK REGISTER
BALANCE?

• HAVE YOU CARRIED THE CORRECT BALANCE FORWARD FROM ONE
CHECK REGISTER STUB TO THE NEXT?

• HAVE YOU CHECKED ALL ADDITIONS AND SUBTRACTIONS IN YOUR
CHECK REGISTER?

• HAVE YOU REVIEWED LAST MONTH'S RECONCILEMENT TO MAKE
SURE ANY DIFFERENCES WERE CORRECTED?

ANY ERRORS OR EXCEPTIONS SHOULD BE REPORTED IMMEDIATELY TO THE BANK

STEP 3

Tips

*Subtract outstanding
checks.*

Many banks supply their own reconciliation forms. Illustration 29B shows one such form and how the bank reconciliation statement for the Alpha Paging Service would appear in that form. Notice how all of the places are labeled for balances and outstanding items. Like most bank-supplied reconciliation forms, there is no place for a heading; however, this form is usually used by individuals, not businesses.

In this form, you do not begin with two balances, but only with the bank statement balance. After adding outstanding deposits and subtracting outstanding checks, you arrive at an adjusted balance that should agree with your checkbook balance if no errors have been made.

BUILDING YOUR BUSINESS VOCABULARY

On a sheet of paper, write the headings **Statement Number** and **Words**. Next, choose the words that match the statements. Write each word you choose next to the statement number it matches. Be careful; not all the words listed should be used.

Statements	Words
1. Money left in an account per bank's records	bank reconciliation statement
2. Brought into agreement	bank statement
3. The party who is ordered to pay the amount on the check	bank statement balance
4. Detailed record of a checking account from the bank	checkbook balance
	drawee
	drawer

Statements	Words
5. Checks issued by the drawer but not yet paid by the bank	outstanding checks
6. A statement that brings the checkbook and bank statement balances into agreement	outstanding deposit
7. A deposit not shown on the bank statement	payee
8. Money left in an account per depositor's records	reconciled

STEPS REVIEW: Handling Outstanding Deposits

STEP 1 Compare the deposits.

STEP 2 Compare the canceled checks.

STEP 3 Complete the reconciliation.

APPLICATION PROBLEMS

Problem 29-1   You are an assistant accountant for Sunnyvale Transmission. Part of your job is to keep the checkbook and prepare the bank reconciliation statement.

CHECK POINT

29-1

If your work is correct, the adjusted balances should both equal $894.36.

Directions

Prepare the bank reconciliation statement as of March 31 from the following information. Use Illustration 29A (page 234) as a model.

Checkbook balance	$894.36
Bank statement balance	907.87
Outstanding deposit	104.52
Outstanding checks:	
#203	8.23
#205	109.80

Problem 29-2   You are a full-time bookkeeper for Executive Limousine Company. Part of your job is to keep the checkbook and prepare the bank reconciliation statement.

Directions

Prepare the bank reconciliation statement as of November 30 from the following information. Use Illustration 29A (page 234) as a model.

Checkbook balance	$10,160.40
Bank statement balance	9,418.96
Outstanding deposit	1,300.27
Outstanding checks:	
#1006	476.50
#1009	82.33

CHECK POINT

29-2

If your work is correct, the adjusted balances should both equal $10,160.40.

You are preparing your own bank reconciliation statement.

Directions

Use the following information to prepare a February 28 statement. Use a bank-supplied form as shown in Illustration 29B (page 235).

Checkbook balance	$754.16
Bank statement balance	757.21
Outstanding deposit	120.00
Outstanding checks:	
#253	12.42
#256	103.90
#258	6.73

Problems 29-4 and 29-5 may be found in the Working Papers.

applied math preview

Copy and complete these problems.

1.			2.			3.		
Balance	$512.21		Balance	$2,628.42		Balance	$ 734.14	
Service charge	−8.40		Interest	+ 6.27		Check #62	− 128.92	
Balance	$		Balance	$		Balance	$	
Interest	+ 3.09		Deposit	+ 211.83		Service charge	− 6.40	
Balance	$		Balance	$		Balance	$	
Check #17	−131.63		Service charge	−7.00		Deposit	+ 239.74	
Balance	$		Balance	$		Balance	$	
Deposit	+ 51.32		Check #41	− 352.84		Interest	+ 7.08	
Balance			Balance			Balance		

key terms preview

- **Interest**

goals

1 To learn how to prepare a bank reconciliation statement with bank service charges and interest earned.

2 To learn how to correct errors made in recording checks.

⇨ UNDERSTANDING THE JOB

Key Terms

Interest. Money paid for the use of money.

For Your Information

Banks that offer interest-earning checking accounts usually require that you maintain a minimum balance in your account. Sometimes the minimum balance expected at all times is $500 or more.

In the previous two jobs, you have learned how to prepare a bank reconciliation statement when checks and deposits were outstanding. Both outstanding items are recorded on the bank statement balance side of the bank reconciliation statement.

There are two items that are recorded by the bank and appear on the bank statement before the depositor has recorded them. One is the bank service charge, or the bank's fee for handling the account. The amount of the service charge is already deducted from the bank statement balance. You must deduct it from your checkbook balance on a bank reconciliation statement.

The second item is interest earned on your bank account. **Interest** is money paid for the use of money. Many checking accounts earn interest. The amount of interest is added to the bank statement balance. You must add it to your checkbook balance on a bank reconciliation statement.

In summary, four items will usually appear on a bank reconciliation statement. Here is how they are handled:

Item	Treatment
Outstanding checks	Subtract from bank statement balance
Outstanding deposits	Add to bank statement balance
Bank service charge	Subtract from checkbook balance
Interest	Add to checkbook balance

In this job, you will see how all four items are recorded. You will also learn how to handle errors you make in your check stubs.

SAMPLE PROBLEM

You are the record keeper for Golden State Catering. Part of your job is to keep the checkbook and prepare the bank reconciliation statement.

On September 30, the checkbook balance is $6,350.40. The bank statement shown in Illustration 30A (page 240) shows a balance of $6,102.63. After comparing deposits shown on the bank statement with deposits shown on the check stubs, you discover an outstanding deposit of $435.00.

A comparison of canceled checks returned by the bank with checks written by the company shows two outstanding checks:

#616 $64.00   #618 $126.00

You also discover that Check No. 617, a canceled check, was for $65.00. You had incorrectly recorded it in your checkbook as $56.00. You also notice on the bank statement a deduction for a service charge of $13.00 and an addition of $19.23 for interest earned.

Illustration 30B (page 240) shows the bank reconciliation statement you would prepare.

Here are the steps you would follow to prepare the statement:

STEP 1   **Enter the heading and the balances; handle outstanding deposits and checks.**

You are familiar with this step from Jobs 28 and 29.

STEP 2   **Subtract the service charge from the checkbook balance.**

Since the bank has already subtracted the service charge from its balance, you must now subtract $13.00 from your balance. Record the difference, $6,337.40. If there were no more adjustments, $6,337.40 would be your adjusted checkbook balance.

STEP 3   **Add the interest earned to the checkbook balance.**

Since the bank has already added the interest earned to its balance, you must add $19.23 to your balance. Record the total, $6,356.63. If there were no more adjustments, $6,356.63 would be your adjusted checkbook balance.

GULF COAST FEDERAL BANK
16500 REED DRIVE • AUSTIN, TX 78711-3178

ACCOUNT OF:

GOLDEN STATE CATERING
150 BASCOM AVE.
AUSTIN, TX 78711-4025

ACCOUNT NO.: 801-3364

STATEMENT DATE: 09/30/--

BEGINNING BALANCE: 4,970.10
TOTAL DEPOSITS/CREDITS: 2,385.23
TOTAL CHECKS/DEBITS: 1,252.70
ENDING BALANCE: 6,102.63

Date	Checks/Debits	Deposits/Credits	Balance
09/01/--			4,970.10
09/04/--	840.00		4,130.10
09/08/--	209.70		3,920.40
09/11/--		2,366.00	6,286.40
09/18/--	125.00		6,161.40
09/25/--	65.00		6,096.40
09/30/--	13.00 SERVICE CHARGE		6,083.40
09/30/--		19.23 INTEREST	6,102.63

STEP 3   STEP 2   STEP 1

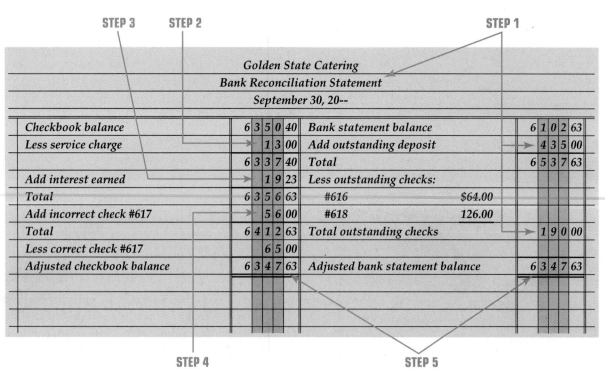

Golden State Catering
Bank Reconciliation Statement
September 30, 20--

Checkbook balance	6 3 5 0 40	Bank statement balance		6 1 0 2 63
Less service charge	1 3 00	Add outstanding deposit		4 3 5 00
	6 3 3 7 40	Total		6 5 3 7 63
Add interest earned	1 9 23	Less outstanding checks:		
Total	6 3 5 6 63	#616	$64.00	
Add incorrect check #617	5 6 00	#618	126.00	
Total	6 4 1 2 63	Total outstanding checks		1 9 0 00
Less correct check #617	6 5 00			
Adjusted checkbook balance	6 3 4 7 63	Adjusted bank statement balance		6 3 4 7 63

STEP 4   STEP 5

STEP 4 Handle any errors.

You wrote a check for $65.00, but recorded it on your check stub as
$56.00. Since it is your error, the correction must be made on the check-
book side of the bank reconciliation statement. There are different ways

to correct the error. One way, shown here, is to *add back* the wrong amount and then *subtract* the right amount. Notice how the $56.00 amount is added and the $65.00 amount is subtracted.

STEP 5 Finish the bank reconciliation statement.

Write your adjusted balances, single rule, and double rule on the same line on both sides of the statement.

STEP 6 Correct your check stubs or check register.

All items that have been listed on the checkbook side of the bank reconciliation statement must now be entered in your check stubs or check register. Illustration 30C shows how your check stub would appear with all items entered.

Illustration 30C

Corrected check stub

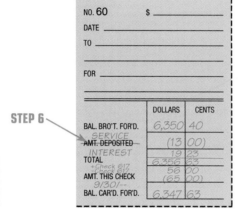

The Bal. Bro't. For'd. is the checkbook balance listed on the bank reconciliation statement, $6,350.40. Each item listed on the left side of the bank reconciliation statement is entered on the check stub, one at a time. Additions are shown without parentheses; subtractions are shown with parentheses. The date is entered by the adjusted checkbook balance, $6,347.63. There is little room for all of these changes. If you had more changes, such as another error correction, you would use the next stub.

Illustration 30D shows how you would record these items in a check register. Notice that additions are entered in the Deposit/Credit column. Subtractions are entered in the Payment/Debit column. Once again, the final balance, $6,347.63, agrees with the adjusted checkbook balance on the bank reconciliation statement.

Illustration 30D

Corrected check register

RECORD ALL CHARGES OR CREDITS THAT AFFECT YOUR ACCOUNT

NUMBER	DATE	DESCRIPTION OF TRANSACTION	PAYMENT/DEBIT (–)	√ T	FEE (IF ANY) (–)	DEPOSIT/CREDIT (+)	BALANCE
							$ 6,350 40
	20--	TO Service charge	$ 13 00	$		$	– 13 00
	9/30	FOR					6,337 40
	9/30	TO Interest earned				19 23	+ 19 23
		FOR					6,356 63
	9/30	TO Check 617 error				56 00	+ 56 00
		FOR					6,412 63
	9/30	TO Check 617 error	65 00				– 65 00
		FOR					6,347 63
		TO					
		FOR					

STEP 6

BUILDING YOUR BUSINESS VOCABULARY

On a sheet of paper, write the headings **Statement Number** and **Words**. Next, choose the words that match the statements. Write each word you choose next to the statement number it matches. Be careful; not all words listed should be used.

Statements	Words
1. A check with a special stub attached	ABA number
2. A number assigned to banks	canceled checks
3. A form instructing a bank not to pay a check	certified check
	insufficient funds
4. A safe form of cash for use when taking a trip	interest
	outstanding checks
5. Checks issued by the drawer but not yet paid by the bank	PIN
	service charge
6. A check that is guaranteed by a bank	stop-payment order
7. Money paid for the use of money	traveler's checks
8. Checks that have been paid by the bank	voucher check
9. Fee for bank services	

STEPS REVIEW: Handling Bank Service Charges, Interest, and Errors

STEP 1 Enter the heading and the balances; handle outstanding deposits and checks.

STEP 2 Subtract the service charge from the checkbook balance.

STEP 3 Add the interest earned to the checkbook balance.

STEP 4 Handle any errors.

STEP 5 Finish the bank reconciliation statement.

STEP 6 Correct your check stubs or check register.

APPLICATION PROBLEMS

Problem 30-1

You are a junior accountant for Bay Plastics Incorporated. Part of your job is to keep the checkbook and prepare a bank reconciliation statement.

CHECK POINT

30-1

If your work is correct, the adjusted balances should both equal $3,463.80.

Directions

Prepare the bank reconciliation statement as of December 31 from the following information. Use Illustration 30B (page 240) as a guide.

Checkbook balance	$3,460.50
Bank statement balance	3,200.45
Service charge	7.00
Interest earned	10.30
Outstanding deposit	483.20
Outstanding checks:	
#136	8.74
#139	211.11

You are a general accounting clerk for the VideoTech Company. Part of your job is to keep the checkbook and prepare a bank reconciliation statement.

Directions

CHECK POINT

30-2

If your work is correct, the adjusted balances should both equal $1,650.58.

Prepare the bank reconciliation statement as of May 31 from the following information:

Checkbook balance	$1,644.28
Bank statement balance	2,249.23
Service charge	5.50
Interest earned	11.80
Outstanding deposit	218.32
Outstanding checks:	
#474	590.93
#478	24.95
#479	201.09

Problem 30-3

You are a record keeper for Tim's Golf Solutions. Part of your job is to keep the checkbook and prepare a bank reconciliation statement.

Directions

a. Prepare a bank reconciliation statement as of November 30 from the following information:

CHECK POINT

30-3

If your work is correct, the adjusted balances should both equal $943.47.

Checkbook balance	$ 945.82
Bank statement balance	1,089.22
Service charge	7.75
Interest earned	5.40
Outstanding deposit	89.43
Outstanding checks:	
#652	148.70
#655	9.08
#657	77.40

b. Enter a balance brought forward of $945.82 in the check register.

c. Record the service charge and the interest earned in the check register. After subtracting the service charge and adding the interest earned, you should record a total that matches the adjusted checkbook balance. (Use Illustration 30D on page 241 as a model.)

Problems 30-4 and 30-5 may be found in the Working Papers.

Chapter 5

CHECK YOUR READING

1. List and explain several advantages of using a checking account. Think of some of the benefits and features discussed in the various Jobs presented in Chapter 5.
2. Why is it important to keep an up-to-date record of the balance in your checking account?
3. What is the difference between a voucher check and a regular check?
4. How is a checkbook with check stubs different from a checkbook with a check register?
5. What does it mean to endorse a check?
6. What is the danger of using a blank endorsement?
7. Explain the terms "outstanding check" and "outstanding deposit."

DISCUSSION

Myles Stanton is your assistant record keeper at work. His job is to keep the check stubs and write the checks. You discover that twice during the past month, Myles has sent out checks but has not filled out the check stubs. What would you say to Myles to explain why it is necessary to fill out the check stubs? Also, tell him how to avoid this error in the future.

ETHICS IN THE WORKPLACE

You are a payroll clerk in charge of checks. As you are getting ready to go home today, you find a check on the floor that you had made out to Brianna Cole, another employee. Brianna had signed a blank endorsement on the check. Write what you would do about this check and what you would tell Brianna.

COMMUNICATION IN THE WORKPLACE

You are an assistant accountant in charge of your company's checking account. You have just read that Kohler Company has gone out of business. The problem that this gives you is that you just wrote a large check along with a completed order for goods to Kohler Company today. You want to stop payment on this check. Write a letter to your bank asking that payment be stopped.

FOCUS ON CAREERS

Most of the jobs written about in this text are record keeping jobs in business. However, record keepers are employed in many public positions as well. For example, schools have record keepers (such as your school clerk). So does the federal government. Many clerks in the federal government are called "civil service clerks." In short, any organization that has an office may have a clerk.

Try to name four other organizations, other than businesses, that would need record keepers.

REVIEWING WHAT YOU HAVE LEARNED

On a sheet of paper, write in the headings **Statement Number** and **Words**. Next, choose the words that best complete the statements. Write each word you choose next to the statement number it completes. Be careful; not all words listed should be used.

Statements	Words
1. A check is written by the _____.	bank reconciliation statement
2. When you endorse by signature only, you make (a, an) _____.	bank statement
3. When you do not have enough money in your account to pay a check, you have _____.	bank statement balance
4. An endorsement which limits the use of a check is the _____.	blank endorsement
	canceled checks
5. When you write on the back of a check, you are making (a, an) _____.	check register
6. The part of a check kept by the depositor is the _____.	check stub
7. A deposit not shown on the bank statement is (a, an) _____.	checkbook balance
	drawee
8. The words "Pay to the order of" make a check _____.	drawer
9. A check that is unusable is marked _____.	endorsement
10. To instruct your bank not to pay a check, use (a, an) _____.	full endorsement
	insufficient funds
11. The detailed record of your checking account sent by the bank is the _____.	negotiable
12. Checks that have been paid by the bank are _____.	outstanding checks
	outstanding deposit
13. Instead of using check stubs to record checks, you can use (a, an) _____.	payee
14. When you cash part of a check and deposit the rest, you have made (a, an) _____.	restrictive endorsement
	split deposit
15. To bring the bank and checkbook balances into agreement, prepare (a, an) _____.	stop-payment order
	void
	voucher
	voucher check

Statements	Words

16. The bank that pays a check is known as the _____.
17. The money in your account per the bank's records is the _____.
18. Checks that you have written, but that are not returned with your bank statement are _____.
19. The money in your account per your records is the _____.
20. A check with a special stub attached is (a, an) _____.

MASTERY PROBLEM

You are a record keeper for the Wright Aviation Company. Part of your job is to keep the checkbook and prepare the bank reconciliation statement. Your bank account is at the Kitty Hawk National Bank.

Directions

a. Enter a balance on June 1, 20--, on Check Stub No. 352 of $6,208.51.
b. Prepare a deposit slip for a June 2 deposit of the following:

Cash:	10	$20.00 bills
	15	$10.00 bills
	31	$ 5.00 bills
	28	$ 1.00 bills
	10	$ 0.50 coins
	42	$ 0.25 coins
	68	$ 0.10 coins
	70	$ 0.05 coins
	86	$ 0.01 coins
Checks:	7-22	$ 631.54
	46-58	1,722.43
	2-29	154.36

c. Record the deposit on Check Stub No. 352.
d. Record and write Checks 352–356 as follows:

Check No.	Date	Payee	For	Amount
352	June 5	Carolina Fuel Corp.	aviation fuel	$ 650.33
353	9	AirWrench, Inc.	tools	179.80
354	12	Aviator Glass Co.	new windshield	423.44
355	23	TBA Supply	spark plugs	29.62
356	27	Big Air Tire	plane tires	263.78

CHECK POINT

(g)
Adjusted checkbook
balance = $8,370.14

e. Record (without preparing a deposit slip) a June 28 deposit of $697.40 on Check Stub No. 357.
f. Write Check No. 357 dated June 30 for $65.83 to Buchanan Office Supplies for letterhead stationery.
g. You receive the following bank statement on June 30, 20--. Prepare a bank reconciliation statement as of June 30. (Find the outstanding checks and deposits.)

Kitty Hawk NATIONAL BANK

17801 Yesler Way, Seattle, WA 98104-0010

ACCOUNT OF:

WRIGHT AVIATION
110 NE ODDFELLOWS ROAD
BAINBRIDGE ISLAND, WA 98110-5055

ACCOUNT NO.: 136-4289

STATEMENT DATE: 06/30/--

BEGINNING BALANCE: 6,208.51
TOTAL DEPOSITS/CREDITS: 3,083.53
TOTAL CHECKS/DEBITS: 1,289.69
ENDING BALANCE: 8,002.35

Date	Checks/Debits	Deposits/Credits	Balance
06/01/--			6,208.51
06/02/--		3,067.99	9,276.50
06/09/--	650.33		8,626.17
06/12--	179.80		8,446.37
06/16/--	423.44		8,022.93
06/28/--	29.62		7,993.31
06/30/--	6.50 SERVICE CHARGE		7,986.81
06/30/--		15.54 INTEREST	8,002.35

h. On Check Stub No. 358, record the service charge and interest earned that appear on the bank statement.

REVIEWING YOUR BUSINESS VOCABULARY

This activity may be found in the Working Papers.

Chapter 6

Petty Cash Records

In Chapter 5, you learned that a check provides a written record for a cash payment. Businesses use these written records, or checks, to help make decisions about how to spend their money. Sometimes, however, it is not convenient or practical to write a check. For example, would you use a check to buy a piece of bubble gum?

In Chapter 6, you will learn how businesses handle small cash payments—through petty cash funds. You will learn how to group these business expenses and prepare special reports for making small cash payments. Finally, you will learn that records of *all* cash payments, whether large or small, are very important to a business. A Calculator Tip will be given for summarizing a petty cash book, which is used to record and classify petty cash payments and receipts.

Modems

Connecting computers to the Internet from home usually requires a special device called a *modem*. That's because you must connect your computer system, which sends and receives data messages, to a phone line, which carries voice messages. The modem converts the messages coming from the computer to messages that the phone line can carry. When your computer receives messages from the phone line, the modem changes those messages back to data that your computer can use.

Modems also have important applications in the business world. Today, businesses must be able to efficiently move electronic information from one place to another. To do so, they rely on the computer and the telephone, with the modem as the link that joins the two. By using modems, business people can send files to one another in a matter of minutes, rather than the hours previously required to send disks by overnight mail. With modems, users can conduct instant online research and gather information from virtually anywhere on the World

Wide Web. In addition, modems allow access to online experts through networking with other computer users.

Modems come in many different types and sizes. Some modems are placed inside your computer system. Other modems can be attached to the outside of your computer system with a cable and look like the one illustrated here.

Some modems are placed into a special slot in a notebook computer. Still other modems connect you to the Internet using the cable TV cable.

applied math preview

Copy and complete these problems.

1.	2.	3.	5.
$ 12.86	$ 17.95	$ 150.00	$ 75.00
17.24	15.80	− 97.75	− 39.97
51.10	33.17		
39.05	4.95		
6.19	18.27	4. $125.00	6. $200.00
+ 18.64	+ 15.91	− 83.16	−171.94

key terms preview

- Currency
- Petty
- Petty cash box
- Petty cash clerk
- Petty cash fund
- Petty cash voucher

goals

1. To learn the use of a petty cash fund.
2. To learn how to record payments made from a petty cash fund.

→ UNDERSTANDING THE JOB

Currency. Bills and coins.

Petty. Small.

Petty cash fund. Currency set aside for making small payments.

Petty cash box. A storage box for petty cash.

Petty cash clerk. Keeps records of petty cash.

Petty cash voucher. Record of payment from petty cash fund.

You learned in Chapter 5 that businesses make most payments by check. Sometimes it is not convenient to write a check to make a small payment. At these and other times, it is necessary to pay in **currency**. Currency means bills and coins. Such payments in currency are made in small, or **petty**, amounts. They are called "petty cash payments."

Petty cash payments are made from a **petty cash fund**. The fund is the actual currency set aside for these payments. To start the fund, the business will estimate how much currency is needed for a certain time period, such as a week or a month. A check will then be written for the amount of the estimate. The check will be cashed and the actual currency placed in a **petty cash box**.

Recording Payments

Careful records must be kept for petty cash payments. The **petty cash clerk** will keep these records. Every time someone is given money from the petty cash fund, that person must sign a printed record. This record is called a **petty cash voucher**.

You are Andrea Neal, and you work for Marie Townes, a lawyer. On July 1, Marie starts a petty cash fund by cashing a check for $100.00. She places the currency in a petty cash box and puts you in charge of the fund. On July 1, Marty Sheehan bought office stationery from Jones Supplies with his own money. On July 2, Marty comes to you and asks for $8.45 in cash to reimburse him. Here are the steps that you will follow to handle Marty's request:

STEP 1 Ask for a receipt to prove the request.

Illustration 31A

Receipt for petty cash request

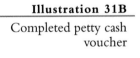

```
JONES SUPPLIES

    07/01/--

STA         5.15
STA         2.67
TAX          .63
TOTAL       8.45
CASH       10.00
CHANGE      1.55

147 2186  9:15 AM
```

Try to collect a receipt for all money paid out of the petty cash fund. For example, when you ask Marty for a receipt, he presents you with the receipt shown in Illustration 31A. (STA stands for stationery.)

STEP 2 Fill out the petty cash voucher.

Complete the petty cash voucher by filling in the following spaces (see Illustration 31B):

Illustration 31B

Completed petty cash voucher

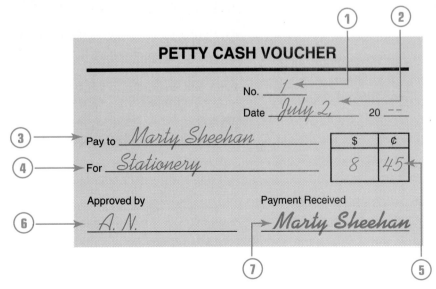

PETTY CASH VOUCHER

No. ___1___ ①
Date _July 2,_ 20 __ ②

③ Pay to _Marty Sheehan_
④ For _Stationery_ $ 8 | ¢ 45 ⑤

Approved by   Payment Received
⑥ _A. N._   _Marty Sheehan_ ⑦

1. **No.**—Write in the number of the voucher, 1. In some cases, the vouchers are printed with numbers, so this step will not be necessary.
2. **Date**—Write "July 2, 20--," the date on which money is being paid out.
3. **Pay to**—Enter Marty Sheehan's name, the person who is being paid.
4. **For**—Write "Stationery," the expense for which you are paying.
5. **$, ¢**—Enter the amount paid out, $8.45. Notice that no dollar sign, cents sign, or decimal point is used.
6. **Approved by**—Enter your initials, A.N.
7. **Payment Received**—Have Marty Sheehan sign his name when he is handed the money.

STEP 3 Attach the receipt to the petty cash voucher.

Attach Marty's receipt to the voucher and file them both in the petty cash box. The receipt is additional proof of payment. There will be times when a receipt is not available, such as for tips or bus fares. But, when there is a receipt, attach it.

Proving the Petty Cash Fund

Another responsibility of the petty cash clerk is to check the balance of the fund daily. At the end of the day, count the currency in the box. Then, add the amounts of the petty cash vouchers in the box and find a total. *The sum of the currency and the vouchers should equal the original balance of the fund.*

You began the day with $100.00 in currency. When you count the currency at the end of the day, you find $79.90. When you add your vouchers, you get a total of $20.10. You then add these two figures.

Currency in box	$ 79.90
Plus: Total of vouchers	20.10
Equals: Original balance	$100.00

Because your total is $100.00, you have done your work accurately. If your total did not add up to $100.00, an error has been made. Handling errors is discussed in Job 34.

BUILDING YOUR BUSINESS VOCABULARY

On a sheet of paper, write the headings **Statement Number** and **Words**. Next, choose the words that match the statements. Write each word you choose next to the statement number it matches. Be careful; not all the words listed should be used.

Statements	Words
1. Currency set aside for making small cash payments	currency
	deposit
2. Quantity times unit price	extension
3. Bills and coins	outstanding check
4. Record of payment from the petty cash fund	petty
	petty cash box
5. Small	petty cash clerk
6. A storage box for petty cash	petty cash fund
7. Keeps records of petty cash	petty cash voucher

STEPS REVIEW: Writing Petty Cash Vouchers

STEP 1 Ask for a receipt to prove the request.

STEP 2 Fill out the petty cash voucher.

STEP 3 Attach the receipt to the petty cash voucher.

APPLICATION PROBLEMS

Problem 31-1   You work for Eileen Stern, an engineer. She puts you in charge of the petty cash fund, which was started on May 1 with a balance of $200.00.

Directions

CHECK POINT

31-1

The money spent plus the money left in the fund should equal $200.00.

a. Fill out a petty cash voucher for each of the following payments made from the petty cash fund. Approve each voucher with your own initials, but do not fill in the signature. Start with Voucher No. 1.

May	4	Paid $21.50 to Ken James, an office clerk, for pencils and pens.
	9	Paid $9.50 to Quick Mail Services for overnight mail.
	16	Paid $12.65 to Ann Couture, a salesperson, for cab fare.
	25	Paid $14.95 to Luis Suarez, an office clerk, for typewriter ribbons.

b. Answer the following questions:
   1. How much money have you spent in May? (Find this amount by adding the vouchers.)
   2. How much money is left in the fund?

Problem 31-2   You work for Melanie Reilly, a real estate agent. She puts you in charge of the petty cash fund, which was started on June 1 with a balance of $100.00.

Directions

CHECK POINT

31-2

The money spent plus the money left in the fund should equal $100.00.

a. Fill out a petty cash voucher for each of the following payments made from the petty cash fund. Approve each voucher with your own initials, but do not fill in the signature. Start with Voucher No. 1.

June	5	Paid $37.40 to Barry Thorne, an office clerk, for mailing packages.
	12	Paid $6.95 to Charlene Ferrer, an agent, for cab fare.
	17	Paid $36.18 to Uptown Caterers for a catered lunch.
	26	Paid $17.12 to Ike Ofoje, an office clerk, for office supplies.

b. Answer the following questions:
   1. How much money have you spent in June?
   2. How much money is left in the fund?

Problem 31-3 may be found in the Working Papers.

applied math preview

Copy and complete these problems.

1. $19.18	2. $18.05	3. $ 19.50	5. $ 11.16
12.21	12.70	37.19	27.91
6.56	1.95	+ 38.55	+ 18.05
31.37	16.80		
19.04	27.10		
4.82	16.05	4. $ 51.10	6. $ 67.16
6.95	21.19	19.11	39.22
+ 0.75	+ 4.95	+ 18.47	+ 24.83

key terms preview

- **Classifications**
- **Petty cash record**

goal

To learn how to classify business expenses using a petty cash record.

→ UNDERSTANDING THE JOB

Classification. The name for a group of similar items.

A petty cash clerk pays out money for business expenses and fills out a petty cash voucher to record each payment. At any time, the petty cash clerk can add up the vouchers to find the total amount spent from the petty cash fund. However, an employer needs to know more than just the total spent. An employer needs to know the amounts spent for each type of expense. For this reason, it is necessary to group or classify the information on the petty cash voucher to find the totals for different kinds of expenses.

For example, money spent for pencils, stamps, computer paper, and other office supplies would be classified as an *office expense*. Money spent for wrapping paper, twine, labels, cartons, and other shipping supplies would be classified as a *shipping expense*. Some typical **classifications** of expenses are:

Office Expense—money spent on supplies used in the office, such as pens, pencils, stationery, printing supplies, computer supplies, and stamps.

Shipping Expense—money spent on supplies used for shipping, such as cartons, tape, wrapping paper, cord, and shipping labels.

Delivery Expense—money spent on delivering packages, such as gas, oil, bridge and highway tolls, repairs for the delivery truck, and bus or taxi fares for employees making deliveries.

General Expense—money spent on items that do not fit under any of the other classifications. Such expenses might include first-aid supplies, window repairs, paper towels, light bulbs for the office or warehouse, cleaning supplies, lock repairs, soap for the washroom, paint, and flowers.

SAMPLE PROBLEM

You are the petty cash clerk for Arnold Taylor, an architect. At the end of the week, you find the following petty cash vouchers in the petty cash box:

Voucher Number	Paid For	Amount
1	Stamps for office	$15.00
2	Gas for truck	15.00
3	Cab fare for delivery	11.25
4	Office light bulbs	7.50
5	Office stationery	15.95
6	Floor cleaning in office	25.00
7	Truck repair	17.50
8	Pencils for office	2.95

Petty cash record. Form used to record and classify petty cash payments.

Mr. Taylor asks you to report how much was spent this week for each of these classifications:

Office Expense
Delivery Expense
General Expense

One way to give this report is to use a form called a **petty cash record**. This form is used to record each petty cash payment and classify it. The data for the petty cash record are taken from the petty cash vouchers. Illustration 32A shows how a petty cash record would look

Illustration 32A

Petty cash record

STEP 1   **STEP 2**

PETTY CASH RECORD

PAID FOR	VO. NO.	TOTAL PAYMENTS	DISTRIBUTION OF PAYMENTS		
			OFFICE EXPENSE	DELIVERY EXPENSE	GENERAL EXPENSE
Stamps for office	1	15 00	15 00		
Gas for truck	2	15 00		15 00	
Cab fare for delivery	3	11 25		11 25	
Office light bulbs	4	7 50			7 50
Office stationery	5	15 95	15 95		
Floor cleaning in office	6	25 00			25 00
Truck repair	7	17 50		17 50	
Pencils for office	8	2 95	2 95		
Totals	—	110 15 / 110 15	33 90 / 33 90	43 75 / 43 75	32 50 / 32 50

STEP 3   **STEP 5**   **STEP 4**

after it was completed. Notice that there is a special column in the petty cash record for each classification. By entering the amount of each payment under one of the classifications and then totaling the columns, you can see how much was spent for each type of expense.

Here are the steps you would follow to complete a petty cash record:

STEP 1 Record vouchers in numerical order.

In the petty cash record shown in Illustration 32A, each voucher is listed in numerical order. The items that the vouchers were issued for are entered in the Paid For column. The number of each petty cash voucher is entered in the Vo. No. column.

STEP 2 Enter the amount of each payment twice.

The amount of each voucher is entered twice on the same line. The Total Payments column is used each time for one entry of the amount. The second entry is in the column that describes the type of expense.

Look at how Voucher No. 1 is recorded. First, $15.00 is entered in the Total Payments column. Then, since stamps are used in the office, it is entered in the Office Expense column.

In the same way, for Voucher No. 2, the $15.00 spent for gas for the truck is entered twice. It is first entered in the Total Payments column and then in the Delivery Expense column.

For Voucher No. 4, the $7.50 is first entered in the Total Payments column. It is then entered in the General Expense column because the payment is neither an office expense nor a delivery expense. You might wonder why the expense is not an office expense, since the light bulbs are for the office. The answer is that Office Expense includes supplies used for the normal, everyday paperwork in the office. Light bulbs are not an everyday expense.

STEP 3 Rule and foot the amount columns.

Each of the four amount columns is single ruled and totaled. A single ruling indicates that all amounts above the ruling are to be added. The totals are first written as footings just below the single ruling. The footings should be written in clear, small figures.

STEP 4 Check totals by crossfooting.

Add the totals of the three Distribution of Payments columns. If your math is accurate, the sum of these three totals should be $110.15, the total of the Total Payments column.

Total of Office Expense column	$ 33.90
Total of Delivery Expense column	43.75
Total of General Expense column	32.50
Total of Total Payments column	$110.15

If the three totals do not equal $110.15, find your error by working in reverse:

Amounts are entered twice on the same line.

Single ruling shows addition.

1. Re-add the three totals.
2. Check that you copied your footed totals correctly.
3. Foot all four amount columns again.
4. Check to see that the amount of each voucher was entered twice.

STEP 5 Record final totals and double rule the amount columns.

After the totals have been checked, they are written again just below the footings. The word "Totals" is written in the Paid For column, and a dash (-) is entered in the Vo. No. column. A double ruling is then drawn across all four amount columns just below the totals. The double ruling shows that the totals have been checked and all work is complete.

Tips

Double ruling shows record is complete.

→ BUILDING YOUR BUSINESS VOCABULARY

On a sheet of paper, write the headings **Statement Number** and **Words**. Next, choose the words that match the statements. Write each word you choose next to the statement number it matches. Be careful; not all the words listed should be used.

Statements

1. Record of payment from the petty cash fund
2. Drawn under a total to show that a record is complete
3. The total of an amount column written in small figures
4. The names for groups of similar items
5. Drawn under an amount column to show addition
6. Currency set aside for making small cash payments
7. Adding a row of figures across a form
8. Form used to record and classify petty cash payments

Words

classifications
crossfooting
currency
double ruling
footing
petty cash box
petty cash fund
petty cash record
petty cash voucher
single ruling

STEPS REVIEW: Using a Petty Cash Fund

STEP 1 Record vouchers in numerical order.

STEP 2 Enter the amount of each payment twice.

STEP 3 Rule and foot the amount columns.

STEP 4 Check totals by crossfooting.

STEP 5 Record final totals and double rule the amount columns.

→ APPLICATION PROBLEMS

Problem 32-1   You are in charge of the petty cash fund for Milly Price, who owns a catering business.

a. Enter the petty cash vouchers listed below in a petty cash record with the same headings shown in Illustration 32A (page 255).

Voucher Number	Paid For	Amount
1	Postage stamps for office	$27.95
2	Office stationery	16.20
3	Gas for truck	14.75
4	Truck repairs	21.90
5	Light bulbs for office	5.05
6	Soap for washroom	7.95
7	Envelopes for office	11.00
8	Printer ribbons for office	23.10

b. Rule and foot the amount columns.
c. Check your totals by crossfooting.
d. If the totals agree, record the final totals and double rule the amount columns.

Problem 32-2

You are in charge of the petty cash fund for the Mason Manufacturing Company.

Directions

a. Enter the petty cash vouchers listed below in a petty cash record with the same headings shown in Illustration 32A (page 255).

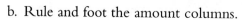

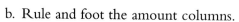

Spreadsheet

Voucher Number	Paid For	Amount
1	Truck tire repair	$15.00
2	File folders for office	12.50
3	Office light bulbs	14.95
4	Gas for truck	28.00
5	Paint for office	25.00
6	Cleaning supplies	12.50
7	Office stationery	11.75
8	Pencils for office	4.75

b. Rule and foot the amount columns.
c. Check your totals by crossfooting.
d. If the totals agree, record the final totals and double rule the amount columns.

Problem 32-3

You are in charge of the petty cash fund for the Hazelton Packing Company.

Directions

a. Prepare a petty cash record with Distribution of Payments columns for Office Expense, Delivery Expense, Shipping Expense, and General Expense. Enter the petty cash vouchers listed on page 259 in this record.

Voucher Number	Paid For	Amount
1	Wrapping paper	$14.75
2	Cab fare for deliveries	15.95
3	Office stationery	27.50
4	Computer paper	18.95
5	Paper towels	14.75
6	Gas for truck	16.50
7	Shipping labels	21.05
8	Flowers	25.00
9	Cartons for shipping	23.75
10	Printer ribbons	19.40

b. Rule and foot the amount columns.

c. Check your totals by crossfooting.

d. If the totals agree, record the final totals and double rule the amount columns.

Problem 32–4 may be found in the Working Papers.

applied math preview

Copy and complete these problems.

1. $ 24.75
   18.60
   11.10
 +19.90

2. $16.30
  57.10
  19.11
+ 4.73

3. $200.00
– 78.93

4. $ 75.00
 –69.18

5. $ 125.00
– 103.95

6. $150.00
 – 97.40

key terms preview

- Petty cash book
- Special column

goal

To learn how to use a petty cash book.

UNDERSTANDING THE JOB

Key Terms

Petty cash book. Form used to record and classify petty cash payments and receipts.

In Job 32, you learned how to use a petty cash record to record and classify petty cash payments. In this job, you will learn how to use a **petty cash book**. As you see in Illustration 33A on page 261, a petty cash book is used to record and classify both petty cash payments and receipts.

A petty cash book may be used by any kind of business. An advertising office may use a petty cash book to record payments for small services, such as printing photographs from slides. A printing plant may use a petty cash book to record the purchase of gas for a delivery truck. A school office may use a petty cash book to record postage for mailing a videotape back to a library. Because any business may make small payments for miscellaneous items, any business may need to use a petty cash book.

The petty cash book is similar to the petty cash record. However, the petty cash book has some additional columns: a Date column, a Receipts column, and the Other Items columns. The Date column is used to record the date of each receipt or payment. The Receipts column is used to record the amount to start the fund, any money added to the fund, and the balance of the fund. You will see how the Other Items columns are used as you study the Sample Problem.

PETTY CASH BOOK

DATE		EXPLANATION	VO. NO.	RECEIPTS		PAYMENTS		OFFICE EXPENSE		DELIVERY EXPENSE		OTHER ITEMS			
												ITEM		AMOUNT	
20-- May	1	Check #306	–	125	00										
	3	Stamps for office	1			15	00	15	00						
	7	Gas for truck	2			15	00			15	00				
	10	Cab fare for delivery	3			11	25			11	25				
	12	Office light bulbs	4			7	50					General Expense		7	50
	16	Office stationery	5			15	95	15	95						
	19	Floor cleaning in office	6			25	00					General Expense		25	00
	20	Truck repair	7			17	50			17	50				
	31	Pencils for office	8			2	95	2	95						
	31	Totals	–	125 125	00 00	110 110	15 15	33 33	90 90	43 43	75 75			32 32	50 50
June	1	Balance	–	14	85										

DISTRIBUTION OF PAYMENTS

STEP 6

STEP 4   STEP 3   STEP 5

Illustration 33A

Petty cash book

→ SAMPLE PROBLEM

You are in charge of the petty cash fund for Arnold Taylor, an architect. In Job 32, you recorded Mr. Taylor's petty cash payments in a petty cash record. Mr. Taylor has now told you that he prefers a petty cash book.

On May 1, he cashed a $125.00 check to start a petty cash fund. The check number was 306. You then made the following payments during May. They are classified as office expense, delivery expense, or general expense.

Illustration 33A above shows how the petty cash book would appear after all the vouchers and other amounts are recorded. You would follow these six steps to complete the petty cash book:

Voucher Number	Date	Paid For	Amount
1	May 3	Stamps for office	$15.00
2	7	Gas for truck	15.00
3	10	Cab fare for delivery	11.25
4	12	Office light bulbs	7.50
5	16	Office stationery	15.95
6	19	Floor cleaning in office	25.00
7	20	Truck repair	17.50
8	31	Pencils for office	2.95

STEP 1 Record the opening balance.

Before you record the vouchers, you must record the $125.00 check that was cashed to start the fund. Since this is the first entry in the petty cash book, you must write the complete date in the Date column. The year is written above the month. The year and the month will not be written again until a new page is started or the year or month changes. After recording the date, "Check #306" is written in the Explanation column. A dash (–) is recorded in the Vo. No. column. The amount, $125.00, is entered in the Receipts column.

STEP 2 Record the payments.

Special column. A column for a specific expense.

For each voucher, enter the date in the Date column. Record what the voucher was paid for in the Explanation column, and enter the voucher number in the Vo. No. column. (Vouchers are always recorded in numerical order.) Next, enter the amount of the voucher twice, once in the Payments column and once in the correct Distribution of Payments column. For example, the payment of $15.00 on May 3 for stamps for the office is extended to the Office Expense column.

Recording the payments on May 12 and May 19 presents a special problem. Each item is a general expense, but there is no column with the heading "General Expense." This is a situation where you use the Other Items columns. The Other Items columns are used whenever there is no **special column** for a payment.

Notice that there are two columns under the heading "Other Items." The Item column is used to enter the classification of the expense. The Amount column is used to enter the amount of the expense.

STEP 3 Rule and foot the amount columns.

Draw a single ruling under all five money columns and foot each column using small figures.

STEP 4 Check the totals by crossfooting.

Check the totals by adding the totals of the columns in the Distribution of Payments section. The sum of these totals should add up to the total of the Payments column, $110.15.

Office Expense column total	$33.90
Delivery Expense column total	43.75
Other Items Amount column total	32.50
Sum of Distribution of Payments totals	$110.15

If the sum did not equal $110.15, you could find the error by following these steps:
1. Re-add the Distribution of Payments totals.
2. Re-add each Distribution of Payments column and the Payments column in the petty cash book.
3. Check to see that each expense was extended correctly from the Payments column to one of the Distribution of Payments columns.

STEP 5 Record the final totals and double rule the amount columns.

After the footings have been checked, write the final totals. Draw a double ruling under the final totals. Enter the same date as the last payment date in the Date column. Write the word "Totals" in the Explanation column, and enter a dash in the Vo. No. column.

STEP 6 Find and enter the new balance.

Calculate the new balance by subtracting total payments from total receipts.

Receipts column total	$ 125.00
Payments column total	−110.15
New balance	$ 14.85

Enter the new balance in the petty cash book on the line below the double ruling. Enter the date in the Date column. Use the day *after* the last payment, June 1. Write the word *Balance* in the Explanation column, and enter a dash in the Vo. No. column. Record the balance, $14.85, in the Receipts column. This balance should be compared with what is actually in the petty cash box on the morning of June 1.

→ BUILDING YOUR BUSINESS VOCABULARY

On a sheet of paper, write the headings **Statement Number** and **Words**. Next, choose the words that match the statements. Write each word you choose next to the statement number it matches. Be careful; not all the words listed should be used.

Statements	Words
1. Form used to record and classify petty cash payments and receipts	classifications
2. Entered again in a special column	crossfooting
3. Types of business expenses	extended
4. A column for a specific expense	petty cash book
5. Record of payment from the petty cash fund	petty cash box
6. Currency set aside for making small cash payments	petty cash fund
7. Form used to record and classify petty cash payments	petty cash record
	petty cash voucher
	special column

STEPS REVIEW: Using a Petty Cash Book

STEP 1 Record the opening balance.

STEP 2 Record the payments.

STEP 3 Rule and foot the amount columns.

STEP 4 Check the totals by crossfooting.

STEP 5 Record the final totals and double rule the amount columns.

STEP 6 Find and enter the new balance.

Problem 33-1

You are in charge of the petty cash fund for the Zenith Food Store. On June 1, your employer cashed Check No. 207 for $150.00 to start the petty cash fund. Each payment from the fund must be classified as an office expense, delivery expense, or general expense.

Directions

a. Prepare a petty cash book with the same headings as shown in Illustration 33A on page 261. (General expenses must be entered in the Other Items columns.)

b. Record the opening balance.

c. Record the following vouchers issued in June:

CHECK POINT

33-1

July 1 Balance = $33.90

Voucher Number	Date	Paid For	Amount
1	June 3	Stamps for office	$ 7.50
2	7	Gas for truck	20.35
3	9	Stationery for office	19.15
4	12	Office cleaning	16.95
5	14	Light bulbs	5.10
6	18	File folders for office	6.10
7	22	Truck repairs	18.95
8	30	Gas for truck	22.00

d. Rule and foot the amount columns.

e. Check the totals by crossfooting.

f. Record the final totals and double rule the amount columns.

g. Find the new balance and enter it in the petty cash book as of July 1.

Problem 33-2

You are in charge of the petty cash fund for Dyer TV Store. On October 1, your employer cashed Check No. 472 for $175.00 to start the petty cash fund. Each payment from the fund must be classified as a shipping expense, delivery expense, office expense, or general expense.

Spreadsheet

Directions

a. Prepare a petty cash book with special column headings for Shipping Expense and Delivery Expense. (Office expenses and general expenses must be entered in the Other Items columns.)

b. Record the opening balance.

c. Record the following vouchers issued in October:

CHECK POINT

33-2

Total Payments = $139.45

Voucher Number	Date	Paid For	Amount
1	Oct. 4	Office cleaning	$17.50
2	6	Shipping labels	15.95
3	7	Light bulbs	4.10
4	10	Truck repairs	21.60
5	14	Gas for truck	18.95
6	17	Shipping supplies	24.10
7	24	Office stationery	21.00
8	31	Cartons for shipping	16.25

d. Rule and foot the amount columns.

e. Check the totals by crossfooting.

f. Record the final totals and double rule the amount columns.

g. Find the new balance and enter it in the petty cash book as of November 1.

Problem 33-3

You are in charge of the petty cash fund for Malden Moving Company. On August 1, your employer cashed Check No. 1047 for $300.00 to start the petty cash fund. Each payment from the fund must be classified into one of these four categories:

Travel Expense—expenses of drivers for meals and tolls while on the road

Van Expense—gas and repairs for delivery vans

Telephone Expense—phone calls made by drivers while on the road

Office Expense—stationery and stamps

Directions

a. Prepare a petty cash book with special column headings for Travel Expense, Van Expense, and Telephone Expense. (Office expenses must be entered in the Other Items columns.)

b. Record the opening balance.

c. Record the following vouchers issued in August:

CHECK POINT

33-3

Total Van Expense = $116.50

Voucher Number	Date	Paid For	Amount
1	Aug. 4	Gas for van	$25.90
2	7	Meals and tolls	61.75
3	12	Driver phone calls	11.65
4	17	Repairs to van	45.10
5	20	Stamps for office	15.00
6	24	Driver phone calls	10.90
7	26	Meals and tolls	83.95
8	31	Tire for van	45.50

d. Rule and foot the amount columns.

e. Check the totals by crossfooting.

f. Record the final totals and double rule the amount columns.

g. Find the new balance and enter it in the petty cash book as of September 1.

Problem 33-4 may be found in the Working Papers.

key terms preview

• **Replenish the fund**

goals

1 To learn how to record the entry for replenishing a petty cash fund.

2 To learn how to calculate and record petty cash shortages and overages.

3 To practice keeping a petty cash book for more than one month.

UNDERSTANDING THE JOB

Replenish the fund. Add an amount to bring the fund back to its original balance.

In this job, you will learn how to keep a petty cash book for more than one month for the same business. In order to do so, you will learn how to compare the money that is supposed to be in the fund at the end of the month with the money that is actually in the petty cash box. If there is less money in the box than the balance shown in the petty cash book, you must record a cash shortage. If there is more money in the box than the balance shown in the petty cash book, you must record a cash overage.

Even when a petty cash clerk makes an effort to be careful, errors may be made. An error may be made in counting the money to reimburse someone who presents a petty cash voucher. Money may be paid out without being recorded in the petty cash book. The money may be recorded, but the wrong amount may be entered. Currency may be lost or mislaid. A person may withdraw petty cash in advance of a purchase, receive too much change from the purchase, and put the extra money in the petty cash fund. There is always the possibility of a cash shortage because of theft, but most petty cash shortages are caused by honest mistakes.

After recording any cash shortage or cash overage, you will receive from your employer a check to **replenish the fund**. This term means to add an amount of money to bring the fund back to its original balance. The Sample Problems will show these procedures.

Replenishing the Fund—No Cash Shortage or Overage

You are in charge of the petty cash fund for West Hot Air Balloons, Inc. The petty cash book for March has just been completed. It is time to start the petty cash book for April. The original balance in the fund was $200.00. On March 31, the balance shown in the petty cash book is $6.50. A count of the currency in the petty cash box shows $6.50. Your employer cashes Check No. 375 for $193.50 to replenish the fund. Here is how you would record these items:

STEP 1 Carry the balance to a new page.

As you see in Illustration 34A, the $6.50 balance from the March petty cash book is entered on the first line of the April petty cash book. The year and month are both recorded, since you are on a new page. The day, 1, is also entered. The word *Balance* is written in the Explanation column and a dash is entered in the Vo. No. column. The amount, $6.50, is then entered in the Receipts column.

Illustration 34A

Starting a new page and replenishing the fund

PETTY CASH BOOK

DATE		EXPLANATION	VO. NO.	RECEIPTS	PAYMENTS	OFFICE EXPENSE	SHIPPING EXPENSE	DELIVERY EXPENSE	OTHER ITEMS – ITEM	OTHER ITEMS – AMOUNT
20-- Mar.	1	Check #279	–	200 00						
	31	Totals	–	200 00 / 200 00	193 50 / 193 50	37 25 / 37 25	46 19 / 46 19	32 41 / 32 41		77 65 / 77 65
Apr.	1	Balance	–	6 50						

STEP 1

PETTY CASH BOOK

DATE		EXPLANATION	VO. NO.	RECEIPTS	PAYMENTS	OFFICE EXPENSE	SHIPPING EXPENSE	DELIVERY EXPENSE	OTHER ITEMS – ITEM	OTHER ITEMS – AMOUNT
20-- Apr.	1	Balance	–	6 50						
	1	Check #375	–	193 50						

STEP 3

STEP 2 Calculate and record cash shortage or cash overage.

Compare the balance recorded in the petty cash book with the amount of currency in the petty cash box. Since both amounts are $6.50, there is no cash shortage or cash overage.

STEP 3 Calculate and record replenishing the fund.

Subtract the new balance from the original balance to find how much is needed to replenish the fund.

Original balance	$200.00
New balance	− 6.50
Amount needed to replenish fund	$193.50

Enter the check cashed for $193.50 in the April petty cash book. Record the day, 1, in the Date column. Write "Check #375" in the Explanation column. Enter a dash in the Vo. No. column and record the amount, $193.50, in the Receipts column. When totaled, the two amounts in the Receipts column will add up to the original balance of $200.00.

SAMPLE PROBLEM 2A

Replenishing the Fund—Cash Shortage

You are still working for West Hot Air Balloons, Inc. The original balance in the petty cash fund was $200.00, and on March 31, the balance shown in the petty cash book is $6.50. But, there is only $5.50 in the petty cash box on April 1. So, Check #375 is written for $194.50 to replenish the fund. Here is how you would record the cash shortage:

STEP 1 Carry the balance to a new page.

Follow the same procedures as in Step 1 of Sample Problem 1.

STEP 2 Calculate and record cash shortage or cash overage.

Compare the balance recorded in the petty cash book with the amount of currency in the petty cash box. They are not the same. Subtract to find the difference.

Balance recorded in petty cash book	$ 6.50
Currency in petty cash box	− 5.50
Cash shortage	$ 1.00

The difference is a shortage because the currency in the box was *less* than the balance in the petty cash book. Record the shortage in the petty cash book as shown in Illustration 34B. Enter the day, 1, in the Date

Cash shortage occurs when balance in book is greater than currency in box.

PETTY CASH BOOK

DATE		EXPLANATION	VO. NO.	RECEIPTS	PAYMENTS	DISTRIBUTION OF PAYMENTS				
						OFFICE EXPENSE	SHIPPING EXPENSE	DELIVERY EXPENSE	OTHER ITEMS	
									ITEM	AMOUNT
20-- Apr.	1	Balance	–	6 50						
	1	Cash shortage	–	(1 00)						
	1	Corrected balance	–	5 50						
	1	Check #375	–	194 50						

Illustration 34B

Recording a cash shortage

column. Write "Cash shortage" in the Explanation column. Enter a dash in the Vo. No. column, and enter the amount, $1.00, in parentheses in the Receipts column. Parentheses show a subtraction. Draw a single rule under ($1.00). On the line below the cash shortage entry, record the day once again. Write "Corrected balance" in the Explanation column, and enter a dash in the Vo. No. column. Subtract and record $5.50 in the Receipts column.

STEP 3 **Calculate and record replenishing the fund.**

Subtract the *corrected balance* from the original balance to find how much is needed to replenish the fund.

Original balance	$200.00
Corrected balance	− 5.50
Amount needed to replenish fund	$194.50

Tips

Original balance − corrected balance = amount needed to replenish fund

Record the replenishment as you did in Sample Problem 1. The amount of the check ($194.50) plus the corrected balance ($5.50) equals the original balance ($200.00).

 SAMPLE PROBLEM 2B

Replenishing the Fund—Cash Overage

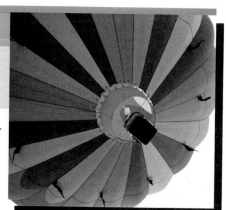

You are still working for West Hot Air Balloons, Inc. All facts remain the same, except there is $8.75 in the petty cash box on April 1 and Check No. 375 is written for $191.25 to replenish the fund. Here is how you would record this cash overage:

STEP 1 **Carry the balance to a new page.**

Follow the same procedures as in Step 1 of Sample Problem 1.

Tips

Cash overage occurs when currency in box is greater than balance in book.

Calculate and record cash shortage or cash overage.

Compare the balance recorded in the petty cash book with the amount of currency in the petty cash box. They are not the same. Subtract to find the difference.

Balance recorded in petty cash book	$ 6.50
Currency in petty cash box	− 8.75
Cash overage	$ 2.25

The difference is an overage because the currency in the box was *more* than the balance in the petty cash book. Record the overage in the petty cash book as shown in Illustration 34C. It is recorded in the same way as a shortage, except the words "Cash overage" are written in the Explanation column, no parentheses are used, and the overage is *added* to the April 1 balance to find the corrected balance of $8.75.

STEP 3 **Calculate and record replenishing the fund.**

Subtract the corrected balance from the original balance to find how much is needed to replenish the fund.

Original balance	$200.00
Corrected balance	− 8.75
Amount needed to replenish fund	$191.25

Record the replenishment as you did in the previous problems. The amount of the check ($191.25) plus the corrected balance ($8.75) equals the original balance ($200.00).

Illustration 34C

Recording a cash overage

STEP 1

STEP 2   STEP 3

PETTY CASH BOOK

DATE		EXPLANATION	VO. NO.	RECEIPTS	PAYMENTS	DISTRIBUTION OF PAYMENTS			OTHER ITEMS	
						OFFICE EXPENSE	SHIPPING EXPENSE	DELIVERY EXPENSE	ITEM	AMOUNT
20-- Apr.	1	*Balance*	–	6 50						
	1	*Cash overage*	–	2 25						
	1	*Corrected balance*	–	8 75						
	1	*Check #375*	–	191 25						

A calculator can help you save time when summarizing a petty cash book. Here is how you can use a calculator to add expense totals and find the ending balance in the petty cash book. Assume that you begin with $100.00 and have expense column totals of $17.95, $12.75, and $31.10.

STEP 1 ▶ *Enter the original balance into memory.*

Enter the original balance into memory by pressing these keys:

| 1 | 0 | 0 | · | 0 | 0 | M+ |

Press the C key to clear the display.

STEP 2 ▶ *Enter the expense column totals.*

Enter each total as follows:

Your display will show 61.8, the sum of the vouchers. Check this total against the total of the Payments column.

STEP 3 ▶ *Place the total of the expense columns into memory.*

Press the M- key. You have placed your total in the memory as a subtraction.

STEP 4 ▶ *Find the ending balance.*

Press the MR or MR/C key. The number 38.2, or 38.20, appears in the display. Enter this amount in the petty cash book as the ending balance.

Remember to press the MC or MR/C key to clear the memory and the C key to clear the display before going on to any other problems.

 BUILDING YOUR BUSINESS VOCABULARY

On a sheet of paper, write the headings **Statement Number** and **Words**. Next, choose the words that match the statements. Write each word you choose next to the statement number it matches. Be careful; not all the words listed should be used.

Statements	Words
1. Actual currency is less than balance in petty cash book	cash overage
2. Currency set aside for making small cash payments	cash shortage
3. Bills and coins	currency
4. Add an amount to bring the fund back to its original balance	petty cash book
5. Actual currency is more than balance in petty cash book	petty cash box
6. Form to record and classify petty cash payments and receipts	petty cash fund
	petty cash record
	replenish the fund

STEPS REVIEW: Replenishing the Petty Cash Fund

STEP 1 Carry the balance to a new page.

STEP 2 Calculate and record cash shortage or cash overage.

STEP 3 Calculate and record replenishing the fund.

APPLICATION PROBLEMS

Problem 34-1

Directions

On each line, calculate the amount of cash overage or cash shortage, the corrected balance, and the amount needed to replenish the fund. The first two lines are done for you as an example.

	Original balance	Balance, petty cash book	Currency in box	(Shortage) Overage	Corrected balance	Amount to replenish
a.	$100.00	$ 5.00	$ 5.00	-0-	$5.00	$ 95.00
b.	$150.00	$ 7.00	$ 6.00	($1.00)	$6.00	$144.00
c.	$200.00	$19.00	$19.00	_____	_____	_____
d.	$150.00	$17.50	$15.50	_____	_____	_____
e.	$ 50.00	$ 9.50	$12.50	_____	_____	_____
f.	$ 75.00	$15.75	$17.95	_____	_____	_____
g.	$125.00	$42.60	$42.60	_____	_____	_____
h.	$250.00	$37.25	$36.95	_____	_____	_____
i.	$175.00	$41.18	$40.98	_____	_____	_____
j.	$100.00	$56.19	$57.22	_____	_____	_____

Problem 34-2

You are the petty cash clerk for Carson's Lumber Yard. On March 1, your employer starts the petty cash fund by cashing Check No. 517 for $175.00. Each payment from the fund is classified as an office expense, delivery expense, shipping expense, or general expense.

Directions

a. Prepare a petty cash book with special column headings for Office Expense, Delivery Expense, and Shipping Expense.
b. Record the opening balance.
c. Record the following vouchers issued in March:

Voucher Number	Date	Paid For	Amount
1	March 3	Postage stamps	$15.00
2	7	Floppy disks for office	15.00
3	12	Gas for truck	12.50
4	16	Filing labels for office	8.75
5	18	Shipping supplies	17.90
6	19	Truck repairs	35.00
7	27	Floor cleaning	25.00
8	31	Cartons for shipping	27.75

CHECK POINT

34-2

May 1 Balance = $40.70.

d. Rule and foot the amount columns.
e. Check your totals by crossfooting.

f. Record the final totals and double rule the amount columns.

g. Find the new balance and enter it as of April 1.

h. Begin a new page of the petty cash book for April and enter the new balance.

i. A count of currency in the box adds to $18.10. Calculate and record any cash shortage or overage and find, if necessary, the corrected balance.

j. Your employer cashes Check No. 619 to replenish the fund. Calculate the amount of this check and record it in the petty cash book.

k. Record the following vouchers issued in April:

Voucher Number	Date	Paid For	Amount
9	April 6	Gas for truck	$14.50
10	10	Printer ribbons	10.25
11	16	Office stationery	15.00
12	17	Shipping supplies	17.40
13	18	Cab fare for deliveries	7.50
14	24	Shipping labels	9.65
15	27	Office door repair	15.00
16	30	Truck tune-up	45.00

l. Rule and foot the amount columns.

m. Check your totals by crossfooting.

n. Record the final totals and double rule the amount columns.

o. Find the new balance and enter it as of May 1.

Problems 34-3 and 34-4 may be found in the Working Papers.

Chapter 6

CHECK YOUR READING

1. Why do businesses start a petty cash fund? Provide an example to support your answer.
2. How does a petty cash clerk document payments made from the petty cash fund?
3. Suppose you are a petty cash clerk and manage a petty cash fund that started with $200.00.
   a. If $60.00 remains in the fund, how would you prove $60.00 is the correct amount?
   b. Suppose the total of all the petty cash vouchers equals $150.00. Is the amount remaining in the petty cash fund short or over? State the amount of the shortage or overage.

DISCUSSION

You are the petty cash clerk for Wilmington Company. Elena Manus, a new employee, asks you why you always prepare a petty cash voucher before you issue any money from the petty cash fund. She wonders why you just don't give out the cash. "After all," she tells you, "it's only small change." What would you say to Elena to explain why you handle petty cash the way that you do?

CRITICAL THINKING

You have learned that in order to make a good decision, it is important to *study all the factors involved*. In the Critical Thinking problem at the end of Chapter 4, you prepared a list of all the factors you would study before buying a new car. This list might have included such items as price, gas mileage, and color. However, some of the items on your list are more important than others when making the decision to buy. For example, you might feel that the price of an automobile is more important than its color. Identifying the most important items on your list can help you make a better decision about which car to buy.

Make a list of all the items that you should consider before buying a car, such as price, gas mileage, and color. List as many as you can. (You may use the same list you created for the Critical Thinking problem at the end of Chapter 4.) Pick the five most important items on your list. Explain why each item is important to you. If you wish, write them in order of importance. These five items are the ones that you must deal with first when deciding which car to buy. Because people are different, not everyone's list will be the same.

REINFORCEMENT ACTIVITIES

 ## COMMUNICATION IN THE WORKPLACE

You are checking the work of your assistant petty cash clerk, Timothy Astor. Tim's job is to arrange vouchers in numerical order and then classify them. The classifications used are office expense, delivery expense, shipping expense, telephone expense, and general expense. Tim has made several errors in classification. Write a letter to Tim, explaining why it is important to classify expenses accurately. Also, explain to him what is classified under office, delivery, shipping, telephone, and general expenses.

 ## FOCUS ON CAREERS

Every worker wants to "move up the ladder." The ladder referred to is a career ladder. A career ladder is a planned series of steps to better and better jobs. Each job higher up the ladder will usually pay more money. It will also require more responsibility on the part of the worker.

An example of a move up the ladder is from assistant petty cash clerk to petty cash clerk and then to head cashier. Moving up usually requires education and experience.

1. Why would education usually be required to climb the ladder?
2. Why would experience usually be required to climb the ladder?
3. Why would a job higher up the ladder require more responsibility by the worker?

 ## GLOBAL BUSINESS: INTERNATIONAL MAIL

You are a record keeper for a financial services company that has clients around the world. You often must send correspondence or your company's newsletters to foreign countries.

There are three categories of international mail:

1. LC mail (initials for the French *lettres* and *cartes postales*—meaning "letters" and "post cards"). LC mail consists mainly of letters and post cards. These items are mailed at the letter rate of postage. This service is airmail delivery.
2. AO mail (initials for the French *Autres Objets*—meaning "other things"). AO mail usually consists of printed materials such as books, periodicals, newsletters, and braille publications. This service is usually by ship and is slower than airmail.
3. CP mail (initials for the French *par Colis Postal*—meaning "by parcel post"). CP mail is the equivalent of parcel post in the U.S. Parcel post is used for items such as merchandise. It is the only class of mail that

can be insured. This service is also usually by ship and, again, is slower than airmail.

If required, there are also special delivery services offered.

1. Express Mail offers a faster delivery than regular airmail, but costs more.
2. International Priority Airmail is intended for bulk items.
3. Registered mail is for items that require a proof of delivery be returned to the sender.

An International Mail Activity can be found in the Working Papers.

REVIEWING WHAT YOU HAVE LEARNED

On a sheet of paper, write in the headings **Statement Number** and **Words**. Next, choose the words that best complete the statements. Write each word you choose next to the statement number it completes. Be careful; not all words listed should be used.

Statements	Words
1. To record and classify petty cash payments and receipts, use (a, an) _____.	cash overage
2. When currency in the petty cash box is more than the balance in the petty cash book, you have (a, an) _____.	cash shortage
3. Expenses are sorted in groups or _____.	classifications
4. Bills and coins are also called _____.	currency
5. When you _____, you are bringing a petty cash fund back to its original balance.	extended
6. An amount that is entered again in a second column is said to be _____.	petty
7. A record of payment from the petty cash fund is the _____.	petty cash book
8. Payments that are not recorded in the Other Items columns of a petty cash book are recorded in (a, an) _____.	petty cash box
9. The person who is in charge of small cash payments is the _____.	petty cash clerk

Words (continued):
- petty cash fund
- petty cash record
- petty cash voucher
- replenish the fund
- special column

MASTERY PROBLEM

You are the petty cash clerk for Coppola Trading Company. On June 1, your employer cashes Check No. 311 for $200.00 to start a petty cash fund. Each payment from the fund must be classified as an office expense, general expense, shipping expense, or delivery expense.

CHECK POINT

(k)
Check No. 412 = $152.05

Directions

a. Prepare a petty cash voucher for each of the following payments made from the petty cash fund. Approve each voucher with your own initials, but do not fill in the signature. Begin with Voucher No. 1.

June	4	Paid $21.95 to Ruth Silverman, office clerk, for a window screen.
	7	Paid $31.60 to Swann Company for shipping supplies.
	9	Paid $14.75 to Bill's Lock Shop for a lock repair.
	12	Paid $25.00 to A-One Cleaning Service for office cleaning.
	16	Paid $17.50 to Main Street Supply Shop for office supplies.
	22	Paid $8.95 to Jose Martinez for cab fare on a delivery.
	27	Paid $10.35 to Jean Pagliano, office clerk, for postage.
	30	Paid $22.05 to Chip Curtis, secretary, for printer ribbons.

b. Prepare a petty cash book with special column headings for Office Expense, General Expense, and Shipping Expense. (Delivery expenses must be entered in the Other Items columns.)

c. Record the opening balance in the petty cash book.

d. Record the petty cash vouchers in the petty cash book.

e. Rule and foot the amount columns.

f. Check your totals by crossfooting.

g. Record the final totals and double rule the amount columns.

h. Find the new balance as of July 1 and enter it in the petty cash book.

i. Begin a new page in the petty cash book and enter the new balance as of July 1.

j. A count of currency in the petty cash box shows $47.95. Calculate and record any cash shortage or overage and find, if necessary, the corrected balance.

k. Your employer cashes Check No. 412 to replenish the fund. Calculate the amount of this check and record it in the petty cash book.

REVIEWING YOUR BUSINESS VOCABULARY

This activity may be found in the Working Papers.

COMPREHENSIVE PROJECT 2

Comprehensive Project 2 has been designed to reinforce major concepts of this and previous chapters. The Comprehensive Project is found in the Working Papers.

Chapter 7

Completing a sales slip is an important task of a sales clerk. Sales clerks need to know how to complete a sales slip manually and by using a computer. They must also learn how to complete a sales slip for a cash sale and for a charge sale.

In Chapter 7, you will learn how to complete a cash sales slip and a charge sales slip. You will also learn how to compute sales taxes and make refunds on charge card sales. Calculator Tips will be given for finding extensions, totaling a sales slip, and calculating sales taxes.

Record Keeping for Sales Clerks

Credit Card Readers

When you use your credit card at most stores, they must make certain that the credit card is good and that your credit is large enough to cover the purchase. In Chapter 1, you learned how to verify credit cards manually. Many businesses today verify the credit card and the credit card balance electronically using credit card readers.

Credit Card Reader

You have probably seen credit card readers in many stores. The customer gives the credit card to the sales clerk. The sales clerk quickly runs the credit card through the slot on the right hand side of the machine. This is called *swiping the card*. The credit card reader reads the information about the credit card holder from the magnetic strip on the back of the card.

The credit card reader then dials another computer system at a bank or other institution to verify that the card is good and that the customer has enough credit. Credit card readers can do this because they have modems inside them that allow them to send data messages over phone lines.

The credit card reader usually takes only about 8–10 seconds to verify the card and the balance. That's a lot faster and easier than doing it manually, isn't it?

Job 35 COMPLETING SALES SLIPS

Tips

Most businesses round off money amounts to the nearest cent. Look at only the third digit to the right of the decimal. If it is 4 or less, leave the first two digits to the right of the decimal and drop off the rest. If the third digit is 5–9, add a one to the second digit to the right of the decimal before dropping off the rest.

UNDERSTANDING THE JOB

Sales slip. Written record of a sale.

Sales slip register. A mechanical device used to record sales.

POS terminal. Point of sale computer.

Most retail store owners keep a written record of each sale. This record is called a **sales slip**. Some stores use blank sales slips that are bound in pads with an original and a copy for each sale. When a sale is made, the sales clerk gives the original to the customer. This is the customer's record of the sale. Many stores require customers to present the sales slip when they exchange or return merchandise. The copy of the sales slip is kept by the store as a record of the sale.

Each sales slip has a printed number. The original and the copy will both have the same number. The numbers on the sales slips are printed in numerical order so that the sales clerk will know if any slips are missing.

Some stores use a mechanical device called a **sales slip register**. Numbered, blank sales slips are locked inside the register. After a sales slip is filled out, the sales clerk gives the original sales slip to the customer, while the copy rolls to where it is safely stored inside the machine.

A common method of recording a sale is to use an electronic register. The advantage of an electronic register is that it automatically completes several parts of the sales slip. An electronic register can compute extensions, determine sales tax, and total purchases. It can even calculate the amount of change due a customer.

USING THE COMPUTER

Many stores use computers to complete sales slips. These computers are usually called point-of-sale terminals or **POS terminals**. POS terminals are special types of electronic cash registers. They include a keyboard, a display screen, a cash drawer, and a printer to print the sales slips.

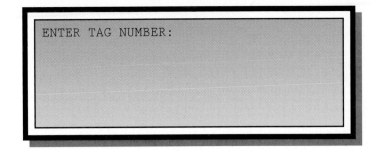

ENTER TAG NUMBER:

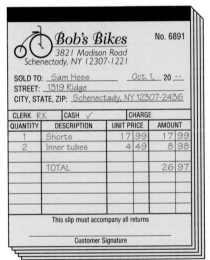

Key Terms

Prompts. Questions or orders on a display screen.

Wand. A scanner that reads bar codes on tags.

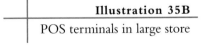

The POS terminal may lead the sales clerk, step by step, through each sales transaction by displaying questions or orders (called **prompts**) on the display screen, like the one shown in Illustration 35A. This ensures that the sales clerk does not forget anything.

POS terminals, like electronic cash registers, may use scanners to read data from bar codes. One type of scanner used by POS terminals is a **wand**. The wand reads bar codes printed on tags attached to merchandise. The wand is attached by wire to the terminal. When a wand is used, the sales clerk does not input the name or price of merchandise being sold. This is done automatically by the computer.

In large stores, the POS terminals may be connected to a central computer in the same way that electronic cash registers in chain stores are connected to central computers. (See Illustration 35B.)

The central computer collects data from each of the POS terminals at the end of the day. The central computer uses the data collected to

1. Prepare a bill to be sent to the customer later if the customer is not paying cash.
2. Keep a record of total sales made.
3. Keep track of the amount of merchandise that the store has on hand. The computer will let the store know when the amount of stock gets low so that more merchandise can be ordered.
4. Keep track of sales taxes and let the store know how much tax must be sent to state and local governments.
5. Compute commissions. If the sales clerk is paid a commission on the sales that are made, the computer will keep track of the total commissions owed to the sales clerk.

Whether you complete sales slips using pads, sales slip registers, electronic registers, or POS terminals, the same data are used. Because these data are used in many ways, it is very important that you enter these data accurately.

In many stores, the selling price is shown on each item. However, some stores do not place the selling price on each article. These stores scan

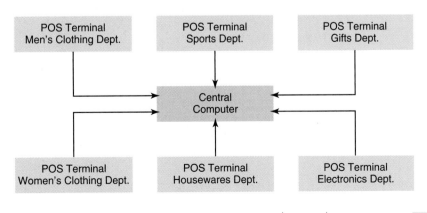

each article, and the computer inputs the price. Other stores provide their sales clerks with a price list so that they can find the price of each item.

 SAMPLE PROBLEM

Adam Pham is a sales associate for Bayview Office Mart. He uses a pad of sales slips and the following price list:

Price List		
Item	**Unit**	**Unit Price**
Pencils	dozen (dz.)	$ 2.10
Paper cutter	each (ea.)	22.79
Index cards	package (pkg.)	.75
Sales slip pads	each (ea.)	3.15
File folders	hundred (C)	7.50
Labels	thousand (M)	1.78
Copy paper	ream (rm.)	4.89
Pencil sharpener	each (ea.)	19.89
Paper clips	box	1.09
Ball-point pens	dozen (dz.)	3.98
Bond paper	ream (rm.)	8.60
Memo pads	dozen (dz.)	2.48
Memo pads	gross (12 dozen)	25.99
3-ring binder	each (ea.)	4.88
Stapler	each (ea.)	9.85

On June 6, Adam sold the following items to Regina Erickson, 121 West Bristol Avenue, Tampa, FL 33606–4136:

6	reams of copy paper
1	pencil sharpener
300	file folders
2000	labels
$3\frac{1}{2}$	dozen pencils
2	gross memo pads

Regina paid for the items with cash. Adam recorded the sale on the sales slip as shown in Illustration 35C.

Illustration 35C

Completed sales slip

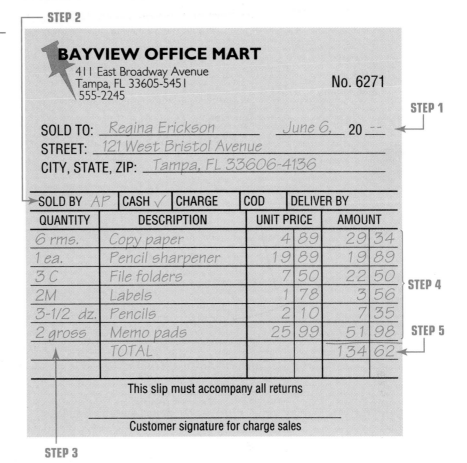

STEP 2

BAYVIEW OFFICE MART

411 East Broadway Avenue
Tampa, FL 33605-5451
555-2245

No. 6271

STEP 1

SOLD TO: _Regina Erickson_   _June 6,_ 20 _--_

STREET: _121 West Bristol Avenue_

CITY, STATE, ZIP: _Tampa, FL 33606-4136_

SOLD BY *AP*	CASH ✓	CHARGE	COD	DELIVER BY	
QUANTITY	DESCRIPTION	UNIT PRICE		AMOUNT	
6 rms.	Copy paper	4	89	29	34
1 ea.	Pencil sharpener	19	89	19	89
3 C	File folders	7	50	22	50
2M	Labels	1	78	3	56
3-1/2 dz.	Pencils	2	10	7	35
2 gross	Memo pads	25	99	51	98
	TOTAL			134	62

STEP 4
STEP 5

This slip must accompany all returns

_____

Customer signature for charge sales

STEP 3

Adam followed these steps to complete the sales slip:

STEP 1 Record the date of the sale and the customer's name and address.

In the spaces provided, Adam wrote the date of the sale (June 6, 20--), the customer's name (Regina Erickson), and her address.

STEP 2 Record the sales clerk's initials and mark the sale as cash or charge.

Adam wrote his initials in the Sold By box to show that he was the sales clerk who made the sale. Some stores give each sales clerk a number to use instead of their initials. Since the customer paid with cash, Adam placed a check mark in the box labeled "Cash." If Regina had paid by check, Adam would have written the word "check" in this space.

STEP 3 Record the quantity, description, and unit price for each item.

Key Terms

In the column headed "Quantity," Adam entered the total number of each item sold. You can see that items on the price list are sold in different units. For example, pencil sharpeners are sold individually, copy paper is sold by the **ream**, file folders are sold by the hundred (**C**), labels are sold by the thousand (**M**), and memo pads are sold by the **gross** (12 dozen or 144).

Adam then recorded the description and the unit price for each item. The **unit price** is the selling price which Adam found on the price list.

Ream. About 500 sheets.

C. Hundred.

M. Thousand.

Gross. 12 dozen or 144.

Unit price. Price for each unit.

Key Terms

Extension. Quantity × unit price.

The total amount for each type of item sold is called the **extension**. It is found by multiplying the quantity by the unit price. Since the unit price of a ream of copy paper is $4.89, Adam found the extension of 6 reams of copy paper by multiplying 6 × $4.89 = $29.34. Extensions are entered in the Amount column.

Adam could have found the extension for 3½ dozen pencils by multiplying the unit price, $2.10, first by ½, then by 3, and adding these totals:

$$
\begin{aligned}
&\text{1. } \$2.10 \times \tfrac{1}{2} = \$1.05\\
&\text{2. } \$2.10 \times 3 \;\; = \;\; \underline{6.30}\\
& \underline{\$7.35}
\end{aligned}
$$

He also could have found the extension by first changing 3½ to a decimal (3.5) and then multiplying $2.10 × 3.5 = $7.35.

Often a solution will not come out evenly in dollars and cents. For example, 2½ × $2.13 = $5.32½. Since you cannot charge someone for a fraction of a cent, you must round the answer to the nearest cent. When the amount is ½ cent or more, drop the fraction and add one cent to the total amount. When the fraction is less than ½ cent, simply drop it. For example:

Rounding With Fractions	Rounding With Decimals
$8.28½ = $8.29	$8.285 = $8.29
$5.16¼ = $5.16	$5.1625 = $5.16
$7.88¾ = $7.89	$7.8875 = $7.89

STEP 5 Total the sales slip.

Adam added the extensions on the sales slip. The total was $134.62.

When he said this amount to the customer, Regina Erickson, she gave him $140.00 in cash. Adam gave the customer $5.38 in change. Since this was a cash sale, Adam did not have to get the customer's signature on the sales slip. Adam gave Regina the original copy of the sales slip along with her change.

Calculator Tips

You can use the calculator to find extensions and the total of a sales slip. You multiply each quantity by the unit price and record the extension. You also store each extension in memory. To find the total of the bill, you recall the amount in memory. Here are the steps to follow:

STEP 1 ▶ Find the first extension.

Multiply the quantity (6) by the unit price ($4.89) by pressing these keys in order:

$$6 \quad \times \quad 4 \quad \cdot \quad 8 \quad 9 \quad =$$

The extension, 29.34, will appear in the display. Record this extension in the Amount column of the sales slip.

STEP 2 ▶ Add the extension to the calculator's memory.

Press the M+ key to add the extension, 29.34, to memory.

STEP 3 ▶ Find and record the extensions for the other items bought and add the extensions to memory.

Now find the extension for each of the other items bought. Record the extensions in the Amount column of the sales slip. When you find each extension, press the M+ key to add it to memory.

STEP 4 ▶ Find the total bill.

When you have added each extension to memory, press the MR (memory recall) or MR/C (memory recall/clear) key once. When you do, the display will show 134.62. This is the total of all the extensions. Draw a line under the extensions on the sales slip. Write the word "Total" in the Description column and record the total, $134.62, in the Amount column.

STEP 5 ▶ Clear memory.

To clear the calculator's memory for the next sales slip, press the MC (memory clear) key. If your calculator has a MR/C key, press that key twice. When you press the MR/C key once, the display shows the contents of memory. When you press it twice, you clear or erase memory.

➡ BUILDING YOUR BUSINESS VOCABULARY

On a sheet of paper, write the headings **Statement Number** and **Words**. Next, choose the words that match the statements. Write each word you choose next to the statement number it matches. Be careful; not all the words listed should be used.

Statements	Words
1. The price for each unit	C
2. A computer for completing sales slips	crossfoot
3. Thousand	estimate
4. A written record of a sale	extension

Statements	Words
5. Quantity times unit price	gross
6. A mechanical device used to record a sale	M
7. About 500 sheets of paper	POS terminal
8. An input device attached by wire to a POS terminal and used to read bar codes	prompts
	ream
9. Questions or orders on a display screen of a computer	sales slip
	sales slip register
10. Hundred	unit price
11. Twelve dozen or 144	wand

STEPS REVIEW: Completing Sales Slips

STEP 1 Record the date of the sale and the customer's name and address.

STEP 2 Record the sales clerk's initials and mark the sales as cash or charge.

STEP 3 Record the quantity, description, and unit price for each item.

STEP 4 Extend the amount for each item.

STEP 5 Total the sales slip.

APPLICATION PROBLEMS

Problem 35-1

Adam Pham is still a sales associate for Bayview Office Mart. He completes a sales slip for each sale he makes. He uses a sales slip form like the one in the Sample Problem.

CHECK POINT

35-1

Sale #1
Total = $98.42

Directions

On June 7, Adam made the following eight sales. Complete a sales slip for each sale using the price list found in the Sample Problem. If needed, use two lines for an item. Every customer paid cash. Begin numbering the sales slips with 6283.

Sale #1

Customer's name   Baypointe Automotive
Address   1261 West Bay Avenue
           Tampa, FL 33611-7133
Items sold   10 boxes paper clips
              4 pencil sharpeners
              2 dz. ball-point pens

Sale #2

Customer's name   Brett Frye
Address   124 East Caracas Street
           Tampa, FL 33603-6218
Items sold   6 C file folders
              2 rms. bond paper
              1 stapler

Sale #3

Customer's name   Lewis Medical Mart
Address   2150 North Branch Avenue
           Tampa, FL 33603-4840
Items sold $5\frac{1}{2}$ dz. pencils
              2 gross memo pads
              2 rms. copy paper

Sale #4

Customer's name   Angela Grimes
Address   263 Brentwood Drive
           Tampa, FL 33617-2236
Items sold   8 ea. 3-ring binders
              7 pkgs. index cards
              3 M labels

Sale #5

Customer's name   Huff Dental Group
Address   1104 West Burke Street
           Tampa, FL 33604-1844
Items sold   20 sales slip pads
              3 paper cutters
              $4\frac{1}{4}$ dz. ball-point pens

Sale #6

Customer's name   Mission Painting
Address   1441 Barry Road
           Tampa, FL 33634-7208
Items sold   6 rms. bond paper
              5 rms. copy paper
              2 gross memo pads

Sale #7

Customer's name   Silva's Custom Tailoring
Address   68 West Bird Street
           Tampa, FL 33604-1080
Items sold   12 dz. pencils
              6 dz. ball-point pens
              20 boxes paper clips

Sale #8

Customer's name   MTS Enterprise
Address   1229 Barclay Road
           Tampa, FL 33612-3911
Items sold   4 pencil sharpeners
              7 pkgs. index cards
              1 stapler

Job 36 COMPUTING SALES TAXES ON MERCHANDISE

Convert fractions to decimals before multiplying. Example:
$4\frac{1}{2} = 4.5$
$2\frac{1}{4} = 2.25$

applied math preview

Copy and complete these problems. Round your answers to the nearest cent.

1. $ 0.82 × 6 =	5. $ 6.20 × $2\frac{1}{4}$ =
2. $ 2.12 × 4 =	6. $10.33 × $7\frac{1}{2}$ =
3. $15.04 × 5 =	7. $ 0.88 × $3\frac{1}{4}$ =
4. $ 6.19 × 3 =	8. $ 5.34 × $6\frac{1}{2}$ =

key terms preview

• Retailers   • Sales tax

goals

1 To learn how to find the amount of sales tax on a retail sale.

2 To learn how to complete sales slips when sales taxes are charged.

➡ UNDERSTANDING THE JOB

Retailers. Store owners who sell directly to consumers.

Sales tax. Percent of selling price collected by retailer for governments.

There are many places where **retailers** must collect a **sales tax** from each customer on all or certain types of sales. The tax is based on the selling price of the merchandise sold.

The sales tax collected is usually a state sales tax. All retailers in the state must collect the tax from each customer and send it to the state government. Tax rates vary from state to state because the tax laws are not the same in each state.

In many places, there is also a local (city or county) sales tax. The money collected for local taxes is turned over to the local government. Where both state and local sales taxes are charged, the taxes are usually combined so that the retailer may collect them as one amount.

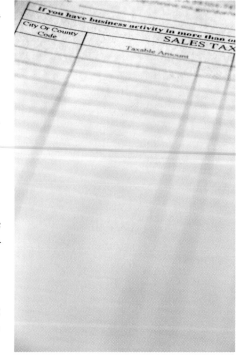

Each sales slip must show the amount of the sale and the amount of the sales tax. Sales tax charts like the one shown in Illustration 36B (page 290) help sales clerks determine the amount of sales tax to charge for each sale.

SAMPLE PROBLEM

You are a sales clerk for McAbee Electronics in a state which charges a 5% sales tax. You sold three surge protectors for $3.29 each and one two-button wheel mouse for $24.88. The sales slip you completed is shown in Illustration 36A.

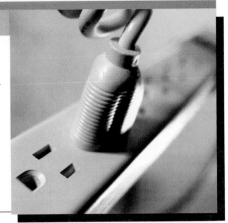

STEP 1 **Compute the sales tax.**

The sales tax of $1.74 on the sale of $34.75 was found by using the sales tax chart (Illustration 36B) in this way:

Tax on $34.00 (34 x $.05)	$ 1.70
Tax on $.75 (Tax chart, $.70-$.89)	+ 0.04
Total tax	$ 1.74

Illustration 36A

Completed sales slip showing sales tax

No. **786**

McAbee Electronics
13089 Franklin Road
Boise, ID 83709-5162
555-3939

SOLD TO: _Brach Engineering_   _April 12,_ 20 __
STREET: _211B 1st Street, Apt. 24_
CITY, STATE, ZIP: _Boise, ID 83705-1928_

SOLD BY 04	CASH ✓	CHECK	CHARGE	DELIVER BY	
QUANTITY	DESCRIPTION		UNIT PRICE	AMOUNT	
3 ea.	Surge protectors		3 29	9 87	
1 ea.	Two-button				
	wheel mouse		24 88	24 88	← STEP 1
	Amount of sale			34 75	
	5% sales tax			1 74	←
	Total			36 49	← STEP 2

Customer signature for charge sales

THIS SLIP MUST ACCOMPANY ALL RETURNS

5% Sales Tax Chart	
Amount of Sale	**Tax**
$.00 - $.09	No Tax
.10 - .29	$.01
.30 - .49	.02
.50 - .69	.03
.70 - .89	.04
.90 - 1.00	.05

On a sale over $1.00, take $.05 for each full dollar plus the tax given in the chart above for the amount over an even dollar.

If you do not have a tax chart, you must find the tax by multiplying the amount of the sale, $34.75, by the tax rate of 5%:

Amount of sale	$ 34.75
Tax rate, 5%	× 0.05
Sales tax	$ 1.7375 = $1.74

You must round to the nearest cent.

STEP 2 Add the sales tax to the amount of the sale.

Amount of sale	$34.75
Sales tax	+ 1.74
Total	$36.49

You can use the calculator to complete sales slips that include sales taxes. Here is how you would use the calculator to complete the sales slip in the Sample Problem.

STEP 1 ▶ *Find the extensions.*

Multiply the unit price ($3.29) times the quantity (3) to find the extension for the surge protectors by pressing these keys in order:

$$\boxed{3}\ \boxed{\cdot}\ \boxed{2}\ \boxed{9}\ \boxed{\times}\ \boxed{3}\ \boxed{=}$$

The extension, 9.87, will appear in the display. Enter this amount on the sales slip. Then, add the extension to memory by pressing the M+ key.

Now find the second extension in the same way. When you do, add the extension to memory by pressing the M+ key.

STEP 2 ▶ *Find the amount of the sale.*

Press the MR or MR/C key once. The total of the extensions, 34.75, now appears in the display. Enter this amount on the sales slip.

STEP 3 ▶ *Find the amount of the sales tax.*

The total, 34.75, is still in the display. Multiply the total by the sales tax rate, 5%, by pressing these keys in order:

The amount of the sales tax, 1.7375, will appear in the display. Round the amount to the nearest whole cent, 1.74, and enter the rounded amount on the sales slip. Now add the unrounded amount of the sales tax to memory by pressing the M+ key.

STEP 4 ▶ *Find the total of the sales slip.*

Press the MR or MR/C key once. The total amount of the sales slip, 36.4875, will appear in the display. Round the amount off to the nearest cent, 36.49, and enter it on the Total line of the sales slip.

STEP 5 ▶ *Clear memory.*

Press the MC key once or the MR/C key twice. This will clear memory and prepare you for the next sales slip.

⇨ BUILDING YOUR BUSINESS VOCABULARY

On a sheet of paper, write the headings **Statement Number** and **Words**. Next, choose the words that match the statements. Write each word you choose next to the statement number it matches. Be careful; not all the words listed should be used.

Statements	Words
1. A store owner who sells directly to the consumer	crossfoot
2. Quantity times unit price	extension
3. The price of each unit	merchandise
4. A written record of a sale	ream
5. A percentage of the selling price collected by the retailer for the state and/or local government	retailer
6. An input device attached to a POS terminal and used to read bar codes	sales slip
7. A mechanical device used to record a sale	sales slip register
	sales tax
	unit price
	wand

STEPS REVIEW: Computing Sales Tax on Merchandise

STEP 1 Compute the sales tax.

STEP 2 Add the sales tax to the amount of the sale.

Problem 36-1 | **Directions**

Complete the following form by finding the sales tax and the total amount for each sale. Use the 5% sales tax chart in Illustration 36B (page 290) to find the sales tax.

CHECK POINT

36-1 (1)

Sales Tax = $0.02

No.	Amount of Sale		Amount of Sales Tax		TOTAL	
1		40				
2		09				
3		42				
4		91				
5	3	64				
6	10	12				
7	4	53				
8	19	82				
9	20	30				
10	135	48				

Problem 36-2 | **Directions**

Complete the following form by finding the sales tax and the total amount for each sale. Use the 5% sales tax chart in Illustration 36B (page 290) to find the sales tax.

CHECK POINT

36-2 (1)

Total = $0.79

Spreadsheet

No.	Amount of Sale		Amount of Sales Tax		TOTAL	
1		75				
2		90				
3		07				
4	6	30				
5	5	27				
6	28	66				
7	47	99				
8	321	37				
9	405	44				
10	612	53				

Problem 36-3 | You are a retail clerk for San Juan Bookstore in Spartanburg, South Carolina.

Automated Accounting

Sales Slip No. 8041
Total = $46.38

Directions
Complete the following four sales slips. Find the sales tax by multiplying the amount of the sale by the sales tax rate of 7%.

San Juan Bookstore
66 N. Pine Street
Spartanburg, SC 29302-7145
DATE _February 3,_ 20 _--_
SOLD TO: _Stacey Moynihan_
STREET: _6892 North Street_
CITY, STATE, ZIP: _Spartanburg, SC 29301-8861_

SOLD BY 06	CASH ✓	CHECK	DELIVER BY	
QUANTITY	DESCRIPTION			AMOUNT
3	Book covers @ .79			
2	Dictionaries @ $20.49			
	Amount of sale			
	7% sales tax			
	Total			

8041

San Juan Bookstore
66 N. Pine Street
Spartanburg, SC 29302-7145
DATE _February 3,_ 20 _--_
SOLD TO: _Tommy Prak_
STREET: _2809 Oak Street_
CITY, STATE, ZIP: _Spartanburg, SC 29316-7201_

SOLD BY 06	CASH	CHECK ✓	DELIVER BY	
QUANTITY	DESCRIPTION			AMOUNT
1	Nonfiction @ $17.36			
3	Mystery paperbacks			
	@ $4.88			
	Amount of sale			
	7% sales tax			
	Total			

8042

San Juan Bookstore
66 N. Pine Street
Spartanburg, SC 29302-7145
DATE _February 3,_ 20 _--_
SOLD TO: _Tamara Preston_
STREET: _7280 Peachtree Road_
CITY, STATE, ZIP: _Spartanburg, SC 29302-0060_

SOLD BY 06	CASH ✓	CHECK	DELIVER BY	
QUANTITY	DESCRIPTION			AMOUNT
4	Book holders @ $6.99			
5	Leather bookmarks			
	@ $3.08			
	Amount of sale			
	7% sales tax			
	Total			

8043

San Juan Bookstore
66 N. Pine Street
Spartanburg, SC 29302-7145
DATE _February 3,_ 20 _--_
SOLD TO: _REI Industries_
STREET: _919 Ranch Road_
CITY, STATE, ZIP: _Spartanburg, SC 29316-7848_

SOLD BY 06	CASH ✓	CHECK	DELIVER BY	
QUANTITY	DESCRIPTION			AMOUNT
2	Teen paperbacks @ $4.98			
1	Video cassette @ $10.99			
	Amount of sale			
	7% sales tax			
	Total			

8044

Problem 36–4 may be found in the Working Papers.

Tips

Before multiplying, convert percents to decimals by moving the decimal two places to the left and dropping the percent sign.
Example:
12% = .12
5% = .05
8.25% = .0825

applied math preview

Copy and complete these problems. Round your answers to the nearest cent.

1. $385.00 × 0.02 =
2. $157.40 × 0.08 =
3. $212.42 × 6% =
4. $472.82 × 3% =
5. $209.40 × .065 =
6. $183.91 × .0425 =
7. $311.14 × 6.3% =
8. $72.71 × 8.25% =

key terms preview

• Bill

goals

1 To learn how to find the amount of sales tax on sales of goods and services.

2 To learn how to complete sales slips that include goods, services, and sales taxes.

UNDERSTANDING THE JOB

Some states charge a sales tax on both retail goods and services. For example, if you had your car repaired in New York, you would have to pay a sales tax on the total amount charged for the repair. This would include the amount charged for goods (materials and parts), as well as the amount charged for services (labor).

Many states do not charge sales taxes on everything sold to consumers. For example, some states do not charge sales taxes on food or prescription drugs. Other states do not tax services. In these states, you must separate the charges that are to be taxed from those that are not taxed. For example, in states that do not tax services, you must separate the charges for labor from the charges for parts when you prepare a car repair bill. Then you compute the sales tax only on the charge for parts.

SAMPLE PROBLEM 1

Key Terms

Bill. Sales slip.

Tax on Goods and Services

You are a cashier for Sterling VCR and Camcorder Repair in Poughkeepsie, New York. You complete a sales slip, or **bill**, for Kim Thorpe. Kim had her video cassette recorder repaired and must be charged for parts and labor. Poughkeepsie has a 7% sales tax on *both goods and services*. The completed bill is shown in Illustration 37A.

STERLING VCR AND CAMCORDER REPAIR
2023 Forbus Street
Poughkeepsie, NY 12603-4041

NO. **6247**

NAME _Kim Thorpe_
ADDRESS _428 Ferris Lane_
Poughkeepsie, NY 12603-0052

MAKE	MODEL	SERIAL NO.		DATE
RCA	XR-96	2649118		4/18/--

DESCRIPTION	PARTS		LABOR	
Repair damaged video head	26	45	54	00
Replace switch	2	95	10	00
TOTALS	29	40	64	00
PARTS FORWARD ⟶			29	40
SUBTOTAL			93	40
SALES TAX — 7%			6	54
TOTAL BILL			99	94

STEP 1   STEP 2

STEP 1 Compute the sales tax.

The sales tax of $6.54 was based on the total charge for parts and labor. The tax on $93.40 is $6.538, or $6.54 ($93.40 × 0.07).

STEP 2 Add the sales tax to the amount of the sale.

The amount of the sale was $93.40 for parts and labor. The sales tax is $6.54 on parts and labor. The total bill is $99.94 ($93.40 + $6.54).

➡ SAMPLE PROBLEM 2

Tax Only on Goods

You work for Lexington Automotive in Santa Clara, California. You must complete a bill for Peter Johansen, who had his car repaired. In Santa Clara, a 8.25% sales tax is charged *only on goods*. Services are not taxed. The completed bill is shown in Illustration 37B on page 296.

STEP 1 Compute the sales tax.

The sales tax, $2.05, was based only on the charge for parts. The tax on $24.89 is $2.05 ($24.89 × 0.0825).

STEP 2 Add the sales tax to the amount of the sale.

The amount of the sale is $85.54 for parts and labor. The sales tax is $2.05 on parts only. The total bill is $87.59 ($85.54 + $2.05).

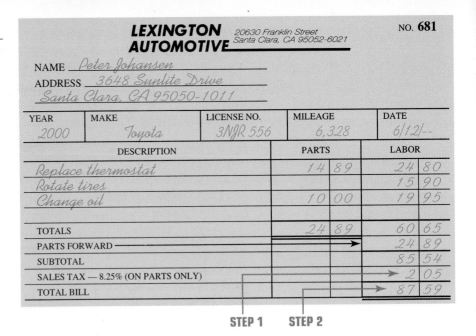

LEXINGTON AUTOMOTIVE 20630 Franklin Street, Santa Clara, CA 95052-6021

NO. **681**

NAME _Peter Johansen_
ADDRESS _3648 Sunlite Drive_
Santa Clara, CA 95050-1011

YEAR	MAKE	LICENSE NO.	MILEAGE	DATE
2000	Toyota	3NJR 556	6,328	6/12/--

DESCRIPTION	PARTS		LABOR	
Replace thermostat	14	89	24	80
Rotate tires			15	90
Change oil	10	00	19	95
TOTALS	24	89	60	65
PARTS FORWARD			24	89
SUBTOTAL			85	54
SALES TAX — 8.25% (ON PARTS ONLY)			2	05
TOTAL BILL			87	59

STEP 1   STEP 2

BUILDING YOUR BUSINESS VOCABULARY

On a sheet of paper, write the headings **Statement Number** and **Words**. Next, choose the words that match the statements. Write each word you choose next to the statement number it matches. Be careful; not all the words listed should be used.

Statements

1. A store owner who sells directly to the consumer
2. A sales slip
3. A total on which other calculations will be made
4. A percentage of the selling price collected by retailers for state or local governments
5. Quantity times unit price
6. A mechanical device used to record a sale

Words

bill
extension
merchandise
retailer
sales slip register
sales tax
subtotal
unit price

STEPS REVIEW: Computing Sales Taxes on Goods and Services

STEP **1** Compute the sales tax.

STEP **2** Add the sales tax to the amount of the sale.

APPLICATION PROBLEMS

Problem **37-1**   You work for a store in a state with a 6% sales tax. The tax is charged on both goods and services. On the following page is a chart to help you find the tax.

Directions

Complete the table shown below by finding the subtotal, sales tax, and final total for each sale. Use the 6% sales tax chart to find the sales tax.

6% SALES TAX CHART	
Sale	**Tax**
$ .01 – $ .08	No tax
.09 – .24	$ .01
.25 – .41	.02
.42 – .58	.03
.59 – .74	.04
.75 – .91	.05
.92 – 1.00	.06

On a sale over $1.00, take $ .06 for each full dollar plus the tax given in the chart above for the amount over an even dollar.

Bill No.	Labor		Parts		Total Labor and Parts (Subtotal)		Sales Tax		FINAL TOTAL	
Example	20	00	6	20	26	20	1	57	27	77
1	6	30	32	10						
2	58	79	6	89						
3	103	42	46	70						
4	212	36	83	45						
5	421	71	108	38						

Problem 37-2

You work in the cashier's office of Gibraltar Auto Repair, in Poughkeepsie, New York. As part of your job, you complete bills for auto repairs. The sales tax is 7%. The sales tax is charged for both goods and services.

CHECK POINT

37-2

Bill #1
Total = $215.82

Directions

Copy and complete the four bills below and on the next page. Find the sales tax by multiplying the total sale by 7%.

Bill #1

GIBRALTAR AUTO REPAIR
1701 Main Street
Poughkeepsie, NY 12601-7280

NO. **00201**
NAME _Yoshihiro Ihara_
ADDRESS _470 Innis Avenue_
Poughkeepsie, NY 12603-1560

YEAR	MAKE	LICENSE NO.	MILEAGE	DATE
1999	Dodge Viper	O5R-736	20,752	10/21/--

DESCRIPTION	PARTS		LABOR	
20,000 mile checkup			70	00
Replace front brake pads	40	95	90	75
TOTALS				
PARTS FORWARD				
SUBTOTAL				
SALES TAX — 7%				
TOTAL BILL				

Bill #2

GIBRALTAR AUTO REPAIR
1701 Main Street
Poughkeepsie, NY 12601-7280

NO. **00202**
NAME _Christine Campoy_
ADDRESS _27086 Gifford Avenue_
Poughkeepsie, NY 12601-2243

YEAR	MAKE	LICENSE NO.	MILEAGE	DATE
1998	Chevrolet	MNX-824	41,260	10/21/--

DESCRIPTION	PARTS		LABOR	
Replace radiator hose	19	99	31	50
Repair air conditioner	62	39	76	00
TOTALS				
PARTS FORWARD				
SUBTOTAL				
SALES TAX — 7%				
TOTAL BILL				

Bill #3

GIBRALTAR AUTO REPAIR
1701 Main Street
Poughkeepsie, NY 12601-7280

NO. **00203**

NAME _Kevin McGuire_
ADDRESS _36805 Poplar Street_
Poughkeepsie, NY 12601-2032

YEAR	MAKE	LICENSE NO.	MILEAGE	DATE
2000	Saturn	NXL-829	12,311	10/21/--

DESCRIPTION	PARTS		LABOR	
Change oil and filter	16	90	19	00
Replace defective water pump	61	49	65	00
TOTALS				
PARTS FORWARD ⟶				
SUBTOTAL				
SALES TAX — 7%				
TOTAL BILL				

Bill #4

GIBRALTAR AUTO REPAIR
1701 Main Street
Poughkeepsie, NY 12601-7280

NO. **00204**

NAME _Erin Foglia_
ADDRESS _9847 Montgomery Street_
Poughkeepsie, NY 12601-3161

YEAR	MAKE	LICENSE NO.	MILEAGE	DATE
1968	Ford Mustang	AYE-741	147,211	10/21/--

DESCRIPTION	PARTS		LABOR	
Replace belts	41	66	52	50
Service transmission	29	00	46	00
TOTALS				
PARTS FORWARD ⟶				
SUBTOTAL				
SALES TAX — 7%				
TOTAL BILL				

Problem 37-3

You are an accounting clerk for Cheswick Small Engine and Appliance Repair in Naperville, Illinois. It is part of your job to complete the bills for appliance repairs. The sales tax that you must charge is 6.5% on parts only. No sales tax is charged on services.

Directions

Copy and complete the following four bills. Find the sales tax by multiplying the total sale of parts by 6.5%.

CHECK POINT

37-3

Bill #1
Total = $35.93

Bill #1

Cheswick Small Engine and Appliance Repair
3982 South Naper Blvd.
Naperville, IL 60565

NO. **7542**

NAME _Karen Hoffman_
APPLIANCE _Floor waxer/polisher_   ADDRESS _2136 N. Loomis St._
DATE _April 12,_ 20 _--_   _Naperville, IL 60563-5101_

DESCRIPTION	PARTS		LABOR	
Repair floor waxer/polisher			19	25
Replace wax container	10	50	5	50
TOTALS				
PARTS FORWARD ⟶				
SUBTOTAL				
SALES TAX — 6.5% (ON PARTS ONLY)				
TOTAL BILL				

Bill #2

Cheswick Small Engine and Appliance Repair
3982 South Naper Blvd.
Naperville, IL 60565

NO. **7543**

NAME _William Proteau_
APPLIANCE _Snow blower_   ADDRESS _4370 N. Mill Street_
DATE _April 12,_ 20 _--_   _Naperville, IL 60563-2148_

DESCRIPTION	PARTS		LABOR	
Replace rotor	16	29	20	55
Replace chain	18	98	7	00
TOTALS				
PARTS FORWARD ⟶				
SUBTOTAL				
SALES TAX — 6.5% (ON PARTS ONLY)				
TOTAL BILL				

Bill #3

Cheswick Small Engine and Appliance Repair
3982 South Naper Blvd.
Naperville, IL 60565

NO. **7544**

NAME _Selby McDade_
APPLIANCE _Log splitter_   ADDRESS _5081 Olympus Drive_
DATE _April 12,_ 20 _--_   _Naperville, IL 60565-3001_

DESCRIPTION	PARTS		LABOR	
Tune up	21	66	28	60
Replace wheel	8	79	6	95
TOTALS				
PARTS FORWARD ⟶				
SUBTOTAL				
SALES TAX — 6.5% (ON PARTS ONLY)				
TOTAL BILL				

Bill #4

Cheswick Small Engine and Appliance Repair
3982 South Naper Blvd.
Naperville, IL 60565

NO. **7545**

NAME _Eric Hicklin_
APPLIANCE _Chain saw_   ADDRESS _3791 Ogden Avenue_
DATE _April 12,_ 20 _--_   _Naperville, IL 60540-6843_

DESCRIPTION	PARTS		LABOR	
Replace blade	9	49	7	25
Clean fuel system	10	60	9	60
TOTALS				
PARTS FORWARD ⟶				
SUBTOTAL				
SALES TAX — 6.5% (ON PARTS ONLY)				
TOTAL BILL				

Spreadsheet

Job 38   HANDLING CHARGE SALES

applied math preview

Copy and complete these problems. Round your answers to the nearest cent.

1. $\$100.20 \times 0.10 =$
2. $\$200.40 \times 0.05 =$
3. $\$760.48 \times 0.075 =$
4. $\$393.36 \times 0.0725 =$
5. $\$82.00 \times 8\frac{1}{2}\% =$
6. $\$796.55 \times 1\% =$
7. $\$796.55 \times 10\% =$
8. $\$147.38 \times 8\frac{1}{4}\% =$

key terms preview

- Authorization number
- Bank credit cards
- Charge sales
- Credit card sales slip
- Credit card verification terminal
- Expiration date
- Triplicate
- Warning bulletin

goal

To learn how to handle charge sales in a retail business.

Tips

Credit cards authorize customers to buy on credit.

Key Terms

Charge sales. Sales on credit. Buy now, pay later.

Bank credit cards. Credit cards issued by banks.

For Your Information

Some stores will allow you to pay for your purchases with a debit card. Remember, however, if you use a debit card for a purchase, the amount is immediately deducted from your checking account.

➡ UNDERSTANDING THE JOB

You have already learned, as a customer, how to apply for credit and to verify your credit card statements. In this job, you will learn how to handle credit sales as a retail store clerk.

Many retail stores, such as department stores, encourage their customers to buy on credit; that is, to buy now and pay later. Retailers call these sales **charge sales**.

You have already learned that large department stores may issue their own credit cards. The customer's name and charge account number are usually embossed in OCR on the card. There is also a space, usually on the back of the card, for the customer's signature.

The sales clerk must always compare the signature on the card with the customer's signature on the sales slip. This is to make sure that someone is not unlawfully using someone else's credit card and forging the signature.

Stores that issue their own credit cards must keep careful records of how much each customer owes and bill them accordingly. Customers who use a store credit card send their payments directly to the store.

Many stores also accept **bank credit cards**, such as VISA or MasterCard. When a customer charges sales using a bank credit card, copies of the sales slips are sent to the bank that issued the card. The bank pays the store the amount owed by the customer less a fee for the bank's service. The bank then sends a monthly statement to the charge customer. The customer sends payments for the amount due directly to the bank that issued the card.

Store Credit Cards

You are a sales associate in the children's apparel department of Shop Fair Department Store. A customer, Jessica Vargas, is purchasing a pair of infant pajamas. When you ask, "Cash or charge?" Jessica says, "Charge," and gives you a Shop Fair credit card shown in Illustration 38A.

Illustration 38A

Store credit card

Here are the steps you take to complete the sale:

STEP 1 Imprint the sales slip.

You place the credit card and a blank sales slip into an imprinter. All the letters and numbers on the card are transferred or *imprinted* onto the sales slip. Some stores pass the credit card through a special credit card terminal instead of an imprinter. This special terminal reads customer information from a magnetic strip on the back of the credit card. If the credit card terminal is connected to a computer, a POS terminal will print the customer name and account number on a sales slip.

STEP 2 Complete the sales slip.

You complete the sales slip as you learned to do in Jobs 35 and 36. However, for charge sales, you place a check mark in the box for charge sales and ask the customer to sign the sales slip.

Illustration 38B shows how the completed sales slip looks after Jessica Vargas signs it. Jessica's name and account number (A-724-6118) are imprinted from her charge card.

If a computer were used, a POS terminal would print out a sales slip for the charge sale like the one shown in Illustration 38C.

STEP 3 Verify the customer's signature.

You must verify the customer's signature by comparing the signature on the sales slip to the signature on the credit card. If the signatures are different, give the card to your supervisor who will handle the problem.

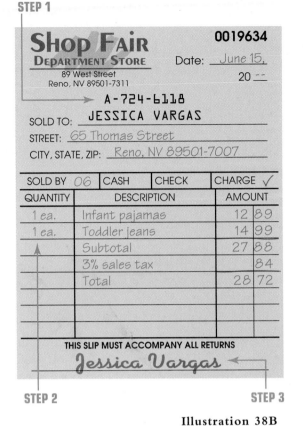

STEP 1

Shop Fair
DEPARTMENT STORE
89 West Street
Reno, NV 89501-7311

0019634

Date: June 15,
20 --

A-724-6118

SOLD TO: JESSICA VARGAS

STREET: 65 Thomas Street

CITY, STATE, ZIP: Reno, NV 89501-7007

SOLD BY 06	CASH	CHECK		CHARGE ✓	
QUANTITY	DESCRIPTION			AMOUNT	
1 ea.	Infant pajamas			12	89
1 ea.	Toddler jeans			14	99
	Subtotal			27	88
	3% sales tax				84
	Total			28	72

THIS SLIP MUST ACCOMPANY ALL RETURNS

Jessica Vargas

STEP 2   STEP 3

Illustration 38B
Sales slip for charge sale

STEP 1   STEP 3

Shop Fair
DEPARTMENT STORE
89 West Street
Reno, NV 89501-7311

C H A R G E T O	A-724-6118 JESSICA VARGAS
	PURCHASER'S SIGNATURE X *Jessica Vargas*

TYPE OF SALE	SALES PERSON	STORE LOC.	TERM	TRANS
CHARGE	000006	07 019	00347	10892
	DATE 06/15/--		TIME	06:45 PM

DEPT.		DESCRIPTION	QTY.	AMOUNT	
9/3	30799	INFANT MDSE.	1	12.89	C U S T O M E R C O P Y
9/3	30720	TODDLER MDSE.	1	14.99	
		SUBTOTAL		27.88	
		3.00 TAX		.84	
		TOTAL CHARGE		28.72	

AUTH. SIG AND NO. 3392	CR. AUTH.	$28.72

STEP 2

Illustration 38C
Sales slip printed by POS terminal

You find that the signatures for Jessica Vargas match, so you give her a copy of the sales slip and return her credit card. The store's copy of the sales slip will be used by the bookkeeping department to keep a record of the amount due.

→ SAMPLE PROBLEM 2

Bank Credit Cards

You are a sales clerk at Daley Furniture Mart. Nick Barrett, a customer, is purchasing a sofa, Stock Number 5721, for $1,200.00. When you ask how he wants to pay for the sofa, he says, "By credit card," and gives you the bank credit card shown in Illustration 38D.

Illustration 38D
A bank credit card

Lakota
STATE BANK

VISA

7417 4611 8263 8809

1167

VALID FROM ► 06/99   GOOD THRU ► 06/03

NICK BARRETT

STEP 1

Here are the steps you take to complete the sale:

STEP 1 Check the expiration date.

Check the last day on which the card can be used. This is called the **expiration date**. Nick's card shows "GOOD THRU 06/03," which means that the card may be used up to the last day in June of 2003.

STEP 2 Check for lost or stolen cards.

A list of lost or stolen card numbers is printed in a booklet called a **warning bulletin**. You compare the numbers on Nick's card, 7417-4611-8263-8809, with the list of numbers in the warning bulletin and find that Nick's card number is not on the list. If you had found that the card was listed as lost or stolen, you would have given the card to your supervisor who would have handled the problem.

Expiration date. Last day card can be used.

Warning bulletin. List of lost or stolen bank credit cards.

Authorization number. Means customer's credit is good.

Credit card sales slip. Special slip used for credit card sales.

Triplicate. Three copies.

STEP 3 Obtain the authorization number.

If the amount of the sale is over a certain amount, usually $50.00, you must get authorization from the bank to charge the sale. You do this by telephoning a special number. If the customer's credit is good, you will be given an **authorization number** to record in the proper space on the sales slip. Nick's credit is good, so you are given authorization number 721156.

STEP 4 Imprint the bank credit card sales slip.

You use the imprinter to transfer Nick's name and bank credit card number and also the store's name and identification number to a special sales slip form used with bank credit cards. This special form is called a **credit card sales slip** and is prepared in **triplicate** (three copies):

Copy 1 is kept by the store owner.
Copy 2 is sent to the bank that issued the card.
Copy 3 is given to the customer.

STEP 5 Complete the credit card sales slip and verify the customer's signature.

After you fill in all the information on the sales slip, you ask the customer, Nick Barrett, to sign the slip. Illustration 38E shows how the completed

Illustration 38E
Completed bank credit card slip

STEP 1 Check expiration date.
STEP 2 Check warning bulletin.
STEP 3
STEP 5

STEP 4

Credit card verification terminal. Automatically checks credit card.

sales slip looks after Nick signs it. Notice that the VISA symbol was circled to show that a VISA card was used.

You then compare Nick's signature with the signature on the back of his bank credit card. If the signatures match, you give Nick the copy of the sales slip marked "customer copy" and return his card to him. If the signatures do not match, you would turn the problem over to your supervisor.

So, the sales clerk must check the customer's bank credit card for

1. The expiration date.
2. Whether or not the card is lost or stolen.
3. Whether or not the customer's credit is good.

This checking takes time and keeps the customer waiting. To speed up the checking of the credit card, many businesses use a special **credit card verification terminal** that does this automatically. This special terminal is hooked up by telephone to a computer at the bank.

Some credit card verification terminals allow the sales clerk to insert the credit card into the terminal. Others require the sales clerk to key in the customer's card number. The terminal then automatically checks the customer's card number. If everything is all right, the terminal displays an authorization number for the sales clerk to use. If there is a problem with the card, the computer will display the reason for the problem on the screen.

BUILDING YOUR BUSINESS VOCABULARY

On a sheet of paper, write the headings **Statement Number** and **Words**. Next, choose the words that match the statements. Write each word you choose next to the statement number it matches. Be careful; not all the words listed should be used.

Statements	Words
1. A machine that transfers data from a credit card to a sales slip	authorization number
2. Means customer's credit is good	bank credit cards
3. Credit cards issued by banks	bill
4. Credit sales	charge sales
5. The last day on which a credit card can be used	credit card sales slip
6. A total on which other calculations will be made	credit card verification terminal
7. A special form used with credit card sales	expiration date
8. A list of lost and stolen bank credit cards	imprinter
9. Automatically checks credit cards	subtotal
10. Three copies	triplicate
	warning bulletin

STEPS REVIEW: Handling Charge Sales on Bank Credit Cards

STEP 1 Check the expiration date.

STEP 2 Check for lost or stolen cards.

STEP 3 Obtain the authorization number.

STEP 4 Imprint the bank credit card sales slip.

STEP 5 Complete the credit card sales slip and verify the customer's signature.

Problem 38-1

You are a sales clerk for Beck's Automotive, 99 Statler St., Tacoma, WA 98409–2298. Your sales clerk number is 43.

CHECK POINT

38-1

Sale #1
Total = $27.18

Directions

a. Complete sales slips for the following four charge sales made on November 15. Each customer used a Beck's store credit card. The customer's name and credit card number are imprinted on the sales slip from the credit card. All other information must be filled in manually. Fill in all data except the customer's signature. Find the sales tax by multiplying the amount of the sale by 6.5%.

Sale #1	Sale #2
Address 150 Breckenridge St. Tacoma, WA 98466-4847	Address 860 Hosmer Street Tacoma, WA 98405-6712
Items sold 2 pr. Wiper blades @ $8.29 6 qt. Motor oil @ $1.49	Items sold 4 ea. Wheel rim @ $165.00 4 ea. Tire stem @ $1.50
Sale #3	**Sale #4**
Address 63 Morgan Lane Tacoma, WA 98404-5621	Address 642 York Avenue Tacoma, WA 98466-0891
Items sold 1 dz. 15 amp fuse @ $11.88 2 ea. Gas treatment @ $1.89 1 ea. Floor mat set @ $36.99	Items sold 2 ea. Replacement lamp @ $2.61 1 ea. Battery @ $65.50 2 dz. Chrome nuts @ $21.49

b. Answer this question: After completing the sales slip and obtaining the customer's signature, what should you do?

Problem 38-2

You are a sales clerk for the GolfPro Store of Morgan Hill, California. GolfPro accepts MasterCard or VISA for charge sales. However, you must get an authorization number for all charge sales over $50.00. Your sales clerk number is 009, and you work in department number 3.

CHECK POINT

38-2

Total = $617.95

Directions

Complete credit card sales slips for the following four charge sales made on May 1. Each customer used a VISA card. The customer's name and credit card number, the invoice number, and the store name and identification number are imprinted on the sales slip from the credit card and the imprinter. All other information must be filled in manually. Fill in all data except the customer's signature. Find the sales tax by multiplying the amount of the sale by 8.25%.

Sale #1

Items sold	3 dz. Spin 90 balls
	@ $26.95
	(#590X11)
	1 ea. Titanium driver
	@ $490.00
	(#TD 810)

Authorization No.   311658

Card used   VISA

Sale #2

Items sold	1 ea. Travel cover
	@ $79.95
	(TC 17995)
	1 ea. Ripstop golf bag
	@ $160.90
	(GB 1690)

Authorization No.   000637

Card used   VISA

Sale #3

Items sold	3 packages Pro Wrap
	@ $9.95
	(PW 95)
	1 ea. Hitting net
	@ $99.99
	(H 99)

Authorization No.   312764

Card used   VISA

Sale #4

Items sold	1 pair Golf shoes
	@ $89.95
	(F 70077)

Authorization No.   203611

Card used   VISA

applied math preview

Copy and complete these problems. Round your answers to the nearest cent.

1. $350.00 × 0.01 =
2. $272.00 × 0.10 =
3. $463.51 × 0.0325 =
4. $170.68 × 0.065 =
5. $918.44 × 1% =
6. $918.44 × 10% =
7. $630.09 × 6½% =
8. $ 24.83 × 7¼% =

key terms preview

- **Credit slip**

goal

To learn how to complete a credit slip.

→ UNDERSTANDING THE JOB

Key Terms

Credit slip. Gives customer credit for return.

If a customer pays cash for merchandise and later decides to return it, the store will usually give the customer the money back. If the customer used a bank charge card to buy the goods, returning merchandise is not quite so simple.

When a customer buys goods using a bank credit card, the customer does not pay the store cash. Instead, the customer is billed for the purchase by the credit card company. When the customer returns goods, the store usually will not give the customer cash back. Instead, it will give the customer a **credit slip** like the one shown in Illustration 39A.

The form is called a credit slip because the customer will receive credit for the return on the customer's next credit card statement. That means that

Illustration 39A

A bank credit card credit slip

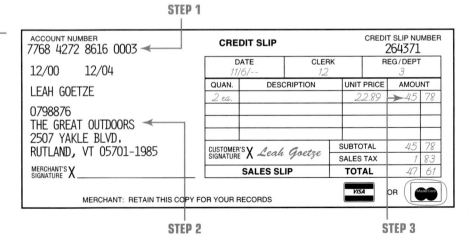

GREAT EASTERN BANK

Transaction Date	Reference	Transaction Description		New Loans, Fees, & Purchases	Payments & Credits
11/02/--	07139827	Summit Ski Lodge	Rutland, VT	35.89	
11/03/--	82647362	Boulevard Motors	Rutland, VT	138.95	
11/04/--	15243416	Payment -- Thank You			103.44
11/06/--	60798986	The Great Outdoors	Rutland, VT		47.61
11/11/--	10183928	Fifth Street Station	Rutland, VT	18.86	
11/17/--	38563847	Cleremont TV	Rutland, VT	19.76	

Illustration 39B

Section of credit card statement showing credit

it will be recorded in the Payments and Credits column of the statement and reduce the balance owed. (See Illustration 39B.)

Completing a credit slip for returned merchandise is very much like completing a credit card sales slip for a sale of merchandise. The Sample Problem will show you how.

 SAMPLE PROBLEM

James Merlino is a sales associate at The Great Outdoors. Leah Goetze purchased merchandise from the shop two days ago and wants to return two of the items today. Here are the steps James followed to handle the return:

STEP 1 Check the sales slip.

James asked for Leah's copy of the credit card sales slip, which was prepared when Leah purchased the merchandise. James also asked for Leah's MasterCard credit card. James verified that the customer name and account number shown on the sales slip were the same as those shown on the card. James also verified that the goods that Leah wanted to return were listed on the sales slip.

STEP 2 Imprint the credit slip.

James used the imprinter to transfer Leah's name, account number, and the store's name and identification number to the credit slip. Like the credit card sales slip, the credit slip is prepared in triplicate. Copy 1 is given to the customer. Copy 2 is sent to the bank that issued the card. Copy 3 is kept by the store.

STEP 3 Complete the credit slip.

James filled in the information on the credit slip and asked Leah to sign it. The completed credit slip is shown in Illustration 39A on page 306. Notice that James figured the extension for the items returned and also

calculated the sales tax. Since the customer had been charged for the item plus the sales tax, the total amount deducted from the customer's account must include both the amount of the return and the sales tax. Notice also that the MasterCard symbol at the bottom right of the form was circled.

James compared the signature on the credit slip to the signature on Leah's card. Since the signatures matched, he gave Leah the copy of the credit slip marked "customer copy" and returned her card. If the signatures had not matched, James would have turned the problem over to his supervisor.

Some stores require that sales clerks fill out one or more additional forms for each return of merchandise. These forms usually require that the sales clerk find out why the goods were returned. This information helps the store owner decide what merchandise to buy and where to buy it in the future.

→ BUILDING YOUR BUSINESS VOCABULARY

On a sheet of paper, write the headings **Statement Number** and **Words**. Next, choose the words that match the statements. Write each word you choose next to the statement number it matches. Be careful; not all the words listed should be used.

Statements	Words
1. Credit cards issued by banks	bank credit cards
2. A form used to return merchandise bought with a bank credit card	bill
	charge sales
3. A machine that transfers data from a credit card to a sales slip	credit card sales slip
4. A total on which other calculations will be made	credit card verification terminal
	credit slip
5. A special form used with credit card sales	expiration date
6. Automatically checks credit cards	imprinter
7. The last day on which a credit card can be used	subtotal
	triplicate
8. Three copies	warning bulletin
9. Credit sales	
10. A list of lost and stolen bank credit cards	

STEPS REVIEW: Making Refunds on Charge Card Sales

STEP 1 Check the sales slip.

STEP 2 Imprint the credit slip.

STEP 3 Complete the credit slip.

Problem 39-1   Debbie Cole is a sales clerk for Edison Electric, Inc., of Edison, New Jersey. Her sales clerk number is 5, and she works at register no. 2.

Directions

Complete credit slips for the following four VISA charge sale returns made on July 7 for Debbie. The customer's name and credit card number are already imprinted on the credit slip from the credit card. All other information must be filled in manually. Fill in all data except the customer's signature. Sign Debbie's name in the blank for merchant's signature. Find the sales tax by multiplying the amount of the sale by 6%.

Return #1
Items returned   2 ea. Extension cord
                    @ $3.99

Return #2
Items returned   6 ea. Frost bulbs
                    @ $1.29

Return #3
Items returned   2 dz. Switch plates
                    @ $11.49

Return #4
Items returned   1 ea. Light fixture
                    @ $57.00

Problem 39-2   Loren Nisaki is a sales clerk for Bayside Gift Shop. The shop is located in Friday Harbor, Washington. Her sales clerk number is 4, and she works at register no. 1.

Directions

Complete credit slips for the following four MasterCard charge sale returns made on June 22 for Loren. The customer's name and credit card number are already imprinted on the credit slip from the credit card. All other information must be filled in manually. Fill in all data except the customer's signature. Sign Loren's name in the blank for merchant's signature. Find the sales tax by multiplying the amount of the sale by 6.5%.

Return #1
Items returned   1 ea. Music box
                    @17.50

Return #2
Items returned   1 ea. Carved figurine
                    @ $39.89

Return #3
Items returned   2 ea. Woven baskets
                    @11.99

Return #4
Items returned   2 ea. Ceramic pots
                    @ $15.49

Chapter 7

CHECK YOUR READING

1. List at least three different options for preparing sales slips. Hint: One is manual, one is mechanical, and two are electronic.
2. What are the advantages of connecting a company's POS terminals to a central computer?
3. a. What is the percent of sales tax charged in your community?
   b. If a local sales tax is added to your state's sales tax, what is the local sales tax rate and what is it used for?
   c. Does your community charge sales tax on both retail goods and services?
4. What is the difference between a store credit card and a bank credit card? Provide several examples of each.

DISCUSSION

Retailers do not usually receive the full amount of each sale made using a bank credit card. The bank credit card company keeps a small percentage of the total sale as a fee for its services. This fee may be as much as 5% of the total amount of the sale.

Suppose that a customer purchased a $700.00 mountain bike using a bank credit card and the credit card company charged a 5% fee. Suppose also that the sales clerk must verify the customer's available credit for all sales over $50.00.

1. How much would the store owner receive from the sale?
2. How much would the customer have to pay the credit card company for the lamp?
3. Since the credit card company charges a fee, why do you think a store would let customers use a bank credit card?
4. Why do you think sales clerks are required to check the customer's credit only on sales over $50.00? Why are they not required to check the customer's credit on all sales?

CRITICAL THINKING

You are a manager of a store that accepts bank credit cards. The store is in a city that has an 8% sales tax. The store requires that sales clerks get an authorization number for all sales over $50.00.

An angry customer shows you the credit card sales slip shown on page 311. The slip shows that the customer had just bought two items from the store using his VISA card. After leaving the store, the customer noticed that the slip had not been completed correctly.

REINFORCEMENT ACTIVITIES

The sales clerk who completed the slip is on lunch break. There are three errors on the sales slip. What are they? What would you say to the customer?

ACCOUNT NUMBER		SALE AMOUNT		INVOICE NUMBER
4205 6271 8800 9109		00068.52		179322

DATE	AUTHORIZATION NO.	SALES CLERK	DEPT.
5/9/--		D1	2

3/00   3/04

DAN MORGAN

0191228
VALLEY PET STORE
324 JANWAY DRIVE
EL PASO, TX 79925-1922

QUAN.	DESCRIPTION	PRICE	AMOUNT
2 ea.	Leashes	4.98	9 96
2 ea.	Cat shelters	24.89	49 78

SIGN HERE X *Dan Morgan*

SUBTOTAL	59 74
SALES TAX	4 78
SALES SLIP TOTAL	68 52

VISA OR MasterCard

MERCHANT COPY

MERCHANT: RETAIN THIS COPY FOR YOUR RECORDS

COMMUNICATION IN THE WORKPLACE

If you were the manager of the store in the Critical Thinking Activity, what would you say to the sales clerk when the sales clerk returns from lunch?

FOCUS ON CAREERS

People who complete sales slips may work in many different types of stores. They may also work in many different types of departments within a business and have many different job titles.
For example:

1. A person who sells goods over the counter at a department store completes sales slips and may be called a *salesclerk* or sales associate.
2. A person who sells goods to customers by visiting the customer's home or business may complete sales slips and be called a *field representative*.
3. A person who sells goods to customers who order the goods by telephone may complete sales slips and be called an *order entry clerk*.
4. A person at a cash register in a restaurant may complete bank credit card sales slips for customers who pay for their meals by bank credit cards. This person may be called a *cashier*.
5. A person who sells computer equipment for a dealer may complete sales slips and be called a *customer service representative*.

On a separate sheet of paper, write these two headings: (1) Business or Place and (2) Job Description. Then choose five jobs that you know about in which workers complete sales slips. For each job, list the name of the business where the job is found, and describe each job by listing some of the duties of the worker in the job.

REVIEWING WHAT YOU HAVE LEARNED

On a sheet of paper, write the headings **Statement Number** and **Words**. Next, choose the words that best complete the statements. Write each word you choose next to the statement number it completes. Be careful; not all the words listed should be used.

Statements	Words
1. Most stores require the customer to present (a, an) _____ in order to return or exchange merchandise.	authorization number
	customer
	extension
2. The original of the sales slip should be given to the _____.	retailer
3. For credit card sales over a certain amount, sales clerks must get (a, an) _____.	sales slip
	sales tax
4. In some states, sales taxes are charged on both goods and _____.	services
	wand
5. Sales clerks usually check a customer's credit card by looking up the card number in (a, an) _____.	warning bulletin
6. A device which is attached to a POS terminal by a cable and reads bar codes is called (a, an) _____.	
7. Sales clerks multiply the unit price by the quantity to find the _____.	

MASTERY PROBLEM

You are a sales clerk for Harte's Arts and Crafts Store in Charleston, West Virginia. Your sales clerk number is 03 and your register number is 5. On April 2, 20--, you handle the following sales and returns. Use a sales tax rate of 5% on all goods.

Sales Slip #1

Type of sale: Cash

Customer name: Gerald Leavitt

Address: 56-24 Visitor Street

Charleston, WV 25302-7892

Items sold: 2 dz. Votive candles @ $6.98

1 ea. Glue gun @ $24.99

Return #1

Type of return: VISA

Items returned: 1 ea. Ceramic vase @ $11.55

1 ea. 8"x10" Photo frame @ 8.99

Sales Slip #2

Type of sale: VISA

Items sold: 3 ea. Eucalyptus bunches @ $4.99

2 Packages dried flowers @ $3.98

CHECK POINT

(a) Sales Slip (#1) Total = $40.90

Directions

a. Complete a sales slip for each sale. If a customer uses a bank credit card, the following information is imprinted on the sales slip from the credit card and the imprinter: the customer's name and credit card number, the invoice number, and the store name and identification number. All other information must be filled in manually. Fill in all data except the customer's signature.

b. Complete a credit slip for the VISA charge sale return. The customer's name and credit card number, the credit slip number, and the store name and identification number are imprinted on the credit slip from the credit card and the imprinter. All other information must be filled in manually. Fill in all data except the customer's signature. Sign your name in the blank for merchant's signature.

REVIEWING YOUR BUSINESS VOCABULARY

This activity may be found in the Working Papers.

Chapter 8

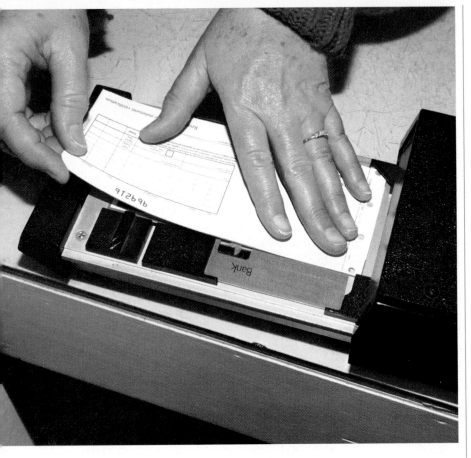

Record Keeping for Retail Charge Sales

Stores that sell on credit must keep careful records to know how much each charge customer owes. Stores do this by keeping a separate record for each customer showing the customer's purchases, payments, and returns. In addition, retailers usually send each charge customer a monthly statement showing all the transactions recorded in the customer's account during the month and requesting a payment.

In Chapter 8, you will learn how to keep records for charge customers. You will learn how to record purchases, payments, and returns. You will also learn how to prepare customer statements. A Calculator Tip will be given for finding running balances in customer accounts.

Notebook Computers

Many sales people sell their products to customers at the customer's place of business. Sales people call on the customer, show the customer their products, and take the customer's order. Obviously, they can't take along a cash register to record the sale. But, they can bring along a notebook computer, like the one shown here, which they can use to record the sale.

Notebook Computer

You learned about modems in Chapter 6. At the customer's store or factory, the salesperson can use the notebook computer's modem to connect to the main computer back at the salesperson's office. The salesperson can then record the sale immediately just as if the salesperson was back in the office.

key terms preview

- Account balance
- Accounts receivable account
- Accounts receivable clerk
- Credit
- Debit
- Payment on account
- Running balance
- Three-column account

goal

To learn how to keep records for charge customers.

UNDERSTANDING THE JOB

Accounts receivable account. A record of a charge customer's purchases and payments.

Accounts receivable clerk. An employee who keeps records for charge customers.

Three-column account. An account that has debit, credit, and balance columns.

Debit. An increase in a customer account.

Credit. A decrease in a customer account.

Account balance. Amount owed by customer.

Running balance. Balance found after each entry.

The record that stores keep of a customer's purchases and payments is called an account. For charge customers, these records are called **accounts receivable accounts**. The word *receivable* is used to show that the amounts due from customers are to be *received*.

If you are employed to help keep records for charge customers, you may be called an **accounts receivable clerk**. You may keep accounts receivable records manually or with a computer. Regardless of the way you keep the records, the same concepts of recording are used. You will learn these concepts in this job.

One form of account used by many businesses to keep track of charge customers is the **three-column account**. This type of account has three amount or money columns: a Debit column, a Credit column, and a Balance column. A three-column account is shown in Illustration 40A. Notice that special columns are provided for the date, item, and amounts.

Charge sales, or increases in a customer account, are recorded in the **Debit** column. Payments from customers, or decreases in a customer account, are recorded in the **Credit** column.

The advantage of the three-column account is that it has a special column for the **account balance**, or the amount owed by the customer. Each time a debit is recorded, it is added to the balance. Each time a credit is recorded, it is subtracted from the balance. As a result, the account always shows an up-to-date balance. This is called a **running balance**.

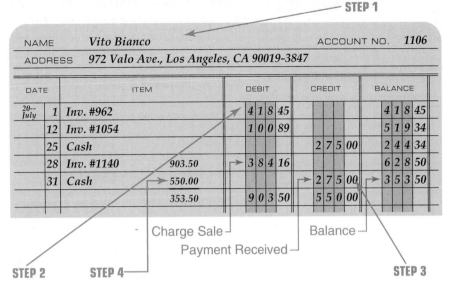

Tips

- Add debits.
- Subtract credits.
- Inv. = Invoice

Computers are often used to process customer accounts. If a computer were used to keep accounts, Vito Bianco's account might look like the display screen shown in Illustration 40B.

Illustration 40B

Customer account on a display screen

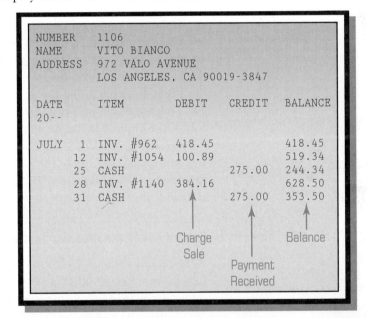

SAMPLE PROBLEM

Rose Jung is an accounts receivable clerk for King's Department Store. On July 1, the store opened a charge account for Vito Bianco. The following charge sales and payments were made by Vito during July:

Payment on account. Part payment.

July 1 Sold merchandise on credit to Vito Bianco for $418.45; invoice no. 962.
     12 Sold merchandise on credit to Vito Bianco for $100.89; invoice no. 1054.
     25 Received a check from Vito Bianco for $275.00 in **payment on account**.
     28 Sold merchandise on credit to Vito Bianco for $384.16; invoice no. 1140.
     31 Received a check from Vito Bianco for $275.00 in payment on account.

Illustration 40A (page 317) shows how Rose recorded these facts in Vito Bianco's account. Here are the steps Rose followed:

STEP 1 Record the account heading.

Rose opened the account by recording the customer's name, address, and account number at the top of the account form.

STEP 2 Record charge sales in the Debit column.

Rose entered the date in the Date column. Since the charge sale on July 1 was the first transaction in the account, she recorded the year (20--), month (July), and day (1). Rose will not record the year or month in that account again until the year or month changes or she goes on to a new page.

Rose also recorded the number of the invoice (962) in the Item column to show that merchandise was sold. She recorded the number of the invoice in the account so that if any one questioned the transaction, she could refer back to the original invoice.

Next, Rose recorded the amount of the charge sale ($418.45) in the *Debit column* of the account. Since there was no balance in the account on July 1, she entered the same amount into the Balance column.

When Rose recorded the charge sale on July 12, however, she *added* the amount ($100.89) to the old balance in the account ($418.45) and recorded the new balance ($519.34) in the Balance column. Rose recorded the other charge sale in the same way.

Debits increase customer accounts.

STEP 3 Record payments received in the Credit column.

Rose recorded the day (25) in the Date column and amount of the first cash payment received ($275.00) in the *Credit column* of the account. She wrote the word *Cash* in the Item column to show that it was a cash receipt. She then *subtracted* the payment from the old balance ($519.34) and entered the new balance ($244.34) in the Balance column. Rose recorded each payment received in the same way.

Notice that every time Rose recorded an amount in the Debit or Credit column, she also entered the new balance the customer owed into the Balance column. Notice also that Rose always (1) added debits to the old balance and (2) subtracted credits from the old balance to find the new balance.

Credits decrease customer accounts.

STEP 4 Prove the balance.

At the end of the month, Rose checked the balance in the account to make sure that it was correct. She footed the Debit and Credit columns to get the totals for the month. Rose subtracted the total credits from the total debits.

Total debits − Total credits = Account balance

Total debits	$ 903.50
Less: Total credits	−550.00
Final balance	$ 353.50

Notice that Rose proved the balance in small figures in the Items column of Vito Bianco's account. If the total debits had been equal to the total credits, the account balance would have been zero. She would have written the zero balance in the Balance column as 0.00 or drawn a line through the Balance column as shown:

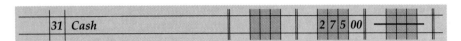

In that case, Rose would only have footed the Debit and Credit columns. She would not have written the totals in the Item column (as shown in Illustration 40A, page 317). Also, if there had been only one amount in a column, Rose would not have needed to foot that column.

Many record keepers use calculators to find the running balances in customer accounts. If Rose Jung used a calculator to find the running balances in Vito Bianco's account, here is how she would do it:

STEP 1 ▶ **Add the sale on account for July 1 to the sale on account for July 12.**

Press these keys in order:

[4][1][8][.][4][5][+][1][0][0][.][8][9][=]

The answer, 519.34, will appear in the display. This is the balance Rose would enter into the Balance column of the customer's account.

STEP 2 ▶ **Subtract the cash received on July 25.**

Without clearing the calculator, press these keys in order:

[−][2][7][5][.][0][0][=]

The balance for July 25, 244.34, will appear in the display.

STEP 3 ▶ **Add the amount sold on account on July 28.**

Without clearing the calculator, press these keys in order:

[+][3][8][4][.][1][6][=]

The balance for July 28, 628.50, will appear in the display.

STEP 4 ▶ **Subtract the cash received on July 31.**

Without clearing the calculator, press these keys in order:

[−][2][7][5][.][0][0][=]

The balance for July 31, 353.50, will appear in the display.

On a sheet of paper, write the headings **Statement Number** and **Words**. Next, choose the words that match the statements. Write each word you choose next to the statement number it matches. Be careful; not all the words listed should be used.

Statements	Words
1. Record of charge customer's purchases and payments	account balance
2. Total debits minus total credits	accounts receivable account
3. An increase in a customer account	accounts receivable clerk
4. A decrease in a customer account	authorization
5. Part payment of the amount due	credit
6. Has debit, credit, and balance columns	debit
7. The balance found after each entry is made	payment on account
8. An employee who keeps records for charge customers	running balance
	subtotal
	three-column account

STEPS REVIEW: Keeping Records for Charge Customers

STEP 1 Record the account heading.

STEP 2 Record charge sales in the Debit column.

STEP 3 Record payments received in the Credit column.

STEP 4 Prove the balance.

⇒ | **APPLICATION PROBLEMS**

Problem 40-1 You are an accounts receivable clerk for the Gingerbread Store. It is your job to keep the accounts for charge customers. The data for each customer shown was taken from copies of sales slips and from the record of payments received from the charge customers.

Directions

a. Open a three-column account for each charge customer listed by writing the customer's name, address, and account number at the top of an account form.

b. Record in each customer account the charge sales made and the payments received.

c. Find the new balance after each debit or credit is recorded.

d. At the end of the month, foot the Debit and Credit columns of each account. Prove the balance of each account by subtracting the total credits from the total debits. Write your proofs in the Item column of the accounts.

CHECK POINT
40-1 (1)

Balance = $153.45

Account #1   Customer's name   Calvin Cray
              Address   2150 Kane Street, Anchorage, AK 99501-3120
              Account number   1304

Feb.   2   Sold merchandise on credit to Calvin Cray for $268.50; invoice #271.
        8   Sold merchandise on credit to Calvin Cray for $106.20; invoice #342.
       18   Received a check from Calvin Cray for $250.00 in payment on account.
       26   Received a check from Calvin Cray for $100.00 in payment on account.
       27   Sold merchandise on credit to Calvin Cray for $128.75; invoice #556.

CHECK POINT
40-1 (2)

Balance = $134.74

Account #2   Customer's name   Leslie Herbst
              Address   5212 Lexow Street, Anchorage, AK 99503-1201
              Account number   1305

Feb.   3   Sold merchandise on credit to Leslie Herbst for $192.75; invoice #288.
        8   Sold merchandise on credit to Leslie Herbst for $216.90; invoice #351.
       21   Received a check from Leslie Herbst for $300.00 in payment on account.
       23   Sold merchandise on credit to Leslie Herbst for $325.09; invoice #537.
       28   Received a check from Leslie Herbst for $300.00 in payment on account.

Account #3   Customer's name   Luis Reos
              Address   249 Krone Street, Anchorage, AK 99502-7283
              Account number   1306

Feb.   5   Sold merchandise on credit to Luis Reos for $86.50; invoice #299.
       12   Sold merchandise on credit to Luis Reos for $263.80; invoice #375.
       18   Received a check from Luis Reos for $100.00 in payment on account.
       25   Sold merchandise on credit to Luis Reos for $112.75; invoice #549.
       28   Received a check from Luis Reos for $100.00 in payment on account.

Account #4   Customer's name   Lilly Frances
              Address   1625 Bellon Street, Anchorage, AK 99507-4605
              Account number   1307

Feb.   1   Sold merchandise on credit to Lilly Frances for $297.75; invoice #265.
        8   Received a check from Lilly Frances for $150.00 in payment on account.
       15   Sold merchandise on credit to Lilly Frances for $187.50; invoice #411.
       21   Received a check from Lilly Frances for $150.00 in payment on account.
       26   Sold merchandise on credit to Lilly Frances for $119.65; invoice #553.

Account #5   Customer's name   Irving Fleigle
              Address   25 Rane Boulevard, Anchorage, AK 99516-5975
              Account number   1308

Feb.   3   Sold merchandise on credit to Irving Fleigle for $606.15; invoice #291.
        9   Sold merchandise on credit to Irving Fleigle for $285.90; invoice #356.
       15   Received a check from Irving Fleigle for $600.00 in payment on account.
       24   Sold merchandise on credit to Irving Fleigle for $376.70; invoice #541.

Account #6   Customer's name   John O'Brien
                     Address   1101 Torre Street, Anchorage, AK 99504-6758
                     Account number   1309

Feb.	4	Sold merchandise on credit to John O'Brien for $175.60; invoice #298.
	6	Sold merchandise on credit to John O'Brien for $187.50; invoice #312.
	10	Sold merchandise on credit to John O'Brien for $196.25; invoice #362.
	24	Received a check from John O'Brien for $300.00 in payment on account.
	28	Received a check from John O'Brien for $100.00 in payment on account.

Account #7   Customer's name   Ivy Rustin
                     Address   16 Lakely Drive, Anchorage, AK 99502-2162
                     Account number   1310

Feb.	7	Sold merchandise on credit to Ivy Rustin for $145.90; invoice #315.
	9	Sold merchandise on credit to Ivy Rustin for $178.85; invoice #357.
	20	Received a check from Ivy Rustin for $175.00 in payment on account.
	22	Sold merchandise on credit to Ivy Rustin for $208.00; invoice #523.
	27	Received a check from Ivy Rustin for $357.75 as full payment of the amount due.

Account #8   Customer's name   Larry Todd
                     Address   316 Clar Avenue, Anchorage, AK 99502-7683
                     Account number   1311

Feb.	7	Sold merchandise on credit to Larry Todd for $115.85; invoice #318.
	12	Sold merchandise on credit to Larry Todd for $224.70; invoice #370.
	25	Received a check from Larry Todd for $200.00 in payment on account.
	26	Sold merchandise on credit to Larry Todd for $217.40; invoice #555.
	28	Received a check from Larry Todd for $250.00 in payment on account.

Problem 40-2 may be found in the Working Papers.

key terms preview

• **Credit memo**

goal

To learn how to record merchandise returned by charge customers.

→ UNDERSTANDING THE JOB

Key Terms

Credit memo. Shows that a charge customer has returned merchandise and owes less money.

Tips

CR = credit

You have learned that sales clerks give credit slips when customers return goods bought with bank credit cards. When customers buy with store credit cards or have accounts with a store, sales clerks usually give them a form called a credit memorandum or **credit memo**.

A credit memo is shown in Illustration 41A on page 324. A credit memo shows that the customer owes less money than before. The retailer will keep a copy of the credit memo so that the amount of the return can be recorded in the customer's account.

Many department stores that use point-of-sale (POS) terminals do not use special credit memorandum forms. Instead, the terminals print the credit to the customer account on a regular sales slip, like the one in Illustration 41B on page 324. The amount may be shown on the sales slip as a negative number with the letters *CR* printed beside it. The letters *CR* show that the amount is to be recorded in the Credit column of the customer account.

You have learned that you record a payment from a charge customer in the Credit column of the customer's account to show that the customer owes less. Since a return of merchandise also means that the customer owes less, it is also recorded in the Credit column.

CREDIT MEMO

BRIGG'S BEST STORES

831 Malow Street • Akron, OH 44319-2127

NO. **381**

CUSTOMER NAME *Rhoda Lewis*   ACCOUNT NO. *2153*

ADDRESS *1611 Wanda Avenue*
Akron, OH 44306-8249

CLERK NO. 21	REG. NO. 3	DATE 10/17/20--

We have credited your account as follows:

DESCRIPTION	UNIT PRICE	AMOUNT
2 pr. Jeans	29 99	59 98
4% Sales tax		2 40
Total credit		62 38

BRIGG'S BEST STORES

831 Malow Street • Akron, OH 44319-2127

CHARGE TO
2153
RHODA LEWIS

PURCHASER'S SIGNATURE   X *Rhoda Lewis*

TYPE OF SALE	SALES PERSON	STORE LOC.	TERM	TRANS
RETURN	021	016 17	00675	41029

DATE 10/17/20--   TIME 02:15 PM

DEPT.	DESCRIPTION	QTY.	AMOUNT
3	61135426 JEANS		
		2 29.99	59.98CR

SUBTOTAL   59.98CR
4.00 TAX   2.40CR
TOTAL CREDIT   62.38CR

CUSTOMER COPY

AUTH. SIG AND NO.	CR. AUTH. *R. Stewart*	-62.38CR

Remember: Charge sales are recorded in the Debit column, while cash received and merchandise returned are recorded in the Credit column. (See Illustration 41C.)

Tips

Record returns in the Credit column.

NAME					ACCOUNT NO.	
ADDRESS						
DATE	ITEM		DEBIT	CREDIT	BALANCE	

Charge sales are recorded in this column. Debits increase the balance of a customer's account.

Payments and returns are recorded in this column. Credits decrease the balance of a customer's account.

Cultural Notes

In the ancient Incan civilization in what is now Peru, South America, record keepers memorized business transactions and recited them when necessary. Using small ropes of different colors and sizes, the Incan record keepers tied knots and joined the ropes in different ways to help remember financial data. These ropes were called *quipu*.

Tips

Inv. = invoice

Tom Yount, a sales clerk at Brigg's Best Stores, opened a charge account for Rhoda Lewis. The following charge sales, returns, and payments were made during October:

Oct. 8   Sold merchandise on credit to Rhoda Lewis for $320.78; Inv. #281.
     11   Received a check from Rhoda Lewis for $100.00 in payment on account.
     17   Issued Credit Memo #381 to Rhoda Lewis for $62.38 for merchandise returned. (See Illustration 41A, page 324.)
     21   Sold merchandise on credit to Rhoda Lewis for $98.89; Inv. #493.

Illustration 41D shows how Tom recorded these transactions in the accounts receivable account for Rhoda Lewis.

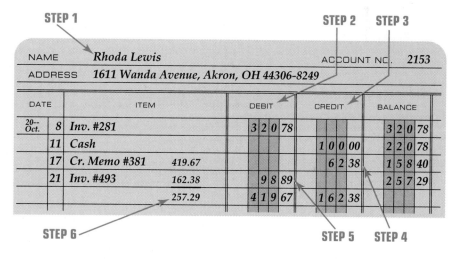

STEP 1   **STEP 2** **STEP 3**

| NAME | Rhoda Lewis | | ACCOUNT NO. | 2153 |
| ADDRESS | 1611 Wanda Avenue, Akron, OH 44306-8249 | | | |

DATE	ITEM		DEBIT	CREDIT	BALANCE
20-- Oct. 8	Inv. #281		3 2 0 78		3 2 0 78
11	Cash			1 0 0 00	2 2 0 78
17	Cr. Memo #381	419.67		6 2 38	1 5 8 40
21	Inv. #493	162.38	9 8 89		2 5 7 29
		257.29	4 1 9 67	1 6 2 38	

STEP 6   **STEP 5** **STEP 4**

Illustration 41D

Accounts receivable account

Here is how Tom did it:

STEP 1 **Record the account heading.**

Tom opened the account by recording Rhoda Lewis's name, address, and account number at the top of the account form.

STEP 2 **Record charge sales in the Debit column.**

Tom entered the date in the Date column. Since the charge sale on October 8 was the first transaction in the account, he recorded the year (20--), month (October), and day (8). Tom did not record the year or month in that account again during October since neither the year nor month changed and no new page was required.

Tom also recorded "Inv. #281" in the Item column to provide a reference to the original sales invoice. Were there to be any question about the charge sale later, the original invoice could be examined.

Tips

Charge sales are recorded in the debit column.

Next, Tom recorded the amount of the charge sale ($320.78) in the *Debit column* of the account. Since there was no balance in the account on October 8, he entered the same amount in the Balance column.

Subtract credits.

STEP 3 Record payments received in the Credit column.

Tom recorded the day (11) in the Date column and amount of the cash payment received ($100.00) in the *Credit column* of the account. He wrote the word *Cash* in the Item column to show that it was a cash receipt. He then *subtracted* the payment from the old balance ($320.78) and entered the new balance ($220.78) in the Balance column.

Payments and returns are recorded in the credit column.

STEP 4 Record the merchandise returned in the Credit column.

Tom recorded the day (17) in the Date column and amount of the return ($62.38) in the *Credit column* of the account. He wrote "Credit Memo #381" in the Item column to show that it was a return of merchandise and to provide a reference to the original credit memo in case there should be any question about the transaction later. He then *subtracted* the amount of the return from the old balance ($220.78) and entered the new balance ($158.40) in the Balance column.

STEP 5 Record the other charge sale.

Tom recorded the other charge sale made on October 21 in the Debit column. Since there was a balance this time ($158.40), he *added* the charge sale ($98.89) to that balance and entered the total ($257.29) in the Balance column.

Add debits.

STEP 6 Prove the balance.

At the end of the month, Tom checked the balance in the account to make sure that it was correct. He started with the opening balance at the beginning of the month. He then footed the Debit and Credit columns to get the totals for the month. Tom added the total debits to the opening balance and subtracted the total credits.

Opening balance	$ 0.00
Plus: Total debits	+419.67
Total	$ 419.67
Less: Total credits	−162.38
Final balance	$ 257.29

➡ BUILDING YOUR BUSINESS VOCABULARY

On a sheet of paper, write the headings **Statement Number** and **Words**. Next, choose the words that match the statements. Write each word you choose next to the statement number it matches. Be careful; not all the words listed should be used.

Statements	Words
1. The column used to record a charge sale in a customer account	account balance
	accounts receivable
2. The column used to record a payment or a return in a customer account	account
	credit
3. Part payment of the amount due	credit memo
4. Total debits minus total credits	debit
5. Record of charge customer's purchases and payments	payment on account
	running balance
6. A form that shows that a charge customer has returned merchandise and owes less money	sales returns
	subtotal
7. The balance found after each entry is made	

STEPS REVIEW: Handling Sales and Returns

STEP 1 Record the account heading.

STEP 2 Record charge sales in the Debit column.

STEP 3 Record payments received in the Credit column.

STEP 4 Record the merchandise returned in the Credit column.

STEP 5 Record the other charge sales.

STEP 6 Prove the balance.

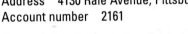

APPLICATION PROBLEMS

Problem 41-1   You are employed in the bookkeeping department of Lenora's department store. Your job is to keep the accounts for charge customers.

Spreadsheet

Directions
a. Open an account for each charge customer by writing the customer's name, address, and account number at the top of an account form.
b. Record in each customer's account the charge sales made, the payments received, and the merchandise returned.
c. Prove the balance of each account by footing the columns and subtracting the total credits from the total debits.

Account #1   Customer's name   Anne Rich
Address   4130 Rale Avenue, Pittsburgh, PA 15212-8346
Account number   2161

CHECK POINT

41-1 (1)

Balance = $81.30

August	1	Sold merchandise on credit to Anne Rich for $356.78; Inv. #301.
	3	Sold merchandise on credit to Anne Rich for $188.60; Inv. #378.
	9	Issued Credit Memo #21 to Anne Rich for $22.29 for merchandise returned.
	15	Received a check from Anne Rich for $300.00 in payment on account.
	21	Sold merchandise on credit to Anne Rich for $59.27; Inv. #709.
	28	Issued Credit Memo #41 to Anne Rich for $51.06 for merchandise returned.
	31	Received a check from Anne Rich for $150.00 in payment on account.

CHECK POINT

41-1 (2)

Balance = $183.97

Account #2   Customer's name   Rob Tate
Address   2162 Belser Street, Pittsburgh, PA 15214-1146
Account number   2162

August	2	Sold merchandise on credit to Rob Tate for $188.97; Inv. #362.
	5	Sold merchandise on credit to Rob Tate for $147.85; Inv. #417.
	7	Issued Credit Memo #17 to Rob Tate for $57.80 for merchandise returned.
	19	Received a check from Rob Tate for $175.00 in payment on account.
	23	Received a check from Rob Tate for $100.00 in payment on account.
	24	Sold merchandise on credit to Rob Tate for $209.16; Inv. #861.
	30	Issued Credit Memo #52 to Rob Tate for $29.21 for merchandise returned.

Account #3   Customer's name   Roger Simm
Address   1289 Reeder Avenue, Pittsburgh, PA 15221-6736
Account number   2163

August	3	Sold merchandise on credit to Roger Simm for $29.99; Inv. #391.
	5	Sold merchandise on credit to Roger Simm for $239.50; Inv. #421.
	8	Issued Credit Memo #19 to Roger Simm for $35.45 for merchandise returned.
	19	Received a check from Roger Simm for $150.00 in payment on account.
	23	Sold merchandise on credit to Roger Simm for $227.55; Inv. #808.
	27	Issued Credit Memo #39 to Roger Simm for $45.90 for merchandise returned.
	30	Received a check from Roger Simm for $175.00 in payment on account.

Account #4   Customer's name   Lavonda Keen
Address   12489 Rasche Blvd. Pittsburgh, PA 15236-7091
Account number   2164

August	5	Sold merchandise on credit to Lavonda Keen for $248.73; Inv. #436.
	7	Sold merchandise on credit to Lavonda Keen for $125.65; Inv. #503.
	19	Received a check from Lavonda Keen for $300.00 in payment on account.
	20	Sold merchandise on credit to Lavonda Keen for $75.66; Inv. #673.
	23	Issued Credit Memo #35 to Lavonda Keen for $28.25 for merchandise returned.
	29	Received a check from Lavonda Keen for $75.00 in payment on account.
	31	Sold merchandise on credit to Lavonda Keen for $228.50; Inv. #1107.

Account #5   Customer's name   Ian Reese
Address   8451 Falen Road, Pittsburgh, PA 15224-5582
Account number   2165

August	1	Sold merchandise on credit to Ian Reese for $89.89; Inv. #305.
	3	Sold merchandise on credit to Ian Reese for $47.88; Inv. #398.
	6	Issued Credit Memo #12 to Ian Reese for $8.30 for merchandise returned.
	17	Received a check from Ian Reese for $65.00 in payment on account.
	28	Received a check from Ian Reese for $50.00 in payment on account.
	29	Sold merchandise on credit to Ian Reese for $76.30; Inv. #1096.
	31	Issued Credit Memo #54 to Ian Reese for $12.76 for merchandise returned.

Account #6   Customer's name   Cora Banks
Address   8512 Mannel Street, Pittsburgh, PA 15221-8657
Account number   2166

August	6	Sold merchandise on credit to Cora Banks for $294.50; Inv. #482.
	9	Sold merchandise on credit to Cora Banks for $241.89; Inv. #532.
	12	Issued Credit Memo #26 to Cora Banks for $72.68 for merchandise returned.
	24	Received a check from Cora Banks for $245.00 in payment on account.
	25	Sold merchandise on credit to Cora Banks for $314.20; Inv. #883.
	28	Issued Credit Memo #40 to Cora Banks for $93.30 for merchandise returned.
	30	Sold merchandise on credit to Cora Banks for $61.15; Inv. #1099.

Account #7   Customer's name   Sonja Heidel
Address   9445 Toomas Ave., Pittsburgh, PA 15236-3428
Account number   2167

August	5	Sold merchandise on credit to Sonja Heidel for $151.67; Inv. #442.
	9	Issued Credit Memo #24 to Sonja Heidel for $18.90 for merchandise returned.
	12	Sold merchandise on credit to Sonja Heidel for $468.50; Inv. #617.
	22	Received a check from Sonja Heidel for $275.00 in payment on account.
	26	Received a check from Sonja Heidel for $300.00 in payment on account.
	28	Sold merchandise on credit to Sonja Heidel for $62.25; Inv. #1002.
	31	Issued Credit Memo #55 to Sonja Heidel for $16.29 for merchandise returned.

Account #8   Customer's name   Frank Bell
Address   3445 Seemac Road, Pittsburgh, PA 15241-9466
Account number   2168

August	2	Sold merchandise on credit to Frank Bell for $256.12; Inv. #363.
	4	Issued Credit Memo #6 to Frank Bell for $25.90 for merchandise returned.
	6	Sold merchandise on credit to Frank Bell for $310.88; Inv. #495.
	14	Issued Credit Memo #29 to Frank Bell for $132.70 for merchandise returned.
	19	Received a check from Frank Bell for $200.00 in payment on account.
	25	Sold merchandise on credit to Frank Bell for $225.50; Inv. #879.
	30	Sold merchandise on credit to Frank Bell for $72.42; Inv. #1103.

Problem 41-2 may be found in the Working Papers.

Job 42 PREPARING CUSTOMER STATEMENTS

key terms preview

- Billing clerks
- Customer statement
- Cycle billing
- Previous balance

goal

To learn how to prepare customer statements.

→ UNDERSTANDING THE JOB

Customer statement. A monthly report of customer transactions.

Cycle billing. Billing groups of customers at different times.

Billing clerks. Workers who prepare customer statements.

You have learned how to keep records of the amounts owed by charge customers in forms called accounts. Retailers usually send each charge customer a monthly report showing all the transactions recorded in the customer's account during the month. This report is called a **customer statement**, or simply a statement. The customer statement:

1. Allows customers to check their own records against the store's records.
2. Reminds customers of the amounts they owe.

Customer statements are usually prepared and mailed at the end of each month. However, stores with thousands of customers will spread out this work over the month. They divide their customers into groups, and prepare and mail a portion of the customer statements on different days of the month. For example, if your last name begins with the letter *A*, you might receive your customer statement at the beginning of the month. Customers with last names beginning with the letter *K* might receive customer statements in the middle of the month, and so forth. This method of preparing and mailing customer statements is called **cycle billing**.

Accounts receivable clerks may prepare the customer statements or bills. Or, specialized employees may prepare the customer statements. Employees who spend most of their time preparing customer statements are called **billing clerks**.

You are employed in the accounts receivable department of the Moreno Department Store. The store sends customer statements to each charge customer at the end of every month. Statements were sent to all charge customers at the end of June. It is now the end of July. You are asked to prepare a customer statement for July for Kim Garbe. The customer account is shown in Illustration 42A along with the statement you will prepare. Here is how you prepare the statement:

STEP 1 Record the statement heading.

Date the statement as of the last day of the month, July 31. Copy the customer's name, address, and account number from the account heading.

Illustration 42A

Customer account and customer statement

NAME *Kim Garbe* **ACCOUNT NO.** *2106*
ADDRESS *419 Secas Avenue, Miami, FL 33165-9337*

DATE		ITEM	DEBIT	CREDIT	BALANCE
20-- June	4	Inv. #1062	1 3 7 16		1 3 7 16
	14	Cash		1 0 0 00	3 7 16
July	5	Inv. #1131	1 0 8 99		1 4 6 15
	18	Credit Memo #417		1 8 89	1 2 7 26
	25	Cash		1 0 0 00	2 7 26
	31	Inv. #1723	1 6 8 19		1 9 5 45

STEP 1

Moreno DEPARTMENT STORE
5 Cade Street, Miami, Fl 33160-7823

CUSTOMER STATEMENT

TO: Kim Garbe   July 31,   20 - - -
419 Secas Avenue
Miami, FL 33165-9337   **ACCOUNT NO.** 2106

DATE		ITEM	DEBIT	CREDIT	BALANCE
20-- July	1	PREVIOUS BALANCE			37 16
	5	Inv. #1131	108 99		146 15
	18	Credit Memo #417		18 89	127 26
	25	Cash		100 00	27 26
	31	Inv. #1723	168 19		195 45

LAST AMOUNT IN THIS COLUMN IS THE BALANCE DUE

STEP 2   STEP 3

STEP 2 Record the date and previous balance.

Record the date, July 1, on the line for the **previous balance** on the customer statement.

Find the amount of the previous balance by looking at the last balance for June ($37.16) in the customer's account. Record this balance in the Balance column on the line for the previous balance. This was the ending account balance shown in the customer statement for June. This balance becomes the opening balance in the customer statement for July.

STEP 3 Copy the entries for the month.

After recording the opening balance of $37.16, copy all the entries in the account for July, starting with July 5. The last amount in the Balance column, $195.45, is the balance due at the end of July.

BUILDING YOUR BUSINESS VOCABULARY

On a sheet of paper, write the headings **Statement Number** and **Words**. Next, choose the words that match the statements. Write each word you choose next to the statement number it matches. Be careful; not all the words listed should be used.

Statements	Words
1. The balance of the account at the end of last month	billing clerks
2. The column used to record a charge sale in a customer account	credit
3. A monthly report listing all transactions in a customer account during the month	credit memo
4. A form which shows that a charge customer has returned merchandise and owes less money	customer statement
5. The column used to record a payment or a return in a customer account	cycle billing
6. Billing groups of customers at different times during the month	debit
7. The balance found after each entry is made	previous balance
8. Employees who spend most of their time preparing customer statements	running balance
	subtotal
	transaction

STEPS REVIEW: Preparing Customer Statements

STEP 1 Record the statement heading.

STEP 2 Record the date and previous balance.

STEP 3 Copy the entries for the month.

Problem **42-1** You work in the accounting department of Devoe's, a department store in Dayton, Ohio. Your job is to prepare customer statements for charge customers. Customer statements were sent to all charge customers at the end of March. It is now the end of April.

Directions

Prepare customer statements for April for the following customer accounts. Date all statements April 30. Remember to start each statement with the previous balance.

CHECK POINT

42-1 (1)

Balance due = $331.52

Account #1

NAME	Lisa Hays			ACCOUNT NO.	2617
ADDRESS	3023 Fairview Avenue, S., Dayton, OH 45405-9337				

DATE		ITEM	DEBIT	CREDIT	BALANCE
20-- March	4	Inv. #208	432 81		432 81
	14	Cash		380 00	52 81
April	8	Inv. #223	193 15		245 96
	18	Credit Memo #25		76 16	169 80
	25	Cash		50 00	119 80
	30	Inv. #231	211 72		331 52

Account #2

NAME	Martin Bobb			ACCOUNT NO.	2618
ADDRESS	16 Montro Street, N., Dayton, OH 45416-1377				

DATE		ITEM	DEBIT	CREDIT	BALANCE
20-- March	5	Inv. #211	65 61		65 61
	15	Cash		25 00	40 61
April	6	Inv. #217	213 41		254 02
	17	Credit Memo #23		32 07	221 95
	23	Cash		200 00	21 95
	27	Inv. #224	103 27		125 22

Account #3

NAME	John Meyer			ACCOUNT NO.	2619
ADDRESS	12106 Main Street, N., Dayton, OH 45415-6593				

DATE		ITEM	DEBIT	CREDIT	BALANCE
20-- March	6	Inv. #213	1205 15		1205 15
	14	Cash		850 00	355 15
April	6	Inv. #218	147 93		503 08
	19	Credit Memo #26		53 47	449 61
	25	Cash		350 00	99 61
	29	Inv. #228	242 27		341 88

Account #4

NAME	Shane Reitz									ACCOUNT NO.		2620	
ADDRESS	9612 Webster Street, S., Dayton, OH 45414-3165												

DATE		ITEM	DEBIT			CREDIT			BALANCE		
20-- March	6	Inv. #214	5 2 8 82						5 2 8 82		
	12	Cash				3 0 0 00			2 2 8 82		
April	7	Inv. #219	2 1 1 54						4 4 0 36		
	16	Credit Memo #22				1 2 35			4 2 8 01		
	27	Cash				2 5 0 00			1 7 8 01		
	30	Inv. #229	4 0 1 11						5 7 9 12		

Account #5

NAME	Stacey Rist									ACCOUNT NO.		2621	
ADDRESS	4163 Pritz Avenue, N., Dayton, OH 45410-2878												

DATE		ITEM	DEBIT			CREDIT			BALANCE		
20-- March	7	Inv. #215	9 2 66						9 2 66		
	12	Cash				8 0 00			1 2 66		
April	5	Inv. #216	1 7 7 15						1 8 9 81		
	19	Credit Memo #27				1 6 23			1 7 3 58		
	27	Cash				1 3 0 00			4 3 58		
	28	Inv. #226	2 0 1 27						2 4 4 85		

Account #6

NAME	Craig Ory									ACCOUNT NO.		2622	
ADDRESS	793 Oak Street, N., Dayton, OH 45410-4459												

DATE		ITEM	DEBIT			CREDIT			BALANCE		
20-- March	4	Inv. #209	3 3 71						3 3 71		
	11	Cash				2 5 00			8 71		
April	7	Inv. #220	2 1 15						2 9 86		
	15	Credit Memo #21				3 84			2 6 02		
	22	Cash				2 0 00			6 02		
	28	Inv. #227	1 0 2 22						1 0 8 24		

Account #7

| NAME | Michele Page | | | ACCOUNT NO. | 2623 |

ADDRESS 6476 Castle Drive, N., Dayton, OH 45424-9199

DATE		ITEM	DEBIT	CREDIT	BALANCE
20-- March	5	Inv. #212	1 8 4 42		1 8 4 42
	13	Cash		1 2 5 00	5 9 42
April	7	Inv. #221	1 0 3 91		1 6 3 33
	17	Credit Memo #24		2 8 45	1 3 4 88
	26	Cash		1 2 5 00	9 88
	30	Inv. #230	1 1 3 02		1 2 2 90

Account #8

| NAME | Crystal Paslay | | | ACCOUNT NO. | 2624 |

ADDRESS 4618 Fauver Avenue, S., Dayton, OH 45420-4152

DATE		ITEM	DEBIT	CREDIT	BALANCE
20-- March	4	Inv. #210	2 4 1 07		2 4 1 07
	13	Cash		2 0 0 00	4 1 07
April	7	Inv. #222	1 2 3 12		1 6 4 19
	20	Credit Memo #28		5 7 47	1 0 6 72
	24	Cash		1 0 0 00	6 72
	27	Inv. #225	3 3 1 16		3 3 7 88

 CHECK YOUR READING

1. Why do stores refer to the records kept for charge customers as accounts receivable? Explain the use of both "account" and "receivable."

2. a. What type(s) of transaction(s) is (are) recorded in the debit column of a customer's account?

    b. What type(s) of transaction(s) is (are) recorded in the credit column of a customer's account?

    c. Are cash sales recorded in charge customer accounts? Explain.

    d. Are cash payments received from charge customers recorded in a charge customer accounts?

3. What is a customer statement?

 DISCUSSION

Vallow's Department Store does not send out all of its customer statements at the end of the month. Instead, it uses the plan shown below:

Customer's Last Name Begins With	Working Day Statement Sent	Customer's Last Name Begins With	Working Day Statement Sent
A	1	L	15
B	2	M	16
C	3	N	17
D	4	O	18
E	5	P, Q	19
F	8	R	22
G	9	S	23
H	10	T, U	24
I, J	11	V	25
K	12	W, X, Y, Z	26

Explain how this plan helps the store.

 ETHICS IN THE WORKPLACE

You are an accounts receivable clerk. Part of your job is to open the mail and make a list of the checks that come in from customers. One of the checks that you received today is from Ralph Weisel, as indicated by the printed name and address on the check. However you discover that Mr. Weisel, in error, wrote in the word Cash following the words Pay to the order of. You realize that anyone can use this check, which is in the amount of $2,000. What should you do with this check? What should you not do with this check?

 ## COMMUNICATION IN THE WORKPLACE

1. Look at the customer account and customer statement shown below. The customer account is correct. However, the customer statement has several errors in it. List and describe each error you find in the customer statement.
2. Suppose that the incorrect customer statement was accidentally sent to the customer before it was corrected. Suppose also that you find the errors before the customer calls or writes. Prepare a corrected customer statement to send to the customer.
3. Write a letter of apology to the customer for the errors found in the customer statement.

NAME	Susan Lange				ACCOUNT NO.	17211

ADDRESS	2134 Cartel Street, Baltimore, MD 21227-2933

DATE		ITEM	DEBIT	CREDIT	BALANCE
20-- Oct.	3	Inv. #7812	234 28		234 28
	5	Inv. #7934	88 79		323 07
	14	Cash		250 00	73 07
	15	Credit Memo #23		18 98	54 09
	30	Inv. #8567	195 49		249 58

ZUGGIE'S, INC. 16 Wetzler Street
San Antonio, TX 78237-8823

CUSTOMER STATEMENT

TO: Susan Lange
2134 Cartel Street
Baltimore, MD 21227-2933

October 31, 20 --

ACCOUNT NO. 17211

DATE		ITEM	DEBIT	CREDIT	BALANCE
20-- Oct.	1	PREVIOUS BALANCE ⟶			0 00
	5	Inv. #7934	188 79		332 07
	14	Cash	.	250 00	82 07
	15	Credit Memo #23	18 98		101 05
	30	Inv. #8567	195 49		296 54

LAST AMOUNT IN THIS COLUMN IS THE BALANCE DUE ⟶

Specialization of labor.
Employees are responsible for a limited range of work.

One of the advantages of being a large business is that a firm can have **specialization of labor**. When labor is specialized, employees have a limited range of tasks to do or work for which they are responsible. For example, a very small firm may have one record keeper to keep all the records for the firm. A larger business may have cash clerks, sales clerks, accounts receivable clerks, and other employees who keep records for only one part of the business. An even larger business may have accounts receivable clerks and billing clerks who work with only part of the firm's customers. For example, one accounts receivable clerk may be responsible only for customers whose last names begin with A through E. Another accounts receivable clerk may be responsible only for customers whose last names begin with F through J, and so on through the alphabet.

1. How might specialization of labor make employees more efficient?
2. How might specialization of labor make it easier for firms to train employees?
3. How might specialization of labor make it easier for firms to find new employees?
4. What disadvantages might specialization of labor hold for employees?

REVIEWING WHAT YOU HAVE LEARNED

On a sheet of paper, write the headings **Statement Number** and **Words**. Next, choose the words that best complete the statements. Write each word you choose next to the statement number it completes. Be careful; not all the words listed should be used. Some words may be used more than once.

Statements	Words
1. Many large department stores use _____ terminals to record each sale.	account
	added
2. Charge sales are recorded in the _____ column of a customer's account.	credit
	credit memo
3. Merchandise returns are recorded in the _____ column of a customer's account.	cycle billing
	debit
4. Cash payments are recorded in the _____ column of a customer's account.	decrease
	increase
5. Debits _____ the balance of customer accounts.	POS
6. Credits _____ the balance of customer accounts.	specialization of labor
	subtracted
7. Debits are always _____ to the balance of a customer's account.	
8. Credits are always _____ from the balance of a customer's account.	
9. A plan to mail customer statements to groups of customers at different times during the month is called _____ .	
10. Making employees responsible for a limited range of work is called _____ .	

MASTERY PROBLEM

You are an accounts receivable clerk for Bailey's, Inc. Your job is to keep accounts for charge customers and prepare customer statements at the end of each month.

Directions

a. Copy the following data onto a three-column account for each charge customer.

NAME	Joshua Reynolds				ACCOUNT NO.	109
ADDRESS	7612 Raitt Street, Chattanooga, TN 37411-8879					

DATE		ITEM	DEBIT	CREDIT	BALANCE
20-- May	6	Inv. #811	2 5 1 89		2 5 1 89
	15	Inv. #945	3 6 19		2 8 8 08

NAME	Janice O'Clair				ACCOUNT NO.	183
ADDRESS	6133 Toro Street, Chattanooga, TN 37404-2617					

DATE		ITEM	DEBIT	CREDIT	BALANCE
20-- May	3	Inv. #536	2 0 7 82		2 0 7 82
	12	Inv. #794	3 2 1 64		5 2 9 46

b. Record the following charge sales, payments, and merchandise returns for May in the customer accounts.

June	2	Sold merchandise on account to Joshua Reynolds for $19.78; Invoice #1061.
	3	Sold merchandise on account to Janice O'Clair for $222.19; Invoice #1255.
	5	Sold merchandise on account to Joshua Reynolds for $207.87; Invoice #1416.
	6	Issued Credit Memo #25 for $25.90 to Joshua Reynolds for merchandise returned.
	7	Received a check from Joshua Reynolds for $350.00 in payment on account.
	10	Sold merchandise on account to Janice O'Clair for $218.62; Invoice #1739.
	12	Issued Credit Memo #31 for $43.19 to Janice O'Clair for merchandise returned.
	14	Sold merchandise on account to Joshua Reynolds for $256.45; Invoice #1887.
	18	Received a check from Janice O'Clair for $800.00 in payment on account.
	19	Received a check from Joshua Reynolds for $75.00 in payment on account.
	23	Sold merchandise on account to Janice O'Clair for $181.15; Invoice #1982.
	25	Received a check from Janice O'Clair for $200.00 in payment on account.
	28	Sold merchandise on account to Joshua Reynolds for $78.47; Invoice #2174.
	30	Received a check from Joshua Reynolds for $150.00 in payment on account.

CHECK POINT

(c)
Joshua Reynolds
Balance due = $249.75

c. Prepare customer statements for June for the two accounts.

REVIEWING YOUR BUSINESS VOCABULARY

This activity may be found in the Working Papers.

Chapter 9

Record Keeping for Accounts Receivable Clerks

Wholesalers are businesses that sell in large quantities to retailers. The wholesaler gets orders for merchandise from the retailer by mail, by telephone, or through the wholesaler's salesperson. Most wholesalers first record all merchandise ordered by the retailer on a special form called a sales order. Also, because most merchandise sold in a wholesale business is sold on credit, wholesalers must keep records of how much each customer owes. This bookkeeping is done in accounts receivable records.

In Chapter 9, you will learn how to prepare sales invoices from sales orders and how to keep accounts receivable records. You will learn how to use a sales journal, a cash receipts journal, and a sales returns and allowances journal.

Handheld Computing

Computers continue to shrink. One popular small computer is the *handheld computer*. One such computer is only about the length and width of a 3″ x 5″ card, although it's almost $\frac{1}{2}$″ thick and weighs just 4 ounces.

Handheld computers are not toys. They offer many features, including letting you:

- Store names, addresses, and phone numbers
- Schedule appointments
- Keep track of your "to do" list
- Read and write e-mail messages
- Write memos, letters, and other documents
- Transfer information to/from a desktop computer

Some handhelds let you attach a modem to access the Internet and send and receive faxes. Others run word processors and spreadsheet programs. Still others let you record sales orders and send them to the office using a modem. These devices are very useful to a sales representative or other business person on the road.

Handheld Computer with Keyboard

Handheld Computer without Keyboard

Job 43 PREPARING SALES INVOICES

When multiplying by multiples of ten (10, 100, 1000, 10,000, etc.) move the decimal in the number being multiplied to the right the same number of "0's" contained in the multiplier. Ex: 4.71 × 100 (2 zeros in multiplier) = 471 (decimal moved two places to the right) Ex: 12.30 × 1000 (3 zeros in multiplier) = 12,300 (decimal moved three places to the right)

applied math preview

Copy and complete these problems.

1. $ 16.50 × 10 =   7. 60 × $ 6.30 =
2. $422.79 × 10 =   8. 75 × $27.20 =
3. $ 0.32 × 100 =   9. 50 × $16.40 =
4. $ 6.74 × 100 =   10. 130 × $21.20 =
5. $ 22.49 × 1,000 =   11. 110 × $15.80 =
6. $ 8.37 × 1,000 =   12. 125 × $3.40 =

key terms preview

- **Due date**
- **Sales invoice**
- **Sales order**
- **Terms**
- **Wholesaler**

goals

1 To learn how sales orders are used in business.

2 To learn how to prepare sales invoices from sales orders.

3 To learn how to find the due dates of invoices from the terms of the sale.

→ UNDERSTANDING THE JOB

For Your Information

Wholesalers do not collect sales tax from retailers. Only the final consumer pays sales tax.

You have learned how to prepare sales slips for a retail store where merchandise is sold directly to the consumer. Retailers get the merchandise they sell from **wholesalers**. In this job, you will learn about the sales records of a wholesale business.

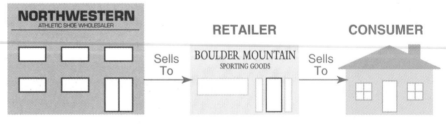

Illustration 43A

Wholesalers, retailers, and consumers

Key Terms

Wholesaler. A firm that sells to retailers.

Sales order. Form on which order is first recorded.

Sales invoice. A bill.

When you make a sale in a retail store, you prepare a sales slip. In a wholesale business, two forms may be prepared. The first form is a **sales order**. The second form is a **sales invoice**, or bill.

Wholesalers usually sell their goods on credit. Therefore, after the sales order is completed, it is sent to the credit department. The credit department checks to see if the customer is a good credit risk. If the credit department decides the customer is not a good credit risk, the customer will be asked to pay cash or the order will be canceled.

If the credit department decides the customer is a good credit risk, a copy of the sales order is sent to the stock department. The stock department checks to see if the merchandise ordered is on hand. If it is, the sales order will be sent to the billing department where the sales invoice will be prepared.

The information for the sales invoice is copied from the sales order. Usually, at least three copies of the sales invoice are prepared. The original is mailed to the customer when the order is shipped. The second copy is sent to the shipping department to be used to select and ship the merchandise. The third copy is sent to the accounting department so that they will know how much the customer owes.

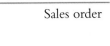 **SAMPLE PROBLEM**

You are employed by NorthWestern Athletic Shoe Wholesaler. It is part of your job to complete sales invoices from completed sales order forms. Boulder Mountain Sporting Goods, a retailer of sports-related products, ordered 20 pairs of cross trainers and 30 pairs of basketball shoes. Illustration 43B shows the completed sales order form.

Illustration 43B

Sales order

SALES ORDER

NORTHWESTERN
ATHLETIC SHOE WHOLESALER
1600 Dallas Parkway • Dallas, TX 75240-0810 • 555-3285

SOLD TO Boulder Mountain Sporting Goods
707 Central Avenue
San Antonio, TX 78219-6401

OUR ORDER NO. 5741
DATE October 1, 20--
CUSTOMER ORDER NO. 11734B

TERMS 30 days

SHIP VIA Truck

QUANTITY	STOCK NO.	DESCRIPTION	UNIT PRICE
20 pairs	CT6001	Cross trainer	39	99
30 pairs	BB7400	Basketball shoes	51	70

Notice the following information recorded on the sales order:

1. *Our order number.* Sales order forms are usually numbered in consecutive order. The number used for Boulder Mountain Sporting Goods order was 5741. The next sales order form will be numbered 5742.
2. *The date.* The date (October 1, 20--) shows when the order was received.
3. *The customer's order number.* The customer's order number, 11734B, is the number the customer, Boulder Mountain Sporting Goods, assigned to the order for its records. It is important to record this number because Boulder Mountain Sporting Goods will use this order number when calling or writing about the merchandise ordered.
4. *The customer's name and address.* The customer's name and address shows where the merchandise and the invoice are to be sent.

5. *The terms.* The **terms** of the sale are 30 days. This means that the customer should pay for the merchandise within 30 days from the date of the invoice. If the invoice is dated October 1, payment will be due 30 days later (October 31).

6. *Method of shipment.* Boulder Mountain Sporting Goods wanted the merchandise shipped by truck. This fact is shown on the sales order with the words "ship via truck."

7. *The merchandise ordered.* The quantity, stock number, description, and unit price of the merchandise are recorded on the sales order. Notice that no extensions or totals are shown. You will show the extensions and the total on the sales invoice when the customer is billed.

The sales invoice you would prepare from the sales order for Boulder Mountain Sporting Goods is shown in Illustration 43C. Like sales orders, sales invoices are also usually numbered in consecutive order. The invoice for Boulder Mountain Sporting Goods is numbered 4663.

Here are the steps to follow to prepare the sales invoice from the sales order:

STEP 1 Copy the information from the sales order.

Copy the same information that was recorded on the sales order form onto the sales invoice.

STEP 2 Extend and total the invoice.

Find the extensions by multiplying the quantity times the unit price for each item. Record the extensions in the Amount column. Draw a single ruling and add the extensions. Record the total and write the words "Total invoice" in the Description column.

It is important to check the figures on the invoice for accuracy. Any error in the total means that you are asking the customer to pay an incorrect amount.

Large companies use computers for electronic billing systems. Computers process and print invoices at rapid speeds. The computers use the data on the invoices to update customer accounts and stock records.

Illustration 43C

Sales invoice

Tips

Sales invoices show extensions and totals.

┌─ STEP 1

SALES INVOICE

NORTHWESTERN
ATHLETIC SHOE WHOLESALER
1600 Dallas Parkway • Dallas, TX 75240-0810 • 555-3285

SOLD TO	Boulder Mountain Sporting Goods 707 Central Avenue San Antonio, TX 78219-6401	INVOICE NO. 4663
		DATE Oct. 1, 20--
		OUR ORDER NO. 5741
		CUSTOMER ORDER NO. 11734B
TERMS	30 days	SHIP VIA Truck

QUANTITY	STOCK NO.	DESCRIPTION	UNIT PRICE	AMOUNT
20 pairs	CT6001	Cross trainer	39 99	799 80
30 pairs	BB7400	Basketball shoes	51 70	1,551 00
		Total invoice		2,350 80

STEP 2

Finding Due Dates

The terms of the sale to Boulder Mountain Sporting Goods are 30 days. This means that the customer has 30 days from the date of the invoice to pay the bill. The date that this invoice should be paid, the **due date**, is October 31.

$$\underset{\text{(Date of Invoice)}}{\text{October 1}} + \underset{\text{(Terms)}}{\text{30 days}} = \underset{\text{(Due Date)}}{\text{October 31}}$$

It is not always this easy to find the due date. For example, if an invoice is dated October 11 and the terms are 30 days, the due date would be November 10. This due date is found this way:

1. Find the number of days left in the month in which the invoice is dated. Since this invoice is dated October 11 and there are 31 days in October, there will be 20 days left in the month of October.

$$
\begin{array}{rl}
31 & \text{(days in October)} \\
-\ 11 & \text{(date of invoice, October 11)} \\
\hline
20 & \text{(days from October 11 to October 31)}
\end{array}
$$

2. Add the number of days in the following month or months until the total equals the terms of the invoice. Since you found that there are 20 days left in October, you need 10 days more in the next month (November) to get a total of 30 days.

20 days	10 days

October 11 ⟶ to October 31 ⟶ to November 10
(Date of Invoice)   (End of Month)   (Due Date)

$$
\begin{array}{lr}
\text{October 11 to October 31} & 20 \text{ days} \\
\text{Needed to reach 30 days} & +\ 10 \text{ days} \quad \text{(to November 10)} \\
\text{Total according to terms} & \overline{30 \text{ days}}
\end{array}
$$

To find the correct due date, you must know the exact number of days in each month. If you are not sure of the days in each month, the following rhyme may help you:

> Thirty days hath September,
> April, June, and November.
> All the rest have thirty-one
> Except February alone
> To which we twenty-eight assign,
> But leap year gives it twenty-nine.

Now test yourself and see if you agree with the due dates in the following example:

Date of Invoice	Terms of Invoice	Due Date
August 11	15 days	August 26
March 21	15 days	April 5
June 20	30 days	July 20
November 26	30 days	December 26
August 20	60 days	October 19
June 26	60 days	August 25

On a sheet of paper, write the headings **Statement Number** and **Words**. Next, choose the words that match the statements. Write each word you choose next to the statement number it matches. Be careful; not all the words listed should be used.

Statements	Words
1. The date by which an invoice should be paid	accounts receivable
2. The price for one unit	accounts
3. Quantity times the unit price	charges
4. A business that sells in large quantities to retailers	due date
5. A bill	extension
6. The length of time the customer has to pay a bill, such as 30 days	retailer
7. Accounts for charge customers	sales invoice
8. A form on which a customer's request for merchandise is first recorded	sales order
9. A business that sells directly to the consumer	terms
	transaction
	unit price
	wholesaler

STEPS REVIEW: Preparing Sales Invoices

STEP 1 Copy the information from the sales order.

STEP 2 Extend and total the invoice.

 APPLICATION PROBLEMS

Problem 43-1 **Directions**

Find the due date of each invoice.

CHECK POINT

43-1

(a) Feb. 14
(c) April 20

	Date of Invoice	Terms of Invoice	Due Date		Date of Invoice	Terms of Invoice	Due Date
a.	Feb. 4	10 days	_____	i.	March 8	15 days	_____
b.	Sept. 7	20 days	_____	j.	Jan. 17	20 days	_____
c.	March 21	30 days	_____	k.	July 27	30 days	_____
d.	April 3	30 days	_____	l.	Nov. 23	30 days	_____
e.	Nov. 17	30 days	_____	m.	Jan. 16	30 days	_____
f.	July 19	60 days	_____	n.	March 3	75 days	_____
g.	Dec. 12	60 days	_____	o.	May 19	90 days	_____
h.	March 22	90 days	_____	p.	Sept. 11	90 days	_____

Problem 43-2

You are employed by PhoneCom, Inc., a wholesaler of phones and related equipment. It is part of your job to prepare sales invoices from copies of sales orders.

 **CHECK POINT**

43-2

(Sale No. 1)
Invoice total = $339.85

Directions

The information for the sales that follow was taken from the sales orders. Prepare a sales invoice for each sale. Date each invoice January 8. Terms

allowed each customer are 30 days. All merchandise is to be shipped by truck. Start numbering invoices with 17053.

Sale #1

Sold to: Phone Store, Inc.
78 River Road
Bismark, ND 58504-6131
Our order no. 1710
Customer's order no. 66B
10 ea. Big Button Phone, #43-781 @ $12.99
5 ea. 32-Memory SpeakerPhone, #43-629
@ $41.99

Sale #2

Sold to: Phone Electronics, Inc.
6759 White Oak Drive
Gadsden, AL 35907-6244
Our order no. 1711
Customer's order no. 6-483
10 ea. Surface-Mount Dual Jack, #279-11 @ $3.99
10 ea. Modular Jack with Wiring Block, Ivory,
#279-12 @ $2.99
10 ea. Quick-Connect Jack, White, #279-15 @ $1.99

Sale #3

Sold to: Phone Hut
91 Washington Square
Wilmington, DE 19802-2584
Our order no. 1712
Customer's order no. 11-803
5 ea. 900MHz Cordless Phone, #43-109,
@ $59.99
5 ea. All-Digital Answer Machine,
#43-5811 @ $39.99

Sale #4

Sold to: TeleMart, Inc.
1100 Webster Street
Yakima, WA 98902-1217
Our order no. 1713
Customer's order no. 729
2 ea. 90-Memory Caller ID, #43-972 @ $11.95
5 ea. Dual-Band PCS Phone, #17-8116 @ $69.90

Sale #5

Sold to: Fone Mart
8870 E. Clay Street
Richmond, VA 23223-5510
Our order no. 1714
Customer's order no. A-66
6 ea. Maxion 30-Number Pager,
#M30-1712 @ $15.80
5 ea. Lightweight Headset Phone,
#LH-600 @ $39.50
2 dz. 25 ft. Phone Cord, White,
#279-600 @ $18.79

Sale #6

Sold to: Cellular Six
52946 Glenside Avenue
Baton Rouge, LA 70808-5626
Our order no. 1715
Customer's order no. 17312
2 dz. Leather Phone Case, #17-435 @ $19.50
1 dz. Car DC Adapters, #273-1217 @ $21.00
10 ea. Extended Service Battery, #23-1019
@ $29.98

You may find it easier to multiply by some fractions if you change them to decimals. For example: $1/2 = 0.50$, $1/4 = 0.25$, $3/4 = 0.75$, $1\,1/2 = 1.50$, and $2\,1/4 = 2.25$.

applied math preview

Copy and complete these problems.

1. $1/4 \times \$30.16 =$
2. $1/2 \times \$ 7.54 =$
3. $1/3 \times \$ 7.89 =$
4. $3/4 \times \$ 9.24 =$
5. $2/3 \times \$ 3.63 =$

6. $4\,1/4 \times \$ 7.56 =$
7. $2\,2/3 \times \$15.21 =$
8. $1\,3/4 \times \$ 8.52 =$
9. $5\,1/2 \times \$ 4.82 =$
10. $3\,1/3 \times \$ 6.33 =$

key terms preview

- **Accounts receivable ledger**
- **Schedule of accounts receivable**

goals

1 To learn how to keep accounts receivable records for a wholesale business.

2 To learn how to prepare a schedule of accounts receivable.

 ## UNDERSTANDING THE JOB

Accounts receivable ledger. A group of customer accounts.

Since most merchandise sold in a wholesale business is sold on credit, wholesalers must keep records of how much each customer owes. This is done by keeping a separate account for each customer in the same way you learned to keep accounts for retail charge customers in Chapter 8. The customer accounts are usually kept together in an **accounts receivable ledger**.

In a manual system, a loose-leaf binder or a set of ledger cards may be used for the ledger. Customer accounts may be put in alphabetical order by customer name or numerical order by customer account number. New accounts can be added easily.

Many companies use computers for their accounts receivable records. When computers are used, the accounts receivable ledger may be stored on disks.

Remember that when you keep accounts for customers, all sales of merchandise on account are recorded in the Debit column of the customer's account. All cash received from the customer and merchandise returned are recorded in the Credit column of the account.

NAME			ACCOUNT NO.		
ADDRESS			TERMS		
DATE	ITEM	DEBIT	CREDIT	BALANCE	

Sales (from duplicate sales invoices) ⌐

Cash received in payment
(from a list of cash
received from customers)

Merchandise returned
(from duplicate credit
memos)

 ## SAMPLE PROBLEM

You work as an accounts receivable
clerk in the accounting department of
Pacific Wholesale Packing and
Crating. You record data in customer
accounts from duplicate sales invoices,
duplicate credit memos, and a list of
cash collected.

Here is a list of the duplicate sales
invoices:

Date	Invoice Number	Customer	Amount
Oct. 5	2306	PDM Industrial	$2,480.00
9	2307	Quement Promotions, Inc.	6,140.60
12	2308	Tafoya Distributors, Inc.	2,265.45
24	2309	Quement Promotions, Inc.	8,758.28
27	2310	PDM Industrial	3,976.70

Here is a list of the duplicate credit memos issued for merchandise
returned:

Date	Credit Memo No.	Customer	Amount
Oct. 12	141	PDM Industrial	$630.00
16	142	Tafoya Distributors, Inc.	245.00

Here is a list of the cash received from customers:

Date	Customer	Amount
Oct. 19	PDM Industrial	$1,850.00
20	Quement Promotions, Inc.	6,140.60
23	Tafoya Distributors, Inc.	2,020.45

Illustration 44A shows how the customer accounts would look after the sales, merchandise returns, and cash receipts were recorded. Notice how the final balances were checked.

Illustration 44A

Customer accounts

NAME *PDM Industrial* ACCOUNT NO. **120**

ADDRESS *1200 Paragon Road, Dayton, OH 45459-6004* TERMS **20 days**

DATE		ITEM		DEBIT	CREDIT	BALANCE
20-- Oct.	5	Invoice #2306		2 4 8 0 00		2 4 8 0 00
	12	Credit Memo #141			6 3 0 00	1 8 5 0 00
	19	Cash	6,456.70		1 8 5 0 00	—
	27	Invoice #2310	2,480.00	3 9 7 6 70		3 9 7 6 70
			3,976.70	6 4 5 6 70	2 4 8 0 00	

NAME *Quement Promotions, Inc.* ACCOUNT NO. **125**

ADDRESS *960 Quail Lane, Dayton, OH 45434-2501* TERMS **20 days**

DATE		ITEM		DEBIT	CREDIT	BALANCE
20-- Oct.	9	Invoice #2307		6 1 4 0 60		6 1 4 0 60
	20	Cash	14,898.88		6 1 4 0 60	—
	24	Invoice #2309	6,140.60	8 7 5 8 28		8 7 5 8 28
			8,758.28	14 8 9 8 88		

When numbering accounts in the accounts receivable ledger, it is recommended that you assign account numbers by 5's or 10's, such as #110, #120, #130, etc. By doing so, new accounts can be added easily. New numbers can be assigned between existing account numbers without renumbering all the accounts in the accounts receivable ledger.

NAME *Tafoya Distributors, Inc.* ACCOUNT NO. **130**

ADDRESS *4692 Poplar Street, Dayton, OH 45415-5025* TERMS **20 days**

DATE		ITEM		DEBIT	CREDIT	BALANCE
20-- Oct.	12	Invoice #2308		2 2 6 5 45		2 2 6 5 45
	16	Credit Memo #142			2 4 5 00	2 0 2 0 45
	23	Cash			2 0 2 0 45	—
					2 2 6 5 45	

Remember: When working with accounts receivable, *debits* are always *added* to the old balance to find the new balance. *Credits* are always *subtracted* from the old balance to find the new balance.

In the Sample Problem, there are only three customers. In a real business, there would be many more customers. A separate account would be kept for each customer.

At the end of the month, your employer asks you for a list of customers and the amount each customer owes. This list is called a **schedule of accounts receivable**. The schedule of accounts receivable you would prepare is shown in Illustration 44B.

Schedule of accounts receivable. A list of customers who owe money.

STEP 1

STEP 2

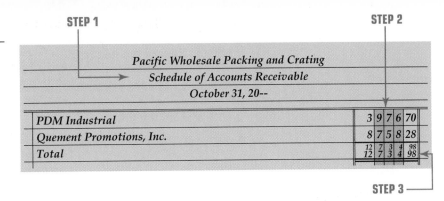

Pacific Wholesale Packing and Crating		
Schedule of Accounts Receivable		
October 31, 20--		
PDM Industrial		3 9 7 6 70
Quement Promotions, Inc.		8 7 5 8 28
Total		12 7 3 4 98
		12 7 3 4 98

STEP 3 —

These are the steps you would follow to prepare the schedule of accounts receivable:

STEP 1 Record the heading.

The heading you record for the schedule of accounts receivable must answer these questions:

WHO?   Pacific Wholesale Packing and Crating
WHAT?   Schedule of Accounts Receivable
WHEN?   October 31, 20--

STEP 2 List the accounts with balances due.

The name and the balance due for each customer are listed in the schedule. If no account numbers are shown on the schedule, accounts are usually listed in alphabetical order. Notice that the Tafoya Distributors, Inc., account was not listed because this account had no balance due.

STEP 3 Find the total.

Rule and foot the money column. Verify your work by re-adding the amounts. Then write the total again and double rule the money column. The total of $12,734.98 is the total amount due from all customers on October 31.

BUILDING YOUR BUSINESS VOCABULARY

On a sheet of paper, write the headings **Statement Number** and **Words**. Next, choose the words that match the statements. Write each word you choose next to the statement number it matches. Be careful; not all the words listed should be used.

Statements	Words
1. The length of time the customer has to pay a bill, such as 20 days	accounts receivable ledger
2. The date by which an invoice should be paid	credit memo
3. A business that sells directly to the consumer	due date
4. A form on which a customer's request for merchandise is first recorded	menu retailer
5. A form which shows that a customer has returned merchandise and owes less money	sales order schedule of accounts receivable
6. A group of customer accounts	terms
7. A list of customers who owe money	wholesaler

APPLICATION PROBLEMS

Problem 44-1

You are employed in the accounting department of Burton's Party Supply Wholesalers. Your job is to take care of the accounts receivable records.

Directions

a. Open an account for each of the following customers. The terms for all customers are 15 days.

Allison Special Events, 1826 Hamilton Street, Sacramento, CA 95841-3233, Acct. #130

Party Town, Inc., 4401 Gerber Road, Sacramento, CA 95828-7240, Acct. #140

Williams Card and Party Supply, 1072 Franklin Boulevard, Sacramento, CA 95818-0060, Acct. #150

b. Record the following transactions in the order in which they occurred:

List of Duplicate Sales Invoices

Date	Invoice Number	Customer	Amount
August 5	472	Party Town, Inc.	$ 530.00
6	473	Williams Card & Party Supply	1,125.00
10	474	Allison Special Events	793.00
12	475	Allison Special Events	471.00
18	476	Williams Card & Party Supply	597.00
24	477	Party Town, Inc.	228.00
27	478	Party Town, Inc.	404.00

List of Duplicate Credit Memos

Date	Credit Memo No.	Customer	Amount
August 17	136	Party Town, Inc.	$140.00
20	137	Williams Card & Party Supply	84.00

CHECK POINT

44-1

Allison Special Events
balance = $0.00

List of Cash Received

Date	Customer	Amount
August 19	Allison Special Events	$ 600.00
22	Party Town, Inc.	390.00
24	Allison Special Events	300.00
25	Williams Card & Party Supply	1,125.00
30	Allison Special Events	364.00

c. To check the final balance of each account, foot the Debit and Credit columns at the end of the month. Subtract the total credits from the total debits. Show your math in the Item column.

d. Prepare a schedule of accounts receivable on August 31.

Problem 44-2

You are an accounts receivable clerk for the EyeCare Wholesale Company. Your job is to keep the records of charge customers.

Directions

a. Open an account for each of the following customers. The terms for all customers are 20 days.

O'Brien Optical, 4221 Lindell Avenue, Eugene, OR 97402-5324, Acct. #120
Secure Vision, 18 Polka Street, Eugene, OR 97404-7222, Acct. #140
Visual Insight, 152992 Jefferson Avenue, Eugene, OR 97401-1918, Acct. #160

b. Record the following transactions in the order in which they occurred:

List of Duplicate Sales Invoices

Date	Invoice Number	Customer	Amount
July 2	565	Visual Insight	$950.75
4	566	O'Brien Optical	426.35
8	567	Secure Vision	506.50
11	568	Secure Vision	751.00
12	569	O'Brien Optical	204.20
14	570	Visual Insight	390.10
24	571	Secure Vision	62.80

List of Duplicate Credit Memos

Date	Credit Memo No.	Customer	Amount
July 21	91	Secure Vision	$150.30
28	92	Visual Insight	90.10

List of Cash Received

Date	Customer	Amount
July 22	Visual Insight	$950.75
24	O'Brien Optical	426.35
28	Secure Vision	670.00
31	Secure Vision	437.20
31	O'Brien Optical	204.20

CHECK POINT

44-2

Secure Vision balance = $62.80

c. To check the final balance of each account, foot the Debit and Credit columns at the end of the month. Subtract the total credits from the total debits. Show your math in the Item column.

d. Prepare a schedule of accounts receivable on July 31.

Problem 44-3 may be found in the Working Papers.

applied math preview

Find the due dates of these invoices.

	Date of Invoice	Terms		Date of Invoice	Terms
1.	June 3	15 days	6.	August 23	60 days
2.	April 20	15 days	7.	November 10	60 days
3.	May 21	20 days	8.	April 12	90 days
4.	March 5	30 days	9.	March 11	90 days
5.	October 18	30 days	10.	July 4	90 days

key terms preview

- Journalize
- Post
- Posting references
- Sales journal

goals

1 To learn how to record sales in a sales journal.

2 To learn how to post to customer accounts from a sales journal.

→ UNDERSTANDING THE JOB

Sales journal. Record of charge sales.

So far, you have learned to record the totals of sales invoices directly in customer accounts as debits. This method is used in many businesses. However, some businesses record all charge sales invoices first in a separate record called a **sales journal**, like the one shown in Illustration 45A (page 355).

Here are the steps that you would follow to make the entry in the sales journal:

STEP 1 Copy the date.

Copy the date, May 1, from the duplicate sales invoice.

STEP 2 Copy the customer's name.

Copy the customer's name, Electronic Solutions, into the Customer's Name column.

STEP 3 Copy the invoice number.

Write the invoice number, 691, in the Invoice No. column.

STEP 4 Copy the amount.

Write the invoice amount, $275.94, in the Amount column.

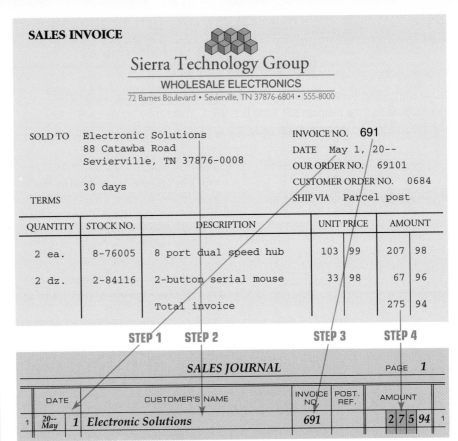

SALES INVOICE

Sierra Technology Group

WHOLESALE ELECTRONICS
72 Barnes Boulevard • Sevierville, TN 37876-6804 • 555-8000

SOLD TO   Electronic Solutions
88 Catawba Road
Sevierville, TN 37876-0008

30 days

TERMS

INVOICE NO. **691**
DATE May 1, 20--
OUR ORDER NO. 69101
CUSTOMER ORDER NO. 0684
SHIP VIA Parcel post

QUANTITY	STOCK NO.	DESCRIPTION	UNIT PRICE	AMOUNT
2 ea.	8-76005	8 port dual speed hub	103 99	207 98
2 dz.	2-84116	2-button serial mouse	33 98	67 96
		Total invoice		275 94

STEP 1   STEP 2   STEP 3   STEP 4

SALES JOURNAL   PAGE **1**

	DATE		CUSTOMER'S NAME	INVOICE NO.	POST. REF.	AMOUNT	
1	20-- May	1	*Electronic Solutions*	691		2 7 5 94	1

Post. To transfer data from one record to another.

Sales invoice
↓
recorded in
↓
sales journal
↓
posted to
↓
customer account

After you have recorded the sales invoice in the sales journal, you then record the sales invoice in the customer account to show how much the customer owes. To do this, you must transfer, or **post**, data from the sales journal to the customer accounts. Postings should be made daily to keep the accounts up-to-date.

This means that two records are used to record sales on account. The first record is the sales journal, where you first record sales invoices. The second record is the accounts receivable ledger, to which you post from the sales journal. You must post carefully so that the correct amount is transferred from the sales journal to the customer account. Also, you must be sure that the amount is posted to the correct customer account.

Illustration 45B on page 356 shows an entry in a sales journal posted to a customer account. Here are the six steps you would follow to make this posting:

STEP 1 Copy the date.

Copy the date, May 1, from the sales journal into the Date column of the customer account.

STEP 2 Copy the invoice number.

Copy the invoice number, 691, into the Item column of the customer account. The invoice number will help you find the invoice if any question comes up about the sale.

Key
Terms

Posting references.
Abbreviations which show
where entries were posted
from.

STEP 6

		SALES JOURNAL		PAGE	1

	DATE		CUSTOMER'S NAME	INVOICE NO.	POST. REF.	AMOUNT	
1	20-- May	1	Electronic Solutions	691	120	2 7 5 94	1

STEP 1   STEP 2   STEP 3   STEP 4

NAME	Electronic Solutions			ACCOUNT NO.	120	
ADDRESS	88 Catawba Road, Sevierville, TN 37876-0008			TERMS	30 days	

DATE		ITEM	POST. REF.	DEBIT	CREDIT	BALANCE
20-- May	1	Invoice #691	S1	2 7 5 94	STEP 5	2 7 5 94

STEP 3 **Record the posting reference in the customer account.**

Record the **posting reference**, S1, in the Post. Ref. column of the customer account. The abbreviation, S1, shows that the entry was posted from page *1* of the sales journal. When you post from the second page of the sales journal, you will use S2.

STEP 4 **Post the amount.**

Write the amount, $275.94, in the Debit column of the account because all sales are recorded in the Debit column.

STEP 5 **Find the new balance.**

Find the new balance and record it in the Balance column. Since the amount posted in the Debit column is the only amount in the account, the new balance is the same as the debit amount.

STEP 6 **Enter the account number in the sales journal.**

Put the account number 120 in the Post. Ref. column of the sales journal to show that the entry has been posted to the customer account. If you are interrupted while you are posting, the account numbers will let you know where you left off.

⇨ | **SAMPLE PROBLEM**

You are the accounts receivable clerk for Sierra Technology Group. The duplicate sales invoices show these sales for the month:

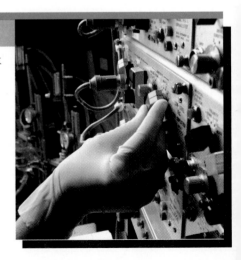

May	1	Sold merchandise on account to Electronic Solutions for $275.94. (Start with Invoice #691.)
	6	Sold merchandise on account to Phi-Alpha Electronics, for $970.00.
	18	Sold merchandise on account to Tech Mart Corporation for $1,510.00.
	19	Sold merchandise on account to Phi-Alpha Electronics, for $2,461.00.
	24	Sold merchandise on account to Phi-Alpha Electronics, for $843.00.
	30	Sold merchandise on account to Electronic Solutions for $2,008.06.

Illustration 45C shows how these sales would be recorded in the sales journal and posted to the customer accounts.

Here are the steps that you would follow:

STEP 1 Record the sales in the sales journal.

Record the sales in the sales journal using the data from the duplicate sales invoices. Recording data in a journal is called **journalizing**.

Illustration 45C

Sales journal and accounts receivable ledger

┌─ STEP 1   STEP 3 ─┐

SALES JOURNAL   PAGE 1

	DATE		CUSTOMER'S NAME	INVOICE NO.	POST. REF.	AMOUNT	
1	20-- May	1	Electronic Solutions	691	120	2 7 5 94	1
2		6	Phi-Alpha Electronics	692	140	9 7 0 00	2
3		18	Tech Mart Corporation	693	160	1 5 1 0 00	3
4		19	Phi-Alpha Electronics	694	140	2 4 6 1 00	4
5		24	Phi-Alpha Electronics	695	140	8 4 3 00	5
6		30	Electronic Solutions	696	120	2 0 0 8 06	6
7		31	Total			8 0 6 8 00	7

STEP 2   STEP 2

NAME	Electronic Solutions			ACCOUNT NO. 120		
ADDRESS	88 Catawba Road, Sevierville, TN 37876-0008			TERMS 30 days		

DATE		ITEM	POST. REF.	DEBIT	CREDIT	BALANCE
20-- May	1	Invoice #691	S1	2 7 5 94		2 7 5 94
	30	Invoice #696	S1	2 0 0 8 06		2 2 8 4 00
				2 2 8 4 00		

NAME	Phi-Alpha Electronics			ACCOUNT NO. 140		
ADDRESS	150 Burridge Drive, Sevierville, TN 37862-2404			TERMS 30 days		

DATE		ITEM	POST. REF.	DEBIT	CREDIT	BALANCE
20-- May	6	Invoice #692	S1	9 7 0 00		9 7 0 00
	19	Invoice #694	S1	2 4 6 1 00		3 4 3 1 00
	24	Invoice #695	S1	8 4 3 00		4 2 7 4 00
				4 2 7 4 00		

NAME	Tech Mart Corporation			ACCOUNT NO. 160		
ADDRESS	22701 Beach Front Drive, Sevierville, TN 37876-1150			TERMS 30 days		

DATE		ITEM	POST. REF.	DEBIT	CREDIT	BALANCE
20-- May	18	Invoice #693	S1	1 5 1 0 00		1 5 1 0 00

At the end of each day, post the amounts in the sales journal to the customer accounts in the accounts receivable ledger. Enter the account number in the Post. Ref. column of the sales journal as you complete each posting.

STEP 3 Total the sales journal.

At the end of the month, rule and foot the Amount column of the sales journal. Re-add the column before writing the final total. Draw a double ruling under the final total. Write the word *Total* in the Customer's Name column. Date the total as the last day of the month.

 BUILDING YOUR BUSINESS VOCABULARY

On a sheet of paper, write the headings **Statement Number** and **Words**. Next, choose the words that match the statements. Write each word you choose next to the statement number it matches. Be careful; not all the words listed should be used.

Statements	Words
1. To record in a journal	accounts receivable
2. A business that sells in large quantities to retailers	ledger
	credit
3. A group of customer accounts	debit
4. A bill	journalize
5. To transfer data from one record to another	post
	posting references
6. A record of all charge sales	retailer
7. A list of customers who owe money	sales invoice
8. Abbreviations, such as S1, which show where entries were posted from	sales journal
	schedule of accounts
9. The column used to record a charge sale in a customer account	receivable
	wholesaler

STEPS REVIEW: Recording in the Sales Journal

STEP 1 Record the sales in the sales journal.

STEP 2 Post to the customer accounts.

STEP 3 Total the sales journal.

 APPLICATION PROBLEMS

Problem 45-1 You are employed by TelCom Wholesale Company as an accounts receivable clerk. Part of your job is to record sales in the sales journal and post to the customer accounts.

Directions

a. Open an account for each customer. The terms for all customers are 30 days.

American Communications, Inc., 26 NW 31st Avenue, Ft. Lauderdale, FL 33311-6404, Acct. #110

Byington Corporation, 9020 Riverside Drive, Danville, VA 24541-9373, Acct. #115

Escobar & Evans, Inc., 7200 Floyd Road, Dallas, TX 75243-7898, Acct. #120

b. Record the following sales in a sales journal. Number the journal page 1.

Aug. 5 Sold merchandise on account to Byington Corporation for $540.00. (Start with Invoice #1082.)

9 Sold merchandise on account to Escobar & Evans, Inc. for $472.00.

21 Sold merchandise on account to American Communications, Inc., for $987.00.

24 Sold merchandise on account to Escobar & Evans, Inc. for $653.00.

27 Sold merchandise on account to Byington Corporation for $1,229.00.

29 Sold merchandise on account to American Communications, Inc., for $810.00.

c. Post daily from the sales journal to the customer accounts. Do not forget to enter an account number in the sales journal and the posting reference S1 in the accounts as you post.

d. Foot, total, and rule the sales journal for the month.

e. Check the balance in each customer account by footing the Debit column.

Problem 45-2 You work as an accounts receivable clerk for Calvetti Wholesale Distributors, Inc.

Directions

a. Open an account for each customer. The terms for all customers are 30 days.

Unitex United Corporation, 12317 Lee Road, Tampa, FL 33612-2278, Acct. #160

Van Rooy & Company, 481 Beachview Road, Tampa, FL 33624-5061, Acct. #170

Viking Semiconductor, Inc., 12322 Tampania Pky., Tampa, FL 33615-4188, Acct. #180

b. Record the following sales in a sales journal. Number the journal page 4.

Jan. 3 Sold merchandise on account to Van Rooy & Company for $1,260.00. (Start with Invoice #602.)

12 Sold merchandise on account to Viking Semiconductor, Inc., for $723.40.

17 Sold merchandise on account to Unitex United Corporation for $632.55.

22 Sold merchandise on account to Viking Semiconductor, Inc., for $106.30.

25 Sold merchandise on account to Unitex United Corporation for $490.10.

29 Sold merchandise on account to Van Rooy & Company for $382.24.

c. Post daily from the sales journal to the customer accounts. Do not forget to enter an account number in the sales journal and the posting reference S4 in the accounts as you post.

d. Foot, total, and rule the sales journal for the month.

e. Check the balance in each customer account by footing the Debit column.

Problems 45-3, 45-4, and 45-5 may be found in the Working Papers.

Job 46 USING A CASH RECEIPTS JOURNAL

applied math preview

Find the due dates of these invoices.

Date of Invoice	Terms	Date of Invoice	Terms
1. March 4	15 days	6. September 24	60 days
2. February 13	15 days	7. October 19	60 days
3. January 10	30 days	8. November 1	60 days
4. April 10	30 days	9. May 15	90 days
5. June 6	30 days	10. July 11	90 days

key terms preview

- **Cash receipts journal**

goals

1 To learn how to record cash received from customers in a cash receipts journal.

2 To learn how to post to customer accounts from a cash receipts journal.

→ UNDERSTANDING THE JOB

Cash receipts journal. A record of cash received.

You have just learned to enter sales in a record called a sales journal. A sales journal is a record of all charge sales. It is used to record sales of merchandise that have been charged by customers. These sales are posted to the customer accounts. In this case, *posted* means that the data are transferred from the sales journal to the customer accounts. Charge sales increase the amounts that customers owe.

On or before the due dates shown on their invoices, the customers will pay for the charge sales. When the payments are received, they are recorded in a record called the **cash receipts journal**.

You will now learn how to record cash received from customers in the cash receipts journal. Entries recorded in the cash receipts journal are posted to the customer accounts. In this case, *posted* means that the data are transferred from the cash receipts journal to the customer accounts. Cash receipts from charge customers decrease the amounts that customers owe. The amounts are recorded as credits. Postings are made daily to keep the accounts up-to-date.

The customer accounts in Illustration 46A show the sales made by Henderson's Wholesale Tire & Wheel Company during May. The terms show that customers should pay their bills within 45 days. Since the sales were made in May, payments for these sales should begin to be received by Henderson's Wholesale Tire & Wheel Company during June.

Illustration 46A

Customer accounts

NAME	Discount Tire		ACCOUNT NO.	110	
ADDRESS	2640 Signal Hill Road, Manassas, VA 20111-7252		TERMS	45 days	

DATE	ITEM	POST. REF.	DEBIT	CREDIT	BALANCE
20-- May 4	Invoice #561	S1	1 2 0 4 60		1 2 0 4 60
24	Invoice #565	S1	6 2 4 50		1 8 2 9 10

NAME	Morris Tire & Wheel Outlet		ACCOUNT NO.	120	
ADDRESS	4890 Sudley Road, Manassas, VA 20109-1310		TERMS	45 days	

DATE	ITEM	POST. REF.	DEBIT	CREDIT	BALANCE
20-- May 7	Invoice #562	S1	2 7 8 45		2 7 8 45
16	Invoice #564	S1	6 2 3 10		9 0 1 55
25	Invoice #566	S1	8 4 6 53		1 7 4 8 08

NAME	Tire Warehouse		ACCOUNT NO.	130	
ADDRESS	93 River Road, Manassas, VA 20111-6347		TERMS	45 days	

DATE	ITEM	POST. REF.	DEBIT	CREDIT	BALANCE
20-- May 9	Invoice #563	S1	6 3 0 15		6 3 0 15

The following is a record of the money collected during June:

June 18   Received a check for $1,204.60 from Discount Tire for the invoice of May 4.

     21   Received a check for $278.45 from Morris Tire & Wheel Outlet, for the invoice of May 7.

     23   Received a check for $630.15 from Tire Warehouse for the invoice of May 9.

     30   Received a check for $623.10 from Morris Tire & Wheel Outlet, for the invoice of May 16.

     30   Received a check for $200.00 from Discount Tire in partial payment on account.

Illustration 46B on page 362 shows how these cash receipts were recorded in the cash receipts journal and posted to the customer accounts.

STEP 1 STEP 3

CASH RECEIPTS JOURNAL PAGE **1**

	DATE		RECEIVED FROM	FOR	POST. REF.	AMOUNT	
1	20-- June	18	Discount Tire	Invoice, 5/4	110	1 2 0 4 60	1
2		21	Morris Tire & Wheel Outlet	Invoice, 5/7	120	2 7 8 45	2
3		23	Tire Warehouse	Invoice, 5/9	130	6 3 0 15	3
4		30	Morris Tire & Wheel Outlet	Invoice, 5/16	120	6 2 3 10	4
5		30	Discount Tire	On account	110	2 0 0 00	5
6		30	Total			2 9 3 6 30 2 9 3 6 30	6

STEP 2   STEP 2

ACCOUNTS RECEIVABLE LEDGER

NAME	*Discount Tire*		ACCOUNT NO.	**110**
ADDRESS	*2640 Signal Hill Road, Manassas, VA 20111-7252*	TERMS	**45 days**	

DATE		ITEM	POST. REF.	DEBIT	CREDIT	BALANCE
20-- May	4	Invoice #561	S1	1 2 0 4 60		1 2 0 4 60
	24	Invoice #565	S1	6 2 4 50		1 8 2 9 10
June	18	Cash 1,829.10	CR1		1 2 0 4 60	6 2 4 50
	30	Cash 1,404.60	CR1		2 0 0 00	4 2 4 50
		424.50		1 8 2 9 10	1 4 0 4 60	

STEP 4 ———————— Matches ————————

NAME	*Morris Tire & Wheel Outlet*		ACCOUNT NO.	**120**
ADDRESS	*4890 Sudley Road, Manassas, VA 20109-1310*	TERMS	**45 days**	

DATE		ITEM	POST. REF.	DEBIT	CREDIT	BALANCE
20-- May	7	Invoice #562	S1	2 7 8 45		2 7 8 45
	16	Invoice #564	S1	6 2 3 10		9 0 1 55
	25	Invoice #566	S1	8 4 6 53		1 7 4 8 08
June	21	Cash 1,748.08	CR1		2 7 8 45	1 4 6 9 63
	30	Cash 901.55	CR1		6 2 3 10	8 4 6 53
		846.53		1 7 4 8 08	9 0 1 55	

NAME	*Tire Warehouse*		ACCOUNT NO.	**130**
ADDRESS	*93 River Road, Manassas, VA 20111-6347*	TERMS	**45 days**	

DATE		ITEM	POST. REF.	DEBIT	CREDIT	BALANCE
20-- May	9	Invoice #563	S1	6 3 0 15		6 3 0 15
June	23	Cash	CR1		6 3 0 15	—

Tips

Post from the cash receipts journal daily.

Post from the cash receipts journal to the Credit column of customer accounts.

Subtract credits.

CR1 = cash receipts journal page 1.

Here are the steps to follow:

STEP 1 Record the receipts in the cash receipts journal.

As money is received from each customer, record the date, the customer's name, an explanation, and the amount in the cash receipts journal. For example, in Illustration 46B, the first entry shows that on June 18 a payment was received from Discount Tire for the invoice dated May 4 for $1,204.60.

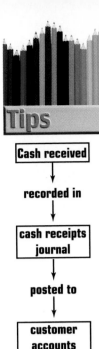

Tips

Cash received
↓
recorded in
↓
cash receipts journal
↓
posted to
↓
customer accounts

Total debits
− Total credits
Final balance

STEP 2 Post to the customer accounts.

At the end of each day, post from the cash receipts journal to the customer accounts in the accounts receivable ledger. The $1,204.60 received from Discount Tire on June 18 was posted as a credit to the customer account. Credits are subtracted from the account balance to show that the customer owes less than before. The $1,204.60 credit was subtracted from the old balance of $1,829.10 to get a new balance of $624.50.

As each posting is made, enter the posting reference CR1 in the customer account. The posting reference CR1 shows that the entry was posted from page *1* of the *c*ash *r*eceipts journal. Enter an account number in the Post. Ref. column of the cash receipts journal to show that the posting has been made.

STEP 3 Total the cash receipts journal.

After you finish posting for the month, total the Amount column of the cash receipts journal. The total is the amount of cash collected from all customers for the month. The cash receipts journal in Illustration 46B (page 362) shows that $2,936.30 was collected from customers during June. Notice that the total was first written as a footing and then re-added before the final total was written. After recording the final total, double rule the Amount column and write the word *Total* in the Received From column. Date the total as the last day of the month.

STEP 4 Check the account balances.

Check the balance in each customer account by footing the Debit and Credit columns. Subtract the total credits from the total debits. The answer should agree with the final balance shown in the account. Notice how the math is done in the accounts in Illustration 46B.

BUILDING YOUR BUSINESS VOCABULARY

On a sheet of paper, write the headings **Statement Number** and **Words**. Next, choose the words that match the statements. Write each word you choose next to the statement number it matches. Be careful; not all the words listed should be used.

Statements	Words
1. To transfer data from one record to another	accounts receivable ledger
2. Abbreviations, such as CR1, which show where entries were posted from	cash receipts journal
3. To record in a journal	credit
4. A business that sells in large quantities to retailers	debit
5. The date by which an invoice should be paid	due date
6. A record of all cash received	duplicate
7. A group of customer accounts	journalize
8. The column in which increases in a customer account are recorded	post
9. The column in which decreases in a customer account are recorded	posting references
	retailer
	wholesaler

STEPS REVIEW: Using a Cash Receipts Journal

STEP 1 Record the receipts in the cash receipts journal.

STEP 2 Post to the customer accounts.

STEP 3 Total the cash receipts journal.

STEP 4 Check the account balances.

APPLICATION PROBLEMS

Problem 46-1 You work for Franklin Furnace, Inc., as an accounts receivable clerk.

Directions

a. Copy the following customer accounts, which show the sales recorded in March.

CHECK POINT

46-1

Cash receipts journal
total = $3,265.00

NAME	Allied Heating, Inc.			ACCOUNT NO.		105	
ADDRESS	63 Ash Street, Scranton, PA 18509-3721			TERMS		30 days	
DATE	ITEM	POST. REF.	DEBIT	CREDIT		BALANCE	
20-- Feb. 13	Invoice #182	S2	9 8 0 00			9 8 0 00	

NAME	Brady Heating & Cooling			ACCOUNT NO.		115	
ADDRESS	274 Delaware Street, Scranton, PA 18512-2402			TERMS		30 days	
DATE	ITEM	POST. REF.	DEBIT	CREDIT		BALANCE	
20-- Feb. 6	Invoice #180	S2	1 0 0 8 00			1 0 0 8 00	
23	Invoice #184	S2	4 2 1 00			1 4 2 9 00	

NAME	Dali Brothers' Furnace & Heating			ACCOUNT NO.		125	
ADDRESS	16 Erie Street, Scranton, PA 18510-7658			TERMS		30 days	
DATE	ITEM	POST. REF.	DEBIT	CREDIT		BALANCE	
20-- Feb. 10	Invoice #181	S2	1 9 0 00			1 9 0 00	
21	Invoice #183	S2	6 6 6 00			8 5 6 00	

b. Record the following cash receipts in a cash receipts journal. Number the journal page 5.

Mar. 5 Received a check for $1,008.00 from Brady Heating & Cooling for the invoice of February 6.

8 Received a check for $190.00 from Dali Brothers' Furnace & Heating for the invoice of February 10.

12 Received a check for $980.00 from Allied Heating, Inc., for the invoice of February 13.

20 Received a check for $666.00 from Dali Brothers' Furnace & Heating for the invoice of February 21.

22 Received a check for $421.00 from Brady Heating & Cooling for the invoice of February 23.

c. Post daily from the cash receipts journal to the Credit column of the customer accounts. Enter the posting reference CR3 in the accounts and an account number in the cash receipts journal as you post.

d. Foot, total, and rule the Amount column of the cash receipts journal.

e. Check the balance in each customer account by footing the Debit and Credit columns. Subtract the total credits from the total debits. The answer should agree with the final balance shown in the account.

Problem 46-2 You are employed as an accounts receivable clerk by Tuxedo Warehouse, Inc.

Directions

a. Copy the following customer accounts, which show the sales recorded in April.

CHECK POINT

46-2

Cash receipts journal total = $2,947.00

NAME **Eli Johnson Formalwear**   ACCOUNT NO. **160**
ADDRESS **171 Memorial Drive, Waycross, GA 31501-9322**   TERMS **45 days**

DATE		ITEM	POST. REF.	DEBIT	CREDIT	BALANCE
20-- Apr.	5	Invoice #262	S1	6 2 0 00		6 2 0 00

NAME **Milo's Tuxedos**   ACCOUNT NO. **170**
ADDRESS **99 State Street, Waycross, GA 31501-6253**   TERMS **45 days**

DATE		ITEM	POST. REF.	DEBIT	CREDIT	BALANCE
20-- Apr.	2	Invoice #260	S1	3 9 0 00		3 9 0 00
	20	Invoice #264	S1	1 1 4 2 00		1 5 3 2 00

NAME **South City Tux Shoppe**   ACCOUNT NO. **180**
ADDRESS **231 Mary Street, Waycross, GA 31501-7082**   TERMS **45 days**

DATE		ITEM	POST. REF.	DEBIT	CREDIT	BALANCE
20-- Apr.	3	Invoice #261	S1	4 8 1 00		4 8 1 00
	13	Invoice #263	S1	5 0 6 00		9 8 7 00
	24	Invoice #265	S1	7 7 4 00		1 7 6 1 00

b. Record the following cash receipts in a cash receipts journal. Number the journal page 1.

May 16   Received a check for $390.00 from Milo's Tuxedos for the invoice of April 2.

18   Received a check for $481.00 from South City Tux Shoppe for the invoice of April 3.

20   Received a check for $620.00 from Eli Johnson Formalwear for the invoice of April 5.

26   Received a check for $506.00 from South City Tux Shoppe for the invoice of April 13.

27   Received a check for $600.00 from Milo's Tuxedos in partial payment on account.

28   Received a check for $350.00 from South City Tux Shoppe in partial payment on account.

c. Post daily from the cash receipts journal to the Credit column of the customer accounts. Enter the posting reference CR1 in the accounts and an account number in the cash receipts journal as you post.

d. Foot, total, and rule the Amount column of the cash receipts journal.

e. Check the balance in each customer account by footing the Debit and Credit columns. Subtract the total credits from the total debits. The answer should agree with the final balance shown in the account.

Problems 46-3 and 46-4 may be found in the Working Papers.

Job 47   USING SALES AND CASH RECEIPTS JOURNALS

applied math preview

Copy and complete these problems.

1. $ 60.00 + $40.00 = $ 2. $ 52.00 − $30.00 = $
   75.00 +   30.00 =   81.00 −   18.00 =
   112.40 +   64.00 =   90.00 −   72.00 =
   72.50 +   22.30 =   200.00 −   40.00 =
   34.90 +   62.10 = _____   110.00 −   90.00 = _____
   $ _____ + $ _____ = $ _____ $ _____ − $ _____ = $ _____

goals

To practice using the
1 **sales journal.**
2 **cash receipts journal.**
3 **accounts receivable ledger.**

⇨ UNDERSTANDING THE JOB

You have learned how to use three records to record transactions with customers who buy merchandise on account. The three records are
1. The *sales journal,* in which you record all sales invoices.
2. The *cash receipts journal,* in which you record all cash received from customers.
3. The *accounts receivable ledger,* in which you keep the customer accounts. Debits in the customer accounts are posted from the sales journal. Credits in these accounts are posted from the cash receipts journal.

Look at Illustration 47A.

Illustration 47A

How sales invoices and cash receipts are recorded

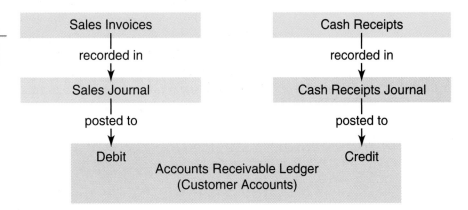

In this job, you will use all three records. You will be posting from both the sales journal and the cash receipts journal to the customer accounts. Remember: *Postings are made each day and must follow the order of the dates.*

SAMPLE PROBLEM

You are an accounts receivable clerk for American Florist. During September you recorded the following transactions:

Sept. 3 Sold merchandise on account to Village Floral for $700.00 (Invoice #1120).
      13 Received a check for $700.00 from Village Floral for the invoice of September 3.
      15 Sold merchandise on account to Village Floral for $900.00 (Invoice #1121).
      25 Received a check for $900.00 from Village Floral for the invoice of September 15.
      26 Sold merchandise to Village Floral for $600.00 (Invoice #1122).

Illustration 47B shows how you recorded these entries in both journals and posted to the customer account.

Illustration 47B

Posting from the sales journal and the cash receipts journal

STEP 1   STEP 3

SALES JOURNAL — PAGE 1

	DATE		CUSTOMER'S NAME	INVOICE NO.	POST. REF.	AMOUNT	
1	20-- Sept.	3	Village Floral	1120	180	7 0 0 00	1
2		15	Village Floral	1121	180	9 0 0 00	2
3		26	Village Floral	1122	180	6 0 0 00	3
4		30	Total			2 2 0 0 00	4

CASH RECEIPTS JOURNAL STEP 2 — PAGE 1

	DATE		RECEIVED FROM	FOR	POST. REF.	AMOUNT	
1	20-- Sept.	13	Village Floral	Invoice, 9/3	180	7 0 0 00	1
2		25	Village Floral	Invoice, 9/15	180	9 0 0 00	2
3		30	Total			1 6 0 0 00	3

NAME	Village Floral			ACCOUNT NO.	180		
ADDRESS	5362 Avalon Lane, Oklahoma City, OK 73118-2170			TERMS	10 days		

DATE		ITEM		POST. REF.	DEBIT	CREDIT	BALANCE
20-- Sept.	3	Invoice #1120		S1	7 0 0 00		7 0 0 00
	13	Cash		CR1		7 0 0 00	—
	15	Invoice #1121		S1	9 0 0 00		9 0 0 00
	25	Cash	2,200.00	CR1		9 0 0 00	—
	26	Invoice #1122	1,600.00	S1	6 0 0 00		6 0 0 00
			600.00		2 2 0 0 00	1 6 0 0 00	

STEP 4 ——————————————— Matches ———————

Here are the steps you took:

STEP 1 Record the transactions in the proper journals.

When you received a sales invoice or a check, you decided in which journal you should record it. You recorded all sales invoices in the sales journal and all checks received in the cash receipts journal.

STEP 2 Post daily to the customer accounts.

After you entered each transaction in the proper journal, you posted the transaction to the customer account. It is important to post daily to customer accounts so that customer balances are up-to-date.

STEP 3 Foot, total, and rule each journal.

At the end of the month, you footed, totaled, and ruled the sales and cash receipts journals.

STEP 4 Check the account balances.

At the end of the month, you verified the balances in the customer account by footing the Debit and Credit columns. You subtracted the total credits from the total debits and compared that amount to the balance in the account. You showed your math in the Item column of the account.

BUILDING YOUR BUSINESS VOCABULARY

On a sheet of paper, write the headings **Statement Number** and **Words**. Next, choose the words that match the statements. Write each word you choose next to the statement number it matches. Be careful; not all the words listed should be used.

Statements	Words
1. A list of customers who owe money	accounts receivable
2. A group of customer accounts	ledger
3. To transfer data from one record to another	credit
	credit memo
4. A record of all charge sales	debit
5. The date by which an invoice should be paid	due date
	journalize
6. The column used to record a charge sale in a customer account	post
	sales invoice
7. The column used to record a cash receipt in a customer account	sales journal
	sales order
8. To record in a journal	schedule of accounts
9. The length of time the customer has to pay a bill, such as 10 days	receivable
	terms
10. A form which shows that the balance of an account has been reduced because merchandise was returned	

STEP **1** Record the transactions in the proper journals.

STEP **2** Post daily to the customer accounts.

STEP **3** Foot, total, and rule each journal.

STEP **4** Check the account balances.

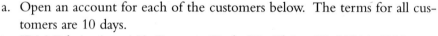

APPLICATION PROBLEMS

Problem **47-1**   You are employed in the accounting department of Discount Wholesale Distributors, Inc. to handle accounts receivable records.

CHECK POINT

47-1

Sales journal
total = $3,927.75

Directions

a. Open an account for each of the customers below. The terms for all customers are 10 days.
IDM Fabrication, 162 Concert Circle, Big Plains, ID 83814-6052, Acct. #125
Spectrum Manufacturing, 7277 Lindbergh Boulevard, St. Louis, MO 63125-0612, Acct. #130
Titan Construction, 402 Wilco Street, Indianapolis, IN 46222-1146, Acct. #135

b. Record the following sales and cash receipts in the proper journals. As you read each transaction, decide if it should be recorded in the sales journal or in the cash receipts journal. Use page 1 for both journals. Post to the customer accounts as soon as you have recorded each transaction.

Nov. 2	Sold merchandise on account to IDM Fabrication for $490.60. Since this is a sale, it must be recorded in the sales journal. (Start with Invoice #920.)
6	Sold merchandise on account to Spectrum Manufacturing for $506.30.
9	Sold merchandise on account to IDM Fabrication for $717.20.
12	Received a check for $490.60 from IDM Fabrication for the invoice of November 2. Since this is a cash receipt, it must be entered in the cash receipts journal.
14	Sold merchandise on account to Titan Construction for $472.10.
16	Received a check for $506.30 from Spectrum Manufacturing for the invoice of November 6.
19	Received a check for $717.20 from IDM Fabrication for the invoice of November 9.
21	Sold merchandise on account to Titan Construction for $846.75.
24	Received a check for $472.10 from Titan Construction for the invoice of November 14.
27	Sold merchandise on account to Spectrum Manufacturing for $404.20.
29	Sold merchandise on account to Titan Construction for $490.60.

c. Foot, total, and rule the sales and the cash receipts journals.
d. Check the balance at the end of the month in each account. Show all footings.
e. Prepare a schedule of accounts receivable on November 30. If necessary, refer back to Illustration 44B (page 351) as a guide.

Directions

a. Open an account for each of the following customers. The terms for all customers are 10 days.

Alliance MicroSystems, Inc., 3647 Gervais Street, Columbia, SC 29204-4321, Acct. #125

Sonitrol Imaging Corporation, 2801 Clark Street, Eugene, OR 97402-6058, Acct. #150

XioTech, Inc., 6230 Kurchel Avenue, Paterson, NJ 07514-0015, Acct. #175

b. Record the following transactions using a sales journal and a cash receipts journal. Use page 4 for both journals. Post to the customer accounts as soon as you have recorded each transaction.

CHECK POINT

Accounts receivable
total = $2,608.75

Aug. 3 Sold merchandise on account to Alliance MicroSystems, Inc. for $492.80. (Start with Invoice #342.)

7 Sold merchandise on account to Sonitrol Imaging Corporation for $1,120.50.

11 Sold merchandise on account to Alliance MicroSystems, Inc. for $700.40.

13 Received a check for $492.80 from Alliance MicroSystems, Inc. for the invoice of August 3.

16 Sold merchandise on account to XioTech, Inc. for $892.00.

17 Received a check for $1,120.50 from Sonitrol Imaging Corporation for the invoice of August 7.

21 Received a check for $700.40 from Alliance MicroSystems, Inc. for the invoice of August 11.

24 Sold merchandise on account to Sonitrol Imaging Corporation for $622.70.

26 Received a check for $892.00 from XioTech, Inc. for the invoice of August 16.

28 Sold merchandise on account to XioTech, Inc. for $1,480.30.

31 Sold merchandise on account to Sonitrol Imaging Corporation for $505.75.

c. Foot, total, and rule the sales and cash receipts journals.

d. Check the balance at the end of the month in each account. Show all footings.

e. Prepare a schedule of accounts receivable on August 31.

Problem 47-3 may be found in the Working Papers.

applied math preview

Copy and complete these problems.

1.		2.	
$ 30.00 + $52.00 = $		$ 84.00 − $34.00 = $	
24.00 + 40.00 =		60.00 − 15.00 =	
20.00 + 17.60 =		28.70 − 6.30 =	
54.60 + 5.10 =		176.45 − 128.20 =	
106.20 + 21.55 =		42.00 − 31.40 =	
$ ____ + $ ____ = $ ____		$ ____ − $ ____ = $ ____	

key terms preview

- Allowance
- Overcharge
- Sales returns and allowances journal

goals

1 To learn how to record credit memos in a sales returns and allowances journal.

2 To practice posting from the sales journal, the sales returns and allowances journal, and the cash receipts journal to the accounts receivable ledger.

UNDERSTANDING THE JOB

Allowance. A price reduction.

Overcharge. A price on the invoice is more than it should be.

Sales returns and allowances journal. Record of all duplicate credit memos.

An allowance is given to:
1. reduce the price.
2. correct an overcharge.
Credit memos are issued for:
1. returns.
2. allowances.

You have learned that when a credit customer returns merchandise, the seller prepares a form called a credit memo. (See Illustration 48A on page 373.) Occasionally, the customer may want to keep damaged merchandise if the wholesaler will reduce the price. Reducing the price for damaged merchandise is called giving an **allowance**. An allowance may also be given to correct an **overcharge** on a sales invoice. When an allowance is given, a credit memo is issued for the amount of the allowance. So, credit memos may be issued for two reasons:

1. To show that a customer owes less money because merchandise was *returned*.
2. To show that a customer owes less money because an *allowance* was given.

Two copies of the credit memo are prepared. In a wholesale business, the original is sent to the customer to show that a record has been made of the return or allowance. The duplicate is kept by the wholesaler, and the information on it is recorded in a **sales returns and allowances journal**. The entry recorded in the sales returns and allowances journal is posted to the customer account in the accounts receivable ledger. The amount of the credit memo is recorded in the *Credit* column. Postings are made daily.

CREDIT MEMO NO. **93**

McKenzie's
Wholesale Jewelry
1290 Parklane, Rockville, RI 02873-6407

TO San Juan Jewelers **DATE** March 16, 20--
1700 Northland Drive
Rockville, RI 02873-1511

We have credited your account as follows:

DESCRIPTION	UNIT PRICE	TOTAL
Allowance for damaged goods: 2 Blue Topaz pendant, 056-7211	20 00	40 00

SAMPLE PROBLEM

You are an accounts receivable clerk
for McKenzie's Wholesale Jewelry
The customer accounts in Illustration
48B show the sales made by the
company during March.

NAME	*San Juan Jewelers*		ACCOUNT NO.	*160*	
ADDRESS	*1700 Northland Drive, Rockville, RI 02873-1511*		TERMS	*30 days*	

DATE	ITEM	POST. REF.	DEBIT	CREDIT	BALANCE
20-- Mar. 5	*Invoice #1172*	*S1*	1 7 0 0 00		1 7 0 0 00
13	*Invoice #1174*	*S1*	9 8 0 00		2 6 8 0 00

NAME	*Taylor's Jewelry & Design*		ACCOUNT NO.	*180*	
ADDRESS	*1229 Avery Avenue, Buffalo, NY 14216-1780*		TERMS	*30 days*	

DATE	ITEM	POST. REF.	DEBIT	CREDIT	BALANCE
20-- Mar. 2	*Invoice #1171*	*S1*	1 2 6 0 00		1 2 6 0 00
12	*Invoice #1173*	*S1*	8 1 0 00		2 0 7 0 00

The following sales returns and allowances were made during the
month:

Mar. 16 Issued Credit Memo #93 for $40.00 to San Juan Jewelers as an
allowance for damaged merchandise. (The credit memo is shown in
Illustration 48A above.)

17 Issued Credit Memo #94 for $100.00 to Taylor's Jewelry & Design as an
allowance to correct an overcharge on the invoice of March 12.

Illustration 48C

Sales returns and allowances
journal and customer
accounts

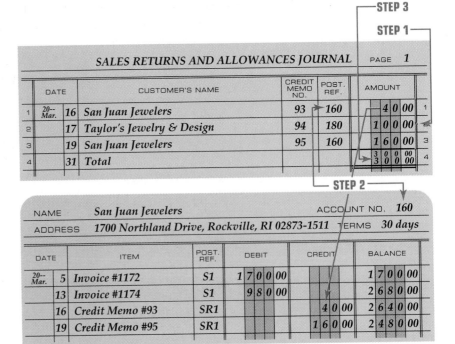

STEP 3
STEP 1
STEP 2

SALES RETURNS AND ALLOWANCES JOURNAL PAGE **1**

	DATE		CUSTOMER'S NAME	CREDIT MEMO NO.	POST. REF.	AMOUNT	
1	20-- Mar.	16	San Juan Jewelers	93	160	4 0 00	1
2		17	Taylor's Jewelry & Design	94	180	1 0 0 00	2
3		19	San Juan Jewelers	95	160	1 6 0 00	3
4		31	Total			3 0 0 00 / 3 0 0 00	4

NAME **San Juan Jewelers** ACCOUNT NO. **160**
ADDRESS **1700 Northland Drive, Rockville, RI 02873-1511** TERMS **30 days**

DATE		ITEM	POST. REF.	DEBIT	CREDIT	BALANCE
20-- Mar.	5	Invoice #1172	S1	1 7 0 0 00		1 7 0 0 00
	13	Invoice #1174	S1	9 8 0 00		2 6 8 0 00
	16	Credit Memo #93	SR1		4 0 00	2 6 4 0 00
	19	Credit Memo #95	SR1		1 6 0 00	2 4 8 0 00

NAME **Taylor's Jewelry & Design** ACCOUNT NO. **180**
ADDRESS **1229 Avery Avenue, Buffalo, NY 14216-1780** TERMS **30 days**

DATE		ITEM	POST. REF.	DEBIT	CREDIT	BALANCE
20-- Mar.	2	Invoice #1171	S1	1 2 6 0 00		1 2 6 0 00
	12	Invoice #1173	S1	8 1 0 00		2 0 7 0 00
	17	Credit Memo #94	SR1		1 0 0 00	1 9 7 0 00

19 Issued Credit Memo #95 for $160.00 to San Juan Jewelers for merchandise returned.

After you recorded these transactions, the sales returns and allowances journal and customer accounts looked as shown in Illustration 48C.

Here are the steps to follow to record the transactions:

STEP 1 Record the credit memos in the sales returns and allowances journal.

Record returns and allowances in the sales returns and allowances journal from the data you find on the duplicate credit memos.

STEP 2 Post to the customer accounts.

After you record the returns and allowances in the journal, post the entries to the customer accounts. Each amount should be posted to the Credit column of the customer account. Subtract to find the new balance.

You can see how this is done by looking at the San Juan Jewelers account in Illustration 48C. On March 16, the store received an allowance of $40.00 for damaged merchandise. The amount was posted to the Credit column of the account. The $40.00 was then subtracted from the old balance of $2,680.00 to get the new balance of $2,640.00.

As you post each transaction, enter the posting reference SR1 in the customer account. The posting reference SR1 shows that the entry was posted from page *1* of the sales returns and allowances journal. Also, enter an account number in the sales returns and allowances journal to show that the posting has been made.

STEP 3 Total the sales returns and allowances journal.

After you finish all the postings for the month, add the amounts in the sales returns and allowances journal. The journal in Illustration 48C (page 374) shows that the total returns and allowances for June were $300.00. This total was footed and re-added before the final total was written. Date the final total as the last day of the month, and write the word *Total* in the Customer's Name column.

Handling Customer Payments

When customers return goods or receive an allowance on goods, they do not owe as much as before. Thus, they pay the amount of the invoice less the amount of the credit memo. For example, Taylor's Jewelry & Design purchased $810.00 on March 12 (Invoice #1173). On March 17, it was issued Credit Memo #94 for $100.00. This means that the company owed only $810.00 − $100.00, or $710.00, as the balance on Invoice #1173.

When you received the $710.00 payment for this invoice, you recorded it in the cash receipts journal in this way:

	DATE	RECEIVED FROM	FOR	POST. REF.	AMOUNT	
1	20-- Apr. 21	Taylor's Jewelry & Design	Bal. Inv., 3/12	180	7 1 0 00	1

CASH RECEIPTS JOURNAL — PAGE 1

Notice that the reason for the receipt was shown as "Bal. Inv., 3/12." This means that the receipt was for the balance of the invoice dated March 12.

You are now using four records to keep track of transactions with customers to whom merchandise is sold on credit. The four records are

1. *The sales journal*, in which you record all the duplicate charge sales invoices.
2. *The cash receipts journal*, in which you record all cash collections from customers.
3. *The sales returns and allowances journal*, in which you record all the duplicate credit memos.
4. *The accounts receivable ledger*, in which you keep the customer accounts.

The debits in the customer accounts are posted from the sales journal. The credits in these accounts are posted from the cash receipts journal and from the sales returns and allowances journal. When you use all of these books, it is important to remember to post in the order of the dates of the transactions.

Look at Illustration 48D on page 376.

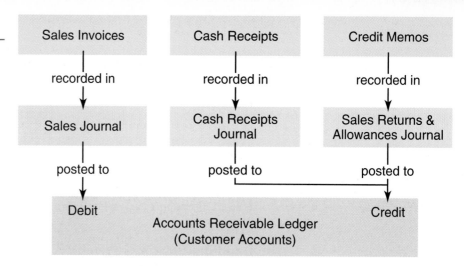

BUILDING YOUR BUSINESS VOCABULARY

On a sheet of paper, write the headings **Statement Number** and **Words**. Next, choose the words that match the statements. Write each word you choose next to the statement number it matches. Be careful; not all the words listed should be used.

Statements	Words
1. To transfer data from one record to another	allowance
2. A record of all cash received	cash receipts journal
3. The column used to record a charge sale in a customer account	credit
4. The column used to record a receipt, return, or allowance in a customer account	credit memo
5. A bill	debit
6. A record in which you record credit memos	original
7. A form that shows that the balance of an account has been reduced because of a return or allowance	overcharge
8. A reduction in price given for damaged merchandise or to correct an overcharge	post
9. When the price on a sales invoice is more than it should be	sales invoice
	sales returns and allowances journal

STEPS REVIEW: Using a Sales Returns and Allowances Journal

STEP 1 Record the credit memos in the sales returns and allowances journal.

STEP 2 Post to the customer accounts.

STEP 3 Total the sales returns and allowances journal.

You are employed in the accounting department of Evergreen Wholesale Company.

Directions

a. Copy the following customer accounts. Include the amounts already posted.

NAME	Cypress Landscape, Inc.		ACCOUNT NO.	120	
ADDRESS	2650 Brighton Drive, Valencia, CA 91355-0606		TERMS	30 days	

DATE		ITEM	POST. REF.	DEBIT	CREDIT	BALANCE
20-- Oct.	6	Invoice #1202	S1	4 3 0 00		4 3 0 00
	13	Invoice #1205	S1	1 6 3 00		5 9 3 00

Check Point

48-1(e)

Cypress Landscape, Inc. ending balance = $553.00

NAME	Gish Landscape Design & Installation		ACCOUNT NO.	140	
ADDRESS	1742 Calvello Drive, Valencia, CA 91354-2242		TERMS	30 days	

DATE		ITEM	POST. REF.	DEBIT	CREDIT	BALANCE
20-- Oct.	10	Invoice #1204	S1	3 6 2 00		3 6 2 00
	14	Invoice #1206	S1	4 0 3 00		7 6 5 00

NAME	Valley Pride Landscaping		ACCOUNT NO.	160	
ADDRESS	360 Decoro Drive, Valencia, CA 91354-6242		TERMS	30 days	

DATE		ITEM	POST. REF.	DEBIT	CREDIT	BALANCE
20-- Oct.	8	Invoice #1203	S1	5 1 1 00		5 1 1 00
	18	Invoice #1207	S1	3 2 2 00		8 3 3 00

b. Use a sales returns and allowances journal to record the following data taken from the credit memos issued during the month. Number the journal page 1.

Date		Customer's Name	Credit Memo No.	Amount
Oct.	15	Cypress Landscape, Inc.	85	$40.00
	17	Gish Landscape Design & Installation	86	22.00
	20	Valley Pride Landscaping	87	175.00
	23	Gish Landscape Design & Installation	88	36.00
	26	Valley Pride Landscaping	89	80.00

c. Post from the sales returns and allowances journal to the customer accounts. Enter the posting reference SR1 in the accounts and an account number in the sales returns and allowances journal as you post.

d. Foot, total, and rule the sales returns and allowances journal.

e. Check the balance at the end of the month in each account. Show all footings in each account.

You are the assistant bookkeeper for Almaden Valley Pool Supplies and Chemicals.

Directions

a. Copy the following customer accounts. Include the amounts already posted.

NAME	AquaClear Pool Service				ACCOUNT NO. 105	
ADDRESS	63421 Berrent Street, Houston, TX 77003-8045				TERMS 30 days	

DATE	ITEM	POST. REF.	DEBIT	CREDIT	BALANCE
20-- July 6	Invoice #639	S7	9 2 0 00		9 2 0 00
18	Invoice #643	S7	4 7 2 00		1 3 9 2 00

NAME	Diablo Pool & Spa Service				ACCOUNT NO. 125	
ADDRESS	2715 Rancho Verde Drive, Houston, TX 77078-6004				TERMS 30 days	

DATE	ITEM	POST. REF.	DEBIT	CREDIT	BALANCE
20-- July 10	Invoice #641	S7	8 9 1 00		8 9 1 00
21	Invoice #644	S7	6 4 6 00		1 5 3 7 00

NAME	Saratoga Pool Treatment				ACCOUNT NO. 145	
ADDRESS	10 Market Square, Houston, TX 77078-4368				TERMS 30 days	

DATE	ITEM	POST. REF.	DEBIT	CREDIT	BALANCE
20-- July 9	Invoice #640	S7	6 0 2 00		6 0 2 00
15	Invoice #642	S7	2 3 0 00		8 3 2 00

b. Use a sales returns and allowances journal to record the following data taken from the credit memos issued during the month. Number the journal page 7.

CHECK POINT

48-2(d)

Journal total = $339.00

Date	Customer's Name	Credit Memo No.	Amount
July 19	AquaClear Pool Service	206	$100.00
20	Saratoga Pool Treatment	207	42.00
22	Diablo Pool & Spa Service	208	58.00
26	Saratoga Pool Treatment	209	64.00
29	AquaClear Pool Service	210	75.00

c. Post from the sales returns and allowances journal to the customer accounts. Use the posting reference SR7.

d. Foot, total, and rule the sales returns and allowances journal.

e. Check the balance at the end of the month in each account. Show all footings in each account.

You are employed by Ampac Business Systems. It is part of your job to handle the accounts for customers.

Directions

a. Copy the following customer accounts. Include the amounts already posted.

NAME	Allied Business Solutions				ACCOUNT NO.	110	
ADDRESS	99 Moorefield Bridge Road, Danville, VA 24540-6021				TERMS	30 days	

DATE		ITEM	POST. REF.	DEBIT	CREDIT	BALANCE
20-- Jan.	11	Invoice #1235	S11	7 6 2 40		7 6 2 40
	19	Invoice #1237	S11	8 8 1 33		1 6 4 3 73

NAME	Golden State Office Systems				ACCOUNT NO.	115	
ADDRESS	9640 Koch Lane, San Jose, CA 95125-5010				TERMS	30 days	

DATE		ITEM	POST. REF.	DEBIT	CREDIT	BALANCE
20-- Jan.	5	Invoice #1233	S11	3 9 0 12		3 9 0 12
	22	Invoice #1238	S11	6 8 3 63		1 0 7 3 75

NAME	Premier Copier Sales & Services				ACCOUNT NO.	120	
ADDRESS	38902 Blue Heron Road, Corvallis, OR 97330-1822				TERMS	30 days	

DATE		ITEM	POST. REF.	DEBIT	CREDIT	BALANCE
20-- Jan.	8	Invoice #1234	S11	9 8 99		9 8 99
	15	Invoice #1236	S11	6 4 1 60		7 4 0 59

b. Use a sales returns and allowances journal to record the following data taken from the credit memos issued during the month. Number the journal page 6.

Date		Customer's Name	Credit Memo No.	Amount
Jan.	23	Golden State Office Systems	630	$ 60.18
	24	Premier Copier Sales & Services	631	81.35
	26	Allied Business Solutions	632	103.42
	28	Golden State Office Systems	633	77.93
	29	Allied Business Solutions	634	38.40

CHECK POINT

48-3(e)

Premier Copier Sales & Services ending balance = $659.24

c. Post from the sales returns and allowances journal to the customer accounts. Use the posting reference SR6.
d. Foot, total, and rule the sales returns and allowances journal.
e. Check the balance at the end of the month in each account. Show all footings in each account.

Problems 48-4, 48-5, and 48-6 may be found in the Working Papers.

CHECK YOUR READING

1. What are some of the differences between a wholesaler and a retailer?
2. Describe two different systems for keeping and maintaining an accounts receivable ledger.
3. a. What transaction(s) is(are) recorded in the Debit column of a customer's account?
   b. What transaction(s) is(are) recorded in the Credit column of a customer's account?
4. Describe the entries or transactions recorded in the following journals: sales journal, cash receipts journal, and the sales returns and allowances journal.
5. a. Design a sales invoice for a company you have created. Make sure you include the appropriate spaces and titles for important information such as your company's name and logo, dates, prices, product descriptions, etc.
   b. Create a customer and list several items your company has sold. Use the invoice you designed to record the sales order. Be sure to list prices and a total amount.

DISCUSSION

You are the supervisor of a group of order clerks. The clerks take orders over the phone and use a computer program to record each order.

Your manager wants to pay higher wages to clerks who produce more than other workers. Your manager has asked you to suggest a way to measure the productivity of each of your order clerks. That is, your manager wants you to find a way to measure how much each clerk produces.

You decide to ask your order clerks for ideas. One clerk feels that the number of hours each clerk spends working is a good measure of productivity. Another feels that the number of orders completed should be used as the measure. Still another feels that productivity should be measured by how "hard" each clerk works.

List one advantage and one disadvantage for each of the three ideas.

CRITICAL THINKING

You are an order clerk for Northern Sunwear, Inc. Northern Sunwear's customers order merchandise by phone using a catalog that the company has sent them. The catalog contains a description and the stock number for each item of merchandise the company sells. Your job is to take customer orders over the telephone and enter the data into a computer.

Answer the questions listed below. Keep in mind that you may be the

REINFORCEMENT ACTIVITIES

only person from Northern Sunwear, Inc., that the customer ever meets or talks to. How the customer feels about the company may depend on what you say and do. Also keep in mind that you should not waste time idly chatting with a customer over the telephone. Other customers may be waiting to call in orders.

1. What would you say when you first answered the telephone?
2. If the customer said, "I'd like to order some merchandise," what would you ask the customer?
3. What would you say when you finish taking the order?

COMMUNICATION IN THE WORKPLACE

Bao Vy is a new order clerk with Northern Sunwear, Inc., the same company as in the Critical Thinking exercise. You are her supervisor and are responsible for training her in her new job. Write what you would say to Bao Vy to explain why

1. She should not chew gum or eat food while talking with customers.
2. She should be as pleasant to customers as possible.
3. She must be accurate when recording orders from customers.

FOCUS ON CAREERS

Order clerks who take orders over the telephone are important to the business for which they work. They must have certain skills and knowledge to do their work well. What are two special skills or areas of knowledge that order clerks should have to succeed at their work?

GLOBAL BUSINESS: FOREIGN CURRENCY

Kimika Embree is an accounts receivable clerk for a book wholesaler. The company has many international customers. The payments that she receives are of two types. Sometimes they are in U.S. dollars; other times they are in foreign currency. If the payment is in foreign currency, Kimika

must convert that currency into U.S. dollars before she records it in the cash receipts journal.

A new type of foreign currency is the Euro. The Euro is a type of money used by most European companies. To convert the Euro to U.S. dollars, Kimika must know the exchange rate, or the value of the Euro in relation to the U.S. dollar. She can find the exchange rate in the newspaper, on the Internet, or by calling her local bank. For example, the exchange rate of the Euro is 1.07078 U.S. dollars on a certain date.

This value is how many Euros it would take to convert to one U.S. dollar. If Kimika receives 350 Euros, she would multiply the exchange rate by 350 to find out how many U.S. dollars 350 Euros were worth. In other words:

$$1.07078 \times 350 = 374.773, \text{ rounded to } \$374.77$$

Sometimes the exchange rate is more than one U.S. dollar, as the Euro is. Other times it is less. For example, the exchange rate for Italian lira is very small—0.00055. The following table shows some exchange rates. These rates do change daily, so the current rates could differ from those shown here.

Country	Currency	U.S. Dollar Equivalent
Belgium	franc	0.02660
Canada	dollar	0.66578
	Euro	1.07078
Italy	lira	0.00055
Greece	drachma	0.00328
Japan	yen	0.00821
South Korea	won	0.00089

REVIEWING WHAT YOU HAVE LEARNED

On a sheet of paper, write the headings **Statement Number** and **Words**. Next, choose the words that best complete the statements. Write each word you choose next to the statement number it completes. Be careful; not all the words listed should be used.

Statements	Words
	accounts receivable ledger
1. To find out if there is enough merchandise to fill an order, a copy of a sales order is sent to the _____ department.	allowance
2. When the seller gives you 30 days to pay for the goods you bought, the 30 days are known as the _____.	April 1 credit
3. You should post _____ to charge customer accounts so that the account balances are kept up-to-date.	daily debit extension
4. At the end of the period, the accounts receivable clerk prepares a list of all charge customers who have balances in their accounts. This list is called (a, an) _____.	March 31 schedule of accounts receivable
5. A customer may want to keep damaged merchandise if the wholesaler will give (a, an) _____.	stock terms weekly
6. The amount of a sale on account is posted to the _____ column of the customer's account.	
7. The amount of a cash receipt is posted to the _____ column of the customer's account.	
8. The amount of a return of merchandise is posted to the _____ column of the customer's account.	
9. When you multiply the unit price by the quantity, you are finding the _____.	

→ MASTERY PROBLEM

CHECK POINT

✓

(a) Atlantic Technologies invoice total = $2,487.25

You are employed by Quasar Electronics, a wholesale computer equipment firm. Part of your job is to prepare sales invoices from copies of sales orders. You also record sales invoices in a sales journal.

Directions

a. The data from the sales that follow were taken from sales orders. Prepare a sales invoice for each sale. Date each invoice January 15. Terms for each customer are 30 days. All merchandise is to be shipped by parcel post.

Sale #1

Sold To: Atlantic Technologies
        3408 Delaware Street
        Mobile, AL 36604-1983
Our Order No. 701
Customer Order No. 307988
15 Color printers, #DM144
@ $119.89
50 Diskette caddies, #DC108
@ $3.78
10 Fax modems, #M0120
@ $49.99

Sale #2

Sold To: Computer Warehouse
        9183 Bell Road
        Montgomery, AL 36116-7348
Our Order No. 702
Customer Order No. 3078-45
10 Tape backup units, #TB110
@ $329.89
25 Serial boards, #SB960
@ $24.88
30 Memory boards, #MB300
@ $149.99

Sale #3

Sold To: Southern Computer, Inc.
        6319 Goode Street
        Montgomery, AL 36105-3366
Our Order No. 703
Customer Order No. A781
25 Star computers, #C286
@ $1,799.80
15 Milan hard drives, #HD40
@ $268.90
15 Star floppy drives, #FD36
@ $59.99

Sale #4

Sold To: Mobile.com, Inc.
        6891 Lake Drive
        Mobile, AL 36613-3361
Our Order No. 704
Customer Order No. 10444
20 VGA boards, #VB233
@ $169.79
15 Color monitors, #VT137
@ $148.90
10 Mouse kits, #MK991
@ $39.59

b. Record the sales invoices in a sales journal. Number the journal page 1. Do not foot the journal since other sales invoices must be recorded for January.

REVIEWING YOUR BUSINESS VOCABULARY

This activity may be found in the Working Papers.

COMPREHENSIVE PROJECT 3

Comprehensive Project 3 has been designed to reinforce major concepts of this and previous chapters. The Comprehensive Project is found in the Working Papers.

A Business Simulation

The following activities are included in the Get Inline Skate Shop simulation:

1. Completing source documents for cash and for charge sales and returns.
2. Completing and recording petty cash vouchers.
3. Proving cash.
4. Recording transactions in a cash receipts journal, sales journal, and sales returns journal from source documents.
5. Counting cash.
6. Making a bank deposit.
7. Writing checks and check stubs.
8. Posting to the accounts receivable ledger from the cash receipts journal, from the sales journal, and from the sales returns journal.
9. Completing customer statements.
10. Making a schedule of accounts receivable.
11. Recording petty cash.
12. Analyzing a budget.

Get Inline Skate Shop is a store that sells inline skates and skating equipment to individuals, roller hockey clubs, and businesses. This business simulation requires students to use the skills and procedures presented in the first semester of record keeping. Students get hands-on experience working with realistic business documents such as sales slips, petty cash vouchers, bank deposit slips, sales journal, cash receipts journal, checks, and more. This simulation is available in manual and automated versions, for use with *Automated Accounting* software.

Chapter 10

Record Keeping for Stock Record Clerks

Most stores have a large selection of merchandise. Have you ever wondered how business people

1. Keep a record of the merchandise they have on hand?
2. Know which merchandise sells fast and should be reordered?
3. Know which merchandise moves slowly and should be reduced in price for a quick sale?

Successful businesses are able to answer these questions by keeping accurate records of their merchandise.

In Chapter 10, you will learn how to keep, use, and check a stock record. You will also learn how to prepare a purchase requisition and an open order report. A Calculator Tip will be given for verifying the ending balance on a stock record.

Handheld Computers

You learned in the last chapter how handheld computers can be used in sales work. Handheld computers can also be used by stock record clerks to keep track of inventory items.

Using bar code scanner

Some companies place bar codes on each item of stock or on the edges of the shelves on which the stock are stored. Stock record clerks use handheld computers that read the bar codes. The handheld computers might have *wands* attached to them that scan, or read, the bar codes. You probably have seen wands used in grocery and department stores. Some handheld computers do not have wands. Instead, the scanner is built right into the handheld computer, as illustrated here. The stock record clerk simply points the handheld computer at the bar code to read it.

For example, a stock record clerk might point the scanner at the bar code on a stock item to identify the stock item. Then the stock record clerk would count the items on the shelf and enter the amount using the handheld computer's keyboard. When the stock record clerk finished counting the stock, he or she would transfer the information from the handheld to the main computer system.

key terms preview

- Balance
- Issue
- Logging on
- Maximum
- Menu bar
- Minimum
- Option
- Passwords
- Periodic inventory
- Perpetual inventory system
- Stock
- Stock record
- Stock record clerk

goals

1 To learn how to record the receipt and issuance of merchandise on a stock record.

2 To learn how to use the information on a stock record.

⇨ UNDERSTANDING THE JOB

As you know, merchandise is also called **stock**. It is stored in a stockroom.

Businesses are able to keep accurate records of their stock by using a form called a **stock record**. A stock record shows stock received, stock issued, and how much there is on hand for any one item of stock. A stock record is shown in Illustration 49A on page 389.

Key Terms

Stock. Merchandise.

Stock record. A record of each item in the stockroom.

Illustration 49A

Stock record

STOCK RECORD

ITEM _Soccer Balls_   MAXIMUM _180_

STOCK NO. _1110_   MINIMUM _75_

UNIT _Each_

← STEP 1

DATE		QUANTITY RECEIVED	QUANTITY ISSUED	BALANCE
20-- AUG.	1	140		140 ←
	5		30	110 ←
	12		20	90 ←
	16	55		145 ←

The balance changes after each entry

STEP 2

Cultural Notes

Around 630 B.C., an important contribution to record keeping was made in Greece in Europe. The Greeks invented coined money, making it easier to assign values to transactions. An example of Greek financial records is the Zenon papyri (transactions recorded on papyrus). These records date back to 256 B.C. when Egypt was a Greek province. The papyri are named after Zenon, who was an Egyptian manager.

Key Terms

Stock record clerk. A worker who keeps track of goods received or issued.

SAMPLE PROBLEM 1

You are employed as a **stock record clerk** by the Lenzi Sports Equipment Company. This company only sells wholesale. This means that it sells only to retail stores and not to the general public. You work in the stockroom where all the merchandise is stored. You are handed some stock records that were filled in by another clerk, Shirley Lord. Each record is for a different item of equipment, such as footballs, baseball gloves, or soccer balls. Each item in the stockroom must have its own record. The first record you look at is shown in Illustration 49A above.

Here are the steps Shirley followed to complete the record:

STEP 1 Complete the heading.

Shirley first filled in the heading. Next to the word *Item* she wrote Soccer Balls, since this record will be used only to keep track of soccer balls.

Each item is given a stock number to identify it. In the space for Stock No., Shirley recorded 1110, the number assigned to soccer balls.

Unit refers to the measure in which items are sold. Those sold individually, including soccer balls, have the word *Each* recorded as the unit. Some items are sold by the dozen (12). Some are sold by the gross (12 dozen or 144). Each record must show what the unit of measure is.

The word **maximum** means the most that should ever be on hand. Your employer thinks that you will never need more than 180 soccer balls on hand, so 180 was recorded next to the word *Maximum*.

Minimum refers to the least that should ever be on hand. You always want to have on hand the merchandise your customers need. Your employer thinks that at least 75 soccer balls should be in stock, so 75 was entered next to the word *Minimum*.

STEP 2 Record the merchandise received and issued and calculate the balances.

Maximum. The most.

Minimum. The least.

Balance. The amount of stock on hand.

Issue. To give out or ship out.

Perpetual inventory system. Running balance is kept for each item of stock.

On August 1, 140 soccer balls were received in the stockroom. Shirley entered the year 20-- and Aug. 1 on the first line of the Date column. Then she wrote 140 in the Quantity Received column. Since there was no previous **balance**, the amount on hand was also 140. Shirley wrote 140 in the Balance column.

On August 5, 30 soccer balls were shipped out, or **issued**. Since the month was still August, only the new day, 5, was written in the Date column. The amount issued, 30, was entered in the Quantity Issued column. Shirley then figured the new balance this way:

Previous balance	140
Less: Quantity issued	− 30
Equals: New balance	110

Shirley entered 110 in the Balance column below the old balance of 140.

The entry on August 12 was handled in the same way as the entry on August 5.

On August 16, 55 soccer balls were received. Shirley entered 55 in the Quantity Received column. This time, she figured the new balance a little differently:

Previous balance	90
Plus: Quantity received	+ 55
Equals: New balance	145

She entered 145 in the Balance column to complete her recording.

Remember: Every time you receive or issue merchandise, the balance changes. When you receive, the balance *increases*; when you issue, the balance *decreases*. Be sure to check carefully each addition or subtraction before you enter it in the Balance column.

There is a special name given to a system in which the new balance is found after each entry. It is called a **perpetual inventory system**. In a perpetual inventory system, the new or running balance is calculated after each receipt or issuance of stock. Thus, the balance will always be up-to-date.

One problem with a perpetual inventory system is that the longer it is kept, the more errors there are in the stock balances in the system. There are a number of reasons why the stock balances in a perpetual inventory system can be wrong:

Key Terms

Periodic inventory. Actual count of stock on hand.

1. The wrong amount of stock may have been entered when a sale or receipt of merchandise was recorded.
2. The wrong amount may have been sent to a customer, and the customer may not have notified the company of the error.
3. Some stock may have been damaged in the stockroom and removed from the shelves.
4. Some stock may have been stolen.
5. Some stock may have been placed on the wrong shelves.

To correct the balances in a perpetual inventory system, most companies take an actual count of the stock on hand at least once each year. This actual count is called a **periodic inventory**. A periodic inventory is also referred to as a physical inventory.

The stock balances from the periodic inventory are then compared to the balances on the stock records. When differences are found, the balances on the stock records are corrected. It is very important to every business to have an accurate list of each stock item and the balance of that item on hand.

 SAMPLE PROBLEM 2

Shirley Lord has worked at Lenzi Sports Equipment for the month of August. On September 1, her stock record for soccer balls is full, so she must start a new record. The new record is shown in Illustration 49B on page 392.

Here are the steps Shirley followed in preparing the new record:

STEP 1 **Complete the heading.**

Shirley filled in the heading by copying all of the information from the heading of the August record.

STEP 2 **Record the balance on hand.**

The August record showed that there were 145 soccer balls on hand after the last entry. Shirley wrote the year and Sept. 1 in the Date column and 145 in the Balance column of the new record. Notice that the amount, 145, was written *only* in the Balance column. This is always done when a balance is carried forward from a previous record. No additional soccer balls were purchased on September 1, so no amount was entered in the Quantity Received column on September 1.

STEP 3 **Record the merchandise received and issued and calculate the balances.**

Shirley recorded the receipt and issuance of stock as she did in Sample Problem 1.

STOCK RECORD

ITEM ___Soccer Balls___   MAXIMUM ___180___

STOCK NO. ___1110___   MINIMUM ___75___

UNIT ___Each___

DATE		QUANTITY RECEIVED	QUANTITY ISSUED	BALANCE
20-- SEPT.	1			145
	7	30		175
	17		60	115
	22		40	75
	27	50		125

Key Terms

Passwords. Secret words that let you use the terminal.

Logging on. Identifying yourself as an authorized user.

If you study the stock record in Illustration 49B, you will find valuable information on it. For example, you can add the amounts on September 17 (60) and September 22 (40) from the Quantity Issued column to get a total of 100. This tells you that 100 soccer balls were sold in September. If you total the Quantity Received column, you find that 30 + 50 = 80 soccer balls were purchased in September.

You can also see why the company decided to make a purchase in late September. The balance went down to 75, which is just at minimum. Notice also the day of the highest number of soccer balls on hand, September 7. All the information that you record helps your business to make good decisions about buying and selling.

 ## USING THE COMPUTER

Many businesses use computers to keep stock records. When you keep stock records using a computer, you follow many of the same steps used in a manual system. For example, if Shirley Lord were to use a computer in her job, here are the steps that she might follow to keep records of soccer balls:

STEP 1 Log on to the computer.

Shirley enters her employee number, her password, and the date in order to log on to the computer. **Passwords** are secret words that are given to each clerk. Only persons who have a password can use the computer. This prevents unauthorized persons from using the computer. When Shirley keys her employee number, password, and the date, she is **logging on** to the computer. Log-on procedures are those steps you take to identify yourself to the computer as an authorized user.

STEP 1

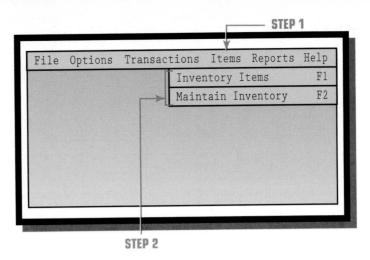

```
File  Options  Transactions  Items  Reports  Help
                            Inventory Items      F1
                            Maintain Inventory   F2
```

STEP 2

Menu bar. List of choices or options.

Option. A choice from a menu.

After logging on and selecting Inventory, a **menu bar** appears on the screen. The Items option is selected from the menu bar and appears as shown in Illustration 49C above.

STEP 2 Choose an option from the menu.

The Items menu shows two choices or **options**. Shirley wants to create a stock record for soccer balls. So, she chooses Option 2, Maintain Inventory. In this example, the Maintain Inventory option is used to add, change, or delete inventory items.

STEP 3 Enter the stock number.

The computer asks Shirley to key the stock number of the record she wants to add, so she keys 1110.

STEP 4 Enter the description.

The description is the name of the item. So, Shirley enters the words *Soccer balls*.

STEP 5 Enter the unit of measure.

The unit of measure defines how the soccer balls are ordered. The word *Each* is keyed here.

STEP 6 Enter the reorder point.

The reorder point is the minimum number of soccer balls in stock when the new order is placed. Shirley keys 75 for this line.

STEP 7 Enter the retail price.

Shirley must go to the bill for the soccer balls to find the retail price. She checks and it is $50.00, so that is what she keys. The screen appears as shown in Illustration 49D on page 394.

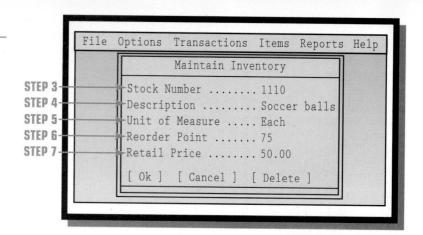

STEP 3 ⎯⎯ Stock Number 1110
STEP 4 ⎯⎯ Description .... Soccer balls
STEP 5 ⎯⎯ Unit of Measure ..... Each
STEP 6 ⎯⎯ Reorder Point 75
STEP 7 ⎯⎯ Retail Price 50.00

BUILDING YOUR BUSINESS VOCABULARY

On a sheet of paper, write the headings **Statement Number** and **Words**. Next, choose the words that match the statements. Write each word you choose next to the statement number it matches. Be careful; not all the words listed should be used.

Statements	Words
1. The least	balance
2. To give out or ship out	gross
3. 12 dozen or 144	issue
4. A worker who keeps track of goods received and issued	logging on
5. The amount of stock on hand	maximum
6. A record of each item in the stockroom	menu bar
7. Merchandise	minimum
8. A choice from a menu	option
9. A system in which a running balance is kept of each item in stock	password
10. Actual count of stock on hand	periodic inventory
	perpetual inventory system
	stock
	stock record
	stock record clerk

Tips

Use the Steps Review as a reminder when you are working on the Application Problems or studying for a test.

STEPS REVIEW: Preparing a New Stock Record

STEP 1 Complete the heading.

STEP 2 Record the balance on hand.

STEP 3 Record the merchandise received and issued and calculate the balances.

APPLICATION PROBLEMS

Problem 49-1   You are the stock record clerk for Zelinski Skate Company.

Directions

a. Enter the following information at the top of a stock record:

   1. The item is men's figure skates.
   2. The stock number is 3.
   3. The unit is pair.
   4. The maximum is 250.
   5. The minimum is 50.

b. Record the following:

Apr. 1   The balance on hand is 77. (Enter 77 only in the Balance column.)
     3   Received 175 pairs of men's figure skates.
     8   Issued 83 pairs of men's figure skates.
   10   Issued 112 pairs of men's figure skates.
   12   Received 210 pairs of men's figure skates.
   16   Issued 76 pairs of men's figure skates.
   19   Issued 59 pairs of men's figure skates.
   22   Issued 83 pairs of men's figure skates.
   27   Received 211 pairs of men's figure skates.
   30   Issued 59 pairs of men's figure skates.

CHECK POINT

49-1

Final balance = 201

c. Answer the following questions:

   1. On what date did you have the largest quantity of men's figure skates?
   2. On what date did you have the smallest quantity?
   3. On what dates did you go above maximum?
   4. On what dates did you go below minimum?
   5. How many pairs of men's figure skates were received during April?
   6. How many pairs of men's figure skates were sold during April?

Problem 49-2   You are the stock record clerk for Zelinski Skate Company.

Directions

a. Open a stock record for each of the following items. Enter all information listed in this table. Sort the stock records numerically.

Item	Stock No.	Unit	Maximum	Minimum	Balance on May 1
Men's figure skates	3	Pair	250	50	201
Women's figure skates	2	Pair	275	75	90
Children's figure skates	4	Pair	175	60	72
Adult hockey skates	1	Pair	300	70	67
Children's hockey skates	6	Pair	100	20	96
Double runner skates	5	Pair	150	40	46

b. Record the following in the order in which they are shown:

May	2	Received 200 pairs of women's figure skates.
	2	Issued 42 pairs of children's hockey skates.
	2	Received 19 pairs of children's figure skates.
	7	Received 203 pairs of adult hockey skates.
	7	Issued 37 pairs of children's hockey skates.
	7	Received 65 pairs of double runner skates.
	10	Issued 72 pairs of men's figure skates.
	10	Issued 76 pairs of women's figure skates.
	10	Received 35 pairs of double runner skates.
	15	Issued 83 pairs of men's figure skates.
	15	Received 55 pairs of children's hockey skates.
	17	Issued 29 pairs of children's figure skates.
	17	Issued 83 pairs of women's figure skates.
	17	Issued 31 pairs of adult hockey skates.
	20	Received 30 pairs of children's hockey skates.
	20	Issued 18 pairs of children's figure skates.
	20	Received 190 pairs of men's figure skates.
	20	Issued 48 pairs of double runner skates.
	21	Issued 47 pairs of adult hockey skates.
	21	Issued 54 pairs of women's figure skates.
	21	Received 9 pairs of double runner skates.
	26	Issued 38 pairs of children's hockey skates.
	26	Issued 62 pairs of men's figure skates.
	26	Received 150 pairs of women's figure skates.
	29	Received 84 pairs of children's figure skates.
	29	Issued 77 pairs of adult hockey skates.

CHECK POINT

49-2

Stock No. 3 final
balance = 174

c. Answer the following questions. (Remember that each item has a different maximum and minimum.)
1. Which items were below the minimum during May?
2. Which items were above the maximum during May?
3. Which item sold the most during May?
4. Which item sold the least during May?

Problem 49-3 may be found in the Working Papers.

Job 50 CHECKING STOCK RECORDS

UNDERSTANDING THE JOB

Stock record clerks must be accurate when they record new balances on stock records. If you worked carefully on Job 49, you always checked your addition or subtraction before you entered each new balance. To check your addition, you should add the numbers again in the opposite direction. For example, suppose that you added 70 + 55 and got 125. To check the addition, 55 + 70 = 125. To check your subtraction, you should add the answer you got to the number you subtracted. For example, 140 − 30 = 110. To check the subtraction, 110 + 30 = 140.

In this job, you will learn another method to check the accuracy of your math, for you may one day be in charge of a large supply of stock.

SAMPLE PROBLEM

You are a stock record clerk for Mindy's Sock Shop. Refer to Illustration 50A on page 398. To check the accuracy of the May 31 final balance of 42 pairs of socks, follow these 4 steps:

STEP 1 Foot the Quantity Received column.

Add the numbers in the Quantity Received column. The total is 82. Write this total in small figures under the line on which the last amount was recorded. You have now footed the column.

STEP 2 Foot the Quantity Issued column.

Add the numbers in the Quantity Issued column. The total is 110. Write this total in small figures on the same line as you wrote the footing of the Quantity Received column.

STEP 3 Find the ending balance.

On another sheet of paper, write the amount of the opening balance, 70, shown on the stock record. Add the total Quantity Received (from Step 1) to this balance. Then, from this total, subtract the total Quantity Issued (from Step 2). This difference will give you the ending balance.

Opening balance	70
Add: Total quantity received	+ 82
Total	152
Less: Total quantity issued	− 110
Ending balance	42

STEP 4 Verify the ending balance.

Compare your calculation from Step 3 with the ending balance on the stock record. In this case, 42 = 42. This tells you that your work is correct. You have verified it.

Illustration 50A
Stock record

STOCK RECORD

ITEM _Socks_   MAXIMUM _75_

STOCK NO. _KH43_   MINIMUM _25_

UNIT _Pair_

DATE		QUANTITY RECEIVED	QUANTITY ISSUED	BALANCE	
20-- MAY	1			(70)	← STEP 3
	5		15	55	
	7		25	30	
	15	50 +		80	
	16		42	38	
	22	15		53	
	27		28	25	
	31	17		(42)	← STEP 4
		(82)	(110)		

STEP 1   STEP 2

A calculator can be an aid in verifying the ending balance on a stock record in two ways. First, you can use it, as you already know, to add the Quantity Received and Quantity Issued columns.

There is also another way to use the calculator. If there is an error, your calculator can aid you in rapid correction. Suppose you were checking the stock record in Illustration 50A (on page 398). By hand, you are doing this: 70 − 15 = 55; 55 − 25 = 30; 30 + 50 = 80; 80 − 42 = 38; and so forth. With a calculator, you do not have to enter each new balance again. You just keep adding or subtracting. Here's how:

STEP 1 ▶ *Enter the opening balance.*

Enter the opening balance by pressing these keys:

$$\boxed{7}\ \boxed{0}$$

STEP 2 ▶ *Subtract the first issuance.*

Subtract the first issuance by pressing these keys:

$$\boxed{-}\ \boxed{1}\ \boxed{5}$$

The balance of 55 will appear in the display. Check it off on your stock record.

STEP 3 ▶ *Enter the remaining issuances and receipts.*

Do not clear your answer. Do not re-enter 55. Simply press these keys to enter the next issuance:

$$\boxed{-}\ \boxed{2}\ \boxed{5}$$

A new balance of 30 will appear in the display. Check it off.
Add the receipt on May 15 by pressing these keys:

$$\boxed{+}\ \boxed{5}\ \boxed{0}$$

A balance of 80 will appear in the display. Check it off.
Subtract 42, the next issuance, by pressing these keys:

$$\boxed{-}\ \boxed{4}\ \boxed{2}$$

A balance of 38 will appear in the display.

STEP 4 ▶ *Continue to the end.*

You are using the idea of **chaining** on a calculator. Chaining means that you can continue adding or subtracting without clearing and re-entering your previous answer. It saves a lot of time and chance of error.

What if the two figures do not agree? First, go back through the four steps. If you find that the two balances still do not agree, there is a math error on the stock record. You must now check each calculation on the stock record.

Chaining. Continuous calculation without clearing.

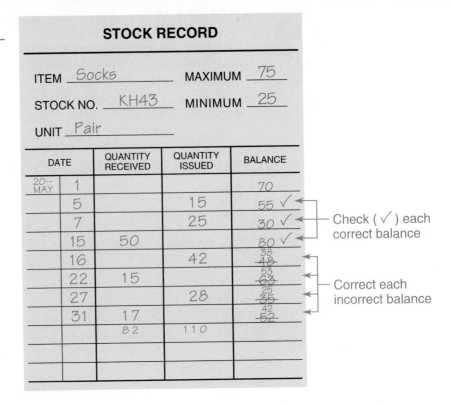

STOCK RECORD

ITEM _Socks_   MAXIMUM _75_

STOCK NO. _KH43_   MINIMUM _25_

UNIT _Pair_

DATE		QUANTITY RECEIVED	QUANTITY ISSUED	BALANCE
20-- MAY	1			70
	5		15	55 ✓
	7		25	30 ✓
	15	50		80 ✓
	16		42	38 ~~48~~
	22	15		53 ~~63~~
	27		28	25 ~~35~~
	31	17		42 ~~52~~
		82	110	

Check (✓) each correct balance

Correct each incorrect balance

Look at Illustration 50B. It is the same record from Illustration 50A (on page 398) but with an error made on May 16. A line was drawn through the incorrect balance of 48, and the correct figure of 38 was written above it. Since the May 16 balance was incorrect, all remaining balances had to be changed.

If you want to avoid this extra work, be careful and check your math before you record each new balance.

BUILDING YOUR BUSINESS VOCABULARY

On a sheet of paper, write the headings **Statement Number** and **Words**. Next, choose the words that match the statements. Write each word you choose next to the statement number it matches. Be careful; not all the words listed should be used.

Statements	Words
1. To check for accuracy	balance
2. The most	chaining
3. A list of choices or options	foot
4. The amount of stock on hand	issue
5. To add a column and record the total	maximum
6. A record of each item in the stockroom	menu bar
7. Continuous calculation without clearing	minimum
8. A system in which a running balance is kept of each item in stock	perpetual inventory system
	stock record
	verify

STEPS REVIEW: Checking Stock Records

STEP 1 Foot the Quntity Received column.

STEP 2 Foot the Quantity Issued column.

STEP 3 Find the ending balance.

STEP 4 Verify the ending balance.

APPLICATION PROBLEMS

 Problem 50-1   You are a stock record clerk for Best Supply Company.

CHECK POINT

 50-1

The first record is correct.

Directions

a. Follow the four steps in the Sample Problem to check the accuracy of the following stock records. If the ending balances are correct, you are finished with this problem. If not, then continue with part "b."

DATE		QUANTITY RECEIVED	QUANTITY ISSUED	BALANCE
20-- JUNE	1			86
	3	31		117
	6	15		132
	7	·	19	113
	12		36	77
	15	29		106
	18		15	91
	22		12	79
	27	42		121
	30		37	84

DATE		QUANTITY RECEIVED	QUANTITY ISSUED	BALANCE
20-- JUNE	1			59
	6		19	40
	8	38		78
	12	54		132
	15		26	106
	17		29	77
	19	41		118
	22	22		150
	26		37	113
	30		18	95

b. Go back through the four steps. If the balances still do not agree, check each daily balance on each stock record. If a balance is incorrect, draw a line through it and write the correct figure above it. (Use Illustration 50B on page 400 as an example.)

Problem 50-2   You are a stock record clerk for Best Supply Company.

CHECK POINT

 50-2

First record's correct balance = 146

Directions

a. Follow the four steps in the Sample Problem to check the accuracy of the stock records on page 402. If the ending balances are correct, you are finished with this problem. If not, then continue with part "b."

b. Go back through the four steps. If the balances still do not agree, check each daily balance on each stock record. If a balance is incorrect, draw a line through it and write the correct figure above it. (Use Illustration 50B on page 400 as an example.)

DATE	QUANTITY RECEIVED	QUANTITY ISSUED	BALANCE
20-- MAY 1			207
7		99	108
9	57		165
14	44		209
15		37	172
17		86	86
27	130		216
29		59	167
30	31		198
31		42	156

DATE	QUANTITY RECEIVED	QUANTITY ISSUED	BALANCE
20-- MAY 1			107
3		42	65
8	39		94
10		27	67
12	41		108
17		33	75
20		21	54
22	85		139
28	45		184
31		109	75

Problem 50-3   You are a stock record clerk for the Bright Lamp Company.

CHECK POINT

50-3

Desk lamps final
balance = 106

Directions

a.   Open a separate stock record for each of the four items listed in the following table:

Item	Stock No.	Unit	Maximum	Minimum	Balance May 1
Desk lamps	DL 141	Each	200	50	71
Floor lamps	FL 063	Each	175	30	84
Hanging lamps	HL 119	Each	125	20	33
Table lamps	TL 003	Pair	250	40	56

b.   Record the following in the order in which they are shown:

May 2   Received 120 desk lamps.
    2   Received 50 hanging lamps.
    5   Issued 61 floor lamps.
    5   Received 185 pairs of table lamps.
    5   Issued 59 desk lamps.
    8   Issued 57 hanging lamps.
    8   Received 150 floor lamps.
    8   Issued 67 pairs of table lamps.
    12   Received 95 hanging lamps.
    12   Issued 43 desk lamps.
    17   Received 40 pairs of table lamps.
    17   Issued 36 floor lamps.
    17   Issued 83 hanging lamps.
    22   Issued 79 pairs of table lamps.
    22   Issued 29 floor lamps.
    25   Received 90 desk lamps.
    25   Issued 51 pairs of table lamps.
    29   Received 50 hanging lamps.
    29   Issued 47 floor lamps.
    29   Issued 73 desk lamps.

c.   Check the accuracy of the ending balance on each record with the method you used in Problems 50-1 and 50-2. If the balance is incorrect, make the necessary corrections on each record.

402 | Chapter 10 | Record Keeping for Stock Record Clerks

applied math preview

Copy and complete the following problems.

1. 250	2. 175	3. 1,050	4. 975
$-\ 83$	$-\ 96$	$-\ 827$	$-\ 346$

5. 800	6. 750	7. 1,275	8. 2,185
$-\ 111$	$-\ 269$	$-\ 297$	$-\ 996$

key terms preview

- **Open order**
- **Open order report**
- **Purchase requisition**
- **Purchasing agent**

goals

1. To learn how to complete a purchase requisition.
2. To learn how to prepare an open order report.

⟹ UNDERSTANDING THE JOB

Purchasing agent. The buyer for a business.

Purchase requisition. A form telling the purchasing agent to place an order.

So far, you have learned to record information on stock records and to check the accuracy of your work. However, there is more to a stock record clerk's position. You must let the person who buys stock know when more stock is needed. This person has the job title of **purchasing agent** or buyer.

To be able to tell the purchasing agent when to buy, you must watch carefully three numbers on the stock records:

1. The balance
2. The maximum
3. The minimum

When the balance gets close to the minimum, it is time to order. To find out how much to order, subtract the balance from the maximum. Then, tell the purchasing agent to place an order by preparing a **purchase requisition**. Sample Problem 1 will show you how to prepare a purchase requisition.

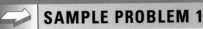
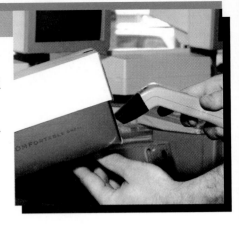

Mary Johnson is a stock record clerk for the LaSalle Shoe Store. Illustration 51A shows a stock record that she has been working on.

After finding the balance of 55, Mary compared it to the minimum of 50. Because the balance was getting close to the minimum, she decided to request more merchandise.

To find out how much to request, she subtracted the balance from the maximum.

Maximum	150
Balance	− 55
Amount to Request	95

Illustration 51A

Stock record

STOCK RECORD

ITEM __Athletic shoes__   MAXIMUM __150__

STOCK NO. __A14__   MINIMUM __50__ ←

UNIT __Pair__

DATE	QUANTITY RECEIVED	QUANTITY ISSUED	BALANCE
20-- MAY	1		107
	9	52	55 ←

When the balance nears the minimum, it is time to prepare a purchase requisition.

The amount of 95 is the most that she should request, since she does not want to go above the maximum. Mary then prepared the purchase requisition shown in Illustration 51B (page 405) in five steps.

STEP 1 Record the name of the department.

Next to the words *For Department*, Mary wrote Shoes to show that the merchandise is needed for the Shoe Department.

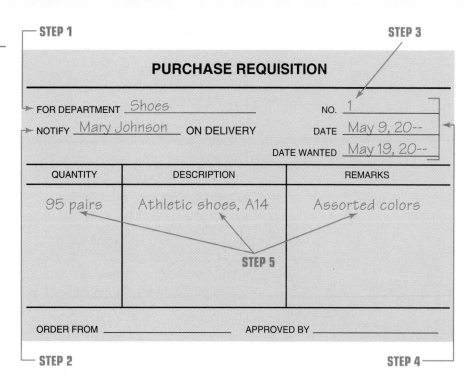

STEP 1

STEP 3

PURCHASE REQUISITION

FOR DEPARTMENT _Shoes_   NO. _1_

NOTIFY _Mary Johnson_ ON DELIVERY   DATE _May 9, 20--_

DATE WANTED _May 19, 20--_

QUANTITY	DESCRIPTION	REMARKS
95 pairs	Athletic shoes, A14	Assorted colors

STEP 5

ORDER FROM _____ APPROVED BY _____

STEP 2

STEP 4

STEP 2   Record the name of the stock clerk who needs the stock.

Mary wrote her own name next to the word *Notify*. Because she is the person requesting the stock, she should be notified when it arrives.

STEP 3   Number the requisition.

Since this is the first requisition prepared by Mary, it is numbered 1. The next will be numbered 2, and so forth.

STEP 4   Record the dates.

Two dates must be recorded on a purchase requisition. The first is the date on which the requisition was prepared, May 9, 20--. Mary recorded May 9, 20--, by the word *Date*.

The second date is when the stock is needed. Mary wants the new shoes by May 19, 20--, so she recorded this date in the Date Wanted space.

STEP 5   Record the merchandise details.

Mary must let the purchasing agent know exactly what she needs. In the Quantity column, she wrote 95 pairs, the amount calculated from the stock record. (It is possible that the purchasing agent will order a different quantity to get a better price, but it is Mary's duty to request up to the maximum.)

In the Description column, she recorded what was needed—athletic shoes, (stock number) A14. Since she wants a variety of colors, she wrote Assorted colors in the Remarks column.

The spaces at the bottom, Order From and Approved By, are used by the purchasing agent. Mary sends the original purchase requisition to that agent after making a copy for her records. From the copies of all the purchase requisitions that she keeps, she prepares an **open order report**. This form lists all of the requisitions that she has prepared and when they are filled. In Sample Problem 2, you will see how this report is prepared.

SAMPLE PROBLEM 2

Mary issued five purchase requisitions during May. Illustration 51C below shows the open order report that Mary prepared in two steps.

STEP 1 **Fill in the first three columns from copies of the purchase requisitions.**

The information for the first three columns of the open order report is filled in when the requisitions are made out. All of the information is contained on the requisitions. The requisitions are recorded in numerical order.

Open order report. List of filled and unfilled purchase requisitions.

Open order. Order not yet received.

STEP 2 **Fill in the last two columns when the merchandise is received.**

The date of receipt and any information about the order are filled in when the merchandise is received.

Look at the remark for Purchase Requisition 1 in Illustration 51C. While 95 pairs were requested, only 93 were received. The stock record clerk, Mary, must notify the purchasing agent immediately. Perhaps the purchasing agent ordered only 93, so there is no problem. But if 95 were ordered, then the purchasing agent must ask the seller why only 93 were sent.

The remark for Purchase Requisition 2 is None, indicating that what was requested was received. Mary need take no action about properly filled orders. However, she must notify the purchasing agent about Purchase Requisition 4, since 2 of the cartons were damaged.

Notice also that Purchase Requisitions 3 and 5 are not yet received. They are **open orders**, or orders not yet received. Mary can tell which orders are still out by looking at the open order report.

Illustration 51C

Open order report

OPEN ORDER REPORT

DATE OF REQUISITION	PURCHASE REQUISITION NO.	DATE WANTED	DATE RECEIVED	REMARKS
20-- MAY 9	1	May 19	May 17	Only 93 pairs
12	2	May 20	May 19	None
17	3	May 25		
22	4	May 30	May 30	2 cartons damaged
29	5	June 8		
	STEP 1		STEP 2	

On a sheet of paper, write the headings **Statement Number** and **Words**. Next, choose the words that match the statements. Write each word you choose next to the statement number it matches. Be careful; not all the words listed should be used.

Statements	Words
1. A record of each item in the stockroom	chaining
2. Check for accuracy	foot
3. A form telling the purchasing agent to place an order	issue
	open order
4. A list of filled and unfilled purchase requisitions	open order report
5. Continuous calculation without clearing	perpetual inventory system
6. A system in which a running balance is kept of each item in stock	purchase requisition
	purchasing agent
7. An order not yet received	stock record
8. The buyer for a business	verify

STEPS REVIEW: Preparing Purchase Requisitions

STEP 1 Record the name of the department.

STEP 2 Record the name of the stock clerk who needs the stock.

STEP 3 Number the requisition.

STEP 4 Record the dates.

STEP 5 Record the merchandise details.

STEPS REVIEW: Preparing Open Order Reports

STEP 1 Fill in the first three columns from copies of the purchase requisitions.

STEP 2 Fill in the last two columns when the merchandise is received.

Problem 51-1   You are a stock record clerk for Fen Auto Supply Company.

Directions

Complete the following table:

CHECK POINT

51-1(1)

Amount needed = 559

Item No.	Balance, May 1	Maximum	Amount needed to bring the balance up to maximum
1	891	1,450	
2	237	900	
3	394	750	
4	1,188	1,875	
5	404	475	
6	177	650	
7	196	700	
8	947	2,150	

Tips

Maximum
− Balance
_____
Amount
Needed

Problem 51-2   You are a stock record clerk for the Drummond Toy Store.

CHECK POINT

51-2

Stuffed animals to be
ordered = 243.

Directions

a. For each of the items listed, find the amount that you must order to
    bring the balance up to maximum. (To do this, subtract the June 1
    balance from the maximum.)

Description	Unit of Measure	Maximum	Date Wanted	Balance on June 1	Amount to be Ordered
Stuffed animal, #A 6	Each	275	June 15	32	
Electric train, #T 4	Set	190	June 20	82	
Jigsaw puzzle, #P 7	Each	500	June 24	113	
Rocking horse, #H 9	Each	150	June 27	74	

b. Prepare a purchase requisition for each item that needs to be ordered in part "a." You work for Department B. Start with purchase requisition no. 62. Date all requisitions June 6, 20--. (Use Illustration 51B on page 405 as an example.)

c. Record each of the four requisitions on an open order report. (Use Illustration 51C on page 406 as an example.)

d. Enter the following information about stock received on the open order report.

Purchase Requisition No.	Date Received	Remarks
62	June 14	None
63	June 19	Only 105 received
65	June 28	One doesn't rock

Problems 51-3 and 51-4 may be found in the Working Papers.

CHECK YOUR READING

1. What is the name of the business form companies use to keep track of their inventories? Describe the information shown on this form.
2. a. Describe the difference between a perpetual inventory system and a periodic inventory.
   b. What is another name for a periodic inventory?
3. Many companies request that stock record clerks complete a purchase requisition and send it to the purchasing agent when it is time to reorder. Why do companies follow this procedure instead of allowing stock record clerks to do all the ordering when necessary?

DISCUSSION

You work for a ski shop as a stock record clerk. Randy Miller has just begun to work with you. He is a stock record clerk also. Randy does not understand why the stock records need to have maximum and minimum amounts recorded. He has asked you to explain. What would you say to him?

ETHICS IN THE WORKPLACE

You are working as a stock record clerk for a wholesaler of television sets. You keep a perpetual inventory record. Once a month you go to the stockroom to count the sets on hand. The purpose of manually counting is to see if the number of sets in the stockroom matches what is supposed to be there.

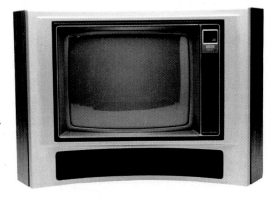

REINFORCEMENT ACTIVITIES

You notice over a three-month period that your records are always off. You seem to have three or four less sets in stock than are on the records. One evening, you happen to notice a good friend taking a set home. Two days later, you notice it again and conclude that your friend is stealing television sets. You mention it to that friend, who offers to split the money with you on the sale of the stolen sets if you don't say anything about it.

Write what you would do in this situation.

 ## COMMUNICATION IN THE WORKPLACE

Part of your job is preparing an open order report. You record purchase requisitions when they are made out. You then fill in the last two columns of the report when merchandise is received. Look at Illustration 51C (page 406) to see your finished work.

When merchandise received is damaged, you must notify the purchasing agent. Purchase Requisition 4, which was for 12 cartons of socks, included 2 damaged cartons. Write the body of the note that you would send to the purchasing agent to indicate what is damaged. Be sure to include all details about the shipment that are found in the open order report in Illustration 51C (on page 406). Be as brief as possible.

 ## FOCUS ON CAREERS

You read the following ad found in your local newspaper.

Answer the following questions:
1. Is this an entry-level job? Explain your answer.
2. How do you go about applying for this job?
3. Is the job a temporary one or a permanent one? Explain your answer.

Inventory Clerks

Earn extra cash during our semi-annual store-wide inventory. Immediate part-time positions (day, evening, and weekend schedules) are available for individuals to conduct our inventory (that is, organize, count and check prices of merchandise). Potential for regular placement. Please apply in person, Monday through Saturday, 10 AM to 6 PM. No experience necessary.

 ## REVIEWING WHAT YOU HAVE LEARNED

On a sheet of paper, write the headings **Statement Number** and **Words**. Next, choose the words that best complete the statements. Write each word you choose next to the statement number it completes. Be careful; not all the words listed should be used.

Statements	Words
1. A record of each item in the stockroom is called (a, an) _____.	balance
	issue
2. The form used to tell the purchasing agent to place an order is the _____.	maximum
	menu bar
3. The lowest amount of stock that should be on hand is the _____.	merchandise
	minimum
4. A list of filled and unfilled purchase requisitions is the _____.	open order report
	option
5. When an order received contains goods that are damaged, the person to notify is the _____.	perpetual inventory system
6. The amount of stock on hand is the _____.	purchase requisition
	purchasing agent
7. Another name for stock is _____.	stock record
8. The highest amount of stock that should be on hand is the _____.	verify
9. When you keep a running balance of each item of stock, you are using a(an) _____.	

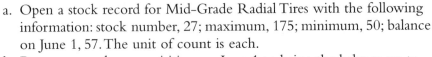

MASTERY PROBLEM

You are the stock record clerk for Tirrell's Tire Company.

Directions

a. Open a stock record for Mid-Grade Radial Tires with the following information: stock number, 27; maximum, 175; minimum, 50; balance on June 1, 57. The unit of count is each.

b. Prepare a purchase requisition on June 1 to bring the balance up to maximum. Your department is Department 2. You want the tires in 3 days. The purchase requisition number is 37.

c. Enter the purchase requisition on an open order report.

d. Record receipt of the order of tires on June 4 on the open order report. Only 115 were received.

e. Enter the receipt of 115 tires on the stock record.

f. Record the remaining receipts and issues of tires for June on your stock record.

June	5	Issued 36 tires.
	10	Issued 49 tires.
	12	Received 81 tires.
	15	Issued 27 tires.
	17	Received 20 tires.
	19	Issued 29 tires.
	22	Issued 62 tires.
	28	Received 95 tires.

g. Verify the balance of tires by footing the Quantity Received and Quantity Issued columns.

REVIEWING YOUR BUSINESS VOCABULARY

This activity may be found in the Working Papers.

Chapter 11

Record Keeping for Purchase Order Clerks

You make wise purchases by checking out information and prices on the same product from different companies. Think about how you might select a backpack for hiking. You do not buy one at the first store that you visit. You "shop around" at many stores.

A purchasing agent also shops around and gets prices from vendors. The agent uses a price quotation record to record the prices. When merchandise is ready to be ordered, the purchasing agent will have a purchase order prepared. Receiving reports and purchase invoices are forms that are also part of the purchasing cycle.

In Chapter 11, you will learn how to prepare a price quotation record, a purchase order, and a receiving report. You will also learn how to check and file purchase invoices. A Calculator Tip will show you how to check the extensions and totals on purchase invoices.

FOCUS ON TECHNOLOGY

Electronic Data Interchange

In Chapter 10 you learned to prepare stock records, price quotation records, and purchase requisitions. In Chapter 11, you will learn how to prepare purchase orders and verify purchase invoices. There is a lot of paperwork involved in buying stock.

Instead of having people spot when stock is low and prepare purchase requisitions, purchase orders, invoices, and checks for payment, many firms have worked out agreements with their major vendors to let their computers do these tasks. Let's say that Bell, Inc. sells color printers to Carr, Inc., which sells computer equipment to its customers. Each day Bell's computer asks Carr's computer how many color printers Carr, Inc. has on hand and Carr's computer answers the question.

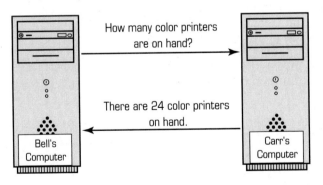

When Bell's computer finds that the stock of color printers at Carr, Inc. is low (below 25), it tells Carr's computer to issue a purchase order to Bell for enough printers to bring the stock level back to the correct level (50).

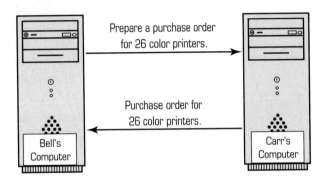

When Bell delivers the printers to Carr, Bell's computer sends a purchase invoice to Carr's computer. A receiving report is completed in the usual way on Carr's computer. If the shipment is OK, Carr's computer sends a check to Bell, Inc. to pay for it.

As you can see, many purchasing forms are never printed out at all. In fact, some may never be seen by record keepers at all.

This process is called *electronic data interchange*, or EDI. EDI is the computer-to-computer exchange of business forms, such as price quotations, purchase orders, invoices, and payments. EDI allows companies to reduce paperwork substantially by letting business transactions occur with little or no human input.

key terms preview

- Price quotation record
- Purchase order clerk

goals

1 To learn how to keep records of prices that different companies charge for the same item.

2 To learn how to choose the best price for the same item.

➡ UNDERSTANDING THE JOB

Purchase order clerk. Assists purchasing agent.

Price quotation record. Record of vendors, information, and prices relating to one stock item.

In Chapter 10, you learned how to compare the balance on a stock record with its minimum amount. You also learned that when the balance neared the minimum (or went below it), it was time to prepare a purchase requisition. The purchase requisition is used to notify the purchasing agent that more merchandise is needed.

In this chapter, you will learn the duties of the **purchase order clerk**. This clerk assists the purchasing agent in his or her duties. In this job, you will learn how to keep records that help the purchasing agent make wise purchases.

A purchasing agent gets information and prices from several vendors, or sellers. The purchase order clerk records the information and prices on a form called a **price quotation record**, like the ones shown in Illustration 52A below and on page 417. In this job, you will learn how to prepare price quotation records from which the purchasing agent can make wise purchases.

Illustration 52A

Completed price quotation records

PRICE QUOTATION RECORD

STEP 1

ITEM: _High performance tire_   STOCK NO. _HP 45_   UNIT _Dozen_

DATE		FIRM AND ADDRESS	PRICE		TERMS	ADDITIONAL INFORMATION
20-- MAY 1		Akers Tire Company				
		2010 Redal Road				
		Peoria, IL 61606-2010	1,620	00	60 days	
	1	Kim Rubber Company				
		25 Alba Street				
		Cedar Rapids, IA 52405-0025	1,843	20	30 days	
	1	LaRouse Tires, Inc.				
		107 Keril Avenue				
		South Bend, IN 46625-0107	1,706	40	45 days	

STEP 2

PRICE QUOTATION RECORD

STOCK NO. _SB 11_

ITEM _Steel belted tire_   UNIT _Set of 4_

DATE		FIRM AND ADDRESS	PRICE		TERMS	ADDITIONAL INFORMATION
20-- MAY	1	Akers Tire Company				
		2010 Redal Road				
		Peoria, IL 61606-2010	331	20	60 days	
	1	Kim Rubber Company				
		25 Alba Street				
		Cedar Rapids, IA 52405-0025	244	80	30 days	
	1	North Tire and Rubber, Inc.				
		4211 Meade St., N				
		South Bend, IN 46614-4211	307	28	20 days	

→ SAMPLE PROBLEM

You are a purchase order clerk for the Guedo Tire Shop. On May 1, you are asked by the purchasing agent to open a separate price quotation record for each item in the table below.

Since you are given prices for two different items, High performance tires, HP 45, and Steel belted radials, SB 11, you will open two price quotation records. Illustration 52A (above and on page 416) shows how the completed records will look. Here are the steps you would follow in preparing the price quotation records:

STEP 1 Complete the headings.

Fill in three items in the heading of each record: the item, the stock number, and the unit of count.

Firm Name and Address	Stock No.	Item	Unit	Price	Terms
Akers Tire Company 2010 Redal Road Peoria, IL 61606-2010	HP 45 SB 11	High performance tire Steel belted tire	Dozen Set of 4	$1,620.00 $331.20	60 days 60 days
Kim Rubber Company 25 Alba Street Cedar Rapids, IA 52405-0025	HP 45 SB 11	High performance tire Steel belted tire	Dozen Set of 4	$1,843.20 $244.80	30 days 30 days
La Rouse Tires, Inc. 107 Keril Avenue South Bend, IN 46625-0107	HP 45	High performance tire	Dozen	$1,706.40	45 days
North Tire & Rubber, Inc. 4211 Meade St., N. South Bend, IN 46614-4211	SB 11	Steel belted tire	Set of 4	$307.28	20 days

Record the date, firm name and address, price, terms, and any additional information.

In the columns provided, record the date (May 1), the name and address of each company, the price, the terms, and any additional information that might be provided.

Notice that Akers Tire Company is on both records. This is because Akers Tire Company sells both kinds of tires.

From each record, the purchasing agent can answer such questions as who offers the lowest price and who offers the longest terms. For high performance tires, Akers Tire Company offers the lowest price. Akers Tire Company offers the longest terms. What the records do not show are such things as quality of tires and service by the company. Thus, the purchasing agent will not always choose the lowest price. Terms, quality, and service must be considered. You know from your own experience that there are many reasons to buy from one store rather than another.

→ USING THE COMPUTER

As you can see, keeping price quotation records manually takes a lot of work. When a new price quotation is received from a vendor, the correct price quotation record must be found in the filing system. Then, the new quotation must be added to the record. This will usually mean recopying the vendor's name and address as well as the terms. This work is much easier when using a computer.

For example, suppose a new quotation is received from Roberts Tire Company for steel belted tires. The price is $267.80 per set for stock number SB 11. The purchase order clerk will enter the vendor's name into the computer to bring up the vendor's record. When the clerk does this, the computer will search its files for the vendor's record and automatically show the vendor's address beneath the name. (See Illustration 52B, below.) The clerk will check the address to see that the correct record is on the screen.

Illustration 52B

Bringing the record up on the screen

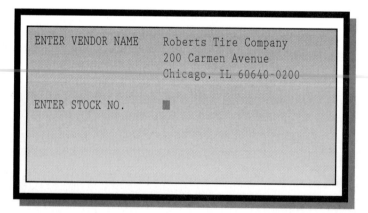

```
ENTER VENDOR NAME     Roberts Tire Company
                      200 Carmen Avenue
                      Chicago, IL 60640-0200


ENTER STOCK NO.       ▪
```

The clerk will then enter the stock number, SB 11. When this is done, the last quotation made by Roberts Tire Company for steel belted tires will appear on the screen. (See Illustration 52C on page 419.)

All the clerk has to do now is to move the cursor down to the price line which shows $274.90. The clerk simply types in $267.80 over the old

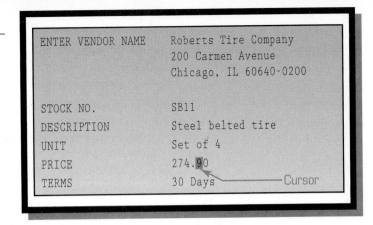

```
ENTER VENDOR NAME    Roberts Tire Company
                     200 Carmen Avenue
                     Chicago, IL 60640-0200


STOCK NO.            SB11
DESCRIPTION          Steel belted tire
UNIT                 Set of 4
PRICE                274.90
TERMS                30 Days ————————— Cursor
```

price and the price is changed. As you can see, the computer lets you keep accurate and up-to-date records of price quotations easily.

BUILDING YOUR BUSINESS VOCABULARY

On a sheet of paper, write the headings **Statement Number** and **Words**. Next, choose the words that match the statements. Write each word you choose next to the statement number it matches. Be careful; not all the words listed should be used.

Statements	Words
1. Seller	minimum
2. The buyer for a business	open order report
3. A record of each item of stock	price quotation record
4. Assists the purchasing agent	purchase order clerk
5. A request to the buyer to place an order	purchase requisition
6. The length of time a customer has to pay a bill, such as 30 days	purchasing agent
	stock record
7. Record of vendors, information, and prices relating to one stock item	stock record clerk
	terms
8. The least	vendor

STEPS REVIEW: Preparing Price Quotation Records

STEP 1 **Complete the headings.**

STEP 2 **Record the date, firm name and address, price, terms, and any additional information.**

APPLICATION PROBLEMS

Problem 52-1   You are a purchase order clerk for the East Mall Appliance Store.

Directions

a. Open a price quotation record for each item listed in the table on page 420. You will need five records. Fill in the records with the information from the table. Use October 1 as the date. Remember, each record is used to record information about all the companies that sell that one item.

Firm Name and Address	Stock No.	Item	Unit	Price	Terms
R. Taylor Company 712 Anderson Road Duluth, MN 55811-0712	KS 3 MW 1	Knife sharpener Microwave ovens	Ea. Ea.	$ 14.95 118.95	60 days 60 days
Regent, Inc. 3102 Grant Street, S. Denver, CO 80210-3102	HV 6 CO 4 BL 9	Hand vacuum Electric can openers Blenders	Ea. Ea. Ea.	$ 11.10 7.95 29.90	45 days 45 days 45 days
W. W. Baxter Company 16 Broadway Street Kansas City, MO 64105-0016	MW 1 HV 6 BL 9	Microwave ovens Hand vacuum Blenders	Ea. Ea. Ea.	$165.10 12.55 26.15	30 days 30 days 30 days
Stein Distributors, Inc. 412 Jones Street Little Rock, AR 72205-0412	KS 3 CO 4	Knife sharpener Electric can openers	Ea. Ea.	$ 16.95 6.25	60 days 60 days
Siever Company 103 Melrose Avenue Batavia, NY 14020-0030	MW 1 BL 9	Microwave ovens Blenders	Ea. Ea.	$149.90 31.40	20 days 20 days
Belmont, Inc. Wilson Road Luray, VA 22835-1036	CO 4 KS 3 HV 6	Electric can openers Knife sharpener Hand vacuums	Ea. Ea. Ea.	$ 8.50 15.50 14.95	90 days 90 days 90 days

CHECK POINT

52-1(b.1)

W. W. Baxter Company

b. Answer the following questions:
1. Which firm sells blenders at the lowest price?
2. Which firm sells knife sharpeners at the lowest price?
3. Which firm offers the longest terms on hand vacuums?

Problem 52-2   You are a purchase order clerk for the Hi-Tech Store.

Directions

a. Open a price quotation record for each item listed in the table below and on page 421. You will need six records. Fill in the information from the table. Use February 1 as the date. Remember, each record is used to record information about all the companies that sell that one item.

Firm Name and Address	Stock No.	Item	Unit	Price	Terms
CompuBuy Company 15 Garry Avenue W. Santa Ana, CA 92907-0150	DH 6 SS 3 MO 7	Hard drive Speaker set Modem	Ea. Ea. Ea.	$105.50 59.50 38.00	30 days 30 days 30 days
IT Supply Company 9117 Dolph Street, S.W. Portland, OR 97223-9117	MS 8 KB 4	Mouse Keyboard	Ea. Ea.	$ 7.50 6.00	20 days 20 days
Nu Tech Company 5166 13th Avenue New York, NY 10031-5166	SS 3 MO 7 DF 2	Speaker set Modem Floppy drive	Ea. Ea. Ea.	$ 54.50 37.50 14.95	90 days 90 days 90 days

Firm Name and Address	Stock No.	Item	Unit	Price	Terms
Sanford, Inc.	DH 6	Hard drive	Ea.	$ 72.95	45 days
1503 Arlington Street	DF 2	Floppy drive	Ea.	12.90	45 days
Ames, IA 50010-1503					
RT Distributors, Inc.	MO 7	Modem	Ea.	$ 40.00	15 days
86 Mountain Street	MS 8	Mouse	Ea.	7.95	15 days
Murdo, SD 57559-0086	KB 4	Keyboard	Ea.	8.00	15 days
The Rausch Company	SS 3	Speaker set	Ea.	$ 52.10	60 days
5613 Oliver Street	DH 6	Hard drive	Ea.	81.95	60 days
Ft. Wayne, IN 46806-5613	DF 2	Floppy drive	Ea.	10.90	60 days

CHECK POINT

52-(b.1)

The Rausch Company

b. Answer the following questions:
   1. Which firm sells speaker sets at the lowest price?
   2. Which firm sells modems at the lowest price?
   3. Which firm sells floppy drives at the lowest price?
   4. Which firm offers the longest terms on hard drives?

Problem 52-3 may be found in the Working Papers.

Job 53 PREPARING PURCHASE ORDERS

applied math preview

Copy and complete the following problems.

1. $219 \times \$7.76 =$
2. $5,045 \times \$15.29 =$
3. $318 \times \$0.45 =$
4. $3,345 \times \$0.51 =$
5. $8,007 \times \$18.09 =$
6. $4,900 \times \$27.60 =$
7. $4,120 \times \$5.17\frac{1}{2} =$
8. $1,576 \times \$3.09\frac{1}{4} =$

key terms preview

- **Prenumbered**
- **Purchase order**
- **Reorder level**
- **Triplicate**

goals

To learn how to prepare purchase orders.

UNDERSTANDING THE JOB

Purchase order. A form used to order merchandise.

Prenumbered. Numbered in advance.

Triplicate. Three copies.

You have learned that a stock record clerk prepares

1. Stock records, which tell when more merchandise is needed.
2. Purchase requisitions, which tell the purchasing agent that more merchandise is needed.

You have also learned that a purchase order clerk prepares

3. Price quotation records, which help the purchasing agent choose the best vendor.

When merchandise is ordered, the purchasing agent will ask the purchase order clerk to prepare a **purchase order**. Purchase order forms are usually **prenumbered**, or numbered in advance. They are also usually prepared in three copies, which is called in **triplicate**. Illustration 53A shows where each copy goes.

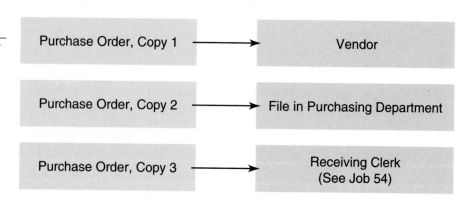

Illustration 53A

Flow of three copies of purchase order

Purchase Order, Copy 1 →	Vendor
Purchase Order, Copy 2 →	File in Purchasing Department
Purchase Order, Copy 3 →	Receiving Clerk (See Job 54)

You are a purchase order clerk for Guedo Tire Shop. On May 5, you are asked by the purchasing agent, Tom Shen, to prepare a purchase order for the following items from Akers Tire Company:

3 dozen High performance tires,
Stock No. HP 45
3 sets of Steel belted tires,
Stock No. SB 11

Cultural Notes

By around 1000 B.C., the Chinese had developed one of the most complex accounting systems in the world. They used a system of currency and had a central bank. The Office of the Superintendent of Records produced for the government lists of receipts and payments, maps, totals of the number of workers in each occupation, kinds and quantities of production tools, and estimates of natural resources.

The items are wanted by May 20. The order is to be shipped by truck to the stockroom. According to your price quotation records, HP 45 costs $1,620.00 per dozen; SB 11 costs $331.20 per set of 4. Akers allows 60 days for payment. Their address is found in Illustration 52A (pages 416–417). The order is your first—number 1.

Illustration 53B below shows the purchase order that was completed in three steps.

STEP 1 **Complete the top part of the form.**

Copy the name, address, and terms from the price quotation records. Then, fill in the order number, date of the order, ship via, ship to, and date wanted. Make sure that all blanks are filled in.

STEP 2 **Complete the bottom part of the form.**

Fill in the quantity, description (including stock number), and unit price of each item. The unit prices will come from the price quotation records. The quantity can be each, dozen, pair, dozen pair, gross, or some other unit of count.

Illustration 53B
Completed purchase order

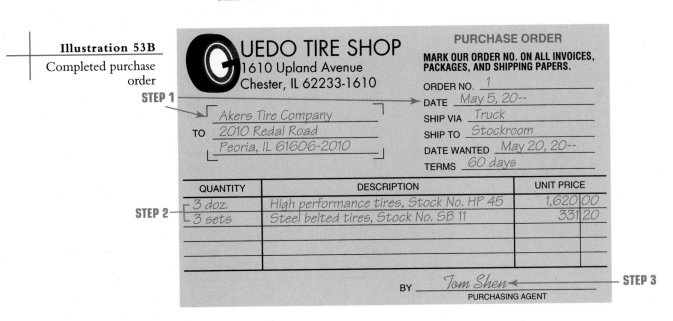

GUEDO TIRE SHOP
1610 Upland Avenue
Chester, IL 62233-1610

PURCHASE ORDER

MARK OUR ORDER NO. ON ALL INVOICES, PACKAGES, AND SHIPPING PAPERS.

STEP 1

ORDER NO. _1_
DATE _May 5, 20--_

TO _Akers Tire Company_
2010 Redal Road
Peoria, IL 61606-2010

SHIP VIA _Truck_
SHIP TO _Stockroom_
DATE WANTED _May 20, 20--_
TERMS _60 days_

QUANTITY	DESCRIPTION	UNIT PRICE
3 doz.	High performance tires, Stock No. HP 45	1,620 00
3 sets	Steel belted tires, Stock No. SB 11	331 20

STEP 2

BY _Tom Shen_ ◄——— STEP 3
PURCHASING AGENT

Give the purchase order to Tom Shen, the purchasing agent, for his signature. Usually, you would give a batch of purchase orders at one time for him to sign. Once signed, the triplicate copies are separated and sent where they need to go.

USING THE COMPUTER

Key Terms

Reorder level. Point at which stock reaches minimum.

If a computer is used, purchase orders can be prepared automatically when stock levels become low. The computer searches the stock records for any item that has reached its **reorder level**. The reorder level is reached when an item falls to or below its minimum amount.

For example, the computer searches the stock records and finds that item SB 11 has fallen below the minimum and must be reordered. This information is shown in Illustration 53C.

The computer subtracts the balance (17) from the maximum (30). The difference (13) is the amount that will be ordered. If price quotation records are also computerized, the computer may select the vendor if the purchasing agent has indicated the preferred vendor in advance.

By combining data from the stock record with data from the price quotation record, the computer generates a purchase order. Illustration

Illustration 53C

Stock record on display screen

```
                    STOCK RECORD
STOCK NO.           SB 11
STOCK ITEM          Steel belted tires
UNIT                Set of 4
MINIMUM             20
MAXIMUM             30
BALANCE             17
ISSUED
RECEIVED
```

Maximum 30
Balance −17
Ordered   13

Illustration 53D

Purchase order prepared by computer

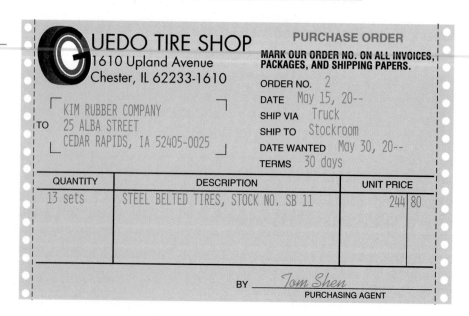

53D (page 424) shows the purchase order prepared by the computer system.

BUILDING YOUR BUSINESS VOCABULARY

On a sheet of paper, write the headings **Statement Number** and **Words**. Next, choose the words that match the statements. Write each word you choose next to the statement number it matches. Be careful; not all the words listed should be used.

Statements

1. Assists the purchasing agent
2. Record of vendors, information, and prices relating to one stock item
3. Numbered in advance
4. Seller
5. Point at which stock reaches minimum
6. The buyer for a business
7. A form used to order merchandise
8. A request to the buyer to place an order
9. Three copies

Words

prenumbered
price quotation record
purchase order
purchase order clerk
purchase requisition
purchasing agent
reorder level
stock record clerk
terms
triplicate
vendor

STEPS REVIEW: Preparing Purchase Orders

STEP 1 Complete the top part of the form.

STEP 2 Complete the bottom part of the form.

STEP 3 Request the purchasing agent's signature.

APPLICATION PROBLEMS

Problem 53-1 You are a purchase order clerk for Greenbrier Inn, 419 South Street, Santee, SC 29142-0419. It is your job to help the purchasing agent prepare purchase orders.

CHECK POINT

53-1

There should be two items of merchandise entered on each purchase order.

Directions

Prepare purchase orders from the following information. Fill in all spaces except the purchasing agent's signature. All merchandise is to be shipped by truck to the stockroom.

Purchase Order No. 61
Date: April 7
Date Wanted: April 17
To: Colfax Company
210 Monely Avenue
High Point, NC 27260-1210
Terms: 30 days
30 pair Curtains—Stock No. C5 @ $19.99
30 ea. Pillows—Stock No. P6 @ $5.99

Purchase Order No. 62
Date: April 9
Date Wanted: April 19
To: Allen Motel Suppliers
110 Regalia Avenue
Columbus, GA 31906-6110
Terms: 45 days
20 ea. Bed spreads—Stock No. BS 5 @ $19.95
20 ea. Mattress covers—Stock No. MC 7 @ $16.89

Purchase Order No. 63
Date: April 17
Date Wanted: April 27
To: Clarkson Linens
103 Muney Street
Nashville, TN 37209-5103
Terms: 60 days
10 dz. Towels—Stock No. T6 @ $42.95
10 dz. Wash cloths—Stock No. W8 @ $13.88

Problem 53-2

You are a purchase order clerk for Castelli Specialties, Inc., 2212 Gage Blvd., Topeka, KS 66610-7212. You help the purchasing agent prepare purchase orders.

CHECK POINT

53-2

There should be two items of merchandise entered on each purchase order.

Directions

Prepare purchase orders from the following information. Fill in all spaces except the purchasing agent's signature. All merchandise is to be shipped by air freight to the stockroom.

Purchase Order No. 201
Date: June 8
Date Wanted: June 15
To: Imber's Bridal Shoppe
3031 Stalle Blvd.
Plaistow, NH 03865-3031
Terms: 60 days
20 ea. Black jackets—Stock No. BJ 7 @ $85.50
2 dz. Bow ties—Stock No. BT 12 @ $69.88

Purchase Order No. 203
Date: June 17
Date Wanted: June 24
To: Glen's Boutique
3708 Bonde Street
Presque Isle, ME 04769-3708
Terms: 20 days
10 dz. pr. Black shoes—Stock No. B 17 @ $613.00
50 ea. Cummerbunds—Stock No. CB 3 @ $9.85

Purchase Order No. 202
Date: June 12
Date Wanted: June 19
To: R & D Tuxedo Rentals
257 14th Street, W.
Juneau, AK 99801-0257
Terms: 45 days
26 ea. White jackets—Stock No. WJ 8 @ $66.99
2 gr. Invitations—Stock No. IN 4 @ $24.87

Problem 53-3 may be found in the Working Papers.

applied math preview

Copy and complete the following problems.

1. 10 x $ 5.16 =
2. 10 x $26.99 =
3. 100 x $ 7.52 =
4. 100 x $28.31 =
5. 1,000 x $ 5.14 =

6. 20 x $ 5.10 =
7. 30 x $ 7.00 =
8. 40 x $ 8.20 =
9. 50 x $10.50 =
10. 60 x $12.00 =

key terms preview

- Backordered
- Delivery receipt
- Discontinued

- Over
- Packing slip
- Receiving clerk

- Receiving report
- Short

goals

1 To learn how to compare stock received to stock ordered.

2 To learn how to prepare receiving reports.

UNDERSTANDING THE JOB

You have learned that one copy of each purchase order is sent to the receiving department. The receiving department records are kept by a **receiving clerk**. It is the job of the receiving clerk to compare what was ordered with what was actually received. The form used to show this comparison is the **receiving report**, which is shown in Illustration 54C on page 429.

Sample Problem 1 describes how to prepare a receiving report in a manual system. Sample Problem 2 shows how to prepare a receiving report in a computer system.

SAMPLE PROBLEM 1

Manual System

Key Terms

Receiving clerk. Receives goods and compares with goods ordered.

Receiving report. Form that shows goods ordered and received.

Guedo Tire Shop sells, mounts, and balances car and truck tires. Guedo Tire Shop also sells and installs brake pads and shock absorbers for cars and trucks. When Guedo Tire Shop receives a shipment of tires, the tires are simply stacked on the bed of the delivery truck. Since the tires are large, they are not shipped in cartons. When Guedo Tire Shop receives brake pads or shock absorbers, they are delivered in cartons.

STEP 1

DELIVERY RECEIPT
Akers Tire Company
2010 Redal Road
Peoria, IL 61606-2010

SHIP TO	Guedo Tire Shop	INVOICE NO. 1410
	1610 Upland Avenue	DATE May 19, 20--
	Chester, IL 62233-1610	OUR ORDER NO. 171
		CUSTOMER'S ORDER NO. 1
TERMS	60 days	SHIP VIA Truck

QUANTITY	STOCK NO.	DESCRIPTION	UNIT PRICE	TOTAL AMOUNT
2 dozen	HP 45	High performance tires		
3 sets	SB 11	Steel belted tires		
		Note: 1 dozen HP 45 on backorder		

Vera Long is a receiving clerk for Guedo Tire Shop. Her job is to compare the stock received with the purchase order and prepare a receiving report. Here is how she does her job.

STEP 1 Compare the stock received with the delivery receipt or packing slip.

Key Terms

Packing slip. Form which describes contents of a shipment.

Delivery receipt. Form which describes contents of a shipment

When Vera receives a shipment of brake pads or shock absorbers, she opens the cartons and unpacks the stock. Included in the cartons is a packing slip. When Vera receives a shipment of tires, there are no cartons to unpack. Instead of a **packing slip**, the truck driver gives her a **delivery receipt**. Both the packing slip and the delivery receipt describe the contents of the shipment and contain the same types of information. The difference is that a packing slip is put inside the carton when it is filled by the vendor and the delivery receipt is usually handed to Vera by the person who delivers the stock.

A delivery receipt for the delivery of tires is shown in Illustration 54A. A packing slip that Vera received for a delivery of brake pads is shown in Illustration 54B. Vera will compare the stock received in cartons with

PACKING SLIP
Benson Auto Parts, Inc.
504 Grand Avenue
Elgin, IL 60120-0504

SOLD TO	Guedo Tire Shop	INVOICE NO. 3012
	1610 Upland Avenue	DATE May 19, 20--
	Chester, IL 62233-1610	OUR ORDER NO. 1427
		CUSTOMER'S ORDER NO. 2
TERMS	30 days	SHIP VIA Truck

QUANTITY	STOCK NO.	DESCRIPTION	UNIT PRICE	TOTAL AMOUNT
30 pr.	BP 6	Brake pads		
3 dz. pr.	SA 4	Shock absorbers		
		Note: 6 LC 3 on backorder		

Key Terms

Backordered. Out of stock temporarily.

Discontinued. No longer sold.

Short. Less than ordered.

Over. More than ordered.

what is printed on the packing slip. She will compare the tires received with what is printed on the delivery receipt. Vera decides to check the delivery of tires first.

Vera first compares the quantity received with the quantity listed on the delivery receipt. She counts 2 dozen high performance tires, which agrees with the delivery receipt. As the driver unloads the tires, Vera verifies that each tire is a high performance tire and inspects them to see if any are damaged. When she had verified the count and the condition of the tires, she places a check mark on the delivery receipt next to "2 dozen."

If Vera finds damaged stock or errors in the shipment, she notes the errors or damages on the delivery receipt. For example, if she had found 3 tires damaged, she would write "3 tires damaged" on the delivery receipt.

Vera uses the same procedures when comparing the stock in cartons with what is printed on the packing slip.

Notice that the Unit Price and Total Amount columns on the delivery receipt are blackened out. The receiving clerk deals only with quantity, not with price.

Notice also that 1 dozen HP 45 is on **backorder**. Backorder means that the vendor is temporarily out of stock on that item. The stock will be sent as soon as possible. If the goods ordered are never to be sold again by the vendor, they are called **discontinued** goods. Vera will record information about backordered and discontinued goods in Step 3.

STEP 2 **Compare the packing slip or delivery receipt with the purchase order.**

Vera compares the checked delivery receipt with the purchase order (Illustration 54C). She finds that 3 dozen of HP 45 were ordered. The delivery receipt shows that 2 dozen of HP 45 were received and 1 is on backorder, so HP 45 checks out. She finds that 3 sets of SB 11 were ordered and were received. No goods are **short** (less than ordered) or **over** (more than ordered). She is now ready to prepare a receiving report.

Illustration 54C

Completed purchase order for tires

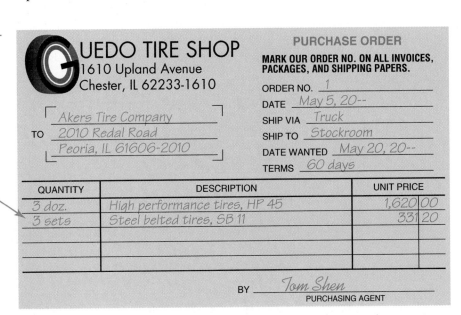

STEP 2

GUEDO TIRE SHOP
1610 Upland Avenue
Chester, IL 62233-1610

PURCHASE ORDER

MARK OUR ORDER NO. ON ALL INVOICES, PACKAGES, AND SHIPPING PAPERS.

TO
Akers Tire Company
2010 Redal Road
Peoria, IL 61606-2010

ORDER NO. _1_
DATE _May 5, 20--_
SHIP VIA _Truck_
SHIP TO _Stockroom_
DATE WANTED _May 20, 20--_
TERMS _60 days_

QUANTITY	DESCRIPTION	UNIT PRICE	
3 doz.	High performance tires, HP 45	1,620	00
3 sets	Steel belted tires, SB 11	331	20

BY _Tom Shen_
PURCHASING AGENT

STEP 3 Prepare the receiving report.

The receiving report that Vera prepares is shown in Illustration 54D (below).

On the report, Vera writes in the date on which the shipment was received and fills in the vendor name and number. She also fills in the purchase order number used by the purchasing department and the vendor's invoice number that she found on the delivery receipt.

Vera copies the item numbers, descriptions, units, and quantities ordered from the purchase order. She then lists the quantities actually received. Since only 2 dozen of item HP 45 were received, Vera records only 2 in the Quantity Received column. She writes "1 backordered" in the Remarks column to explain the difference between the Quantity Ordered and Quantity Received columns.

She then records the sets of SB 11 that were received. She enters "3" in the Quantity Received column. Vera then signs the receiving report to indicate that it is she who has prepared it.

STEP 4 Send copies of the receiving report to the accounting clerk and the stock record clerk.

Vera sends two copies of the receiving report. One goes to the accounting department so that they can pay the vendor. The second goes to the stock record clerk who can then update two records:

1. The stock records, by adding the amounts received to the balance on hand.
2. The open order report, by recording an order now filled.

Vera will now follow the same steps to verify the shipment of brake pads and shock absorbers.

Illustration 54D

Completed receiving report for tires

STEP 3 ⟶

QUEDO TIRE SHOP
1610 Upland Avenue
Chester, IL 62233-1610

RECEIVING REPORT

Date Received __May 20__ 20 __-__

Vendor Name __Akers Tire Company__   Vendor No. __714__

Our Purchase Order No. __1__   Vendor Invoice No. __1410__

Item No.	Item Description	Unit	Quantity Ordered	Quantity Received	Remarks
HP45	High performance tires	Doz.	3	2	1 backordered
SB11	Steel belted tires	Sets	3	3	

Receiving Clerk __V. Long__

In some companies, a copy of the purchase order is used as the receiving report. The receiving clerk places a check mark on the purchase order next to each item that has been received in the quantity ordered and in good condition. If there are any differences (such as damage, backorder, over, or short), the clerk writes these remarks next to the quantity ordered on the purchase order. Copies of the purchase order are then sent to the accounting clerk and the stock record clerk.

SAMPLE PROBLEM 2

Computer System

In many companies, the receiving report is prepared using a computer. When the computer is used, the same steps are followed as in a manual system, but much of the work is done automatically. If Vera used a computer, here is how she would record the shipment of the two types of tires:

STEP 1 Compare the stock received with the delivery receipt.

Even though she is using a computer, Vera must still examine the stock received and compare it with the delivery receipt. In other words, Step 1 will remain unchanged when using a computer.

STEP 2 Compare the delivery receipt with the purchase order.

Step 2 also remains unchanged when using a computer. The packing slip and the purchase order must be compared to see if what was received was what the company ordered. But, Vera completes this step as part of Step 3.

STEP 3 Prepare the receiving report.

It is at this point that the computer becomes a timesaver. Instead of copying data by hand onto a receiving report, Vera brings up the receiving report form on the screen of her computer. Illustration 54E (page 432) shows this report.

Vera keys the purchase order number, 1, and the computer automatically fills in the facts about the purchase order. These facts were stored in the computer files when the purchase order was prepared.

The cursor, next to Vendor Invoice No., is asking Vera to enter the vendor invoice number, so she keys 1410, as shown in Illustration 54F (page 432). The cursor then moves to the Quantity Received column, asking Vera to key the amount of stock that was received. There were 3 dozen of HP45 ordered, but since only 2 were received, Vera keys in 2.

The cursor moves under the Remarks column. Vera uses the codes at the bottom of the screen and keys in 1B to show that one dozen are on backorder.

She then enters the quantity received for SB11, 3 sets. Illustration 54F shows a completed receiving report.

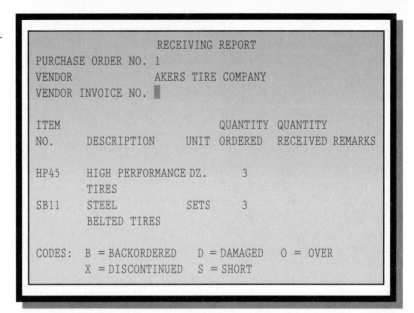

```
                    RECEIVING REPORT
PURCHASE ORDER NO. 1
VENDOR             AKERS TIRE COMPANY
VENDOR INVOICE NO.

ITEM                          QUANTITY QUANTITY
NO.     DESCRIPTION    UNIT   ORDERED  RECEIVED REMARKS

HP45    HIGH PERFORMANCE DZ.     3
        TIRES
SB11    STEEL          SETS      3
        BELTED TIRES

CODES:  B = BACKORDERED   D = DAMAGED   O = OVER
        X = DISCONTINUED  S = SHORT
```

```
                    RECEIVING REPORT
PURCHASE ORDER NO. 1
VENDOR             AKERS TIRE COMPANY
VENDOR INVOICE NO. 1410

ITEM                          QUANTITY QUANTITY
NO.     DESCRIPTION    UNIT   ORDERED  RECEIVED REMARKS

HP45    HIGH PERFORMANCE DZ.     3        2       1B
        TIRES
SB11    STEEL          SETS      3        3
        BELTED TIRES

CODES:  B = BACKORDERED   D = DAMAGED   O = OVER
        X = DISCONTINUED  S = SHORT
```

The computer will print the receiving report if asked to do so. Copies do not need to be sent to the accounting clerk and the stock record clerk since each can bring it up on his or her own screen.

As you can see, the computer makes the job of the receiving clerk much easier. The work of the stock record clerk is also reduced. The computer will automatically update the stock records and the open order report. However, you must be careful when entering data into a computer, for a wrong entry will make several different records incorrect.

BUILDING YOUR BUSINESS VOCABULARY

On a sheet of paper, write the headings **Statement Number** and **Words**. Next, choose the words that match the statements. Write each word you choose next to the statement number it matches. Be careful; not all the words listed should be used.

Statements	Words
1. Three copies	backordered
2. Form that shows goods ordered and received	delivery receipt
	discontinued
3. No longer sold	over
4. Less than ordered	packing slip
5. Receives goods and compares with goods ordered	prenumbered
	receiving clerk
6. Out of stock temporarily	receiving report
7. More than ordered	reorder level
8. Point at which stock reaches minimum	short
9. Form in a carton which describes contents of a shipment	terms
	triplicate
10. Form which describes contents of a shipment	

STEPS REVIEW: Receiving Goods and Preparing Receiving Reports— Manual System

STEP 1 Compare the stock received with the packing slip or delivery receipt.

STEP 2 Compare the packing slip or delivery receipt with the purchase order.

STEP 3 Prepare the receiving report.

STEP 4 Send copies of the receiving report to the accounting clerk and the stock record clerk.

APPLICATION PROBLEMS

Problem 54-1

In the table that follows, stock ordered appears in the left column. Stock received appears in the right column.

CHECK POINT

54-1

There should be 4 check marks in the Agree column.

Directions

On a sheet of paper, write the numbers 1 through 10 and two column headings, Agree and Disagree. If the information about stock ordered agrees with the information about stock received, place a check mark in the Agree column. If the information about stock ordered and stock received disagrees, place a check mark in the Disagree column.

	Ordered		Received	
1.	26	BL575	26	BL575
2.	175	SB82	173	SB82
3.	198	LLA15	198	LLA15
4.	117	DY27	171	DY27
5.	37	M3766	37	M3676
6.	63 pr.	L182	63 pr.	L182
7.	15 dz.	RP599	15 dz.	RP599
8.	18	J2077	18	J2076
9.	2 gr.	RZ1388	2 gr.	RZ1338
10.	106 pr.	BN4399	105 pr.	BN4399

Problem 54-2   You are the shipping clerk for Ellis Home Store. Your job is to check shipments of stock received and prepare receiving reports.

Directions

Prepare a receiving report from the information that follows. Use Illustration 54D (page 430) as a model.

On August 8 you receive a shipment of merchandise from Dallas Company, Vendor No. 31. The purchase order number for this shipment is 613; the vendor's invoice number is 107.

The delivery receipt sent with the shipment lists the following:

Qty.	Unit	Item No.	Description
25	Each	WD 06	Window doors
20	Rolls	RF 19	Roofing felt
125	Bundles	RS 12	Roofing shingles
80	Sections	PF 24	Picket fencing

When you examine the shipment, you discover that 4 rolls of roofing felt are damaged and cannot be placed in inventory. You also find a note telling you that 5 window doors are on backorder.

Purchase Order No. 613 lists the following order:

Qty.	Unit	Item No.	Description
30	Each	WD 06	Window doors
20	Rolls	RF 19	Roofing felt
125	Bundles	RS 12	Roofing shingles
80	Sections	PF 24	Picket fencing

CHECK POINT

54-2(d)

Two items need to be entered in the Remarks column.

a. On the top part of the receiving report, enter the date received, vendor name and number, our purchase order number, and the vendor invoice number.
b. Fill in the Item No., Item Description, Unit, and Quantity Ordered columns using information from the purchase order.
c. Fill in the Quantity Received column from the information given on the delivery receipt. Remember to enter only stock that has actually been received in good condition.
d. Explain any differences between the amounts in the Quantity Ordered and Quantity Received columns. Use the Remarks column.
e. Sign your name as receiving clerk.

Problem 54-3   You are the receiving clerk for Cullen Hotel. Your job is to check shipments of stock received and prepare receiving reports.

Directions

Prepare a receiving report from the information that follows. Use Illustration 54D (page 430) as a model. Follow steps *a.* through *e.* listed in Problem 54-2.

You have received today, January 9, a shipment of merchandise from Dillon Supply Company, Vendor No. 471. The purchase order number for this shipment is 1047; the vendor's invoice number is 3166.

CHECK POINT

54-3(d)

Four items need to be entered in the Remarks column.

The packing slip sent with the shipment lists the following:

Qty.	Unit	Item No.	Description
30	Each	TL 07	Towels
5	Dozen	LB 15	Light bulbs
50	Each	LK 21	Locks
0	Each	SB 09	Waste baskets

When you examine the shipment, you discover that three towels are damaged and cannot be placed in inventory. You also find a note telling you that 10 locks are on backorder. A second note tells you that SB 09 waste baskets are no longer available.

Purchase Order No. 1047 lists the following order:

Qty.	Unit	Item No.	Description
30	Each	TL 07	Towels
6	Dozen	LB 15	Light bulbs
60	Each	LK 21	Locks
50	Each	SB 09	Waste baskets

No reason was given for the 1 dozen missing light bulbs.

Problem 54-4 may be found in the Working Papers.

→ UNDERSTANDING THE JOB

Purchase invoice. What buyer calls bill from vendor.

Cash discount. Small discount given for early payment.

You have learned in Job 53 that a purchase order is sent by a purchasing agent to a vendor. After shipping the merchandise ordered, the vendor sends a bill to the buyer. The vendor calls this bill a sales invoice. The buyer calls this bill a **purchase invoice**.

A clerk in the accounting department will need to check the accuracy of the math on the invoice before it is paid. The clerk will then need to file the invoice by its due date, which is the date by which it must be paid. By using this filing process, invoices can be pulled from the file and paid when they are due.

As you learned in Job 43, invoices have terms of sale, which tell when an invoice is due. An example of terms is 60 days (also expressed as n/60), which means that the invoice must be paid by 60 days after its date. Thus, the invoice in Illustration 55A (page 437) dated August 9 with terms of 60 days is due by October 8. (You can review how to figure the due date in Job 43.) The clerk will file the invoice under the date of October 5 or 6 to be sure that payment reaches the seller by the due date of October 8.

Sometimes, the seller will want to give the buyer a reason to pay the invoice earlier than its due date. In such cases, the seller will offer the buyer a **cash discount**. A cash discount is a small discount given for early payment of an invoice. Cash discounts are usually 1 percent, 2 percent, or 3 percent.

If terms include a cash discount, they are written in this form: 2/10, n/60. This expression means that a 2 percent discount will be given for payment within 10 days of the date of the invoice, or the full amount of the invoice must be paid by 60 days after its date.

If the invoice in Illustration 55A (below) had terms of 2/10, n/60, then payment by 10 days after August 9, which is August 19, would entitle the buyer to a 2 percent discount. The discount would be figured as follows:

Corrected amount of invoice	$8,208.00
Rate of cash discount	× .02
Amount of cash discount	$ 164.16

The amount to be paid within the discount period would not be the full amount of $8,208.00, but $164.16 less.

Corrected amount of invoice	$8,208.00
Less: amount of cash discount	− 164.16
Amount to be paid	$8,043.84

SAMPLE PROBLEM

Bea Shea is an accounting clerk at the Guedo Tire Shop. She receives the invoice shown in Illustration 55A (below).

These are the steps Bea followed to check and file this invoice:

STEP 1 Compare the invoice with the purchase order.

Bea compared the invoice with the purchase order to see if the quantities, stock numbers, descriptions, and unit prices agreed. If they did not agree, she would have notified the purchasing agent.

Illustration 55A

Approved purchase invoice

STEP 1
Compare invoice with purchase order.

STEP 2
Compare invoice with receiving report.

STEP 3

Akers Tire Company
2010 Redal Road
Peoria, IL 61606-2010

SOLD TO Guedo Tire Shop	INVOICE NO. 1578
1610 Upland Avenue	DATE August 9, 20--
Chester, IL 62233-1610	OUR ORDER NO. 1642
	CUSTOMER'S ORDER NO. 25
TERMS 60 days	SHIP VIA Truck

QUANTITY	STOCK NO.	DESCRIPTION	UNIT PRICE	TOTAL AMOUNT
15 sets	SB 11	Steel belted tires	331 20	4,968 00 ~~4,981 50~~
2 doz.	HP 45	High performance tires	1,620 00	3,240 00
		Total invoice		8,208 00 ~~8,221 50~~

Approved Bea Shea

STEP 5

STEP 4

STEP 6 File the invoice for payment.

STEP 2   Compare the invoice with the receiving report.

Bea compared the quantities listed on the invoice with the receiving report to see if the quantities agreed. If they did not agree, she would have notified the purchasing agent.

STEP 3   Check the extensions.

The invoice shows that 15 × $331.20 = $4,981.50. Bea used her calculator to check the extension. She found that it was incorrect. The product of 15 × $331.20 = $4,968.00. Bea crossed out the wrong extension, $4,981.50, and entered the correct extension, $4,968.00, just above it.

She then checked the second extension, 2 × $1,620.00 = $3,240.00 and found that it was correct.

STEP 4   Check the total.

After Bea checked both extensions and corrected the first one, she added them in order to check the total of $8,221.50. Because of the error in the first extension, she needed to correct the total to $8,208.00. She did so by crossing out the incorrect total and writing in the correct total above it.

STEP 5   Approve the invoice for payment.

After correcting the invoice, Bea wrote the word *Approved* and signed her name. Her signature means that the invoice can be paid when it is due. Bea **vouched** the invoice, which means that she guaranteed its correctness.

STEP 6   File the invoice for payment.

The invoice will then be filed for payment. Guedo Tire Shop follows the practice of filing by a date three days before the due date in order to pay it on time. Since the due date is October 8, it will be filed under October 5.

If there were a cash discount available, the invoice would be filed by a date three days before the last date for discount. Thus, if terms were 2/10 for a discount, it would be filed for payment three days before August 19, which is August 16.

Key Terms

Vouch. To guarantee that something is correct.

➡ USING THE COMPUTER

If Bea used a computer to check an invoice, she would select the invoice approval option from the menu. She would key the information from the purchase invoice. The computer would automatically check this information against the purchase order and the receiving report records. In the case of any differences, the computer would indicate a problem. Bea would then notify the purchasing agent. The computer would then check and correct the extensions and the total, and display them on the screen. Bea would approve and sign the invoice as in a manual system.

A calculator can be useful in verifying purchase invoices. Both extensions and the total can be checked. Here's how to check the invoice shown in Illustration 55A (page 437) with a calculator:

STEP 1 ▶ Find the first extension.

Enter the first quantity by pressing these keys:

| 1 | 5 |

Next, multiply by the first unit price by pressing these keys:

| × | 3 | 3 | 1 | . | 2 | 0 |

Now, store the extension, 4,968, in memory by pressing the M+ key. Correct the incorrect extension at this point.

STEP 2 ▶ Find the second extension.

Enter the second quantity by pressing this key:

| 2 |

Next, multiply by the second unit price by pressing these keys:

| × | 1 | 6 | 2 | 0 | . | 0 | 0 |

Store the extension, 3,240.00, in memory by pressing the M+ key.

STEP 3 ▶ Check the total on the invoice.

Press the MR/C or MR key. This will display the total in the memory, 8208, or $8,208.00. Correct the incorrect total on the invoice.

Press the MR/C or MC key to clear the memory. Now, press the C key. This will clear your calculator for the next operation.

➡ BUILDING YOUR BUSINESS VOCABULARY

On a sheet of paper, write the headings **Statement Number** and **Words**. Next, choose the words that match the statements. Write each word you choose next to the statement number it matches. Be careful; not all the words listed should be used.

Statements	Words
1. Record of vendors, information, and prices relating to one stock item	cash discount
	extension
2. Assists the purchasing agent	issue
3. A form used to order merchandise	menu
4. Quantity times unit price	prenumbered
5. Seller	price quotation record

Statements	Words
6. Length of time a customer has to pay a bill	purchase invoice
7. To guarantee that something is correct	purchase order
8. What the vendor calls the bill to the buyer	purchase order clerk
9. What the buyer calls the bill from the vendor	sales invoice
10. Numbered in advance	terms
11. A reduction in price for early payment of an invoice	vendor
	vouch

STEPS REVIEW: Checking and Filing Purchase Invoices

STEP 1 Compare the invoice with the purchase order.

STEP 2 Compare the invoice with the receiving report.

STEP 3 Check the extensions.

STEP 4 Check the total.

STEP 5 Approve the invoice for payment.

STEP 6 File the invoice for payment.

APPLICATION PROBLEMS

Problem 55-1

A group of extensions follows. Your job is to check the extensions.

CHECK POINT

55-1

There are 5 incorrect extensions.

Directions

On a sheet of paper, write the numbers 1 through 10 and two column headings, Correct and Incorrect. If the extension is correct, place a check mark in the Correct column. If it is not correct, calculate the correct extension and write the correct amount in the Incorrect column.

1.	425	× $16.12 =	$ 6,889.25
2.	371	× $ 9.08 =	$ 3,368.68
3.	17	× $ 1.39 =	$ 32.81
4.	109	× $ 2.16 =	$ 253.44
5.	48	× $ 2.97 =	$ 142.56
6.	517	× $10.95 =	$ 5,661.15
7.	1,004	× $ 1.89 =	$ 1,897.65
8.	271½	× $ 0.52 =	$ 141.18
9.	181	× $19.68 =	$ 3,562.08
10.	2,137	× $ 8.17 =	$174,592.90

Problem 55-2   You are responsible for figuring the amount to be paid for invoices. Round your answers to the nearest cent.

CHECK POINT

55-2(2)

Amount to be Paid = $4,410

Directions
Copy and complete the following table by:
a. Calculating the amount of cash discount, if one is offered.
b. Figuring the amount to be paid.

	Amount of Invoice	Terms	Cash Discount	Amount to be Paid
1.	$2,500.00	n/30		
2.	$4,500.00	2/10, n/30		
3.	$4,600.00	n/60		
4.	$ 850.00	2/10, n/60		
5.	$ 355.00	3/10, n/30		
6.	$ 745.00	n/90		
7.	$ 654.75	1/10, n/60		
8.	$2,575.40	n/45		
9.	$3,324.05	2/10, n/30		
10.	$ 675.95	3/20, n/60		

You are working in the accounting department of Herbert's Company, a department store. Your job is to check purchase invoices. You have received the following invoices and have already compared them with purchase orders and receiving reports.

Directions

a. Copy the following partial invoices. Check each extension and each total. If you find an error, draw a line through the incorrect amount and write the correct amount above it. Remember, if an extension is incorrect, the total will also need to be corrected.

b. After making the necessary corrections, write the word *Approved* on each invoice and sign your name.

c. Indicate the due date and the date under which you would file to pay each invoice. Assume that invoices should be filed by a date three days before they are due.

Invoice #1 (Date March 17, 20--; Terms: n/30)

QUANTITY	STOCK NO.	DESCRIPTION	UNIT PRICE		TOTAL AMOUNT	
150 ea.	AR 12	Area rugs	37	16	1,486	40
50 ea.	SC 3	Slipcover sets	42	89	1,586	93
		Total invoice			3,073	33

Invoice #2 (Date May 30, 20--; Terms: n/30)

QUANTITY	STOCK NO.	DESCRIPTION	UNIT PRICE		TOTAL AMOUNT	
45 ea.	QB 6	Quilt bedspreads	99	75	4,488	75
9 dz.	DP 15	Down pillows	34	70	312	30
		Total invoice			4,523	45

Invoice #3 (Date July 7, 20--; Terms: n/60)

QUANTITY	STOCK NO.	DESCRIPTION	UNIT PRICE	TOTAL AMOUNT
37 ea.	BB 14	Boom boxes	34 15	1,263 55
19 ea.	PR 01	Portable radios	22 25	422 75
52 ea.	AN 16	Antennas	19 98	1,083 96
		Total invoice		2,770 26

Invoice #4 (Date April 10, 20--; Terms: 60 days)

QUANTITY	STOCK NO.	DESCRIPTION	UNIT PRICE	TOTAL AMOUNT
30 ea.	BC 8	Beauty cases	39 55	1,186 50
15 ea.	WC 6	Weekend cases	66 90	1,003 50
19 ea.	PC 4	Pullman cases	51 45	977 55
		Total invoice		3,167 55

Invoice #5 (Date October 14, 20--; Terms: 90 days)

QUANTITY	STOCK NO.	DESCRIPTION	UNIT PRICE	TOTAL AMOUNT
28 ea.	SC 12	Suitcases	72 94	2.042 32
40 ea.	EB 19	Executive bags	86 12	3,444 80
		Total invoice		5,487 12

Invoice #6 (Date August 22, 20--; Terms: n/90)

QUANTITY	STOCK NO.	DESCRIPTION	UNIT PRICE	TOTAL AMOUNT
20 ea.	CW 4	Cookware sets	87 27	1,754 40
19 ea.	MO 11	Microwave ovens	63 20	1,200 80
50 ea.	SI 10	Spray irons	7 62	381 00
		Total invoice		3,336 20

Chapter 11

CHECK YOUR READING

1. What is the advantage of using a computer to update price quotations?
2. a. How many copies of a purchase order are usually prepared?
   b. Where does each copy of the purchase order go?
3. What are the advantages of using a computer to reorder stock?
4. a. What is the job of the receiving clerk?
   b. What forms does the receiving clerk use to complete her/his job?

DISCUSSION

You and Vern Knabe work together as receiving clerks. Vern cannot understand why it is necessary to use both the delivery receipt and the purchase order before preparing a receiving report. He has asked you to explain. What would you say to him?

CRITICAL THINKING

You are a receiving clerk. Your supervisor has complained to you recently that too many damaged goods are being found in the inventory. You know that you are not responsible for these because you carefully unpack each shipment and look for damage. If goods are damaged, you put them aside for return. You report only undamaged goods on your receiving report.

However, there is a new worker in the department. You watch him unpack goods and discover that he counts them, but does not inspect them for damage. You decide to talk to him directly. Write two reasons that you would give him for inspecting shipments for damage.

COMMUNICATION IN THE WORKPLACE

You are the purchasing agent for your school store. You need a price quotation for a school sweatshirt. Prepare a letter that you would write to a vendor to obtain a price quotation. Include the following in your letter:

REINFORCEMENT ACTIVITIES

a. A description of the item in detail (such as color, size, material, and so forth)
b. A request for the price
c. A request for terms
d. A request for information about discounts if a large quantity is purchased

Your letter should not be more than one page in length.

➡ FOCUS ON CAREERS

Key Terms

Clerk. Person who keeps records as a major part of his or her work.

A **clerk** is defined in most dictionaries as a person who is employed to keep records as the major part of his or her daily work. The reason that different clerks have different titles is that they keep different kinds of records.

1. What record does a stock record clerk keep?
2. What record does a purchase order clerk keep?
3. What record does a receiving clerk keep?

Sometimes you can tell the title of the clerk if you know the record kept.

4. What title would be given to a clerk who keeps payroll records?
5. What title would be given to a clerk who keeps records of accounts receivable?

However, a clerk sometimes keeps so many records that a more general title is given. The title "general clerk" is often used for this person.

6. If a general clerk were in charge of all of the activities discussed in this chapter, list all of the records that he or she might keep.

➡ REVIEWING WHAT YOU HAVE LEARNED

On a sheet of paper, write the headings **Statement Number** and **Words**. Next, choose the words that best complete the statements. Write each word you choose next to the statement number it completes. Be careful; not all the words listed should be used.

Statements	Words
1. The form used to order merchandise is the _____.	backordered
2. Goods that are out of stock temporarily are said to be _____.	cash discount
	delivery receipt
3. The form that shows goods ordered and received is the _____.	discontinued
	packing slip
4. Goods no longer sold by a vendor are said to be _____.	price quotation record
	purchase invoice

Statements	Words
5. A record of vendors, information, and prices relating to one item is a _____.	purchase order
6. The form in a carton that describes the contents of a shipment is the _____.	receiving report
	reorder level
7. The point at which stock reaches its minimum level is the _____.	vendor
	vouch
8. The term that means to guarantee that something is correct is _____.	
9. A _____ is a reduction in the amount of an invoice for early payment.	
10. The form which describes the contents of a shipment is the _____.	

MASTERY PROBLEM

You work for Appliance World, located at 3509 A Avenue, Columbus, OH 43207-3509. Because you are the only clerk in the business, you perform a variety of jobs.

CHECK POINT

(d)
The invoice is incorrect.

Directions

a. You are acting as a purchase order clerk. You have requested price quotations from three companies for food processors, item no. FP 7. The quotations are as follows:

Vendor No.	Co. Name and Address	Unit	Price	Terms
167	J & N Company 6317 Frank Avenue Flint, MI 48507-6317	Ea.	$49.95	60 days
192	Pete's Kitchen Goods 21 Indian Drive Hobbs, NM 88240-0021	Ea.	$52.75	30 days
413	Southeast Food Equipment Company 191 7th Avenue Dothan, AL 36301-1917	Ea.	$51.99	45 days

Prepare a price quotation record and enter this information. The date is July 9, 20--.

b. It is now July 12, 20--. You have the authority to select the vendor who offered the lowest price. Do so and prepare Purchase Order No. 419 for 75 food processors. You want the goods in 20 days, shipped by truck to your stockroom.

c. You are now acting as a receiving clerk. The goods ordered arrive on July 31, 20--. The packing slip that accompanies the goods indicates the following:

65 FP 7 food processors; 10 backordered

You count the goods and find 65 present. All are in good condition. Prepare a receiving report. Remember to include under Quantity Received only those goods actually received. The vendor invoice number is 1897.

d. You are now acting as accounting clerk. Copy the following partial invoice. Check the invoice and guarantee it for payment.

QUANTITY	STOCK NO.	DESCRIPTION	UNIT PRICE	TOTAL AMOUNT
65 ea.	FP 7	Food processors	49 95	3,264 75

REVIEWING YOUR BUSINESS VOCABULARY

This activity may be found in the Working Papers.

Chapter 12

Wholesalers purchase merchandise in large quantities from manufacturers and other suppliers. Because most merchandise purchased by a wholesale business is bought on credit, wholesalers must keep records of how much they owe to each manufacturer or supplier.

In Chapter 12, you will learn how to keep accounts payable records. You will also learn how to use a purchases journal, a cash payments journal, and a purchases returns and allowances journal.

Record Keeping for Accounts Payable Clerks

Web Phones

You can use the Internet for more than just e-mail and Web browsing. You can also use it to telephone friends. One advantage of using *Web phones*, as they are called, is that many people connect to the Internet for a flat monthly rate. That means that you can use the Internet for long distance calls for long periods of time with no increase in your Internet bills.

Right now, the quality of sound of Web phones is not as good as regular phones. There may be delays between when you speak and when your caller hears what you said. Also, the caller's voice may sound thin and wavering at times.

What is a Web phone? It may be a special phone with a screen. But more likely it is simply software that you run on your computer system. Two companies offer the software free as part of their Internet browser software. For example, both Microsoft and Netscape offer Web phone software as part of their browsers. Microsoft's Web phone is called NetMeeting. Netscape's is called CoolTalk.

To use the software, you must have speakers and a microphone attached to your computer. If you have a camera also attached, you can view your caller. Presently, Web phone software works only when both parties are using the same software, and of course, you both must have your computers running.

Major telephone companies have been buying cable TV companies. Many experts predict that telephone companies will soon use that cable TV wiring to provide customers with cable TV, telephone service, and Internet access and that we will use our computer systems for telephone calls, Internet access, and TV viewing.

applied math preview

Copy and complete these problems. Pay close attention to the + and − signs.

1.	2.	3.	4.
+477	+785	+5,177	+2,414
−218	+724	−3,987	+ 987
+104	−319	− 104	+3,621
−196	−508	+2,166	+ 473
+355	− 97	+1,045	−1,476
−127	+206	+ 919	−2,990

key terms preview

- **Accounts payable ledger**
- **Creditors**
- **Purchase on account**
- **Schedule of accounts payable**

goals

1 To learn how to keep a record of the amounts owed to creditors.

2 To learn how to prepare a schedule of accounts payable.

UNDERSTANDING THE JOB

Key Terms

Creditors. People or businesses to whom money is owed.

Accounts payable ledger. Group of creditor accounts.

Purchase on account. Buying merchandise on credit.

You have learned to keep accounts for customers. In this job, you will learn to keep accounts for **creditors**. Creditors are people or businesses to whom your company owes money. A group of creditor accounts is called the **accounts payable ledger**.

When your company buys merchandise from another company on credit, this is called a **purchase on account**. The company from which you buy merchandise on credit is the creditor. When merchandise is purchased on credit, the record keeper must do the following:

1. Open a separate account for each creditor from whom merchandise is purchased.
2. Keep the accounts in a separate book or file called the accounts payable ledger.
3. Record information in the accounts using the rules shown in Illustration 56A.

Illustration 56A

Rules for recording in a creditor account

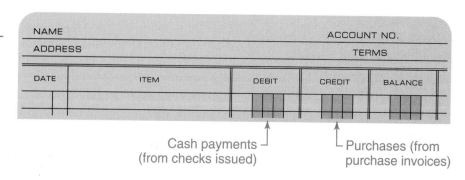

Cash payments (from checks issued) — DEBIT

Purchases (from purchase invoices) — CREDIT

NAME		ACCOUNT NO.		
ADDRESS		TERMS		
DATE	ITEM	DEBIT	CREDIT	BALANCE

When using accounts for creditors, all purchases are recorded in the Credit column of the account. Credits increase the balance of the creditor account. All cash payments are recorded in the Debit column of the account. Debits decrease the balance of a creditor account.

Illustration 56B shows how BW Supply Company's creditor account (number 2116) would look after recording a purchase for $710.00 on May 3, Invoice No. 112. Terms of the purchase were 20 days.

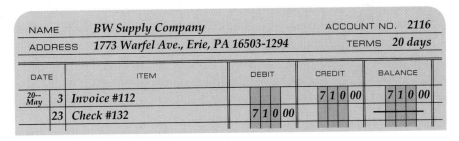

NAME	*BW Supply Company*		ACCOUNT NO.	*2116*	
ADDRESS	*1773 Warfel Ave., Erie, PA 16503-1294*		TERMS	*20 days*	

DATE		ITEM	DEBIT	CREDIT	BALANCE
20-- May	3	*Invoice #112*		7 1 0 00	7 1 0 00

Notice the following about the recording shown in Illustration 56B:

1. The heading shows the name and address of the creditor, as well as the account number and terms of sale.
2. The date of the invoice, May 3, was recorded in the Date column.
3. The invoice number, 112, was entered in the Item column.
4. The amount of the purchase invoice, $710.00, was entered in the Credit column. Amounts owed to creditors are always entered in the Credit column of a creditor account.
5. The amount of the credit, $710.00, was *added* to the previous balance, $0.00 (not shown), to find the new balance of $710.00. Credits are always added to the previous balance to find the new balance of a creditor account. The new balance was recorded in the Balance column.

Illustration 56C shows how BW Supply Company's creditor account would look after recording a cash payment of $710.00 on May 23, check no. 132.

NAME	*BW Supply Company*		ACCOUNT NO.	*2116*	
ADDRESS	*1773 Warfel Ave., Erie, PA 16503-1294*		TERMS	*20 days*	

DATE		ITEM	DEBIT	CREDIT	BALANCE
20-- May	3	*Invoice #112*		7 1 0 00	7 1 0 00
	23	*Check #132*	7 1 0 00		———

Notice the following about the recording shown in Illustration 56C:

1. The date of the payment, May 23, was entered in the Date column. Only the number 23 was entered, since the year and month were already there and did not change.
2. The check number, 132, was written in the Item column.
3. The amount of the payment, $710.00, was entered in the Debit column. Payments to creditors are always entered in the Debit column of a creditor account.
4. The amount of the debit, $710.00, was *subtracted* from the previous balance, $710.00, to find the new balance of $0.00. Debits are always subtracted from the previous balance to find the new balance of a creditor

account. The new balance of $0.00 was entered as a line drawn through the Balance column.

The account now shows all of the dealings with BW Supply Company in May. No money is owed to that company as of May 23. Since the debits and credits are equal, the balance is zero.

A company will have many creditor accounts in the accounts payable ledger. These accounts may be kept in a loose-leaf binder, on a floppy disk, or on a hard drive. Whether there are 2 or 1,000 creditor accounts, a list of what all creditors are owed must be prepared monthly. This list is called a **schedule of accounts payable**. A schedule that goes along with the Sample Problem is shown in Illustration 56E on page 454.

SAMPLE PROBLEM

You are an accounts payable clerk for P. O'Reilly Construction Company. Your company purchased materials and other items from three companies:

Creditor	Address	Account No.	Terms
R. Dixon Company	2199 Bowne Road Reno, NV 89511-1472	2101	15 days
P. Nogales Company	2540 Enterprise Road Reno, NV 89512-3712	2102	20 days
N. Ramirez Company	5406 Mill Street Reno, NV 89502-5406	2103	30 days

During March, your company made the following purchases and payments. Illustration 56D (page 453) shows how you recorded them in the creditor accounts.

Mar. 3   Received Purchase Invoice No. 137 from P. Nogales Company for $765.00.

    4   Received Purchase Invoice No. 297 from N. Ramirez Company for $995.00.

    5   Received Purchase Invoice No. 505 from R. Dixon Company for $865.00.

    7   Received Purchase Invoice No. 509 from R. Dixon Company for $410.00.

  20   Issued Check No. 271 to R. Dixon Company in payment of the invoice dated March 5.

  22   Issued Check No. 272 to R. Dixon Company in payment of the invoice dated March 7.

  23   Issued Check No. 273 to P. Nogales Company in payment of the invoice dated March 3.

  28   Received Purchase Invoice No. 317 from N. Ramirez Company for $416.00.

  31   Received Purchase Invoice No. 159 from P. Nogales Company for $905.00.

Notice the pencil footings in the three accounts to prove the final balances. Only columns with at least two numbers were footed. This is why the P. Nogales Company Debit column was not footed.

NAME	R. Dixon Company			ACCOUNT NO. **2101**	
ADDRESS	2199 Bowne Rd., Reno, NV 89511-1472			TERMS **15 days**	

DATE		ITEM	DEBIT	CREDIT	BALANCE
20-- Mar.	5	Invoice #505		865 00	865 00
	7	Invoice #509		410 00	1275 00
	20	Check #271	865 00		410 00
	22	Check #272	410 00		———
			1275 00	1275 00	

NAME	P. Nogales Company			ACCOUNT NO. **2102**	
ADDRESS	2540 Enterprise Rd., Reno, NV 89512-3712			TERMS **20 days**	

DATE		ITEM	DEBIT	CREDIT	BALANCE
20-- Mar.	3	Invoice #137		765 00	765 00
	23	Check #273	1,670.00	765 00	———
	31	Invoice #159	-765.00	905 00	905 00
			905.00	1670 00	

NAME	N. Ramirez Company			ACCOUNT NO. **2103**	
ADDRESS	5406 Mill St., Reno, NV 89502-5406			TERMS **30 days**	

DATE		ITEM	DEBIT	CREDIT	BALANCE
20-- Mar.	4	Invoice #297		995 00	995 00
	28	Invoice #317		416 00	1411 00
				1411 00	

To prove the final balance of the P. Nogales Company account, the following math was done:

Total credits	$1,670.00
Less: Total debits	− 765.00
Final balance	$ 905.00

Illustration 56E (page 454) shows the schedule of accounts payable you prepared for P. O'Reilly Construction Company. It was prepared in three steps:

STEP 1 **Record the heading.**

The standard three-line heading was entered to answer the questions Who?, What?, and When? The schedule is prepared as of the last day of the month.

Each creditor account with a balance was entered. Notice that since the R. Dixon Company account had a zero balance, it was left out of the schedule. Accounts are listed in alphabetical order, as they appear in the accounts payable ledger.

Illustration 56E

Schedule of accounts payable

Tips

List only accounts with balances other than zero.

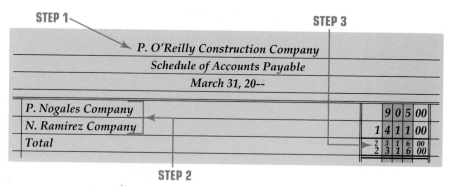

STEP 1

STEP 3

P. O'Reilly Construction Company
Schedule of Accounts Payable
March 31, 20--

P. Nogales Company	9 0 5 00
N. Ramirez Company	1 4 1 1 00
Total	2 3 1 6 00
	2 3 1 6 00

STEP 2

STEP 3 Find the total.

The money column was ruled and footed. The footed total, after being checked by re-adding, was entered again as a final total. The word *Total* was written under the creditor names, and a double ruling was drawn under the money column.

➡ BUILDING YOUR BUSINESS VOCABULARY

On a sheet of paper, write the headings **Statement Number** and **Words**. Next, choose the words that match the statements. Write each word you choose next to the statement number it matches. Be careful; not all the words listed should be used.

Statements	Words
1. The column used to record an increase in a creditor account	accounts payable ledger
2. Buying merchandise on credit	accounts receivable account
3. A group of creditor accounts	accounts receivable ledger
4. A record of a charge customer's purchases and payments	credit
5. A list of creditors with the amounts owed to them	creditors
6. The column used to record a decrease in a creditor account	debit
7. People or businesses to whom money is owed	purchase on account
	schedule of accounts payable
	three-column account

STEPS REVIEW: Preparing a Schedule of Accounts Payable

STEP 1 Record the heading.

STEP 2 List the creditor names and balances.

STEP 3 Find the total.

Problem 56-1   You are employed by the Walters Appliance Company as an accounts payable clerk. Your job is to record purchase invoices and checks written to pay these invoices in creditor accounts.

Directions

a. Open a creditor account for M. Windsor Company, 1632 Park Avenue, Jackson, MS 39212-4846, Account Number 2361. Terms of purchase are 20 days.

b. Record the following items in the M. Windsor Company account. Remember to find the new balance after each debit or credit is recorded.

CHECK POINT

56-1(c)

Final balance = $2,994.60

June	4	Received Purchase Invoice No. 506 for $8,142.20.
	9	Received Purchase Invoice No. 509 for $2,116.80.
	17	Received Purchase Invoice No. 527 for $975.50.
	24	Issued Check No. 277 in payment of the invoice dated June 4.
	27	Received Purchase Invoice No. 546 for $2,019.10.
	29	Issued Check No. 291 in payment of the invoice dated June 9.

c. Prove the balance at the end of the month. Show all footings in the account.

Problem 56-2   You are employed by the Pineiro Vacuum Cleaner Company as an accounts payable clerk. Your job is to record purchase invoices and checks written to pay these invoices in creditor accounts.

Directions

a. Open a creditor account for W. Lopez Company, 110 Calle Caribe, Bayamon, PR 00959-0110, Account Number 2270. Terms of purchase are 10 days.

b. Record the following items in the W. Lopez Company account. Remember to find the new balance after entering each amount.

CHECK POINT

56-2(c)

Final balance = $4,220.01

Oct.	3	Received Purchase Invoice No. 809 for $863.84.
	8	Received Purchase Invoice No. 821 for $1,604.37.
	13	Issued Check No. 411 in payment of the invoice dated October 3.
	15	Received Purchase Invoice No. 837 for $1,047.82.
	18	Issued Check No. 417 in payment of the invoice dated October 8.
	26	Received Purchase Invoice No. 856 for $3,172.19.

c. Prove the balance at the end of the month. Show all footings in the account.

Problem 56-3   You are employed by the M. Arend Company as an accounts payable clerk. Your job is to record purchase invoices and checks written to pay these invoices in creditor accounts.

Directions

a. Open accounts for the following creditors:

Creditor	Address	Account No.	Terms
J. Cernak Company	502 SE Long Street Topeka, KS 66607-8054	2101	10 days
D. Hahn Company	491 Morton Avenue Des Moines, IA 50313-7120	2102	20 days
F. Schwartz Company	612 Colonial Avenue Waterbury, CT 06708-4208	2103	15 days

b. Record the following information in the creditor accounts. Remember to find the new balance after entering each amount.

CHECK POINT

56-3(d)

Total = $1,029.97

Aug. 3   Received Purchase Invoice No. 112 from J. Cernak Company for $310.85.
   5   Received Purchase Invoice No. 511 from D. Hahn Company for $511.81.
   8   Received Purchase Invoice No. 701 from F. Schwartz Company for $408.19.
   11   Received Purchase Invoice No. 705 from F. Schwartz Company for $511.12.
   13   Issued Check No. 104 to J. Cernak Company in payment of the invoice dated August 3.
   17   Received Purchase Invoice No. 119 from J. Cernak Company for $416.47.
   18   Received Purchase Invoice No. 721 from F. Schwartz Company for $317.81.
   19   Received Purchase Invoice No. 514 from D. Hahn Company for $712.16.
   23   Issued Check No. 119 to F. Schwartz Company in payment of the invoice dated August 8.
   25   Issued Check No. 121 to D. Hahn Company in payment of the invoice dated August 5.
   26   Issued Check No. 124 to F. Schwartz Company in payment of the invoice dated August 11.
   27   Issued Check No. 126 to J. Cernak Company in payment of the invoice dated August 17.

c. Prove the balances at the end of the month. Show all footings in the accounts.

d. Prepare a schedule of accounts payable as of August 31.

Problem 56–4 may be found in the Working Papers.

applied math preview

Find the due date of these invoices.

Date of Invoice	Terms	Date of Invoice	Terms
1. July 24	10 days	5. August 7	15 days
2. May 10	20 days	6. June 13	45 days
3. March 17	30 days	7. October 4	60 days
4. April 9	60 days	8. November 14	30 days

key terms preview

- Purchases journal

goals

1. To learn how to record purchase invoices in a purchases journal.
2. To learn how to post from the purchases journal to the accounts payable ledger.
3. To learn how purchase invoices are filed.

→ UNDERSTANDING THE JOB

Key Terms

Purchases journal. A record of purchases on account.

Tips

Entry date goes in Date column.

You have learned how to record amounts due to creditors directly from the purchase invoices into the accounts payable ledger. Many accounts payable clerks do not record directly into the creditor accounts. Instead, they first enter purchase invoices in a special record called a **purchases journal**. The purchases journal lists all purchases from creditors by date. Illustration 57A on page 458 shows how data from a purchase invoice are recorded in a purchases journal.

Here are the steps you would follow to make the entry in the purchases journal shown in Illustration 57A (page 458):

STEP 1   Copy the date of entry.

Copy the date of entry (date of approval) in the Date column. This will usually be a date *after* the date of the invoice, since a few days are needed to check and approve an invoice.

STEP 2   Copy the creditor's name.

Copy the name on the top of the invoice, D. Phillips Company, into the Creditor's Name column.

STEP 3   Copy the invoice number.

Write the invoice number, 117, in the Invoice No. column.

Illustration 57A

Recording a purchase
invoice in a purchases
journal

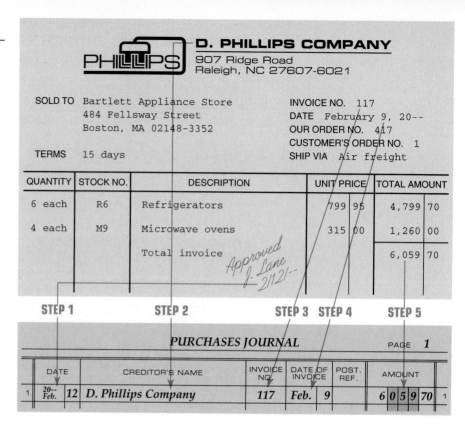

PHILLIPS

D. PHILLIPS COMPANY
907 Ridge Road
Raleigh, NC 27607-6021

SOLD TO   Bartlett Appliance Store
          484 Fellsway Street
          Boston, MA 02148-3352

TERMS   15 days

INVOICE NO. 117
DATE February 9, 20--
OUR ORDER NO. 417
CUSTOMER'S ORDER NO. 1
SHIP VIA Air freight

QUANTITY	STOCK NO.	DESCRIPTION	UNIT PRICE	TOTAL AMOUNT
6 each	R6	Refrigerators	799 95	4,799 70
4 each	M9	Microwave ovens	315 00	1,260 00
		Total invoice		6,059 70

Approved
J. Lane
2/12/--

STEP 1   STEP 2   STEP 3   STEP 4   STEP 5

PURCHASES JOURNAL   PAGE   **1**

	DATE	CREDITOR'S NAME	INVOICE NO.	DATE OF INVOICE	POST. REF.	AMOUNT	
1	20-- Feb. 12	*D. Phillips Company*	117	*Feb.* 9		6 0 5 9 70	1

STEP 4 Copy the date of invoice.

Write the date of the invoice, February 9, in the Date of Invoice column. Of the two dates entered in the purchases journal, February 9 and February 12, the 9th is the more important date. Since the terms are 15 days, the due date is 15 days after February 9, or February 24.

STEP 5 Copy the amount.

The total amount of the invoice, $6,059.70, is written in the Amount column.

Recording in the purchases journal is only part of the process. A record still needs to be made in the creditor accounts in the accounts payable ledger. To do this, you must post from the purchases journal to the creditor accounts.

Posting must be done with great care and accuracy. The correct amounts must be posted to the correct accounts. Illustration 57B (page 459) shows how the purchase already recorded in the purchases journal is posted to the D. Phillips Company account. Here are the steps followed:

STEP 1 Copy the date.

Be very careful here. The *date of invoice* is the date that is written in the Date column of the creditor account. February 9 is the date written in the account.

STEP 2 Copy the invoice number.

Write Invoice #117 in the Item column.

STEP 3 Record the posting reference in the creditor account.

The posting reference is P1. P stands for *purchases journal*; 1 stands for page *1*. A posting from the second page of the purchases journal would be written as P2. Enter P1 in the Post. Ref. column of the D. Phillips Company account.

STEP 4 Post the amount.

Write the amount, $6,059.70, in the Credit column of the account, since all purchases are recorded in the Credit column.

Illustration 57B

Posting from purchases journal to creditor account

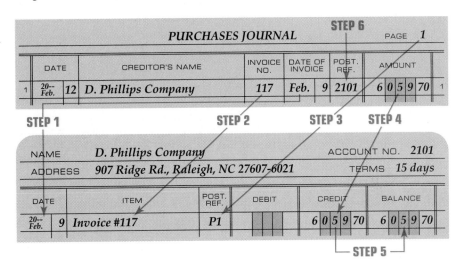

Tips

Date of invoice is recorded in Date column of creditor account.

Post purchases to the Credit column of a creditor account. Add credits to previous balance.

STEP 5 Find the new balance.

Find the new balance of the account and record it in the Balance column. Since there was no previous balance, the balance is $6,059.70.

STEP 6 Enter the account number in the purchases journal.

Put the number of the creditor account, 2101, in the Post. Ref. column of the purchases journal to show that the entry has been posted to creditor account number 2101.

SAMPLE PROBLEM

You are the accounts payable clerk for the M & T Wholesale Company. Your purchase invoices show these purchases for the month:

Apr. 4 Received Purchase Invoice No. 106 from L. Dexter Company, dated April 3, for $1,075.10.

7 Received Purchase Invoice No. 219 from J. Rollins Company, dated April 4, for $963.85.

13 Received Purchase Invoice No. 123 from L. Dexter Company, dated April 11, for $805.91.

Apr. 21 Received Purchase Invoice No. 229 from J. Rollins Company, dated April 18, for $1,517.90.

27 Received Purchase Invoice No. 245 from J. Rollins Company, dated April 25, for $701.12.

Illustration 57C (below) shows how these purchases would be recorded in the purchases journal and posted to the creditor accounts. The creditor accounts show the terms for each creditor. Here are the steps that you would follow:

STEP 1 Record the purchases in the purchases journal.

Record the purchases in the purchases journal, using the data from the purchase invoices.

STEP 2 File the invoices.

Once an invoice has been recorded in the purchases journal, it is ready for filing. There are many different ways to file purchase invoices. As you learned in Job 55, some clerks file purchase invoices two or three days

Illustration 57C

Purchases journal and accounts payable ledger

STEP 1

PURCHASES JOURNAL   PAGE **7**

	DATE		CREDITOR'S NAME	INVOICE NO.	DATE OF INVOICE		POST. REF.	AMOUNT	
1	20-- Apr.	4	*L. Dexter Company*	106	*Apr.*	3	201	1 0 7 5 10	1
2		7	*J. Rollins Company*	219		4	202	9 6 3 85	2
3		13	*L. Dexter Company*	123		11	201	8 0 5 91	3
4		21	*J. Rollins Company*	229		18	202	1 5 1 7 90	4
5		27	*J. Rollins Company*	245		25	202	7 0 1 12	5
6		30	*Total*					5 0 6 3 88 5 0 6 3 88	6

STEP 3 —— STEP 4

ACCOUNTS PAYABLE LEDGER

NAME	*L. Dexter Company*				ACCOUNT NO. **201**
ADDRESS	*1300 Oak St., Mobile AL 36604-2147*				TERMS **10 days**

DATE		ITEM	POST. REF.	DEBIT	CREDIT	BALANCE
20-- Apr.	3	*Invoice #106*	P7		1 0 7 5 10	1 0 7 5 10
	11	*Invoice #123*	P7		8 0 5 91	1 8 8 1 01
					1 8 8 1 01	

STEP 5

NAME	*J. Rollins Company*				ACCOUNT NO. **202**
ADDRESS	*1630 Pecan St., Mobile, AL 36617-3119*				TERMS **25 days**

DATE		ITEM	POST. REF.	DEBIT	CREDIT	BALANCE
20-- Apr.	4	*Invoice #219*	P7		9 6 3 85	9 6 3 85
	18	*Invoice #229*	P7		1 5 1 7 90	2 4 8 1 75
	25	*Invoice #245*	P7		7 0 1 12	3 1 8 2 87
					3 1 8 2 87	

STEP 3

before the due date. Another common method is to file them according to the dates they are due. When filing according to due date, 31 folders would be used—one for each day of the month. Illustration 57D (below) shows this type of filing system.

Using this system, L. Dexter Invoice No. 106 would be filed under the 13 folder, since April 3 (date of invoice) plus 10 days (terms) equals April 13 (due date). J. Rollins Invoice No. 219 would be filed under 29. (April 4 plus 25 days equals April 29.) This system lets the accounts payable clerk pay invoices on the due date.

STEP 3 Post to the creditor accounts.

At the end of each day, post the amounts in the purchases journal to the creditor accounts in the accounts payable ledger. Notice P7 was entered in the Post. Ref. column, since page 7 of the purchases journal was used. The account number was entered in the purchases journal *after* each posting. New account balances were calculated after each posting.

STEP 4 Total the purchases journal.

At the end of the month, rule and foot the Amount column of the purchases journal. Re-add the column before writing the final total. Draw a double ruling under the final total. Write the word Total in the Creditor's Name column. Date the total as of the last day of the month.

Illustration 57D
A due date filing system

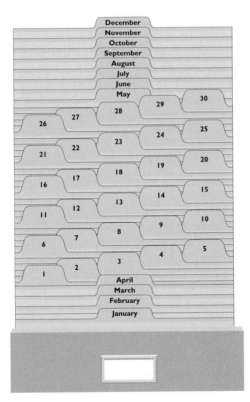

STEP 5 Prove the account balances and prepare a schedule of accounts payable.

Each account was footed to prove its balance, and then a schedule of accounts payable was prepared for M & T Wholesale Company. (See Illustration 57E, page 462.)

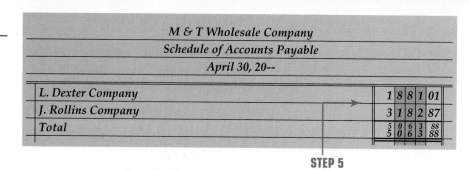

M & T Wholesale Company
Schedule of Accounts Payable
April 30, 20--

L. Dexter Company	1 8 8 1 01
J. Rollins Company	3 1 8 2 87
Total	5 0 6 3 88

STEP 5

BUILDING YOUR BUSINESS VOCABULARY

On a sheet of paper, write the headings **Statement Number** and **Words**. Next, choose the words that match the statements. Write each word you choose next to the statement number it matches. Be careful; not all the words listed should be used.

Statements

1. The column used to record an increase in a creditor account
2. People or businesses to whom money is owed
3. A group of customer accounts
4. Buying merchandise on credit
5. A record of purchases on account
6. A list of creditors with the amounts owed to them
7. The account column in which payments to creditors are recorded
8. A group of creditor accounts

Words

accounts payable ledger
accounts receivable
 ledger
credit
creditors
debit
purchase on account
purchases journal
schedule of accounts
 payable
schedule of accounts
 receivable
terms

STEPS REVIEW: Using a Purchases Journal and an Accounts Payable Ledger

STEP 1 Record the purchases in the purchases journal.

STEP 2 File the invoices.

STEP 3 Post to the creditor accounts.

STEP 4 Total the purchases journal.

STEP 5 Prove the account balances and prepare a schedule of accounts payable.

APPLICATION PROBLEMS

Problem 57-1
You are employed as an accounts payable clerk at K & P Lumber Company. Your job is to record approved purchase invoices in the purchases journal.

CHECK POINT

57-1(e)

Total = $6,506.42

Directions

a. Open a purchases journal for April. Number the journal page 1.
b. Record the following approved purchase invoices in the purchases journal:

Apr. 3   Received Purchase Invoice No. 137 from J. Hobbs Company, dated April 1, for $847.16.

6   Received Purchase Invoice No. 701 from K. Urbach Company, dated April 2, for $916.32.

9   Received Purchase Invoice No. 142 from J. Hobbs Company, dated April 6, for $1,710.93.

12   Received Purchase Invoice No. 603 from C. McMahon Company, dated April 9, for $104.17.

15   Received Purchase Invoice No. 155 from J. Hobbs Company, dated April 11, for $497.82.

17   Received Purchase Invoice No. 706 from K. Urbach Company, dated April 14, for $1,121.05.

22   Received Purchase Invoice No. 813 from C. McMahon Company, dated April 19, for $711.18.

30   Received Purchase Invoice No. 717 from K. Urbach Company, dated April 27, for $597.79.

c. Total the Amount column of the purchases journal.
d. Verify the footing of the purchases journal by re-adding.
e. Record the final total in the Amount column of the purchases journal. Double rule the journal, and write the date and the word *Total* in the proper places.

Problem 57-2   You are employed as an accounts payable clerk by R. Guillaume Company. Your job is to record approved purchase invoices in the purchases journal and post to the creditor accounts in the accounts payable ledger.

Directions

a. Open a purchases journal for July. Number the journal page 1.
b. Open ledger accounts for the creditors below:

Creditor	Address	Account No.	Terms
C. Brooks Company	162 Kenneth Street Detroit, MI 48203-0162	201	10 days
W. Navarro Company	1328 SW Douglas Street Portland, OR 97219-3208	202	30 days
N. Salazar Company	3117 Hartford Avenue Providence, RI 02919-3117	203	20 days

CHECK POINT

57-2(f)

Total = $4,928.99

c. Record the following approved purchase invoices in the purchases journal. Post daily from the purchases journal to the Credit column of the creditor accounts. Do not forget to enter P1 as a posting reference in the accounts and an account number as a posting reference in the journal.

July 5   Received Purchase Invoice No. 917 from W. Navarro Company, dated July 1, for $439.17.

8   Received Purchase Invoice No. 308 from C. Brooks Company, dated July 6, for $2,104.19.

July 11 Received Purchase Invoice No. 417 from N. Salazar Company, dated July 8, for $147.65.

17 Received Purchase Invoice No. 320 from C. Brooks Company, dated July 15, for $711.02.

22 Received Purchase Invoice No. 946 from W. Navarro Company, dated July 19, for $731.04.

26 Received Purchase Invoice No. 329 from C. Brooks Company, dated July 23, for $618.34.

30 Received Purchase Invoice No. 477 from N. Salazar Company, dated July 27, for $177.58.

d. Total the Amount column of the purchases journal.

e. Verify the footing of the purchases journal by re-adding.

f. Record the final total in the Amount column of the purchases journal. Double rule the journal, and write the date and the word *Total* in the proper places.

g. Prove the account balances at the end of the month by footing the Credit column in each creditor account.

h. Prepare a schedule of accounts payable as of July 31. Use Illustration 57E (page 462) as a guide.

Problem 57–3 may be found in the Working Papers.

applied math preview

Copy and complete these problems. Pay close attention to the + and − signs.

1.	2.	3.	4.
+611	+5,176	+$511.25	+$1,571.08
−317	+2,093	− 37.95	+ 1,396.12
+209	−1,277	+ 206.10	− 1,471.08
−167	−1,094	− 199.40	+ 2,099.16
+410	− 472	+ 146.81	− 1,396.12
−377	+ 389	− 209.94	− 2,199.16

key term preview

- Cash payments journal

goals

1 To learn how to record payments to creditors in a cash payments journal.

2 To learn how to post from the cash payments journal to the accounts payable ledger.

⇨ UNDERSTANDING THE JOB

Key Terms

Cash payments journal. A record of cash payments.

You have learned how to record approved purchase invoices in the purchases journal. You have also learned how to post from the purchases journal to the creditor accounts in the accounts payable ledger. In this job, you will learn how to record payments made to creditors in a **cash payments journal**. The cash payments journal lists all cash payments by date. The data for entries in the cash payments journal come from check stubs. Illustration 58A shows how data from a check stub are recorded in a cash payments journal.

Here are the steps you would follow to make the entry in the cash payments journal shown in Illustration 58A:

Illustration 58A

Recording a check stub in a cash payments journal

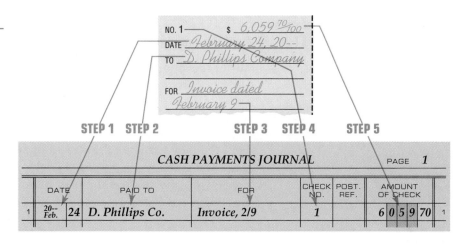

STEP 1   Copy the date of the check.

Copy the date, February 24, in the Date column.

STEP 2   Copy the creditor's name.

Write the name, D. Phillips Co., in the Paid To column. You should abbreviate as needed to fit data in the space provided.

STEP 3   Copy the invoice date.

Write the words *Invoice, 2/9* in the For column to show which invoice was paid with this check.

STEP 4   Copy the check number.

Write the number of the check, 1, in the Check No. column.

STEP 5   Enter the amount.

Copy the amount of the check, $6,059.70, in the Amount of Check column of the cash payments journal.

After recording the check in the cash payments journal, you must post to the D. Phillips Company account in the accounts payable ledger. Illustration 58B (page 467) shows how this posting is done. Here are the steps followed:

STEP 1   Copy the date.

Enter the day, 24, in the Date column of the account. The year and month do not need to be repeated.

STEP 2   Enter the check number.

Write *Check #1* in the Item column.

STEP 3   Record the posting reference in the creditor account.

Enter CP1 for *C*ash *P*ayments Journal, page *1* in the Post. Ref. column of the account.

STEP 4   Post the amount.

Write the amount, $6,059.70, in the Debit column of the account, since all payments are recorded in the Debit column.

STEP 5   Find the new balance.

Find the new balance of the account and enter it in the Balance column. Since the amount was recorded in the Debit column, *subtract* it from the previous balance to find the new balance. The zero balance in the account is calculated as follows:

Tips

Post payments to the Debit column of a creditor account.

Previous balance	$ 6,059.70
Debit on February 24	−6,059.70
New balance	$ 0.00

Use a blank line in the Balance column to show a zero balance.

Tips

Subtract a debit from the previous balance.

STEP 6 Enter the account number in the cash payments journal.

Enter the account number, 2101, in the Post. Ref. column of the cash payments journal to show that the entry has been posted to the creditor account.

Illustration 58B

Posting from cash payments journal to creditor account

CASH PAYMENTS JOURNAL — STEP 6 — PAGE 1

	DATE	PAID TO	FOR	CHECK NO.	POST. REF.	AMOUNT OF CHECK	
1	20-- Feb. 24	D. Phillips Co.	Invoice, 2/9	1	2101	6 0 5 9 70	1

STEP 1   STEP 2   STEP 3   STEP 4

NAME	D. Phillips Company		ACCOUNT NO.	2101
ADDRESS	907 Ridge Rd., Raleigh, NC 27607-6021		TERMS	15 days

DATE	ITEM	POST. REF.	DEBIT	CREDIT	BALANCE
20-- Feb. 9	Invoice #117	P1		6 0 5 9 70	6 0 5 9 70
24	Check #1	CP1	6 0 5 9 70		

— STEP 5 —

SAMPLE PROBLEM

You are the accounts payable clerk for M & T Wholesale Company. The creditor accounts in your accounts payable ledger already contain postings from the purchases journal. You make the following cash payments during April:

Apr. 13 Issued Check No. 57 to L. Dexter Company for $1,075.10 in payment of the invoice dated April 3.

21 Issued Check No. 58 to L. Dexter Company for $805.91 in payment of the invoice dated April 11.

29 Issued Check No. 59 to J. Rollins Company for $963.85 in payment of the invoice dated April 4.

Illustration 58C (page 468) shows how these cash payments would be recorded in the cash payments journal and posted to the creditor accounts. Here are the steps you would follow:

STEP 1 Record the cash payments in the cash payments journal.

Record the payments in the cash payments journal, using the data from the check stubs.

STEP 2 File the paid invoices.

Pull the purchase invoices paid from the due date folders and file them under each creditor's name.

STEP 3 Post to the creditor accounts.

At the end of each day, post the amounts in the cash payments journal to the creditor accounts in the accounts payable ledger. Notice CP6 in the Post. Ref. column, since page 6 of the cash payments journal was used. An account number was entered in the cash payments journal after each posting. New account balances were calculated after each posting.

Tips

Post daily to creditor accounts.

STEP 4 Total the cash payments journal.

At the end of the month, rule and foot the Amount of Check column of the cash payments journal. Re-add the column before writing the final total. Draw a double ruling under the final total. Write the word *Total* in the Paid To column. Date the total as of the last day of the month.

Illustration 58C

Cash payments journal and accounts payable ledger

STEP 1

CASH PAYMENTS JOURNAL — PAGE 6

	DATE		PAID TO	FOR	CHECK NO.	POST. REF.	AMOUNT OF CHECK	
1	20-- Apr.	13	L. Dexter Co.	Invoice, 4/3	57	201	1 0 7 5 10	1
2		21	L. Dexter Co.	Invoice, 4/11	58	201	8 0 5 91	2
3		29	J. Rollins Co.	Invoice, 4/4	59	202	9 6 3 85	3
4		30	Total				2 8 4 4 86 / 2 8 4 4 86	4

ACCOUNTS PAYABLE LEDGER   STEP 3   STEP 4

NAME **L. Dexter Company**   ACCOUNT NO. **201**
ADDRESS **1300 Oak St., Mobile, AL 36604-2147**   TERMS **10 days**

DATE		ITEM	POST. REF.	DEBIT	CREDIT	BALANCE
20-- Apr.	3	Invoice #106	P7		1 0 7 5 10	1 0 7 5 10
	11	Invoice #123	P7		8 0 5 91	1 8 8 1 01
	13	Check #57	CP6	1 0 7 5 10		8 0 5 91
	21	Check #8	CP6	8 0 5 91		———
				1 8 8 1 01	1 8 8 1 01	

NAME **J. Rollins Company**   ACCOUNT NO. **202**
ADDRESS **1630 Pecan St., Mobile, AL 36617-5119**   TERMS **25 days**

DATE		ITEM		POST. REF.	DEBIT	CREDIT	BALANCE
20-- Apr.	4	Invoice #219		P7		9 6 3 85	9 6 3 85
	18	Invoice #229		P7		1 5 1 7 90	2 4 8 1 75
	25	Invoice #245	3,182.87	P7		7 0 1 12	3 1 8 2 87
	29	Check #59	-963.85	CP6	9 6 3 85		2 2 1 9 02
			2,219.02			3 1 8 2 87	

STEP 3   STEP 5

STEP 5 Prove the account balances and prepare a schedule of accounts payable.

Each account was footed to prove its balance, and then a schedule of accounts payable was prepared. Since only J. Rollins Company has a balance other than zero, the schedule is not shown here.

 ## BUILDING YOUR BUSINESS VOCABULARY

On a sheet of paper, write the headings **Statement Number** and **Words**. Next, choose the words that match the statements. Write each word you choose next to the statement number it matches. Be careful; not all the words listed should be used.

Statements

1. A group of creditor accounts
2. A record of cash payments
3. To transfer data from one record to another
4. A record of all cash received
5. A record of purchases on account
6. A list of creditors with the amounts owed to them
7. Buying merchandise on credit
8. People or businesses to whom money is owed

Words

accounts payable ledger
cash payments journal
cash receipts journal
creditors
post
purchase on account
purchases journal
sales journal
schedule of accounts payable
schedule of accounts receivable

STEPS REVIEW: Using a Cash Payments Journal and an Accounts Payable Ledger

STEP 1 Record the cash payments in the cash payments journal.

STEP 2 File the paid invoices.

STEP 3 Post to the creditor accounts.

STEP 4 Total the cash payments journal.

STEP 5 Prove the account balances and prepare a schedule of accounts payable.

 ## APPLICATION PROBLEMS

Problem 58-1
You are employed as an accounts payable clerk at Winslow Wholesale Company. Your job is to record cash payments in a cash payments journal.

Directions
a. Open a cash payments journal. Number the journal page 1.
b. Record the following data taken from the check stubs for October:

Oct. 12 Issued Check No. 1 for $812.90 to J. Normandin Company in payment of the invoice dated October 2.

19 Issued Check No. 2 for $711.75 to K. Bohan Company in payment of the invoice dated October 4.

22 Issued Check No. 3 for $577.12 to B. Smith Company in payment of the invoice dated October 7.

26 Issued Check No. 4 for $1,261.35 to J. Poisson Company in payment of the invoice dated October 6.

28 Issued Check No. 5 for $1,124.10 to S. Rosen Company in payment of the invoice dated October 8.

29 Issued Check No. 6 for $1,077.18 to K. Conway Company in payment of the invoice dated October 19.

30 Issued Check No. 7 for $539.63 to A. Partridge Company in payment of the invoice dated October 5.

CHECK POINT

58-1(c)

Total = $6,104.03

c. Find the total cash paid for the month by footing the Amount of Check column. Check your footing, write the final total, double rule the column, write the word *Total* in the Paid To column, and enter the date.

Problem 58-2   You are an accounts payable clerk for Digennero Computer Company. Your job is to keep the accounts payable records.

Directions

a. Open a cash payments journal for June. Number the journal page 1.

b. Copy the creditor accounts below. Include the amounts that have already been posted.

NAME	J. Asbury Company		ACCOUNT NO.	210		
ADDRESS	106 Hills Rd., Sioux Falls, SD 57103-2469		TERMS	20 days		

DATE		ITEM	POST. REF.	DEBIT	CREDIT	BALANCE
20-- June	3	Invoice #47	P1		4 0 1 10	4 0 1 10
	9	Invoice #51	P1		3 9 6 85	7 9 7 95
	20	Invoice #56	P1		5 1 8 17	1 3 1 6 12

NAME	M. Durocher Company		ACCOUNT NO.	211		
ADDRESS	66 Lawn Ave., St. Louis, MO 63144-8216		TERMS	10 days		

DATE		ITEM	POST. REF.	DEBIT	CREDIT	BALANCE
20-- June	11	Invoice #614	P1		1 0 2 6 19	1 0 2 6 19
	14	Invoice #619	P1		4 1 8 02	1 4 4 4 21

NAME	S. Gatlin Company		ACCOUNT NO.	212		
ADDRESS	1240 Custer Ave., Billings, MT 59101-3227		TERMS	15 days		

DATE		ITEM	POST. REF.	DEBIT	CREDIT	BALANCE
20-- June	4	Invoice #301	P1		8 1 7 11	8 1 7 11
	10	Invoice #310	P1		2 9 1 73	1 1 0 8 84
	18	Invoice #327	P1		5 1 5 27	1 6 2 4 11

c. Record the following data taken from the check stubs for June. Post daily from the cash payments journal to the creditor accounts. Do not forget to record CP1 and account numbers in the proper Post. Ref. columns.

June 19 Issued Check No. 1 for $817.11 to S. Gatlin Company in payment of the invoice dated June 4.
21 Issued Check No. 2 for $1,026.19 to M. Durocher Company in payment of the invoice dated June 11.
23 Issued Check No. 3 for $401.10 to J. Asbury Company in payment of the invoice dated June 3.
24 Issued Check No. 4 for $418.02 to M. Durocher Company in payment of the invoice dated June 14.
25 Issued Check No. 5 for $291.73 to S. Gatlin Company in payment of the invoice dated June 10.
29 Issued Check No. 6 for $396.85 to J. Asbury Company in payment of the invoice dated June 9.

CHECK POINT

✔ 58-2(f)

Total = $1,033.44

d. Find the total cash paid for the month by footing the Amount of Check column in the cash payments journal. Check your footing, write the final total, double rule the column, write the word *Total* in the Paid To column, and enter the date.
e. Prove the balance at the end of the month in each creditor account. Show all footings.
f. Prepare a schedule of accounts payable as of June 30.

Problem 58-3   You are an accounts payable clerk for Ricard Chemical Company. Your job is to keep the accounts payable records.

Directions
a. Open a cash payments journal for January. Number the journal page 1.
b. Copy the creditor accounts on page 472. Include the amounts that have already been posted.
c. Record the data below and on page 472 taken from the check stubs for January. Post daily from the cash payments journal to the creditor accounts. Record the proper posting reference marks.

NAME	R. Crowley Company			ACCOUNT NO. 251	
ADDRESS	957 Elm St., Birmingham, AL 35206-1716			TERMS	20 days

DATE		ITEM	POST. REF.	DEBIT	CREDIT	BALANCE
20-- Jan.	5	Invoice #68	P1		3 7 2 80	3 7 2 80
	8	Invoice #74	P1		5 7 7 16	9 4 9 96
	10	Invoice #81	P1		4 1 2 20	1 3 6 2 16

NAME	C. Dowling Company			ACCOUNT NO. 252	
ADDRESS	88 Seale Ave., Palo Alto, CA 94301-2203			TERMS	15 days

DATE		ITEM	POST. REF.	DEBIT	CREDIT	BALANCE
20-- Jan.	3	Invoice #94	P1		9 0 6 37	9 0 6 37
	9	Invoice #99	P1		6 9 5 70	1 6 0 2 07
	17	Invoice #117	P1		5 9 9 85	2 2 0 1 92

NAME	S. Marquis Company			ACCOUNT NO.	253	
ADDRESS	376 Maple Ave., Lexington, KY 40508-7370			TERMS	10 days	

DATE		ITEM	POST. REF.	DEBIT	CREDIT	BALANCE
20-- Jan.	13	Invoice #312	P1		7 5 6 35	7 5 6 35
	16	Invoice #319	P1		8 0 1 12	1 5 5 7 47
	22	Invoice #327	P1		4 3 7 65	1 9 9 5 12

Jan. 18   Issued Check No. 1 for $906.37 to C. Dowling Company in payment of the invoice dated January 3.

   23   Issued Check No. 2 for $756.35 to S. Marquis Company in payment of the invoice dated January 13.

   24   Issued Check No. 3 for $695.70 to C. Dowling Company in payment of the invoice dated January 9.

   25   Issued Check No. 4 for $372.80 to R. Crowley Company in payment of the invoice dated January 5.

   26   Issued Check No. 5 for $801.12 to S. Marquis Company in payment of the invoice dated January 16.

   28   Issued Check No. 6 for $577.16 to R. Crowley Company in payment of the invoice dated January 8.

   30   Issued Check No. 7 for $412.20 to R. Crowley Company in payment of the invoice dated January 10.

CHECK POINT

58-3(d)

Total = $4,521.70

d. Find the total cash paid for the month by footing the Amount of Check column in the cash payments journal. Check your footing, write the final total, double rule the column, write the word *Total* in the Paid To column, and enter the date.

e. Prove the balance at the end of the month in each creditor account. Show all footings.

f. Prepare a schedule of accounts payable as of January 31.

applied math preview

Copy and complete these problems.

1. $ 3,771.27	2. $ 5,136.90	3. $ 7,299.04
−1,639.81	+1,039.06	−6,301.99
−1,045.12	+ 795.18	− 712.77
+3,776.18	−3,172.12	+6,096.88

goals

1 To practice using the purchases journal, the cash payments journal, and the accounts payable ledger.

2 To learn how accounts payable records are kept with a computer.

UNDERSTANDING THE JOB

You have learned to use three records to enter transactions with creditors from whom you buy merchandise on credit. The three records are

1. The *purchases journal*, in which you record all approved invoices.
2. The *cash payments journal*, in which you record all cash payments to creditors.
3. The *accounts payable ledger*, in which you keep the creditor accounts. Credits to these creditor accounts are posted from the purchases journal. Debits to these accounts are posted from the cash payments journal.

Illustration 59A shows the flow of data for these three records.

In this job, you will use all three records. You will be posting from both the purchases journal and the cash payments journal to the creditor accounts. *Remember:* Postings must be made each day.

Illustration 59A

How purchase invoices and cash payments are recorded

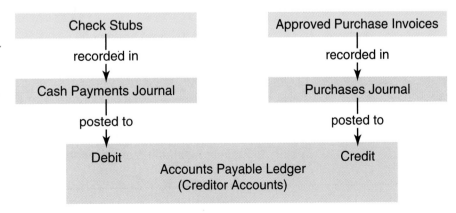

You are an accounts payable clerk for Stafford Company. During June, you recorded the following transactions:

June   5   Received Purchase Invoice No. 477 from P. Walker Company, dated June 3, for $463.89.

         9   Received Purchase Invoice No. 482 from P. Walker Company, dated June 6, for $704.60.

        13   Issued Check No. 1 for $463.89 to P. Walker Company in payment of the invoice dated June 3.

        16   Issued Check No. 2 for $704.60 to P. Walker Company in payment of the invoice dated June 6.

        27   Received Purchase Invoice No. 499 from P. Walker Company, dated June 24, for $715.95.

Illustration 59B (page 475) shows how you recorded these transactions in the two journals and then posted to the creditor account. Here are the steps that you followed:

STEP 1 Record the transactions in the proper journals.

When you received an approved purchase invoice or a check stub, you decided in which journal you should record it. You recorded the purchase invoices in the purchases journal and the check stubs in the cash payments journal.

STEP 2 Post daily to the creditor account(s).

Tips

Post in the order of transactions.

After you recorded each transaction in the proper journal, you posted each transaction to the creditor account. It is important to post daily so that creditor account balances are up-to-date. Post in the order of the transactions.

STEP 3 Total and rule each journal.

At the end of the month, you footed, totaled, and ruled the purchases and cash payments journals.

STEP 4 Check the account balance(s).

At the end of the month, you verified the running balance of the account by footing the Debit and Credit columns. You subtracted the Debit total from the Credit total and compared that amount to the balance in the account.

STEP 5 Prepare a schedule of accounts payable.

You did not prepare a schedule of accounts payable in this problem because there is only one creditor account. You would usually do this as your final step.

Illustration 59B

Recording purchases and cash payments in two journals and a creditor account

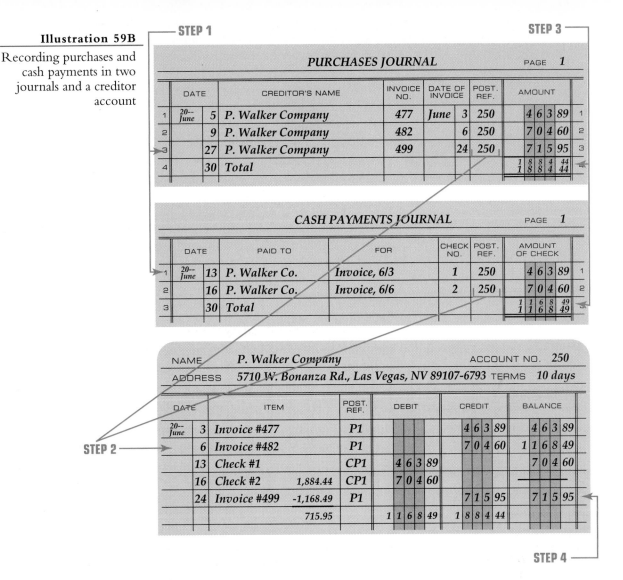

PURCHASES JOURNAL   PAGE 1

	DATE		CREDITOR'S NAME	INVOICE NO.	DATE OF INVOICE		POST. REF.	AMOUNT	
1	20-- June	5	P. Walker Company	477	June	3	250	4 6 3 89	1
2		9	P. Walker Company	482		6	250	7 0 4 60	2
3		27	P. Walker Company	499		24	250	7 1 5 95	3
4		30	Total					1 8 8 4 44	4

CASH PAYMENTS JOURNAL   PAGE 1

	DATE		PAID TO	FOR	CHECK NO.	POST. REF.	AMOUNT OF CHECK	
1	20-- June	13	P. Walker Co.	Invoice, 6/3	1	250	4 6 3 89	1
2		16	P. Walker Co.	Invoice, 6/6	2	250	7 0 4 60	2
3		30	Total				1 1 6 8 49	3

NAME   **P. Walker Company**   ACCOUNT NO. **250**

ADDRESS   **5710 W. Bonanza Rd., Las Vegas, NV 89107-6793** TERMS **10 days**

DATE		ITEM		POST. REF.	DEBIT	CREDIT	BALANCE
20-- June	3	Invoice #477		P1		4 6 3 89	4 6 3 89
	6	Invoice #482		P1		7 0 4 60	1 1 6 8 49
	13	Check #1		CP1	4 6 3 89		7 0 4 60
	16	Check #2	1,884.44	CP1	7 0 4 60		———
	24	Invoice #499	-1,168.49	P1		7 1 5 95	7 1 5 95
			715.95		1 1 6 8 49	1 8 8 4 44	

STEP 2

STEP 4

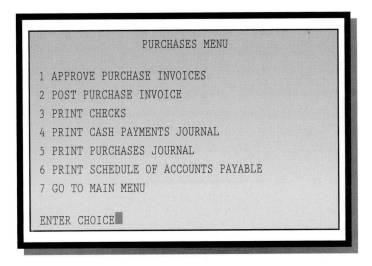

→ USING THE COMPUTER

The computer can be a useful tool to assist the accounts payable clerk in his or her job. Illustration 59C shows a purchases menu.

The clerk would have already used menu item 1, APPROVE

Illustration 59C

Purchases menu

```
                    PURCHASES MENU

    1 APPROVE PURCHASE INVOICES

    2 POST PURCHASE INVOICE

    3 PRINT CHECKS

    4 PRINT CASH PAYMENTS JOURNAL

    5 PRINT PURCHASES JOURNAL

    6 PRINT SCHEDULE OF ACCOUNTS PAYABLE

    7 GO TO MAIN MENU


    ENTER CHOICE▮
```

PURCHASE INVOICES, before recording an invoice in the creditor accounts. In order to record in the creditor accounts, the clerk will use menu item 2, POST PURCHASE INVOICES. The computer will then post automatically to the correct creditor account.

In a computerized, or automated, accounts payable system, journals are not prepared directly. If a journal is needed, the computer will print the data from the purchase invoices or the check stubs by date. Using menu items 4 and 5 can get this job done.

No additional work is needed to prepare a schedule of accounts payable. The computer will respond to menu item 6, PRINT SCHEDULE OF ACCOUNTS PAYABLE, by printing out the schedule.

A computer can also print checks to pay invoices. By selecting menu item 3, PRINT CHECKS, and inserting check forms into the printer, a check such as the one shown in Illustration 59D will be prepared. The check is a voucher check, since it has the explanation of the check attached.

Accuracy in entering data is vital when a computer is used to process accounts payable. A single error in entering an invoice quantity, for example, will cause errors in every other menu item. The creditor account, journals, check, and schedule of accounts payable will all be incorrect.

Illustration 59D

Check to creditor printed by computer

STAFFORD COMPANY
1110 9th Avenue
Wilmington, DE 19808-4108

			CONTROL NO.	PAYEE NO.	CHECK DATE	CHECK NO.
			30775	1823	6/13/--	000001

INVOICE NUMBER	INVOICE DATE	GROSS AMOUNT	DISCOUNT	NET AMOUNT	COMMENTS
477	6/3/--	$463.89	$0.00	$463.89	
	TOTAL	$463.89	$0.00	$463.89	

DETACH HERE BEFORE DEPOSITING CHECK

STAFFORD COMPANY
1110 9th Avenue
Wilmington, DE 19808-4108

			CONTROL NO.	PAYEE NO.	CHECK DATE	CHECK NO.
			30775	1823	6/13/--	000001

62-7578
2311

	CHECK AMOUNT
	$463.89

Pay Exactly FOUR HUNDRED SIXTY-THREE 89/100 DOLLARS

TO THE ORDER OF
P. WALKER COMPANY
5710 W. BONANZA RD.
LAS VEGAS, NV 89107-6793

HAMILTON NATIONAL BANK
Wilmington, DE 19808-4444

Elmer Sturgeon, Treasurer

⑆231175788⑆ 564⑈5423⑆

⇨ BUILDING YOUR BUSINESS VOCABULARY

On a sheet of paper, write the headings **Statement Number** and **Words**. Next, choose the words that match the statements. Write each word you choose next to the statement number it matches. Be careful; not all the words listed should be used.

Statements	Words
1. The column used to record an increase in a creditor account	accounts payable ledger
2. A list of programs	accounts receivable ledger
3. A group of creditor accounts	cash payments journal
4. A check with a special stub attached	credit
5. The column used to record a decrease in a creditor account	creditors
6. A record of cash payments	debit
7. People or businesses to whom money is owed	menu
8. A record of purchases on account	post
	purchases journal
	voucher check

STEPS REVIEW: Using a Purchases Journal, a Cash Payments Journal, and an Accounts Payable Ledger

STEP 1 Record the transactions in the proper journals.

STEP 2 Post daily to the creditor account(s).

STEP 3 Total and rule each journal.

STEP 4 Check the account balance(s).

STEP 5 Prepare a schedule of accounts payable.

APPLICATION PROBLEMS

Problem 59-1   You are an accounts payable clerk for the Rollins Tool Company.

Directions

a. Open a purchases journal and a cash payments journal for September. Number each journal page 1.

b. Record the following transactions. You must decide if each transaction is to be recorded in the purchases journal or the cash payments journal.

Sept. 5 Received Purchase Invoice No. 517, dated September 4, from J. Berger Company, for $906.45.

10 Received Purchase Invoice No. 519, dated September 9, from J. Berger Company, for $811.80.

13 Received Purchase Invoice No. 972, dated September 12, from W. Beliveau Company, for $475.85.

14 Issued Check No. 1 for $906.45 to J. Berger Company in payment of the invoice dated September 4.

19 Issued Check No. 2 for $811.80 to J. Berger Company in payment of the invoice dated September 9.

22 Received Purchase Invoice No. 136, dated September 20, from S. Marchant Company, for $581.70.

25 Received Purchase Invoice No. 979, dated September 23, from W. Beliveau Company, for $209.60.

27 Issued Check No. 3 for $475.85 to W. Beliveau Company in payment of the invoice dated September 12.

Sept. 29 Received Purchase Invoice No. 144, dated September 27, from
S. Marchant Company, for $1,041.10.
30 Issued Check No. 4 for $581.70 to S. Marchant Company in payment of
the invoice dated September 20.

c. Foot, total, and rule the journals.

Problem 59-2

You are an accounts payable clerk for Rigby Storage Company.

Directions

a. Open a purchases journal and a cash payments journal for May.
Number each journal page 1.

b. Open accounts for the following creditors:

Creditor	Address	Account No.	Terms
P. Choates Company	496 Morton Avenue Des Moines, IA 50313-7121	200	10 days
L. Eliot Company	375 NE Long Street Topeka, KS 66607-8055	201	20 days
S. Parzuch Company	59 Ridge Road Richmond, VA 23229-7582	202	15 days

c. Record the following transactions. You must decide if each transaction
is to be recorded in the purchases journal or the cash payments journal.
Post daily to the creditor accounts.

May 5 Received Purchase Invoice No. 55, dated May 3, from P. Choates
Company, for $311.76.
7 Received Purchase Invoice No. 97, dated May 5, from S. Parzuch
Company, for $585.12.
12 Received Purchase Invoice No. 105, dated May 9, from L. Eliot Company,
for $721.05.
13 Issued Check No. 1 for $311.76 to P. Choates Company in payment of the
invoice dated May 3.
18 Received Purchase Invoice No. 59, dated May 17, from P. Choates
Company, for $1,041.95.
19 Received Purchase Invoice No. 112, dated May 18, from S. Parzuch
Company, for $1,277.19.
20 Issued Check No. 2 for $585.12 to S. Parzuch Company in payment of the
invoice dated May 5.
23 Received Purchase Invoice No. 137, dated May 21, from L. Eliot
Company, for $971.37.
27 Issued Check No. 3 for $1,041.95 to P. Choates Company in payment of
the invoice dated May 17.
29 Issued Check No. 4 for $721.05 to L. Eliot Company in payment of the
invoice dated May 9.
31 Received Purchase Invoice No. 141, dated May 30, from S. Parzuch
Company, for $609.27.

d. Foot, total, and rule the journals.
e. Prove the balance at the end of the month in each account. Show all
footings.
f. Prepare a schedule of accounts payable as of May 31.

You are an accounts payable clerk for Marshall Software Company.

Directions

a. Open a purchases journal and a cash payments journal for June. Number each journal page 1.

b. Open accounts for the following creditors:

Creditor	Address	Account No.	Terms
N. Boyle Company	16 Circle Drive Cleveland, OH 44106-2902	222	20 days
O. Newfield Company	746 Oakwood Drive Charlotte, NC 28205-3746	223	10 days
R. Van Meer Company	333 Maple Street Charleston, SC 29406-1333	224	15 days

c. Record the following transactions. You must decide if each transaction is to be recorded in the purchases journal or the cash payments journal. Post daily to the creditor accounts.

June 4 Received Purchase Invoice No. 94, dated June 2, from O. Newfield Company, for $811.36.

  5 Received Purchase Invoice No. 361, dated June 3, from N. Boyle Company, for $392.07.

  8 Received Purchase Invoice No. 365, dated June 5, from N. Boyle Company, for $516.11.

 11 Received Purchase Invoice No. 99, dated June 9, from O. Newfield Company, for $1,027.95.

 12 Issued Check No. 1 for $811.36 to O. Newfield Company in payment of the invoice dated June 2.

 15 Received Purchase Invoice No. 411, dated June 11, from R. Van Meer Company, for $879.31.

 19 Issued Check No. 2 for $1,027.95 to O. Newfield Company in payment of the invoice dated June 9.

 23 Issued Check No. 3 for $392.07 to N. Boyle Company in payment of the invoice dated June 3.

 25 Received Purchase Invoice No. 435, dated June 24, from R. Van Meer Company, for $413.67.

 25 Issued Check No. 4 for $516.11 to N. Boyle Company in payment of the invoice dated June 5.

 26 Issued Check No. 5 for $879.31 to R. Van Meer Company in payment of the invoice dated June 11.

 29 Received Purchase Invoice No. 113, dated June 28, from O. Newfield Company, for $699.95.

d. Foot, total, and rule the journals.

e. Prove the balance at the end of the month in each account. Show all footings.

f. Prepare a schedule of accounts payable as of June 30.

Problem 59-4 may be found in the Working Papers.

CHECK POINT

59-3(f)

Total = $1,113.62

USING A PURCHASES RETURNS AND ALLOWANCES JOURNAL AND AN ACCOUNTS PAYABLE LEDGER

applied math preview

Copy and complete the following problems.

1.	2.	3.
$ 6,179.44	$ 1,577.26	$ 599.74
−1,496.89	+2,014.91	− 46.87
−3,199.05	− 103.80	− 39.95
+3,172.18	−2,577.26	− 19.83

key terms preview

- Debit memo
- Purchases returns and allowances journal

goals

1 To learn how to record credit memos received from creditors in a purchases returns and allowances journal.

2 To learn how to post from the purchases returns and allowances journal to the accounts payable ledger.

3 To learn how to file credit memos.

UNDERSTANDING THE JOB

Debit memo. A form used by the buyer to notify a creditor of a return or an allowance.

Purchases returns and allowances journal. A record of all credit memos received.

Debit a creditor account for returns and allowances.

You have learned that purchase invoices are recorded in a purchases journal and posted to the Credit column of a creditor account. You have also learned that cash payments are recorded in a cash payments journal and posted to the Debit column of a creditor account. A third transaction with a creditor results from a return of merchandise or an incorrect charge or shortage on an invoice.

When you return merchandise or request an allowance because of an overcharge or a shortage, you may notify the creditor in writing. To do this, you may use a form called a **debit memo** to notify the creditor. Illustration 60A (page 481) shows a debit memo issued by the buyer (Bartlett Appliance Store) to the creditor (D. Phillips Company).

The form is called a debit memo because it tells the creditor that his or her account will be debited. Returns and allowances are recorded in the Debit column of a creditor account.

Illustration 60B (page 481) shows all of the transactions that affect a creditor account. Notice in Illustration 60B that returns and allowances are recorded from either a debit memo or a credit memo.

You learned about credit memos in Job 48. A debit memo is issued by the buyer; the credit memo is issued by the seller after receiving the debit memo. Most buyers do not record a return or an allowance until after receiving the credit memo from the seller. Illustration 60C (page 482) shows the credit memo that Bartlett Appliance Store received from D. Phillips Company in response to its debit memo.

Bartlett Appliance Store will record this credit memo in a **purchases returns and allowances journal** This journal is used to record all

DEBIT MEMO

Bartlett

APPLIANCE STORE

484 Fellsway Street • Boston, MA 02148-3352

NO. 1

TO D. Phillips Company
907 Ridge Road
Raleigh, NC 27607-6021

DATE May 26, 20--

WE HAVE DEBITED YOUR ACCOUNT AS FOLLOWS:

DESCRIPTION	UNIT PRICE	TOTAL
Return of 2 microwave ovens, stock number M9	315 00	630 00

Tips

Debit memo prepared by buyer. Credit memo prepared by seller.

credit memos received. Illustration 60C shows how the credit memo is recorded. Here are the steps you would follow to make the entry in the purchases returns and allowances journal:

STEP 1 Copy the date of the credit memo.

Copy the date, May 31, in the Date column.

STEP 2 Copy the creditor's name.

Enter the name, D. Phillips Company, in the Creditor's Name column.

STEP 3 Copy the credit memo number.

Enter the credit memo number, 17, in the Credit Memo No. column.

STEP 4 Enter the amount.

Enter the total amount, $630.00, in the Amount column of the purchases returns and allowances journal.

After recording the credit memo in the purchases returns and allowances journal, you must now post to the D. Phillips account in the accounts payable ledger. Illustration 60D on page 483 shows how this posting is done.

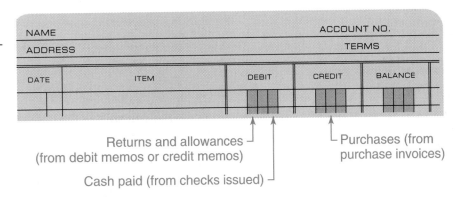

NAME				ACCOUNT NO.	
ADDRESS				TERMS	
DATE	ITEM		DEBIT	CREDIT	BALANCE

Returns and allowances ┘
(from debit memos or credit memos)

└ Purchases (from purchase invoices)

Cash paid (from checks issued) ┘

Illustration 60C

Recording a credit memo in
a purchases returns and
allowances journal

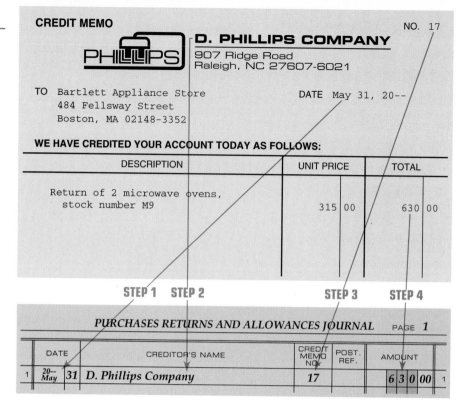

Here are the steps followed:

STEP 1 Copy the date.

Enter the day, 31, in the Date column.

STEP 2 Enter the credit memo number.

Write "Credit Memo #17" in the Item column.

STEP 3 Record the posting reference in the creditor account.

Enter PR1 for *P*urchases *R*eturns and Allowances Journal, page *1* in the Post. Ref. column of the account.

STEP 4 Post the amount.

Write the amount, $630.00, in the Debit column, since all credit memos are recorded in the Debit column.

STEP 5 Find the new balance.

Find the new balance by subtracting the debit amount, $630.00, from the previous balance, $6,300.00. Enter the difference, $5,670.00, in the Balance column.

STEP 6 Enter the account number in the purchases returns and allowances journal.

Write the account number, 2101, in the Post. Ref. column of the journal to show that the posting is complete.

Illustration 60D

Posting from purchases
returns and allowances
journal to creditor account

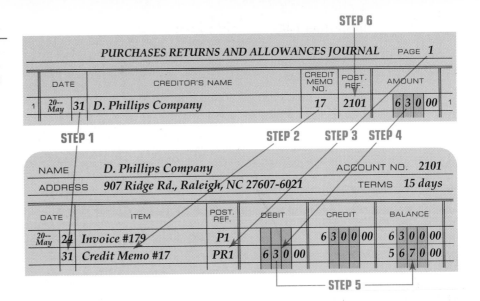

STEP 6

PURCHASES RETURNS AND ALLOWANCES JOURNAL   PAGE *1*

	DATE		CREDITOR'S NAME	CREDIT MEMO NO.	POST. REF.	AMOUNT	
1	20-- May	31	D. Phillips Company	17	2101	6 3 0 00	1

STEP 1   STEP 2   STEP 3   STEP 4

NAME	D. Phillips Company				ACCOUNT NO. **2101**		
ADDRESS	907 Ridge Rd., Raleigh, NC 27607-6021				TERMS **15 days**		

DATE		ITEM	POST. REF.	DEBIT	CREDIT	BALANCE
20-- May	24	Invoice #179	P1		6 3 0 0 00	6 3 0 0 00
	31	Credit Memo #17	PR1	6 3 0 00		5 6 7 0 00

STEP 5

→ SAMPLE PROBLEM

You are the accounts payable clerk for Woburn Supply Company. The creditor accounts in your accounts payable ledger already contain postings from the purchases journal. You receive the following credit memos during May:

May 16   Received Credit Memo No. 46 for $55.00 from C. Wesley Company to correct an overcharge.

      17   Received Credit Memo No. 27 for $195.50 from S. Arnold Company for a shortage in the shipment of goods.

      19   Received Credit Memo No. 51 for $95.10 from C. Wesley Company for damaged merchandise returned.

Illustration 60E on page 484 shows how these credit memos are recorded in the purchases returns and allowances journal and posted to the creditor accounts. Here are the steps you would follow:

STEP 1   **Record the credit memos in the purchases returns and allowances journal.**

Record the data from the credit memos in the purchases returns and allowances journal.

STEP 2   **File the credit memos.**

You have learned that purchase invoices are filed according to due date. A credit memo should be attached to the purchase invoice for which it was received. Credit Memo No. 27, for example, should be attached to Purchase Invoice No. 406.

Illustration 60E

Purchases returns and
allowances journal and
accounts payable ledger

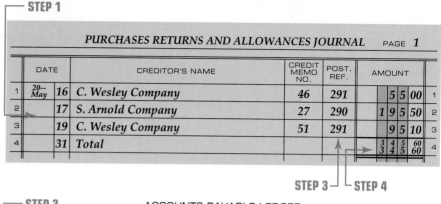

STEP 1

PURCHASES RETURNS AND ALLOWANCES JOURNAL   PAGE **1**

	DATE		CREDITOR'S NAME	CREDIT MEMO NO.	POST. REF.	AMOUNT	
1	20-- May	16	C. Wesley Company	46	291	5 5 00	1
2		17	S. Arnold Company	27	290	1 9 5 50	2
3		19	C. Wesley Company	51	291	9 5 10	3
4		31	Total			3 4 5 60 / 3 4 5 60	4

STEP 3 ⌐ └ STEP 4

STEP 3   ACCOUNTS PAYABLE LEDGER

NAME	S. Arnold Company				ACCOUNT NO. **290**		
ADDRESS	762 14th Avenue, Wilmington, DE 19808-0379				TERMS **20 days**		

DATE		ITEM	POST. REF.	DEBIT	CREDIT	BALANCE
20-- May	12	Invoice #406	P1		5 9 5 00	5 9 5 00
	17	Credit Memo #27	PR1	1 9 5 50		3 9 9 50

NAME	C. Wesley Company				ACCOUNT NO. **291**		
ADDRESS	6210 Byrd Avenue, Racine, WI 53406-9084				TERMS **30 days**		

DATE		ITEM		POST. REF.	DEBIT	CREDIT	BALANCE
20-- May	13	Invoice #51		P1		6 3 5 00	6 3 5 00
	16	Invoice #55		P1		4 1 5 00	1 0 5 0 00
	16	Cr. Memo #46	1,050.00	PR1	5 5 00		9 9 5 00
	19	Cr. Memo #51	- 150.10	PR1	9 5 10		8 9 9 90
			899.90		1 5 0 10	1 0 5 0 00	

On June 1, when Invoice No. 406 is due, it will be removed from the file folder with Credit Memo No. 27 attached. The clerk who writes the check to pay the invoice will see that $195.50 should be subtracted from $595.00 and will write a check for the difference, $399.50.

STEP 3 Post to the creditor accounts.

At the end of each day, post from the purchases returns and allowances journal to the creditor accounts. Notice PR1 in the Post. Ref. column of the accounts and the account numbers in the journal Post. Ref. column. New account balances were calculated after each posting.

STEP 4 Total the purchases returns and allowances journal.

At the end of the month, rule and foot the Amount column of the journal. Re-add the column before writing in the final total. Draw a double ruling under the final total. Write the word *Total* and the last day of the month, 31, in the correct places.

Each account was footed to prove its balance. A schedule of accounts payable was prepared as of May 31. (See Illustration 60F.)

STEP 5

Illustration 60F

Schedule of accounts payable

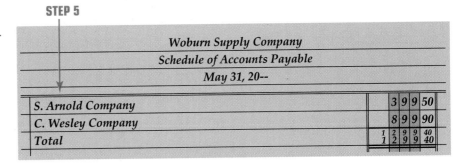

Woburn Supply Company				
Schedule of Accounts Payable				
May 31, 20--				
S. Arnold Company		3	9	9	50
C. Wesley Company		8	9	9	90
Total	1	2	9	9	40

You are now using four records to keep track of transactions with creditors from whom merchandise is bought. They are

1. The *purchases journal,* in which you record approved purchase invoices.
2. The *cash payments journal,* in which you record checks written to creditors.
3. The *purchases returns and allowances journal,* in which you record credit memos received from creditors.
4. The *accounts payable ledger,* in which you keep the creditor accounts.

The debits in the creditor accounts are posted from the cash payments journal and from the purchases returns and allowances journal. The credits in the creditor accounts are posted from the purchases journal. When you use all of the records, it is important to remember to post in the order of the dates of the transactions.

Illustration 60G shows the source documents, the journals, and the postings for creditors.

Illustration 60G

Recording check stubs, credit memos, and purchase invoices

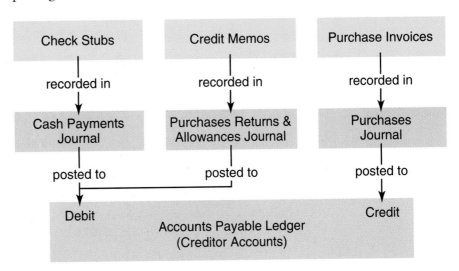

On a sheet of paper, write the headings **Statement Number** and **Words**. Next, choose the words that match the statements. Write each word you choose next to the statement number it matches. Be careful; not all the words listed should be used.

Statements	Words
1. A record of cash payments	accounts payable ledger
2. A form used by the seller to show that the balance of an account has been reduced because of a return or an allowance	cash payments journal credit credit memo
3. A group of creditor accounts	creditors
4. A form used by the buyer to notify a creditor of a return or an allowance	debit debit memo
5. A record of all credit memos received	purchase invoice
6. A record of purchases on account	purchases journal
7. A list of creditors with the amounts owed to them	purchases returns and allowances journal
8. People or businesses to whom money is owed	schedule of accounts payable

STEPS REVIEW: Using a Purchases Returns and Allowances Journal and an Accounts Payable Ledger

STEP 1 Record the credit memos in the purchases returns and allowances journal.

STEP 2 File the credit memos.

STEP 3 Post to the creditor accounts.

STEP 4 Total the purchases returns and allowances journal.

STEP 5 Prove the account balances and prepare a schedule of accounts payable.

Problem 60-1

You are employed as an accounts payable clerk at the Carlton Company.

Directions

a. Open a purchases returns and allowances journal for August. Number the journal page 5.

b. Copy the following creditor accounts. Include the amounts that have already been posted.

NAME **A. Eastman Company**   ACCOUNT NO. **201**
ADDRESS **410 Joseph St., Charleston, WV 25303-9008**   TERMS **30 days**

DATE		ITEM	POST. REF.	DEBIT	CREDIT	BALANCE
20-- Aug.	5	Invoice #1710	P9		6 1 1 75	6 1 1 75
	10	Invoice #1713	P9		1 0 0 4 15	1 6 1 5 90

NAME **S. Jones Company**   ACCOUNT NO. **202**
ADDRESS **3705 Tulsa St., Fort Smith, AR 72903-1210**   TERMS **45 days**

DATE		ITEM	POST. REF.	DEBIT	CREDIT	BALANCE
20-- Aug.	8	Invoice #2104	P9		5 8 5 63	5 8 5 63
	12	Invoice #2172	P9		9 1 0 95	1 4 9 6 58

NAME **N. Perras Company**   ACCOUNT NO. **203**
ADDRESS **13510 W. Flagler St., Miami, FL 33184-4931**   TERMS **60 days**

DATE		ITEM	POST. REF.	DEBIT	CREDIT	BALANCE
20-- Aug.	3	Invoice #591	P9		4 1 2 87	4 1 2 87
	7	Invoice #599	P9		8 3 9 81	1 2 5 2 68

c. Enter the following credit memos in the purchases returns and allowances journal. Post daily to the creditor accounts.

Aug. 8 Received Credit Memo No. 55 for $45.00 from N. Perras Company for a shortage in the shipment of goods.

11 Received Credit Memo No. 106 for $28.75 from A. Eastman Company for damaged merchandise returned.

13 Received Credit Memo No. 27 for $39.60 from S. Jones Company to correct an overcharge.

14 Received Credit Memo No. 58 for $20.75 from N. Perras Company for damaged merchandise returned.

17 Received Credit Memo No. 117 for $32.45 from A. Eastman Company to correct an overcharge.

18 Received Credit Memo No. 30 for $55.00 from S. Jones Company for a shortage in the shipment of goods.

d. Foot, total, and rule the purchases returns and allowances journal. Enter the date and the word *Total.*

e. Check the balance of each creditor account, and prepare a schedule of accounts payable as of August 31.

Problem 60-2   You are employed as an accounts payable clerk at the Morgan Toy Store.

Directions

a. Open a purchases returns and allowances journal for December. Number the journal page 8.

b. Copy the following creditor accounts. Include the amounts that have already been posted.

NAME	T. Dupuis Company				ACCOUNT NO. **271**	
ADDRESS	103 Kenmore Ave., Joliet, IL 60433-4920				TERMS **30 days**	

DATE	ITEM	POST. REF.	DEBIT	CREDIT	BALANCE
20-- Dec. 2	Invoice #771	P12		4 9 0 25	4 9 0 25
9	Invoice #789	P12		6 1 3 46	1 1 0 3 71

NAME	L. Fayette Company				ACCOUNT NO. **272**	
ADDRESS	15 Cherry St., South Bend, IN 46625-0015				TERMS **45 days**	

DATE	ITEM	POST. REF.	DEBIT	CREDIT	BALANCE
20-- Dec. 3	Invoice #512	P12		7 1 2 37	7 1 2 37
8	Invoice #522	P12		2 6 5 48	9 7 7 85

NAME	M. Lannone Company				ACCOUNT NO. **273**	
ADDRESS	99 Beech St., Pueblo, CO 81003-5011				TERMS **90 days**	

DATE	ITEM	POST. REF.	DEBIT	CREDIT	BALANCE
20-- Dec. 10	Invoice #719	P12		1 1 2 0 45	1 1 2 0 45
12	Invoice #726	P12		9 1 3 76	2 0 3 4 21

c. Enter the following credit memos in the purchases returns and allowances journal. Post daily to the creditor accounts.

Dec. 9 Received Credit Memo No. 74 for $42.10 from L. Fayette Company for a shortage in the shipment of goods.

10 Received Credit Memo No. 14 for $57.50 from T. Dupuis Company to correct an overcharge.

12 Received Credit Memo No. 76 for $265.48 from L. Fayette Company for damaged merchandise returned.

15 Received Credit Memo No. 112 for $31.10 from M. Lannone Company for damaged merchandise returned.

16 Received Credit Memo No. 17 for $74.30 from T. Dupuis Company for a shortage in the shipment of goods.

19 Received Credit Memo No. 114 for $36.80 from M. Lannone Company to correct an overcharge.

d. Foot, total, and rule the purchases returns and allowances journal.
e. Check the balance of each creditor account, and prepare a schedule of accounts payable.

Problem 60-3 may be found in the Working Papers.

CHECK POINT

60-2(e)

Total = $3,608.49

Chapter 12

CHECK YOUR READING

1. a. What is a creditor?
   b. List several creditors that you or your parents have.
2. What does it mean to make a purchase on account?
3. a. What transaction(s) is(are) recorded in the Debit column of a creditor's account?
   b. What transaction(s) is(are) recorded in the Credit column of a creditor's
4. Describe the entries or transactions recorded in the following journals: purchases journal, cash payments journal, and purchases returns and allowances journal.

DISCUSSION

You are one of two accounts payable clerks at Bradley Wholesale Company. You noticed in checking through your journals that you owed A. Taylor Company $900.00 and had received a credit memo for $70.00. Yet, when it came time to pay A. Taylor Company, a check was written for $900.00. Your co-worker is responsible for posting from the journals to the creditor accounts. The $70.00 credit memo had never been posted, even though the Post. Ref. column of the journal showed the A. Taylor Company account number. When you asked your co-worker about this, here is the answer you received: "I always write the account number when I record the transaction in the journal. It saves time."

What would you say to your co-worker to explain why the procedure followed is wrong?

ETHICS IN THE WORKPLACE

You are an accounts payable clerk. Another accounts payable clerk works alongside you. The other clerk is not a friend, but just a co-worker. You notice unusual attendance habits by the other clerk. The clerk is 5 to 10 minutes late each morning, 5 to 10 minutes late returning from lunch every day, and leaves work about 10 minutes early each afternoon.

Your company is small, so employees fill out time slips by hand every Friday for the week. You just happen to notice that your co-worker filled out this week's form for a full 40 hours. No lateness was recorded.

You wonder what, if anything, you should do about this situation. Write some of the possible things that you might do. Then, write what you would do.

REINFORCEMENT ACTIVITIES

COMMUNICATION IN THE WORKPLACE

You are the accounts payable clerk for Waltham Company. You recently received a shipment of 10 clock-radios, Stock No. CR 12, @ $45.95 each, from T. Melrose Company. Two of the 10 are damaged, so you want to return the items and ask for a credit memo from T. Melrose Company. Your company does not use debit memos, so a letter is needed. Write a letter to T. Melrose Company asking for the credit memo. Keep your letter to one page.

FOCUS ON CAREERS

The following ad appears in the newspaper:

Accounts Payable

Organized and detail-oriented individual needed to handle all invoicing and check writing responsibilities for a multi-company structure. For this position, you must be hard working and willing to work with our computerized system.

1. What four characteristics must the person who applies for this position possess?
2. Will the person who does this job record in journals? Explain.
3. What do you think is meant by a multicompany structure?
4. Is this job an entry-level job? Explain.

GLOBAL BUSINESS: INTERNATIONAL WEIGHTS AND MEASURES

As an accounts payable clerk for a large hardware wholesaler, you see many purchase invoices from vendors in other countries. The weights and measures of those items are usually given in the metric system, which is used by most industrial countries other than the United States. The metric system is based on a decimal system that is similar to one we use for U.S. currency.

Your company's stock records, however, use the U.S. system of weights and measures. Your boss has asked you to convert the metric quantities shown on the purchase invoices. You use the following table and round to the nearest whole number.

To Change	To	Multiply By
kilograms	pounds	2.205
meters	inches	39.37
centimeters	inches	0.39
millimeters	inches	0.039
liter (dry)	quarts (dry)	0.908
liter (liquid)	quarts (liquid)	1.057

To convert, take the metric weight or measure and multiply by the number shown. For example, 100 kilograms x 2.205 = 220.50 pounds, rounded to 221 pounds.

An International Weights and Measures Activity can be found in the Working Papers.

 ## REVIEWING WHAT YOU HAVE LEARNED

On a sheet of paper, write the headings **Statement Number** and **Words**. Next, choose the words that best complete the statements. Write each word you choose next to the statement number it completes. Be careful; not all the words listed should be used.

Statements	Words
1. Credit memos are recorded in the _____.	accounts payable ledger
2. Posting from any journal to creditor accounts is done _____.	balance
	cash payments journal
3. On a schedule of accounts payable, the _____ of a creditor account is listed.	creditors
	daily
4. To record checks written to creditors, use the _____.	debit memo
	due date
5. Credit memos should be attached to the related _____.	purchase invoice
6. Creditor accounts are found in the _____.	purchase on account
	purchases journal
7. Approved purchase invoices are filed by their _____.	purchases returns and allowances journal
8. A form that can be used to request a reduction in your account from a creditor is the _____.	schedule of accounts payable
9. When you buy merchandise from a creditor with 30 days to pay, you are making (a, an) _____.	

 ## MASTERY PROBLEM

You are employed as an accounts payable clerk for the W. Joyce Company.

Directions

a. Open a purchases journal, a cash payments journal, and a purchases returns and allowances journal. Number each journal page 1.

b. Open accounts for creditors as follows:

Creditor	Address	Account No.	Terms
E. Cronin Company	613 Division Street Baltimore, MD 21207-1613	2101	10 days
K. Delorme Company	276 Emerson Street Erie, PA 16502-3186	2102	20 days

Creditor	Address	Account No.	Terms
R. Watley Company	12357 Bell Road Scottsdale, AZ 85351-2570	2103	15 days

c. Record the following transactions. You must decide in which of the three journals to record each transaction. As soon as you have recorded in the journal, post *immediately* to the creditor account.

June 3 Received Purchase Invoice No. 109, dated June 1, from K. Delorme Company, for $510.90.

5 Received Purchase Invoice No. 46, dated June 3, from E. Cronin Company, for $475.50.

6 Received Purchase Invoice No. 97, dated June 5, from R. Watley Company, for $1,277.40.

7 Received Credit Memo No. 12 for $18.00 from E. Cronin Company for damaged merchandise returned on Invoice No. 46.

9 Received Purchase Invoice No. 114, dated June 7, from K. Delorme Company, for $695.60.

10 Received Credit Memo No. 13 for $151.35 from R. Watley Company for damaged merchandise returned on Invoice No. 97.

11 Received Credit Memo No. 36 for $19.05 from K. Delorme Company to correct an overcharge on Invoice No. 114.

13 Issued Check No. 1 for $457.50 to E. Cronin Company in payment of the balance of the invoice dated June 3.

20 Issued Check No. 2 for $1,126.05 to R. Watley Company in payment of the balance of the invoice dated June 5.

20 Received Purchase Invoice No. 57, dated June 18, from E. Cronin Company, for $912.87.

21 Issued Check No. 3 for $510.90 to K. Delorme Company in payment of the invoice dated June 1.

22 Received Credit Memo No. 15 for $13.95 from E. Cronin Company for a shortage in the shipment of goods on Invoice No. 57.

26 Received Purchase Invoice No. 105, dated June 24, from R. Watley Company, for $811.75.

27 Issued Check No. 4 for $676.55 to K. Delorme Company in payment of the balance of the invoice dated June 7.

28 Issued Check No. 5 for $898.92 to E. Cronin Company in payment of the balance of the invoice dated June 18.

30 Received Purchase Invoice No. 112, dated June 29, from R. Watley Company, for $295.10.

30 Received Purchase Invoice No. 151, dated June 30, from K. Delorme Company, for $1,145.10.

d. Foot, total and rule the journals.

e. Prove the last balance in each account. Show all footings in the accounts.

f. Prepare a schedule of accounts payable as of June 30.

CHECK POINT

(f)
Total = $2,251.95

REVIEWING YOUR BUSINESS VOCABULARY

This activity may be found in the Working Papers.

COMPREHENSIVE PROJECT 4

Comprehensive Project 4 has been designed to reinforce major concepts of this and previous chapters. The Comprehensive Project is found in the Working Papers.

Chapter 13

Record Keeping for Small Businesses

If you were someday to own and operate a small business, such as a computer repair shop, you would receive money from your customers for repairing their computers. You would also have expenses. Expenses include such things as rent for the building in which your shop is located, your telephone bill, your electric bill, truck gas and repairs, and parts and supplies.

In Chapter 13, you will learn how to record income in a cash receipts journal and expenses in a cash payments journal. You will also learn how to post from both journals to a general ledger and how to prepare a trial balance.

Desktop Conferencing

Business people often work in groups to solve business problems. That usually means that they must meet in the same place to plan their work, listen to ideas from other group members, and share the results of their efforts. Often, meetings may be short, but getting to them may take a lot of time. For example, a sales manager may hold a meeting to present a new product to salespeople. The manager may need only 30-60 minutes to present the new product and answer questions; but, some salespeople may have to travel for hours to attend.

To reduce the time needed for meetings, you can use hardware and software like those described in the Chapter 12 Technology Focus. The sales manager and the salespeople can use desktop computers that have speakers, microphones, and cameras to hold meetings. They can talk to each other and share the computer screen of the sales manager. The sales manager can display pictures of the new product and lists of features on his or her screen. They can discuss the product while they are viewing the pictures and features on their desktop computers. Most importantly, the sales manager and the salespeople can be in different locations.

Video camera attached to PC

Desktop conferencing allows people to meet without the expense, inconvenience, and time needed to get to a common meeting site. This means that sales people can stay on the road and get back to selling quickly. It also means that parents can work at home so they can care for their children. Another use is for a sick student to meet with his or her teacher without leaving home.

1. $3,127.85	2. $2,517.50	3. $4,075.50	4. $2,117.19
1,129.75	209.95	2,195.45	101.67
377.15	1,635.71	3,160.10	3,292.92
87.95	412.99	8,177.99	6,483.83
+ 4,081.21	+ 1,037.16	+ 4,059.86	+ 5,754.01

key terms preview

- **Double-entry system**
- **Income**
- **Merchandising business**
- **Service business**

goals

1 To learn how a service business earns income.

2 To learn how to record this income in a cash receipts journal.

UNDERSTANDING THE JOB

Key Terms

Income. Money received.

Merchandising business. One that sells a product.

Service business. One in which a service for a customer is performed.

If you owned your own small business, such as a computer repair shop, the money that you would receive is called **income**. If your small business sold a product, such as computers, you would own a **merchandising business**. But, since your business only repairs computers, it is called a **service business**. In this job, you will learn how to record income for a service business.

In Job 46, you learned how to record cash received for sales of merchandise using a cash receipts journal. In this job, you will learn how to record cash received for services that you perform. You will record cash received for services in a cash receipts journal, also.

Illustration 61A shows a completed cash receipts journal for a service business.

Illustration 61A

A cash receipts journal for a service business

STEP 1   STEP 2

CASH RECEIPTS JOURNAL   PAGE 1

	DATE	ACCOUNT TITLE	DOC. NO.	POST. REF.	INCOME CREDIT WOOD FENCE	INCOME CREDIT METAL FENCE	CASH DEBIT	BANK DEPOSITS	
1	20-- Mar. 1	√	T1	√	2 9 5 00	2 3 0 00	5 2 5 00	5 2 5 00	1
2	8	√	T8	√		3 6 5 00	3 6 5 00	3 6 5 00	2
3	15	√	T15	√		1 0 4 5 00	1 0 4 5 00		3
4	17	√	T17	√	9 7 5 00		9 7 5 00	2 0 2 0 00	4
5	29	√	T29	√	7 1 5 00	4 2 0 00	1 1 3 5 00	1 1 3 5 00	5
6	31	Totals			1 9 8 5 00 1 9 8 5 00	2 0 6 0 00 2 0 6 0 00	4 0 4 5 00 4 0 4 5 00	4 0 4 5 00 4 0 4 5 00	6

STEP 3   STEP 4

Beth Auclair owns and operates Beth's Fence Company. The company installs and repairs wood and metal fences. Beth prepares an invoice for each customer and keeps a duplicate for her records. Payment is made by each customer at the time the service is performed; that is, when the fence is put up.

Cultural Notes

Luca Pacioli, an Italian mathematician, is known as the Father of Accounting. He is called this because he was the first person to explain an accounting system in writing. His book, *The Method of Venice*, which was published in 1494, contained the first description of the double-entry accounting system.

Beth separates income from wood fences and income from metal fences in order to know how much is received from each type of fence. Entries are recorded for each type of income in the cash receipts journal.

At the end of each day, Beth separates her duplicate invoices. She puts the invoices from work on wood fences into one stack. She puts the invoices from work on metal fences into another stack. Beth uses a calculator with a printer. She adds the amounts in the stack of invoices for wood fences, and then adds the amounts in the stack of invoices for metal fences. On March 1, Beth makes the following calculations while adding the amounts of the duplicate invoices:

Income From	Amount	Income From	Amount
Wood fence	$100.00	Metal fence	$125.00
Wood fence	195.00	Metal fence	105.00
Totals	$295.00		$230.00

The printout or tape from the calculator will be Beth's source document for the journal entry. On the calculator tape, she writes *T* (for *tape*) and *1* (for March *1*, the date of the sales). Beth also writes the words *Wood fence* next to the total of wood fence sales and the words *Metal fence* next to the total of metal fence sales. See Illustration 61B.

Illustration 61B

Calculator tape for March 1

```
T1
                    100.00+
                    195.00+
Wood fence          295.00*+


                    125.00+
                    105.00+
Metal fence         230.00*+
```

Total sales for March are listed below:

Date	Income From	Amount
March 1	Wood fence	$ 295.00
	Metal fence	230.00
8	Metal fence	365.00
15	Metal fence	1,045.00
17	Wood fence	975.00
29	Wood fence	715.00
	Metal fence	420.00

Bank deposits were made on March 1, 8, 17, and 29.
Here is how the income was recorded in the cash receipts journal:

STEP 1 Enter the first calculator tape in the journal.

From the calculator tape, the date, tape number, and amount were recorded.

Special amount columns are provided for all acccounts in this transaction. Therefore, a check mark is placed in the Account Title column to show that no account title needs to be written. A check mark is also placed in the Post. Ref. column. The check mark in the Post. Ref. column will be explained in Job 62.

To enter the amounts in the correct columns, examine the calculator tape to determine the type of income. Because two types of fences were installed on March 1, both Income Credit columns were used. *Income is always recorded as a credit.*

The first total on Tape T1 is marked *Wood fence*. The first total, $295.00, was entered in the Wood Fence column under Income Credit. The second total on Tape T1 is marked *Metal fence*. The second total, $230.00, was entered in the Metal Fence column.

The journal being used is part of a **double-entry system**. In a double-entry system, every transaction has at least one debit and one credit. For tape T1, the individual amounts of the sales were entered in the Income Credit columns. The total of $295.00 + $230.00, or $525.00, was entered again in (extended into) the Cash Debit column. *Cash received is always recorded as a debit.* In a double-entry system, debits must always equal credits.

STEP 2 Enter the bank deposits.

Beth deposits all of the money that she receives in her checking account at the bank. She goes to the bank every few days to make a deposit. Each time a deposit is made, she records the amount of the deposit in the Bank Deposits column of the cash receipts journal. The March 1 receipts of $525.00 were deposited on that same day, so $525.00 was entered in the Bank Deposits column.

STEP 3 Record the remaining calculator tapes and bank deposits in the journal.

The income on March 8, $365.00, was from a metal fence, so it was entered in the journal in the Metal Fence column under Income Credit and in the Cash Debit column. A bank deposit was made on that date, so $365.00 was entered in the Bank Deposits column.

Notice that no bank deposit was made on March 15, but one was made on March 17 for the total of the receipts from March 15 and 17. So, the amounts of $1,045.00 on March 15 and $975.00 on March 17 were added to get a total of $2,020.00, which was entered in the Bank Deposits column on March 17.

STEP 4 Total and rule the journal.

Rule and foot all four money columns. Check the totals as shown on page 499:

Tips

Income is always recorded as a credit.

Key Terms

Double-entry system. Each transaction has at least one debit and one credit.

Tips

Cash received is always recorded as a debit.

1. Since debits must equal credits, add the two Income Credit column totals, Wood Fence and Metal Fence. The total of these columns should equal the Cash Debit column total.

Income, Wood Fence	$ 1,985.00
Income, Metal Fence	+ 2,060.00
Cash Debit	$ 4,045.00

2. Since all cash received was deposited in the bank, the total of the Cash Debit column should equal the total of the Bank Deposits column.

After the footings have been checked, enter the final totals and double rule each money column. Date the totals as of the last day of the month, and write the word *Totals* in the Account Title column.

BUILDING YOUR BUSINESS VOCABULARY

On a sheet of paper, write the headings **Statement Number** and **Words**. Next, choose the words that match the statements. Write each word you choose next to the statement number it matches. Be careful; not all the words listed should be used.

Statements	Words
1. How income is always recorded	cash receipts journal
2. Money received from the sale of merchandise or services	credit
	debit
3. A record of income received	double-entry system
4. A business that sells a product	extended
5. A system in which every transaction has at least one debit and one credit	income
	invoice
6. A business in which a service for customers is performed	merchandising business
	post
7. How cash received is always recorded	service business
8. Entered again in a second column	

STEPS REVIEW: Recording Income in a Cash Receipts Journal

STEP 1 Enter the first calculator tape in the journal.

STEP 2 Enter the bank deposit.

STEP 3 Record the remaining calculator tapes and bank deposits in the journal.

STEP 4 Total and rule the journal.

APPLICATION PROBLEMS

Problem 61-1

You are the record keeper for Warren Stern, who owns and operates Warren's Fence Company. Your job is to record income in the cash receipts journal. Warren's income is earned by installing wood and metal fences.

Directions

a. Set up a cash receipts journal identical to the one shown in Illustration 61A (on page 496). Number the journal page 1.

b. Record in the cash receipts journal the following information taken from calculator tapes made by adding the duplicate invoices:

June 3   Received $655.00 for installing a wood fence, T3
     5   Received $385.00 for installing a metal fence, T5.
     5   Deposited all money received from June 3 to 5 in the bank. The deposit amounted to $1,040.00. Enter this amount in the Bank Deposits column on the same line with T5.
    11   Received $1,450.00: $945.00 for a wood fence and $505.00 for a metal fence, T11.
    14   Received $2,110.00: $1,010.00 for wood fences and $1,100.00 for metal fences, T14.
    14   Deposited all money received from June 11 to 14 in the bank. The deposit amounted to $3,560.00.
    18   Received $585.75 for installing a wood fence, T18.
    19   Received $1,035.50 for installing metal fences, T19.
    19   Deposited all cash received from June 18 to 19 in the bank. The deposit amounted to $1,621.25.
    25   Received $1,646.50: $511.75 for wood fences and $1,134.75 for metal fences, T25.
    27   Received $972.85: $312.65 for a wood fence and $660.20 for a metal fence, T27.
    27   Deposited all money received from June 25 to 27 in the bank. The deposit amounted to $2,619.35.

c. Rule and foot all money columns. Check the footings to be sure that the sum of the Income Credit column totals equals the total of the Cash Debit column. Check also to be sure that the total of the Cash Debit column equals the total of the Bank Deposits column.

d. Enter the final totals and double rule the money columns. Date the totals as of the last day of June, and write the word *Totals* in the proper place.

CHECK POINT

61-1(d)

Cash Debit total = $8,840.60

You are employed by Wilma's Window Company, a business owned and operated by Wilma Paine. Wilma earns income by repairing broken windows and broken screens. It is part of your job to transfer information from calculator tapes, made by adding duplicate sales invoices, into the cash receipts journal.

Directions

a. Open a cash receipts journal with the following headings. Number the journal page 1.

				INCOME CREDIT			
DATE	ACCOUNT TITLE	DOC. NO.	POST. REF.	WINDOWS	SCREENS	CASH DEBIT	BANK DEPOSITS

CASH RECEIPTS JOURNAL   PAGE

b. Record in the cash receipts journal the following information taken from calculator tapes:

July 5 Received $17.50 for a window repair, T5
7 Received $31.10 for a window repair, T7.
8 Received $9.75 for a screen repair, T8.
8 Deposited all money received from July 5 to 8 in the bank. The deposit amounted to $58.35. Enter this amount in the Bank Deposits column on the same line as T8.
12 Received $57.50: $46.75 for a window repair and $10.75 for a screen repair, T12.
14 Received $83.45: $61.10 for a window repair and $22.35 for a screen repair, T14.
15 Received $106.35: $47.25 for a window repair and $59.10 for a screen repair, T15.
15 Deposited all money received from July 12 to 15 in the bank. The deposit amounted to $247.30.
22 Received $94.15 for a window repair, T22.
25 Received $31.75 for a window repair, T25.
27 Received $45.20: $36.10 for a window repair and $9.10 for a screen repair, T27.
27 Deposited all money received from July 22 to 27 in the bank. The deposit amounted to $171.10.

CHECK POINT

61-2(d)

Bank Deposits total = $476.75

c. Rule and foot all money columns. Check the footings to be sure that the sum of the Income Credit column totals equals the total of the Cash Debit column. Check also to be sure that the total of the Cash Debit column equals the total of the Bank Deposits column.

d. Enter the final totals and double rule the money columns. Date the totals as of the last day of July, and write the word *Totals* in the proper place.

Problem 61–3 may be found in the Working Papers.

key terms preview

- **Four-column ledger account**
- **General ledger**
- **Memorandum column**

goals

1 To learn how to post from a cash receipts journal to the general ledger.

2 To learn how to use four-column general ledger accounts.

→ UNDERSTANDING THE JOB

Key Terms

General ledger. A group of accounts other than customer and creditor accounts.

Four-column ledger account. A general ledger account with two balance columns.

In earlier jobs, you learned how to post from a journal to a ledger. For example, in Job 46, you posted from a cash receipts journal to customer accounts in an accounts receivable ledger.

In this job, you will learn again how to post from the cash receipts journal. However, you will be posting to a **general ledger**. A general ledger is the place where all accounts, other than those for customers and creditors, are kept.

You will also learn how to use a **four-column ledger account** in this job. Illustration 62A shows this form of account.

The first two money columns, Debit and Credit, are used in the usual way. But, while customer and creditor accounts have only one balance column, general ledger accounts have two balance columns. This is because a general ledger account can have either a debit balance or a credit balance. You will see how all of these columns are used in the Sample Problem.

Illustration 62A

A four-column general ledger account

GENERAL LEDGER

ACCOUNT					ACCOUNT NO.	
		POST.			BALANCE	
DATE	ITEM	REF.	DEBIT	CREDIT	DEBIT	CREDIT

Beth Auclair's cash receipts journal and general ledger are shown in Illustration 62B (on page 504). Here are the steps followed in posting from the cash receipts journal to the general ledger:

STEP 1 Enter the date in the accounts.

The date of the totals in the cash receipts journal is March 31. That date is entered in the Date column of each account as it is posted. Totals are always posted as of the last day of the month. March is written as Mar.

STEP 2 Enter the posting reference in the accounts.

The reference, CR1, for *c*ash *r*eceipts journal, page *1*, is entered in the Post. Ref. column of each account as it is posted.

STEP 3 Post the totals of the journal columns to the accounts.

To save time, only the totals of the debit and credit journal columns will be posted. The column headings in the cash receipts journal tell you where and how to post. Go to the account titled "Income, Wood Fence," and enter a *credit* of $1,985.00. Go to the account titled "Income, Metal Fence," and enter a *credit* of $2,060.00. These are both posted as credits because the column heading in the cash receipts journal is "Income Credit."

Next, go to the Cash account. The column heading in the cash receipts journal is Cash Debit. So, enter a debit of $4,045.00 in the Cash account.

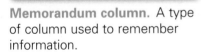

The total of the Bank Deposits column is *not posted*. Its purpose is to help the owner of the business remember important information, such as when was money deposited in the bank. For this reason it is called a **memorandum column**. *You never post from a memorandum column.*

STEP 4 Figure the new balances in each account.

After you post the total to a ledger account, figure the new balance.

All three accounts began with a zero balance, so the new balance is the same as the first amount entered. In the Cash account, since you entered a debit of $4,045.00, the balance is also a debit of $4,045.00. In each income account, you entered a credit. The balance of each income account is also a credit for that amount.

STEP 5 Enter the posting references in the cash receipts journal.

The number of each account is entered in parentheses under each column total as soon as the account has been posted and the new balance figured. Writing the number shows that the posting is complete. Since the Cash

Illustration 62B

Posting from the cash
receipts journal to the
general ledger

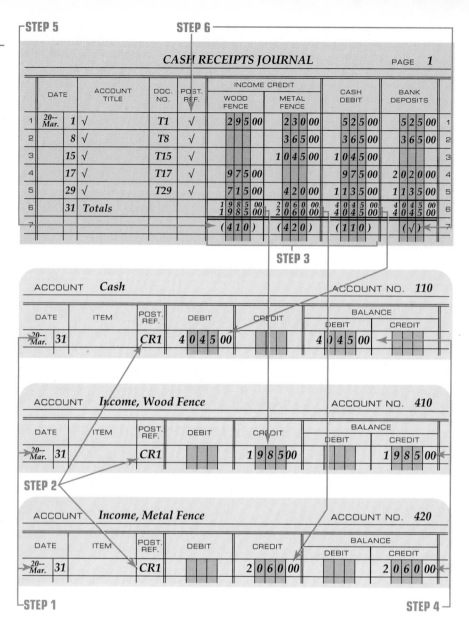

account is Account Number 110, 110 is entered as (110) under the Cash Debit column total. Since the Income, Wood Fence account is Account Number 410, 410 is entered as (410) under the Income Credit, Wood Fence column. For Income Credit, Metal Fence, (420) is entered.

STEP 6 **See that check marks were entered for amounts not posted; add any necessary for memorandum column(s).**

Check marks were already entered in the Post. Ref. column on each date, except on the Totals line. These check marks show that the individual amounts on March 1, 8, 15, 17, and 29 are not to be posted; they are posted as part of the March 31 total.

Now, enter a check mark under the Bank Deposits column total. This check mark is entered because a memorandum column total is not posted.

Illustration 62C (on page 505) shows how the balance columns of the general ledger accounts work. In this illustration, you see how postings for April's totals are made. For the Cash account, a debit of $6,150.00 is

Illustration 62C

General ledger accounts
with balances for two
months

CASH RECEIPTS JOURNAL PAGE 2

| | DATE | ACCOUNT TITLE | DOC. NO. | POST. REF. | INCOME CREDIT | | CASH DEBIT | BANK DEPOSITS | |
					WOOD FENCE	METAL FENCE			
6	30 Totals				3 1 5 0 00	3 0 0 0 00	6 1 5 0 00	6 1 5 0 00	6
7					(4 1 0)	(4 2 0)	(1 1 0)	(√)	7

ACCOUNT	*Cash*					ACCOUNT NO.	110	

| DATE | ITEM | POST. REF. | DEBIT | CREDIT | BALANCE | |
					DEBIT	CREDIT
20-- Mar. 31		CR1	4 0 4 5 00		4 0 4 5 00	
Apr. 30		CR2	6 1 5 0 00		10 1 9 5 00	

ACCOUNT	*Income, Wood Fence*					ACCOUNT NO.	410	

| DATE | ITEM | POST. REF. | DEBIT | CREDIT | BALANCE | |
					DEBIT	CREDIT
20-- Mar. 31		CR1		1 9 8 5 00		1 9 8 5 00
Apr. 30		CR2		3 1 5 0 00		5 1 3 5 00

ACCOUNT	*Income, Metal Fence*					ACCOUNT NO.	420	

| DATE | ITEM | POST. REF. | DEBIT | CREDIT | BALANCE | |
					DEBIT	CREDIT
20-- Mar. 31		CR1		2 0 6 0 00		2 0 6 0 00
Apr. 30		CR2		3 0 0 0 00		5 0 6 0 00

entered on April 30. To find the new balance, add the new debit to the old debit balance:

Previous debit balance	$ 4,045.00
New debit	+ 6,150.00
New debit balance	$10,195.00

For the Income, Wood Fence account, $3,150.00 is entered on April 30. To find the new balance, add the new credit to the old credit balance:

Previous credit balance	$ 1,985.00
New credit	+ 3,150.00
New credit balance	$ 5,135.00

Notice in Illustration 62C that the posting reference CR2 is entered in the accounts. Page 2 of the cash receipts journal was used in April.

BUILDING YOUR BUSINESS VOCABULARY

On a sheet of paper, write the headings **Statement Number** and **Words**. Next, choose the words that match the statements. Write each word you choose next to the statement number it matches. Be careful; not all the words listed should be used.

Statements	Words
1. A group of customer accounts	accounts payable ledger
2. A group of accounts other than customer and creditor accounts	accounts receivable ledger
3. A general ledger account with two balance columns	double-entry system
4. A group of creditor accounts	extend
5. Money received from the sale of merchandise or services	four-column ledger account
6. A type of column used to remember information	general ledger
7. To transfer data from one record to another	income
8. A system in which every transaction has at least one debit and one credit	memorandum column
	post
	three-column account

STEPS REVIEW: Recording Income in the General Ledger

STEP 1 Enter the date in the accounts.

STEP 2 Enter the posting reference in the accounts.

STEP 3 Post the totals of the journal columns to the accounts.

STEP 4 Figure the new balances in each account.

STEP 5 Enter the posting references in the cash receipts journal.

STEP 6 See that check marks were entered for amounts not posted; add any necessary for memorandum column(s).

APPLICATION PROBLEMS

Problem 62-1

You are the record keeper for Jeremy Lindstrom, a consultant and financial manager.

Directions

a. Copy the following cash receipts journal for May, 20--:

CASH RECEIPTS JOURNAL   PAGE **1**

	DATE		ACCOUNT TITLE	DOC. NO.	POST. REF.	INCOME CREDIT — CONSULTING	INCOME CREDIT — MANAGEMENT	CASH DEBIT	BANK DEPOSITS	
1	20-- May	3	√	T3	√	400 00		400 00		1
2		6	√	T6	√		700 00	700 00		2
3		7	√	T7	√	350 00		350 00	1450 00	3
4		15	√	T15	√	500 00	650 00	1150 00		4
5		18	√	T18	√	430 00	250 00	680 00	1830 00	5

b. Open the following general ledger accounts. (Allow three lines for each account.)

Cash	#110
Income, Consulting	#410
Income, Management	#420

c. Rule the money columns in the cash receipts journal and foot the columns.

d. Check the footings to see if total debits equal total credits. Also, check to see that the Cash Debit and Bank Deposits column totals are equal.

e. Write the final totals and double rule the money columns. Enter the date and the word *Totals* in the proper places.

f. Post the totals to the general ledger accounts. Be sure to include posting references in the accounts and in the journal.

g. Insert a check mark in the proper place.

✓ **CHECK POINT**

62-1(e)

Cash Debit total = $3,280.00

Problem **62-2**

You are the record keeper for Move and Groove, a water ski instruction and rental shop.

Directions

a. Copy the following cash receipts journal for June, 20--:

CASH RECEIPTS JOURNAL PAGE 4

	DATE	ACCOUNT TITLE	DOC. NO.	POST. REF.	INCOME CREDIT		CASH DEBIT	BANK DEPOSITS	
					LESSONS	RENTALS			
1	20-- June 3	✓	T3	✓	75 00		75 00		1
2	5	✓	T5	✓		45 00	45 00	120 00	2
3	16	✓	T16	✓	80 00		80 00		3
4	18	✓	T18	✓		125 00	125 00	205 00	4
5	27	✓	T27	✓	350 00		350 00	350 00	5

b. Copy the following general ledger accounts. They show the postings for the past three months. (Allow five lines for each account.)

ACCOUNT   **Cash**   ACCOUNT NO. **110**

DATE	ITEM	POST. REF.	DEBIT	CREDIT	BALANCE	
					DEBIT	CREDIT
20-- Mar. 31		CR1	805 00		805 00	
Apr. 30		CR2	710 00		1515 00	
May 31		CR3	745 00		2260 00	

ACCOUNT   **Income, Lessons**   ACCOUNT NO. **410**

DATE	ITEM	POST. REF.	DEBIT	CREDIT	BALANCE	
					DEBIT	CREDIT
20-- Mar. 31		CR1		520 00		520 00
Apr. 30		CR2		470 00		990 00
May 31		CR3		390 00		1380 00

ACCOUNT	*Income, Rentals*				ACCOUNT NO.	*420*	

DATE		ITEM	POST. REF.	DEBIT	CREDIT	BALANCE	
						DEBIT	CREDIT
20-- Mar.	31		CR1		2 8 5 00		2 8 5 00
Apr.	30		CR2		2 4 0 00		5 2 5 00
May	31		CR3		3 5 5 00		8 8 0 00

CHECK POINT

Cash account final
balance = $2,935.00

c. Rule the money columns in the cash receipts journal and foot the columns.

d. Check the footings to see if total debits equal total credits. Also, check to see that the Cash Debit and Bank Deposits column totals are equal.

e. Write the final totals and double rule the money columns. Enter the date and the word *Totals* in the proper places.

f. Post the totals to the general ledger accounts. Include all posting references. Calculate new account balances.

g. Insert a check mark in the proper place.

Problem 62-3 may be found in the Working Papers.

applied math preview

Copy and complete these problems. In each problem, crossfoot and then add down. Find the grand totals.

1.					2.			
$ 7.56 +	$ 8.12 +	$ 5.95 +	$11.75 =		44 +	53 +	27 +	91 =
19.12 +	0.56 +	11.16 +	31.09 =		37 +	36 +	19 +	81 =
31.15 +	9.71 +	2.75 +	45.04 =		29 +	42 +	35 +	55 =
18.06 +	12.10 +	6.99 +	11.55 =		66 +	57 +	21 +	29 =
19.11 +	75.80 +	31.04 +	82.09 =		18 +	69 +	76 +	42 =
+	+	+	=		+	+	+	=

goals

 1 To practice recording in a cash receipts journal and posting to the general ledger.

 2 To use a cash receipts journal with three income columns.

➡ UNDERSTANDING THE JOB

In Jobs 61 and 62, you learned how to record income in a cash receipts journal and post to the general ledger. In this job, you will have the chance to practice both of these skills. You will use a cash receipts journal with a Cash Debit column and three Income Credit columns, as well as the Bank Deposits column.

➡ SAMPLE PROBLEM

Allen Powell owns and operates a travel agency. He earns income from tours, cruises, and air fares. You are his record keeper. You record his income in a cash receipts journal with three income columns. You also post to his general ledger accounts.

His transactions for May, 20--, are as follows:

May 2 Received $745.60 for a tour, T2.
4 Received $475.15 for cruises, T4.
4 Deposited all cash received from May 2 to 4.
14 Received $1,505.37: $942.12 for cruises and $563.25 for air fare, T14.
16 Received $755.00 for a tour, T16.
16 Deposited all cash received from May 14 to 16.
24 Received $135.00 for air fare and $517.86 for cruises, T24.
25 Received $637.50 for a tour and $812.44 for cruises, T25.
28 Received $475.50 for air fare, $1,144.65 for cruises, and $2,275.00 for a tour, T28.
28 Deposited all cash received from May 24 to 28.

Illustration 63A on page 511 shows how these transactions are recorded in the cash receipts journal and posted to the general ledger. Here are the steps you would follow:

STEP 1 Open the cash receipts journal and the general ledger accounts.

Open a cash receipts journal with three Income Credit columns, a Cash Debit column, and a Bank Deposits column.

Open four general ledger accounts. The Cash account is always first.

STEP 2 Journalize each transaction.

Record each transaction in the cash receipts journal. Look carefully at the data that are given. On May 14, you are given the amounts for cash debit ($1,505.37), cruises ($942.12), and air fare ($563.25).

On May 24, however, you are given the amounts for air fare ($135.00) and cruises ($517.86), but not for cash debit. To find the amount for cash debit, add the two Income Credit column amounts:

Income Credit, Air Fares	$ 135.00
Income Credit, Cruises	+ 517.86
Cash Debit	$ 652.86

Enter a check mark in the Post. Ref. column for each daily transaction, since only totals are posted.

Tips

Extend total credit amounts to the Cash Debit column.

Debits = Credits

STEP 3 Record the bank deposits in the Bank Deposits column.

The first deposit is made on May 4. It is the sum of the cash debits on May 2 and 4. Add $745.60 + $475.15 to get $1,220.75, the first bank deposit.

STEP 4 Rule and foot the cash receipts journal, and check the totals.

On the last day of the month, the columns are ruled, footed, and checked. Totals are checked by crossfooting total debits with total credits to see if they are equal.

Income Credit, Tours	$4,413.10
Income Credit, Cruises	3,892.22
Income Credit, Air Fares	+1,173.75
Cash Debit	$9,479.07

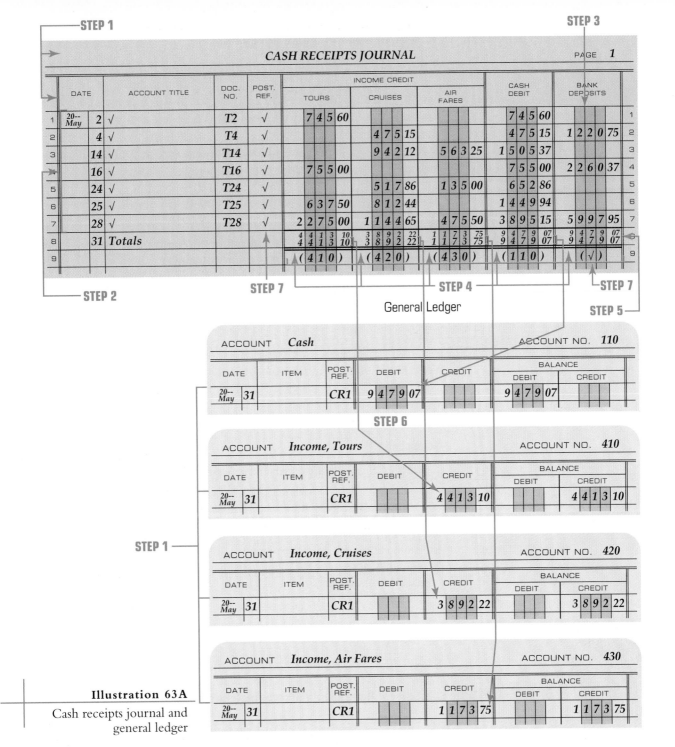

STEP 1

STEP 3

CASH RECEIPTS JOURNAL PAGE 1

	DATE		ACCOUNT TITLE	DOC. NO.	POST. REF.	INCOME CREDIT						CASH DEBIT	BANK DEPOSITS		
						TOURS	CRUISES		AIR FARES						
1	20-- May	2	√	T2	√	7 4 5 60						7 4 5 60			1
2		4	√	T4	√		4 7 5 15					4 7 5 15	1 2 2 0 75		2
3		14	√	T14	√		9 4 2 12		5 6 3 25		1 5 0 5 37				3
4		16	√	T16	√	7 5 5 00						7 5 5 00	2 2 6 0 37		4
5		24	√	T24	√		5 1 7 86		1 3 5 00		6 5 2 86				5
6		25	√	T25	√	6 3 7 50	8 1 2 44				1 4 4 9 94				6
7		28	√	T28	√	2 2 7 5 00	1 1 4 4 65		4 7 5 50		3 8 9 5 15	5 9 9 7 95		7
8		31	Totals			4 4 1 3 10	3 8 9 2 22		1 1 7 3 75		9 4 7 9 07	9 4 7 9 07		8
9						(4 1 0)	(4 2 0)		(4 3 0)		(1 1 0)	(√)		9

STEP 2

STEP 7

STEP 4

STEP 7

STEP 5

General Ledger

ACCOUNT	Cash					ACCOUNT NO.	110
DATE	ITEM	POST. REF.	DEBIT	CREDIT	BALANCE		
					DEBIT	CREDIT	
20-- May 31		CR1	9 4 7 9 07		9 4 7 9 07		

STEP 6

ACCOUNT	Income, Tours					ACCOUNT NO.	410
DATE	ITEM	POST. REF.	DEBIT	CREDIT	BALANCE		
					DEBIT	CREDIT	
20-- May 31		CR1		4 4 1 3 10		4 4 1 3 10	

STEP 1

ACCOUNT	Income, Cruises					ACCOUNT NO.	420
DATE	ITEM	POST. REF.	DEBIT	CREDIT	BALANCE		
					DEBIT	CREDIT	
20-- May 31		CR1		3 8 9 2 22		3 8 9 2 22	

Illustration 63A

Cash receipts journal and general ledger

ACCOUNT	Income, Air Fares					ACCOUNT NO.	430
DATE	ITEM	POST. REF.	DEBIT	CREDIT	BALANCE		
					DEBIT	CREDIT	
20-- May 31		CR1		1 1 7 3 75		1 1 7 3 75	

The Cash Debit column total and the Bank Deposits column total are also compared. They should be equal. If the totals do not agree, re-add the columns. If they still are not equal,

1. Recheck each entry to make sure that the debits and the credits are equal.
2. Recheck your addition for each bank deposit.

STEP 5 **Write in final totals and double rule the columns.**

Date your totals as of the last day of the month, and write the word *Totals* in the Account Title column. Double rule all five money columns.

Credit income accounts. Debit the Cash account for cash received.

STEP 6 Post to the general ledger accounts.

Enter the date (May 31) and posting reference (CR1) in each account. Enter the amount in each account. The column heading of the journal will indicate the name of the account and if it is a debit or a credit. Income accounts are always credited. The Cash account is always debited for cash received.

Enter the balance in each account. Income accounts will have a credit balance. The Cash account will have a debit balance.

Enter the account number in parentheses under each total in the cash receipts journal, except for the Bank Deposits column total.

STEP 7 See that check marks were entered in the journal for items not posted; add any necessary for memorandum column(s).

Enter a check mark under the Bank Deposits column total since the total of a memorandum column is not posted.

➡ BUILDING YOUR BUSINESS VOCABULARY

On a sheet of paper, write the headings **Statement Number** and **Words**. Next, choose the words that match the statements. Write each word you choose next to the statement number it matches. Be careful; not all the words listed should be used.

Statements	Words
1. The side of an account on which income is recorded	credit
2. A general ledger account with two balance columns	debit
3. The side of an account on which cash received is recorded	extended
	four-column ledger account
4. A type of column used to remember information	general ledger
5. Entered again in a second column	income
6. A group of accounts other than customer and creditor accounts	journalize
7. To record in a journal	memorandum column
8. Symbols, such as CR1, that show from where an entry was posted	post
	posting references

STEPS REVIEW: Using a Cash Receipts Journal and a General Ledger

STEP 1 Open the cash receipts journal and the general ledger accounts.

STEP 2 Journalize each transaction.

STEP 3 Record the bank deposits in the Bank Deposits column.

STEP 4 Rule and foot the cash receipts journal, and check the totals.

STEP 5 Write in final totals and double rule the columns.

STEP 6 Post to the general ledger accounts.

STEP 7 See that check marks were entered in the journal for items not posted; add any necessary for memorandum column(s).

Problem 63-1   You are the record keeper for Evangeline Doong, who owns a ticket agency. Evangeline separates income into three types: theater tickets, sports tickets, and concert tickets. Your job is to journalize and post her income transactions.

Directions

a. Open a cash receipts journal with the following headings. Number the journal page 1.

DATE	ACCOUNT TITLE	DOC. NO.	POST. REF.	INCOME CREDIT			CASH DEBIT	BANK DEPOSITS
				THEATER	SPORTS	CONCERTS		

CHECK POINT

63-1(f)

Bank Deposits total = $2,667.10

b. Open the following general ledger accounts. The accounts have no previous balances. (Allow three lines for each account.)

Cash	#110
Income, Theater	#410
Income, Sports	#420
Income, Concerts	#430

c. Record the following information for July in the cash receipts journal:

July 3   Received $195.50 for theater tickets, T3.
    5   Received $57.75 for sports tickets, T5.
    5   Deposited all cash received from July 3 to 5.
   10   Received $127.60 for concert tickets, T10.
   11   Received $217.40: $106.35 for concert tickets and $111.05 for theater tickets, T11.
   11   Deposited all cash received from July 10 to 11.
   15   Received $316.95: $210.90 for theater tickets and $106.05 for sports tickets, T15.
   17   Received $296.10: $45.60 for sports tickets and $250.50 for theater tickets, T17.
   18   Received $217.40 for concert tickets, T18.
   18   Deposited all cash received from July 15 to 18.
   22   Received $103.90 for theater tickets and $75.55 for sports tickets, T22.
   23   Received $64.10 for sports tickets and $104.95 for concert tickets, T23.
   23   Deposited all cash received from July 22 to 23.
   28   Received $45.10 for sports tickets, $95.80 for concert tickets, and $131.10 for theater tickets, T28.
   29   Received $617.90: $204.30 for concert tickets, $96.85 for sports tickets, and $316.75 for theater tickets, T29.
   29   Deposited all cash received from July 28 to 29.

d. Rule and foot all money columns in the cash receipts journal.
e. Check the footings to see if total debits equal total credits. Also, see if the totals of the Cash Debit and Bank Deposits columns agree.
f. Write in final totals and draw a double ruling.
g. Post the totals to the ledger accounts. Be sure to include all posting references and check marks.

Problem 63-2 You are the record keeper for Allen Powell, who runs a travel agency. (See Sample Problem, page 509.) You record his income and post to the general ledger.

CHECK POINT

63-2(g)

Cash account final balance = $22,350.78

Directions

a. Open a cash receipts journal identical to the one used in the Sample Problem (Illustration 63A, page 511). Number the journal page 2.

b. Copy the ledger accounts shown in Illustration 63A. (Allow three lines for each account.)

c. Record the following information for June in the cash receipts journal:

June 2 Received $974.10 for a tour, T2.
   4 Received $645.70 for cruises, T4.
   4 Deposited all cash received from June 2 to 4.
   7 Received $1,710.36: $775.40 for a tour and $934.96 for cruises, T7.
   9 Received $882.40: $511.24 for cruises and $371.16 for air fare, T9.
  10 Received $197.55 for air fare, T10.
  10 Deposited all cash received from June 7 to 10.
  15 Received $408.17 for cruises and $795.99 for a tour, T15.
  16 Received $511.76 for cruises and $204.75 for air fare, T16.
  17 Received $625.94: $108.10 for air fare and $517.84 for cruises, T17.
  17 Deposited all cash received from June 15 to 17.
  21 Received $508.10 for cruises, $795.05 for a tour, and $199.99 for air fare, T21.
  22 Received $1,755.95 for a tour, T22.
  22 Deposited all cash received from June 21 to 22.
  28 Received $2,655.90: $1,045.00 for a tour, $496.86 for cruises and $1,114.04 for air fare, T28.
  28 Deposited all cash received on June 28.

d. Rule and foot all money columns in the cash receipts journal.

e. Check the footings to see if total debits equal total credits. Also, see if the totals of the Cash Debit and Bank Deposits columns agree.

f. Write in final totals and draw a double ruling.

g. Post the totals to the ledger accounts. Calculate new balances after each posting. Be sure to include all posting references and check marks.

Problem 63-3 may be found in the Working Papers.

applied math preview

Copy and complete the following problems.

1.	2.	3.	4.
$4,671.45	$ 7,142.19	$6,244.18	$6,177.09
2,179.84	5,017.36	8,280.92	5,834.11
5,011.36	1,457.21	1,415.15	2,621.17
+ 5,277.19	+10,368.02	+ 4,637.34	+4,117.09

key terms preview

- Drawing
- Expenses
- General columns
- Special columns

goals

1. To learn about the expenses of a service business.
2. To learn how to record these expenses in a cash payments journal.
3. To learn how to record the owner's personal expenses in a cash payments journal.

→ UNDERSTANDING THE JOB

Key Terms

Expenses. Costs of operating a business.

Drawing. Money taken out of a business by the owner.

In Job 61, you learned how to record income earned by a service business. To operate your own business, you will also have **expenses**. Expenses are the costs of operating a business. Expenses include such things as rent for the building, your telephone bill, your electric bill, truck gas and repairs, and parts and supplies.

In addition to these business expenses, most owners of a business take or withdraw money from the business for their personal living expenses. These personal expenses include rent, food, clothing, and other personal expenses. To show the amount withdrawn for personal use, a separate account is used in the general ledger. The account used is called the owner's **drawing** account. If the owner's name is Beth Auclair, the account would be called "Beth Auclair, Drawing."

In this job, you will learn how to record both types of expenses in a journal that you were introduced to in Job 58, the cash payments journal.

Illustration 64A (on page 516) shows a completed cash payments journal for a service business.

STEP 1

CASH PAYMENTS JOURNAL

PAGE 1

	DATE		ACCOUNT TITLE	CHECK NO.	POST. REF.	GENERAL DEBIT	BETH AUCLAIR, DRAWING DEBIT	SUPPLIES EXPENSE DEBIT	CASH CREDIT	
1	20-- Mar.	1	Rent Expense	101		9 5 0 00			9 5 0 00	1
2		4	√	102	√		1 5 0 00		1 5 0 00	2
3		12	√	103	√			7 1 0 00	7 1 0 00	3
4		17	√	104	√			2 4 5 00	2 4 5 00	4
5		22	Telephone Expense	105		1 3 5 00			1 3 5 00	5
6		30	√	106	√		4 0 0 00		4 0 0 00	6
7		31	Totals			1 0 8 5 00	5 5 0 00	9 5 5 00	2 5 9 0 00	7

STEP 2

Illustration 64A

A cash payments journal for
a service business

SAMPLE PROBLEM

Beth Auclair owns and operates Beth's Fence Company. (See Job 61.) Beth uses a checkbook to pay all expenses. She uses the check stubs as the source documents for entries in the cash payments journal.

Beth's cash payments for March, 20--, are as follows:

Mar. 1 Issued Check No. 101 for $950.00 to Nash Realty for March rent.
4 Issued Check No. 102 for $150.00 to Beth Auclair for personal use.
12 Issued Check No. 103 for $710.00 to Briggs Company for supplies.
17 Issued Check No. 104 for $245.00 to Russell Company for supplies.
22 Issued Check No. 105 for $135.00 to County Telephone for the telephone bill for March.
30 Issued Check No. 106 for $400.00 to Central Bank for Beth Auclair's personal car payment.

Here is how the expenses were recorded in the cash payments journal:

STEP 1 Enter each check stub in the journal.

From each check stub, record the date, check number, and amount.

To enter the amounts in the correct column, examine each check stub to see what it was paid for. Then remember the meaning of the double-entry system: each transaction has at least one debit and one credit.

1. Enter the amount first in one of the debit columns.
2. Enter the amount of every check stub again in the Cash Credit column. *Cash paid out is always recorded as a credit.*

The cash payments journal in Illustration 64A has three debit columns: General Debit; Beth Auclair, Drawing Debit; and Supplies

Tips

In a double-entry system, each transaction has at least one debit and one credit. Cash paid out is always recorded as a credit.

Expense Debit. Columns such as Beth Auclair, Drawing Debit and Supplies Expense Debit are called **special columns**. Special columns in a journal are used for only one type of item. Every time there is a personal expense, such as for Check No. 102 and No. 106, the amount will be entered in the Beth Auclair, Drawing column. Every time there is a supplies expense, such as for Check No. 103 and No. 104, the amount will be entered in the Supplies Expense Debit column. A check mark is placed in the Account Title column to show that no account title needs to be written. A check mark is also placed in the Post. Ref. column. The check mark in the Post. Ref. column will be explained in Job 65.

The names of special columns will vary from company to company. Each company will set up a special column for an expense that is paid often. The Cash Credit column is also a special column.

Now, look at how Check No. 101 is extended. There is no special column for rent expense, so the General Debit column must be used. Since there will be many different kinds of other items, the name of the expense, Rent Expense, is written in the Account Title column. The Post. Ref. column is left blank. The amount is then recorded in the General Debit column. Columns like the General Debit column are called **general columns**, since they are used for many different types of items. When recording in a journal with special columns and general columns, use the general columns when there is no special column for your amount.

Look at how Check No. 105 was recorded. There is no special column for telephone expense. The General Debit column was used. The name of the expense, Telephone Expense, was written in the Account Title column, the Post. Ref. column was left blank, and the amount was entered in the General Debit column.

Whether you extend to a special column or to the general column in the cash payments journal, *an expense is always recorded as a debit.*

STEP 2 Rule and foot the money columns.

Rule and foot all four money columns. Check the totals to see if debits equal credits as shown below:

General Debit	$1,085.00
Beth Auclair, Drawing Debit	550.00
Supplies Expense Debit	+ 955.00
Cash Credit	$2,590.00

After the footings have been checked, enter the final totals and draw a double ruling under each money column. Date the totals as of the last day of the month, and write the word *Totals* in the Account Title column.

 BUILDING YOUR BUSINESS VOCABULARY

On a sheet of paper, write the headings **Statement Number** and **Words**. Next, choose the words that match the statements. Write each word you choose next to the statement number it matches. Be careful; not all the words listed should be used.

Statements	Words
1. A record of income received	cash payments journal
2. Money taken out of the business by the owner	cash receipts journal
	credit
3. A column in a journal used for only one type of item	debit
	double-entry system
4. How an expense is always recorded	drawing
5. A record of expenses paid	expenses
6. Columns in a journal used for items that have no special column	general columns
	general ledger
7. Costs of operating a business	special column
8. How cash paid out is always recorded	

STEPS REVIEW: Recording Expenses in a Cash Payments Journal

STEP 1 Enter each check stub in the journal.

STEP 2 Rule and foot the money columns.

APPLICATION PROBLEMS

Problem 64-1

You work in the office of Alex Carney, a lawyer. Part of your job is to record cash payments in a cash payments journal.

Spreadsheet

CHECK POINT

✓ 64-1(c)

Cash Credit total = $3,465.00

Directions

a. Open a cash payments journal with the same headings as in Illustration 64A (page 516), but label the Drawing Debit column "Alex Carney, Drawing." Number the journal page 1.

b. Record the following cash payments in the cash payments journal:

Oct. 3   Issued Check No. 101 for $550.00 to City Stationery Company for office supplies.

7   Issued Check No. 102 for $125.00 to Alex Carney for personal use.

10   Issued Check No. 103 for $95.00 to Main Street Supply Company for mailing supplies.

12   Issued Check No. 104 for $900.00 to Prime Realty for office rent. (Use the account Rent Expense.)

17   Issued Check No. 105 for $245.00 to City Telephone Company for the phone bill. (Use the account Telephone Expense.)

19   Issued Check No. 106 for $450.00 to Alex Carney for personal use.

26   Issued Check No. 107 for $350.00 to City Stationery Company for office supplies.

29   Issued Check No. 108 for $750.00 to Prime Realty for Alex Carney's home rent.

c. Total and rule the journal. Remember to check your totals to be sure that debits equal credits before entering final totals.

Problem 64-2

You work for Jennie Cartwright, a self-employed plumber. Part of your job is to record cash payments in a cash payments journal.

Automated Accounting

Directions

a. Open a cash payments journal with the following column headings. Number the journal page 42.

CASH PAYMENTS JOURNAL							PAGE
DATE	ACCOUNT TITLE	CHECK NO.	POST. REF.	GENERAL DEBIT	PLUMBING SUPPLIES EXPENSE DEBIT	TRUCK EXPENSE DEBIT	CASH CREDIT

CHECK POINT

64-2(c)

Cash Credit total
= $2,055.00

b. Record the cash payments below in the cash payments journal:

Mar. 2 Issued Check No. 1001 for $165.00 to Neptune Company for plumbing supplies.

6 Issued Check No. 1002 for $75.00 to Kay's Garage for truck repairs.

11 Issued Check No. 1003 for $135.00 to Kendall Auto Parts for a truck battery.

14 Issued Check No. 1004 for $200.00 to Jennie Cartwright for personal use. (Use the account J. Cartwright, Drawing.)

17 Issued Check No. 1005 for $175.00 to Acme Tire Company for a new tire for the truck.

20 Issued Check No. 1006 for $675.00 to Neptune Company for plumbing supplies.

22 Issued Check No. 1007 for $355.00 to Lincoln Insurance Company for insurance expense.

28 Issued Check No. 1008 for $275.00 to R & S Supply Company for plumbing supplies.

c. Total and rule the journal. Remember to check your totals to be sure that debits equal credits before entering final totals.

Problem 64-3 You work in the office of Larry Hodgkiss, a printer. Part of your job is to record cash payments in a cash payments journal.

Directions

a. Open a cash payments journal with the following headings. Number the journal page 3.

b. Record the following cash payments in the cash payments journal:

CASH PAYMENTS JOURNAL							PAGE
DATE	ACCOUNT TITLE	CHECK NO.	POST. REF.	GENERAL DEBIT	LARRY HODGKISS, DRAWING DEBIT	PRINTING SUPPLIES EXPENSE DEBIT	CASH CREDIT

CHECK POINT

64-3(c)

General Debit total
= $1,080.00

May 3 Issued Check No. 49 for $175.00 to Larry Hodgkiss for personal use.

7 Issued Check No. 50 for $395.00 to Best Ink Company for printing supplies.

10 Issued Check No. 51 for $250.00 to Wilson Bank for Larry Hodgkiss' car payment.

16 Issued Check No. 52 for $955.00 to James Realty for office rent.

18 Issued Check No. 53 for $425.00 to Best Ink Company for printing supplies.

22 Issued Check No. 54 for $350.00 to Granite Phone Company for Larry Hodgkiss' home phone bill.

27 Issued Check No. 55 for $125.00 to Lee's Garage for truck repair.

29 Issued Check No. 56 for $755.00 to C & J Paper Company for printing paper.

c. Total and rule the journal.

applied math preview

Copy and complete the following problems.

1. $4,627.08	2. $6,327.16	3. $ 57.25	4. $ 206.19
45.27	1,099.19	6,083.11	2,127.35
599.94	6.34	416.12	391.08
8,064.12	975.12	1,935.10	2,077.17
+3,152.06	+2,777.89	+ 46.12	+ 9.19

goal

To learn how to post from the cash payments journal to the general ledger.

UNDERSTANDING THE JOB

In Job 62, you learned how to post from the cash receipts journal to the general ledger. The total cash received was posted to the debit side of the Cash account, and the total amounts of each type of income were posted to the credit side of each income account.

In this job, you will learn how to post from the cash payments journal to the general ledger.

SAMPLE PROBLEM

Beth Auclair's cash payments journal from Job 64 is shown in Illustration 65A on page 522. Also shown are some general ledger accounts on page 522. These accounts include an amount which has been posted from the cash receipts journal to the Cash account.

Here are the steps followed to journalize and post the cash payments journal to these accounts:

STEP 1 Journalize each transaction.

Record each transaction in the journal as you learned to do in Job 64.

STEP 2 Record check marks where necessary.

Make sure that a check mark was put in the Post. Ref. column of the journal for those items that do not require daily posting. Transactions that are recorded in special columns will not be posted daily. They will be posted at the end of the month as part of column totals. There should be check marks for March 4, 12, 17, and 30 in the Post. Ref. column.

STEP 3 Complete the daily postings.

Only entries in the General Debit column are posted daily. On March 1, the $950.00 that was recorded in the General Debit column was posted to the Rent Expense account in the general ledger. The posting was done in these steps:

Tips

Post individual amounts from general columns.

Date individual items on the date of entry.

a. Enter the date, March 1, in the Date column of the Rent Expense account.

b. Enter the posting reference, CP1 (for cash payments journal, page 1), in the Post. Ref. column of the Rent Expense account.

c. Enter the amount, $950.00, in the Debit column of the Rent Expense account.

d. Figure the new balance of the Rent Expense account. Since there was no previous balance, the new balance is a debit of $950.00.

e. Enter the number of the Rent Expense account, 520, in the Post. Ref. column of the cash payments journal.

The debit to the Telephone Expense account on March 22 was posted in the same way.

STEP 4 Rule, foot, and check the totals.

On the last day of the month, rule, foot, and check the totals of the cash payments journal as you learned to do in Job 64.

STEP 5 Post the totals of the special columns to the accounts.

Post the totals of the three special columns to the general ledger accounts. The column headings tell you where and how to post.

Post the total of the Cash Credit column by following these steps:

Tips

Date totals as of the last day of the month.

Subtract a credit from a debit balance.

a. Enter the date, 31, in the Date column of the Cash account.

b. Enter the post reference, CP1, in the Post. Ref. column of the Cash account.

c. Enter the amount, $2,590.00, in the Credit column of the Cash account.

d. Figure the new balance of the Cash account. The Cash account has a previous debit balance. Subtract the credit entered from the debit balance and enter the difference. You still have a debit balance, though it is a smaller one. Here is how it is calculated:

Previous debit balance	$ 4,045.00
Credit	− 2,590.00
New debit balance	$ 1,455.00

e. Enter (110) under the total of the Cash Credit column of the cash payments journal.

Following the same steps used to post to the Cash account, post the totals of the Supplies Expense Debit column ($955.00) and the Beth Auclair, Drawing Debit column ($550.00) to the proper accounts in the general ledger.

CASH PAYMENTS JOURNAL — PAGE 1

	DATE	ACCOUNT TITLE	CHECK NO.	POST. REF.	GENERAL DEBIT	BETH AUCLAIR, DRAWING DEBIT	SUPPLIES EXPENSE DEBIT	CASH CREDIT	
1	20-- Mar. 1	Rent Expense	101	520	9 50 0 00			9 50 0 00	1
2	4	√	102	√		1 50 00		1 50 00	2
3	12	√	103	√			7 10 00	7 10 00	3
4	17	√	104	√			2 45 00	2 45 00	4
5	22	Telephone Expense	105	530	1 35 00			1 35 00	5
6	30	√	106	√		4 00 00		4 00 00	6
7	31	Totals			1 0 85 00	5 50 00	9 55 00	2 5 90 00	7
					(√)	(3 2 0)	(5 1 0)	(1 1 0)	

STEP 1

STEP 2 STEP 5 STEP 4

General Ledger

STEP 3

Illustration 65A

Posting from the cash payments journal to the general ledger

ACCOUNT **Cash** — ACCOUNT NO. 110

DATE	ITEM	POST. REF.	DEBIT	CREDIT	BALANCE DEBIT	BALANCE CREDIT
20-- Mar. 31		CR1	4 0 45 00		4 0 45 00	
31		CP1		2 5 90 00	1 4 55 00	

ACCOUNT **Beth Auclair, Drawing** — ACCOUNT NO. 320

DATE	ITEM	POST. REF.	DEBIT	CREDIT	BALANCE DEBIT	BALANCE CREDIT
20-- Mar. 31		CP1	5 50 00		5 50 00	

ACCOUNT **Supplies Expense** — ACCOUNT NO. 510

DATE	ITEM	POST. REF.	DEBIT	CREDIT	BALANCE DEBIT	BALANCE CREDIT
20-- Mar. 31		CP1	9 55 00		9 55 00	

ACCOUNT **Rent Expense** — ACCOUNT NO. 520

DATE	ITEM	POST. REF.	DEBIT	CREDIT	BALANCE DEBIT	BALANCE CREDIT
20-- Mar. 1		CP1	9 50 00		9 50 00	

ACCOUNT **Telephone Expense** — ACCOUNT NO. 530

DATE	ITEM	POST. REF.	DEBIT	CREDIT	BALANCE DEBIT	BALANCE CREDIT
20-- Mar. 22		CP1	1 35 00		1 35 00	

ACCOUNT	Rent Expense				ACCOUNT NO.	520		
DATE	ITEM	POST. REF.	DEBIT	CREDIT	BALANCE			
					DEBIT		CREDIT	
20-- Mar. 1		CP1	9 5 0 00		9 5 0 00			
Apr. 1		CP2	9 5 0 00		1 9 0 0 00			

Do not post totals of general columns.
Add a debit to a debit balance.

Notice that the total of the General Debit column was not posted. A check mark (✔) was entered under the total to show that the total should not be posted. Since this column is not a special column, the total was not posted.

Illustration 65B shows how an expense account balance column is used. The March 1 debit balance of $950.00 and the April 1 debit of $950.00 were added to get the new balance of $1,900.00.

BUILDING YOUR BUSINESS VOCABULARY

On a sheet of paper, write the headings **Statement Number** and **Words**. Next, choose the words that match the statements. Write each word you choose next to the statement number it matches. Be careful; not all the words listed should be used.

Statements	Words
1. Columns in a journal used for items that have no special column	accounts payable ledger
2. Costs of operating a business	credit
3. A general ledger account with two balance columns	debit
4. The balance of an expense account	drawing
5. The balance of an income account	expenses
6. Money received from the sale of merchandise or services	four-column ledger account
7. A column in a journal used for only one type of item	general columns
8. Money taken out of the business by the owner	general ledger
	income
	memorandum column
	special column

Extra words listed:
- accounts payable ledger
- credit
- debit
- drawing
- expenses
- four-column ledger account
- general columns
- general ledger
- income
- memorandum column
- special column

STEPS REVIEW: Recording Expenses in the General Ledger

STEP 1 Journalize each transaction.

STEP 2 Record check marks where necessary.

STEP 3 Complete the daily postings.

STEP 4 Rule, foot, and check the totals.

STEP 5 Post the totals of the special columns to the accounts.

Problem 65-1   You are the record keeper for Andy Katz, the owner of a tree service company.

Directions

a. Copy the cash payments journal for July, 20--, that follows:

CASH PAYMENTS JOURNAL   PAGE 1

	DATE		ACCOUNT TITLE	CHECK NO.	POST. REF.	GENERAL DEBIT	ANDY KATZ, DRAWING DEBIT	TRUCK EXPENSE DEBIT	CASH CREDIT	
1	20-- July	5	√	101	√			650 00	650 00	1
2		12	√	102	√		1200 00		1200 00	2
3		17	Insurance Expense	103		205 00			205 00	3
4		27	√	104	√			295 00	295 00	4
5		28	√	105	√		350 00		350 00	5
6		30	Office Expense	106		575 00			575 00	6

b. Open the following general ledger accounts. (Allow three lines for each account.)

Cash	#110
Andy Katz, Drawing	#320
Truck Expense	#510
Insurance Expense	#520
Office Expense	#530

c. Enter a debit of $3,550.00 in the Cash account. Date the entry July 31. Write CR1 in the Post. Ref. column. Extend $3,550.00 to the Balance Debit column.

d. Post the individual items from the General Debit column to the general ledger accounts. Enter the correct posting references for each item in the journal and accounts.

CHECK POINT

65-1(g)

Cash Credit total = $3,275.00

e. Rule the money columns in the cash payments journal and foot the columns.

f. Check the footings to see if total debits equal total credits.

g. Write the final totals and double rule the money columns. Enter the date and the word *Totals* in the proper places.

h. Post the totals to the general ledger accounts. Be sure to include posting references in the accounts and in the journal. Calculate the new balance of the Cash account.

i. Enter a check mark under the General Debit column total.

Problem 65-2   You are the record keeper for Ken Watson, who owns and operates a lawn service.

Directions

a. Copy the cash payments journal for May, 20--, on page 525.

b. Copy the general ledger accounts that follow. They show postings for the previous month. (Allow five lines for each account.)

c. Post the individual items from the General Debit column to the general ledger accounts. Enter the correct posting references for each item in the journal and accounts.

CASH PAYMENTS JOURNAL

	DATE		ACCOUNT TITLE	CHECK NO.	POST. REF.	GENERAL DEBIT	KEN WATSON, DRAWING DEBIT	SUPPLIES EXPENSE DEBIT	CASH CREDIT	
1	20-- May	1	Rent Expense	107		8 7 5 50			8 7 5 50	1
2		5	√	108	√		5 2 5 00		5 2 5 00	2
3		9	√	109	√			6 1 1 37	6 1 1 37	3
4		12	Truck Expense	110		3 6 7 92			3 6 7 92	4
5		17	√	111	√			1 0 4 6 12	1 0 4 6 12	5
6		27	√	112	√		3 5 0 00		3 5 0 00	6

ACCOUNT Cash   **ACCOUNT NO.** 110

DATE		ITEM	POST. REF.	DEBIT	CREDIT	BALANCE DEBIT	BALANCE CREDIT
20-- Apr.	30		CR1	5 1 9 2 07		5 1 9 2 07	
	30		CP1		3 7 7 2 64	1 4 1 9 43	
May	31		CR2	6 0 1 7 90		7 4 3 7 33	

ACCOUNT Ken Watson, Drawing   **ACCOUNT NO.** 320

DATE		ITEM	POST. REF.	DEBIT	CREDIT	BALANCE DEBIT	BALANCE CREDIT
20-- Apr.	30		CP1	7 7 5 00		7 7 5 00	

ACCOUNT Supplies Expense   **ACCOUNT NO.** 510

DATE		ITEM	POST. REF.	DEBIT	CREDIT	BALANCE DEBIT	BALANCE CREDIT
20-- Apr.	30		CP1	1 6 1 1 05		1 6 1 1 05	

ACCOUNT Rent Expense   **ACCOUNT NO.** 520

DATE		ITEM	POST. REF.	DEBIT	CREDIT	BALANCE DEBIT	BALANCE CREDIT
20-- Apr.	1		CP1	8 7 5 50		8 7 5 50	

ACCOUNT Truck Expense   **ACCOUNT NO.** 530

DATE		ITEM	POST. REF.	DEBIT	CREDIT	BALANCE DEBIT	BALANCE CREDIT
20-- Apr.	15		CP1	5 1 1 09		5 1 1 09	

CHECK POINT

65-2(g)

Cash account final balance = $3,661.42

d. Rule the money columns in the cash payments journal and foot the columns.

e. Check the footings to see if total debits equal total credits.

f. Write the final totals and double rule the money columns. Enter the date and the word *Totals* in the proper places.

g. Post the totals to the general ledger accounts. Be sure to include posting references in the accounts and in the journal. Calculate new balances in all accounts.

h. Enter a check mark under the General Debit column total.

Problem 65-3 may be found in the Working Papers.

Copy and complete these problems. In each problem, crossfoot and then add down. Find the grand totals.

1. $4.27 + $15.41 + $59.16 + $37.06 =
   15.99 + 22.90 + 5.99 + 59.10 =
   14.76 + 37.10 + 17.44 + 91.04 =
   73.85 + 12.11 + 51.82 + 8.32 =
   10.11 + 6.95 + 36.18 + 61.09 =
   ___+___+___+___=

2. 63 + 16 + 41 + 32 =
   21 + 45 + 26 + 10 =
   30 + 74 + 50 + 75 =
   72 + 86 + 74 + 38 =
   94 + 13 + 99 + 92 =
   ___+___+___+___=

goal

To practice recording in a cash payments journal and posting to the general ledger.

➡ UNDERSTANDING THE JOB

In Jobs 64 and 65, you learned how to record expenses in a cash payments journal and post to the general ledger. In this job, you will have a chance to practice both of these skills.

➡ SAMPLE PROBLEM

Jo Ames owns and operates a ticket agency. You are her record keeper. You record her expenses in the cash payments journal and post to the general ledger accounts. The journal has special columns for Computer Expense and Van Expense. Her transactions for March, 20--, are as follows:

Mar. 1 Issued Check No. 101 for $745.37 to DJ Computers for computer supplies.
     5 Issued Check No. 102 for $145.86 to Ajax Garage for van repairs.
     9 Issued Check No. 103 for $537.50 to West Realty for Jo Ames's home rent.
    12 Issued Check No. 104 for $177.84 to Computown for computer supplies.
    15 Issued Check No. 105 for $975.00 to West Realty for business rent.

Mar. 22   Issued Check No. 106 for $350.00 to Jo Ames for personal expenses.
    27   Issued Check No. 107 for $711.82 to Main Motors for van maintenance
          and repairs.

Illustration 66A on page 528 shows how these transactions would be recorded in the cash payments journal and posted to the general ledger. Here are the steps you would follow:

STEP 1 Set up the cash payments journal and the general ledger accounts.

Set up a cash payments journal with a Cash Credit column, two special columns for expenses, and a General Debit column.

Set up five ledger accounts. The Cash account will already have a debit balance from the March 31 posting from the cash receipts journal.

STEP 2 Journalize each transaction.

Record each transaction in the journal. Be sure to use the Cash Credit column and one debit column for each check written. When the General Debit column is used, remember to write in both the name of the account and the amount. Also, remember to place check marks in the Account Title and Post. Ref. columns for entries made in special columns.

STEP 3 Post the entries in the General Debit column.

Enter the date, CP1, and amount in the ledger accounts, and calculate the new balance. Enter the account number in the Post. Ref. column of the journal.

STEP 4 Rule and foot the cash payments journal, and check the totals.

On the last day of the month, rule, foot, and total the money columns. Check the totals by comparing total debits with total credits to see if they are equal.

General Debit	$1,862.50
Computer Expense Debit	923.21
Van Expense Debit	+ 857.68
Cash Credit	$3,643.39

If debits do not equal credits, re-add your column totals. If they still are not equal, check each entry to see that you recorded equal debits and credits.

STEP 5 Write in final totals and double rule the money columns.

Date your totals as of the last day of the month, and write the word *Totals* in the Account Title column. Double rule all four money columns.

STEP 6 Post the column totals to the general ledger accounts.

Enter March 31, CP1, and the column total in the ledger accounts. The Cash account is always credited for cash paid out. Expense accounts are

Tips

*Debits = Credits
Credit the Cash
account for cash paid
out.
Debit expense
accounts.*

STEP 2

CASH PAYMENTS JOURNAL

PAGE 1

	DATE		ACCOUNT TITLE	CHECK NO.	POST. REF.	GENERAL DEBIT	COMPUTER EXPENSE DEBIT	VAN EXPENSE DEBIT	CASH CREDIT	
1	20-- Mar.	1	√	101	√		7 45 37		7 45 37	1
2		5	√	102	√			1 45 86	1 45 86	2
3		9	Jo Ames, Drawing	103	320	5 37 50			5 37 50	3
4		12	√	104	√		1 77 84		1 77 84	4
5		15	Rent Expense	105	530	9 75 00			9 75 00	5
6		22	Jo Ames, Drawing	106	320	3 50 00			3 50 00	6
7		27	√	107	√			7 11 82	7 11 82	7
8		31	Totals			18 62 50	9 23 21	8 57 68	36 43 39	8
9						(√)	(510)	(520)	(110)	9

STEP 4   **STEP 5**   **STEP 3**   **STEP 6**

General Ledger

ACCOUNT **Cash**   ACCOUNT NO. **110**

DATE		ITEM	POST. REF.	DEBIT	CREDIT	BALANCE DEBIT	BALANCE CREDIT
20-- Mar.	31		CR1	4 13 7 91		4 13 7 91	
	31		CP1		3 64 3 39	4 94 52	

ACCOUNT **Jo Ames, Drawing**   ACCOUNT NO. **320**

DATE		ITEM	POST. REF.	DEBIT	CREDIT	BALANCE DEBIT	BALANCE CREDIT
20-- Mar.	9		CP1	5 37 50		5 37 50	
	22		CP1	3 50 00		8 87 50	

STEP 1

ACCOUNT **Computer Expense**   ACCOUNT NO. **510**

DATE		ITEM	POST. REF.	DEBIT	CREDIT	BALANCE DEBIT	BALANCE CREDIT
20-- Mar.	31		CP1	9 23 21		9 23 21	

ACCOUNT **Van Expense**   ACCOUNT NO. **520**

DATE		ITEM	POST. REF.	DEBIT	CREDIT	BALANCE DEBIT	BALANCE CREDIT
20-- Mar.	31		CP1	8 57 68		8 57 68	

ACCOUNT **Rent Expense**   ACCOUNT NO. **530**

DATE		ITEM	POST. REF.	DEBIT	CREDIT	BALANCE DEBIT	BALANCE CREDIT
20-- Mar.	15		CP1	9 75 00		9 75 00	

Illustration 66A

Cash payments journal and general ledger

always debited. Calculate the new balance of each account. Enter the account number in parentheses under each total that you post. Place a check mark under the total that is not posted—General Debit.

BUILDING YOUR BUSINESS VOCABULARY

On a sheet of paper, write the headings **Statement Number** and **Words**. Next, choose the words that match the statements. Write each word you choose next to the statement number it matches. Be careful; not all the words listed should be used.

Statements

1. A business in which a service for customers is performed
2. Columns in a journal used for items that have no special column
3. A record of expenses paid
4. Costs of operating a business
5. Money taken out of the business by the owner
6. Money received from the sale of merchandise or services
7. A group of accounts other than customer or creditor accounts
8. A column in a journal used for only one type of item

Words

cash payments journal
cash receipts journal
drawing
expenses
general columns
general ledger
income
merchandising business
service business
special column

STEPS REVIEW: Using a Cash Payments Journal and a General Ledger

STEP 1 Set up the cash payments journal and the general ledger accounts.

STEP 2 Journalize each transaction.

STEP 3 Post the entries in the General Debit column.

STEP 4 Rule and foot the cash payments journal, and check the totals.

STEP 5 Write in final totals and double rule the money columns

STEP 6 Post the column totals to the general ledger accounts.

APPLICATION PROBLEMS

Problem 66-1   You are the record keeper for Cindy Forbes, who owns and operates a television repair shop. Your job is to journalize and post her expense transactions.

Directions

a. Open a cash payments journal with the following headings. Number the journal page 1.

DATE	ACCOUNT TITLE	CHECK NO.	POST. REF.	GENERAL DEBIT	TRUCK EXPENSE DEBIT	SUPPLIES EXPENSE DEBIT	CASH CREDIT

b. Open the following general ledger accounts. (Allow three lines for each account.)

Cash	#110
Cindy Forbes, Drawing	#320
Truck Expense	#510
Supplies Expense	#520
Rent Expense	#530

c. Enter a debit of $14,624.19 in the Cash account. Date the entry June 30. Write CR1 in the Post. Ref. column. Extend $14,624.19 to the Balance Debit column.

d. Record the following transactions for June in the cash payments journal. (Enter check marks in the Post. Ref. column for those entries in special columns.)

June 1   Issued Check No. 101 for $614.76 to Carson Supply Company for supplies.

      3   Issued Check No. 102 for $250.00 to Cindy Forbes for personal expenses.

      7   Issued Check No. 103 for $65.70 to Irene's Garage for truck maintenance.

      9   Issued Check No. 104 for $436.09 to Winwood Supply Company for supplies.

    12   Issued Check No. 105 for $416.35 to A & S Auto Company for truck tires.

    15   Issued Check No. 106 for $1,040.00 to Lebel Realty Company for business rent.

    19   Issued Check No. 107 for $850.00 to Lebel Realty Company for Cindy Forbes' home rent.

    21   Issued Check No. 108 for $527.16 to Carson Supply Company for supplies.

    24   Issued Check No. 109 for $361.04 to Irene's Garage for truck repairs.

    27   Issued Check No. 110 for $127.16 to Midwest Telephone Company for Cindy Forbes' home phone bill.

    29   Issued Check No. 111 for $2,126.12 to Winwood Supply Company for supplies.

CHECK POINT

66-1(h)

Cash Credit total = $6,814.38

e. Post daily from the General Debit column, and enter the correct posting references in the journal and ledger.

f. Rule and foot all money columns in the cash payments journal.

g. Check the footings to be sure that total debits equal total credits.

h. Write the final totals and double rule the money columns.

i. Post the totals to the general ledger accounts. Be sure to include all posting references and check marks.

Problem 66-2   You are the record keeper for Jo Ames, who owns a ticket agency. (See Sample Problem, page 526.) Your job is to journalize and post her expense transactions.

Directions

a. Open a cash payments journal identical to the one used in the Sample Problem (Illustration 66A, page 528). Number your journal page 2.

b. Copy the ledger accounts shown in Illustration 66A on page 528. (Allow five lines for each account.)

c. Record an April 30 debit in the Cash account for $7,047.91. Use CR2 as the posting reference.

d. Record the following transactions for April in the cash payments journal. (Enter check marks in the Post. Ref. column for those entries in special columns.)

Apr. 2 Issued Check No. 108 for $612.09 to DJ Computers for computer supplies.
3 Issued Check No. 109 for $199.06 to Ajax Garage for van repairs.
9 Issued Check No. 110 for $537.50 to West Realty for Jo Ames' home rent.
12 Issued Check No. 111 for $1,036.15 to Computown for computer supplies.
15 Issued Check No. 112 for $975.00 to West Realty for business rent.
17 Issued Check No. 113 for $511.04 to DJ Computers for computer supplies.
20 Issued Check No. 114 for $96.34 to Ajax Garage for van repairs and maintenance.
22 Issued Check No. 115 for $300.00 to Jo Ames for personal expenses.
25 Issued Check No. 116 for $477.99 to Computown for computer supplies.
27 Issued Check No. 117 for $117.71 to State Telephone Company for Jo Ames' home phone bill.
28 Issued Check No. 118 for $245.00 to Main Motors for new tires for the van.

CHECK POINT

66-2(i)

Cash account final balance = $2,434.55

e. Post daily from the General Debit column, and enter the correct posting references in the journal and ledger.

f. Rule and foot all money columns in the cash payments journal.

g. Check the footings to be sure that total debits equal total credits.

h. Write the final totals and double rule the money columns.

i. Post the totals to the general ledger accounts. Be sure to include all posting references and check marks.

Problem 66-3 may be found in the Working Papers.

applied math preview

Copy and complete the following problems.

1.	2.	3.	4.
$3,172.04	$7,147.16	$ 511.17	$ 75.12
4,066.19	9,024.71	2,230.15	6,014.16
5,122.11	377.50	3,189.27	371.08
477.06	196.25	424.60	51.14
305.41	6,172.09	955.48	5,709.96
+3,771.19	+ 47.65	+2,767.39	+8,521.79

key terms preview

- Normal balance
- Slide
- Transposition
- Trial balance

goal

To learn how to prepare a trial balance.

→ UNDERSTANDING THE JOB

Key Terms

Trial balance A form used to prove that debits equal credits in the ledger.

It is easy to understand how a record keeper—who may have to record hundreds of transactions in a day—may make mistakes. To catch possible mistakes, the record keeper regularly checks the journals and ledgers. You have learned how to check the footings of a journal to prove that debits equal credits. In this job, you will learn how to check the balances of general ledger accounts to prove that debits equal credits. If you have posted correctly to the general ledger, the total of all debits in the general ledger will equal the total of all credits in the general ledger. The form used to show this proof is called the **trial balance**. The word *trial* is used because the trial balance is a test, or trial, of the accuracy of the general ledger. You are testing to see if total debits equal the total credits. The word *balance* is used because only the balance of each account is listed.

Illustration 67B on page 534 shows a completed trial balance.

Beth Auclair's general ledger accounts for Beth's Fence Company are shown in Illustration 67A, below and on page 534. These include all of her income transactions that you posted in Job 62 and her expense transactions that you posted in Job 65. You now need to prepare a trial balance to check the accuracy of your postings. The trial balance will show you if you have posted equal debits and credits.

Here are the steps you would follow to prepare the trial balance shown in Illustration 67B on page 534:

STEP 1 Enter the heading.

Every business summary has a three-line heading, answering these questions: WHO?, WHAT?, and WHEN?

WHO? Beth's Fence Company
WHAT? Trial Balance
WHEN? March 31, 20--

GENERAL LEDGER

Illustration 67A

General ledger with income and expense accounts

ACCOUNT	Cash				ACCOUNT NO. 110	
DATE	ITEM	POST. REF.	DEBIT	CREDIT	BALANCE DEBIT	BALANCE CREDIT
20-- Mar. 31		CR1	4 0 4 5 00		4 0 4 5 00	
31		CP1		2 5 9 0 00	1 4 5 5 00	

ACCOUNT	Beth Auclair, Drawing				ACCOUNT NO. 320	
DATE	ITEM	POST. REF.	DEBIT	CREDIT	BALANCE DEBIT	BALANCE CREDIT
20-- Mar. 31		CP1	5 5 0 00		5 5 0 00	

ACCOUNT	Income, Wood Fence				ACCOUNT NO. 410	
DATE	ITEM	POST. REF.	DEBIT	CREDIT	BALANCE DEBIT	BALANCE CREDIT
20-- Mar. 31		CR1		1 9 8 5 00		1 9 8 5 00

ACCOUNT	Income, Metal Fence				ACCOUNT NO. 420	
DATE	ITEM	POST. REF.	DEBIT	CREDIT	BALANCE DEBIT	BALANCE CREDIT
20-- Mar. 31		CR1		2 0 6 0 00		2 0 6 0 00

Illustration 67A

General ledger with income
and expense accounts
(continued)

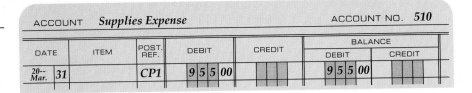

ACCOUNT	Supplies Expense				ACCOUNT NO.	510		
DATE	ITEM	POST. REF.	DEBIT	CREDIT	BALANCE DEBIT		BALANCE CREDIT	
20-- Mar. 31		CP1	9 5 5 00		9 5 5 00			

ACCOUNT	Rent Expense				ACCOUNT NO.	520		
DATE	ITEM	POST. REF.	DEBIT	CREDIT	BALANCE DEBIT		BALANCE CREDIT	
20-- Mar. 1		CP1	9 5 0 00		9 5 0 00			

ACCOUNT	Telephone Expense				ACCOUNT NO.	530		
DATE	ITEM	POST. REF.	DEBIT	CREDIT	BALANCE DEBIT		BALANCE CREDIT	
20-- Mar. 22		CP1	1 3 5 00		1 3 5 00			

A trial balance is always dated as of the last day of the period. Since March has 31 days, March 31 is the date recorded.

Tips

Do not include accounts with balances of zero.

Enter debit balances in the Debit column. Enter credit balances in the Credit column.

STEP 2 Enter the account titles.

Write the names of all accounts in the general ledger in the order they appear in the ledger. Thus, write *Cash* first and *Telephone Expense* last. Do not include any accounts with a balance of zero. Check that an account has a balance other than zero before you list it on the trial balance.

STEP 3 Enter the amounts.

Copy the balances from the accounts to the trial balance. The balance to be copied is the last amount in the Balance column of each account. For the Cash account, you will be copying $1,455.00.

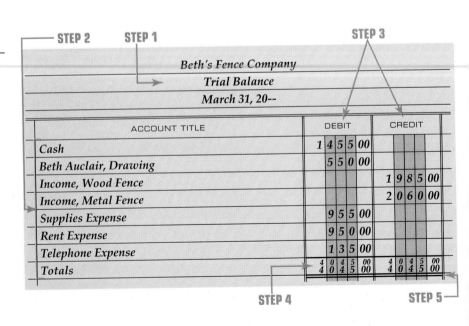

STEP 2   STEP 1   STEP 3

Beth's Fence Company
Trial Balance
March 31, 20--

ACCOUNT TITLE	DEBIT	CREDIT
Cash	1 4 5 5 00	
Beth Auclair, Drawing	5 5 0 00	
Income, Wood Fence		1 9 8 5 00
Income, Metal Fence		2 0 6 0 00
Supplies Expense	9 5 5 00	
Rent Expense	9 5 0 00	
Telephone Expense	1 3 5 00	
Totals	4 0 4 5 00	4 0 4 5 00

STEP 4   STEP 5

Enter the balance of accounts with debit balances in the Debit column of the trial balance. The balances of the cash, drawing, and expense accounts are debit balances.

Enter the balance of accounts with credit balances in the Credit column of the trial balance. The balances of income accounts are credit balances.

STEP 4 Rule and foot the money columns.

Draw a single rule and foot the Debit and Credit columns. If the totals are the same, you have done your work correctly. If the totals are not the same, there is an error. To find the error, work in reverse:

1. Foot the columns again; this time add them from the bottom up. If they still do not agree, go to #2.
2. Check to see if the correct amounts were copied to the trial balance from the general ledger accounts. Also, be sure that you entered the amounts in the correct column—Debit or Credit.

Look for these common errors: **transpositions** (for example, 83 for 38), **slides** (for example, 10 for 100), and balances that are not normal. The **normal balance** of each account is the side of the account (debit or credit) where the balance is usually found. For example, the cash, drawing, and expense accounts normally have debit balances. Income accounts normally have credit balances.

If the columns still do not balance, go to #3.

3. Check the math in each account to see if the balances calculated are correct. If the columns do not balance after this step, go to #4.
4. Check the posting from the journals to the accounts. Were all amounts posted? Were they posted to the correct columns in the correct accounts? If the columns still do not balance, go to #5.
5. Check your journals. Were they footed accurately? If you still have not found the error, go to #6.
6. Check each entry in the journal to see if you entered equal debits and credits.

Transposition. A reversal of digits in a number.

Slide. Entering an amount a column or more off.

Normal balance. Where the balance of an account is usually found.

Normal balance of cash and drawing accounts is debit.
Normal balance of expense accounts is debit.
Normal balance of income accounts is credit.

STEP 5 Enter the totals and double rule the money columns.

When your footings are equal, enter the final totals and double rule the columns. Write the word *Totals* directly under the last account title.

USING THE COMPUTER

If you are doing manual record keeping, you will prepare your trial balance from general ledger accounts. If you are using a computer and you want a trial balance prepared, you ask the computer to prepare one. Illustration 67C on page 536 shows the trial balance for Beth's Fence Company prepared by the computer system.

```
                    Beth's Fence Company
                       Trial Balance
                         03/31/--

Acct.       Account
Number      Title                      Debit      Credit

110         Cash                       1455.00
320         Beth Auclair, Drawing       550.00
410         Income, Wood Fence                    1985.00
420         Income, Metal Fence                   2060.00
510         Supplies Expense            955.00
520         Rent Expense                950.00
530         Telephone Expense           135.00

            Totals                     4045.00    4045.00
```

BUILDING YOUR BUSINESS VOCABULARY

On a sheet of paper, write the headings **Statement Number** and **Words**. Next, choose the words that match the statements. Write each word you choose next to the statement number it matches. Be careful; not all the words listed should be used.

Statements

1. Costs of operating a business
2. Entering an amount a column or more off, such as 10 for 1,000
3. A record of expenses paid
4. A system in which every transaction has at least one debit and one credit
5. The side of an account where the balance is usually found
6. A reversal of digits in a number, such as 67 for 76
7. A form used to prove that debits equal credits in the ledger
8. Money received from the sale of merchandise or services

Words

cash payments journal
cash receipts journal
credit
debit
double-entry system
expenses
income
normal balance
slide
transposition
trial balance

STEPS REVIEW: Preparing a Trial Balance

STEP 1 Enter the heading.

STEP 2 Enter the account titles.

STEP 3 Enter the amounts.

STEP 4 Rule and foot the money columns.

STEP 5 Enter the totals and double rule the money columns.

Problem 67-1

You work for Richard Coleman, owner of Rich's Auto Repair Shop. Richard's accounts as of July 31 are as follows:

ACCOUNT **Cash** ACCOUNT NO. **110**

DATE	ITEM	POST. REF.	DEBIT	CREDIT	BALANCE DEBIT	BALANCE CREDIT
20-- July 31		CR1	11 4 3 9 28		11 4 3 9 28	
31		CP1		7 9 0 4 21	3 5 3 5 07	

ACCOUNT **Richard Coleman, Drawing** ACCOUNT NO. **320**

DATE	ITEM	POST. REF.	DEBIT	CREDIT	BALANCE DEBIT	BALANCE CREDIT
20-- July 31		CP1	1 4 7 5 00		1 4 7 5 00	

ACCOUNT **Income, Truck Repairs** ACCOUNT NO. **410**

DATE	ITEM	POST. REF.	DEBIT	CREDIT	BALANCE DEBIT	BALANCE CREDIT
20-- July 31		CR1		4 7 6 5 19		4 7 6 5 19

ACCOUNT **Income, Car Repairs** ACCOUNT NO. **420**

DATE	ITEM	POST. REF.	DEBIT	CREDIT	BALANCE DEBIT	BALANCE CREDIT
20-- July 31		CR1		6 6 7 4 09		6 6 7 4 09

ACCOUNT **Supplies Expense** ACCOUNT NO. **510**

DATE	ITEM	POST. REF.	DEBIT	CREDIT	BALANCE DEBIT	BALANCE CREDIT
20-- July 31		CP1	5 1 7 2 09		5 1 7 2 09	

ACCOUNT **Rent Expense** ACCOUNT NO. **520**

DATE	ITEM	POST. REF.	DEBIT	CREDIT	BALANCE DEBIT	BALANCE CREDIT
20-- July 1		CP1	9 4 0 00		9 4 0 00	

ACCOUNT **Telephone Expense** ACCOUNT NO. **530**

DATE	ITEM	POST. REF.	DEBIT	CREDIT	BALANCE DEBIT	BALANCE CREDIT
20-- July 30		CP1	3 1 7 12		3 1 7 12	

CHECK POINT

67-1

Total debits and total credits = $11,439.28

Directions

Prepare a trial balance as of July 31, 20--.

You work for Lori Stokes, owner of Lori's Painting Company. Lori's accounts as of June 30 are shown below.

| ACCOUNT | *Cash* | | | | | | ACCOUNT NO. | **110** |

DATE	ITEM	POST. REF.	DEBIT	CREDIT	BALANCE DEBIT	BALANCE CREDIT
20-- May 31		CR1	9 7 3 4 11		9 7 3 4 11	
31		CP1		8 4 3 3 71	1 3 0 0 40	
June 30		CR2	15 3 9 0 23			
30		CP2		9 5 5 5 99		

| ACCOUNT | *Lori Stokes, Drawing* | | | | | | ACCOUNT NO. | **320** |

DATE	ITEM	POST. REF.	DEBIT	CREDIT	BALANCE DEBIT	BALANCE CREDIT
20-- May 12		CP1	4 7 5 00		4 7 5 00	
June 6		CP2	3 8 1 16			
19		CP2	2 9 9 05			

| ACCOUNT | *Income, Home Painting* | | | | | | ACCOUNT NO. | **410** |

DATE	ITEM	POST. REF.	DEBIT	CREDIT	BALANCE DEBIT	BALANCE CREDIT
20-- May 31		CR1		3 5 7 7 09		3 5 7 7 09
June 30		CR2		6 0 1 2 17		

CHECK POINT

67-2(c)

Total credits = $25,124.34

| ACCOUNT | *Income, Business Painting* | | | | | | ACCOUNT NO. | **420** |

DATE	ITEM	POST. REF.	DEBIT	CREDIT	BALANCE DEBIT	BALANCE CREDIT
20-- May 31		CR1		6 1 5 7 02		6 1 5 7 02
June 30		CR2		9 3 7 8 06		

| ACCOUNT | *Supplies Expense* | | | | | | ACCOUNT NO. | **510** |

DATE	ITEM	POST. REF.	DEBIT	CREDIT	BALANCE DEBIT	BALANCE CREDIT
20-- May 31		CP1	4 1 7 2 09		4 1 7 2 09	
June 30		CP2	5 3 6 1 15			

| ACCOUNT | *Truck Expense* | | | | | | ACCOUNT NO. | **520** |

DATE	ITEM	POST. REF.	DEBIT	CREDIT	BALANCE DEBIT	BALANCE CREDIT
20-- May 31		CP1	2 1 7 6 12		2 1 7 6 12	
June 30		CP2	1 9 0 4 13			

ACCOUNT	*Insurance Expense*					ACCOUNT NO. *530*	
DATE	ITEM	POST. REF.	DEBIT	CREDIT	BALANCE		
					DEBIT	CREDIT	
20-- May 10		CP1	4 1 0 50		4 1 0 50		
June 6		CP2	4 1 0 50				

ACCOUNT	*Rent Expense*					ACCOUNT NO. *540*	
DATE	ITEM	POST. REF.	DEBIT	CREDIT	BALANCE		
					DEBIT	CREDIT	
20-- May 1		CP1	1 2 0 0 00		1 2 0 0 00		
June 1		CP2	1 2 0 0 00				

Directions

a. Copy the accounts.
b. Enter the missing balances in the accounts.
c. Prepare a trial balance as of June 30, 20--.

Problem 67-3   You work for Scotch Welding Company. The November 30 account balances are listed below:

CHECK POINT

67-3

Total debits = $25,623.31

```
Account Title                    Balance
--------------------------------------------
Cash                            $ 2,667.36
Joan Scotch, Drawing              1,031.95
Income, Welding                  14,172.06
Income, Finishing                10,147.15
Income, Repairs                   1,304.10
Supplies Expense                 11,501.19
Van Expense                       7,179.21
Insurance Expense                   595.00
Rent Expense                      2,177.50
Telephone Expense                   471.10
```

Directions

Prepare a trial balance as of November 30, 20--.

Problem 67-4   You work for Bestlawn Lawn Care Company. The February 28 account balances are listed below:

CHECK POINT

67-4

Total credits = $14,480.97

```
Account Title                    Balance
--------------------------------------------
Cash                            $ 3,241.88
Sid Ames, Drawing                   525.10
Income, Seeding                   4,173.19
Income, Fertilizing               6,011.97
Income, Shrub Care                4,295.81
Supplies Expense                  6,912.12
Truck Expense                     2,047.17
Insurance Expense                   411.04
Rent Expense                        945.50
Telephone Expense                   398.16
```

Directions

Prepare a trial balance as of February 28, 20--.

Chapter 13

CHECK YOUR READING

1. a. What is the difference between a merchandising business and a service business?
   b. List several names of merchandising businesses in your community.
   c. List several names of service businesses in your community.
2. What does it mean to "post" from a journal to a ledger?
3. What is the difference between "income" and "expenses"?
4. What is the purpose of a trial balance?

DISCUSSION

You are a record keeper at Whittier Trucking Company. You record entries in the cash receipts and cash payments journals, while your assistant does the posting. Your assistant is confused about posting references and asks you these questions:

1. Why am I entering a number on some lines and a check mark on other lines in the Post. Ref. column of the journals?
2. Why am I entering a number below some journal totals and a check mark below others?
3. Can you give me some simple rules to tell me when to use a number and when to use a check mark?

How would you answer these questions?

CRITICAL THINKING

Your company has been using a cash payments journal with a single money column. To save time posting, a journal with special columns will now be used. Your job is to decide which three special columns should be chosen. You count the debits to the different expense accounts over the past year. Here is what you find:

Account Title	Number of Debits
Rent Expense	12
Supplies Expense	42
Telephone Expense	31
Truck Expense	57
Insurance Expense	5

Using this information, write which special columns you would use and explain why you chose them.

REINFORCEMENT ACTIVITIES

 ## COMMUNICATION IN THE WORKPLACE

You are the head record keeper in your firm. A new assistant has just been hired. In the past, your assistants have had difficulty understanding how to use source documents. In order to avoid this problem with the new assistant, you plan to write a note to explain the following:
1. What a source document is.
2. How calculator tapes, check stubs, and bank deposit slips are used as source documents for the cash journals.

Write the note to the new assistant to explain these items. Keep your note to half a sheet of paper.

 ## FOCUS ON CAREERS

A *full-charge record keeper* handles the general ledger. An assistant record keeper handles the other ledgers. Using these definitions, answer the following questions:
1. What ledgers would be kept by the assistant record keeper?
2. How would the full-charge record keeper check his or her ledger?
3. How would the assistant record keeper check his or her ledger?
4. Who would post to the income and expense accounts?
5. Who would use a double-entry system?
6. Who would keep the customer or creditor accounts?

 ## REVIEWING WHAT YOU HAVE LEARNED

On a sheet of paper, write the headings **Statement Number** and **Words**. Next, choose the words that best complete the statements. Write each word you choose next to the statement number it completes. Be careful; not all the words listed should be used.

Statements	Words
1. To prove that debits and credits in the general ledger are equal, prepare (a, an) _____.	double-entry system drawing
2. An expense is always recorded as a debit because that is its _____.	expenses extended
3. The costs of operating a business are its _____.	four-column ledger account
4. Accounts, other than those for creditors and customers, are found in the _____.	general columns general ledger income

Statements	Words
5. Individual amounts are posted from _____ in a journal.	memorandum column
6. A general ledger account with two balance columns is (a, an) _____	merchandising business
	normal balance
7. Only the total is posted from (a, an) _____ in a journal.	post
8. Paying the owner's home phone bill is classified as _____.	service business
	slide
9. A repair business is an example of (a, an) _____.	special column
10. You always make equal debits and credits in (a, an) _____.	trial balance
11. The Bank Deposits column is an example of (a, an) _____.	
12. The money earned from the sale of services or merchandise is the _____ of a business.	
13. A department store is an example of (a, an) _____.	

The words list, aligned to statements:

memorandum column
merchandising business
normal balance
post
service business
slide
special column
trial balance

MASTERY PROBLEM

You are a record keeper for Mona Wellman, owner and operator of Mona's Money Saver Travel Agency. Your job is to record income and expenses in the cash receipts and cash payments journals. You then post to the general ledger and prepare a trial balance.

Directions

a. Open a cash receipts journal with Income Credit columns for Tours, Cruises, and Air Fares. Number the journal page 1.

b. Open a cash payments journal with special columns for Telephone Expense and Computer Expense. Number the journal page 1.

c. Open 8 general ledger accounts as follows:

Account Title	Number
Cash	110
Mona Wellman, Drawing	320
Income, Tours	410
Income, Cruises	420
Income, Air Fares	430
Telephone Expense	510
Computer Expense	520
Rent Expense	530

d. Record the transactions below and on page 543 in the correct journal:

March 1 Received $475.50 for a cruise, T1.
2 Received $1,965.10 for a tour, T2.
4 Received $1,655.80: $397.60 for air fare and $1,258.20 for a tour, T4.
4 Deposited all cash received from March 1 to 4.
5 Issued Check No. 101 for $1,027.91 to Ace Computer Supply Company for computer supplies.
5 Issued Check No. 102 for $1,200.00 to Magnet Realty for March rent.

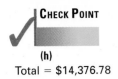
March 9 Received $906.45 for a tour and $499.00 for a cruise, T9.

10 Received $504.70 for a cruise and $417.76 for air fare, T10.

10 Issued Check No. 103 for $310.70 to State Telephone Company for phone calls to date.

11 Received $935.99 for a tour and $675.40 for air fare, T11.

11 Deposited all cash received from March 9 to 11.

14 Issued Check No. 104 for $200.00 to Mona Wellman for personal expenses.

16 Received $602.99 for air fare, T16.

19 Issued Check No. 105 for $991.03 to Carl's Computer Company for computer software.

20 Issued Check No. 106 for $377.91 to State Telephone Company for phone calls to date.

20 Received $2,043.61: $1,247.63 for a cruise and the balance for a tour, T20.

20 Deposited all cash received from March 16 to 20.

24 Issued Check No. 107 for $1,177.62 to Ace Computer Supply Company for computer supplies.

26 Received $757.50 for a tour, $645.93 for air fare, and $699.99 for a cruise, T26.

29 Issued Check No. 108 for $975.00 to Magnet Realty for Mona Wellman's home rent.

29 Received $573.16 for air fare and $1,017.90 for a tour, T29.

29 Deposited all cash received from March 26 to 29.

e. Enter check marks in the Post. Ref. column of the cash payments journal for entries in special columns. Post individual amounts from the cash payments journal.

f. Foot, total, and rule both journals.

g. Make all postings of totals to the general ledger accounts. Post the cash receipts journal first. Enter check marks for totals not posted.

h. Prepare a trial balance as of March 31, 20--.

REVIEWING YOUR BUSINESS VOCABULARY

This activity may be found in the Working Papers.

Chapter 14

1st Quarter

Financial Statements for Small Businesses

Every business has a value to its owner and to potential buyers. This value is what the business is worth. As a business operates, its value changes. A net income makes the value of a business go up. A net loss makes the value of a business go down.

In Chapter 14, you will learn how to calculate net income or loss, prepare an income statement, and compute taxes. You will also learn how to prepare a capital statement, a balance sheet, and a six-column work sheet.

FOCUS ON TECHNOLOGY

Digital Cameras

Digital cameras have become very popular, especially for sending photographs through e-mail. Digital cameras record scenes on digital media, and the scenes can be transferred to a computer system for immediate display. There is no "film" and no "developing" is needed. The media can be used over and over again to record new photos.

At first glance, you might think that digital cameras are just for fun and recreation. However, there are many business uses for digital cameras. They can be used to take photos of products. These photos can be placed on a Web site so that customers can see the products of a company. Product photos can also be inserted into stock records so that new stock clerks don't record information incorrectly. Photos of a store and employees can be placed on a Web site, too. And, employee photos can be inserted into employee records to help human resource department personnel identify people in a large firm.

Photos of products, buildings, and employees can be easily inserted into documents produced by word processing and desktop publishing software. These documents may be advertisements, brochures, or mailing flyers. The photos taken can even be used as screen savers and wallpaper files given to customers as a sales promotion.

applied math preview

Copy and complete these problems.

1.	2.	3.	5.
$4,163.23	$ 742.16	$ 4,684.60	$41,508.48
2,782.09	1,068.52	−3,219.40	−24,647.62
394.51	612.43		
108.60	3,284.79		
490.36	420.60	4. $22,360.24	6. $12,582.40
+5,007.16	+8,609.45	−19,471.02	−11,021.30

key terms preview

- Financial statements
- Income statement
- Net income
- Net loss
- Revenue

goals

1 To learn how to calculate net income for a service business.

2 To learn how to prepare an income statement.

UNDERSTANDING THE JOB

Key Terms

Net income. Income is greater than expenses.

Net loss. Expenses are greater than income.

Financial statements. Summaries of the results of a business.

Income statement. Shows income, expenses, and net income or net loss.

You have learned that income is money received from selling merchandise or performing services. You have also learned that expenses are the costs of operating a business. When expenses are subtracted from income, the difference is your earnings—your **net income**.

For example, if during one month you received $3,500.00 from your customers for repairs that you made and you spent $1,400.00 for expenses, your net income would be $2,100.00.

Income from repairs	$ 3,500.00
Less expenses	−1,400.00
Net income	$ 2,100.00

The $2,100.00 is your earnings for the month. Your earnings may change from month to month as your income and expenses increase or decrease.

If your expenses are greater than your income, you have a **net loss**. For example, if your income is $1,700.00 and your expenses are $1,900.00, you have a net loss of $200.00.

Expenses	$ 1,900.00
Less income	−1,700.00
Net loss	$ 200.00

Business people use **financial statements** to summarize the results of a business. One financial statement is the **income statement**. The income statement shows income, expenses, and net income or net loss for a certain period of time. In this job, you will learn how to prepare an income statement.

Melissa Kadir operates her own auto and boat detail shop, called AutoPro Detailing. She keeps separate records of income from auto detailing and boat detailing.

During the month of June, she received $620.00 from boat detailing and $2,460.00 from auto detailing.

She paid the following business expenses during June: rent, $810.00; insurance, $60.00; supplies, $240.00; truck, $125.00; telephone, $75.00; and electricity, $140.00.

Illustration 68A shows Melissa's income statement for June to summarize this information. Here are the steps to follow to prepare the income statement:

STEP 1 Enter the heading.

The heading answers the three questions that start most business forms:

WHO? AutoPro Detailing
WHAT? Income Statement
WHEN? For the Month Ended June 30, 20--

Notice that the WHO? is the name of the business, not the name of the owner. The WHEN? is for a period of time, not just one day. If the income statement were for a full calendar year, the third line would read "For the Year Ended December 31, 20--."

Illustration 68A

Income statement

STEP 2

STEP 1

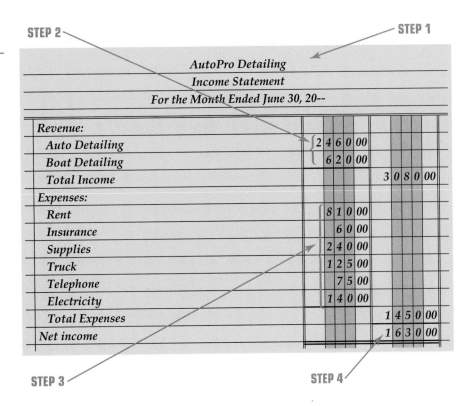

AutoPro Detailing
Income Statement
For the Month Ended June 30, 20--

Revenue:			
Auto Detailing	2 4 6 0 00		
Boat Detailing	6 2 0 00		
Total Income		3 0 8 0 00	
Expenses:			
Rent	8 1 0 00		
Insurance	6 0 00		
Supplies	2 4 0 00		
Truck	1 2 5 00		
Telephone	7 5 00		
Electricity	1 4 0 00		
Total Expenses		1 4 5 0 00	
Net income		1 6 3 0 00	

STEP 3

STEP 4

Key Terms

Revenue. Income.

On income statements, the word **revenue** is often used in place of the word *income*. The words mean the same. So, write the word *Revenue:* on the first line. Indent the next two lines and write the types of income: *Auto Detailing* and *Boat Detailing*. Enter the amount of each type of income in the left money column. Draw a single line, add the two amounts, and enter the total one line below in the right money column. Write the words *Total Income* on the line with the total. Notice that dollar signs are not written because money columns are used.

STEP **3** Record the expenses.

Write the word *Expenses:* on the next line. Then, indent and write the name of each expense on the next several lines. Record each amount in the left money column. Draw a single line, add the amounts, and enter the total one line below in the right money column. Write the words *Total Expenses* on the line with the total.

STEP **4** Enter the net income or net loss.

For Your Information

The left money column on the income statement is used to list individual amounts. The right money column is used to emphasize total amounts.

Rule a single line under the amount of total expenses. Subtract the total expenses from the total income. Enter the difference on the next line in the right money column. If total income is more than total expenses, write the words *Net Income* on the line with the difference. In this example, there is a net income, calculated as follows:

Total income	$ 3,080.00
Less total expenses	−1,450.00
Net income	$1,630.00

If total expenses are greater than total income, there is a net loss. A net loss would be entered by writing the words *Net Loss* and entering the amount of the net loss in parentheses. For example, a loss of $400.00 would be entered as (400.00).

Draw a double ruling across both money columns under the last amount to show that the income statement is complete.

USING THE COMPUTER

Many small businesses with computers use programs that will prepare financial statements automatically. The computer program will pull income and expense account data that has been stored in the computer and print it out as an income statement. Illustration 68B shows how the income statement in Illustration 68A (page 547) might appear if prepared by the computer.

```
                    AutoPro Detailing
                    Income Statement
              For the Month Ended June 30, 20--


Operating Revenue
---------------------------------------------------------------
Income, Auto Detailing                              2,460.00
Income, Boat Detailing                                620.00

Total Operating Revenue                             3,080.00

Operating Expenses
---------------------------------------------------------------
Rent Expense                                          810.00
Insurance Expense                                      60.00
Supplies Expense                                      240.00
Truck Expense                                         125.00
Telephone Expense                                      75.00
Electricity Expense                                   140.00

Total Operating Expenses                            1,450.00

Net Income                                          1,630.00
```

BUILDING YOUR BUSINESS VOCABULARY

On a sheet of paper, write the headings **Statement Number** and **Words**.
Next, choose the words that match the statements. Write each word you
choose next to the statement number it matches. Be careful; not all the
words listed should be used.

Statements	Words
1. Costs of operating a business	expenses
2. Summaries of the results of a business	financial statements
3. Another word for income	income statement
4. When income is greater than expenses	invoice
5. A form that shows income, expenses, and net income or net loss	net income
	net loss
6. When expenses are greater than income	revenue
	withdrawals

STEPS REVIEW: Preparing an Income Statement

STEP 1 Enter the heading.

STEP 2 Record the income.

STEP 3 Record the expenses.

STEP 4 Enter the net income or net loss.

APPLICATION PROBLEMS

Problem 68-1 William Lieberman, CPA, owns and operates Lieberman's Tax &
Bookkeeping Service. He records income received from corporate services and income received from individual services separately.

CHECK POINT

68-1

Net income = $3,220.00

Directions

Prepare an income statement for the month ended May 31, 20--, from the following information:

During May, he received $4,800.00 from corporate services and $2,300.00 from individual services.

He paid these business expenses during May: rent, $2,700.00; electricity, $490.00; telephone, $305.00; insurance, $210.00; and supplies, $175.00.

Problem 68-2

Paula Dempsey owns and operates Cambria Glass Company. Paula's company replaces windows, repairs store fronts, and installs insulated glass. She records income received from commercial installations and income received from residential repairs separately.

CHECK POINT

68-2

Net income = $6,832.01

Directions

Prepare an income statement for the month ended August 31, 20--, from the following information:

During August, she received $9,243.00 from commercial installations and $4,752.00 from residential repairs.

She paid these business expenses during August: advertising, $450.00; electricity, $165.30; glass and supplies, $3,691.50; rent, $2,050.00; truck, $482.75; telephone, $178.44; and insurance, $145.00.

Problem 68-3

Emilio Adriano owns and operates Adriano Concrete Specialists, which specializes in driveways, patios, pool decks, exposed aggregate, stamped concrete, and retaining walls. Emilio records income received from industrial construction and for residential construction separately.

CHECK POINT

68-3

Net loss = ($175.40)

Directions

Prepare an income statement for the month ended December 31, 20--, from the following information:

During December, he received $4,370.00 from industrial construction and $1,660.00 from residential construction.

He paid these business expenses during December: concrete supplies, $3,992.20; rent, $1,080.00; electricity, $174.60; telephone, $96.54; advertising, $350.00; truck, $408.66; and miscellaneous, $103.40.

applied math preview

Copy and complete these problems.

1. $50,000.00 × 0.16 =
2. $42,500.00 × 0.16 =
3. $20,800.00 × 0.16 =
4. $19,700.00 × 0.16 =
5. $38,600.00 × 16% =
6. $30,000.00 × 16% =
7. $27,350.00 × 16% =
8. $ 8,420.00 × 16% =

key terms preview

- Audit
- Balance due
- Estimate
- Estimated tax
- Income tax
- Refund
- Self-employment tax

goals

1 To learn how to use the income statement to compute taxes for people who are self-employed.

2 To practice preparing income statements.

➡ UNDERSTANDING THE JOB

Key Terms

Self-employment tax. Social security tax for self-employed people.

In Job 68, you learned that business people prepare a financial statement called an income statement. The income statement shows income, expenses, and net income or net loss.

You will also learn in later jobs that people who work for others pay two kinds of taxes to the federal government's Internal Revenue Service (IRS). These taxes are income tax and social security tax. If you work for an employer, these taxes are deducted from your pay. The employer then sends them to the IRS for you. However, if you are self-employed, you must figure out your own taxes and send them to the IRS. Both taxes are figured using the net income shown on your income statement.

Self-Employment Taxes

The social security taxes paid by business owners are called **self–employment taxes**. The amount of self-employment tax an owner must pay is found by multiplying the owner's net income by the self-employment tax rate. The rate of self-employment tax is set by Congress and is changed often. In this text, a rate of 16% on the first $70,000.00 of net income will be used. This means that once the self-employment taxes on the first $70,000.00 of the owner's net income have been paid, no more self-employment taxes are paid that year.

For example, if you have a net income of $50,000.00, your self-employment tax would be found this way:

$50,000.00 × 0.16 = $8,000.00   self-employment tax

If your net income is $70,000.00, your self-employment tax would be:

$$\$70,000.00 \times 0.16 = \$11,200.00 \quad \text{self-employment tax}$$

If your net income is over $70,000.00, the tax is still $11,200.00.

Income tax. Tax on net income earned.

Estimate. A careful guess.

Estimated tax. Estimated amount of income tax and self-employment tax paid to IRS during year.

Income Taxes

Business owners must also pay **income taxes** on their net income. The amount of income taxes paid depends on many factors. In this job, you will be given the amounts of income tax that the owner must pay.

Estimated Taxes

A business owner never knows the *exact* amount of income taxes or self-employment taxes that must be paid until the end of the year. That is true because the owner does not know the exact amount of net income until the income statement is prepared at the end of the year. However, the IRS requires owners to **estimate** their net income and send parts of the income and self-employment taxes to them on April 15, June 15, September 15, and January 15. The tax payments made on these dates are called **estimated taxes**.

By April 15 of the next year, the owner must report the net income earned on an income tax return sent to the IRS. On this return, the owner can correct the estimates made and settle up any difference with the IRS.

 SAMPLE PROBLEM

Wesley Larkin owns and operates Class One Limousine Service. At the beginning of the year, Wesley estimated that his income tax and self-employment tax due for the year would be $10,200.00. He sent in the estimated taxes in four equal payments during the year.

At the end of the year, Wesley's income statement for the year showed a net income of $35,000.00. Here is how Wesley would figure what his actual taxes should be for the year and what he must pay the IRS:

STEP 1 Compute the actual income tax.

Wesley's income tax would be found by looking up his net income in a government table provided by the IRS. The amount of income tax Wesley found in the table for his net income was $5,450.00.

STEP 2 Compute the actual self-employment tax.

Wesley would multiply his net income by 16% to get the amount of self-employment tax.

$$\$35,000.00 \times 0.16 = \$5,600.00$$

STEP 3 Figure the total taxes due.

Since self-employed people must pay both income tax and self-employment tax, Wesley would add the answers from Steps 1 and 2 to get the total taxes due.

Income tax	$ 5,450.00
Self-employment tax	+ 5,600.00
Total taxes due	$11,050.00

STEP 4 Settle up with the IRS.

Key Terms

Balance due. Total taxes due are greater than estimated taxes paid.

Refund. Estimated taxes paid are greater than total taxes due.

Audit. To verify or check for accuracy and completeness.

Wesley would compare the total taxes due with the estimated taxes paid. If the total taxes due are greater than the estimated taxes paid, he has a **balance due**. He must then pay this balance. He will send a check for the balance with his tax return. Wesley has a balance due of $850.00, calculated as follows:

Total taxes due	$11,050.00
Estimated taxes paid	−10,200.00
Balance due	$ 850.00

If the estimated taxes paid were greater than the total taxes due, Wesley would receive a **refund**. He would send in his tax return and request that the difference be returned to him. For example, if Wesley paid estimated taxes of $11,400.00 but his total taxes due were only $11,050.00, his refund is calculated as follows:

Estimated taxes paid	$11,400.00
Total taxes due	−11,050.00
Refund	$ 350.00

You can also tell the IRS to keep that difference as part of next year's estimated taxes paid.

Maintaining Records for a Tax Audit

The Internal Revenue Service **audits**, or verifies the tax returns of certain individuals and companies each year. The reasons that the IRS selects certain income tax returns to audit change from time to time.

If your income tax return is selected for audit, it is important that you have records to back up the data you entered on the return you sent to the IRS. For small businesses, these records include source documents, such as sales invoices and check stubs. They also include record keeping forms, such as cash receipts and payments journals, and financial statements.

Usually the IRS does not audit your income tax return in the year you sent it in. You are more likely to be audited for returns you submitted three or four years ago. Most accountants recommend that you keep your source documents, record keeping forms, and financial statements for at least five years. Many businesses keep these records for a much longer time.

BUILDING YOUR BUSINESS VOCABULARY

On a sheet of paper, write the headings **Statement Number** and **Words**. Next, choose the words that match the statements. Write each word you choose next to the statement number it matches. Be careful; not all the words listed should be used.

Statements

1. A careful guess
2. Social security tax for self-employed people
3. A form that shows income, expenses, and net income or net loss
4. When expenses are greater than income
5. When estimated taxes paid are greater than total taxes due
6. When total taxes due are greater than estimated taxes paid
7. When income is greater than expenses
8. A tax on net income
9. Estimated amounts of income tax and self-employment tax paid during the year
10. To verify or check for accuracy and completeness

Words

audit
balance due
estimate
estimated tax
expenses
financial statements
income
income statement
income tax
net income
net loss
refund
self-employment tax

STEPS REVIEW: Using the Income Statement to Compute Taxes

STEP 1 Compute the actual income tax.

STEP 2 Compute the actual self-employment tax.

STEP 3 Figure the total taxes due.

STEP 4 Settle up with the IRS.

APPLICATION PROBLEMS

 Directions

Copy and complete the table that follows in this way:

a. Find the self-employment tax on each net income by using a rate of 16% and a maximum of $70,000.00. Enter your answer in Column A.
b. Add the income tax on each line to your answer in Column A. Enter this total in Column B.
c. Compare the total taxes due in Column B with the estimated taxes paid listed on each line. Enter the difference in Column C.
d. Label the difference that you entered in Column C as either a *balance due* or a *refund*. Enter the words *balance due* or *refund* in Column D.
   Line 1 is filled in for you as an example. (Watch out for the $70,000.00 limit.)

Net Income	A Self-Employment Tax	Income Tax	B Total Taxes Due	Estimated Taxes Paid	C Difference	D Balance Due or Refund
1. $ 30,000.00	$ 4,800.00	$ 4,100.00	$ 8,900.00	$ 8,600.00	$ 300.00	balance due
2. $ 25,000.00	$_____	$ 6,300.00	$_____	$ 9,700.00	$_____	_____
3. $ 60,000.00	$_____	$15,000.00	$_____	$24,800.00	$_____	_____
4. $ 45,000.00	$_____	$10,200.00	$_____	$17,900.00	$_____	_____
5. $ 70,000.00	$_____	$17,100.00	$_____	$28,750.00	$_____	_____
6. $ 11,500.00	$_____	$ 2,200.00	$_____	$ 3,930.00	$_____	_____
7. $ 75,000.00	$_____	$19,400.00	$_____	$31,100.00	$_____	_____
8. $100,000.00	$_____	$32,500.00	$_____	$47,100.00	$_____	_____

Problem 69-2 **Directions**

Complete the following table by using directions *a.* through *d.* given in Problem 1.

Net Income	A Self-Employment Tax	Income Tax	B Total Taxes Due	Estimated Taxes Paid	C Difference	D Balance Due or Refund
1. $ 33,000.00	$_____	$ 7,200.00	$_____	$11,660.00	$_____	_____
2. $ 49,500.00	$_____	$12,400.00	$_____	$20,090.00	$_____	_____
3. $ 18,500.00	$_____	$ 3,175.00	$_____	$ 6,120.00	$_____	_____
4. $ 13,200.00	$_____	$ 2,010.00	$_____	$ 5,069.00	$_____	_____
5. $ 73,000.00	$_____	$17,230.00	$_____	$28,100.00	$_____	_____
6. $ 51,000.00	$_____	$14,150.00	$_____	$22,030.00	$_____	_____
7. $170,000.00	$_____	$68,600.00	$_____	$80,100.00	$_____	_____
8. $200,000.00	$_____	$79,100.00	$_____	$92,100.00	$_____	_____

CHECK POINT

69-2(1b)

Total Taxes Due = $12,480.00

Problem 69-3   Cynthia Sabean owns and operates Vista Green Driving Range. She keeps separate records of income received from operating the driving range and from giving golf lessons.

Directions

a. Prepare an income statement for the year ended December 31, 20--, from the following information:
   During the year, she received $38,730.00 from the driving range and $24,650.00 from golf lessons.
   She paid the following expenses during the year: advertising, $1,250.20; electricity, $3,711.55; rent, $10,930.00; insurance, $1,650.95; office, $1,431.30; supplies, $2,891.65; telephone, $909.45; and miscellaneous, $2,482.50.

CHECK POINT

69-3(d)

Difference = $799.58

b. Calculate her self-employment tax, using a rate of 16% of net income. Round off to the nearest whole cent.
c. If her income taxes are $7,100.00, find the total taxes due.
d. If estimated taxes that she paid during the year are $12,400.00, find the difference between estimated taxes paid and total taxes due.
e. Label the difference in d. as either balance due or refund.

Problem 69-4 may be found in the Working Papers.

applied math preview

Copy and complete the following problems.

1. $ 19,426.83	3. $21,892.17	5. $3,698.02	7. $109,786.97
−12,537.85	−9,746.25	−2,783.44	−63,815.98

2. $143,000.00	4. $36,926.88	6. $10,703.46	8. $12,427.53
+38,724.38	+14,103.62	+13,633.81	+7,680.96

key terms preview

- Capital
- Capital statement
- Net decrease in capital
- Net increase in capital
- Withdrawal

goals

1 To learn how capital changes.
2 To learn how to prepare a capital statement.

UNDERSTANDING THE JOB

Capital. The worth of a business.

Withdrawal. Cash or other items of value taken for the owner's use.

Capital statement A form that shows changes in capital over a period of time.

Net income increases capital.
Net loss decreases capital.
Withdrawals decrease capital.

Every business has a value to its owner and to potential buyers. This value is what the business is worth. The name given to the worth of a business is **capital**.

As a business operates, capital changes. Capital can increase or it can decrease. A net income will cause capital to increase. Net income makes the value of a business go up. A net loss will cause capital to decrease. A net loss makes the value of a business go down.

You learned in earlier jobs that owners of businesses may take cash, or other items of value, from their businesses for their own use. These **withdrawals** will cause capital to decrease. Withdrawals make the value of a business go down.

You have also learned how to prepare one kind of financial statement—the income statement. In this job, you will learn how to prepare another financial statement—the **capital statement**. A capital statement shows the changes in the owner's worth over a period of time. You will find net income, net loss, and withdrawals on a capital statement, since these are the items that cause a change in the value of a business.

Melissa Kadir, owner of AutoPro Detailing, began the month of June with capital of $70,000.00. During June, she earned net income of $1,630.00. (See Illustration 70A, below.) During June, she withdrew $1,400.00. Your job is to prepare her capital statement for June.

Illustration 70A shows Melissa's capital statement for June. Here are the steps you would follow to prepare it:

A double rule across the bottom of a financial statement indicates that the amounts above are accurate and have been verified.

STEP 1 Enter the heading.

As usual, the capital statement has a three-line heading.

WHO? AutoPro Detailing
WHAT? Capital Statement
WHEN? For the Month Ended June 30, 20--

Like the income statement, the capital statement covers a period of time, so the WHEN? reads "For the Month Ended..." For a twelve-month period, it would read "For the Year Ended..."

STEP 2 Record the beginning amount of capital.

Write "Capital, June 1, 20--" on the first line. Enter the amount of capital on June 1 in the right money column. Dollar signs are not needed.

STEP 3 Record the net income or net loss.

Write the words "Net Income" on the next line. Enter the amount of net income in the left money column.

The net income amount comes from the income statement. Look at the final amount in Illustration 68A (page 547), and you will find $1,630.00. Whenever a record keeper prepares both an income statement

Illustration 70A
Capital statement

STEP 3
STEP 2
STEP 1

AutoPro Detailing
Capital Statement
For the Month Ended June 30, 20--

Capital, June 1, 20--			70 0 0 0 00
Net Income	1 6 3 0 00		
Less: Withdrawals	1 4 0 0 00		
Net Increase in Capital			2 3 0 00
Capital, June 30, 20--			70 2 3 0 00

STEP 4
STEP 5
STEP 6

Prepare the income statement before the capital statement.

and a capital statement, the income statement must be done first. The reason for this is that you need the net income figure to prepare the capital statement.

If there was a net loss instead of a net income, the words *Net Loss* would be written instead and the amount would be entered in parentheses.

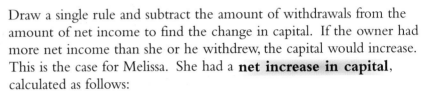

STEP 4 Record the withdrawals.

Since withdrawals decrease capital, they will be subtracted from the amount of net income. Write "Less: Withdrawals" on the next line. The word *Less* tells you to subtract. Enter the amount in the left money column.

STEP 5 Figure the change in capital.

Net increase in capital. Net income is greater than withdrawals.

Net decrease in capital. Withdrawals are greater than net income.

Draw a single rule and subtract the amount of withdrawals from the amount of net income to find the change in capital. If the owner had more net income than she or he withdrew, the capital would increase. This is the case for Melissa. She had a **net increase in capital**, calculated as follows:

Net income	$1,630.00
Less: withdrawals	−1,400.00
Net increase in capital	$ 230.00

Melissa earned a net income of $1,630.00, but she chose to remove $1,400.00 of it from the business. The value of her business, the capital, increased by $230.00. The amount of $230.00 is entered in the right money column. "Net Increase in Capital" is written on the fourth line.

Some business owners withdraw more than they earn. When this happens, you have a **net decrease in capital**. If you have a net income of $1,630.00, but withdraw $1,930.00, the net decrease in capital is calculated as follows:

Net income	$ 1,630.00
Less: withdrawals	− 1,930.00
Net decrease in capital	($ 300.00)

The amount of $300.00 is entered in parentheses in the right money column, and "Net Decrease in Capital" is written on the fourth line.

STEP 6 Find the ending amount of capital.

Rule a single line under the amount of net increase in capital. Add the net increase in capital to the beginning amount of capital to get the ending amount of capital.

Capital, June 1, 20--	$70,000.00
Net increase in capital	+ 230.00
Capital, June 30, 20--	$70,230.00

Enter the total in the right money column and double rule both money columns. Write "Capital, June 30, 20--" on the fifth line.

If there were a net decrease in capital, it would be subtracted from the beginning amount of capital. For example, if you began with capital of $70,000.00 and had a net decrease in capital of $500.00, you would calculate the ending amount of capital as follows:

```
                    AutoPro Detailing
                    Capital Statement
                 For Period Ending 06/30/--

Melissa Kadir, Capital [Beg. of Period]      70,000.00

Net Income                          1,630.00
Less: Withdrawls                    1,400.00

Net Increase in Capital                            230.00

Melissa Kadir, Capital [End of Period]       70,230.00
```

Capital, June 1, 20--	$70,000.00
Net decrease in capital	− 500.00
Capital, June 30, 20--	$69,500.00

You would still write "Capital, June 30, 20--" on the fifth line. You would enter the new amount of capital in the right money column and double rule both money columns.

USING THE COMPUTER

Illustration 70B shows a computer-generated capital statement. All financial statements can be prepared by a computer by selecting the proper menu key.

BUILDING YOUR BUSINESS VOCABULARY

On a sheet of paper, write the headings **Statement Number** and **Words**. Next, choose the words that match the statements. Write each word you choose next to the statement number it matches. Be careful; not all the words listed should be used.

Statements	Words
1. When cash or other items of value of a business are taken for the owner's use	balance due
	capital
2. The worth of a business	capital statement
3. Summaries of the results of a business	estimate
4. When net income is greater than withdrawals	financial statements
	income statement
5. A form that shows income, expenses, and net income or net loss	net decrease in capital
	net increase in capital
6. A form that shows changes in capital over a period of time	revenue
	withdrawal
7. When withdrawals are greater than net income	
8. A careful guess	

STEPS REVIEW: Preparing a Capital Statement

STEP 1 Enter the heading.

STEP 2 Record the beginning amount of capital.

STEP 3 Record the net income or net loss.

STEP 4 Record the withdrawals.

STEP 5 Figure the change in capital.

STEP 6 Find the ending amount of capital.

APPLICATION PROBLEMS

CHECK POINT

70-1

Ending amount of capital = $43,750.00

Problem 70-1

Nellie Zuzich, owner of Nellie's DVD Rentals, begins the month of January, 20--, with capital of $43,000.00. During January, she earns net income of $3,100.00. During March, she withdraws $2,350.00 from the business.

Directions

Using the information given, prepare a capital statement for Nellie's DVD Rentals for the month ended January 31, 20--.

CHECK POINT

70-2

Ending amount of capital = $119,042.70

Problem 70-2

Conner Tierney, owner of Tierney's Financial Services, begins the month of March, 20--, with capital of $115,624.55. During March, he earns net income of $12,794.60. During March, he withdraws $9,376.45 from the business.

Directions

Using the information given, prepare a capital statement for Tierney's Financial Services for the month ended March 31, 20--.

Problem 70-3

Anthony McMahon owns and operates Tony's Child Care Service. He begins the month of April, 20--, with capital of $24,983.57. During April, he earns net income of $5,623.00. During April, he withdraws $6,150.00 from the business.

CHECK POINT

70-3

Ending amount of capital = $24,456.57

Directions

Using the information given, prepare a capital statement for Tony's Child Care Service for the month ended April 30, 20--.

Problem 70-4 may be found in the Working Papers.

applied math preview

Find the missing amount on each line.

1. $ 80,000.00 = $60,000.00 + $_____
2. $ 45,000.00 = $_____ + $ 15,000.00
3. $ _____ = $21,500.00 + $ 40,000.00
4. $ 31,480.70 = $10,630.50 + $_____
5. $ _____ = $28,360.15 + $ 40,600.85
6. $143,711.22 = $_____ + $102,780.80

key term preview

- Accounting equation
- Assets
- Balance sheet
- Liabilities

goals

1 To learn the fundamental equation of accounting.

2 To learn how to prepare a balance sheet.

UNDERSTANDING THE JOB

Key Terms

Assets. Things owned that have money value.

Liabilities. Amounts owed to creditors.

Accounting equation. Assets = liabilities + capital.

Balance sheet. A form that shows that assets equal liabilities plus capital.

Tips

Assets − Liabilities = Capital.

When one person owns a business, the items that are owned are known as the **assets** of that business. Assets are things owned that have money value. Examples of business assets are cash, supplies, equipment, land, and buildings.

Some of the assets that you own will be fully paid for. Some of the assets may not be fully paid for. For example, you may have borrowed money to buy a building. Or, you may owe money for equipment that you purchased on credit. Amounts owed to creditors are called **liabilities**. Examples of liabilities are accounts payable and sales tax payable. A liability usually includes the word *payable* in its title.

If a business has assets of $20,000.00 and liabilities of $5,000.00, the business is actually worth the difference, $15,000.00:

Assets	−	Liabilities	=	Capital
$20,000.00	−	$5,000.00	=	$15,000.00

One way to prove your math is to add the capital to the liabilities. The total should equal the assets, as shown below:

Assets	=	Liabilities	+	Capital
$20,000.00	=	$5,000.00	+	$15,000.00

The statement Assets = Liabilities + Capital is called the **accounting equation**. An equation shows that the amounts on each side of the equals sign are equal, or in balance. In the accounting equation, that means that the total amount of assets must equal the total amount of liabilities and capital for a business.

In this job, you will learn how to prepare another type of financial statement—the **balance sheet**. A balance sheet shows the assets, liabilities, and capital of a business. In other words, a balance sheet shows what a business owns, owes, and is worth. To be correct, the balance sheet must show that the assets of a business are equal to its liabilities and capital. So, the balance sheet shows the accounting equation for a business.

Tips

Balance sheet shows that accounting equation is in balance.

ASSETS   LIABILITIES AND CAPITAL

SAMPLE PROBLEM

Melissa Kadir, owner of AutoPro Detailing, finds that the business has the following asset, liability, and capital balances on June 30, 20--:

Cash	$20,600.00
Supplies	6,340.00
Equipment	31,980.00
Truck	23,400.00
Accounts Payable	12,090.00
Melissa Kadir Capital	70,230.00

Your job is to prepare the balance sheet for the business as of June 30. Illustration 71A shows Melissa's balance sheet. Here are the steps to follow to prepare it:

Illustration 71A

Balance sheet

STEP 2   STEP 1

AutoPro Detailing
Balance Sheet
June 30, 20--

Assets		
Cash	20 6 0 0 00	
Supplies	6 3 4 0 00	
Equipment	31 9 8 0 00	
Truck	23 4 0 0 00	
Total Assets		82 3 2 0 00
Liabilities		
Accounts Payable		12 0 9 0 00
Capital		
Melissa Kadir, Capital		70 2 3 0 00
Total Liabilities and Capital		82 3 2 0 00

STEP 3

STEP 4

562 | Chapter 14 | Financial Statements for Small Businesses

STEP 1 Enter the heading.

The heading again answers three questions:

WHO? AutoPro Detailing
WHAT? Balance Sheet
WHEN? June 30, 20--

Notice that the balance sheet is prepared as of a single date. It does not cover a period of time as the income and capital statements do. A balance sheet tells you balances on that date. Think of the balance sheet as a "snapshot" of a business on a given date.

STEP 2 Prepare the Assets section.

Write the word *Assets* in the center of the first line. Then, list each asset at the left margin. Enter the amount of each asset in the left money column.

Draw a single ruling under the last asset amount. Add the amounts, and enter the total one line down in the right money column. Write the words *Total Assets* at the left margin, on the line with $82,320.00. Draw a double ruling across both money columns under the total.

Melissa has only four assets. Whether a business has four assets or twenty assets, the organization of the Assets section will be the same.

STEP 3 Prepare the Liabilities section.

Write the word *Liabilities* in the center of the next line. Then, list each liability at the left margin. Melissa has only one liability, Accounts Payable. Enter the amount in the right money column.

If there were more than one liability, the Liabilities section would be set up in the same way as the Assets section. Illustration 71B shows how this would look.

Illustration 71B
A liabilities section of a balance sheet

Liabilities												
Accounts Payable	13	4	5	0	00							
Sales Tax Payable	2	8	6	5	00							
Total Liabilities							16	3	1	5	00	

STEP 4 Prepare the Capital section.

Write the word *Capital* in the center of the next line. Write "Melissa Kadir, Capital" on the following line at the left margin. Enter the amount of capital, $70,230.00, in the right money column.

The amount may be familiar to you. You will find it in Illustration 70A (page 557). It is the ending amount of capital from the capital statement. When you are preparing financial statements, you must prepare the capital statement before you prepare the balance sheet. You need that ending capital figure for the balance sheet.

Tips

Prepare the capital statement before the balance sheet.

STEP 5 Complete the balance sheet.

Draw a single ruling under the amount of capital. Add the amount of total liabilities ($12,090.00) to the amount of capital ($70,230.00). The

```
                        AutoPro Detailing
                          Balance Sheet
                            06/30/--

    Assets

    Cash                              20,600.00
    Supplies                           6,340.00
    Equipment                         31,980.00
    Truck                             23,400.00

    Total Assets                                      82,320.00

    Liabilities

    Accounts Payable                  12,090.00

    Total Liabilities                                 12,090.00

    Capital

    Melissa Kadir, Capital            70,230.00

    Total Capital                                     70,230.00

    Total Liabilities & Capital                       82,320.00
```

total should equal the total of the assets ($82,320.00). Since it does, you have proven that the accounting equation is in balance.

Assets	=	Liabilities	+	Capital
$82,320.00	=	$12,090.00	+	$70,230.00

Write "Total Liabilities and Capital" on the line with the total. Draw a double ruling across both money columns under the total.

USING THE COMPUTER

Illustration 71C shows how a computer-generated balance sheet would look. The menu key for balance sheet would display this form on the screen.

BUILDING YOUR BUSINESS VOCABULARY

On a sheet of paper, write the headings **Statement Number** and **Words**. Next, choose the words that match the statements. Write each word you choose next to the statement number it matches. Be careful; not all the words listed should be used.

Statements	Words
1. A form that shows income, expenses, and net income or net loss	accounting equation
	assets
2. Things owned that have money value	balance sheet
3. Summaries of the results of a business	capital
4. A form that shows that assets equal liabilities plus capital	capital statement
	financial statements
5. Assets equal liabilities plus capital	income statement
6. A form that shows changes in capital over a period of time	liabilities
	net income

Statements	Words
7. Amounts owed to creditors	withdrawal
8. The worth of a business	

STEPS REVIEW: Preparing a Balance Sheet

STEP 1 Enter the heading.

STEP 2 Prepare the Assets section.

STEP 3 Prepare the Liabilities section.

STEP 4 Prepare the Capital section.

STEP 5 Complete the balance sheet.

APPLICATION PROBLEMS

Problem 71-1 Javier Hernandez has the following assets, liabilities, and capital on August 31, 20--:

CHECK POINT

71-1

Total assets = $50,488.07

Cash	$ 8,243.51
Office Supplies	894.66
Store Supplies	1,404.70
Office Equipment	15,623.20
Tools	8,722.00
Truck	15,600.00
Accounts Payable	11,780.00
Javier Hernandez, Capital	38,708.07

Directions
Prepare a balance sheet as of August 31, 20--, for Javier's business, Hernandez Construction, Inc.

Problem 71-2 Kathy Harrington owns and operates Harrington Electrical. Her assets, liabilities, and capital on September 30, 20--, are as follows:

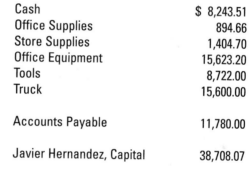

Cash	$15,409.68
Electrical Supplies	6,256.11
Office Furniture	3,790.40
Equipment & Tools	32,601.00
Accounts Payable	20,024.70
Kathy Harrington, Capital	38,032.49

CHECK POINT

71-2

Total assets = $58,057.19

Directions
Prepare her balance sheet as of September 30, 20--.

Jageet Ralad owns and operates Green Dragon Miniature Golf. His assets, liabilities, and capital on December 31, 20--, are as follows:

Cash	$ 4,231.46
Supplies	1,780.59
Golf Equipment	3,007.45
Golf Structures	25,890.00
Vending Machines	5,810.74
Truck	23,670.00
Accounts Payable	19,509.10
Sales Tax Payable	949.83
Jageet Ralad, Capital	43,931.31

CHECK POINT

71-3

Total liabilities =
$20,458.93

Directions

Prepare his balance sheet as of December 31, 20--.

Problem 71-4 may be found in the Working Papers.

Job 72 PREPARING A SIX-COLUMN WORK SHEET

UNDERSTANDING THE JOB

You have learned how to prepare three financial statements in this chapter: the income statement, the capital statement, and the balance sheet. This is the order in which the statements should be prepared. Illustration 72A shows the relationship among the statements.

Illustration 72A shows that income and expense information is used to prepare the income statement. The answer to the income statement, net income or net loss, is used on the capital statement. Beginning capital and withdrawals information is used to prepare the capital statement. The answer to the capital statement, ending capital, is used on the balance sheet. Assets and liabilities information is used to prepare the balance sheet.

The titles listed on the financial statements are actually *names of accounts* found in the general ledger. General ledger account titles and balances are used to prepare the statements.

Illustration 72A

How the financial statements are related

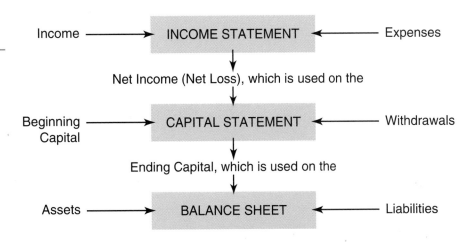

The fastest way to prepare all financial statements from information in the accounts is to use a form called a **work sheet**. A work sheet is not a formal financial statement. It is a form on which you summarize all the information you need for the financial statements. Think of a worksheet as a piece of accounting "scratch paper" or as a piece of paper on which you make notes to prepare a report.

Illustration 72B on page 569 shows a completed work sheet. Sample Problem 1 shows you how it was prepared. Sample Problem 2 shows you how financial statements are prepared from the work sheet.

SAMPLE PROBLEM 1

Melissa Kadir's general ledger account balances for AutoPro Detailing as of June 30, 20--, follow:

Acct. No.	Account Title	Balance Debit	Balance Credit
110	Cash	$20,600.00	
120	Supplies	6,340.00	
130	Equipment	31,980.00	
140	Truck	23,400.00	
210	Accounts Payable		$ 12,090.00
310	Melissa Kadir, Capital		70,000.00
320	Melissa Kadir, Drawing	1,400.00	
410	Income, Auto Detailing		2,460.00
420	Income, Boat Detailing		620.00
510	Rent Expense	810.00	
520	Insurance Expense	60.00	
530	Supplies Expense	240.00	
540	Truck Expense	125.00	
550	Telephone Expense	75.00	
560	Electricity Expense	140.00	

Illustration 72B shows how these account balances were used to prepare a work sheet. Here are the steps to follow:

STEP 1 Enter the heading.

The heading should again answer:

WHO? AutoPro Detailing
WHAT? Work Sheet
WHEN? For the Month Ended June 30, 20--

STEP 2 Prepare a trial balance on the work sheet.

Enter all account titles in the Account Title column. Enter all account numbers in the Acct. No. column. Enter account balances in the Debit

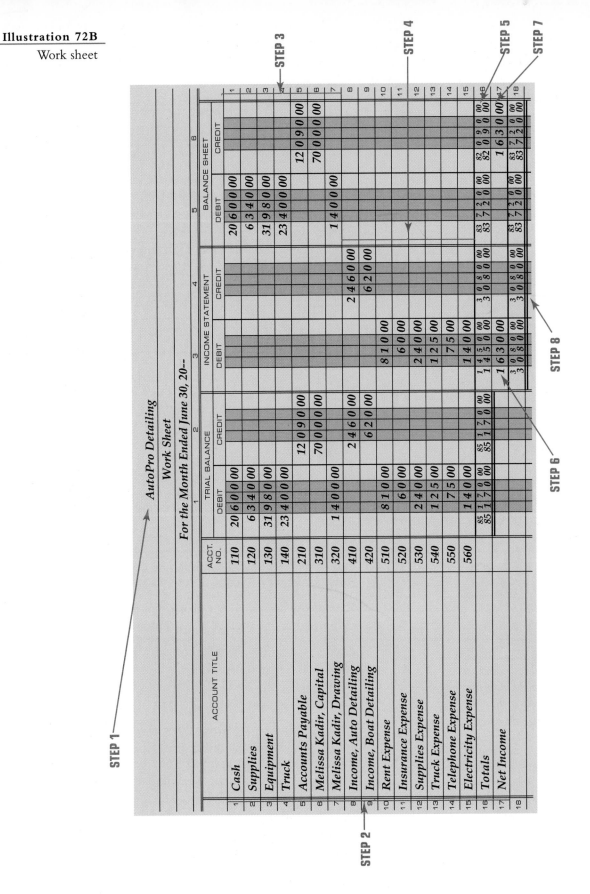

STEP 1

STEP 2

STEP 3

STEP 4

STEP 5

STEP 7

STEP 6

STEP 8

AutoPro Detailing

Work Sheet

For the Month Ended June 30, 20--

ACCOUNT TITLE	ACCT. NO.	TRIAL BALANCE		INCOME STATEMENT		BALANCE SHEET	
		DEBIT	CREDIT	DEBIT	CREDIT	DEBIT	CREDIT
Cash	110	20 6 0 0 00				20 6 0 0 00	
Supplies	120	6 3 4 0 00				6 3 4 0 00	
Equipment	130	31 9 8 0 00				31 9 8 0 00	
Truck	140	23 4 0 0 00				23 4 0 0 00	
Accounts Payable	210		12 0 9 0 00				12 0 9 0 00
Melissa Kadir, Capital	310		70 0 0 0 00				70 0 0 0 00
Melissa Kadir, Drawing	320	1 4 0 0 00				1 4 0 0 00	
Income, Auto Detailing	410		2 4 6 0 00		2 4 6 0 00		
Income, Boat Detailing	420		6 2 0 00		6 2 0 00		
Rent Expense	510	8 1 0 00		8 1 0 00			
Insurance Expense	520	6 0 00		6 0 00			
Supplies Expense	530	2 4 0 00		2 4 0 00			
Truck Expense	540	1 2 5 00		1 2 5 00			
Telephone Expense	550	7 5 00		7 5 00			
Electricity Expense	560	1 4 0 00		1 4 0 00			
Totals		85 1 7 0 00	85 1 7 0 00	1 4 5 0 00	3 0 8 0 00	83 7 2 0 00	82 0 9 0 00
Net Income				1 6 3 0 00			1 6 3 0 00
				3 0 8 0 00	3 0 8 0 00	83 7 2 0 00	83 7 2 0 00

ACCOUNT TITLE	ACCT. NO.	TRIAL BALANCE			
		DEBIT		CREDIT	
1 Cash	110	20 6 0 0 00			
2 Supplies	120	6 3 4 0 00			
3 Equipment	130	31 9 8 0 00			
4 Truck	140	23 4 0 0 00			
5 Accounts Payable	210			12 0 9 0 00	
6 Melissa Kadir, Capital	310			70 0 0 0 00	
7 Melissa Kadir, Drawing	320	1 4 0 0 00			
8 Income, Auto Detailing	410			2 4 6 0 00	
9 Income, Boat Detailing	420			6 2 0 00	
10 Rent Expense	510	8 1 0 00			
11 Insurance Expense	520	6 0 00			
12 Supplies Expense	530	2 4 0 00			
13 Truck Expense	540	1 2 5 00			
14 Telephone Expense	550	7 5 00			
15 Electricity Expense	560	1 4 0 00			
16 Totals		85 1 7 0 00		85 1 7 0 00	
17 Net Income					
18					

STEP 2

or Credit columns of the trial balance. What you are doing is preparing the trial balance on the work sheet.

Draw a single ruling under the Trial Balance columns. Foot each column. When your Debit and Credit totals are equal, write in final totals and double rule under the totals. Write the word *Totals* in the Account Title column. Do not continue to Step 3 until your trial balance is in balance. Illustration 72C shows the completed trial balance.

STEP 3 Extend asset, liability, capital, and drawing account balances to the Balance Sheet columns.

Extend the accounts that belong on the balance sheet and the capital statement to the Balance Sheet columns:

Assets—Cash, Supplies, Equipment, Truck
Liabilities—Accounts Payable
Capital—Melissa Kadir, Capital
Drawing—Melissa Kadir, Drawing

To extend an amount, copy that amount a second time. *Extend a debit as a debit.* Thus, the amount of Cash, $20,600.00, is extended to the Balance Sheet Debit column. The balances of the Supplies, Equipment, Truck, and Melissa Kadir, Drawing accounts are all extended to the Balance Sheet Debit column.

Extend a credit as a credit. The balances of the Accounts Payable and Melissa Kadir, Capital accounts are extended to the Balance Sheet Credit column.

Illustration 72D (page 571) shows the extensions to the Balance Sheet columns.

Tips

Extend balance sheet and capital statement accounts to the Balance Sheet columns.
Extend assets and drawing to the Balance Sheet Debit column.
Extend liabilities and capital to the Balance Sheet Credit column.

	ACCOUNT TITLE	ACCT. NO.	TRIAL BALANCE		BALANCE SHEET		
			DEBIT	CREDIT	DEBIT	CREDIT	
1	Cash	110	20 6 0 0 00		20 6 0 0 00		1
2	Supplies	120	6 3 4 0 00		6 3 4 0 00		2
3	Equipment	130	31 9 8 0 00		31 9 8 0 00		3
4	Truck	140	23 4 0 0 00		23 4 0 0 00		4
5	Accounts Payable	210		12 0 9 0 00		12 0 9 0 00	5
6	Melissa Kadir, Capital	310		70 0 0 0 00		70 0 0 0 00	6
7	Melissa Kadir, Drawing	320	1 4 0 0 00		1 4 0 0 00		7

STEP 3

Illustration 72D

Extending amounts to the
Balance Sheet columns

Tips

*Extend income statement
accounts to the Income
Statement columns.
Extend income accounts to
the Income Statement
Credit column.
Extend expense accounts
to the Income Statement
Debit column.*

STEP 4 Extend income and expense account balances to the Income Statement columns.

Extend the accounts that belong on the income statement to the Income Statement columns. Extend both income accounts and all six expense accounts to the Income Statement columns.

Extend a credit as a credit. Thus, both income accounts are extended to the Income Statement Credit column.

Extend a debit as a debit. Thus, all expense accounts are extended to the Income Statement Debit column.

Illustration 72E shows the extensions to the Income Statement columns.

STEP 5 Foot the Income Statement and Balance Sheet columns.

Draw a single ruling under all four columns to which you have extended amounts. Foot all four columns.

STEP 6 Calculate net income or net loss.

Think about what each of the four columns contains. Illustration 72F on page 572 summarizes the contents of each column.

To find net income or net loss, you subtract expenses from income. Using the work sheet, subtract the total of the Income Statement Debit column (expenses) from the total of the Income Statement Credit column (income). The difference is net income or net loss.

Illustration 72E

Extending amounts to the
Income Statement
Columns

STEP 4

	ACCOUNT TITLE	ACCT. NO.	TRIAL BALANCE		INCOME STATEMENT		
			DEBIT	CREDIT	DEBIT	CREDIT	
8	Income, Auto Detailing	410		2 4 6 0 00		2 4 6 0 00	
9	Income, Boat Detailing	420		6 2 0 00		6 2 0 00	
10	Rent Expense	510	8 1 0 00		8 1 0 00		
11	Insurance Expense	520	6 0 00		6 0 00		
12	Supplies Expense	530	2 4 0 00		2 4 0 00		
13	Truck Expense	540	1 2 5 00		1 2 5 00		
14	Telephone Expense	550	7 5 00		7 5 00		
15	Electricity Expense	560	1 4 0 00		1 4 0 00		

Illustration 72F

Contents of the four
financial statement columns

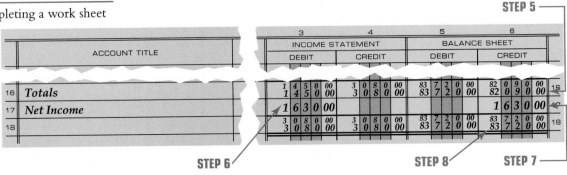

	INCOME STATEMENT		BALANCE SHEET	
	3	4	5	6
	DEBIT	CREDIT	DEBIT	CREDIT
1				
2	EXPENSES	INCOME	ASSETS	LIABILITIES
3			DRAWING	CAPITAL

Tips

*Income Statement
Credit − Income
Statement Debit =
Net Income or Net
Loss*

Income Statement, Credit	$ 3,080.00
Income Statement, Debit	− 1,450.00
Net Income	$ 1,630.00

Since income (Credit) is larger than expenses (Debit), you have a net income. If the total expenses were larger, you would have a net loss.

STEP 7 Check the amount of net income (or net loss).

To check your answer for net income, subtract the Balance Sheet Credit column from the Balance Sheet Debit column. The answer should be the same as in Step 6 if you have done all of your extensions and additions correctly.

Balance Sheet Debit	$ 83,720.00
Balance Sheet Credit	− 82,090.00
Net Income	$ 1,630.00

STEP 8 Complete the work sheet.

You have five more steps to follow to complete the work sheet.

1. Record the totals of the Income Statement and Balance Sheet columns as final totals.
2. Enter the amount of net income twice: in the Income Statement column with the smaller total (Debit) and in the Balance Sheet column with the smaller total (Credit).
3. Draw a single ruling under the four financial statement columns again. Foot one more time. You should have two pairs of equal totals.
4. Write in the four final totals and double rule the four columns.
5. Write the words *Net Income* in the Account Title column on the line where you recorded $1,630.00 twice.

Illustration 72G shows the steps to complete a work sheet.

Tips

*Balance Sheet Debit
− Balance Sheet
Credit = Net Income*

Illustration 72G

Completing a work sheet

STEP 5

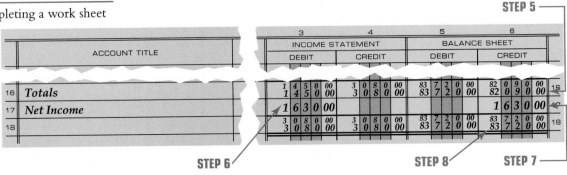

	ACCOUNT TITLE	INCOME STATEMENT		BALANCE SHEET		
		3 DEBIT	4 CREDIT	5 DEBIT	6 CREDIT	
16	Totals	1 4 5 0 00	3 0 8 0 00	83 7 2 0 00	82 0 9 0 00	16
17	Net Income	1 6 3 0 00			1 6 3 0 00	17
18		3 0 8 0 00	3 0 8 0 00	83 7 2 0 00	83 7 2 0 00	18

STEP 6   STEP 8   STEP 7

Melissa Kadir will now prepare her financial statements from the work sheet. Here are the steps she follows:

STEP 1 Prepare the income statement.

To prepare the income statement from the work sheet, Melissa will use all of the information in the Income Statement columns.
Illustration 72H shows how the information is taken from the Income Statement columns and placed on the income statement.

Illustration 72H

Transferring information from the work sheet to the income statement

	ACCOUNT TITLE	ACCT. NO.	3 INCOME STATEMENT DEBIT	4 INCOME STATEMENT CREDIT
1	Cash	110		
2	Supplies	120		
3	Equipment	130		
4	Truck	140		
5	Accounts Payable	210		
6	Melissa Kadir, Capital	310		
7	Melissa Kadir, Drawing	320		
8	Income, Auto Detailing	410		2 4 6 0 00
9	Income, Boat Detailing	420		6 2 0 00
10	Rent Expense	510	8 1 0 00	
11	Insurance Expense	520	6 0 00	
12	Supplies Expense	530	2 4 0 00	
13	Truck Expense	540	1 2 5 00	
14	Telephone Expense	550	7 5 00	
15	Electricity Expense	560	1 4 0 00	
16	Totals		1 4 5 0 00	3 0 8 0 00
17	Net Income		1 6 3 0 00	
18			3 0 8 0 00	3 0 8 0 00

STEP 1

AutoPro Detailing
Income Statement
For the Month Ended June 30, 20--

Revenue:		
Auto Detailing	2 4 6 0 00	
Boat Detailing	6 2 0 00	
Total Income		3 0 8 0 00
Expenses:		
Rent	8 1 0 00	
Insurance	6 0 00	
Supplies	2 4 0 00	
Truck	1 2 5 00	
Telephone	7 5 00	
Electricity	1 4 0 00	
Total Expenses		1 4 5 0 00
Net income		1 6 3 0 00

STEP 2 Prepare the capital statement.

To prepare the capital statement from the work sheet, Melissa will use three figures: beginning capital, net income, and withdrawals. Illustration 72I shows where these figures are found on the work sheet and how they are transferred to the capital statement. Notice that the Melissa Kadir, Drawing account is used for the withdrawals figure.

STEP 3 Prepare the balance sheet.

To prepare the balance sheet from the work sheet, Melissa will use the asset and liability accounts from the Balance Sheet columns.

The capital amount to be used on the balance sheet is *not* found on the work sheet. It is the final figure on her capital statement—the ending capital. (See Illustration 72I.) Illustration 72J shows how information is transferred from the Balance Sheet columns to the balance sheet.

Illustration 72I

Transferring information from the work sheet to the capital statement

	ACCOUNT TITLE	ACCT. NO.	BALANCE SHEET DEBIT	BALANCE SHEET CREDIT	
1	Cash	110	20 6 0 0 00		1
2	Supplies	120	6 3 4 0 00		2
3	Equipment	130	31 9 8 0 00		3
4	Truck	140	23 4 0 0 00		4
5	Accounts Payable	210		12 0 9 0 00	5
6	Melissa Kadir, Capital	310		70 0 0 0 00	6
7	Melissa Kadir, Drawing	320	1 4 0 0 00		7
8	Income, Auto Detailing	410			8
9	Income, Boat Detailing	420			9
10	Rent Expense	510			10
11	Insurance Expense	520			11
12	Supplies Expense	530			12
13	Truck Expense	540			13
14	Telephone Expense	550			14
15	Electricity Expense	560			15
16	Totals		83 7 2 0 00	82 0 9 0 00	16
17	Net Income			1 6 3 0 00	17
18			83 7 2 0 00	83 7 2 0 00	18

STEP 2

AutoPro Detailing
Capital Statement
For the Month Ended June 30, 20--

Capital, June 1, 20--		70 0 0 0 00
Net Income	1 6 3 0 00	
Less: Withdrawals	1 4 0 0 00	
Net Increase in Capital		2 3 0 00
Capital, June 30, 20--		70 2 3 0 00

	ACCOUNT TITLE	ACCT. NO.	BALANCE SHEET	
			DEBIT	CREDIT
1	Cash	110	20 6 0 0 00	
2	Supplies	120	6 3 4 0 00	
3	Equipment	130	31 9 8 0 00	
4	Truck	140	23 4 0 0 00	
5	Accounts Payable	210		12 0 9 0 00
6	Melissa Kadir, Capital	310		70 0 0 0 00
7	Melissa Kadir, Drawing	320	1 4 0 0 00	
8	Income, Auto Detailing	410		
9	Income, Boat Detailing	420		
10	Rent Expense	510		
11	Insurance Expense	520		
12	Supplies Expense	530		
13	Truck Expense	540		
14	Telephone Expense	550		
15	Electricity Expense	560		
16	Totals		83 7 2 0 00	82 0 9 0 00
17	Net Income			1 6 3 0 00
18			83 7 2 0 00	83 7 2 0 00

STEP 3

AutoPro Detailing		
Balance Sheet		
June 30, 20--		
Assets		
Cash	20 6 0 0 00	
Supplies	6 3 4 0 00	
Equipment	31 9 8 0 00	
Truck	23 4 0 0 00	
Total Assets		82 3 2 0 00
Liabilities		
Accounts Payable		12 0 9 0 00
Capital		
Melissa Kadir, Capital		70 2 3 0 00
Total Liabilities and Capital		82 3 2 0 00

BUILDING YOUR BUSINESS VOCABULARY

On a sheet of paper, write the headings **Statement Number** and **Words**. Next, choose the words that match the statements. Write each word you choose next to the statement number it matches. Be careful; not all the words listed should be used.

Statements	Words
1. Entered again in a second column	accounting equation
2. Assets equal liabilities plus capital	assets
3. A form used to summarize information for financial statements	balance sheet
	capital

Statements	Words
4. Things owned with money value	capital statement
5. Amounts owed to creditors	extended
6. When income is greater than expenses	income statement
7. A form that shows changes in capital over a period of time	liabilities
	net income
8. A form that shows income, expenses, and net income or net loss	net loss
	work sheet

STEPS REVIEW: Preparing a Six-Column Work Sheet

STEP 1 Enter the heading.

STEP 2 Prepare a trial balance on the work sheet.

STEP 3 Extend asset, liability, capital, and drawing account balances to the Balance Sheet columns.

STEP 4 Extend income and expense account balances to the Income Statement columns.

STEP 5 Foot the Income Statement and Balance Sheet columns.

STEP 6 Calculate net income or net loss.

STEP 7 Check the amount of net income (or net loss).

STEP 8 Complete the work sheet.

APPLICATION PROBLEMS

Problem 72-1

You are an assistant bookkeeper for Derek Palajac, owner of Top Dawg, a local dog kennel. Derek's account balances on March 31, 20--, are as shown below:

CHECK POINT

72-1

Net Income = $1,365.00

Spreadsheet

			Balance	
Acct. No.	Account Title		Debit	Credit
110	Cash		$3,500.00	
120	Supplies		750.00	
130	Kennel Equipment		23,400.00	
140	Truck		18,900.00	
210	Accounts Payable			$12,500.00
310	Derek Palajac, Capital			33,685.00
320	Derek Palajac, Drawing		1,000.00	
410	Income, Kennel Fees			4,350.00
510	Supplies Expense		840.00	
520	Truck Expense		390.00	
530	Rent Expense		1,500.00	
540	Insurance Expense		160.00	
550	Miscellaneous Expense		95.00	

Directions

Prepare a work sheet for the month ended March 31, 20--.

You are a junior accountant for Vicky Cipolla, owner of Northern Financial Services. Vicky's account balances on July 31, 20--, are as follows:

CHECK POINT

72-2

Net Income = $1,712.05

		Balance	
Acct. No.	Account Title	Debit	Credit
110	Cash	$ 8,560.20	
120	Office Supplies	1,423.50	
130	Computer Supplies	781.65	
140	Office Equipment	22,490.00	
150	Computer Equipment	18,505.00	
210	Accounts Payable		$16,820.00
220	Sales Tax Payable		260.00
310	Vicky Cipolla, Capital		34,288.30
320	Vicky Cipolla, Drawing	1,320.00	
410	Income, Bookkeeping		5,565.00
420	Income, Consulting Fees		3,390.00
510	Computer Expense	3,871.40	
520	Rent Expense	2,050.00	
530	Utilities Expense	1,149.35	
540	Miscellaneous Expense	172.20	

Directions

Prepare a work sheet for the month ended July 31, 20--.

Problem 72-3 **Directions**

Use the completed work sheet from Problem 72-2 to:

CHECK POINT

72-3(b)

Ending amount of capital = $34,680.35

a. Prepare an income statement for the month ended July 31, 20--.
b. Prepare a capital statement for the month ended July 31, 20--.
c. Prepare a balance sheet as of July 31, 20--.

Problem 72-4 may be found in the Working Papers.

Chapter 14

CHECK YOUR READING

1. List the three financial statements you learned to prepare in Chapter 14. List them in the order they should be prepared.
2. Why is it necessary to prepare these financial statements in this order?
3. a. What accounting form is extremely useful in preparing financial statements?
   b. Why is this form useful?
4. a. How does a company determine if there was a net income or net loss for the month?
   b. When does a net loss occur for a company?
5. The value of an owner's investment or worth in a business can be found in the capital account.
   a. What two business activities increase an owner's capital or worth?
   b. What two business activities decrease an owner's capital or worth?

DISCUSSION

1. Your work sheet shows a net income of $1,000.00.
   a. If the Income Statement Debit total is $8,500.00, what is the Income Statement Credit total?
   b. If the Balance Sheet Credit total is $30,000.00, what is the Balance Sheet Debit total?
2. Your work sheet shows a net income of $400.00.
   a. If the Income Statement Credit total is $8,400.00, what is the Income Statement Debit total?
   b. If the Balance Sheet Debit total is $43,800.00, what is the Balance Sheet Credit total?

CRITICAL THINKING

You have learned many times throughout this textbook how important neatness and accuracy are to a record keeper. They are really important when doing a work sheet because so many different types of errors are possible. List five different types of errors that can be made.

COMMUNICATION IN THE WORKPLACE

You are on your first record keeping job as a general ledger clerk. You record in the cash receipts and payments journals, post to the general ledger, and prepare a six-column work sheet. Write a short letter to your record keeping teacher to tell him or her some of the things you learned

REINFORCEMENT ACTIVITIES

in class that you think have helped you on the job. Remind your teacher of who you are in your letter. Keep the letter to 100 words or less.

 FOCUS ON CAREERS

Bring to class 10 want ads for office and record keeping jobs. Find them in your local newspaper or on the Internet. List the titles of those jobs in which the following are required or desired: (1) accuracy, (2) keyboarding/typewriting, (3) previous experience, (4) a high school education, (5) use of computers, and (6) knowledge of record keeping.

 REVIEWING WHAT YOU HAVE LEARNED

On a sheet of paper, write the headings **Statement Number** and **Words**. Next, choose the words that best complete the statements. Write each word you choose next to the statement number it completes. Be careful; not all the words listed should be used.

Statements	Words
1. If your withdrawals are higher than your net income, you have (a, an) _____.	assets
2. The first financial statement to prepare is the _____.	balance due
3. A careful guess is (a, an) _____.	balance sheet
4. To show that debits equal credits in your general ledger accounts, prepare (a, an) _____.	capital
5. The accounting equation is assets equal _____ plus capital.	capital statement
6. Items with money value owned by a business are its _____.	estimate
7. If your estimated taxes are $600.00 and your total tax due is $650.00, you have (a, an) _____ of $50.00.	extended
8. On a work sheet, amounts are _____ from the trial balance columns to the other columns.	income statement
9. The difference between the Income Statement columns on the work sheet is the amount of _____.	liabilities
10. Both beginning and ending capital balances are found on the _____.	net decrease in capital
11. Before preparing your financial statements, it is handy to prepare (a, an) _____.	net income
	net increase in capital
	refund
	revenue
	trial balance
	work sheet

MASTERY PROBLEM

You are a record keeper for Leotta's Engine & Transmission Repair. Leotta Schermer, the owner, separates income into two types: engine repair and transmission repair.

Leotta's account balances as of December 31, 20--, follow:

Acct. No.	Account Title	Balance
110	Cash	$ 4,371.16
120	Supplies	1,779.24
130	Equipment	15,100.00
140	Tools	47,375.00
150	Truck	21,750.00
210	Accounts Payable	19,210.00
220	Sales Tax Payable	4,100.00
310	Leotta Schermer, Capital	51,627.59
320	Leotta Schermer, Drawing	12,500.00
410	Income, Engine Repair	33,950.00
420	Income, Transmission Repair	45,175.50
510	Rent Expense	9,000.00
520	Equipment Repair Expense	5,167.09
530	Heat and Light Expense	7,275.46
540	Telephone Expense	1,510.90
550	Insurance Expense	2,175.00
560	Cleaning Expense	9,378.64
570	Supplies Expense	11,755.17
580	Miscellaneous Expense	4,925.43

Directions

a. Prepare a work sheet for the year ended December 31, 20--. Use your knowledge of normal balance rules to do your trial balance.
b. Prepare an income statement for the year ended December 31, 20--.
c. Prepare a capital statement for the year ended December 31, 20--. Date your beginning capital January 1, 20--.
d. Prepare a balance sheet as of December 31, 20--.
e. Calculate the refund or balance due on Leotta's taxes from the following information:

CHECK POINT

(d)
Total assets = $90,375.40

Estimated tax payments made	$9,950.00
Income tax	$5,690.00
Self-employment tax	net income × 16%

REVIEWING YOUR BUSINESS VOCABULARY

This activity may be found in the Working Papers.

COMPREHENSIVE PROJECT 5

Comprehensive Project 5 has been designed to reinforce major concepts of this and previous chapters. The Comprehensive Project is found in the Working Papers.

A Business Simulation

The following activities are included in the Links Golf Supply simulation:

1. Preparing sales invoices, credit memorandums, and customer statements.
2. Preparing purchase requisitions, price quotation records, and purchase orders.
3. Preparing receiving reports and debit memorandums.
4. Checking purchase invoices.
5. Opening and updating stock records.
6. Reconciling the bank statement with the checkbook.
7. Preparing checks for monthly expenses and for creditor accounts.
8. Endorsing and depositing customer checks.
9. Using and posting from a sales journal, a sales returns and allowances journal, a cash receipts journal, a purchases journal, a purchases returns and allowances journal, and a cash payments journal.
10. Preparing a schedule of accounts receivable, a schedule of accounts payable, a work sheet, an income statement, a capital statement, and a balance sheet.

LINKS GOLF SUPPLY
Daniel H. Passalacqua

MANUAL SIMULATION

FOR USE WITH

SOUTH-WESTERN
KEEPING FINANCIAL RECORDS FOR BUSINESS

Links Golf Supply is a wholesale merchandise operation that sells golf equipment and accessories to retail outlets. This business simulation requires students to use the skills and procedures presented in the second semester of record keeping. Students get hands-on experience preparing and verifying sales invoices, recording in special journals from source documents, posting from special journals, opening and updating stock records, preparing purchasing source documents, preparing financial statements, and more. This simulation is available in manual and automated versions, for use with *Automated Accounting* software.

Chapter **15**

There are many wage plans used to pay workers. Some workers are paid for each hour they work. Others are paid for a fixed number of hours per week. Still others are paid for the number of pieces of work they finish. Many salespeople are paid a percentage of what they sell.

In Chapter 15, you will learn how to handle time cards, compute weekly wages including overtime wages, and use a payroll register. You will also learn how to compute salaries, commissions, and piecework pay. A Calculator Tip will be given for finding regular pay, overtime pay, and gross pay.

Record Keeping for Payroll Clerks: Computing Gross Pay

FOCUS ON TECHNOLOGY

Tracking Employee Start and Stop Times

In Chapter 15, you will learn how employers keep track of when employees start and stop work. Two ways are described in the chapter: using a time clock and using a special machine that reads the badges employees clip to their shirts when they are at work.

Employers use many other ways to record start and stop times today. One way is to use a card much like a credit card. The employee "swipes" the card through a card reader that looks just like a credit card reader. This card reader, however, identifies the employee and then records and displays the date and time instead of a sales amount.

Instead of using an employee card, the employee could also just key his or her employee number into the reader.

Still another way is to use fingerprints. Using fingerprints eliminates having one employee swiping the card of another employee in the machine or from entering another employee's number.

Job 73 HANDLING TIME CARDS

➡ UNDERSTANDING THE JOB

Time clock. A machine that records time worked.

Time card. A record of the hours worked.

Out rack. Where you place your time card when you leave work.

In rack. Where you place your time card when you start work.

Punching in. Having the time printed on your time card when you start work.

Punching out. Having the time printed on your time card when you leave work.

Some businesses use **time clocks** to keep accurate records of the hours each employee works.

Each employee is given a **time card**, like the one shown in Illustration 73A on page 585. Near the time clock, two racks are provided to hold the time cards—an **Out rack** and an **In rack**. Each employee's card is numbered. At the beginning of each week, the payroll clerk arranges the time cards in numerical order in the *Out* rack.

Illustration 73A shows the time card for Rose Reed. Each morning when she arrives, Rose goes to the *Out* rack and removes her card. She inserts the card in the opening in the time clock. The time clock stamps the time on her card. This is called *clocking in* or **punching in**. Look at the In column for Monday on Rose's time card. Notice that the clock has stamped her card for 8:00 a.m. This means that she punched in at 8:00 a.m. on Monday.

After clocking in, Rose takes the time card out of the time clock and puts it in the *In* rack. This shows that she has clocked in for the day's work.

At lunch time, Rose goes to the In rack, removes her card, and inserts it into the clock. The clock prints 12:00 in the first Out column for Monday. This is called *clocking out* or **punching out**. Rose then puts the card in the Out rack to show that she has gone out for lunch.

When she returns from lunch, Rose repeats the steps she went through in the morning. She clocks in and puts her time card in the In

DAY	IN	OUT	IN	OUT	IN	OUT	TOTAL
M	8:00	12:00	1:00	5:00			
T	7:50	12:03	1:00	5:00			
W	7:54	12:04	12:57	5:06			
TH	7:58	12:02	12:58	5:03			
F	8:04	12:07	1:02	5:05			

Name Rose Reed   No. 81

Week Ending May 22, 20--

TOTAL HOURS WORKED

	HOURS	RATE	WAGES
REGULAR			
OVERTIME			
TOTAL			

A time clock records each worker's time in and out.

rack. Rose clocked in at 1:00 p.m. When Rose goes home, she clocks out and puts her time card in the Out rack.

Notice that Rose used her time card four times on Monday. This procedure is repeated daily for the rest of the week.

The other In and Out columns on the time card are used for special situations. For example, an employee may leave to eat dinner and return to work later. Also, an employee may have a dentist appointment or have to run an urgent errand in the afternoon. If the employee returns to work before the day is finished, the other In and Out columns are used.

Rose's employer has these rules for working hours:

1. Employees must start working at 8:00 a.m., go to lunch at 12:00 noon, return by 1:00 p.m., and work until 5:00 p.m.
2. If workers come to work late, their time will be counted from the next quarter hour according to Schedule #1. Notice that in the morning, employees are given a four-minute leeway (up to 8:04) to clock in. Employees are also given a four-minute leeway to clock in after lunch (up to 1:04).

Schedule #1

Morning		Afternoon	
Punches In	Paid From	Punches In	Paid From
8:01- 8:04	8:00	1:01- 1:04	1:00
8:05- 8:15	8:15	1:05- 1:15	1:15
8:16- 8:30	8:30	1:16- 1:30	1:30
8:31- 8:45	8:45	1:31- 1:45	1:45
8:46- 9:00	9:00	1:46- 2:00	2:00
9:01- 9:15	9:15	2:01- 2:15	2:15
9:16- 9:30	9:30	2:16- 2:30	2:30
9:31- 9:45	9:45	2:31- 2:45	2:45
9:46- 10:00	10:00	2:46- 3:00	3:00
And so on			

While companies usually give workers a few minutes leeway for clocking in, they lose a great deal of money when their machines are idle or when workers must wait for latecomers. Leeway is provided for occasional lateness. Continued lateness is a cause for dismissal.

3. If workers must leave early, they will be paid for the time worked through the last quarter of an hour according to Schedule #2:

Schedule #2			
Morning		**Afternoon**	
Punches Out	**Paid To**	**Punches Out**	**Paid To**
9:45- 9:59	9:45	2:45- 2:59	2:45
10:00- 10:14	10:00	3:00- 3:14	3:00
10:15- 10:29	10:15	3:15- 3:29	3:15
10:30- 10:44	10:30	3:30- 3:44	3:30
10:45- 10:59	10:45	3:45- 3:59	3:45
11:00- 11:14	11:00	4:00- 4:14	4:00
11:15- 11:29	11:15	4:15- 4:29	4:15
11:30- 11:44	11:30	4:30- 4:44	4:30
11:45- 11:59	11:45	4:45- 4:59	4:45
And so on			

The payroll clerk figured Rose's time and recorded her hours on the time card shown in Illustration 73B using a set of rules for counting time worked.

These are the rules the payroll clerk used to figure the time that Rose worked:

Monday: Since Rose did not arrive late or leave early on Monday, the payroll clerk found that she worked 8 hours:

From 8:00 a.m. to 12:00 noon = 4 hours (12:00 − 8:00 = 4 hours)
From 1:00 p.m. to 5:00 p.m. = 4 hours (5:00 − 1:00 = 4 hours)

Illustration 73B

Time card showing total hours worked

Name Rose Reed   No. 81

Week Ending May 22, 20--

DAY	IN	OUT	IN	OUT	IN	OUT	TOTAL
M	8:00	12:00	1:00	5:00			8
T	7:50	12:03	1:00	5:00			8
W	7:54	12:04	12:57	5:06			8
TH	7:58	12:02	12:58	5:03			8
F	8:04	12:07	1:02	5:05			8

TOTAL HOURS WORKED			40
	HOURS	**RATE**	**WAGES**
REGULAR			
OVERTIME			
TOTAL			

The payroll clerk added the two amounts together and wrote 8 in the Total column for Monday on Rose's time card.

Tuesday: Rose came to work at 7:50 a.m. However, since she does not start work until 8:00, her time is counted from 8:00 a.m. Rose clocked out at 12:03 for lunch. However, since Rose is paid to work only to 12:00, her time was counted to 12:00. In a large company, many people will wait in line to clock out. It may take a few minutes to reach the time clock.

The payroll clerk figured that Rose worked 8 hours on Tuesday. Check Rose's total hours worked each day to see if you agree with the total hours recorded by the payroll clerk.

Notice that on Friday, Rose clocked in at 8:04. Since 4 minutes are allowed for lateness, she was given 8 hours for the day.

Time cards must be an accurate record of the hours employees work. The record will be used to compute the employees' wages. Also, time cards may be used to prove that employers are meeting government regulations for hours of work and minimum pay.

Most firms have supervisors check the time cards of the employees they supervise. If the supervisors find no errors on the time cards, they sign or initial them and send them to the payroll department.

➡ USING THE COMPUTER

Key Terms

Badge. A special employee card that is read by a badge reader.

Badge reader. A machine that reads employee badges and records the time.

Many businesses now use computers to keep track of employee hours. These firms do not use time cards. Instead, each employee may be given a special coded card or **badge**. On the badge, each employee number is printed in MICR or in another form that the computer can read.

When employees report to and leave work, they insert their badges into a **badge reader**. The badge reader reads the employee number and records the time that each badge was inserted into the machine. The badge reader is connected to a computer.

The computer figures the total hours worked for each employee automatically, using the data recorded by the badge reader. At the end of the week, the computer prints out a list showing the hours each employee worked during the week. The supervisor for each department checks the list for errors. If there are none, the supervisor approves the list by signing it.

➡ SAMPLE PROBLEM

You are the payroll clerk for Rally Games, Inc. The rules for counting time at your company are:

1. There is a five-day workweek starting on Monday and ending on Friday.
2. All employees must start work at 8:00 a.m., leave for lunch at 12:00 noon, return at 1:00 p.m., and work until 5:00 p.m.
3. When employees arrive late, their time is counted from the next quarter hour using Schedule #1 on page 585.

4. Employees who leave early are paid for the time worked through the last quarter hour completed using Schedule #2 on page 586.

You use these rules to find the hours worked by employees during the week of August 14, 20--. Illustration 73C (below) shows how you completed the first time card.

Here are the steps you would follow to find the hours worked by Tony Gito for the week ending August 14, 20--:

STEP 1 Compute the total hours worked each day.

For each day, find the hours worked until lunchtime. Then find the hours worked during the afternoon. Add the two amounts together to get the total hours worked for the day.

Monday
Tony punched in at 7:58 a.m., but is paid from 8:00 a.m. He also left for lunch at 12:02 p.m., but is only paid until 12:00 noon. To find the hours worked Monday morning, subtract the time that Tony started work (8:00) from the time he stopped work for lunch (12:00):

$$12:00 - 8:00 = 4 \text{ hours}$$

Tony punched in at 12:56 p.m., but is paid from 1:00 p.m. He punched out at 5:04 p.m., but is paid only until 5:00 p.m. To find the hours worked Monday afternoon, subtract the time that Tony began work after lunch (1:00) from the time he stopped work (5:00):

$$5:00 - 1:00 = 4 \text{ hours}$$

The total number of hours Tony worked Monday is 4 + 4 = 8 hours.

Tuesday
On Tuesday morning, Tony punched in late, at 9:48 a.m. According to

Illustration 73C

Time card showing total hours daily and for the week.

| Name | Tony Gito | | | | | No. | 34 |

Week Ending __August 14, 20--__   STEP 1

DAY	IN	OUT	IN	OUT	IN	OUT	TOTAL
M	7:58	12:02	12:56	5:04			8
T	9:48	12:03	12:56	5:07			6
W	8:09	12:02	1:48	5:05			6¾
TH	7:57	11:09	1:03	5:04			7
F	9:19	12:03	12:54	4:35			6

STEP 2

| TOTAL HOURS WORKED | | 33¾ |

STEP 3

	HOURS	RATE	WAGES
REGULAR			
OVERTIME			
TOTAL			

Schedule #1, he should be paid from 10:00 a.m. Although he left at 12:03, he is paid only to 12:00 noon. His time for the morning is:

$$12:00 - 10:00 = 2 \text{ hours}$$

On Tuesday afternoon, Tony worked a normal 4 hours. Although he punched in at 12:56, he is only paid from 1:00 p.m. Although he punched out at 5:07, he is only paid to 5:00 p.m. His time for the afternoon is:

$$5:00 - 1:00 = 4 \text{ hours}$$

Tony worked 2 + 4 , or 6 hours on Tuesday.

Wednesday

On Wednesday morning, Tony punched in late, at 8:09 a.m. According to Schedule #1, he should be paid from 8:15 a.m. Although he punched out for lunch at 12:02, he is only paid to 12:00 noon. His time for the morning is:

$$12:00 - 8:15 = 3 \text{ hours and } 45 \text{ minutes, or } 3\tfrac{3}{4} \text{ hours}$$

On Wednesday afternoon, Tony punched in late, returning from lunch at 1:48 p.m. According to Schedule #1, he should be paid from 2:00 p.m. Although he punched out at 5:05, he should be paid only to 5:00 p.m. His time for the afternoon is:

$$5:00 - 2:00 = 3 \text{ hours}$$

Tony worked 3¾ + 3, or 6¾ hours on Wednesday.

Thursday

On Thursday morning, Tony should be paid from 8:00 a.m. He punched out early for lunch, at 11:09. According to Schedule #2, he should be paid until 11:00. His time for the morning is:

$$11:00 - 8:00 = 3 \text{ hours}$$

On Thursday afternoon, Tony punched in at 1:03 p.m., but according to Schedule #1, should be paid from 1:00 p.m. because of the four-minute leeway. He punched out at 5:04 but should only be paid until 5:00 p.m. His time for the afternoon is:

$$5:00 - 1:00 = 4 \text{ hours}$$

Tony worked 3 + 4, or 7 hours on Thursday.

Friday

Tony reported late for work, at 9:19 a.m. According to Schedule #1, he should be paid starting at 9:30 a.m. Although he left at 12:03 for lunch, he should be paid only to 12:00 noon. His time for the morning is:

$$12:00 - 9:30 = 2 \text{ hours and } 30 \text{ minutes, or } 2\tfrac{1}{2} \text{ hours}$$

Tony punched in after lunch at 12:54, but should be paid starting at 1:00 p.m. He punched out early in the afternoon, at 4:35. According to Schedule #2, he should be paid until 4:30 p.m. His time for the afternoon is:

$$4:30 - 1:00 = 3 \text{ hours and } 30 \text{ minutes, or } 3\tfrac{1}{2} \text{ hours}$$

Tony worked $2\tfrac{1}{2} + 3\tfrac{1}{2}$, or 6 hours on Friday.

STEP 2 Enter the total hours worked each day in the proper column on the time card.

As soon as you find the total hours worked on Monday (8 hours), record 8 in the Total column for Monday. In the same way, enter the total hours worked for every day of the week.

STEP 3 Total the hours for the week.

When you finish entering each daily total, add them to find the total for the week. Enter the weekly total ($33\tfrac{3}{4}$ hours) on the Total Hours Worked line of the time card. You will learn how to finish the rest of the card in the next job.

➡ BUILDING YOUR BUSINESS VOCABULARY

On a sheet of paper, write the headings **Statement Number** and **Words**. Next, choose the words that match the statements. Write each word you choose next to the statement number it matches. Be careful; not all the words listed should be used.

Statements	Words
1. A record of the hours worked by an employee	badge
2. A machine that records a worker's time in and out on a time card	badge reader
	employee
3. Having the time printed on your time card when you arrive at work	employer
	in rack
4. Having the time printed on your time card when you leave work	out rack
	punching in
5. A business that hires people	punching out
6. A machine that reads special employee badges and records the time	terms
	time card
	time clock
7. Where you place your time card when you start work	
8. Where you place your time card when you leave work	
9. A special employee card that is read by a badge reader	

STEPS REVIEW: Handling Time Cards

STEP 1 Compute the total hours worked each day.

STEP 2 Enter the total hours worked each day in the proper column on the time card.

STEP 3 Total the hours for the week.

You are a payroll clerk at ABL Products, Inc. The rules in your office are:

CHECK POINT

73-1

(#1)
Total hours worked = 40
(#2)
Total hours worked = 37½

1. Operating hours: Employees start work at 8:00 a.m., leave for lunch at 12:00 noon, return by 1:00 p.m., and work until 5:00 p.m.
2. When employees arrive late, their time is counted from the next quarter hour. (Use Schedule #1 on page 585.)
3. When employees leave early, they are paid for the time they worked through the last quarter hour. (Use Schedule #2 on page 586.)

Directions

a. For each time card, compute the number of hours the employee worked for each day and enter the number in the Total column.
b. Find each employee's total number of hours worked for the week and enter that number on the Total Hours Worked line.

Card #1

DAY	IN	OUT	IN	OUT	IN	OUT	TOTAL
M	8:00	12:02	1:00	5:03			
T	7:57	12:03	1:01	5:03			
W	7:55	12:04	12:54	5:01			
TH	8:02	12:01	1:00	5:02			
F	7:56	12:00	1:03	5:01			

TOTAL HOURS WORKED

Card #2

DAY	IN	OUT	IN	OUT	IN	OUT	TOTAL
M	8:06	12:02	12:59	5:01			
T	7:57	11:56	12:58	5:02			
W	7:58	12:01	12:56	5:02			
TH	8:00	12:00	1:01	3:02			
F	7:55	12:01	12:57	5:04			

TOTAL HOURS WORKED

Card #3

DAY	IN	OUT	IN	OUT	IN	OUT	TOTAL
M	8:02	12:02	2:02	5:04			
T	7:57	12:01	1:01	4:30			
W	7:56	12:02	12:56	4:50			
TH	7:58	12:01	12:55	5:03			
F	7:59	12:01	1:03	5:05			

TOTAL HOURS WORKED

Card #4

DAY	IN	OUT	IN	OUT	IN	OUT	TOTAL
M	7:55	11:08	12:58	5:01			
T	9:08	12:02	12:58	5:01			
W	7:59	12:02	12:59	4:41			
TH	8:27	12:01	12:58	5:02			
F	8:03	12:02	12:59	5:01			

TOTAL HOURS WORKED

Card #5

DAY	IN	OUT	IN	OUT	IN	OUT	TOTAL
M	7:57	10:48	1:01	5:01			
T	8:00	12:00	12:59	3:57			
W	7:54	12:02	12:56	5:03			
TH	8:01	12:02	1:00	4:35			
F	7:57	12:01	12:55	5:04			
TOTAL HOURS WORKED							

Card #6

DAY	IN	OUT	IN	OUT	IN	OUT	TOTAL
M	9:14	12:01	1:00	5:02			
T	9:01	12:02	12:58	5:01			
W	7:57	12:00	1:00	5:02			
TH	9:17	12:02	12:57	5:01			
F	8:01	12:01	12:59	5:03			
TOTAL HOURS WORKED							

Card #7

DAY	IN	OUT	IN	OUT	IN	OUT	TOTAL
M	7:59	12:02	1:58	5:01			
T	8:35	12:01	12:57	5:00			
W	7:59	12:00	1:04	5:02			
TH	8:01	11:25	12:59	5:03			
F	7:58	12:01	12:58	2:50			
TOTAL HOURS WORKED							

Card #8

DAY	IN	OUT	IN	OUT	IN	OUT	TOTAL
M	7:57	12:02	12:58	5:04			
T	8:02	12:00	1:03	4:05			
W	7:55	12:02	12:56	4:48			
TH	8:02	12:01	12:58	5:02			
F	7:59	11:55	1:01	5:03			
TOTAL HOURS WORKED							

Job 74 COMPUTING HOURLY WAGES

applied math preview

Copy and complete these problems.

1.	2.	3.	4.	5.
$8\frac{1}{2}$	$2\frac{1}{2}$	$7\frac{3}{4}$	$8.70	$12.40
$7\frac{1}{2}$	$11\frac{1}{2}$	$4\frac{1}{4}$	$\times 37\frac{1}{2}$	$\times 38\frac{1}{4}$
$10\frac{1}{4}$	$8\frac{1}{4}$	$8\frac{3}{4}$		
7	$4\frac{3}{4}$	$7\frac{3}{4}$		
$+3\frac{1}{4}$	$+6\frac{1}{2}$	$+1\frac{1}{2}$		

key terms preview

- Commission pay
- Gross pay
- Hourly pay
- Piecework pay
- Weekly pay

goal

To learn how to compute the weekly wages of employees.

UNDERSTANDING THE JOB

You now know how to find the total hours worked by an employee. However, this is only the first step in computing a worker's wages. To find a worker's earnings, the payroll clerk must know the wage plan the employer uses to pay the employee.

There are many wage plans used to pay workers. Some workers are paid for each hour they work. These workers are paid on an **hourly pay** plan. Others are paid for a fixed number of hours per week. These workers are paid on a **weekly pay** plan. Still others are paid for the number of pieces of work they finish. These workers are paid on a **piecework pay** plan. Many salespeople are paid a percentage of what they sell. They are paid on a **commission pay** plan.

In this job, you will learn how to compute wages on an hourly basis.

SAMPLE PROBLEM

Hourly pay. Pay workers for each hour they work.

Weekly pay. Pay workers for a fixed number of hours per week.

Piecework pay. Pay workers for each piece of work finished.

Commission pay. Pay workers a percentage of what they sell.

You are still the payroll clerk for Rally Games, Inc., from Job 73. Lee Barr has been hired to work for the company at the rate of $9.50 per hour. You use the same rules for counting time as shown in Schedule #1 and Schedule #2 in Job 73.

Lee's completed time card for the week ending April 12, 20--, is shown in Illustration 74A on page 594. These are the steps you would follow to find the total pay earned by Lee for the week:

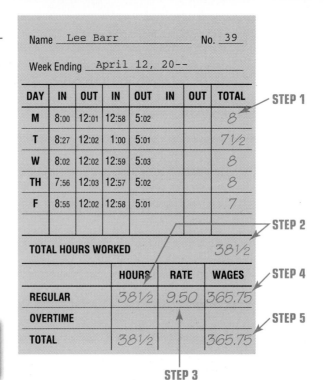

Name Lee Barr   No. 39

Week Ending April 12, 20--

DAY	IN	OUT	IN	OUT	IN	OUT	TOTAL
M	8:00	12:01	12:58	5:02			8
T	8:27	12:02	1:00	5:01			7½
W	8:02	12:02	12:59	5:03			8
TH	7:56	12:03	12:57	5:02			8
F	8:55	12:02	12:58	5:01			7

STEP 1

STEP 2

TOTAL HOURS WORKED			38½
	HOURS	RATE	WAGES
REGULAR	38½	9.50	365.75
OVERTIME			
TOTAL	38½		365.75

STEP 4

STEP 5

STEP 3

Key Terms

Gross pay. Total wages.

Tips

*Hourly rate x Hours
worked = Gross pay*

STEP 1 Enter the hours worked for each day on the time card.

Compute the hours worked for each day and enter each amount in the
Total column of the time card.

STEP 2 Find the total hours for the week.

Add the total hours worked each day and enter the total (38½ hours) on the
Total Hours Worked line of the time card. Also record the total weekly
hours in the Regular Hours box at the bottom of the card.

STEP 3 Enter the rate per hour.

Lee is paid $9.50 an hour. Enter this amount in the Regular Rate box at
the bottom of the time card.

STEP 4 Compute the weekly wages.

Find Lee's total weekly wages, or **gross pay**, for the week by multiplying
the hourly rate by the total hours worked:

$$\$9.50 \times 38\tfrac{1}{2} = \$365.75$$

Enter the gross pay amount in the Regular Wages box of the time
card.

STEP 5 Enter the amounts on the Total line for the Hours and Wages columns.

Enter the total weekly hours worked (38½ hours) and the total
weekly wages ($365.75) on the Total line at the bottom of the card.

BUILDING YOUR BUSINESS VOCABULARY

On a sheet of paper, write the headings **Statement Number** and **Words**. Next, choose the words that match the statements. Write each word you choose next to the statement number it matches. Be careful; not all the words listed should be used.

Statements	Words
1. A wage plan that pays workers for each piece of work finished	badge
	badge reader
2. A wage plan that pays workers for each hour they work	commission pay
3. A wage plan that pays workers a percentage of what they sell	gross pay
	hourly pay
4. A record of the hours worked by an employee	piecework pay
5. A machine that records a worker's time in and out on a time card	punching in
	punching out
6. Having the time printed on your time card when you arrive at work	time card
	time clock
7. A machine that reads special employee badges and records the time	weekly pay
8. A special employee card that is read by a badge reader	
9. Total wages	
10. A wage plan that pays workers for a fixed number of hours per week.	

STEPS REVIEW: Computing Hourly Wages

STEP 1 Enter the hours worked for each day on the time card.

STEP 2 Find the total hours for the week.

STEP 3 Enter the rate per hour.

STEP 4 Compute the weekly wages.

STEP 5 Enter the amounts on the Total line for the Hours and Wages columns.

APPLICATION PROBLEMS

Problem 74-1   You are the payroll clerk for Leland Nursing Center.

Directions
Find the gross pay for each worker.

CHECK POINT

74-1(1)

Gross Pay = $424.00

Name of Worker	Hours Worked	Rate Per Hour		Gross Pay	
1. Cleo Agano	40	10	60		
2. Ronald Berne	39	9	25		
3. Makina Crend	38	11	70		
4. Reginald Davids	37 1/2	8	80		
5. Lois Erthal	38 1/4	9	80		
6. Lu Feng	36 3/4	10	70		
7. Louise Greer	39 1/4	8	90		
8. Alan Hall	37 1/4	9	40		

You are the payroll clerk for Mellico Marts, Inc.

Directions

Find the gross pay for each worker.

Name of Worker	Hours Worked	Rate Per Hour		Gross Pay
1. Ave Angotti	37 1/4	8	40	
2. Harold Benson	38 1/2	9	90	
3. Anne Charles	39 1/4	12	50	
4. Regis Davis	35 1/2	10	38	
5. Nancy Ellers	36 1/4	9	85	
6. Clyde Franke	37 1/2	8	74	
7. Darlene Godo	38 1/4	9	76	
8. Thomas Hatcher	32 3/4	12	68	

Problem 74-3 You are the payroll clerk for Watson Motor Company.

Directions

Complete the following time cards by finding the hours worked each day, the total hours worked for the week, and the gross pay for each worker. Use Schedules #1 and #2 from Job 73 to figure the hours worked each day.

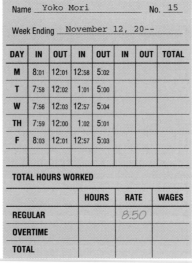

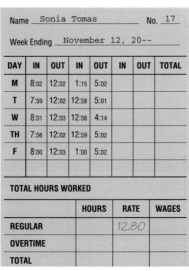

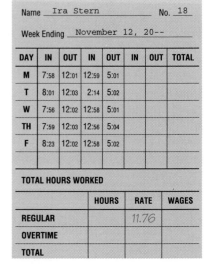

applied math preview

Copy and complete the following problems.

1.	2.	3.	4.	5.
8¼	10½	6¼	$ 9.70	$12.88
6½	4¼	7¾	×37½	×35¼
5¼	12½	8½		
9½	6¼	3½		
+2¼	+11¼	+12½		

key terms preview

• **Payroll register**

goal

To learn how to record time card data in a payroll register.

UNDERSTANDING THE JOB

After hours and wages have been recorded on time cards, payroll clerks may post the data at the end of the week to a **payroll register**.

SAMPLE PROBLEM

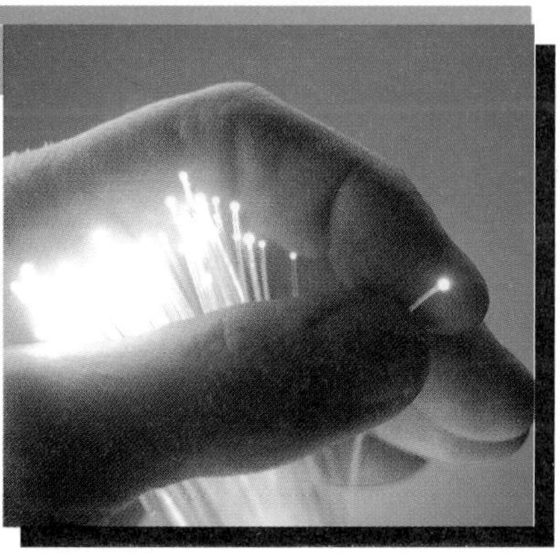

Key Terms

Payroll register. Record of wages earned by employees.

You are a payroll clerk for Craig Technology, Inc. At the end of the week, you took all the time cards and computed the hours and wages for each employee. Illustration 75A on page 598 shows two cards that you completed. Illustration 75B shows how the payroll register looked after you posted the data from the time cards to the payroll register.

Here are the steps you took to record time card data in the payroll register:

STEP 1   **Enter the data from each time card.**

Notice that the hours worked each day by each employee have been entered. Some payroll clerks do not enter the hours for each day in the payroll register. They enter only the weekly total for each employee.

Name	Drew Loften					No. 22
Week Ending	June 24, 20--					

DAY	IN	OUT	IN	OUT	IN	OUT	TOTAL
M	8:03	12:02	12:56	5:01			8
T	7:58	12:03	1:01	5:02			8
W	7:57	12:04	12:58	5:04			8
TH	8:02	12:00	1:02	5:03			8
F	7:56	12:01	12:57	5:02			8
TOTAL HOURS WORKED							40

	HOURS	RATE	WAGES
REGULAR	40	10.50	420.00
OVERTIME			
TOTAL	40		420.00

Name	Esteban Barba					No. 23
Week Ending	June 24, 20--					

DAY	IN	OUT	IN	OUT	IN	OUT	TOTAL
M	7:58	12:03	1:01	5:01			8
T	7:59	12:02	12:57	5:03			8
W	7:56	12:01	12:59	5:01			8
TH	8:01	12:02	12:58	4:03			7
F	7:54	12:05	12:59	5:04			8
TOTAL HOURS WORKED							39

	HOURS	RATE	WAGES
REGULAR	39	11.60	452.40
OVERTIME			
TOTAL	39		452.40

Illustration 75A

Completed time cards

STEP 2 Total and rule the Gross Pay column.

After the data from each time card have been entered, you ruled and footed the Gross Pay column of the register. You then re-added the column and recorded the final total. You drew a double ruling under the final total and wrote the word *Total* in the Name of Employee column. You will use a new page in the payroll register for each week.

→ USING THE COMPUTER TO MAINTAIN PAYROLL

If Craig Technology, Inc., used a computer to maintain payroll records, your job would be somewhat different. If a badge system were used to record employee time, the computer would compute employee time and create the payroll register automatically. There would be no need to keep time cards, compute time cards, or record time card data in a payroll register.

If time cards were used along with a computer, you would still have to find the total hours worked for each employee. Then, you would log on to your computer by keying your employee number, password, and the date.

Illustration 75B

Payroll register with entries

PAYROLL REGISTER   WEEK ENDING *June 24, 20--*

	CARD NO.	NAME OF EMPLOYEE	HOURS WORKED					TOTAL HOURS WORKED	PAY PER HOUR	GROSS PAY	
			M	T	W	TH	F				
1	22	Drew Loften	8	8	8	8	8	40	10 50	420 00	1
2	23	Esteban Barba	8	8	8	7	8	39	11 60	452 40	2
3		Total								872 40	3

STEP 1

STEP 2

After you logged on, the computer screen might look like this:

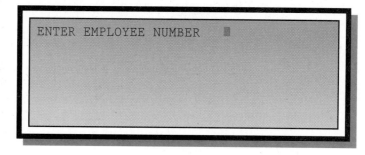

```
ENTER EMPLOYEE NUMBER    ▮
```

The computer is asking you to enter the number of the first employee. You would key the employee number from the first time card (Drew Loften's card). The screen would then change to

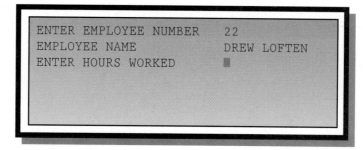

```
ENTER EMPLOYEE NUMBER    22
EMPLOYEE NAME            DREW LOFTEN
ENTER HOURS WORKED       ▮
```

Notice that when you keyed in the employee number, the computer checked its files and displayed Drew Loften's name on the screen. This saved you from having to key the name, and it also let you check to make sure that you keyed the correct number.

The computer is now asking you to key the number of hours that Drew worked. You would check the card and key 40. You would not have to enter the employee's rate of pay. This information would already be in the computer's files. The computer would automatically figure the total weekly wages and then ask you for the next employee number.

So, the only items to enter for each time card are the employee number and the total hours worked. The computer does the rest.

BUILDING YOUR BUSINESS VOCABULARY

On a sheet of paper, write the headings **Statement Number** and **Words**. Next, choose the words that match the statements. Write each word you choose next to the statement number it matches. Be careful; not all the words listed should be used.

Statements	Words
1. To transfer data from one record to another	data
2. A wage plan that pays a worker so much for each piece of work completed	gross pay
3. Information	hourly pay
4. A record of wages earned by employees	payroll register
5. A wage plan that pays a worker so much for each hour worked	piecework pay
6. A machine that records a worker's time in and out on a time card	post
	punching in
	punching out
	time clock
	weekly pay

7. Having the time printed on your time
card when you arrive at work
8. Total wages

STEPS REVIEW: Using a Payroll Register

STEP 1 Enter the data from each time card.

STEP 2 Total and rule the Gross Pay column.

APPLICATION PROBLEMS

Problem 75-1 You are the payroll clerk for O'Brien's Diving Equipment, Inc.

CHECK POINT

75-1(d)

Total Gross Pay =
$2,362.78

Gross pay = hours worked × pay per hour

Directions

a. Copy the data for the week ending September 24, 20--, into a payroll register.

Card No.	Name of Employee	M	T	W	TH	F	Pay Per Hour
1	Tom Adler	8	7	8	7	8	$ 9.50
2	Rose Berner	7½	8	7	8	7½	10.50
3	Tien Chou	8	6¼	8	7	8	12.20
4	Della D'Amato	6½	7	8	7	8	10.70
5	Rob Edgar	7¾	8	6½	7½	8	8.90
6	Gina Flora	8	7½	7	7½	8	11.10

b. Find and enter the total hours worked for each employee in the Total Hours Worked column of the payroll register.
c. Find and enter the gross pay for each employee in the Gross Pay column of the register.
d. Find the total wages for the week (total of the Gross Pay column).

Problem 75-2 You are the payroll clerk for B & C Rug Company.

CHECK POINT

75-2(d)

Total Gross Pay =
$2,196.00

Directions

a. Copy the data for the week ending February 12, 20--, into a payroll register.

Card No.	Name of Employee	M	T	W	TH	F	Pay Per Hour
1	Dell Grant	6	7	7	7½	7¼	$ 8.60
2	Mia Hull	8	6½	8	7½	8	9.70
3	Carl Ingres	7	7	6½	7¼	7¼	11.30
4	Regeana Jarden	7½	8	7	6¼	6½	8.40
5	Edwin Klein	7½	7¼	7½	8½	6	9.80
6	Brad LaMont	8	8	7½	6½	7¼	12.80

b. Find and enter the total hours worked for each employee in the Total Hours Worked column of the payroll register.
c. Find and enter the gross pay for each employee in the Gross Pay column of the register.
d. Find the total wages for the week (Total of the Gross Pay column).

Problem 75-3 may be found in the Working Papers.

Job 76   COMPUTING OVERTIME

applied math preview

Copy and complete these problems.

1.	2.	3.	
$8\frac{1}{4}$	$5\frac{1}{4}$	$12\frac{1}{2}$	4. $\$10.00 \times 1\frac{1}{2} =$
$10\frac{1}{2}$	$14\frac{1}{2}$	$5\frac{3}{4}$	5. $\$ 8.70 \times 1\frac{1}{2} =$
$6\frac{3}{4}$	$7\frac{3}{4}$	$11\frac{1}{2}$	6. $\$14.35 \times 1\frac{1}{2} =$
$2\frac{3}{4}$	$4\frac{1}{2}$	$2\frac{3}{4}$	7. $\$12.64 \times 1\frac{1}{2} =$
$+ 10\frac{1}{4}$	$+ 5\frac{3}{4}$	$+ 8\frac{1}{4}$	8. $\$12.55 \times 1\frac{1}{2} =$
			9. $\$ 8.85 \times 1\frac{1}{2} =$

key terms preview

- Overtime
- Overtime rate of pay
- Regular time
- Regular time rate of pay

goals

1. To learn what overtime means.
2. To learn how to compute the overtime rate.
3. To learn how to compute gross pay including overtime.

➡ UNDERSTANDING THE JOB

Key Terms

Regular time rate of pay. Rate of pay for first 40 hours in a week.

Overtime rate of pay. Rate of pay for any hours beyond 40 hours in a week.

Regular time. First 40 hours of work in a week.

Overtime. Time worked beyond 40 hours in a week.

Tips

Overtime rate =
regular rate $\times 1\frac{1}{2}$

Federal and state laws or union agreements may require that employers pay employees extra if they work more than a certain number of hours in a week. For example, employees may be paid a **regular time rate of pay** for working 40 hours in a week. If they work more than 40 hours in a week, they must be paid an **overtime rate of pay**. In that case, the first 40 hours of the week are called **regular time** and the hours beyond 40 are called **overtime**.

For many workers, the overtime rate that they are paid is $1\frac{1}{2}$ (1.5) times the regular rate. This means that if they are paid $6.00 for each regular hour, they will be paid $9.00 for each overtime hour they work:

$6.00 (regular time rate of pay) $\times$ 1.5 = $9.00 (overtime rate of pay)

Some businesses pay overtime if employees work more than a certain number of hours in a day. For example, employees may be paid overtime if they work more than 8 hours in one day. In this job, you will learn how to compute overtime only for employees who work more than 40 hours in one week.

Employees are paid overtime only if the extra time that they work is authorized by their employers. Employees cannot simply stay on after their normal day in order to earn overtime pay without the approval of their employers.

Figuring overtime hours is much like figuring regular time hours. The same schedules you have already used for punching in and punching out are followed.

You are the payroll clerk for Steifen Lens Company. Joe Carenza is hired at a regular hourly rate of $11.80. Overtime at Steifen is paid at 1½ times the regular hourly rate. Illustration 76A shows Joe's completed time card at the end of his first week.

Here are the steps to follow to find Joe's gross pay:

STEP 1 **Find the total hours worked each day.**

Find the total hours worked each day and record the amounts in the Total column of the time card.

STEP 2 **Find the total hours worked for the week.**

Add the hours worked each day to find the total hours worked for the week. Enter this amount on the Total Hours Worked line of the time card.

STEP 3 **Find the total overtime hours.**

If the total hours worked for the week are more than 40, you must find the number of overtime hours the employee worked. To do this, subtract 40 hours (the total number of regular hours) from the total hours worked:

43	(total hours worked in week)
− 40	(total regular hours)
3	(total overtime hours)

Total hours − Regular hours = Overtime hours

Illustration 76A

Completed time card showing overtime

Name __Joseph Carenza__ No. __15__

Week Ending __March 15, 20--__   ⟋ STEP 1

DAY	IN	OUT	IN	OUT	IN	OUT	TOTAL
M	7:59	12:03	12:57	5:03			8
T	7:58	12:03	12:59	6:04			9
W	7:57	12:02	12:56	6:01			9
TH	7:59	12:00	1:02	5:02			8
F	8:02	12:01	12:59	6:04			9

⟋ STEP 2

TOTAL HOURS WORKED			43

| | HOURS | RATE | WAGES | ⟋ STEP 4
|---|---|---|---|
| REGULAR | 40 | 11.80 | 472.00 | ⟋ STEP 6
| OVERTIME | 3 | 17.70 | 53.10 | ⟋ STEP 7
| TOTAL | 43 | | 525.10 |

STEP 3 ⟋   STEP 5

Enter the number of regular hours (40) in the box for regular hours.
Enter the number of overtime hours (3) in the box for overtime hours.
Enter the total number of hours (43) in the box for total hours worked.

STEP 4 Find the amount of regular pay.

Regular rate ×
Regular hours =
Regular pay

Enter Joe's regular hourly rate of pay ($11.80) in the Regular Rate box of the time card. Then multiply the regular rate by the number of regular hours (40) to find Joe's regular pay:

$$
\begin{array}{ll}
\$\ 11.80 & \text{(regular rate)} \\
\underline{\times\quad 40} & \text{(regular hours)} \\
\$\ 472.00 & \text{(regular pay)}
\end{array}
$$

Enter the amount of regular pay ($472.00) in the Regular Wages box.

STEP 5 Find the overtime rate of pay.

Multiply the regular rate of pay ($11.80) by 1.5 to find the overtime rate of pay:

$$\$11.80 \times 1.5 = \$17.70 \text{ (overtime rate of pay)}$$

Enter the overtime rate of pay in the Overtime Rate box.

STEP 6 Find the amount of overtime pay.

Multiply the overtime rate of pay ($17.70) by the number of overtime hours (3) to find the amount of overtime pay:

$$
\begin{array}{ll}
\$\ 17.70 & \text{(overtime rate)} \\
\underline{\times\quad 3} & \text{(overtime hours)} \\
\$\ 53.10 & \text{(overtime pay)}
\end{array}
$$

Do not round off over-
time rates of pay.

Enter the amount of overtime pay in the Overtime Wages box.

Sometimes the overtime rate of pay does not come out evenly. For example, if Joe's regular rate of pay had been $11.85, his overtime rate of pay would have been $11.85 × 1.5 = $17.775. When this happens, do not round off the overtime rate of pay. You may round off to the nearest cent only after you have multiplied the number of overtime hours by the overtime rate:

$$
\begin{array}{ll}
\$\ 17.775 & \text{(overtime rate)} \\
\underline{\times\quad 3} & \text{(overtime hours)} \\
\$\ 53.325\ , \text{ or } \$53.33 & \text{(overtime pay)}
\end{array}
$$

STEP 7 Find the gross pay.

Find Joe's gross pay for the week by adding the amount of regular pay and the amount of overtime pay:

$$
\begin{array}{ll}
\$\ 472.00 & \text{(regular pay)} \\
\underline{+\quad 53.10} & \text{(overtime pay)} \\
\$\ 525.10 & \text{(gross pay)}
\end{array}
$$

Enter the amount of Joe's gross pay ($525.10) in the Total Wages box.

Calculator
Tips

Many record keepers use calculators to find regular pay, overtime pay, and gross pay. If you wanted to use a calculator to find these amounts for Joe Carenza, here is how you would do it:

STEP 1 ▶ *Multiply the regular time hours by the regular rate of pay.*

Press these keys in order:

$$\boxed{4}\ \boxed{0}\ \boxed{\times}\ \boxed{1}\ \boxed{1}\ \boxed{.}\ \boxed{8}\ \boxed{=}$$

The answer, 472.00, will appear in the display. This is Joe's regular time pay. Enter this in the box for regular wages on the time card.

STEP 2 ▶ *Add regular time pay to memory.*

Press the M+ key to add regular pay ($472.00) to memory.

STEP 3 ▶ *Find the overtime rate of pay.*

Multiply the regular rate of pay, $11.80, by 1.5. Press these keys in order:

$$\boxed{1}\ \boxed{1}\ \boxed{.}\ \boxed{8}\ \boxed{\times}\ \boxed{1}\ \boxed{.}\ \boxed{5}\ \boxed{=}$$

The answer, 17.70, will appear in the display. This is Joe's overtime rate of pay. Enter this in the box for overtime rate on the time card.

STEP 4 ▶ *Find the amount of overtime pay.*

Now, without clearing the calculator, multiply the overtime rate by the number of overtime hours (3). Press these keys in order:

$$\boxed{\times}\ \boxed{3}\ \boxed{=}$$

The answer, 53.10, will appear in the display. Enter this amount in the box for overtime wages on the time card.

STEP 5 ▶ *Add the amount of overtime pay to memory.*

Without clearing the calculator, press the M+ key.

STEP 6 ▶ *Display the amount of gross pay.*

Without clearing memory, press the MR key or the MR/C key once. The amount of gross pay, 525.10, will appear in the display. Enter this amount in the box for total wages on the time card.

Now clear memory for the next problem by pressing the MC key or the MR/C key again.

⇨ BUILDING YOUR BUSINESS VOCABULARY

On a sheet of paper, write the headings **Statement Number** and **Words**. Next, choose the words that match the statements. Write each word you choose next to the statement number it matches. Be careful; not all the words listed should be used.

Statements	Words
1. Time worked beyond 40 hours in a week	badge reader
2. The first 40 hours worked in a week	gross pay
3. A record of wages earned by employees	overtime
4. The rate of pay for the first 40 hours in a week	overtime rate of pay
5. The rate of pay for any hours beyond 40 hours in a week	payroll register
6. Total wages	piecework pay
7. A machine that records a worker's time in and out on a time card	regular time
	regular time rate of pay
	time clock

STEPS REVIEW: Computing Gross Pay Including Overtime

STEP 1 Find the total hours worked each day.

STEP 2 Find the total hours worked for the week.

STEP 3 Find the total overtime hours.

STEP 4 Find the amount of regular pay.

STEP 5 Find the overtime rate of pay.

STEP 6 Find the amount of overtime pay.

STEP 7 Find the gross pay.

Tips

Do not round off overtime rates.

APPLICATION PROBLEMS

Problem 76-1 You are the payroll clerk for Hudson Cement Co. The company pays an overtime rate of 1½ times the regular rate for all hours worked by an employee beyond 40 hours in one week.

Spreadsheet

Directions

a. Copy and complete the following table. The first employee's wages have been computed for you as an example.

Card No.	Total Hours Worked	Regular Time Rate	Regular Hours	Overtime Hours	Regular Time Pay	Overtime Rate	Overtime Pay	Gross Pay
1	42	9 20	40	2	368 00	13 800	27 60	395 60
2	51	8 90						
3	48	11 80						
4	43	12 50						
5	46	7 90						
6	44	9 60						
7	50	9 75						
8	47	10 87						
9	49	11 55						
10	41	12 73						

CHECK POINT

76-1(c)

Total of Gross Pay
column = $5,128.42

b. Foot these columns: Regular Time Pay, Overtime Pay, Gross Pay.
c. Check the totals by crossfooting. The totals of the Regular Time Pay and Overtime Pay columns together should equal the total of the Gross Pay column.

Problem 76-2   You are the payroll clerk for Woodson Publishing Company. The company pays an overtime rate of $1\frac{1}{2}$ times the regular rate for all hours worked by an employee beyond 40 hours in one week.

Directions

a. Copy and complete the following table. Remember not to round off overtime rates of pay.

Card No.	Total Hours Worked	Regular Time Rate	Regular Hours	Overtime Hours	Regular Time Pay	Overtime Rate	Overtime Pay	Gross Pay
1	49	8 93						
2	46	8 57						
3	53	12 53						
4	51	11 79						
5	44	9 71						
6	$41\frac{1}{4}$	9 60						
7	$48\frac{1}{2}$	9 70						
8	$47\frac{1}{4}$	10 80						
9	$50\frac{3}{4}$	11 50						
10	$43\frac{1}{2}$	12 70						

CHECK POINT

76-2(c)

Total of Gross Pay
column = $5,439.28

b. Foot these columns: Regular Time Pay, Overtime Pay, Gross Pay.
c. Check the totals by crossfooting. The totals of the Regular Time Pay and Overtime Pay columns together should equal the total of the Gross Pay column.

Problem 76-3 may be found in the Working Papers.

applied math preview

Copy and complete the following problems. Do not round your answers.

1. $5\frac{1}{4}$	2. $\$\ 9.90 \times 1\frac{1}{2} =$
$7\frac{1}{2}$	3. $\$\ 7.40 \times 1\frac{1}{2} =$
$6\frac{3}{4}$	4. $\$12.27 \times 1\frac{1}{2} =$
$8\frac{1}{4}$	5. $\$13.26 \times 1\frac{1}{2} =$
$+\ 12\frac{3}{4}$	6. $\$11.48 \times 1\frac{1}{2} =$
	7. $\$10.95 \times 1\frac{1}{2} =$

goal

To learn how to record overtime pay in a payroll register.

UNDERSTANDING THE JOB

In this job, you will use a payroll register with columns for regular time pay and overtime pay. The payroll register is shown in Illustrations 77B and 77C on page 609.

SAMPLE PROBLEM

You are the payroll clerk for the Slyvan Brass Company. The company pays overtime for all hours worked beyond 40 hours in one week.

Iona Carr is hired by the company at an hourly rate of $12.75. Illustration 77A on page 608 shows her completed time card for the week ending September 12, 20--.

Here are the steps to follow to record the data from Iona's time card into the payroll register shown in Illustrations 77B and 77C (page 609):

STEP 1 Enter the hours worked daily and the total hours for the week.

Using the data shown on Iona's time card, record the hours she worked each day and the total hours she worked in the week in the proper columns of the payroll register.

Notice that Iona returned to work on Tuesday evening and worked two hours in addition to the eight hours she had worked during the regular day. Her total hours worked on Tuesday were:

DAY	IN	OUT	IN	OUT	IN	OUT	TOTAL
M	7:58	12:01	12:59	5:01			8
T	7:57	12:02	12:57	5:02	5:58	8:01	10
W	7:58	12:03	12:58	5:02			8
TH	7:55	12:02	12:57	6:01			9
F	7:59	12:00	1:01	5:02			8

Name Iona Carr   No. 1

Week Ending   September 12, 20--

TOTAL HOURS WORKED   43

	HOURS	RATE	WAGES
REGULAR	40	12.75	510.00
OVERTIME	3	19.125	57.38
TOTAL	43		567.38

$$12:00 - 8:00 = 4 \quad \text{hours in the morning}$$
$$5:00 - 1:00 = 4 \quad \text{hours in the afternoon}$$
$$8:00 - 6:00 = \underline{2} \quad \text{hours in the evening}$$
$$10 \quad \text{hours total for Tuesday}$$

Notice also that Iona worked until 6:00 p.m. on Thursday. This meant that she worked a total of 9 hours on Thursday. Because she worked more hours on Tuesday and Thursday, her total hours for the week were 43, or 40 regular time hours and 3 overtime hours.

STEP 2 **Enter the regular time pay.**

Look at the bottom section of the time card. Copy the regular hours (40), the regular time rate ($12.75), and the regular time pay ($510.00) in the columns for regular pay in the payroll register.

STEP 3 **Enter the overtime wages.**

Look at the bottom section of the time card. Copy the overtime hours (3), the overtime rate ($19.125), and the overtime pay ($57.38) in the columns for overtime pay in the payroll register.

STEP 4 **Enter the gross pay for the week.**

The bottom section of the time card shows $567.38 as Iona's gross pay for the week. Enter this in the Gross Pay column of the payroll register.

STEP 5 **Foot, rule, and verify the payroll register.**

After you have entered the wages for all employees, foot the Regular Pay Amount column, Overtime Pay Amount column, and Gross Pay column. Verify the register by crossfooting these columns:

PAYROLL REGISTER

	CARD NO.	NAME OF EMPLOYEE	HOURS WORKED					
			M	T	W	TH	F	
1	1	Iona Carr	8	10	8	9	8	1
2	2	Ira Dunne	8	8½	8	9	8	2
3	3	Lamont White	8	7½	8½	10	8	3
4	4	Wesley Yates	8	7	8	8	7	4

STEP 1

STEP 4

PAYROLL REGISTER WEEK ENDING *September 12, 20--*

	TOTAL HOURS WORKED	REGULAR PAY			OVERTIME PAY			GROSS PAY	
		HRS.	RATE	AMOUNT	HRS.	RATE	AMOUNT		
1	43	40	12 75	5 1 0 00	3	19 125	5 7 38	5 6 7 38	1
2	41½	40	8 60	3 4 4 00	1½	12 90	1 9 35	3 6 3 35	2
3	42	40	9 85	3 9 4 00	2	14 775	2 9 55	4 2 3 55	3
4	38	38	10 79	4 1 0 02				4 1 0 02	4
5				1 6 5 8 02 / 1 6 5 8 02			1 0 6 28 / 1 0 6 28	1 7 6 4 30 / 1 7 6 4 30	5

STEP 2   STEP 3   STEP 5

Regular Pay	$1,658.02
Overtime Pay	106.28
Gross Pay	$1,764.30

Since the crossfooted total for gross pay agrees with the total gross pay in your payroll register, double rule the three columns to show that you are finished.

BUILDING YOUR BUSINESS VOCABULARY

On a sheet of paper, write the headings **Statement Number** and **Words**. Next, choose the words that match the statements. Write each word you choose next to the statement number it matches. Be careful; not all the words listed should be used.

Statements	Words
1. A record of wages earned by employees	employee
2. A wage plan that pays workers for each unit of work finished	employer
	gross pay
3. Time worked beyond 40 hours a week	overtime
4. The first 40 hours worked in a week	overtime rate of pay
5. A business that hires people	payroll register
6. The rate of pay for the first 40 hours in a week	piecework pay
	regular time
7. The rate of pay for any hours beyond 40 hours in a week	regular time rate of pay
	time clock
8. Total wages	

STEPS REVIEW: Recording Overtime Wages in the Payroll Register

STEP 1 Enter the hours worked daily and the total hours for the week.

STEP 2 Enter the regular time pay.

STEP 3 Enter the overtime wages.

STEP 4 Enter the gross pay for the week.

STEP 5 Foot, rule, and verify the payroll register.

APPLICATION PROBLEMS

Problem 77-1

You are the payroll clerk for the Beacon Ceramics Company. The company pays overtime (1½ times the regular hourly rate) for all hours worked beyond 40 hours in one week.

Directions

a. Copy the following data for the week ending June 15, 20--, into a payroll register.

Card No.	Name of Employee	Hours Worked					Pay Per Hour
		M	T	W	TH	F	
1	Oki Wakui	8	8	8	10	8	$12.50
2	Edwin Land	8	9	11	9	8	9.80
3	Debra Moore	8	7	9	8	8	11.75
4	Richard Moss	8	9	9	10	8	8.65
5	Ida Steinberg	7	8	7	8	7½	12.90

CHECK POINT

77-1(g)

Total Gross Pay = $2,354.65

b. Find the total hours worked by each employee, and enter the figures in the Total Hours Worked column of the payroll register.
c. Find the regular time hours and pay for each employee, and enter the figures in the Regular Pay columns of the payroll register.
d. Find the overtime hours and pay for each employee, and enter the figures in the Overtime Pay columns of the payroll register.
e. Find the gross pay for each employee, and enter the figures in the Gross Pay column of the payroll register.
f. Rule and foot the two Amount columns and the Gross Pay column.
g. Check your answers by crossfooting. The sum of the totals of the Amount columns should equal the total of the Gross Pay column.
h. Enter the final totals and double rule the columns.

Problem 77-2

You are the payroll clerk for the Cleopatra Pet Store, Inc. The company pays overtime (1½ times the regular hourly rate) for all hours worked beyond 40 hours in one week.

Directions

a. Copy the following data for the week ending December 12, 20--, into a payroll register.

Card No.	Name of Employee	Hours Worked					Pay Per Hour
		M	T	W	TH	F	
1	Candy Allen	8	7	9	10	8	$ 9.90
2	Robert Benez	8	8	10	10	8	12.40
3	Frank Conner	7	7½	8	8½	7	10.75
4	Victor Del Pozo	8½	8½	9	10½	8	8.50
5	Gretchen Reece	8	10¼	9½	8½	8	11.25

b. Complete the payroll register by following steps *b.* through *h.* of Problem 77–1.

Problem 77-3   You are the payroll clerk for Korner Komputer Company. The company pays overtime (1½ times the regular hourly rate) for all hours worked beyond 40 hours in one week.

The following four time cards are for the week ending January 18, 20--. Each card shows the regular hourly rate for the employee.

CHECK POINT

77-3(c)

Total Overtime Pay
= $226.33

Directions

a. Complete each time card. Use Illustration 77A (page 608) as an example.
b. Enter the data from each card in a payroll register.
c. Complete the payroll register. Use Illustrations 77B and 77C (both on page 609) as an example.

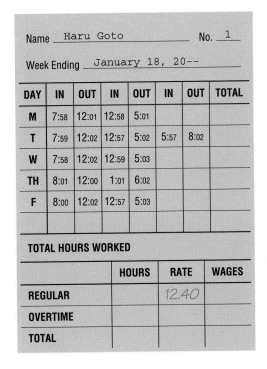

Name	Enid Clark					No.	3

Week Ending January 18, 20--

DAY	IN	OUT	IN	OUT	IN	OUT	TOTAL
M	7:59	12:02	12:58	5:01	5:58	7:02	
T	7:58	12:01	12:56	6:03			
W	8:01	12:02	12:57	5:02	5:57	8:03	
TH	7:58	12:01	12:58	5:34			
F	7:59	12:01	12:59	5:16			

TOTAL HOURS WORKED

	HOURS	RATE	WAGES
REGULAR		12.75	
OVERTIME			
TOTAL			

Name	Karl Shoen					No.	4

Week Ending January 18, 20--

DAY	IN	OUT	IN	OUT	IN	OUT	TOTAL
M	7:57	12:02	1:01	5:31			
T	8:01	12:01	12:56	5:02			
W	7:56	12:02	1:00	5:03			
TH	7:59	12:01	12:59	5:01	5:57	7:35	
F	7:58	12:02	12:57	5:32			

TOTAL HOURS WORKED

	HOURS	RATE	WAGES
REGULAR		10.55	
OVERTIME			
TOTAL			

key terms preview

- **Commissions**
- **Graduated commission**
- **Rate of commission**
- **Salary**
- **Salary plus commission**
- **Straight commission**

goals

1 To learn how to compute commissions.

2 To learn how to compute commissions when the rate of commission increases as sales increase.

3 To learn how to compute gross pay when the employee is paid a salary plus commission.

4 To learn how to complete a payroll register for employees who are paid on a commission pay plan.

⇨ UNDERSTANDING THE JOB

Salary. A fixed amount of pay for a time period.

Employers offer many pay plans to workers in addition to the hourly pay plan. Two types of pay plans, salaries and commissions, are used often in the business world.

Salaries

Many workers, especially office workers, managers, and professional workers, are paid a fixed amount of income, or **salary**, each week or each month. For example, an office worker may be paid $350 a week and work 37½ or 40 hours during the week. A manager may be paid $600 a week in salary but be expected to work as long as is needed during the week to get the work done.

Salaried workers may not have to use time clocks. However, they are expected to be at work for the full amount of time for which they are paid. If some salaried employees work beyond their normal hours, they may be paid overtime. For example, clerical workers and secretaries are usually paid overtime. However, supervisors and managers are not usually paid for any hours they spend beyond the normal work week.

Straight Commission

Many sales workers are paid on the basis of how much they sell. The more they sell, the more they make. For example, Sue Gunn, a salesperson, is paid

5% on all sales she makes during the week. Sue's earnings are called **commissions**. The 5% is called the **rate of commission**.

Sue is paid on a **straight commission** pay plan. This means that her total sales for the week are multiplied by the commission rate to find her total commissions. For example, Sue sold $10,000 last week. Her total commissions would be found this way:

$$
\begin{array}{ll}
\$10,000 & \text{Total sales} \\
\underline{\times\ \ 0.05} & \text{Commission rate} \\
\$500.00 & \text{Total commissions}
\end{array}
$$

Since Sue is only paid commissions, her total commissions of $500 are also her gross pay for the week.

Salary Plus Commission

Key Terms

Commissions. A pay plan based on how much is sold.

Rate of commission. The commission percent.

Straight commission. Sales × commission rate.

Salary plus commission. A fixed amount of pay plus sales × commission rate.

Graduated commission. When the rate of commission increases as the amount of sales increases.

Many workers, especially managers and professional workers, are paid a fixed amount of income, or salary, each week or each month for their work. For example, a manager may be paid $500 a week in salary.

Some salespeople are paid a **salary plus commission** on their sales. For example, Luis Moya is paid a weekly salary of $400 plus a commission of 2% on all sales he makes in a week. Last week Luis sold $5,000.00. His gross pay would be found in two steps:

Step 1
$$
\begin{array}{ll}
\$\ 5,000 & \text{Total sales} \\
\underline{\times\ \ 0.02} & \text{Commission rate} \\
\$100.00 & \text{Total commissions}
\end{array}
$$

Step 2
$$
\begin{array}{ll}
\$\ 400.00 & \text{Weekly salary} \\
\underline{+\ 100.00} & \text{Total commissions} \\
\$\ 500.00 & \text{Gross pay}
\end{array}
$$

Graduated Commission

Some companies try to encourage their workers to sell more by raising the commission rates as the amount of goods sold increases in a week. For example, Reede, Inc., pays its workers commissions according to this schedule:

Total Weekly Sales	Commission Rate
$1–$10,000	5%
$10,001–$20,000	8%
$20,001 and over	10%

This pay plan is called a **graduated commission** pay plan. If you worked for Reede, Inc., and sold $25,000.00 worth of goods last week, here is how your gross pay would be found:

$$
\begin{array}{lll}
\$10,000 \times 0.05 = \$\ \ \ 500.00 & \text{Commission on \$1–\$10,000} \\
\$10,000 \times 0.08 = \$\ \ \ 800.00 & \text{Commission on \$10,001–\$20,000} \\
\underline{\$\ \ 5,000} \times 0.10 = \$\ \ \ \underline{500.00} & \text{Commission on \$20,001 and over} \\
\$25,000 \ \ \ \$\ 1,800.00 & \text{Total commissions or gross pay}
\end{array}
$$

With total sales of $25,000.00, you would earn $1,800.00 in commissions.

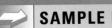

SAMPLE PROBLEM

You maintain the payroll register for salespeople for Ordaz Paper Company. Ordaz pays each of their salespersons a weekly salary plus 2% commission on all sales made in one week.

Last week, the following five salespeople were paid these salaries and made these total sales:

No.	Salesperson	Total Sales	Weekly Salary
1	Cella Valdez	$37,000.00	$400.00
2	Ronald Coles	39,500.00	450.00
3	Frank Ibert	35,678.00	475.00
4	Ashly Kelso	36,197.00	575.00
5	Kevin Streb	44,315.00	525.00

Illustration 78A shows the payroll register you completed for the week ending October 28, 20--. Notice that the payroll register for those paid on commission is somewhat different from those paid on an hourly pay plan. There are no columns for hours worked. There are columns for total weekly sales, commission, and weekly salary.

Illustration 78A

Payroll register for salespeople on commission

STEP 1

STEP 1

NO.	NAME OF SALESPERSON	TOTAL WEEKLY SALES	COMMISSION	WEEKLY SALARY	GROSS PAY
1	Cella Valdez	37 000 00	740 00	400 00	1 140 00
2	Ronald Coles	39 500 00	790 00	450 00	1 240 00
3	Frank Ibert	35 678 00	713 56	475 00	1 188 56
4	Ashly Kelso	36 197 00	723 94	575 00	1 298 94
5	Kevin Streb	44 315 00	886 30	525 00	1 411 30
	Totals	192 690 00	3 853 80	2 425 00	6 278 80
		192 690 00	3 853 80	2 425 00	6 278 80

PAYROLL REGISTER — WEEK ENDING *October 28, 20--*

STEP 2   STEP 3   STEP 4

Here is how you did your work:

STEP 1 Enter the date and the employee numbers, names, total weekly sales, and weekly salaries.

You entered the date on the Week Ending line. Then you entered the number, name, total weekly sales, and weekly salary of each salesperson in the correct columns of the payroll register.

STEP 2 Find and enter the commission for each salesperson.

You found the commission for Cella Valdez this way:

$37,000.00	Total weekly sales
× 0.02	Commission rate
$ 740.00	Total commissions

You entered the amount of her commission in the Commission column and followed the same procedures for the other salespeople.

STEP 3 Find the gross pay for each salesperson.

You then added the commission and weekly salary for each salesperson and entered the total in the Gross Pay column of the payroll register.

STEP 4 Foot, crossfoot, and rule the payroll register.

You footed each of the money columns in the register. Then you verified your work by crossfooting these totals:

$ 3,853.80	Total commissions
+2,425.00	Total weekly salaries
$ 6,278.80	Gross pay

Since the crossfooted total, $6,278.80, agreed with the total of the Gross Pay column, you entered the final totals and double ruled the money columns.

→ BUILDING YOUR BUSINESS VOCABULARY

On a sheet of paper, write the headings **Statement Number** and **Words**. Next, choose the words that match the statements. Write each word you choose next to the statement number it matches. Be careful; not all the words listed should be used.

Statements	Words
1. A pay plan based on how much is sold	commissions
2. The commission percent	graduated commission
3. Total sales multiplied by the commission rate	hourly pay
4. A fixed amount of pay	overtime
5. A fixed amount of pay plus the amount of commission	rate of commission
	salary
6. When the rate of commission increases as the amount of sales increases	salary plus commission
	straight commission

STEPS REVIEW: Using a Payroll Register with Salaries Plus Commissions

STEP 1 Enter the date and the employee numbers, names, total weekly sales, and weekly salaries.

STEP 2 Find and enter the commission for each salesperson.

STEP 3 Find the gross pay for each salesperson

STEP 4 Foot, crossfoot, and rule the payroll register.

Problem 78-1   You are the payroll clerk for Kriege Auto Parts, Inc. The company pays its salespersons a 3% straight commission on all sales made in one week.

Directions

a. Complete the pay chart for the week ending May 17, 20--, by finding the total commission, or gross pay, for each worker.

b. Find the total sales and the total commissions paid for the week by the company.

c. Verify your work by multiplying the total of the Total Sales column by the rate of commission. This amount should agree with the total of the Gross Pay column.

Weekly Pay Chart		
Salesperson	Total Sales	Commission (Gross Pay)
Clara Andulisa	$40,000	
Claire Bennett	28,000	
Frank Carter	35,700	
Nadia Dinencio	29,500	
Sarah Esterman	31,250	
Benjamin Faulk	51,178	
Ina Ginsberg	55,645	
Sally Harmon	57,247	
Theodore Isert	41,211	
Yancy Jesterman	37,890	
Totals		

Problem 78-2   You are the payroll clerk for Ribkins Toy Sales, Inc. The company pays its salespersons a weekly salary plus a 2% commission on all sales made in one week.

Directions

a. Complete the pay chart for the week ended April 2, 20--, by finding the total commission and gross pay for each worker.

b. Find the totals of all the money columns.

Weekly Pay Chart				
Salesperson	Total Sales	Commission	Weekly Salary	Gross Pay
Edward Keller	$35,000		$400.00	
Evelyn Lammert	38,000		450.00	
Lisa Meng	45,850		500.00	
Hawazan Mutair	52,750		650.00	
Robert Nolan	63,512		425.00	
Glenda O'Malley	61,548		675.00	
James Peludat	48,648		540.00	
Laticia Rollins	64,877		585.00	
Samuel Summer	55,406		485.00	
Tina Tillman	59,316		625.00	
Totals				

c. Verify your work by crossfooting the totals of the Commission, Weekly Salary, and Gross Pay columns.

Problem 78-3 You are the payroll clerk for Carrollton Company. The company pays its salespeople using the following graduated commission pay plan:

CHECK POINT

78-3(a)

Aaron Best's commission = $900.00

Total Weekly Sales	Commission Rate
$1 - $10,000	2%
$10,001 - $20,000	4%
$20,001 and over	6%

Directions

a. Complete the pay chart for the week ended May 6, 20--, by finding the total commission, or gross pay, for each worker.
b. Find the total sales and the total commissions paid for the week by the company.

Weekly Pay Chart		
Salesperson	Total Sales	Commission (Gross Pay)
Aaron Best	$25,000	
Trent Blake	41,000	
Timothy Cook	17,560	
Maria Dent	31,160	
Jaron Ellers	43,500	
George Frank	47,140	
Lucy Gantt	31,567	
Patrick Herr	17,472	
Louisa Ivanov	31,514	
Regina James	41,873	
Totals		

Problem 78-4 You are the payroll clerk who maintains the payroll register for all salespeople for Kintral, Inc. The company pays a weekly salary plus a 2% commission on total weekly sales to each salesperson.

CHECK POINT

78-4(a)

Jean Short's gross pay = $872.00

Directions

a. Enter these data for the week ending October 14, 20--, into a payroll register with the same headings as in Illustration 78A (page 615).

No.	Salesperson	Total Sales	Weekly Salary
1	Jean Short	$18,600.00	$500.00
2	Lester Trump	19,500.00	550.00
3	Richard Uber	21,430.00	575.00
4	Lena Vander	14,358.00	580.00
5	Elsa West	22,192.00	520.00

b. Find and enter the commission for each salesperson.
c. Find the gross pay for each salesperson.
d. Foot each of the money columns.
e. Verify your work by crossfooting the Commission, Weekly Salary, and Gross Pay columns.
f. Enter the final totals and double rule the register.

Job 79 PIECEWORK PAY

applied math preview

Copy and complete these problems.

1. 500 × $ .20 =
2. 250 × $ .45 =
3. 415 × $ .26 =
4. 128 × $ .75 =
5. 227 × $ .23 =

6. 400 × $1.22 =
7. 320 × $2.35 =
8. 498 × $3.23 =
9. 200 × $ .23 $\frac{1}{2}$ =
10. 130 × $ .15 $\frac{1}{4}$ =

key terms preview

- Graduated piecework pay
- Piecerate

- Straight piecework pay

goals

1 To learn how to compute an employee's gross pay when the employee is paid on a piecework pay plan.

2 To learn how to compute piecework pay when the rate for each piece increases as the number of pieces increases.

3 To learn how to complete a payroll register for piecework employees.

→ UNDERSTANDING THE JOB

Key Terms

Straight piecework pay. Same pay for each piece.

Piecerate. The rate paid for each piece.

Some employees are paid an amount for each unit or piece of work that they complete and that is accepted. For example, Richard Lee is paid $.80 for each table lamp he assembles correctly. During the work day, another employee inspects each of the lamps he assembles to make sure that they have been completed correctly. Richard is not paid for any lamps that have been improperly assembled.

Straight Piecework

Since Richard is paid the same amount for each unit or piece of work he completes properly, he is paid on a **straight piecework pay** plan. The $.80 he receives for each properly assembled table lamp is called the **piecerate**. If Richard assembled 500 table lamps properly in one week, his gross pay would be found this way:

$$
\begin{array}{rl}
500 & \text{Pieces} \\
\times \ \$.80 & \text{Piecerate} \\
\hline
\$400.00 & \text{Gross pay}
\end{array}
$$

Graduated Piecework

To encourage employees to produce more products, many employers increase the piecerate as the number of accepted units of work increases.

Key Terms

Graduated piecework pay.
Higher rate paid as number of pieces increases.

For example, the Altoona Needle Company pays its employees using the following piecerate schedule:

Number of Accepted Units in One Week	Piecerate
1 - 500	$.40
501 - 800	.50
801 - 1,100	.60
1,101 and over	.70

This pay plan is called a **graduated piecework pay** plan. If you worked for Altoona Needle Company and completed 1,300 pieces last week, here is how you would find your gross pay:

$$500 \times \$.40 = \$200.00 \quad \text{Pay for 1–500 pieces}$$
$$300 \times \$.50 = 150.00 \quad \text{Pay for 501–800 pieces}$$
$$300 \times \$.60 = 180.00 \quad \text{Pay for 801–1,100 pieces}$$
$$\underline{200 \times \$.70} = \underline{140.00} \quad \text{Pay for 1,101 and over pieces}$$
$$1,300 \qquad\qquad \$670.00 \quad \text{Gross pay}$$

If you completed 1,300 pieces, you would earn $670.00 in gross pay.

SAMPLE PROBLEM

You are the payroll clerk for H & R, Inc. H & R pays its factory employees a straight piecerate for each accepted unit of work they complete. Since some work is more difficult than other work, different piecerates are paid. Last week, six factory employees completed these pieces:

		No. of Pieces Completed					
No.	Employee Name	M	T	W	TH	F	Piecerate
1	Jerome Munie	20	21	20	19	19	$4.80
2	Leigh Nadler	17	19	18	17	19	4.82
3	Darren Orr	19	20	20	18	19	4.82
4	Kyong Oh	25	23	24	24	21	4.91
5	David Pacatte	26	25	24	25	24	4.95
6	Amy Patel	27	25	26	28	27	$4.98\frac{1}{2}$

Illustration 79A on page 621 shows the payroll register you completed for the week ending May 15, 20--. Notice that the payroll register for a piecework pay plan is different from the one used for an hourly pay plan. The columns for hours worked are replaced by columns for pieces completed. Also, the column for pay per hour is replaced by one for piecerate.

	NO.	NAME OF EMPLOYEE	PIECES COMPLETED					TOTAL NO. OF PIECES	PIECERATE			GROSS PAY				
			M	T	W	TH	F									
1	1	Jerome Munie	20	21	20	19	19	99		4	80	4	7	5	20	1
2	2	Leigh Nadler	17	19	18	17	19	90		4	82	4	3	3	80	2
3	3	Darren Orr	19	20	20	18	19	96		4	82	4	6	2	72	3
4	4	Kyong Oh	25	23	24	24	21	117		4	91	5	7	4	47	4
5	5	David Pacatte	26	25	24	25	24	124		4	95	6	1	3	80	5
6	6	Amy Patel	27	25	26	28	27	133		4	98½	6	6	3	01	6
7		Total						659				3 2 2 3			00	7

PAYROLL REGISTER — WEEK ENDING **May 15, 20--**

STEP 1 STEP 3 STEP 2 STEP 4

Illustration 79A

Payroll register for piecerate employees

Here is how you did your work:

STEP 1 Enter the date and the employee numbers, names, daily number of pieces completed, and piecerate.

You entered the date on the Week Ending line. Then you entered the number, name, daily number of pieces completed, and piecerate for each factory employee in the proper columns of the payroll register.

STEP 2 Find and enter the total number of pieces completed in the week.

You added the completed units of work for each employee and entered these amounts in the Total No. of Pieces column of the payroll register.

STEP 3 Find the gross pay for each employee.

You found and entered the gross pay for each employee in the Gross Pay column of the payroll register. For example, you found the gross pay for Jerome Munie this way:

$$\begin{array}{r} 99 \quad \text{Total number of pieces} \\ \times\$4.80 \quad \text{Piecerate} \\ \hline \$475.20 \quad \text{Gross pay} \end{array}$$

Sometimes the piecerate contains a fraction. For example, Amy Patel's piecerate is $4.98\frac{1}{2}$, or $4.985. Do not round off piecerates that contain less than one cent. Round off only the final gross pay:

$$\begin{array}{r} 133 \quad \text{Total number of pieces} \\ \times\$4.985 \quad \text{Piecerate} \\ \hline \$663.005 \text{ , or } \$663.01 \quad \text{Gross pay} \end{array}$$

STEP 4 Foot and rule the payroll register.

You footed the Total No. of Pieces and the Gross Pay columns in the register. After you re-added the columns, you entered the final totals and double ruled the columns.

On a sheet of paper, write the headings **Statement Number** and **Words**. Next, choose the words that match the statements. Write each word you choose next to the statement number it matches. Be careful; not all the words listed should be used.

Statements	Words
1. A pay plan based on how much is sold	commission pay
2. A pay plan which pays the same amount for each unit of work completed	graduated commission
	graduated piecework pay
3. A pay plan which increases the amount paid as the units of work completed increase	hourly pay
4. The percent of commission paid	overtime
5. The rate paid for each piece completed	piecerate
6. Total sales multiplied by the commission rate	rate of commission
	salary
7. A fixed amount of pay	salary plus commission
8. A fixed amount of pay plus the amount of commission	straight commission
	straight piecework pay
9. When the rate of commission increases as the amount of sales increases	

STEPS REVIEW: Using a Payroll Register with Piecework

STEP 1 Enter the date and the employee numbers, names, daily number of pieces completed, and piecerate.

STEP 2 Find and enter the total number of pieces completed in the week.

STEP 3 Find the gross pay for each employee.

STEP 4 Foot and rule the payroll register.

APPLICATION PROBLEMS

Problem 79-1   You are a payroll clerk for Rally Electronics Company. The company pays its factory employees $.87 for each unit of work completed properly.

Directions

CHECK POINT

79-1(1)

Gross Pay = $505.47

a. Find the total number of pieces completed by each employee.
b. Find the gross pay for each employee.

Spreadsheet

Employee	No. of Pieces Completed					Total Pieces	Gross Pay
	M	T	W	TH	F		
1	115	117	118	115	116	_____	$_____
2	105	107	106	109	105	_____	_____
3	120	121	125	124	121	_____	_____
4	128	127	124	128	128	_____	_____
5	131	129	130	128	129	_____	_____
6	135	132	134	132	135	_____	_____

You are a payroll clerk for Burton Lawn Products, Inc. Burton pays its assembly-line employees according to the following graduated piecerate schedule:

Number of Accepted Units in One Week	Piecerate
1 - 300	$ .65
301 - 500	.80
501 - 600	.95
601 and over	1.10

Directions
a. Find the total number of pieces completed by each employee.
b. Find the gross pay for each employee.

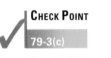

CHECK POINT

79-2(1)

Gross Pay = $339.00

Employee	M	T	W	TH	F	Total Pieces	Gross Pay
1	90	90	110	90	100	_____	$_____
2	81	82	89	81	85	_____	_____
3	113	114	112	113	116	_____	_____
4	124	119	118	125	122	_____	_____
5	99	95	99	92	99	_____	_____
6	102	99	97	104	103	_____	_____

Problem 79-3

You are the payroll clerk for Crestwood Manufacturing Company. The company pays its factory employees a straight piecerate for each completed and accepted piece of work.

Directions
a. Copy the following information for the week ended September 22, 20--, into a payroll register with the same headings as in Illustration 79A (page 621).

CHECK POINT

79-3(c)

Total of Gross Pay
column = $4,003.20

No.	Employee Name	M	T	W	TH	F	Piecerate
1	Ridge Galena	65	68	69	64	67	$1.85
2	Maria Palotta	75	76	74	78	72	1.85
3	Richard Quincy	70	71	75	72	71	1.85
4	Susanna Valencia	35	36	37	34	38	3.50
5	Benjamin Rutman	38	39	38	40	42	3.50
6	Ida Fleig	25	36	34	36	36	4.25

b. Find the total number of pieces completed and the gross pay for each employee.
c. Foot and rule the Total No. of Pieces and Gross Pay columns of the payroll register.

Problem 79-4 may be found in the Working Papers.

CHECK YOUR READING

1. List and explain four different types of wage plans.
2. List and explain three different types of commission pay plans.
3. Why do some companies offer their salespeople a graduated commission pay plan?
4. If your employer offered you a choice of any of the pay plans discussed in this chapter, which one would you select? Explain your answer.

DISCUSSION

1. Why do you think supervisors should check time cards or a list of the times and hours each employee worked before an employee is paid? Give two reasons why you think checking is necessary.
2. Why do you think business firms should have a late schedule? Give two reasons why you think a late schedule is needed.

ETHICS IN THE WORKPLACE

You are a payroll clerk for Lima Products Company. Ron Wilson, who works in the billing department at Lima, is a friend of yours. He calls you on the phone and asks you how much Lisa Ackers, who also works in the billing department, is paid an hour.

What should you tell Ron? Write down what you would say. Do not use more than half a sheet of paper.

COMMUNICATION IN THE WORKPLACE

You are the supervisor of five accounts receivable clerks who work in the accounting department of a large wholesaling firm. One employee, Mia Simms, has been late for the first three mornings of this week. Mia has punched in at 8:04 a.m., 8:05 a.m., and 8:09 a.m. on Monday, Tuesday, and Wednesday, respectively.

When you talk to Mia about the late arrivals, she says, "I've only been a few minutes late. Give me a break! It doesn't hurt anybody."

As her supervisor, what would you say to Mia? Write what you would say on no more than one sheet of paper.

FOCUS ON CAREERS

Some firms make it possible for employees to have a say about when they arrive and leave work. Employees may be able to schedule times to arrive and leave that are earlier or later than usual. These work plans are called

REINFORCEMENT ACTIVITIES

Key Terms

Flextime. A plan that allows employees to vary the time they arrive and leave work.

flextime plans. Flextime permits employees to vary their arrival and departure times to suit their needs. For example, some firms may allow employees responsible for picking up or dropping off their children at school to leave and arrive at times which make this possible.

1. What are two other reasons why employees may wish to vary the time they arrive and leave work?
2. Why do you think employers decide to offer flextime plans?

 ## GLOBAL BUSINESS: INTERNATIONAL MAIL SERVICES

You are a record keeper for a company that does business with many international firms. You often have to send letters and packages to customers located in other countries.

The U.S. Post Office offers businesses a number of international mail services. These services can be grouped into three basic categories:

1. International Correspondence and Transactions for sending letters, memos, invoices, customer statements, and other correspondence.
2. International Direct Mail for sending mass advertising mail to customers, catalogs, books and other publications.
3. International Package Solutions for sending packages that contain merchandise, samples, replacements, and other items.

An International Mail Services Activity can be found in the Working Papers.

 ## REVIEWING WHAT YOU HAVE LEARNED

On a sheet of paper, write the headings **Statement Number** and **Words**. Next, choose the words that best complete the statements. Write each word you choose next to the statement number it completes. Be careful; not all the words listed should be used.

Statements	Words
1. A device that records the time when a worker reports to work or leaves work on a time card is called (a, an) _____.	badge reader commission pay flextime
2. A record of the hours worked by a single employee is called (a, an) _____.	gross pay one and one-half
3. An employee who processes payroll data for a business is called (a, an) _____.	overtime payroll clerk
4. Regular pay plus overtime pay is called _____.	payroll register piecework pay

Statements	Words
5. A wage plan that pays an employee by the number of items completed or produced is called (a, an) _____ plan.	punching in
	punching out
	time card
	time clock
6. A wage plan that pays an employee a percentage of the total amount the employee sells is called (a, an) _____ plan.	
7. The number of hours you work beyond 40 hours a week is called _____.	
8. A record of wages paid to a group of employees is called (a, an) _____.	
9. The overtime rate of pay is _____ times the regular time rate of pay.	
10. Having the time printed on your time card when you leave work is called _____.	
11. A plan that allows employees to vary the time they arrive and leave work is called _____.	

 ## MASTERY PROBLEM

CHECK POINT

(4)
Total wages = $441.51

You are the payroll clerk for Barlow Corporation. The four time cards on page 627 are for the week ending May 14, 20--. Each card shows the regular hourly rate for the employee.

Directions

a. Complete each time card. Use the work schedules found in Job 73 on pages 585 and 586.

b. Enter the data for each time card in the payroll register.

c. Complete the payroll register for the week.

Name Connie Padilla   **No.** 1

Week Ending May 14, 20--

DAY	IN	OUT	IN	OUT	IN	OUT	TOTAL
M	7:59	12:01	12:58	5:01			
T	8:02	12:00	12:57	4:02			
W	7:56	11:32	12:59	5:02			
TH	7:57	12:03	12:56	5:03			
F	7:59	12:01	1:58	5:01			

TOTAL HOURS WORKED

	HOURS	RATE	WAGES
REGULAR		10.50	
OVERTIME			
TOTAL			

Name Jason Reid   **No.** 2

Week Ending May 14, 20--

DAY	IN	OUT	IN	OUT	IN	OUT	TOTAL
M	7:59	12:02	12:58	6:01			
T	7:57	12:03	12:57	5:02			
W	7:59	12:01	12:59	5:01			
TH	7:57	12:02	12:58	5:03	5:58	8:02	
F	7:56	12:03	12:56	5:00			

TOTAL HOURS WORKED

	HOURS	RATE	WAGES
REGULAR		10.80	
OVERTIME			
TOTAL			

Name Ernest Sisson   **No.** 3

Week Ending May 14, 20--

DAY	IN	OUT	IN	OUT	IN	OUT	TOTAL
M	7:57	12:02	1:01	5:00	5:28	7:01	
T	7:58	12:01	12:59	5:02	5:58	8:01	
W	8:01	12:00	12:58	5:03	5:58	8:02	
TH	8:00	12:01	12:59	6:00			
F	7:57	12:02	12:58	5:01			

TOTAL HOURS WORKED

	HOURS	RATE	WAGES
REGULAR		11.80	
OVERTIME			
TOTAL			

Name Kelly Thiel   **No.** 4

Week Ending May 14, 20--

DAY	IN	OUT	IN	OUT	IN	OUT	TOTAL
M	7:57	12:02	12:57	5:01			
T	8:01	12:01	12:59	6:32			
W	8:00	12:02	1:00	5:02			
TH	7:56	12:01	12:58	5:03			
F	7:57	12:02	12:57	5:02			

TOTAL HOURS WORKED

	HOURS	RATE	WAGES
REGULAR		10.45	
OVERTIME			
TOTAL			

REVIEWING YOUR BUSINESS VOCABULARY

This activity may be found in the Working Papers.

Chapter 16

Record Keeping for Payroll Clerks: Computing Net Pay

Employers pay wages to their workers. Employers also make deductions from the wages of their workers. The deductions are for social security tax, federal withholding tax, any state or city income taxes, and other special reasons, such as health insurance.

In Chapter 16, you will learn how to find social security and withholding taxes. You will learn how to use a payroll register and an employee earnings record. You will also learn about the Wage and Tax Statement (W-2 form). A Calculator Tip will be given for finding the amount of social security (FICA) tax and an employee's net pay.

Electronic Commerce

The Web has become a major place through which business can do business. Electronic commerce, or e-commerce, has grown rapidly in the last few years. Some types of e-commerce have been especially popular on the Web, such as paying bills; buying airplane tickets; buying books, CDs and DVDs, and buying and selling stocks and bonds.

However, buying products on the Web has its dangers. Experts suggest these tips for your safety:

- Stick with well-known and established businesses.

- Use your credit card, which often provides a means of getting your money back if something goes wrong.

- Don't enter your credit card number on a Web screen unless the Web site guarantees that it will be secure from the prying eyes of others.

- Write down the firm's address and phone number so you can contact it if a problem arises.

- Make sure you know the total cost of the product after taxes, handling charges, and delivery costs have been added.

- Take the same precautions that you would when buying over the phone, from a catalog, or at a store, including doing comparison shopping. The Web makes shopping around for better prices and deals easy.

Before multiplying a number by a percent, change the percent to a decimal. For example, before multiplying $478.00 by 8%, change 8% to a decimal. You can do this by moving the decimal two places to the left and dropping the percent sign: 8% = 0.08.

applied math preview

Copy and complete each problem. Round your answers to the nearest cent.

1. $327.00
   × 0.08

2. $344.80
   × 0.08

3. $ 463.75
   × 0.08

4. $ 581.97
   × 0.08

5. $307.00 × 8% =

6. $424.89 × 8% =

key terms preview

- **Deductions**
- **Federal Insurance Contributions Act (FICA)**
- **FICA tax**
- **Net pay**
- **Social Security Act**
- **Social security number**

goals

1 To learn about social security.

2 To learn how to figure deductions for social security.

→ UNDERSTANDING THE JOB

Social Security Act. Law that allows qualified persons to receive monthly payments from the federal government.

FICA. Federal Insurance Contributions Act.

FICA Tax. Tax collected to pay for social security program.

Deductions. Amounts subtracted from wages.

In 1935, Congress passed the **Social Security Act**. This law allows people to receive monthly payments from the federal government if they qualify. Since 1935, there have been many changes in the law that have increased the amount people receive. There have also been changes as to the kinds of people who can qualify for benefits.

In general, workers may retire at 62 years of age and receive benefits. Benefits may also be received by widows and widowers, dependent children, and permanently disabled workers. Since 1966, the law has also provided medical care (called *Medicare*) for persons over 65 years of age.

Another law, the **Federal Insurance Contributions Act (FICA)**, was passed by Congress to cover the cost of the social security program. Under this law, the government gets the money to pay social security benefits by collecting taxes from employers and employees. The employee's **FICA tax** is collected as a **deduction** from the employee's wages. The employer must contribute the same amount as is deducted from the employee's wages.

The tax rate is a certain percent of the employee's wages. This tax is deducted each payday until the worker's wages reach a certain amount for the year. Both the rate and the amount are set by Congress and can be changed by Congress at any time. They are changed often. But even though the rate and the amount change, the method of computing the FICA tax is the same.

In this chapter, you will use a FICA tax rate of *8%*. The maximum amount of wages taxable for the year will be *$70,000.00*. The FICA tax

Key Terms

Social security number. An account number in the social security system.

Net pay. Take-home pay.

will be deducted from the worker's wages until the worker has contributed $5,600.00 ($70,000.00 x 8%) of FICA tax.

Since the employer must match the amount contributed by the employee, the employer's FICA tax rate used will also be *8%*. On certain dates, the employer sends the FICA tax money collected from the employer's and the employees' contributions to the government. For example, if a total of $300.00 has been collected from all of the employees, the employer must match this $300.00 and send $600.00 to the government.

The federal government keeps an individual record for each worker. The record shows the wages earned and all the taxes collected for that worker. This record is started when the government is notified that a person has become a member of the social security system.

Everyone must have a **social security number**. You can get an application for a social security number at any social security office or your local post office. Most students already have a social security number like the one shown on the card in Illustration 80A. Your parents had to get you a number for income tax reasons.

Since both your name and social security number are needed for an employer's payroll records, your card must be shown to an employer when you are hired. The employer sends in a report of the name, social security number, gross pay, and social security deduction for each employee. When the government receives this information, your record is updated.

Illustration 80A

Social Security card

SAMPLE PROBLEM

Ray Hirsch is employed by Benson Furniture Company. He earned $575.00 last week. Here are the steps to find how much will be deducted from his wages for social security and the amount he will actually take home, or **net pay**:

STEP 1 **Multiply the gross pay by the FICA, or social security, rate.**

Multiply Ray's gross pay ($575.00) by the FICA rate (8%). To multiply a number by a percent, first change the percent to a decimal. To change 8% to a decimal, drop the percent sign and move the decimal point two places to the left.

$$8\% = 0.08$$

Now multiply the gross pay ($575.00) by the FICA rate (0.08).

$575.00   (gross pay)
× 0.08   (8% changed to a decimal)
$ 46.00   (social security deduction)

STEP 2   **Deduct the social security tax from gross pay to find net pay.**

$575.00   (gross pay)
−46.00   (social security deduction)
$529.00   (net pay)

Many payroll clerks use a calculator to find the amount of FICA tax and an employee's net pay. This is how they might do it to find Ray Hirsch's FICA tax and net pay:

STEP 1 ▶ **Enter gross pay into memory.**

First enter Ray's gross pay into memory by pressing these keys in order:

| 5 | 7 | 5 | M+ |

Do not clear the display. Leave the amount of gross pay in the display.

STEP 2 ▶ **Find the amount of FICA tax.**

Multiply Ray's gross pay ($575.00) by the FICA rate (8%) by pressing these keys in order:

| × | . | 0 | 8 | = |

The amount of the FICA tax, $46.00, will appear in the display.

STEP 3 ▶ **Find the amount of net pay.**

Subtract the FICA tax from gross pay by pressing these keys in order:

| MR | − | 4 | 6 | = |

The amount of net pay, $529.00, will appear in the display. You should now clear the display and memory to prepare for the next problem.

⇒ BUILDING YOUR BUSINESS VOCABULARY

On a sheet of paper, write the headings **Statement Number** and **Words**. Next, choose the words that match the statements. Write each word you choose next to the statement number it matches. Be careful; not all the words listed should be used.

Statements	Words
1. Tax collected to pay for social security	commissions
2. A machine that records a worker's time in and out	deductions
3. Gross pay less deductions, or take-home pay	Federal Insurance Contributions Act (FICA)
4. Time worked beyond 40 hours a week	FICA tax
5. Amounts subtracted from your wages	net pay
6. A record of wages earned by employees	overtime
7. Law passed by Congress to cover the cost of the social security program	payroll register
8. A wage plan that pays workers for each unit of work finished	piecework pay
9. An account number in the social security system	Social Security Act
	social security number
10. Law that allows qualified persons to receive monthly payments from the federal government.	time clock

STEPS REVIEW: Computing Social Security Taxes

STEP 1 Multiply the gross pay by the FICA, or social security, rate.

STEP 2 Deduct the social security tax from gross pay to find net pay.

APPLICATION PROBLEMS

Problem 80-1   You are the payroll clerk for Tolance Books, Inc.

Directions
a. Copy the following table:

CHECK POINT

80-1

Total net pay = $2,675.36

Week Ending March 6, 20--							
Name of Employee	Gross Pay		FICA Tax		Net Pay		
L. Arroyo	359	00					
W. Borland	508	00					
P. Coblitz	388	00					
N. Dubarr	613	00					
S. Ellery	478	00					
T. Feng	562	00					
Totals							

b. Find the net pay for each employee using 8% as the FICA tax rate. Enter the FICA tax and net pay for each worker in the proper columns.

c. Foot the columns. Check your work by adding the totals of the Net Pay and FICA Tax columns. The total should equal the total of the Gross Pay column. If your work is correct, enter the final totals.

Problem 80-2   You are the payroll clerk for the Laidlaw Company.

Directions

a. Copy the following table:

CHECK POINT

80-2

Total net pay =
$2,307.40

Week Ending April 24, 20--						
Name of Employee	Gross Pay		FICA Tax		Net Pay	
T. Garello	378	38				
E. Hua	451	24				
N. Isenberg	301	88				
A. Jones	557	28				
K. Kellog	345	67				
M. Leiber	473	59				
Totals						

b. Find the net pay for each employee using 8% as the FICA tax rate. Enter the FICA tax and net pay for each worker in the proper columns.

c. Foot the columns. Check your work by adding the totals of the Net Pay and FICA Tax columns. The total should equal the total of the Gross Pay column. If your work is correct, enter the final totals.

Problem 80-3 may be found in the Working Papers.

applied math preview

Copy and complete each problem. Round your answers to the nearest cent.

1. $589.58
   × 0.08

2. $476.94
   × 0.08

3. $ 508.31
   × 0.08

4. $562.77
   × 0.08

key terms preview

- Take-home pay

goal

To learn how to use a table to find the social security (FICA) tax deduction.

UNDERSTANDING THE JOB

Key Terms

Take-home pay. Net pay.

In Job 80, you learned how to compute the deduction for social security tax by multiplication. Payroll clerks who must manually compute the deduction for many workers need a fast and easy way to do it. These workers may use a social security tax table.

A table for social security tax deductions can be found in a booklet issued by the Internal Revenue Service called the *Employer's Tax Guide*. New tables are published every time the tax rate changes but the method of using the tax table remains the same.

Part of a social security tax table for an 8% FICA tax rate is shown in Illustration 81A (page 636). Use this table to solve the problems in this job.

SAMPLE PROBLEM

You are the payroll clerk for the Felster & Eades Paper Company. Your duties include calculating net pay, or **take-home pay**, for each employee for the week ending May 12. The first time card for the week shows that Ralph Marsh has earned gross pay of $401.89. The social security tax table shows that the social security tax deduction from Ralph Marsh's wages should be $32.15. Here is how you would find the tax using the table:

Find where the employee's wages fall within the Wages section of the table.

When you look at the table, you will find the word *Wages* above two columns. The figures in the column headed "At least" are the ones you look at first to locate an amount that the employee's actual wages are *close to but not less than.* Then you look at the amount in the second column headed "But less than." The employee's wages should fall somewhere between the amounts in these two columns.

For example, when you look for the amount of Ralph Marsh's wages in the table, you will find that it falls between $401.82 and $401.94. It is close to but not less than $401.82, the amount on the second line of the "At least" column. It is also less than $401.94, the amount on the second line of the "But less than" column.

STEP 2 **Find the amount of FICA tax in the "Tax to be withheld" column.**

Once you locate the correct line in the table, look at the amount shown in the next column headed "Tax to be withheld." You will see $32.15. This is the amount of FICA tax to be withheld from Ralph Marsh's wages.

You can see that any wages that fall between $401.82 and $401.94 will have the same FICA tax of $32.15. If you multiplied $401.82 by 8%, your answer would be rounded off to $32.15. If you multiplied $401.93 by 8%, your answer would be rounded off to $32.15. In fact, you would get the same answer of $32.15 if you multiplied any number that is at least $401.82 but less than $401.94 by 8%. The rounded off amount would change to $32.16 only when you multiplied $401.94 by 8%. That is why the columns are headed "At least" and "But less than."

If you had to find the tax on $402.07, would you choose $32.16 or $32.17? You should choose $32.17. Notice that even though $402.07 is shown in the second column, the column is headed "But less than." That means it does not include $402.07. You must go to the next line and

Illustration 81A

Partial social security tax table

Partial Social Security Tax Table
8% Employee Tax Deduction

Wages		Tax to	Wages		Tax to
At least	But less than	be withheld	At least	But less than	be withheld
$401.69	$401.82	$32.14	$410.69	$410.82	$32.86
401.82	401.94	32.15	410.82	410.94	32.87
401.94	402.07	32.16	410.94	411.07	32.88
402.07	402.19	32.17	411.07	411.19	32.89
402.19	402.32	32.18	411.19	411.32	32.90
$402.32	$402.44	$32.19	$411.32	$411.44	$32.91
402.44	402.57	32.20	411.44	411.57	32.92
402.57	402.69	32.21	411.57	411.69	32.93
402.69	402.82	32.22	411.69	411.82	32.94
402.82	402.94	32.23	411.82	411.94	32.95

STEP 1

STEP 2

look at the "At least" column where you also see \$402.07. This column includes \$402.07, so the tax is \$32.17.

To help you learn to use the social security tax table, the table in Illustration 81B shows wages with the correct FICA tax deductions. Look at the social security tax table and see if you find the same amount of tax for each wage amount. Place a ruler underneath the proper wage amount to prevent your eyes from shifting to the wrong line in the table.

Illustration 81B

Using a table to find social security taxes

Time Card No.	Wages		Social Security Tax (FICA Tax) From Table	
1	401	98	32	16
2	402	79	32	22
3	411	47	32	92
4	401	82	32	15
5	411	69	32	94
6	410	72	32	86
7	402	82	32	23
8	410	93	32	87
9	402	41	32	19
10	411	20	32	90

USING THE COMPUTER TO FIND FICA TAXES

If a computer is used to handle payroll, all employee and employer payroll tax data are stored on disks. You would not use the FICA table. You also would not have to multiply the employee's weekly wage by the FICA rate. The computer will automatically:

1. Check the total FICA taxes paid by the employee to make sure that the total FICA taxes paid so far this year do not exceed the maximum. (If the FICA rate is 8% and the maximum wages are \$70,000.00, \$5,600.00 is the most FICA taxes an employee must pay in one year.)
2. Multiply the weekly wages by the FICA tax rate.

This saves you a great deal of time, and it also makes the payroll more accurate.

BUILDING YOUR BUSINESS VOCABULARY

On a sheet of paper, write the headings **Statement Number** and **Words**. Next, choose the words that match the statements. Write each word you choose next to the statement number it matches. Be careful; not all the words listed should be used.

Statements	Words
1. Tax collected for social security	commission pay
2. A fixed amount of pay	deductions
3. Net pay	FICA tax

Statements	Words
4. Amounts subtracted from your wages	Federal Insurance Contributions Act (FICA)
5. Law which allows qualified persons to receive monthly payments from the federal government	gross pay
	salary
6. A pay plan based on how much is sold	Social Security Act
	take-home pay

STEPS REVIEW: USING THE SOCIAL SECURITY TAX TABLE

STEP 1 Find where the employee's wages fall withing the Wages section of the table.

STEP 2 Find the amount of FICA tax in the "Tax to be withheld" column.

APPLICATION PROBLEMS

Problem 81-1 You are the payroll clerk for Rita Voroff Designs, Inc.

Directions
Copy and complete the following table. Find the social security tax for each wage using the social security tax table in Illustration 81A (page 636).

CHECK POINT
81-1(1)

FICA tax amount
= $32.20

Time Card No.	Wages		Social Security Tax (FICA Tax) From Table	
I	402	50		
2	402	75		
3	411	26		
4	411	40		
5	410	95		
6	401	99		
7	411	58		
8	411	51		
9	402	05		
10	411	03		

Problem 81-2 You are the payroll clerk for the Rolla Cycle Shop.

CHECK POINT
81-1(1)

FICA tax amount
= $32.94

Directions
Copy and complete the following table. Find the social security tax for each wage using the social security tax table in Illustration 81A (page 636).

Time Card No.	Wages		Social Security Tax (FICA Tax) From Table	
1	411	81		
2	410	71		
3	402	37		
4	401	98		
5	411	00		
6	402	18		
7	410	87		
8	402	09		
9	401	89		
10	402	93		

Problem 81-3 may be found in the Working Papers.

Job 82 FINDING WITHHOLDING TAXES

→ UNDERSTANDING THE JOB

Withholding tax. Income tax deducted from wages each payday.

Biweekly. Every two weeks.

Semimonthly. Twice a month.

Withholding allowance. A deduction claimed for the support of another person.

To pay for the expenses of operating the federal government, people earning more than a certain amount of income must pay a federal income tax. In general, a person who earns more than someone else will pay a larger tax. Our tax system is based upon the ability of people to pay the tax.

Federal income taxes used to be paid once a year. To make paying the tax easier, the government passed a withholding tax law. This law requires employers to deduct money for federal income tax from the wages of their employees each payday. Because the tax is withheld from employee wages, it is often called a **withholding tax**.

The amount that must be deducted can be found in the *Employer's Tax Guide*, published by the Internal Revenue Service. The tax guide has tables for finding the federal withholding tax and the social security tax. There are separate tables for making deductions from wages that are paid daily, weekly, **biweekly** (every two weeks), **semimonthly** (twice a month), and monthly to both single and married workers. Since businesses use different pay periods, they need tables for these different pay periods.

In Illustration 82C on pages 642 and 643, you will find an example of a withholding tax table for married persons for a weekly pay period. Once you understand how to use this table, you should be able to use the tables for other pay periods, for single workers, or for any changes that the government may make to withholding amounts.

At the top of the table, you will notice column headings that read from 0 to 10. These figures show the number of **withholding allowances** a worker expects to claim in figuring income tax at the end of the year. A withholding allowance is a deduction a worker may claim for the support of another person, such as a child or spouse.

The United States has many different kinds of people and cultures. In addition to a large population of Caucasians from various European backgrounds, there are also large groups of people with African, Asian, and Hispanic backgrounds. The original residents of North America, the Native Americans, make up another cultural group. It is no surprise, then, that the work force also has many different kinds of people who understand and appreciate cultures from around the world. American businesses can use the knowledge and talents of their diverse work force to expand global trade.

Form **W-4**	Employee's Withholding Allowance Certificate	OMB No. 1545-0010
Department of the Treasury Internal Revenue Service	▶ For Privacy Act and Paperwork Reduction Act Notice, see reverse.	

1 Type or print your first name and middle initial Last name	2 Your social security number
Olive R. Berrios	386-92-9748

Home address (number and street or rural route) 3892 Newton Street	**3 Marital Status**	☐ Single ☒ Married ☐ Married, but withhold at higher Single rate.
City or town, state, and ZIP code Allentown, PA 18104-3892		**Note:** If married, but legally separated, or spouse is a nonresident alien, check the Single box

4 Total number of allowances you are claiming (from line G above or from the Worksheets on back if they apply)	**4**	4
5 Additional amount, if any, you want deducted from each pay	**5**	$ -0-

6 I claim exemption from withholding and I certify that I meet ALL of the following conditions for exemption:
- Last year I had a right to a refund of ALL Federal income tax withheld because I had NO tax liability; AND
- This year I expect a refund of ALL Federal income tax withheld because I expect to have NO tax liability; AND
- This year if my income exceeds $500 and includes nonwage income, another person cannot claim me as a dependent.

If you meet all of the above conditions, enter the year effective and "EXEMPT" here . . . . ▶ **6** | 20

7 Are you a full-time student? (**Note:** Full-time students are not automatically exempt.) . . . . | **7** ☐ Yes ☒ No

Under penalties of perjury, I certify that I am entitled to the number of withholding allowances claimed on this certificate or entitled to claim exempt status.

Employee's signature ▶ *Olive R. Berrios*   Date ▶ March 22   , 20 – –

8 Employer's name and address (**Employer:** Complete 8 and 10 **only if sending to IRS**) Ralis Plastics Corporation 2135 River Road, Allentown, PA 18104-2135	**9** Office code (optional)	**10** Employer identification number 87-8629483

In general, a single worker has one allowance—himself or herself. A married worker with no children has two allowances, one for the husband and one for the wife. A married worker with two children can claim four allowances—one for the husband, one for the wife, and one for each of the two children. A worker who is single and who supports a parent may claim two allowances—one for the worker and one for the parent.

Sometimes a worker may claim no allowances because that worker is claimed as an allowance by someone else. For example, a wife may claim her husband as an allowance. So, he would claim no allowance for himself or his wife.

When you are hired, your employer will ask you to fill out a **W-4 form**. The W-4 form tells the employer how many allowances a worker claims. A completed W-4 form is shown in Illustration 82A above.

 SAMPLE PROBLEM

W-4 form. A form which tells an employer how many allowances a worker claims.

You are the payroll clerk for Centrix Telephone Company. Olive Berrios, whose W-4 form is shown in Illustration 82A, claims 4 allowances and has a gross pay of $507.80. Here are the steps that you would follow to find her withholding tax deduction:

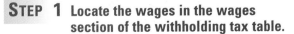

STEP 1 Locate the wages in the wages section of the withholding tax table.

Look at the withholding tax table in Illustration 82C on pages 642 and 643. Find the columns headed "At least" and "But less than." Read down these columns until you come to the amounts within which Olive's wages of $507.80 fall. You will find that her wages fall between the amounts $500.00 and $510.00 in the table.

STEP 2 Find the withholding tax deduction in the correct allowance column.

Olive has claimed 4 allowances. Once you have found the correct wages line, read across the table until the column for 4 allowances is reached. Use a ruler to keep your eyes from straying to the wrong line. You will

Time Card No.	Number of Allowances	Wages		Federal Withholding Tax	
1	1	235	00	9	00
2	2	370	00	22	00
3	5	1,038	00	97	00
4	0	436	85	47	00
5	8	731	73	28	00

MARRIED Persons–WEEKLY Payroll Period

(For Wages Paid in —)

If the wages are—		And the number of withholding allowances claimed is—										
At least	But less than	0	1	2	3	4	5	6	7	8	9	10
		The amount of income tax to be withheld is—										
$0	$125	$0	$0	$0	$0	$0	$0	$0	$0	$0	$0	$0
125	130	1	0	0	0	0	0	0	0	0	0	0
130	135	1	0	0	0	0	0	0	0	0	0	0
135	140	2	0	0	0	0	0	0	0	0	0	0
140	145	3	0	0	0	0	0	0	0	0	0	0
145	150	4	0	0	0	0	0	0	0	0	0	0
150	155	4	0	0	0	0	0	0	0	0	0	0
155	160	5	0	0	0	0	0	0	0	0	0	0
160	165	6	0	0	0	0	0	0	0	0	0	0
165	170	7	0	0	0	0	0	0	0	0	0	0
170	175	7	0	0	0	0	0	0	0	0	0	0
175	180	8	0	0	0	0	0	0	0	0	0	0
180	185	9	1	0	0	0	0	0	0	0	0	0
185	190	10	2	0	0	0	0	0	0	0	0	0
190	195	10	2	0	0	0	0	0	0	0	0	0
195	200	11	3	0	0	0	0	0	0	0	0	0
200	210	12	4	0	0	0	0	0	0	0	0	0
210	220	14	6	0	0	0	0	0	0	0	0	0
220	230	15	7	0	0	0	0	0	0	0	0	0
230	240	17	9	1	0	0	0	0	0	0	0	0
240	250	18	10	2	0	0	0	0	0	0	0	0
250	260	20	12	4	0	0	0	0	0	0	0	0
260	270	21	13	5	0	0	0	0	0	0	0	0
270	280	23	15	7	0	0	0	0	0	0	0	0
280	290	24	16	8	0	0	0	0	0	0	0	0
290	300	26	18	10	2	0	0	0	0	0	0	0
300	310	27	19	11	3	0	0	0	0	0	0	0
310	320	29	21	13	5	0	0	0	0	0	0	0
320	330	30	22	14	6	0	0	0	0	0	0	0
330	340	32	24	16	8	0	0	0	0	0	0	0
340	350	33	25	17	9	1	0	0	0	0	0	0
350	360	35	27	19	11	3	0	0	0	0	0	0
360	370	36	28	20	12	4	0	0	0	0	0	0
370	380	38	30	22	14	6	0	0	0	0	0	0
380	390	39	31	23	15	7	0	0	0	0	0	0
390	400	41	33	25	17	9	1	0	0	0	0	0
400	410	42	34	26	18	10	2	0	0	0	0	0
410	420	44	36	28	20	12	4	0	0	0	0	0
420	430	45	37	29	21	13	5	0	0	0	0	0
430	440	47	39	31	23	15	7	0	0	0	0	0
440	450	48	40	32	24	16	8	1	0	0	0	0
450	460	50	42	34	26	18	10	2	0	0	0	0
460	470	51	43	35	27	19	11	4	0	0	0	0
470	480	53	45	37	29	21	13	5	0	0	0	0
480	490	54	46	38	30	22	14	7	0	0	0	0
490	500	56	48	40	32	24	16	8	0	0	0	0
500	510	57	49	41	33	25	17	10	2	0	0	0
510	520	59	51	43	35	27	19	11	3	0	0	0
520	530	60	52	44	36	28	20	13	5	0	0	0
530	540	62	54	46	38	30	22	14	6	0	0	0
540	550	63	55	47	39	31	23	16	8	0	0	0
550	560	65	57	49	41	33	25	17	9	1	0	0
560	570	66	58	50	42	34	26	19	11	3	0	0
570	580	68	60	52	44	36	28	20	12	4	0	0
580	590	69	61	53	45	37	29	22	14	6	0	0
590	600	71	63	55	47	39	31	23	15	7	0	0
600	610	72	64	56	48	40	32	25	17	9	1	0
610	620	74	66	58	50	42	34	26	18	10	2	0
620	630	75	67	59	51	43	35	28	20	12	4	0
630	640	77	69	61	53	45	37	29	21	13	5	0
640	650	78	70	62	54	46	38	31	23	15	7	0
650	660	80	72	64	56	48	40	32	24	16	8	0
660	670	81	73	65	57	49	41	34	26	18	10	2
670	680	83	75	67	59	51	43	35	27	19	11	3
680	690	84	76	68	60	52	44	37	29	21	13	5
690	700	86	78	70	62	54	46	38	30	22	14	6
700	710	87	79	71	63	55	47	40	32	24	16	8
710	720	89	81	73	65	57	49	41	33	25	17	9
720	730	90	82	74	66	58	50	43	35	27	19	11
730	740	92	84	76	68	60	52	44	36	28	20	12

STEP 1 →

STEP 2 →

Illustration 82C

Federal income tax withholding table (continued)

MARRIED Persons—WEEKLY Payroll Period
(For Wages Paid in —)

If the wages are—		And the number of withholding allowances claimed is—										
At least	But less than	0	1	2	3	4	5	6	7	8	9	10
		The amount of income tax to be withheld is—										
$740	$750	93	85	77	69	61	53	46	38	30	22	14
750	760	95	87	79	71	63	55	47	39	31	23	15
760	770	96	88	80	72	64	56	49	41	33	25	17
770	780	98	90	82	74	66	58	50	42	34	26	18
780	790	99	91	83	75	67	59	52	44	36	28	20
790	800	101	93	85	77	69	61	53	45	37	29	21
800	810	102	94	86	78	70	62	55	47	39	31	23
810	820	104	96	88	80	72	64	56	48	40	32	24
820	830	105	97	89	81	73	65	58	50	42	34	26
830	840	107	99	91	83	75	67	59	51	43	35	27
840	850	108	100	92	84	76	68	61	53	45	37	29
850	860	110	102	94	86	78	70	62	54	46	38	30
860	870	111	103	95	87	79	71	64	56	48	40	32
870	880	113	105	97	89	81	73	65	57	49	41	33
880	890	114	106	98	90	82	74	67	59	51	43	35
890	900	116	108	100	92	84	76	68	60	52	44	36
900	910	117	109	101	93	85	77	70	62	54	46	38
910	920	119	111	103	95	87	79	71	63	55	47	39
920	930	122	112	104	96	88	80	73	65	57	49	41
930	940	124	114	106	98	90	82	74	66	58	50	42
940	950	127	115	107	99	91	83	76	68	60	52	44
950	960	130	117	109	101	93	85	77	69	61	53	45
960	970	133	118	110	102	94	86	79	71	63	55	47
970	980	136	121	112	104	96	88	80	72	64	56	48
980	990	138	124	113	105	97	89	82	74	66	58	50
990	1,000	141	126	115	107	99	91	83	75	67	59	51
1,000	1,010	144	129	116	108	100	92	85	77	69	61	53
1,010	1,020	147	132	118	110	102	94	86	78	70	62	54
1,020	1,030	150	135	120	111	103	95	88	80	72	64	56
1,030	1,040	152	138	123	113	105	97	89	81	73	65	57
1,040	1,050	155	140	126	114	106	98	91	83	75	67	59
1,050	1,060	158	143	128	116	108	100	92	84	76	68	60
1,060	1,070	161	146	131	117	109	101	94	86	78	70	62
1,070	1,080	164	149	134	119	111	103	95	87	79	71	63
1,080	1,090	166	152	137	122	112	104	97	89	81	73	65
1,090	1,100	169	154	140	125	114	106	98	90	82	74	66
1,100	1,110	172	157	142	128	115	107	100	92	84	76	68
1,110	1,120	175	160	145	130	117	109	101	93	85	77	69
1,120	1,130	178	163	148	133	118	110	103	95	87	79	71
1,130	1,140	180	166	151	136	121	112	104	96	88	80	72
1,140	1,150	183	168	154	139	124	113	106	98	90	82	74
1,150	1,160	186	171	156	142	127	115	107	99	91	83	75
1,160	1,170	189	174	159	144	130	116	109	101	93	85	77
1,170	1,180	192	177	162	147	132	118	110	102	94	86	78
1,180	1,190	194	180	165	150	135	120	112	104	96	88	80
1,190	1,200	197	182	168	153	138	123	113	105	97	89	81
1,200	1,210	200	185	170	156	141	126	115	107	99	91	83
1,210	1,220	203	188	173	158	144	129	116	108	100	92	84
1,220	1,230	206	191	176	161	146	132	118	110	102	94	86
1,230	1,240	208	194	179	164	149	134	120	111	103	95	87
1,240	1,250	211	196	182	167	152	137	122	113	105	97	89
1,250	1,260	214	199	184	170	155	140	125	114	106	98	90
1,260	1,270	217	202	187	172	158	143	128	116	108	100	92
1,270	1,280	220	205	190	175	160	146	131	117	109	101	93
1,280	1,290	222	208	193	178	163	148	134	119	111	103	95
1,290	1,300	225	210	196	181	166	151	136	122	112	104	96
1,300	1,310	228	213	198	184	169	154	139	124	114	106	98
1,310	1,320	231	216	201	186	172	157	142	127	115	107	99
1,320	1,330	234	219	204	189	174	160	145	130	117	109	101
1,330	1,340	236	222	207	192	177	162	148	133	118	110	102
1,340	1,350	239	224	210	195	180	165	150	136	121	112	104
1,350	1,360	242	227	212	198	183	168	153	138	124	113	105
1,360	1,370	245	230	215	200	186	171	156	141	126	115	107
1,370	1,380	248	233	218	203	188	174	159	144	129	116	108
1,380	1,390	250	236	221	206	191	176	162	147	132	118	110

$1,390 and over — Use Table 1(b) for a **MARRIED** person on page 34. Also see the instructions on page 32.

find an amount of $25.00. This tells you that you must deduct $25.00 from Olive's wages for federal withholding tax.

To help you learn to use the table, Illustration 82B shows some wages and their correct withholding tax amounts. Look at Illustration 82C and see if you can find the same answers.

USING THE COMPUTER FOR WITHHOLDING TAXES

If a computer is used for payroll, you do not need to look up and record each employee's federal withholding tax. The computer stores the federal

Illustration 82D

The top part of a paycheck printed by a computer showing the withholding tax for the week and the total paid for the year

| Period Ended | 03/04/-- | Employee No. | 1078 |
| Name | EVERETT LANDON | Social Security No. | 334-87-1029 |

	Totals This Period	Totals Year-to-Date
Total Pay	$389.89	$3,509.01
Fed. With.	31.00	375.00
FICA Tax	31.19	280.71
Net Pay	$327.70	$2,853.30

withholding tax tables in its memory and automatically looks up and records each employee's withholding tax. This saves the payroll office a great deal of work and also makes the calculations more accurate.

BUILDING YOUR BUSINESS VOCABULARY

On a sheet of paper, write the headings **Statement Number** and **Words**. Next, choose the words that match the statements. Write each word you choose next to the statement number it matches. Be careful; not all the words listed should be used.

Statements	Words
1. An income tax deducted from a worker's wages each payday	biweekly
2. Time worked beyond 40 hours a week	commission
3. Gross pay less deductions	deductions
4. Twice a month	FICA tax
5. A deduction a worker may claim for the support of another person	net pay
6. Amounts subtracted from wages	overtime
7. A form which shows how many withholding allowances a worker claims	regular time pay
8. Every two weeks	semimonthly
9. A tax collected to pay for social security	W-4 form
	withholding allowance
	withholding tax

STEPS REVIEW: Finding Withholding Taxes

STEP 1 Locate the wages in the wages section of the withholding tax table.

STEP 2 Find the withholding tax deduction in the correct allowance column.

APPLICATION PROBLEMS

Problem 82-1

You work as a payroll clerk for Integrated Systems Corporation.

Directions

Copy and complete the following table. Find the federal withholding tax for each wage amount using the withholding tax table found in Illustration 82C (pages 642–643).

Time Card No.	Number of Allowances	Wages		Federal Withholding Tax	
1	2	310	00		
2	6	578	00		
3	0	489	17		
4	1	1,040	89		
5	7	839	27		
6	3	628	51		
7	1	293	15		
8	4	764	63		
9	0	1,128	85		
10	3	375	45		

Problem 82-2 You are the payroll clerk for Jolor Alloy Company.

Directions

Copy and complete the following table. Find the federal withholding tax for each wage amount using the withholding tax table found in Illustration 82C (pages 642–643).

CHECK POINT

82-2(1)

Withholding
amount = $160.00

Time Card No.	Number of Allowances	Wages		Federal Withholding Tax	
1	4	1,272	37		
2	6	271	39		
3	1	516	07		
4	0	463	91		
5	7	361	20		
6	3	609	75		
7	5	834	51		
8	0	708	64		
9	1	372	34		
10	2	1,011	26		

Problem 82-3 You are a payroll clerk for Sea Trailers, Inc.

Directions

Copy and complete the following table. Find the social security tax and the federal withholding tax for each wage amount. Use the social security tax table found in Illustration 81A on page 636 in Job 81. Use the withholding tax table found in Illustration 82C on pages 642–643 in this job. Remember that the withholding tax is based on the gross pay, or total wages.

CHECK POINT

82-3(3)

FICA tax amount =
$32.16

Withholding amount
= $2.00

Time Card No.	Number of Allowances	Wages		FICA Tax		Federal Withholding Tax	
1	1	401	80				
2	0	411	90				
3	5	402	02				
4	9	410	95				
5	3	401	91				
6	2	411	01				

goals

 To learn how to find a worker's take-home pay after making social security and withholding tax deductions.

 To learn how to enter the information in a payroll register.

UNDERSTANDING THE JOB

In the previous chapter, you learned to record payroll data, including gross pay, in a payroll register. In the last two jobs, you learned how to find the amounts for social security and federal withholding taxes. In this job, you will learn how to record all these data in a payroll register.

SAMPLE PROBLEM

You work as a payroll clerk for Regis Glass Company. You just completed the payroll register shown in Illustrations 83A and 83B on page 647. Here are the steps you followed to record the payroll data in the payroll register:

STEP 1 Enter the time card data.

From the time cards, you filled in the columns for card number, name of employee, hours worked, wage rates, wage amounts, and gross pay.

STEP 2 Enter the number of allowances.

In the No. of Allow. column, you entered the number of allowances the employee claimed on the W-4 form.

STEP 3 Enter the social security tax deduction.

You found the social security tax deduction (FICA tax) for each employee by multiplying the gross pay by 8%, the FICA tax rate used in this chapter. You entered the amount in the FICA Tax column.

STEP 4 Enter the federal withholding tax deduction.

You found the federal withholding tax deduction for each employee by using the table in Illustration 82C on pages 642–643 in Job 82. You entered the amount in the federal withholding tax (Fed. With.) column.

STEP 5 Enter the total deductions for each employee.

You added the amounts in the FICA Tax and Fed. With. tax columns together for each employee and entered the total deductions in the total deductions (Total Ded.) column.

For example, in Illustration 83B, Michelle Levy's total deductions were found this way:

Social security (FICA) tax	$ 32.64
Federal withholding tax	+ 34.00
Total deductions	$ 66.64

You entered the amount of Michelle's total deductions, $66.64, in the Total Ded. column.

STEP 6 Find the net pay, or take-home pay, for each employee.

You found net pay by subtracting the total deductions from the gross pay. You entered the amount of net pay in the Net Pay column. For example, in Illustration 83B, Michelle's net pay was found this way:

Gross pay	$408.00
Less: Total deductions	−66.64
Net pay	$341.36

Illustration 83A
Payroll register (left page)

STEP 1

STEP 2

Illustration 83B
Payroll register (right page)

STEP 7

STEP 3   STEP 4   STEP 5   STEP 6   STEP 8

STEP 7 Foot each money column and check the totals.

You ruled and footed all the money columns. You checked the total of the Gross Pay column by adding the total of the Regular Pay column to the total of the Overtime Pay column.

Regular pay	$748.00
Overtime pay	+ 25.50
Gross pay	$773.50

The total of the Total Ded. column was checked this way:

Total FICA tax	$ 61.88
Total federal withholding tax	+ 46.00
Total deductions	$107.88

The total of the Net Pay column was checked as follows:

Gross pay	$ 773.50
Total deductions	− 107.88
Total net pay	$ 665.62

STEP 8 Record the final totals and double rule the money columns.

After checking the totals by crossfooting, you recorded the final totals. Then, you double ruled the money columns, as shown in Illustrations 83A and 83B (page 647).

BUILDING YOUR BUSINESS VOCABULARY

On a sheet of paper, write the headings **Statement Number** and **Words**. Next, choose the words that match the statements. Write each word you choose next to the statement number it matches. Be careful; not all the words listed should be used.

Statements	Words
1. The amount left after deductions; take-home pay	biweekly
2. Twice a month	FICA tax
3. Social security tax	net pay
4. Every two weeks	overtime
5. A deduction a worker may claim for the support of another person	semimonthly
6. An income tax deducted from a worker's wages each payday	total wages
7. A form which shows how many withholding allowances a worker claims	W-4 form
	withholding allowance
	withholding tax

STEPS REVIEW: Preparing the Payroll

STEP 1 Enter the time card data.

STEP 2 Enter the number of allowances.

STEP 3 Enter the social security tax deduction.

STEP 4 Enter the federal withholding tax deduction.

STEP 5 Enter the total deductions for each employee.

STEP 6 Find the net pay, or take-home pay, for each employee.

STEP 7 Foot each money column and check the totals.

STEP 8 Record the final totals and double rule the money columns.

APPLICATION PROBLEMS

Problem 83-1   You are employed as a payroll clerk by Yanaka Major Leagues, Inc.

Directions

a. Copy and complete the following table. Find the social security tax using an 8% FICA tax rate. Find the federal withholding tax using the income tax withholding table shown in Illustration 82C on pages 642–643 in Job 82.

CHECK POINT

83-1(b)

Total net pay = $1,975.86

Time Card No.	No. of Allow.	Total Wages		Social Security (FICA) Tax		Federal With. Tax		Total Deductions		Net Pay	
1	1	289	78								
2	5	402	78								
3	0	473	59								
4	4	511	38								
5	3	634	27								
	Totals										

b. Foot each money column and check your totals.

Problem 83-2   You are the payroll clerk for Herbst Appliance Company.

Directions

a. Prepare a payroll register with the same column headings as shown in Illustrations 83A and 83B (page 647).

b. Enter the following information for the week ending October 18, 20--, in the payroll register:

Total net pay = $1,957.79

Time Card No.	Name of Employee	No. of Allow.	M	T	W	TH	F	Wages Per Hour
1	T. Howard	1	8	8	8	8	8	$ 8.80
2	V. Hyslip	0	7½	8¼	8½	8	8	13.50
3	B. Ivany	3	8	9	8¼	8¾	9	9.57
4	C. Johnsen	2	8	8½	9½	8	7½	12.45
5	D. Keller	8	10	9½	10	9½	10½	8.25

c. Complete the payroll register. Use a FICA tax rate of 8% and the income tax withholding table shown in Illustration 82C on pages 642–643 in Job 82.

d. Foot each money column and check your totals.

Problem 83-3   You are the payroll clerk for Chiang's Tour Company.

Directions

a. Prepare a payroll register with the same column headings as shown in Illustrations 83A and 83B (page 647).

b. Enter the following information for the week ending June 24, 20--, in the payroll register:

Total net pay = $1,701.74

Time Card No.	Name of Employee	No. of Allow.	M	T	W	TH	F	Wages Per Hour
1	D. Toussant	1	8½	8	8½	8½	8	$ 7.80
2	L. Tunile	0	8	10¼	8½	8	7	10.10
3	S. Tyler	6	8	8	9¼	8	10½	10.65
4	O. Underwood	3	7½	8	7½	7	7½	8.95
5	Y. Vander	1	8	8½	8	7½	8½	9.70

c. Complete the payroll register. Use a FICA tax rate of 8% and the income tax withholding table shown in Illustration 82C on pages 642–643 in Job 82.

d. Foot each money column and check your totals.

applied math preview

Copy and complete these problems.

1. $ 387.91
    712.83
    567.34
    907.78
    297.08
    + 674.98

2. Crossfoot and then add down:
    26 + 83 + 40 + 62 =
    65 + 20 + 56 + 49 =
    28 + 15 + 29 + 48 =
    87 + 17 + 54 + 42 =
    201 + 307 + 74 + 3 =

key terms preview

- **Employee earnings record**
- **FWT**
- **Quarter**

goal

To learn how to keep a record of each employee's earnings and deductions.

 UNDERSTANDING THE JOB

Key Terms

Employee earnings record. A record of an employee's earnings and deductions.

Quarter. 13 weeks or ¼ of a year.

You have learned how social security and federal withholding taxes are deducted from an employee's wages. Employers must pay the money deducted to the federal government at certain times during the year. Employers must also give federal and state agencies information about the earnings and deductions of each employee. To have this information ready when it is needed, payroll clerks keep an **employee earnings record** for each employee, like the one shown in Illustration 84B on page 653.

The information for the top part of the record is recorded when the employee is hired. At the end of each week, the payroll clerk enters data from the payroll register into the employee earnings record. The employee earnings record is totaled and summarized at the end of thirteen weeks, or each **quarter**.

 SAMPLE PROBLEM

Keiko Saburo is the payroll clerk for Rand Insurance Company. The payroll register for the week ending January 4 is shown in Illustration 84A.

Illustration 84B (page 653) shows an employee earnings record for Ari Shaheen. Look at the entry for the week ending January 4. Notice how these data were taken from the payroll register shown in Illustration 84A.

TIME CARD NO.	NAME OF EMPLOYEE	GROSS PAY	DEDUCTIONS			NET PAY	
			FICA TAX	FED. WITH.	TOTAL DED.		
1	102	Ari Shaheen	387 20	30 98	15 00	45 98	341 22	1
2	103	Sally Skelly	528 92	42 31	44 00	86 31	442 61	2
3	104	Todd Skinner	476 31	38 10	53 00	91 10	385 21	3
4	105	Vi Stein	610 42	48 83	58 00	106 83	503 59	4
5		Totals	2002 85	160 22	170 00	330 22	1672 63	5

Illustration 84A

Partial payroll register

Keiko Saburo followed these steps to complete the employee earnings record:

STEP 1 Record the data on the top part of the record when the employee is hired.

Ari Shaheen was hired at a salary of $387.20 a week (40 hours). Keiko recorded this information on the employee earnings record. Ari Shaheen was also asked a number of personal questions. His answers were entered on the top part of his employee earnings record.

STEP 2 Post data from the payroll register to the employee earnings record each payday.

For each employee, the amount of gross pay, FICA tax, and federal withholding tax is posted from the payroll register to the employee earnings record each payday. Compare Illustration 84A to Illustration 84B (page 653). Notice how the information for Ari Shaheen in the payroll register was copied to the employee earnings record for the week ending January 4.

At the end of the second week, January 11, the information was again posted to the employee earnings record from the payroll register. Notice that the gross pay on January 11 differs from the gross pay on January 4. During that week, Ari worked more than 40 hours (42 hours) and received overtime wages for the two hours worked beyond 40 hours.

STEP 3 Total each money column at the end of the quarter.

At the end of the 13 weeks, or quarter, Keiko footed the amount columns of the employee earnings record. After checking the footings, Keiko entered the final totals. The employee earnings record in Illustration 84B shows data about Ari's earnings and deductions for the first quarter of the year.

STEP 4 Record the totals for each quarter in the Summary section.

At the end of each quarter, the totals for the quarter are recorded in the Summary section of the employee earnings record. At the end of the year, the totals for each quarter are added together to find the totals for the year. The amounts are recorded on the Yearly Total line at the bottom of the card. Illustration 84C on page 653 shows the completed Summary section of Ari Shaheen's employee earnings record at the end of the year.

STEP 2
STEP 1

EMPLOYEE EARNINGS RECORD

Name ___Ari Shaheen___   Time Card No. ___102___
Address ___25 Woodley Road___   Social Security No. ___352-82-1872___
___Rockford, IL 61111-0025___   No. of Allowances ___3___
Date of Birth _2_/_23_/_--_   Single ___   Married ___✓___
Job Title ___Administrative Assistant___   Department ___Investments (8)___
Wage Rate $ ___387.20___   Wage Plan ___Weekly Salary___
Date Hired _5_/_17_/_--_   Termination Date ___/___/___

FIRST QUARTER

	Week Ending	Gross Pay				FICA Tax				Fed. With. Tax			
1	20-- Jan. 4		3	8	7	20		3	0	98		1	5	00
2	11		4	1	6	24		3	3	30		2	0	00
3	18		3	8	7	20		3	0	98		1	5	00
4	25		3	8	7	20		3	0	98		1	5	00
5	Feb. 1		4	4	5	28		3	5	62		2	4	00
6	8		3	8	7	20		3	0	98		1	5	00
7	15		3	8	7	20		3	0	98		1	5	00
8	22		3	8	7	20		3	0	98		1	5	00
9	Mar. 1		3	8	7	20		3	0	98		1	5	00
10	8		4	1	6	24		3	3	30		2	0	00
11	15		3	8	7	20		3	0	98		1	5	00
12	22		3	8	7	20		3	0	98		1	5	00
13	29		3	8	7	20		3	0	98		1	5	00
	Totals	5	1	4	9	76	4	1	2	02	2	1	4	00

SUMMARY

Quarters	Gross Pay				FICA Tax				Fed. With. Tax			
First	5	1	4	9	76	4	1	2	02	2	1	4	00
Second													
Third													
Fourth													
Yearly Total													

STEP 3

Total each money column at the end of the quarter.

STEP 4

Totals												

SUMMARY

Quarters	Gross Pay				FICA Tax				Fed. With. Tax			
First	5	1	4	9	76	4	1	2	02	2	1	4	00
Second	5	0	3	3	60	4	0	2	74	2	0	5	00
Third	5	0	6	2	64	4	0	5	06	2	0	9	00
Fourth	5	0	3	3	60	4	0	2	74	2	0	5	00
Yearly Total	20	2	7	9	60	16	2	2	56	8	3	3	00

USING THE COMPUTER

Key Terms

In a computerized payroll system, an employee earnings record is also kept. A printout of Ari Shaheen's employee earnings data produced by a computer at the end of the first quarter is shown in Illustration 84D. You will learn more about computerized payroll systems in Job 85.

Notice that to save space, federal withholding taxes are abbreviated to Federal W/H. Some reports use **FWT**.

FWT. Federal withholding tax.

```
                    Rand Insurance Company
                       Payroll Report
                         03/29/--

                                     Current    Quarterly    Yearly

  102-Ari Shaheen         Gross Pay    387.20     5149.76    5149.76
  25 Woodley Road         Federal W/H   15.00      214.00     214.00
  Rockford, IL 61111-0025 State W/H
  352-82-1872             FICA W/H       30.98      412.02     412.02
  W/H Allow  3  Married   Medicare
  Department  8           Deduction 1
  Pay Periods             Deduction 2
  Reg. Hrs.               Deduction 3
  O. T. Hrs.              Net Pay      341.22
  Extra Pay
  Salary  387.20
```

Illustration 84D

Printout of employee
earnings record

While some of the data in the employee earnings record must be entered by record keepers, much of the data are kept current automatically by the computer.

BUILDING YOUR BUSINESS VOCABULARY

On a sheet of paper, write the headings **Statement Number** and **Words**. Next, choose the words that match the statements. Write each word you choose next to the statement number it matches. Be careful; not all the words listed should be used.

Statements	Words
1. A record of an employee's earnings and deductions	biweekly
2. 1/4 year or 13 weeks	deductions
3. A deduction a worker may claim for the support of another person	employee earnings record
4. Every two weeks	FICA tax
5. Social security tax	FWT
6. The amount of wages left after deductions	gross pay
7. Amounts subtracted from your wages	net pay
8. A fixed amount of pay	quarter
9. Federal withholding tax	salary
	semimonthly
	withholding allowance

STEPS REVIEW: Keeping an Employee Earnings Record

STEP 1 Record the data on the top part of the record when the employee is hired.

STEP 2 Post data from the payroll register to the employee earnings record each payday.

STEP 3 Total each money column at the end of the quarter.

STEP 4 Record the totals for each quarter in the Summary section.

APPLICATION PROBLEMS

Problem 84-1   You are a payroll clerk for Ferral Graphics Company.

CHECK POINT

84-1

Rhonda Lorey's total gross pay = $1,640.00

Directions

a. Open separate employee earnings records for the following people. Use Illustration 84B (page 653) as a guide. You will need four records.
   1. Rhonda Lorey lives at 1425 Kyle Street, San Antonio, TX 78224-1425. She is married and claims 3 allowances. Her date of birth is August 21, 19--. Her social security number is 361-72-7615. She is employed in the art department as a designer. She was hired at a weekly salary of $410.00 on January 2 and was given Time Card No. 1.
   2. Roger Monet lives at 3145 Iowa Street, San Antonio, TX 78203-3145. He is married and claims 2 allowances. His date of birth is May 12, 19--. His social security number is 322-87-5612. He is employed in the production department as a keyboard operator. He was hired at an hourly rate of $9.87 on January 2 and was given Time Card No. 2.
   3. Edith Nunnes lives at 2871 Kendalia Avenue, San Antonio, TX 78224-2871. She is married and claims 1 allowance. Her date of birth is November 15, 19--. Her social security number is 472-81-4578. She is employed in the editorial office as an office manager. She was hired at a weekly salary of $485.00 on January 2 and was given Time Card No. 3.
   4. Wallies O'Hare lives at 623 Mclane Street, San Antonio, TX 78212-0623. He is married and claims 1 allowance. His date of birth is June 16, 19--. His social security number is 507-67-8263. He is employed in the sales department as a sales manager. He was hired at a weekly salary of $540.00 on January 2 and was given Time Card No. 4.

b. The pages of the payroll register that follow show data for the first four weeks of the first quarter. Post the data in the payroll register to the proper employee earnings records.

c. Foot each column on the employee earnings records to show the totals for the month of January.

PAYROLL REGISTER   WEEK ENDING **January 7, 20--**

	TIME CARD NO.	NAME OF EMPLOYEE	GROSS PAY	DEDUCTIONS			NET PAY	
				FICA TAX	FED. WITH.	TOTAL DED.		
1	1	*Rhonda Lorey*	4 1 0 00	3 2 80	2 0 00	5 2 80	3 5 7 20	1
2	2	*Roger Monet*	3 9 4 80	3 1 58	2 5 00	5 6 58	3 3 8 22	2
3	3	*Edith Nunnes*	4 8 5 00	3 8 80	4 6 00	8 4 80	4 0 0 20	3
4	4	*Wallies O'Hare*	5 4 0 00	4 3 20	5 5 00	9 8 20	4 4 1 80	4
5		*Totals*	1 8 2 9 80	1 4 6 38	1 4 6 00	2 9 2 38	1 5 3 7 42	5

PAYROLL REGISTER — WEEK ENDING January 14, 20--

	TIME CARD NO.	NAME OF EMPLOYEE	GROSS PAY	DEDUCTIONS FICA TAX	DEDUCTIONS FED. WITH.	DEDUCTIONS TOTAL DED.	NET PAY	
1	1	Rhonda Lorey	410 00	32 80	20 00	52 80	357 20	1
2	2	Roger Monet	439 22	35 14	31 00	66 14	373 08	2
3	3	Edith Nunnes	485 00	38 80	46 00	84 80	400 20	3
4	4	Wallies O'Hare	540 00	43 20	55 00	98 20	441 80	4
5		Totals	1 874 22	149 94	152 00	301 94	1 572 28	5

PAYROLL REGISTER — WEEK ENDING January 21, 20--

	TIME CARD NO.	NAME OF EMPLOYEE	GROSS PAY	DEDUCTIONS FICA TAX	DEDUCTIONS FED. WITH.	DEDUCTIONS TOTAL DED.	NET PAY	
1	1	Rhonda Lorey	410 00	32 80	20 00	52 80	357 20	1
2	2	Roger Monet	394 80	31 58	25 00	56 58	338 22	2
3	3	Edith Nunnes	485 00	38 80	46 00	84 80	400 20	3
4	4	Wallies O'Hare	540 00	43 20	55 00	98 20	441 80	4
5		Totals	1 829 80	146 38	146 00	292 38	1 537 42	5

PAYROLL REGISTER — WEEK ENDING January 28, 20--

	TIME CARD NO.	NAME OF EMPLOYEE	GROSS PAY	DEDUCTIONS FICA TAX	DEDUCTIONS FED. WITH.	DEDUCTIONS TOTAL DED.	NET PAY	
1	1	Rhonda Lorey	410 00	32 80	20 00	52 80	357 20	1
2	2	Roger Monet	468 83	37 51	35 00	72 51	396 32	2
3	3	Edith Nunnes	485 00	38 80	46 00	84 80	400 20	3
4	4	Wallies O'Hare	540 00	43 20	55 00	98 20	441 80	4
5		Totals	1 903 83	152 31	156 00	308 31	1 595 52	5

Problem 84-2 You continue to work as the payroll clerk for Ferral Graphics Company.

Directions

a. Record the data from the pages of the payroll register shown on page 657 into the same employee earnings records you used in Application Problem 84–1.

b. Foot each column on the employee earnings records to show the totals for the quarter thus far.

CHECK POINT

84-2(b)

Roger Monet's total
FICA tax = $271.61

PAYROLL REGISTER — WEEK ENDING February 4, 20--

	TIME CARD NO.	NAME OF EMPLOYEE	GROSS PAY	DEDUCTIONS			NET PAY	
				FICA TAX	FED. WITH.	TOTAL DED.		
1	1	Rhonda Lorey	471 50	37 72	29 00	66 72	404 78	1
2	2	Roger Monet	394 80	31 58	25 00	56 58	338 22	2
3	3	Edith Nunnes	485 00	38 80	46 00	84 80	400 20	3
4	4	Wallies O'Hare	540 00	43 20	55 00	98 20	441 80	4
5		Totals	1891 30	151 30	155 00	306 30	1585 00	5

PAYROLL REGISTER — WEEK ENDING February 11, 20--

	TIME CARD NO.	NAME OF EMPLOYEE	GROSS PAY	DEDUCTIONS			NET PAY	
				FICA TAX	FED. WITH.	TOTAL DED.		
1	1	Rhonda Lorey	486 88	38 95	30 00	68 95	417 93	1
2	2	Roger Monet	483 63	38 69	38 00	76 69	406 94	2
3	3	Edith Nunnes	485 00	38 80	46 00	84 80	400 20	3
4	4	Wallies O'Hare	540 00	43 20	55 00	98 20	441 80	4
5		Totals	1995 51	159 64	169 00	328 64	1666 87	5

PAYROLL REGISTER — WEEK ENDING February 18, 20--

	TIME CARD NO.	NAME OF EMPLOYEE	GROSS PAY	DEDUCTIONS			NET PAY	
				FICA TAX	FED. WITH.	TOTAL DED.		
1	1	Rhonda Lorey	410 00	32 80	20 00	52 80	357 20	1
2	2	Roger Monet	394 80	31 58	25 00	56 58	338 22	2
3	3	Edith Nunnes	485 00	38 80	46 00	84 80	400 20	3
4	4	Wallies O'Hare	540 00	43 20	55 00	98 20	441 80	4
5		Totals	1829 80	146 38	146 00	292 38	1537 42	5

PAYROLL REGISTER — WEEK ENDING February 25, 20--

	TIME CARD NO.	NAME OF EMPLOYEE	GROSS PAY	DEDUCTIONS			NET PAY	
				FICA TAX	FED. WITH.	TOTAL DED.		
1	1	Rhonda Lorey	456 13	36 49	26 00	62 49	393 64	1
2	2	Roger Monet	424 41	33 95	29 00	62 95	361 46	2
3	3	Edith Nunnes	485 00	38 80	46 00	84 80	400 20	3
4	4	Wallies O'Hare	540 00	43 20	55 00	98 20	441 80	4
5		Totals	1905 54	152 44	156 00	308 44	1597 10	5

Problem 84-3 may be found in the Working Papers.

PREPARING THE WAGE AND TAX STATEMENT

applied math preview

Copy and complete these problems.

1. $18,267.92
   31,078.31
   4,645.15
   978.54
   1,534.81
   36,827.76
   86.42
   606.33
   75,497.64
   +16,423.12

2. Crossfoot and then add down:
   45 + 51 + 63 + 93 =
   63 + 53 + 27 + 81 =
   34 + 24 + 17 + 29 =
   266 + 30 + 61 + 80 =
   126 + 75 + 301 + 52 =

key terms preview

- **Wage and Tax Statement**   • **W-2 form**

goals

1 To learn why the Wage and Tax Statement (W-2 form) is prepared.
2 To learn how a W-2 form is prepared.

→ UNDERSTANDING THE JOB

Wage and Tax Statement. W-2 form.

W-2 form. A record of total wages and deductions for a year.

You have learned that the employee earnings records are used to provide employees and government agencies with information when needed. In this job, you will learn to use the records to give the government and employees a record of total wages and deductions for the year. This record is called a **Wage and Tax Statement** or **W-2 form**. An example of this form is shown in Illustration 85B on page 660.

The W-2 form must be filed by the employer within one month after the close of each year (that is, by January 31 of the following year). The data for this form can be taken from the employee earnings record. The data needed are in the Summary section of the employee earnings record. Look at Illustration 85A. Notice that the total wages, total social security tax, and total federal withholding tax for the year can be found easily.

The payroll clerk prepares four copies of the W-2 form for each employee. One copy is sent to the Social Security Administration. The Social Security Administration records the employee's FICA data and sends the FICA and income tax data to the Internal Revenue Service. One copy is kept by the employer for the files. Two copies are given to each employee. The employee attaches one of the copies to the federal income tax return and keeps the other copy.

If the employee works in a city or state which has an income tax, the payroll clerk prepares six copies of the form. The additional copies are for the state and city and for the employee to attach to the state or local income tax return. Items 17 through 21 of the W-2 form are filled out for state and local governments.

As an employee, you should always compare all the data on the W-2 forms with your records of weekly earnings and deductions. If they do not agree, the payroll clerk should be notified so that corrections can be made immediately.

Roland Moore owns a computer consulting firm called Computer Helper, Inc. It is located at 5726 South Street, Salem, NH 03079-5726, and employs two workers. His employer federal identification number is 67-8162735. His employer state identification number is 1766-8653.

Illustration 85A shows the Summary section of the employee earnings record of one of the firm's employees, Lisa M. Goldmeir, who lives at 3704 Gold Avenue, Salem, NH 03079-3704. Lisa is married and earns $414.40 for a 40-hour week. Her social security number is 389-62-1070.

Illustration 85A

Summary section of employee earnings record

Totals																
SUMMARY																
Quarters	Gross Pay					FICA Tax					Fed. With. Tax					
First	5	3	8	7	20	4	3	0	95		4	6	8	00		
Second	5	3	8	7	20	4	3	0	95		4	6	8	00		
Third	5	4	3	3	52	4	3	4	66		4	7	1	00		
Fourth	5	3	8	7	20	4	3	0	95		4	6	8	00		
Yearly Total	21	5	9	5	12	1	7	2	7	51	1	8	7	5	00	

Illustration 85B (page 660) shows the W-2 form that the payroll clerk prepared at the end of the year. Notice that boxes 16 through 21 have been left blank since New Hampshire has no state income tax and Salem has no local income tax. Other boxes that did not apply to Lisa were also left blank.

Here are the steps that the payroll clerk followed to complete the form:

STEP 1 Record the employer's name, address, and federal and state identification numbers.

The employer's name, address, and identification numbers were entered in Boxes b, c, and 16, as shown in Illustration 85B.

STEP 2 Record the employee's social security number, name, and address.

These data were copied from Lisa's employee earnings record and entered in Boxes d and e of the W-2 form.

STEP 3 Record the total wages, social security tax, and federal withholding tax.

These data were copied from the Summary section of the employee earnings record (Illustration 85A), which shows the total wages, social security

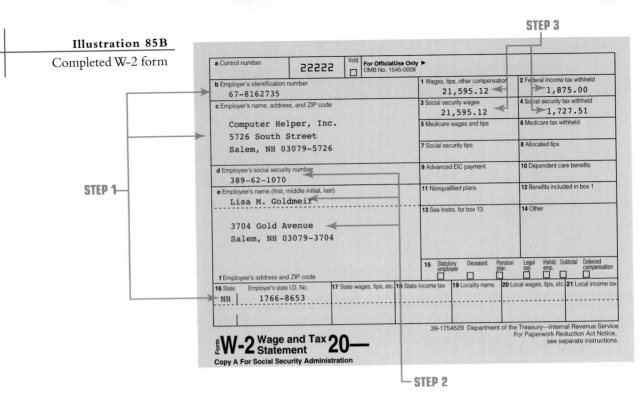

STEP 1

STEP 2

tax, and federal withholding tax for the year. The information was entered in Boxes 1, 2, 3, and 4 as shown in Illustration 85B.

Using the Computer

In a computerized payroll system, W-2 forms are prepared automatically when the payroll clerk orders the computer to do so. In one computerized system, the payroll clerk does this by selecting W-2 statements from the payroll reports menu like the one shown in Illustration 85C. The payroll clerk must first load the computer printer with blank W-2 forms.

Illustration 85C

Payroll menu

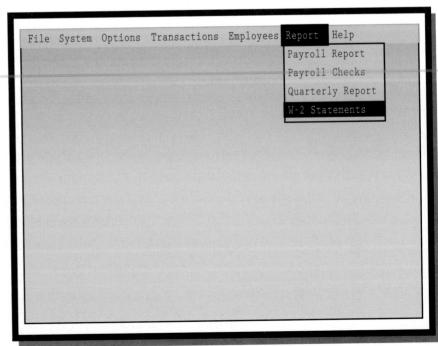

Other Payroll Forms

At the end of each quarter, employers are required to file a Form 941, or the Employer's Quarterly Federal Tax Return. This form is shown in Illustration 85D. The form shows the total wages earned by all employees, total federal income taxes withheld, and total FICA taxes collected from both the employee and the employer.

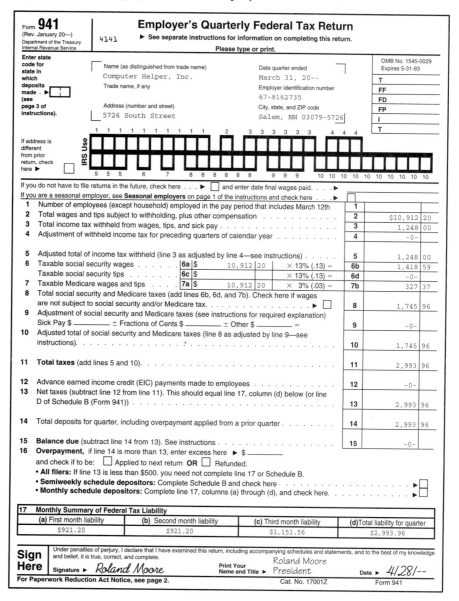

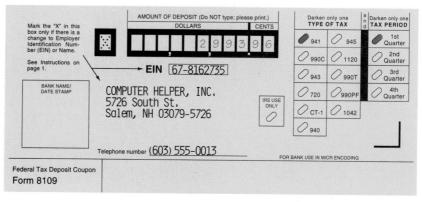

The amounts deducted for federal income taxes and for FICA taxes must then be paid to the federal government. This is done by depositing the funds at a bank using Form 8109, the Federal Tax Deposit Coupon. This form is shown in Illustration 85E on page 661.

BUILDING YOUR BUSINESS VOCABULARY

On a sheet of paper, write the headings **Statement Number** and **Words**. Next, choose the words that match the statements. Write each word you choose next to the statement number it matches. Be careful; not all the words listed should be used.

Statements	Words
1. An income tax deducted from a worker's wages each payday	biweekly
2. A form which shows how many withholding allowances a worker claims	FWT
	menu
3. Twice a month	net pay
4. 1/4 year or 13 weeks	quarter
5. A statement showing the total wages and deductions for an employee for a year	semimonthly
	social security tax
6. FICA tax	W-2 form (Wage and
7. A list of computer programs	Tax Statement)
8. Gross pay less deductions	W-4 form
	withholding tax

STEPS REVIEW: Preparing the Wage and Tax Statement (W-2 Form)

STEP 1 Record the employer's name, address, and federal and state identification numbers.

STEP 2 Record the employee's social security number, name, and address.

STEP 3 Record the total wages, social security tax, and federal withholding tax.

APPLICATION PROBLEMS

Problem 85-1

You are the payroll clerk for Rivas Excavating Company located at 9722 Canal Street, Manchester, NH 03101-9722. The employer's federal identification number is 82-2970816. The employer's state identification number is 6291-4357. Manchester does not have a state or local income tax.

The names, addresses, social security numbers, and Summary sections for three employees follow:

Employee #1   Evelyn A. Wooks
5104 West Street
Concord, NH 03301-5104
Social security #378-98-7561

Totals															

SUMMARY

Quarters	Gross Pay					FICA Tax				Fed. With. Tax			
First	5	8	4	4	80	4	6	7	61	4	1	6	00
Second	5	8	4	4	80	4	6	7	61	4	1	6	00
Third	5	8	4	4	80	4	6	7	61	4	1	6	00
Fourth	5	8	4	4	80	4	6	7	61	4	1	6	00
Yearly Total													

Employee #2

Reed E. Sanford
32 St. James Avenue
Conway, NH 03818-3724
Social security #410-54-8273

Totals															

SUMMARY

Quarters	Gross Pay					FICA Tax				Fed. With. Tax			
First	4	5	2	4	00	3	6	1	92	2	2	1	00
Second	4	5	2	4	00	3	6	1	92	2	2	1	00
Third	4	7	8	4	52	3	8	2	72	2	6	0	00
Fourth	4	7	8	4	52	3	8	2	72	2	6	0	00
Yearly Total													

Employee #3

Dana V. Rodriguez
2114 State Street
Lebanon, NH 03766-2114
Social security #397-61-1452

Totals															

SUMMARY

Quarters	Gross Pay					FICA Tax				Fed. With. Tax			
First	5	0	7	0	00	4	0	5	60	4	2	9	00
Second	5	0	7	0	00	4	0	5	60	4	2	9	00
Third	5	0	7	0	00	4	0	5	60	4	2	9	00
Fourth	5	2	0	0	00	4	1	6	00	4	4	2	00
Yearly Total													

CHECK POINT

85-1(a)

Employee #1 gross pay =
$23,379.20

Directions

a. Copy and complete each Summary section by totaling the columns.
b. Prepare W-2 forms for each employee. Use Illustration 85B (page 660) as an example.

Problem 85-2

You are the payroll clerk for the A & D Auto Company located at 8499 Amherst Street, Nashua, NH 03060-8499. The employer's federal identification number is 28-8675933. The employer's state identification number is 6735-9173. Nashua does not have a state or local income tax.

The names, addresses, social security numbers, and Summary sections for three employees follow:

Employee #1   Evan R. Wakely
6067 Central Road
Portsmouth, NH 03801-6067
Social security #289-65-2867

Totals																					

SUMMARY

Quarters	Gross Pay					FICA Tax					Fed. With. Tax				
First	4	0	5	6	00		3	2	4	48		2	7	3	00
Second	4	2	1	8	20		3	3	7	42		2	8	6	00
Third	4	2	1	8	20		3	3	7	42		2	8	6	00
Fourth	4	2	6	4	00		3	4	1	12		2	8	6	00
Yearly Total															

Employee #2   Doreen R. Brown
1306 Fournier Road
Littleton, NH 03561-1306
Social security #533-42-5241

Totals																					

SUMMARY

Quarters	Gross Pay					FICA Tax					Fed. With. Tax				
First	5	9	8	0	00		4	7	8	40		6	6	3	00
Second	5	9	8	0	00		4	7	8	40		6	6	3	00
Third	5	9	8	0	00		4	7	8	40		6	6	3	00
Fourth	5	9	8	0	00		4	7	8	40		6	6	3	00
Yearly Total															

Employee #3   Vince L. Gibrelli
8551 Wirth Avenue
Tilton, NH 03276-8551
Social security #329-55-9787

Totals																					

SUMMARY

Quarters	Gross Pay					FICA Tax					Fed. With. Tax				
First	5	5	9	0	00		4	4	7	20		6	1	1	00
Second	5	5	9	0	00		4	4	7	20		6	1	1	00
Third	5	5	9	0	00		4	4	7	20		6	1	1	00
Fourth	5	5	9	0	00		4	4	7	20		6	1	1	00
Yearly Total															

✓ **CHECK POINT**

85-2(a)

Employee #2 FICA tax = $1,913.60

Directions

a. Copy and complete each Summary section by totaling the columns.

b. Prepare W-2 forms for each employee. Use Illustration 85B (page 660) as an example.

Job 86   HANDLING OTHER DEDUCTIONS

applied math preview

Copy and complete these problems.

1. $ 8,907.52
    15,816.91
    20,549.08
    17,050.69
    39,468.20
    1,395.87
    24,634.76
    +   183.45

2. Crossfoot and then add down:

    29 + 49 + 60 + 89 =
    68 + 98 + 18 + 30 =
    70 + 106 + 504 + 216 =
    302 + 603 + 720 + 437 =
    130 + 870 + 365 + 908 =

key terms preview

• **Pegboard**

goals

1 To learn about wage deductions other than social security and federal withholding taxes.

2 To learn how to record these deductions in a payroll register.

➡ UNDERSTANDING THE JOB

You have learned that deductions are made from a worker's wages for federal withholding tax and social security tax. You may have wondered why the column in the payroll register is headed "Fed. With." for federal withholding tax instead of just "Withholding Tax." The reason is that some states and cities also require employers to withhold money for state and city income taxes.

To separate the federal from other withholding taxes, one column is headed "Fed. With." for federal withholding tax and the others are headed "State Withholding Tax" and "City Withholding Tax." Separate withholding tax tables are published by the state and city income tax departments for use by the payroll clerk in computing the amounts to be deducted. You use these withholding tax tables the same way you use federal withholding tax tables.

Some employers make other deductions from wages with the approval of the worker. Examples of other deductions include union dues, United States savings bonds, health insurance, life insurance, or private pension plans. The deductions may be made each payday or on certain paydays. The payroll clerk must be careful to make these deductions according to the plan agreed on by the worker and the organization to which the money is to be sent.

Most payroll registers have columns for social security and federal withholding tax deductions. They also usually have two or three columns with no headings. The payroll clerk fills in the headings needed for other deductions.

To learn how to use these other columns, you will complete problems that include monthly deductions for union dues and health insurance.

Jane Feng is the payroll clerk for the Lippold Company. The company is located in a state with no state income tax. The following shows the payroll data for Jerry DiMato, an employee at the company, for the week ending August 26, 20--:

Regular pay	$346.00	
Overtime pay	38.93	
Gross pay		$384.93
Less:		
Social security tax	$ 30.79	
Federal withholding tax	23.00	
Union dues	17.00	
Health insurance	41.17	
Total deductions		111.96
Net pay		$272.97

STEP 1 Record the payroll data in the payroll register.

Illustrations 86A and 86B show how Jane entered these data in the payroll register.

STEP 2 Foot, verify, and rule the payroll register.

Jane would enter the data for other employees in the same way. After all the data have been entered, she would foot, verify, and rule the money columns just as you have learned to do before. When all data have been recorded in the payroll register, Jane will post some of the data to the employee earnings records.

Illustration 86A

Payroll register (left page)

PAYROLL REGISTER

	TIME CARD NO.	NAME OF EMPLOYEE	NO. OF ALLOW.	TOTAL HOURS WORKED	REGULAR PAY			OVERTIME PAY		
					HRS.	RATE	AMOUNT	HRS.	RATE	AMOUNT
1	1	Jerry DiMato	2	43	40	8 65	3 4 6 00	3	12 975	3 8 93

Illustration 86B

Payroll register (right page)

STEP 1 ⌐

PAYROLL REGISTER   WEEK ENDING *August 26, 20--*

	GROSS PAY	DEDUCTIONS					NET PAY
		FICA TAX	FED. WITH.	UNION DUES	INSURANCE	TOTAL DED.	
1	3 8 4 93	3 0 79	2 3 00	1 7 00	4 1 17	1 1 1 96	2 7 2 97

Key Terms

Pegboard. Special writing board which allows you to prepare many forms in one writing.

Using Pegboards to Prepare the Payroll

To speed up the process of preparing the payroll manually, some small businesses use **pegboards**, like the one shown in Illustration 86C. These are specially designed writing boards which will allow you to, all at once:

1. Record data in a payroll register.
2. Record data on the employee earnings record.
3. Write a paycheck for the employee.

Pegboards allow you to line up the columns on the three forms so that the data are entered in the correct place on all three forms at once. Carbon paper or special carbonless paper is used between the forms so that the data are written only once. They are called pegboards because pegs are located along the sides of the board. These pegs allow you to line up the forms correctly.

Since the information is written only once and not recopied, errors that may be made in recopying are eliminated. However, be really careful, because any error in entering data will be made on all forms.

Using Computers to Prepare the Payroll

Today, many businesses, even small businesses, use computers to keep and prepare payroll records. If a computerized payroll system is used, the paycheck, employee earnings record, and payroll register will be prepared automatically by the computer.

Illustration 86C
A pegboard

→ BUILDING YOUR BUSINESS VOCABULARY

On a sheet of paper, write the headings **Statement Number** and **Words**. Next, choose the words that match the statements. Write each word you choose next to the statement number it matches. Be careful; not all the words listed should be used.

Statements	Words
1. Amounts subtracted from wages	biweekly
2. Gross pay less deductions	deductions
3. Every two weeks	manually
4. Every three months	net pay

Statements	Words
5. A deduction a worker may claim for the support of another person	pegboard
6. A form which shows how many withholding allowances a worker claims	quarterly
	gross pay
7. The Wage and Tax Statement prepared from the employee earnings record at the end of the year	W-2 form
	W-4 form
	withholding allowance
8. By hand	withholding tax
9. A special writing board which allows you to prepare the payroll check, employee earnings record, and payroll register in one writing	

STEPS REVIEW: Handling Other Deductions

STEP 1 Record the payroll data in the payroll register.

STEP 2 Foot, verify, and rule the payroll register.

APPLICATION PROBLEMS

Problem 86-1 You are the payroll clerk for Palermo Ceramics, Inc.

Directions

a. Copy this table:

Time Card No.	No. of Allow-ances	Gross Pay		Deductions					Net Pay	
				FICA Tax	Federal With. Tax	Union Dues	Health Insurance	Total Deductions		
I	2	405	89							
2	I	387	80							
3	0	270	00							
4	4	453	78							
5	2	609	00							
	Totals									

CHECK POINT

86-1(c)

Total net pay = $1,462.46

b. Complete the payroll. Use a FICA tax rate of 8% and the federal withholding tax table in Job 82 (pages 642–643). Deduct $19.23 for union dues and $48.75 for health insurance from each worker's pay.

c. Check your totals.

Problem 86-2 You work as a payroll clerk for Tomahawk Craft Company.

Directions

a. Copy this table:

Time Card No.	No. of Allow- ances	Gross Pay		Deductions										Net Pay	
				FICA Tax		Federal With. Tax		Union Dues		Health Insurance		Total Deductions			
1	0	329	80												
2	1	402	30												
3	3	573	86												
4	2	500	70												
5	4	590	95												
	Totals														

CHECK POINT

86-2(c)

Total net pay = $1,682.10

b. Complete the payroll. Use a FICA tax rate of 8% and the federal withholding tax table in Job 82 (pages 642–643). Deduct $27.25 for union dues and $39.89 for health insurance from each worker's pay.

c. Check your totals.

Problem 86-3   You are the payroll clerk for Legion Microtechnology Company.

Directions

a. Copy this table:

Time Card No.	No. of Allow- ances	Gross Pay		Deductions										Net Pay	
				FICA Tax		Federal With. Tax		Union Dues		Health Insurance		Total Deductions			
1	4	1,085	00												
2	5	1,118	90												
3	3	956	78												
4	3	795	60												
5	4	1,168	08												
	Totals														

CHECK POINT

86-3(c)

Total net pay = $3,869.30

b. Complete the payroll. Use a FICA tax rate of 8% and the federal withholding tax table found in Job 82 (pages 642–643). Deduct $31.50 for union dues from each worker's pay and $52.87 for health insurance from the following workers' pay: 1, 2, and 5. Since 3 and 4 did not join the health insurance plan, do not make any deductions for health insurance from their pay.

c. Check your totals.

Problem 86-4 may be found in the Working Papers.

Chapter 16

CHECK YOUR READING

1. Assume you received two employment offers that offered identical benefits and working conditions. Zylar Corporation, however, offers you a biweekly wage of $1,800.00. Mylex Company offers you a semi-monthly wage of $1,875.00. Which employment offer would you accept? Explain your answer.
2. Explain the difference between a W-4 Employee's Withholding Allowance Certificate and a W-2 Wage and Tax Statement.
3. In addition to federal, state, and local income taxes, employees may have other deductions subtracted from their checks. List several examples of "other" deductions.

DISCUSSION

The following errors were made in an employee earnings record. Describe one possible problem that could be caused by each error.
1. The social security number was incorrect.
2. The date hired was wrong by one week.
3. The hourly pay rate was wrong by ten cents.

ETHICS IN THE WORKPLACE

You are a human resources clerk and have discovered that one employee, Aaron Rogers, Employee No. 127, has been receiving $8.61 an hour instead of $6.81 an hour because of an error in his payroll records. The first paycheck with the error was issued on April 1. The last paycheck with the error was issued April 15. Aaron worked 40 hours each of those weeks.

One of your co-workers suggests correcting Aaron Rogers' future paychecks, but saying nothing about the incorrect paychecks. Your co-worker feels that the amount of dollars incorrectly paid is too small to bother with.

Write a memo to your co-worker about your reaction to the suggestion. Use no more than a half sheet of paper for your memo.

COMMUNICATION IN THE WORKPLACE

You are a payroll clerk for the Agar Company. The company is growing rapidly. At a payroll department meeting, Ivy Johnson, the department head, announced that she is considering recommending that the payroll operation be computerized to save time and money. After the announcement, the recommendation was heatedly discussed. Some people felt that

REINFORCEMENT ACTIVITIES

the computer would eliminate their job. Others felt that the computer was needed because of the increase in work that the department was doing.

1. What advantages do you think that the computer might bring to the payroll operation? (List three advantages.)
2. What disadvantages do you think there might be if a computer is used for payroll? (List two disadvantages.)
3. What might you recommend that the company do for its employees to make the changes brought about by the computer as easy to cope with as possible? (List two recommendations.)

Write a memo that summarizes these advantages, disadvantages, and recommendations. Use no more than one sheet of paper for your memo.

FOCUS ON CAREERS

Many record keepers must continue their education while they are working. This advanced education is often called adult education, because it is for adults. It is also called continuing education, because it is education that continues after a person's formal education is completed and often while a person is actually working at a job.

There are many reasons why continuing education is important to record keepers. If a company acquires new technology, the workers may need to retrain. If a company adds new products or services, workers may need to retrain. If workers want promotions to more advanced positions, they may need to retrain.

Most communities provide numerous opportunities for continuing education. These may include evening and weekend classes offered by

1. Your high school.
2. A nearby community college.
3. Nearby business colleges.
4. Professional training organizations.

On a sheet of paper:

a. List the names of two organizations in your area that offer adult or continuing education classes for adults.
b. List the names of those classes, offered by the two organizations, that might provide training in record keeping skills or topics.

On a sheet of paper, write the headings **Statement Number** and **Words**. Next, choose the words that best complete the statements. Write each word you choose next to the statement number it completes. Be careful; not all the words listed should be used.

Statements	Words
1. A record in which the total pay, deductions, and net pay for all workers in a business is recorded is called (a, an) _____.	employee employer FICA taxes four
2. The Wage and Tax Statement is called (a, an) _____.	FWT payroll register
3. The amount paid in social security taxes by an employee must be matched by the _____.	take-home pay three two
4. The form an employee uses to tell an employer how many withholding allowances the employee has is called (a, an) _____.	W-2 form W-4 form withholding allowance
5. A married employee with two dependent children may claim up to _____ withholding allowances.	withholding tax
6. Net pay may also be called _____.	
7. One reason for keeping an employee earnings record for each worker is to tell when that worker has paid the maximum amount of _____.	
8. Federal income tax deducted from an employee's pay is called _____.	

You are the payroll clerk for Reliable Technology, Inc. The payroll information for the week ending March 3, 20-- is shown below:

Card No.	Name of Employee	No. Allow.	M	T	W	TH	F	Pay Per Hour
1	Lee Chun	1	8	8	8	9	7	$ 9.80
2	Lea Maloney	2	8	10	8	8	8	8.60
3	Yun Sun	0	8	8	8	7	8	8.40
4	Valerie Telos	2	$9^1/_2$	8	8	$8^1/_2$	$8^1/_2$	9.75
5	Regina Vitale	1	8	$7^1/_4$	$7^1/_4$	$8^1/_2$	$7^1/_4$	10.60

Directions

a. Prepare a payroll register with the same column headings as shown in Illustrations 86A and 86B (page 666).

b. Enter the date for the week ending at the top of the payroll register.

c. For each employee, enter the card number, name of the employee, number of allowances, and pay per hour in the correct columns of the payroll register.

d. Find the total hours worked for each employee and enter the amount in the Total Hrs. Worked column.

e. Complete the payroll. Use a FICA tax rate of 8% and the federal withholding tax table found in Job 82 (pages 642–643). Deduct $18.00 for union dues and $31.50 for health insurance from each worker's pay.

f. Foot and rule the register. Check the totals by crossfooting.

 REVIEWING YOUR BUSINESS VOCABULARY

This activity may be found in the Working Papers.

 COMPREHENSIVE PROJECT 6

Comprehensive Project 6 has been designed to reinforce major concepts of this and previous chapters. The Comprehensive Project is found in the Working Papers.

Appendix A

PAYING YOUR INCOME TAXES

applied math preview

Copy and complete the problem below. Check your work by crossfooting.

1. $32,786.83 − $4,760.00 =	5. $12,607.82	6. $23,721.84
2. $21,307.62 − $7,709.51 =	3,184.60	3,006.72
3. $ 5,142.47 − $4,298.26 =	478.91	589.19
4. $ 3,340.58 − $1,974.32 =	+ 19.46	+ 76.49

key terms preview

- Adjusted gross income
- Adjustments to gross income
- Exemptions
- Federal income tax
- File
- Form 1099

- Income tax return
- Internal Revenue Service (IRS)
- Itemized deductions
- Standard deduction
- Taxable income

goals

1 To learn how to calculate gross income, adjusted gross income, and taxable income.

2 To learn when to itemize deductions and when to use the standard deduction.

3 To learn how to find federal income taxes from a table.

4 To learn how to use various records to calculate federal income taxes.

→ UNDERSTANDING THE WORK

Key Terms

Federal income tax. Federal government's tax on income.

Internal Revenue Service (IRS). Collects federal income tax.

The federal government taxes the incomes of U.S. citizens and others each year. The tax paid on income is called the **federal income tax** and is collected by the **Internal Revenue Service**, or IRS. Many states and some cities also tax incomes.

You have learned that a certain amount of federal income taxes are withheld from your paycheck each pay period. This tax is called the federal withholding tax, or FWT. You have also learned that the amount of FWT withheld from your paycheck for the year is reported on a Form W-2. Copies of Form W-2 are sent to you (the employee) and the IRS soon after the year ends.

File. Send in your return to the IRS.

Income tax return. Shows how income taxes were calculated.

The federal withholding tax you pay is an estimate of how much you actually owe in federal income taxes. Neither you nor the IRS will know what your real tax for the year is until the year is over. At that time, the IRS requires you to calculate your actual income taxes. You must **file**, or send in a report showing how you calculated the actual taxes owed on your income for last year. This report must be filed no later than April 15 and is called an **income tax return**, or simply a return. You file your return at the nearest office of the Internal Revenue Service.

If the amount of income taxes withheld from your paycheck is larger than the amount of taxes you actually owe, you will get a refund. If the amount withheld is smaller than what you actually owe, you must pay the balance due.

SAMPLE PROBLEM 1

Arianna Reyes is a single person who works two jobs. She is a full-time accounts receivable clerk at Quasar Electronics during the week. On weekends, she is a cashier at Mill Station Theaters.

On February 1, Arianna receives two Forms W-2 in the mail: one for her full-time job and the other for her weekend job. Arianna knows that she does not have to file her federal income tax return until April 15. However, she would like to complete and file her return as soon as possible because she believes that she may get a refund from the government. Arianna's Form W-2 from Quasar Electronics is shown in Illustration A1. Her form from Mill Station Theaters is similar.

Like many other people, Arianna uses an income tax work sheet to help her gather income tax data and calculate her federal income taxes (see Illustration A2 on page 676). She uses a pencil to complete the work sheet so that she can make changes and correct errors.

Illustration A1

Form W-2 for full-time job

a Control number 18901		Void ☐	**For OfficialUse Only ▶** OMB No. 1545-0008	
b Employer's identification number 38-7211846X			**1** Wages, tips, other compensation 14,620.00	**2** Federal income tax withheld 1,508.00
c Employer's name, address, and ZIP code			**3** Social security wages 14,620.00	**4** Social security tax withheld 906.36
Quasar Electronics 1515 Newhall Road Springfield, IL 62702-1515			**5** Medicare wages and tips 14,620.00	**6** Medicare tax withheld 212.16
			7 Social security tips	**8** Allocated tips
d Employee's social security number 415-66-7788			**9** Advanced EIC payment	**10** Dependent care benefits
e Employee's name (first, middle initial, last) Ariana E. Reyes			**11** Nonqualified plans	**12** Benefits included in box 1
f Employee's address and ZIP code 7001 Branch Drive Springfield, IL 62703-7001			**13** See Instrs. for box 13	**14** Other

			15 Statutory employee ☐	Deceased ☐	Pension plan ☐	Legal rep. ☐	Hshld. emp. ☐	Subtotal ☐	Deferred compensation ☐

16 State IL	Employer's state I.D. No. 38-7211846X	**17** State wages, tips, etc. 14,620.00	**18** State income tax 438.60	**19** Locality name	**20** Local wages, tips, etc.	**21** Local income tax

39-1754529 Department of the Treasury—Internal Revenue Service
For Paperwork Reduction Act Notice, see separate instructions.

Form **W-2** **Wage and Tax Statement** **20—**

Copy B To Be Filed With Employee's Federal Income Tax Return

Income:

Salary, Full-time Job	$14,620.00
Salary, Weekend Job	4,744.00
Commissions, Weekend Job	1,946.27
Savings Account Interest	+ 105.65
Gross Income	$21,415.92

Adjustments:

Less: Retirement Deposits	− 438.60
Adjusted Gross Income	$20,977.32

Deductions:

Less: Standard Deduction	− 4,250.00
	$16,727.32

Exemptions:

Less: 1 @ $2,700.00	− 2,700.00
Taxable Income	$14,027.32

Income Tax from Tax Table		$2,104.00
Federal Income Taxes Withheld:		
Full-time Job	$1,508.00	
Weekend Job	+ 104.00	
Total Income Taxes Withheld		−1,612.00
Balance Due		$ 492.00

Illustration A2

Income tax work sheet

Here is how Arianna completes the work sheet and finds the amount of her federal income tax:

STEP 1 Find gross income.

Nearly all types of income are taxable by the federal government. For example, income from salaries and wages, tips, bonuses, interest, prize money, rent receipts, and profits from a business are all taxable. On the other hand, gifts, most kinds of money received from inheritance, and most kinds of money received from life and health insurance are not usually taxable.

Arianna has kept careful records of the amounts of money she has received and spent during the last year. One record of income is the Form W-2 that she receives from each employer. Another is her check register. Arianna deposits all money received in her checking account and writes a brief explanation of each deposit. So, her check register provides a record of all money she receives during the year (see Illustration A3). You can see that recording all money received in your check register will make finding the amount of your income tax a lot easier.

Illustration A3

Part of Arianna's check register

Key Terms

Form 1099-INT. Report of interest earned on savings.

RECORD ALL CHARGES OR CREDITS THAT AFFECT YOUR ACCOUNT								
NUMBER	DATE	DESCRIPTION OF TRANSACTION	PAYMENT/DEBIT (−)	√ T	FEE (IF ANY) (−)	DEPOSIT/CREDIT (+)	BALANCE	246 55
—	20-- 6/3	TO Interest on svgs. acct. FOR	$		$	$ 25 72	+ 25 72	
							272 27	
542	6/4	TO Red Cross FOR donation	15 00				- 15 00	
							257 27	

Still another record that Arianna uses to find her total income is a **Form 1099-INT**. Arianna received a copy of a Form 1099-INT from her bank (see Illustration A4). The Form 1099-INT showed the amount of interest that she earned on her savings account for the year. The bank also sent a copy of the Form 1099-INT to the Internal Revenue Service.

☐ CORRECTED (if checked)		

PAYER'S name, street address, city, state, and ZIP code	Payer's RTN (optional)	OMB No. 1545-0112	
Market Street Bank 5055 Ballwin Avenue Springfield, IL 62702-5055		Form **1099-INT**	**Interest Income**

PAYER'S Federal identification number 37-1978-4455	RECIPIENT'S identification number 415-66-7788	1 Interest income not included in box 3 $ 105.65	**Copy B** **For Recipient**
RECIPIENT'S name Arianna E. Reyes		2 Early withdrawal penalty $ 0.00	3 Interest on U.S. Savings Bonds and Treas. obligations $ 0.00	This is important tax information and is being furnished to the Internal Revenue Service. If you are
Street address (including apt. no.) 7001 Branch Drive		4 Federal income tax withheld $ 0.00		required to file a return, a negligence penalty or
City, state, and ZIP code Springfield, IL 62703-7001		5 Foreign tax paid	6 Foreign country or U.S. possession	other sanction may be imposed on you if this income is taxable and the IRS determines that
Account number (optional) 3829783-3	2nd TIN Not. ☐	$ 0.00		it has not been reported.

Form **1099-INT**   (Keep for your records.)   Department of the Treasury – Internal Revenue Service

---

Illustration A4

A Form 1099-INT showing the interest earned

By looking at her check register, Forms W-2, and Form 1099-INT, Arianna finds that her gross income is $21,415.92 (see Illustration A2 on page 676).

Arianna records each type of income on her work sheet. She then adds the income amounts and records the total, Gross Income.

STEP 2   Find adjusted gross income.

Key Terms

Adjustments to gross income. Amounts subtracted from gross income.

Adjusted gross income. Amount remaining after subtracting adjustments from gross income.

Taxable income. Amount on which you pay federal income taxes.

From your gross income, the federal government allows you to subtract certain kinds of expenses. These amounts include losses from a business, payments you make to approved retirement plans, alimony, and penalties for early withdrawal of savings. Amounts that you subtract from gross income are called **adjustments to gross income**.

Arianna deposits 3 percent of her full-time salary into an approved individual retirement account at her bank. This amount ($14,620.00 × .03 = $438.60) is an adjustment to her gross income. Arianna subtracts the retirement amount from her gross taxable income to find her **adjusted gross income** of $20,977.32 (see Illustration A2 on page 676).

Arianna records the retirement deposits under the title *Adjustments* on the work sheet. She subtracts the amount from her gross income.

STEP 3   Find taxable income.

Taxable income is the amount on which you will pay federal income taxes. Taxable income is your adjusted gross income less deductions and exemptions.

Deductions are those expenses that the federal government lets you subtract from your adjusted gross income. What the federal government lets you claim as deductions changes from time to time. Currently, these expenses include interest paid on a home mortgage, property taxes, state and local income taxes, contributions you make to charities, and part of your medical and dental expenses.

To claim the deductions, you must list, or itemize, each deduction on the income tax return. For example, Arianna could list the donation that she made to the Red Cross as a deduction (see Illustration A3 on page 676). If you itemize your deductions, you must be careful to keep your canceled checks and receipts so that you can verify these deductions to the IRS, if they ask you to do so.

Arianna lists each of her **itemized deductions** by examining her Forms W-2, check register, and the receipts of her expenses she had saved during the year. Her itemized deductions are

Donations	$105.00
State income taxes withheld from full-time job	438.60
State income taxes withheld from part-time job	158.71
Total itemized deductions	$702.31

However, you are alternatively allowed to deduct a fixed amount, called a **standard deduction**, no matter what the dollar amount of your actual deductions is. If the amount of your actual deductions is more than the standard deduction, you can itemize the deductions. If your itemized deductions are less than the standard deduction, you take the standard deduction.

The amounts allowed for the standard deduction and for each exemption are changed often by the federal government. In this text, the amount used for the standard deduction will be $4,250.00 for a single person. Since the standard deduction is more than her itemized deductions, Arianna decides to take the standard deduction.

Arianna records the standard deduction under the heading *Deductions*. She then subtracts the standard deduction from adjusted gross income.

If Arianna had itemized her deductions, she would have listed each one under the heading *Deductions*. She would then have subtracted the total from adjusted gross income.

Exemptions are amounts you may deduct from adjusted gross income based on the number of dependents you list on your tax form. You may list, or claim, one exemption for yourself, unless another person claims you as an exemption on her or his income tax return. For example, suppose that you are working part-time but are still a dependent of your mother and father. If your parents claim you as an exemption on their income tax return, you may not claim an exemption for yourself on your income tax return.

The amount allowed for an exemption is changed often by the federal government. In this text, the amount used for each exemption will be $2,700.00.

Arianna records her exemption under the heading *Exemptions*. She subtracts the amount of the exemption from the amount above it. The result is her taxable income of $14,027.32 (see Illustration A2 on page 676).

Key Terms

Itemized deductions. List of expenses you subtract from adjusted gross income.

Standard deduction. Fixed amount you can deduct.

Exemptions. Deductions based on number of dependents claimed.

STEP 4 Find the amount of income tax.

If your taxable income is not over a certain amount, you can use a tax table to figure your income tax. Part of a federal income tax table is shown in Illustration A5.

To use the table, Arianna finds the amount of her taxable income in the table under the headings labeled with the words "At least" and "But

20-- Tax Table—Continued

If Form 1040A, line 24, is—		And you are—			
At least	But less than	Single	Married filing jointly	Married filing sepa-rately	Head of a house-hold
				Your tax is—	
14,000					
14,000	14,050	2,104	2,104	2,104	2,104
14,050	14,100	2,111	2,111	2,111	2,111
14,100	14,150	2,119	2,119	2,119	2,119
14,150	14,200	2,126	2,126	2,126	2,126
14,200	14,250	2,134	2,134	2,134	2,134
14,250	14,300	2,141	2,141	2,141	2,141
14,300	14,350	2,149	2,149	2,149	2,149
14,350	14,400	2,156	2,156	2,156	2,156

less than." Her taxable income is found on the very first line of the table—"At least 14,000", "But less than 14,050." Since Arianna is single, she looks across the table to the Single column. The amount there, 2,104 (or $2,104.00), is the federal income tax she owes for the year.

Arianna records the taxes owed on the work sheet on a line labeled *Income Tax from Table.*

STEP 5 Find the refund or balance due.

Arianna must now find out if the income taxes that were withheld from her wages during the year were less than or more than the amount of tax she actually owes. To do that, she looks at Box 2 of her Forms W-2. When she does, she finds that her total income taxes withheld are $1,612.00 (see Illustration A2 on page 676).

Arianna records the withholding amounts for each job under the heading *Federal Income Taxes Withheld* and enters the total withholding amount.

Arianna realizes unhappily that the actual amount of taxes owed are more than the estimated amounts withheld from her pay during the year. Arianna subtracts the total amount of withholding from the income taxes that she owes. She is going to have to pay the balance due, $492.00 (see Illustration A2 on page 676).

If the income tax amounts withheld from her paychecks had been larger than the amount of taxes she owed, Arianna would have received a refund. For example, if the total taxes withheld from Arianna's pay had been $2,230.00, Arianna would have received a refund of

$ 2,230.00	Federal income taxes withheld
− 2,104.00	Federal income taxes owed
$ 126.00	Refund

Arianna uses the data from the work sheet (and other forms) to complete the federal income tax return form shown in Illustration A6 on page 680. She mails the return, along with a check for $492.00, to the office of Internal Revenue Service in her area.

1040A | Department of the Treasury—Internal Revenue Service
U.S. Individual Income Tax Return | 20-- (O) IRS Use Only—Do not write or staple in this space.

Label

(See page 18.)

Use the IRS label. Otherwise, please print or type.

L A B E L   H E R E

Your first name and initial	Last name	OMB No. 1545-0085
Arianna E.	Reyes	**Your social security number**
		415 66 7788
If a joint return, spouse's first name and initial	Last name	**Spouse's social security number**

Home address (number and street). If you have a P.O. box, see page 19. | Apt. no.
7001 Branch Drive

City, town or post office, state, and ZIP code. If you have a foreign address see page 19.
Springfield, IL 62703-7001

▲ **IMPORTANT** ▲
You **must** enter your SSN(s) above.

Presidential Election Campaign Fund (See page 19.)

	Yes	No
Do you want $3 to go to this fund?	X	
If a joint return, does your spouse want $3 to go to this fund?		

Note: Checking "Yes" will not change your tax or reduce your refund.

Filing status

Check only one box.

1 ☒ Single
2 ☐ Married filing joint return (even if only one had income)
3 ☐ Married filing separate return. Enter spouse's social security number above and full name here. ▶
4 ☐ Head of household (with qualifying person). (See page 20.) If the qualifying person is a child but not your dependent, enter this child's name here. ▶
5 ☐ Qualifying widow(er) with dependent child (year spouse died ▶ 19   ). (See page 21.)

Exemptions

Check only one box.

6a ☒ **Yourself.** If your parent (or someone else) can claim you as a dependent on his or her tax return, **do not** check box 6a.
b ☐ **Spouse**

No. of boxes checked on 6a and 6b	1

c Dependents:

(1) First name Last name	(2) Dependent's social security number	(3) Dependent's relationship to you	(4) ✔ If qualified child for child tax credit (see page 22)
			☐
			☐
			☐
			☐
			☐
			☐
			☐

No. of your children on 6c who:
• lived with you
• did not live with you due to divorce or separation (see page 23)
Dependents on 6c not entered above

Add numbers entered on lines above	1

d ☐ Total number of exemptions claimed.

Income

Attach Copy B of your Forms W-2 and 1099-R here.

If you did not get a W-2, see page 24.

Enclose, but do not staple, any payment.

7	Wages, salaries, tips, etc. Attach Form(s) W-2.	7	21,310 27
8a	**Taxable** interest. Attach Schedule 1 if required.	8a	105 65
b	**Tax-exempt** interest. DO NOT include on line 8a. 8b		
9	Ordinary dividends. Attach Schedule 1 if required.	9	
10a	Total IRA distributions. 10a	**10b** Taxable amount (see page 24). 10b	
11a	Total pensions and annuities. 11a	**11b** Taxable amount (see page 25). 11b	
12	Unemployment compensation.	12	
13a	Social security benefits 13a	**13b** Taxable amount (see page 27). 13b	
14	Add lines 7 through 13b (far right column). This is your **total income.**	14	21,415 92

Adjusted gross income

15	IRA deduction (see page 28). 15 438 60		
16	Student loan interest deduction (see page 28). 16		
17	Add lines 15 and 16. These are your **total adjustments.**	17	438 60
18	Subtract line 17 from line 14. This is your **adjusted gross income.** If under $30,095 (under $10,030 if a child did not live with you), see the EIC instructions on page 36. ▶ 18		20,977 32

For Disclosure, Privacy Act, and Paperwork Reduction Act Notice, see page 49.   Cat. No. 11327A   **20-- Form 1040A**

Illustration A6

Federal income tax return

STEP 1   STEP 2

Taxable income	19	Enter the amount from line 18.	19	20,977	32

	20a	Check if: ☐ **You** were 65 or older ☐ Blind ☐ **Spouse** was 65 or older ☐ Blind } **Enter number of boxes checked** ▶ 20a
	b	If you are married filing separately and your spouse itemizes deductions, see page 30 and check here .... ▶ 20b ☐

	21	Enter the **standard deduction** for your filing status. **But** see page 31 if you checked any box on line 20a or 20b **OR** if someone can claim you as a dependent. •Single—$4,250 •Married filing jointly or Qualifying widow(er)—$7,100 •Head of household—$6,250 •Married filing separately—$3,550	21	4,250	00
	22	Subtract line 21 from line 19. If line 21 is more than line 19 enter -0-.	22	16,727	32
	23	Multiply $2,700 by the total number of exemptions claimed on line 6d.	23	2,700	00
	24	Subtract line 23 from line 22. If line 23 is more than line 22, enter -0- This is your **taxable income**. ▶	24	14,027	32

STEP 3   STEP 4

Tax, credits, and payments	25	Find the tax on the amount on line 24 (see page 31).	25	2,104	00
	26	Credit for child and dependent care expenses. Attach Schedule 2.	26		
	27	Credit for the elderly or the disabled. Attach Schedule 3.	27		
	28	Child tax credit (see page 32).	28		
	29	Education credits. Attach Form 8863.	29		
	30	Adoption credit. Attach Form 8839.	30		
	31	Add lines 26 through 30. These are your **total credits.**	31		
	32	Subtract line 31 from line 25. If line 31 is more than line 25, enter -0-.	32	2,104	00
	33	Advance earned income credit payments from Form(s) W-2.	33		
	34	Add lines 32 and 33. This is your **total tax.** ▶	34	2,104	00
	35	Total Federal income tax withheld from Forms W-2 and 1099.	35	1,612	00
	36	1998 estimated tax payments and amount applied from 1997 return.	36		
	37a	**Earned income credit.** Attach Schedule EIC if you have a qualifying child.	37a		
	b	Nontaxable earned income: amount ▶ _____ and type ▶ _____			
	38	Additional child tax credit. Attach Form 8812.	38		
	39	Add lines 35, 36, 37a, and 38. These are your **total payments.** ▶	39	1,612	00

Refund Have it directly deposited! See page 43 and fill in 41b, 41c, and 41d.	40	If line 39 is more than line 34, subtract line 34 from line 39. This is the amount you **overpaid.**	40		
	41a	Amount of line 40 you want **refunded to you.**	41a		
	b	Routing number ☐☐☐☐☐☐☐☐☐ c Type: ☐ Checking ☐ Savings			
	d	Account number ☐☐☐☐☐☐☐☐☐☐☐☐☐☐☐☐☐			
	42	Amount of line 40 you want **applied to your 1999 estimated tax.**	42		

STEP 5

Amount you owe	43	If line 34 is more than line 39, subtract line 39 from line 34. This is the **amount you owe.** For details on how to pay, see page 44.	43	492	00
	44	Estimated tax penalty (see page 44).	44		

Sign here Joint return? See page 19. Keep a copy for your records.	Under penalties of perjury, I declare that I have examined this return and accompanying schedules and statements, and to the best of my knowledge and belief, they are true, correct and accurately list all amounts and sources of income I received during the tax year. Declaration of preparer (other than the taxpayer) is based on all information of which the preparer has any knowledge.

Your signature	Date	Your occupation	Daytime telephone number (optional)
Arianna E. Reyes	2/1/--	Accts. Rec. Clerk	
Spouse's signature. If joint return, BOTH must sign.	Date	Spouse's occupation	( )

Paid preparer's use only	Preparer's signature ▶	Date _____ Check if self-employed ☐	Preparer's social security no.
	Firm's name (or yours if self-employed) and address ▶	EIN _____ ZIP code _____

Illustration A6

(continued)

Federal income tax return

Paul Nguyen is a full-time high school student in Gilroy, California. He lives at home with his parents, sister, and two brothers. He also works as a cashier two evenings a week and all day Saturday at the Shoe Sport factory outlet in town.

Paul receives a paycheck every two weeks. Since Paul plans on attending the local community college in two years, he deposits 30% of each paycheck into a special savings account. Paul uses the remainder of his check to pay for clothing, entertainment, food, and automobile expenses.

During the month of January, Paul received a Form W-2 from Shoe Sport and a Form 1099-INT from his bank. These two forms are shown in Illustration A7. Last year in his Record Keeping class, Paul learned how to complete a 1040EZ tax form. Paul knows that he meets all the requirements for using a 1040EZ to file his tax return. He uses the following steps to complete the 1040EZ form.

a Control number 17048	w/s 050	Void ☐	For Official Use Only ▶ OMB No. 1545-0008	

b Employer's identification number 94–611211734		1 Wages, tips, other compensation 3,842.15	2 Federal income tax withheld 271.30
c Employer name, address, and ZIP code Shoe Sport, Inc. 12136 Curtner Avenue San Jose, CA 95125-7204		3 Social security wages 3,842.15	4 Social security tax withheld 247.63
		5 Medicare wages and tips 3,842.15	6 Medicare tax withheld 58.76
		7 Social security tips	8 Allocated tips
d Employee's social security number 721–66–3468		9 Advanced EIC payment	10 Dependent care benefits
e Employee's name (first, middle initial, last) Paul E. Nguyen		11 Nonqualified plans	12 Benefits included in box 1
f Employee's address and ZIP code 17201 Dryden Avenue Gilroy, CA 95020-6033		13 See Instrs. for box 13	14 Other

15	Statutory employee ☐	Deceased ☐	Pension plan ☐	Legal rep. ☐	Hshld. emp. ☐	Subtotal ☐	Deferred compensation ☐

16 State	Employer's state I.D. No.	17 State wages, tips, etc.	18 State income tax	19 Locality name	20 Local wages, tips, etc.	21 Local income tax
CA	800–3791–82	3,842.15	21.54			

39-1754529 Department of the Treasury—Internal Revenue Service
For Paperwork Reduction Act Notice, see separate instructions.

Form **W-2** Wage and Tax Statement **20—**

Copy B To Be Filed With Employee's State, City, or Local Income Tax Return

Illustration A7
Form W2

☐ CORRECTED (if checked)

PAYER'S name, street address, city, state, and ZIP code	Payer's RTN (optional)	OMB No. 1545-0112	
Western Savings and Loan Assoc. 7241 First Street Gilroy, CA 95020-5130		Form **1099-INT**	**Interest Income**

PAYER'S Federal identification number	RECIPIENT'S identification number	1 Interest income not included in box 3	**Copy B**
24-6271-4788	721-66-3468	$ 74.55	**For Recipient**

RECIPIENT'S name	2 Early withdrawal penalty	3 Interest on U.S. Savings Bonds and Treas. obligations	This is important tax information and is being furnished to the Internal Revenue Service. If you are required to file a return, a negligence penalty or other sanction may be imposed on you if this income is taxable and the IRS determines that it has not been reported.
Paul E. Nguyen	$ 0.00	$ 0.00	
Street address (including apt. no.) 17201 Dryden Avenue	4 Federal income tax withheld $ 0.00		
City, state, and ZIP code Gilroy, CA 95020-6033	5 Foreign tax paid	6 Foreign country or U.S. possession	
Account number (optional) 0220-43607811	2nd TIN Not. ☐	$ 0.00	

Form **1099-INT**   (Keep for your records.)   Department of the Treasury – Internal Revenue Service

Illustration A7
(continued)
Form 1099-INT

STEP 1   Fill in name, address, and social security number

This is the first time Paul has filed a return. Paul prints his name, address, and social security at the top of the form shown in Illustration A8 on page 684. He is not married, so he does not complete the lines requesting information for a spouse. Since Paul estimates that he will have not have to pay federal income tax this year, he checks the top "No" box regarding a contribution to the Presidential Election Campaign fund.

STEP 2   Find adjusted gross income

Paul's total wages earned for the year are shown in Box 1 of his Form W-2. Paul enters the amount shown in Box 1, $3,842.15, on line 1 of the 1040EZ form. Since the 1040EZ is read by an optical scanner, Paul writes his numbers very neatly.

On line 2, Paul reports the interest he received on his savings account. He enters $74.55, the amount shown in Box 1 of his 1099-INT form.

Paul did not receive unemployment compensation during the year. He leaves line 3 blank and adds the amounts on lines 1 & 2 & 3 ($3,842.15 + $74.55 + $0.00 = $3,916.70). Paul enters the total, $3,916.70, on line 4.

STEP 3   Find taxable income

Paul qualifies as a dependent of his parents. Since Paul is claimed on his parents' tax return, Paul checks the "Yes" box on line 5.

Before Paul can compute his taxable income, he must complete the worksheet on the back of the 1040EZ form. Paul writes the amount from line 1, $3,842.15, adds $250.00, and enters the total ($4,092.15) on line A. Paul compares the amounts on line A and line B and writes the larger amount, $4,092.15, on line C. Since Paul is single, he enters $4,250.00 on line D. After comparing lines C and D, Paul writes the smaller amount, $4,092.15, on line E. Paul is single and enters "0" on line F. He then adds the amounts on lines E & F ($4,092.15 + 0) and enters the total,

1040EZ

Department of the Treasury—Internal Revenue Service

Income Tax Return for Single and Joint Filers With No Dependents (o)

OMB No. 1545-0675

Use the IRS label here	Your first name and initial Paul E.	Last name Nguyen
	If a joint return, spouse's first name and intital	Last name
	Home address (number and street). If you have a P.O. box, see page 7. 17201 Dryden Avenue	Apt. no.
	City, town or post office, state, and ZIP code. If you have a foreign address, see page 7. Gilroy, CA 95020-6033	

Your social security number

7 2 1 | 6 6 | 3 4 6 8

Spouse's social security number

▲ **IMPORTANT!** ▲
You **must** enter your SSN(s) above.

Presidential Election Campaign (See page 7.)

Note: *Checking "Yes" will not change your tax or reduce your refund.*
Do you want $3 to go to this fund? ▶   Yes ☐   No ☒

If a joint return, does your spouse want $3 to go to this fund? ▶   Yes ☐   No ☐

		Dollars	Cents

Income

Attach Copy B of Form(s) W-2 here. Enclose, but do not staple, any payment.

1 Total wages, salaries, and tips. This should be shown in box 1 of your W-2 form(s). Attach your W-2 form(s).   **1**   3 | 8 4 2 . 1 5

2 Taxable interest income. If the total is over $400, you cannot use Form 1040EZ.   **2**   7 4 . 5 5

3 Unemployment compensation (see page 8).   **3**

4 Add lines 1, 2, and 3. This is your **adjusted gross income.** If under $10,030, see page 9 to find out if you can claim the earned income credit on line 8a.   **4**   3 , 9 1 6 . 7 0

Note: *You* **must** *check Yes or No.*

5 Can your parents (or someone else) claim you on their return?

Yes. Enter amount ☒ from worksheet on back.   **No.** If **single**, enter 6,950.00 ☐ If **married**, enter 12,500.00. See back for explanation.   **5**   4 , 0 9 2 . 1 5

6 Subtract line 5 from line 4. If line 5 is larger than line 4, enter 0. This is your **taxable income.** ▶ **6**   , 0 . 0 0

Payments and tax

7 Enter your Federal income tax withheld from box 2 of your W-2 Form(s).   **7**   2 7 1 . 3 0

8a Earned income credit (see page 9).
b Nontaxable earned income: enter type and amount below.

Type		$		**8a**

9 Add lines 7 and 8a. These are your **total payments.**   **9**   2 7 1 . 3 0

10 Tax. Use the amount on **line 6 above** to find your tax in the tax table on pages 20–24 of the booklet. Then, enter the tax from the table on this line.   **10**   , 0 . 0 0

Refund

Have it directly deposited! See page 12 and fill in 11b, 11c, and 11d.

11a If line 9 is larger than line 10, subtract line 10 from line 9. This is your **refund.**   **11a**   2 7 1 . 3 0

▶ **b** Routing number
▶ **c** Type: Checking ☐   Savings ☐

d Account number

Amount you owe

12 If line 10 is larger than line 9, subtract line 9 from line 10. This is the **amount you owe.** See page 14 for details on how to pay.   **12**

I have read this return. Under penalties of perjury, I declare that to the best of my knowledge and belief, the return is true, correct, and accurately lists all amounts and sources of income I received during the tax year.

Sign here ▶
Keep copy for your records.

Your signature *Paul E. Nguyen*	Spouse's signature if joint return. See page 7.
Date 2/1/--	Your occupation *student*	Date	Spouse's occupation

For Official Use Only

For Disclosure, Privacy Act, and Paperwork Reduction Act Notice, see page 18.

Cat. No. 11329W   **Form 1040EZ**

Illustration A8

1040EZ federal income tax return

Form 1040EZ page 2

Use this form if

- Your filing status is single or married filing jointly
- You do not claim any dependents
- You do not claim a student loan interest deduction or an education credit. See page 3.
- You had **only** wages, salaries, tips, taxable scholarship or fellowship grants, unemployment compensation, or Alaska Permanent Fund dividends, and your taxable interest income was not over $400. **But** if you earned tips, including allocated tips, that are not included in box 5 and box 7 of your W-2, you may not be able to use Form 1040EZ. See page 8.
- You did not receive any advance earned income credit payments.

- You (and your spouse if married were under 65 on January 1, 20-- and not blind at the end of 20--.
- Your taxable income (line 6) is less than $50,000.

If you are not sure about your filing status, see page 7. If you have questions about dependents, use TeleTax topic 354 (see page 17). If you **cannot use this form,** use TeleTax topic 352 (see page 17).

Filling in your return

For tips on how to avoid common mistakes, see page 25.

Enter your (and your spouse's if married) social security number on the front. Because this form is read by a machine, please print your numbers inside the boxes like this:

| 9 | 8 | 7 | 6 | 5 | 4 | 3 | 2 | 1 | 0 |

Do not type your numbers. Do not use dollar signs.

If you received a scholarship or fellowship grant or tax-exempt interest income, such as on municipal bonds, see the booklet before filling in the form. Also, see the booklet if you received a Form 1099-INT showing Federal income tax withheld or if Federal income tax was withheld from your unemployment compensation or Alaska Permanent Fund dividends.

Remember, you must report all wages, salaries, and tips even if you do not get a W-2 form from your employer. You must also report all your taxable interest income, including interest from banks, savings and loans, credit unions, etc., even if you do not get a Form 1099-INT.

Worksheet for dependents who checked "Yes" on line 5

Use this worksheet to figure the amount to enter on line 5 if someone can claim you (or your spouse if married) as a dependent, even if that person chooses not to do so. To find out if someone can claim you as a dependent, use TeleTax topic 354 (see page 17).

A. Amount, if any, from line 1 on front **3,842.15**
+ 250.00 Enter total ▶ A. **4,092.15**

B. Minimum standard deduction... B. 700.00

C. Enter the LARGER of line A or line B here .... C. **4,092.15**

D. Maximum standard deduction. If **single,** enter 4,250.00; if **married,** enter 7,100.00 .... D. **4,250.00**

E. Enter the SMALLER of line C or line D here. This is your standard deduction .... E. **4,092.15**

F. Exemption amount.
- If single, enter 0.
- If married and—
  —both you and your spouse can be claimed as dependents, enter 0.
  —only one of you can be claimed as a dependent, enter 2,700.00.
F. **0**

G. Add lines E and F. Enter the total here and on line 5 on the front.... G. **4,092.15**

If you checked "No" on line 5 because no one can claim you (or your spouse if married) as a dependent, enter on line 5 the amount shown below that applies to you.

- Single, enter 6,950.00. This is the total of your standard deduction (4,250.00) and your exemption (2,700.00).
- Married, enter 12,500.00. This is the total of your standard deduction (7,100.00), your exemption (2,700.00), and your spouse's exemption (2,700.00).

Mailing return

Mail your return by **April 15, 20--.** Use the envelope that came with your booklet. If you do not have that envelope, see page 28 for the address to use.

Paid preparer's use only

See page 14.

Under penalties of perjury, I declare that I have examined this return, and to the best of my knowledge and belief, it is true, correct, and accurately lists all amounts and sources of income received during the tax year. This declaration is based on all information of which I have any knowledge.

| Preparer's signature ▶ | | Date | | Preparer's SSN |

Check if self-employed ☐

| Firm's name (or yours if self-employed) and address ▶ | | | EIN | |
| | | | ZIP code | |

Illustration A8

(continued)

1040EZ federal income tax return

$4,092.15, on line G. Paul returns to the front page of the Form 1040EZ and enters the same amount, $4,092.15, on line 5.

Paul compares the amount on line 5 with the amount on line 4. Since the amount on line 5, $4,092.15, is larger than the amount on line 4, $3,916.70, Paul enters "0.00" on line 6. This means that Paul has no taxable income for the year and will not have to pay income tax on any of his earnings.

STEP 4 Determine payments and amount of tax

Paul enters the amount of income tax withheld from his paychecks during the year on line 7. The amount, $271.30, is shown in Box 2 on Paul's Form W-2.

He skips line 8 since he does not qualify for the Earned Income Credit.

Paul then enters $271.30 again on line 9 to show his total income tax payments.

Paul verifies that he owes no income tax this year by looking up his taxable income as shown on line 6, $0.00, in the federal tax tables. Part of the federal tax table Paul used is shown in Illustration A9. Paul finds the amount of his taxable income in the table under the headings labeled with the words "At least" and "But less than." His taxable income is found on the very first line of the table— "At least 0", "But less than 5." Since Paul is single, he looks across the table to the Single column. The amount there, 0 (or $0.00), is the federal income tax he owes for the year. Paul enters $0.00 on line 10.

Paul subtracts line 10, $0.00, from the amount shown on line 9, $271.30, and enters the total, $271.30, on line 11a. $271.30 is the amount of Paul's refund this year.

STEP 5 Complete the tax form

Paul signs the form at the bottom, enters the current date, and lists his occupation as "student." He attaches Copy B of his Form W-2 to the left side of the 1040EZ form as indicated and mails his return to the Internal Revenue Service Center in his area.

Paperless Electronic Filing

The Internal Revenue Service now allows you to file your return electronically. Electronic filing reduces processing time and will allow you to obtain your refund in half the time. You can use an authorized IRS e-file provider who will prepare and e-file your return or you can file electronically from home. Before using an authorized e-file provider, check on the fee for the service. Some companies will e-file their employees' tax returns for free.

If you use your home computer, you will need to use special tax preparation software and a modem to send your completed tax return. You can obtain tax preparation software from your neighborhood computer store or over the Internet. You can even pay your balance due electronically or use direct deposit to obtain an even faster refund.

If you have a touch-tone telephone, you can file your 1040EZ by phone 24 hours a day, toll free. The IRS calls this option the TeleFile pro-

Tax Table
For persons with taxable income of less than $50,000

Example. Mr. Brown is single. His taxable income on line 6 of Form 1040EZ is $23,850. First, he finds the $26,250-26,300 income line. Next, he finds the "Single" column and reads down the column. The amount shown where the income line and filing status meet is $4,062. This is the tax amount he should enter on line 10 of Form 1040EZ.

At least	But less than	Single	Married filing jointly
26,200	26,250	4,048	3,934
26,250	26,300	4,062	3,941
26,300	26,350	4,049	3,949
26,350	26,400	4,090	3,956

If Form 1040EZ line 6, is—		And you are—		If Form 1040EZ line 6, is—		And you are—		If Form 1040EZ line 6 is—		And you are—		If Form 1040EZ line 6 is—		And you are—	
At least	But less than	Single	Married filing jointly	At least	But less than	Single	Married filing jointly	At least	But less than	Single	Married filing jointly	At least	But less than	Single	Married filing jointly
		Your tax is—				Your tax is—		3,000		Your tax is—		6,000		Your tax is—	
0	5	0	0	1,500	1,525	227	227	3,000	3,050	454	454	6,000	6,050	904	904
5	15	2	2	1,525	1,550	231	231	3,050	3,100	461	461	6,050	6,100	911	911
15	25	3	3	1,550	1,575	234	234	3,100	3,150	469	469	6,100	6,150	919	919
25	50	6	6	1,575	1,600	238	238	3,150	3,200	476	476	6,150	6,200	926	926
50	75	9	9	1,600	1,625	242	242	3,200	3,250	484	484	6,200	6,250	934	934
75	100	13	13	1,625	1,650	246	246	3,250	3,300	491	491	6,250	6,300	941	941
100	125	17	17	1,650	1,675	249	249	3,300	3,350	499	499	6,300	6,350	949	949
125	150	21	21	1,675	1,700	253	253	3,350	3,400	506	506	6,350	6,400	956	956
150	175	24	24	1,700	1,725	257	257	3,400	3,450	514	514	6,400	6,450	964	964
175	200	28	28	1,725	1,750	261	261	3,450	3,500	521	521	6,450	6,500	971	971
200	225	32	32	1,750	1,775	264	264	3,500	3,550	529	529	6,500	6,550	979	979
225	250	36	36	1,775	1,800	268	268	3,550	3,600	536	536	6,550	6,600	986	986
250	275	39	39												

Illustration A9

Part of a Federal 1040EZ income tax table

gram. The average TeleFile call takes about 10 minutes. If you use TeleFile and are expecting a return, you can ask the IRS to deposit your refund directly to your checking or savings account. If you select the direct deposit option, call your bank to verify the correct routing number and account number for your checking or savings account. The IRS publishes a special booklet containing all the instructions needed for completing your return using the TeleFile program. A number of frequently used tax forms are available at selected post offices and libraries. Call your local IRS office for information. You can also download forms, instructions, and publications from the IRS's Internet web site at *www.irs.ustreas.gov.*

BUILDING YOUR BUSINESS VOCABULARY

On a sheet of paper, write the headings **Statement Number** and **Words**. Next, choose the words that match the statement. Write each word you choose next to the statement number it matches. Be careful, not all the words listed will be used.

Statements

1. An alternative fixed amount that you can deduct from your adjusted gross income no matter what the dollar amount of your actual deductions is.
2. The amount left after subtracting adjustments from gross income.
3. The tax paid on income; it is collected by the Internal Revenue Service.
4. When used in connection with income tax return, it means to send or mail.
5. Amounts that the IRS lets you subtract from your gross income.
6. Total income before adjustments, deductions, and exemptions are subtracted.

Words

adjusted gross income
adjustments to
  gross income
deductions
exemptions
federal income tax
file
Form 1099
gross income
income tax return
Internal Revenue
  Service (IRS)
itemized deductions
refund

Statements	Words
7. The agency of the United States Government that collects income taxes.	standard deduction
8. A list of expenses that you are allowed to deduct on your income tax return.	taxable income
9. Amounts deducted from adjusted gross income based on the number of dependents claimed.	trial balance
10. The result when the amount of income taxes withheld during a year is larger than the amount of income taxes actually owed.	withholding taxes
11. A report filed with a government agency that shows how income taxes owed were computed.	
12. Adjusted gross income less deductions and exemptions; the amount on which you pay federal income taxes.	
13. A report of other income, such as interest and dividends, sent to the taxpayer and IRS by the firm paying income.	

STEPS REVIEW: Completing the Income Tax Work Sheet

STEP 1 Find gross income.

STEP 2 Find adjusted gross income.

STEP 3 Find taxable income.

STEP 4 Find the amount of income tax.

STEP 5 Find the refund or balance due.

APPLICATION PROBLEMS

Problem A-1 Find the taxable income for each person below by completing the table. The first one is done for you to show you how.

Name	Gross Income	Adjustments to Income	Adjusted Gross Income	Total Deductions	Total Exemptions	Taxable Income
Ex. Alvarez	19,000.00	2,800.00	16,200.00	4,250.00	2,700.00	9,250.00
(a) O'Brien	18,400.00	1,500.00		4,250.00	2,700.00	
(b) Nguyen	21,750.00	425.00		4,145.00	5,400.00	
(c) Prasaad	31,600.00	975.00		4,683.00	5,400.00	
(d) Muriyama	26,842.00	0.00		4,250.00	2,700.00	
(e) Cipelli	22,369.26	387.24		4,250.00	2,700.00	

Problem A-2 Brett Perryman uses a tax work sheet to find the federal income tax he owes. Complete a work sheet for Brett by following the steps below. Use Illustration A2 (page 676) as a guide.

a. Find Brett's gross income. Brett's Forms W-2 show that he earned $18,302.00 from a full-time job and $3,245.00 from a part-time job. Brett's Form 1099-INT shows that he also earned $235.00 in interest on a savings account.

b. Find Brett's adjusted gross income. Brett's check register shows that he deposited $500.00 in an approved individual retirement account at his bank.

c. Find Brett's deductions and exemptions. Brett's check register shows that he can itemize these deductions: donations, $350.00; state income taxes paid on full-time job, $691.17; state income taxes paid on part-time job, $138.70. Instead of itemizing his deductions, Brett could use the standard deduction of $4,250.00. Brett is single and claims one exemption for himself.

d. Find Brett's taxable income.

e. Use the income tax table in Illustration A5 (page 679) to find the federal income taxes owed.

f. Find the refund or balance due. Brett's Form W-2 shows that he had the following amounts withheld from his paychecks last year: federal income taxes withheld from full-time job, $1,820.00; federal income taxes withheld from part-time job, $104.00.

CHECK POINT

A-2

Tax due = $225.00

Problem A-3 Complete the table below using the instructions for completing a 1040EZ tax form. Notice that the column headings for the table below match specific line numbers from the 1040EZ. Find the Adjusted Gross Income, Taxable Income, Income Tax, and the Refund Amount or Amount Owed. Use the 1040EZ tax table provided in Illustration A9 on page 687. The individuals listed in the table below are single and are claimed on their parents' tax returns. The first one is done for you.

Name	Line 1 Form W-2 Wages	Line 2 1099-INT Int. Income	Line 4 Adj. Gross Income	Line 5 Standard Ded./Exemp.	Line 6 Taxable Income	Line 7 Form W-2 Fed. Tax W/H	Line 10 Income Tax	Line 11a Amount of Refund	Line 12 Amount Owed
Ex. Dan	4,321.00	62.00	4,383.00	4,250.00	133.00	284.00	21.00	263.00	
a. Bob	5,922.00	104.00		4,250.00		201.00			
b. Carol	1,736.40	15.24		1,986.40		164.15			
c. Burt	957.68	311.25		1,207.68		88.60			
d. Larissa	7,302.26	185.72		4,250.00		372.00			
e. Serena	1,296.80	79.43		1,546.80		133.09			

Problem A-4 Katie Delores is a full-time high school student, works part-time, and lives at home. Use the information from the following Form W-2 and 1099-INT to complete a 1040EZ tax return. Use the tax table presented in Illustration A9 on page 687 to determine Katie's tax for the year. Katie is single, is claimed on her parents' tax return, and does not wish to contribute to the Presidential Election Campaign Fund. After completing the 1040EZ, sign the form for Katie. Date the form February 15 of the current year.

a Control number		Void ☐	For OfficialUse Only ▶ OMB No. 1545-0008		

b Employer's identification number 94-78294362		1 Wages, tips, other compensation 1,642.71	2 Federal income tax withheld 209.40
c Employer's name, address, and ZIP code Saratoga Roasting Company 86 Pierre Road Saratoga, CA 95070-0622		3 Social security wages 1,642.71	4 Social security tax withheld 106.94
		5 Medicare wages and tips 1,642.71	6 Medicare tax withheld 25.15
		7 Social security tips	8 Allocated tips
d Employee's social security number 946-11-1802		9 Advanced EIC payment	10 Dependent care benefits
e Employee's name (first, middle initial, last) Katie A. Delores		11 Nonqualified plans	12 Benefits included in box 1
f Employee's address and ZIP code 5207 Congress Springs Road Saratoga, CA 95070-5081		13 See Instrs. for box 13	14 Other

15	Statutory employee ☐	Deceased ☐	Pension plan ☐	Legal rep. ☐	Hshld. emp. ☐	Subtotal ☐	Deferred compensation ☐

16 State	Employer's state I.D. No.	17 State wages, tips, etc.	18 State income tax	19 Locality name	20 Local wages, tips, etc.	21 Local income tax
CA	800-629-1664	1,642.71	31.76			

39-1754529 Department of the Treasury—Internal Revenue Service
For Paperwork Reduction Act Notice,
see separate instructions.

Form **W-2** **Wage and Tax Statement** **20—**

Copy B To Be Filed With Employee's State, City, or Local Income Tax Return

---

☐ CORRECTED (if checked)

PAYER'S name, street address, city, state, and ZIP code Pacific First National 14780 Saratoga-Sunnyvale Road Saratoga, CA 95070-0640	Payer's RTN (optional)	OMB No. 1545-0112 **Interest Income** Form **1099-INT**
PAYER'S Federal identification number 24-8279-4688	RECIPIENT'S identification number 946-11-1802	1 Interest income not included in box 3 $ 343.15	Copy B For Recipient
RECIPIENT'S name Katie A. Delores	2 Early withdrawal penalty $ 0.00	3 Interest on U.S. Savings Bonds and Treas. obligations $ 0.00	This is important tax information and is being furnished to the Internal Revenue Service. If you are required to file a return, a negligence penalty or other sanction may be imposed on you if this income is taxable and the IRS determines that it has not been reported.
Street address (including apt. no.) 5207 Congress Springs Road	4 Federal income tax withheld $ 0.00		
City, state, and ZIP code Saratoga, CA 95070-5081	5 Foreign tax paid	6 Foreign country or U.S. possession	
Account number (optional) 163-7899-42	2nd TIN Not. ☐	$ 0.00	

Form **1099-INT** (Keep for your records.) Department of the Treasury – Internal Revenue Service

Appendix B

APPLIED MATH SKILLS

goal

To review the basic math skills needed to solve the problems in the text.

 UNDERSTANDING THE WORK

The basic math skills needed to solve the problems in the text are presented on this and the following pages. You may wish to review these skills before you begin the study of record keeping. You may also wish to review these skills as you find the need for them.

MATH SKILL 1 Finding the place value of numbers

Every number contains digits. For example, the number 5433.198 has seven digits in it. Each of these digits has a place value. That is, the value of a digit depends on the position it occupies in a number.

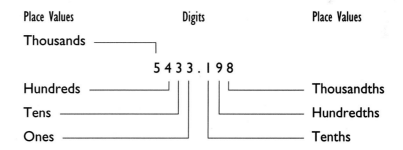

Place Values	Digits	Place Values
Thousands		
	5 4 3 3 . 1 9 8	
Hundreds		Thousandths
Tens		Hundredths
Ones		Tenths

Application Problems

Write the place value of each digit underlined below.
1. 194.5<u>9</u>7
2. $5<u>8</u>3.12
3. <u>3</u>.419
4. <u>1</u>2.021
5. 0.07<u>8</u>
6. $25.<u>6</u>7

MATH SKILL 2 Rounding money amounts

In business, money amounts are usually rounded to the nearest whole cent, or hundredths of a dollar. Rounding to the nearest cent means that an amount *less* than one-half cent ($0.005) is ignored. An amount of *one-half cent or more* is rounded to a whole penny. For example:

Problem		Explanation

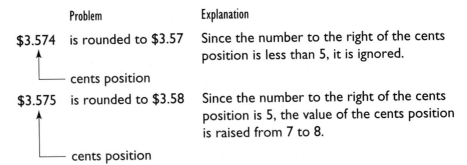

$3.574   is rounded to $3.57 — Since the number to the right of the cents position is less than 5, it is ignored.

cents position

$3.575   is rounded to $3.58 — Since the number to the right of the cents position is 5, the value of the cents position is raised from 7 to 8.

cents position

Application Problems

Round these amounts to the nearest cent.

1. $3.685
2. $14.8925
3. $5.093
4. $25.191
5. $4,003.2865
6. $0.049

MATH SKILL 3 Adding whole numbers

When you add, you combine two or more numbers to get one number. The result is called the sum, or total. For example:

```
     1 1  ←——— carries
   3,295
 + 4,137
   7,432  ←——— sum or total
```

When the total of a column adds to more than 9, you must carry the tens' digit to the next column to the left. For example, in the problem above, 5 + 7 = 12. The 2 of the 12 is written in the first column. The 10 of the 12 is carried to the next column to the left and added to the 9 and 3 to get 13. Likewise, the 3 of the 13 is written in the second column, and the 10 of the 13 is carried over to the next column to the left and added to the 2 and 1 to get 4.

Application Problems

Add these columns.

1.	2.	3.	4.	5.
398	1,058	3,729	10,786	23,498
+ 167	+ 988	73	308	963
		+ 4,198	2,118	6,071
			+ 63	55
				+ 8,207

MATH SKILL 4 Adding decimals

When adding decimal and money amounts, the important thing to remember is to line up the numbers by the decimal points. Otherwise, the numbers added will not be of the same place value. For example, to add $0.03, $107.35, and $5, write:

```
$   0.03
  107.35
+   5.00
$ 112.38
```

Notice that a decimal point and two zeros were added to $5 to make the whole number, 5, line up with the other decimal amounts.

Application Problems

Add the numbers below. Line up the numbers by the decimal points first:

1. $68.315 + 54.905 + 4.1 =$
2. $1,089.76 + 0.62 + 42.73 + 732.676 =$
3. $\$31,649.87 + \$31.89 + \$2,018.87 + \$506.73 + \$9.75 + \$0.21 =$
4. $\$201.33 + \$0.45 + \$1,083.95 + \$42,298.51 + \$0.72 =$
5. $\$0.93 + \$659.21 + \$4.51 + \$46,829.31 + \$65.74 =$

MATH SKILL   5 Adding numbers with the fractions $\frac{1}{4}$, $\frac{1}{2}$, and $\frac{3}{4}$

In business, you often have to add numbers that have these fractions: $\frac{1}{4}$, $\frac{1}{2}$, and $\frac{3}{4}$. For example, you may have to add $9 + 7\frac{1}{2} + 8\frac{1}{4} + 7\frac{3}{4}$. To do so, it is usually easiest to convert these fractions to decimals first. The decimal equivalents of these fractions are

$\quad \frac{1}{4} = 0.25 \qquad \frac{1}{2} = 0.5 \qquad \frac{3}{4} = 0.75$

To find the total of $9 + 7\frac{1}{2} + 8\frac{1}{4} + 7\frac{3}{4}$, convert the fraction in each number to a decimal and add:

9.00	Notice that a decimal point and two zeros were
7.50	added to the 9 to make it line up with the
8.25	numbers. Notice that a zero was also added to 7.5
<u>7.75</u>	to make it line up with the other numbers.
32.50	

Application Problems

Find the total for each problem. Convert any fraction in a number to a decimal first.

1. $7\frac{1}{2} + 8\frac{1}{2} + 9\frac{1}{4} =$
2. $8\frac{1}{2} + 7\frac{1}{4} + 9\frac{1}{2} + 8\frac{3}{4} =$
3. $8 + 7\frac{1}{2} + 9\frac{1}{4} + 8 + 7\frac{1}{4} =$
4. $8 + 8 + 7\frac{3}{4} + 8\frac{3}{4} + 10\frac{1}{2} =$

MATH SKILL   6 Checking addition

To check your addition, you should add the numbers again in the opposite direction. For example, suppose that you added $9 + 4$ and got 13. To check your work, you would add $4 + 9$. Since the answer you got the second time is also 13, you know that you have added correctly.

Application Problems

Add to find the totals. Convert any fractions you find to decimals first. Be careful to line up the numbers by the decimal points. Check each problem by adding the numbers in the opposite direction.

1. $40 + 145 + 6 + 1,459 =$
2. $40.009 + 6.23 + 0.03 + 780.345 =$
3. $\$17.78 + \$9.87 + \$0.56 + \$301.73 =$
4. $\$1,042.08 + \$51.64 + \$0.95 + \$112.23 =$
5. $8\frac{1}{2} + 5\frac{3}{4} + 7\frac{1}{2} + 9\frac{1}{4} + 8 =$

MATH SKILL 7 Subtracting whole numbers

Subtraction is the reverse of addition. When you subtract, you find the difference between two amounts. For example:

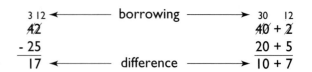

When the bottom number in one column is too large to subtract from the number above it, you must borrow from the column to the left. For example, in the problem just illustrated, 5 is too large to subtract from 2. So, you borrow 10 from the second column. The 2 then becomes 12 and the 40 in the second column is reduced to 30. Now you can subtract 5 from 12 to get 7. To finish the problem, you subtract the twenty in the second column from the 30 in the same column to get 10.

Application Problems

Find the difference in the numbers of each problem by subtracting.

1.	98	2.	139	3.	1,082	4.	3,134	5.	9,215	6.	21,365
	−14		−103		− 76		−1,486		−4,857		−19,739

MATH SKILL 8 Subtracting decimal numbers

When you subtract decimal numbers, be careful to line up the numbers by the decimal points first. For example, to subtract $0.03 from $3.50:

$$\begin{array}{r} {}^{4\,10} \\ \$3.\cancel{50} \\ -0.03 \\ \hline \$3.47 \end{array}$$

Notice that since 3 could not be subtracted from 0 in the first column, 10 was borrowed from 50 in the column to the left. Then, 3 was subtracted from 10 to get 7. The 50 in the second column was reduced to 40. Since 0 was subtracted from it, 4 was written in the second column of the answer.

Application Problems

Find the difference in the numbers of each problem by subtracting.

1. $4.75	2. $6.32	3. $530.19	4. $3,721.73	5. $32,597.83	6. $42,014.23
−1.43	−3.76	−209.73	−2,945.86	−24,638.95	−39,983.56

MATH SKILL 9 Checking subtraction

To check your answer when subtracting, add the difference to the amount subtracted. The total you get should be the same as the top number. For example:

```
$3.50 ◄──── top number          $3.47 ◄──── difference
- 0.03 ◄──── amount subtracted    +0.03 ◄──── amount subtracted
$3.47 ◄──── difference          $3.50 ◄──── top number
```

Application Problems

Find the difference in the numbers of each problem. Check your work by adding the difference and the amount subtracted.

1. 458	2. 1,390	3. 12,513	4. $193.65	5. $7,414.76	6. $61,452.31
−329	−887	−9,978	− 73.78	−3,583.89	−45,625.53

MATH SKILL 10 Multiplying whole numbers

Multiplication is a quick way to add two or more numbers. For example, instead of adding $6 + 6 + 6 + 6$, you multiply 6×4. The answer is the same for both methods: 24. But, multiplication is much faster.

Application Problems

Find the product of the numbers in each problem by multiplying.

1. $8 \times 2 =$ 3. $12 \times 9 =$ 5. $132 \times 14 =$
2. $9 \times 6 =$ 4. $23 \times 6 =$ 6. $320 \times 10 =$

MATH SKILL 11 Multiplying decimal numbers

When you multiply decimal numbers, you must place the decimal point in the product correctly. To do that, point off to the left in the product as many decimal places as there are in *both* numbers multiplied. For example, to multiply 23.56×1.5:

```
$ 23.56      Notice that three places were pointed off in the product
×    1.5     because there are 2 decimal places in one of the numbers
  11780      ($23.56) and 1 decimal place in the other (1.5). However,
   2356      since the last number in the product is less than 5 and
$35.340      you are working with cents, it should be dropped.
```

Application Problems

Find the product by multiplying. Round answers to Problems 3 through 6 to the nearest cent.

1. $132.8 \times 7.3 =$ 3. $\$12.725 \times 6.5 =$ 5. $\$235.45 \times 52 =$
2. $39.334 \times 5.21 =$ 4. $\$9.418 \times 5.25 =$ 6. $\$437.89 \times 52 =$

MATH SKILL 12 Multiplying by ¼, ½, and ¾

In business, you will often have to multiply by the fractions ¼, ½, and ¾. To do this, it is usually easiest to convert the fractions to their decimal equivalents. Then, multiply. If the product is a dollar amount, you may have to round to the nearest cent.

For example, to multiply $24.65 by ¼: first change ¼ to 0.25; then, multiply; finally, round off the product to the nearest whole cent.

$$\begin{array}{r} \$\ 24.65 \\ \times\ \ \ 0.25 \\ \hline 12325 \\ 4930\ \ \\ \hline \$6.1625\ \text{, or }\$6.16 \end{array}$$

Application Problems

Find the product by multiplying. Round answers to the nearest cent, if necessary.

1. $45.80 × ½ =
2. $1,345.23 × ½ =
3. $8.95 × 1½ =
4. $12.56 × 2¾ =
5. $7.54 × 37½ =
6. $12.45 × 39¾ =

Math Skill 13 Multiplying by a percent

Many business problems require you to multiply amounts by a percent. Sometimes the percent has a fraction in it. The easiest way to multiply by a percent is to change it to a decimal first. To change a percent to a decimal, move the decimal place in the percent two places to the left and drop the percent sign. For example:

12.5% = 0.12.5 = 0.125   8 ½% = 8.5% = 0.08.5 = 0.085

8% = 0.08.0 = 0.08   7.51% = 0.07.51 = 0.0751

Original Problem	Suggested Problem
1. $458.97 × 8% =	1. $458.97 × 0.08 = $36.7176, or $36.72
2. $500.00 × 8 ½% =	2. $500.00 × 0.085 = $42.50

Notice that in the first problem, the product was rounded to the nearest cent because you are working with an amount of money and the product did not come out to an even cent.

Application Problems

Find the product of the numbers in each problem. Change any percents and fractions to decimals before multiplying. Round answers to the nearest cent, if necessary.

1. $567.43 × 8% =
2. $1,489.64 × 8% =
3. $93.89 × 3.5% =
4. $3,078.76 × 7.5% =
5. $48.76 × 4½% =
6. $5,918.74 × 7¼% =

Math Skill 14 Checking multiplication

To check your multiplication work, reverse the two numbers you multiplied and multiply again. For example, to check that 5 × 8 = 40, do this: 8 × 5 = 40. Since the product you got when you checked your work was the same as the original product, you know that you have multiplied correctly.

You can also check your multiplication by dividing the product by one of the two numbers. The answer should be the other number. For example, 40 ÷ 8 = 5. Also, 40 ÷ 5 = 8.

Application Problems

Find the product of the numbers in each problem. Change any percents and fractions to decimals before multiplying. Check each answer by reversing the numbers and multiplying again. Round answers to the nearest cent, if necessary.

1. $39 \times 7 =$
2. $184 \times 5 =$
3. $\$6.48 \times 1.5 =$
4. $\$14.78 \times 2\frac{1}{2} =$
5. $\$928.78 \times 5\% =$
6. $\$657.42 \times 8\frac{1}{2}\% =$

MATH SKILL 15   Dividing whole numbers

Division is the opposite of multiplication. When you divide one number by another, you are finding how many times one number is contained within another. For example, dividing 200 by 50 shows that 50 is contained 4 times within 200. The answer, 4, is called the quotient.

When one number is not divisible by another evenly, there is a remainder. For example, 200 divided by 48 shows that 48 is contained 4 times within 200 with a remainder of 8.

When you are dealing with dollar amounts, you will usually round to the nearest cent. To do that, you must divide until you reach the third place to the right of the decimal place, or the thousandths position. For example, to divide $150.00 by 16:

Solution	Explanation
``` 9.375 16)150.000 144 60 48 1 20 1 12 80 80 0 ```	The quotient shows that 16 is contained within 150, 9.375 times. The quotient, $9.375, should be rounded to the nearest cent, or to $9.38.

Application Problems

Find the quotient of the numbers in each problem. Round answers to the nearest cent, if necessary.

1. $\$23,678.00 \div 12 =$
2. $\$31,048.00 \div 12 =$
3. $\$946.00 \div 40 =$
4. $\$45.64 \div 8 =$
5. $\$32,750.64 \div 52 =$
6. $\$348.39 \div 6 =$

MATH SKILL 16   Checking division

To check division, you may rework the problem. You may also check division by multiplying the quotient by the number you divided by and then adding the remainder. For example, $200 \div 48 = 4$, with a remainder of 8. To check this division:

Solution	Explanation
$4 \times 48 = 192$	Multiply the quotient by the number you divided by.
$192 + 8 = 200$	Add the remainder.

Application Problems

Find the quotient of the numbers in each problem. Check your division by reworking each problem.

1. $487.00 \div 40 =$
2. $\$26{,}862.00 \div 12 =$
3. $\$27{,}944.80 \div 52 =$

4. $\$18{,}943.60 \div 52 =$
5. $\$758.40 \div 40 =$
6. $\$15{,}499.80 \div 12 =$

Appendix C

INTERNET BASICS

 WHAT IS A NETWORK?

A *network* is a group of computer systems that are connected. Sometimes a computer is connected to a *local area network*, or LAN (see Illustration C1). A LAN connects computer systems that are close together, such as those in one room or on one floor of a building. For example, the computer lab in your school may be a LAN because it connects all the personal computers, or PCs, in the lab. Most networks are controlled by a server. A *server* is a computer system that manages the network and provides services to other computers on the network. These services might include making printers and document storage space available to the other computers.

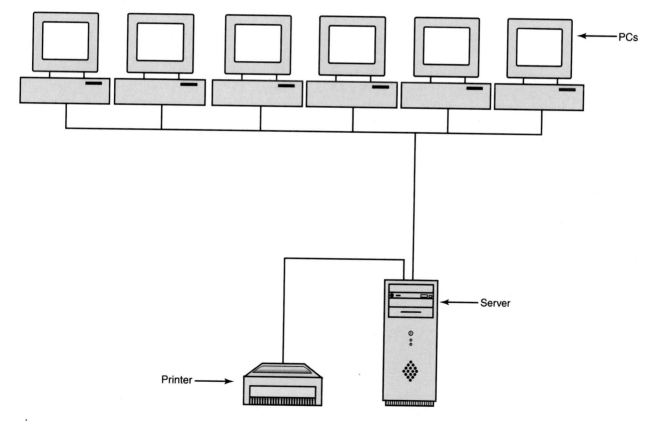

PCs

Server

Printer

Illustration C1
A local area network, or LAN

As shown in Illustration C2, sometimes LANs are also connected to each other to connect the computer systems of an entire organization. For example, all the computer systems at a university, a government agency, or a business may be connected.

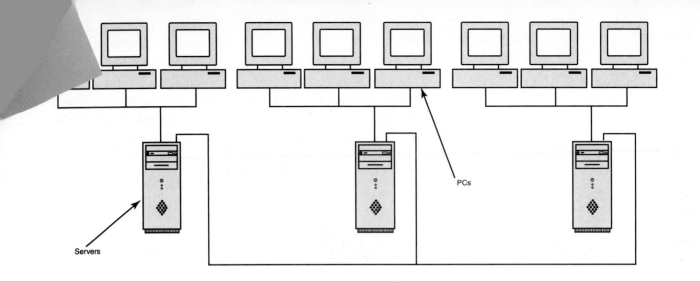

PCs

Illustration C2

Networks connected to networks

Then there are *wide area networks*, or WANs, that connect computer systems across great distances, such as entire cities, states, countries, or more. Illustration C3 shows a WAN.

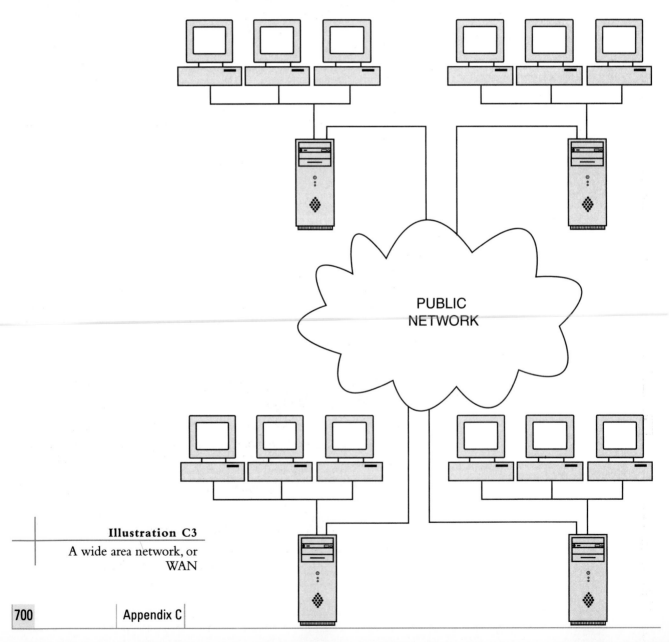

PUBLIC
NETWORK

Illustration C3

A wide area network, or WAN

WHAT IS THE INTERNET?

The *Internet* is a network of all of these networks (see Illustration C4). The Internet provides a means by which computers and computer networks at schools, universities, companies, government agencies, military installations, and other organizations can connect to each other. That means that when you connect your computer to the Internet, you can then connect to computer systems around the world—at universities, government agencies, military installations, and other organizations.

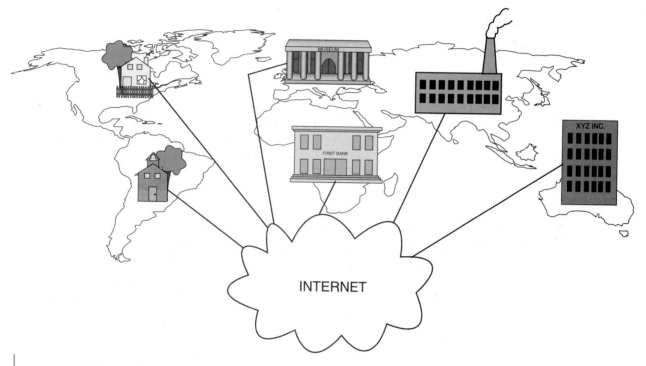

Illustration C4

The Internet

Whether you are a school, business, government agency, or just a computer user at home, to connect to the Internet you must first connect to an *Internet Service Provider*, or ISP. An ISP is a company that connects computers and networks to the Internet.

The Internet is always changing. People and organizations are constantly connecting to the Internet or disconnecting themselves from it. In fact, no one is in charge of the entire Internet. It is just a very large group of people and organizations who have agreed to share information and computer power.

WHAT CAN I DO ON THE INTERNET?

The Internet has become very useful to millions of people. You can:
- Use the Internet to send messages electronically to others around the world. These messages are called *electronic mail*, or e-mail. E-mail is one of the most popular uses of the Internet.
- Download or copy computer files and computer software from other computers on the Internet.
- Run a computer program on another computer miles away or a continent away while sitting at home.
- Discuss or "chat" about topics with others in your class, in your

country, or in another country. Chat groups are a very popular use of the Internet.

- View exhibits at museums and galleries throughout the world by connecting to the computer systems of those museums and galleries.
- Search for information on millions of computer systems. The ability to find, view, or listen to information on other computer systems is an important use of the Internet, not only to home users but to business users.
- Buy products and services on the Internet. For example, you can do your banking, buy books or airline tickets, or even buy stocks and bonds on the Internet.

WHAT IS THE WORLD WIDE WEB?

The *World Wide Web* (WWW)—or more simply, the Web—is part of the Internet. It is an ever-changing collection of millions of documents stored on many computers found throughout the world. These documents may contain text, images, sound, and even video clips. The computers that store Web documents are called *Web servers*. These computers run special software that lets you connect to the Web server and view the documents on them.

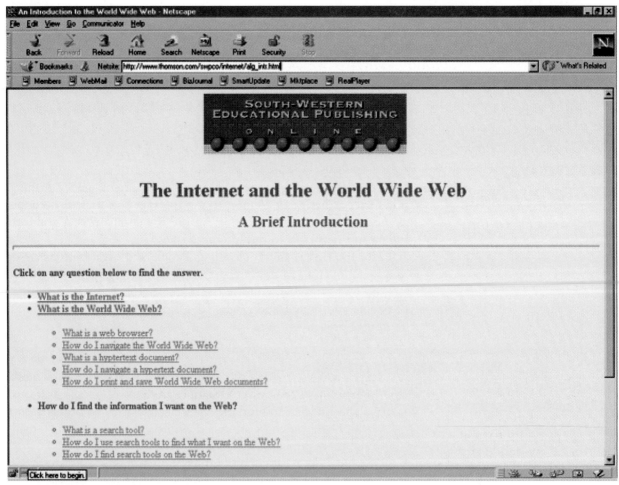

Illustration C5

A Web browser displaying a Web page

WHAT IS A WEB BROWSER?

The software that lets you view Web pages or documents is called a *Web browser.* You need to be running a Web browser to read a Web page, just like you need to be running a word processor to view a document created by that word processor. Browsers let you view text, images, and videos as well as to listen to voice messages, music, or other sounds. Illustration C5 shows a Web browser displaying a Web page.

HOW DO I NAVIGATE THE WEB?

When you connect to a Web site, the first document you view is called the *home page* (see Illustration C6). Businesses, government agencies, schools, and even individuals have home pages. Every home page has a Web address so that you can find it. A Web address is also called a uniform resource locator, or *URL.*

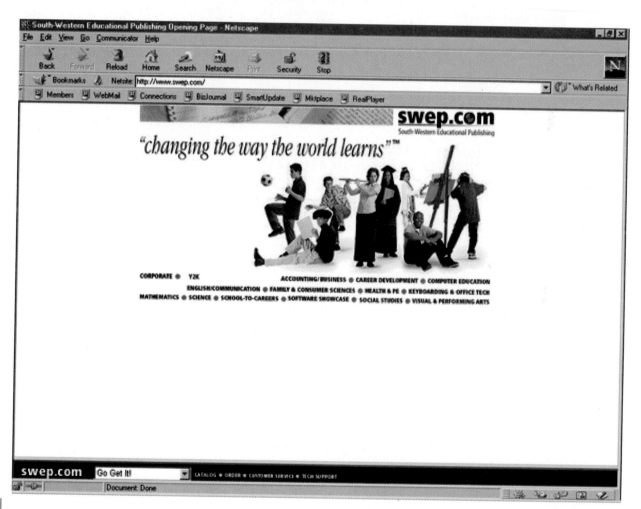

Illustration C6

South-Western Educational Publishing's home page

To go to a Web page, enter the Web address in the address line of your browser. To go to the page shown in Illustration C6, enter the following in the address line: http://www.swep.com

Most browsers let you skip "http://" and enter only www.swep.com. The "www" stands for the World Wide Web. The "swep" stands for *South-Western Educational Publishing.* The ".com" stands for commercial, or a web site owned by a company. Schools usually have web addresses that end in ".edu" (which stands for education). For example, www.siue.edu is the web address for Southern Illinois University at Edwardsville.

In some cases you only have to enter the name of the company, organization, or school. For example, if you enter only "swep" or "siue," your browser may still find those Web sites.

Web documents usually are *hypertext* documents. That is, they are documents that contain links to other documents. These links may be text that is underlined or highlighted in some way, or the links may be images. If you click on a link with your mouse, you will be transported to another document and the linked document is displayed.

The document you go to when you click on a link may be stored on the same Web server or another Web server somewhere else in the world. Moving from one document to another by clicking on links or moving from one Web server to another by entering a new Web address into a browser is called navigating or "surfing the net."

HOW DO I PRINT OR SAVE THE DOCUMENTS I FIND ON THE INTERNET?

When you find an interesting document on the Web, you can print it out or save it as a file on your own computer system. To save a document, click on File and then Save from the menu bar of your Web browser. Your Web browser software may use different menu commands to print or save documents, but all browsers let you do these tasks.

HOW DO I FIND INFORMATION ON THE WEB?

To find documents on the Web, you usually use a search tool. One type of search tool is called a *search engine*. A search engine is a computer program that looks for information for you on the Web. You enter words to search for, and the program scours the Web to find documents that contain those words. The words you enter are called "search terms." For example, you might enter the term "modem" to find documents about modems. You might also enter "Eiffel Tower" to find documents on the tower.

Another type of search tool is a WWW *directory*, like that provided by Yahoo! Web directories are lists of Web pages classified into categories. For example, the Yahoo! Web site uses these categories:

- Arts and Humanities
- Business and the Economy
- Computers and the Internet
- Education
- Entertainment
- Government
- Health
- News and Media
- Recreation and Sports
- Reference
- Regional
- Science
- Social Science
- Society and Culture

When you click on one category, you are usually shown a page of topics within that category. For example, clicking on Education will get you a list of some 30 or more topics, including Adult and Continuing Education, Higher Education, and Special Education. Clicking on Higher Education will get you another, more specific list of Web sites pertaining to colleges and university education.

Sometimes you will find that using a Web directory is faster and easier than using a search engine, and sometimes using a search engine will produce better results. Often you start looking for information using one search tool and strike out; so, you use the other. Many Web sites that offer search tools provide both directories and search engines. For example, Yahoo! provides both search tools: a search engine and a Web directory.

 ## HOW DO I USE A SEARCH TOOL?

The kind of search tool you use should depend on the kind of information that you are looking for on the Web. Search directories are suited for searches for information about broad topics, such as higher education or taxes. When you know a lot about the topic, you are usually able to come up with more specific terms to enter into a search engine, such as Michigan State University or the flat tax.

 ## SAMPLE PROBLEM

You are an office assistant to Dr. Alice Newberry, the Director of Instructional Technology at the Morrisville School District. Dr. Newberry is planning a new computer lab, and you need to learn more about modems to help her. So, you decide to find some Web sites about modems. Here are the steps you follow.

STEP 1 Run your browser.

Move your mouse pointer to the Internet Explorer *icon*, or symbol, on your screen. Then double click on the icon. Once you have done that, the browser Internet Explorer is displayed on your screen.

 Internet Explorer icon

 If you wish to use the browser Netscape Communicator, click this icon:
Netscape Communicator icon

STEP 2 Navigate to a search engine.

Enter the Web address of the search engine Infoseek in the address line of the browser. Instead of entering the full Web address, simply enter www.infoseek.com.

There are many other search engines—for example:

Name of Search Engine	Full Web Address
Infoseek	http://www.infoseek.com
Excite	http://www.excite.com
HotBot	http://www.hotbot.com
Yahoo!	http://www.yahoo.com
Northern Light	http://www.northernlight.com

STEP 3 Enter the search term into the search line.

Enter the word "modem" in the search line, and click on the search button at the end of the search line. (Refer to Illustration C7.)

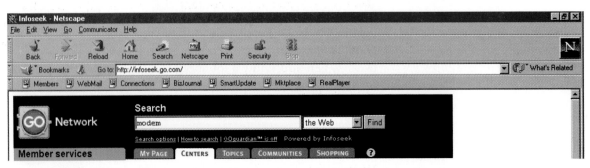

Illustration C7

Part of a search engine page showing the search line and search button

After clicking the search button, your computer displays a search results page that looks similar to Illustration C8.

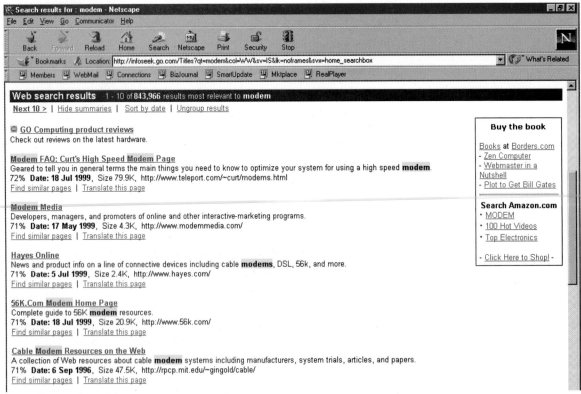

Illustration C8

Part of a search results page that shows the first 10 Web sites

What the search engine has done is display the first 10 Web sites about modems. Four Web sites can be seen on the screen. You can see the rest of the 10 by scrolling down the screen.

Illustration C9

Part of a search results page that shows how to display another 10 Web sites

Each listing contains a link to a Web document. Each link is underlined and in blue. The first link starts with "Modem FAQ." It also briefly describes the document's content, date, size in kilobytes, and full Web address (http://www.teleport.com/~curt/modems.html). The percent (72%) indicates how relevant the Web document is to your search. A score of 100% would mean that it is very relevant.

You can locate the next 10 Web documents found by the search by scrolling to the bottom of the page and clicking on "Next 10." (Refer to Illustration C9.)

STEP 4 Navigate to the web sites listed and read the documents.

Click on the first Web site listed and begin reading the document you find. That means moving your mouse pointer to the line that is underlined and in blue and starts with "Modem FAQ" and clicking on it. You can continue to look at other Web sites and print out those documents you wish to save for later use.

There are several items you should note:
1. If you choose another search engine, your search results will be different. Each search engine searches the Web differently.
2. If you search a few days later using the same search engine and the same search terms, your results may be different. The Web is constantly changing. Both individual documents and whole Web sites are constantly added and deleted from the Web.
3. When you do not find what you want using one search engine, try others until you get the information you need.
4. You may not get the results you want because of the search terms you use. When that happens, try other terms. For example, if you enter "laptop computer" and do not find what you want, enter "notebook computer."
5. Some topics are not covered well on the Web, and you may find little or no information about them.

➡ APPLICATION PROBLEMS

Problem C-1

You have been assigned to write a short paper on how to complete the federal tax Form 1040EZ. Use a search engine to find 10 Web addresses that contain information about the tax form. *Hint:* Use one or more of the following search words or phrases:

1. Form 1040EZ
2. 1040EZ
3. Completing Form 1040EZ

Answer the following:

1. What search engine did you use?
2. What is the search engine's full Web address?
3. What search terms did you enter into the search line of the search engine?
4. Copy down the first 10 Web addresses you find, or print out the search results page that contains the first 10 Web sites.

Problem **C-2**   You need to learn more about stock receiving reports. Use a search engine to find 10 Web addresses that contain information about receiving reports.

Answer the following:

1. What search engine did you use?
2. What is the search engine's full Web address?
3. What search terms did you enter into the search line of the search engine?
4. Copy down the first 10 Web addresses you find, or print out the search results page that contains the first 10 Web sites.

Appendix D

USING CALCULATOR KEYBOARDS AND COMPUTER KEYPADS

 KINDS OF CALCULATORS

There are many different types of calculators available today. Some are powered by electricity, others by batteries, and still others by light. Some are small enough to fit in your hand, and others are better used on a desktop. Because calculators differ, you may have to read the manual that came with your calculator to learn how to operate it properly.

Typical keyboards of handheld calculators and desktop calculators are shown in Illustration D1.

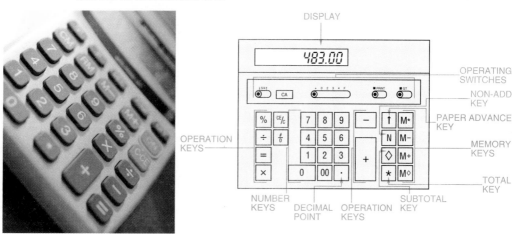

Illustration D1

The keyboards of (a) handheld and (b) desktop calculators

Because instructions for the use of handheld calculators are included throughout the textbook, Appendix D emphasizes instructions for desktop calculators and computer keyboards.

 DESKTOP CALCULATOR SETTINGS

Desktop calculators may have switches that must be set to get the results you want. For example, *decimal selector* sets the decimal places used. If you set the decimal selector to 2, the numbers you enter and the answer shown will have two decimal places. The decimal selector switch may also have a rounding <u>off</u> setting. When this setting is selected, the answer is not rounded. It is carried out to the maximum number of decimal places possible on the calculator.

Some desktop calculators also have *decimal rounding selector* switches. These switches let you choose how to round numbers. Usually rounding a number means to raise the last digit if the following digit is 5 or more. If the following digit is 4 or less, the last digit is not raised. Many desktops let you round up the last digit if there are <u>any</u> following digits. They may also let you round down by dropping any digits beyond the last digit you want.

Many desktop calculators also have a GT or *grand total* switch. If this switch is on, totals that you calculate are saved and accumulated. If you were calculating the extensions on a sales invoice, for example, the total charge for each item purchased would be saved, providing you with the grand total of the sales invoice automatically.

 ## KINDS OF COMPUTER KEYBOARDS

Desktop computer keyboards have a group of keys on the right side called the *numeric keypad*. There are two basic layouts for the numeric keypad: standard and enhanced. On the standard keypad, the directional arrows keys are found on the number keys. To enter numbers, you must press the *Num Lock* key, usually found over the "7" key. When the Num Lock key is on, all the numbers printed at the top of each key work. When the Num Lock key is off, all the items printed at the bottom of each key work, including the directional arrow keys.

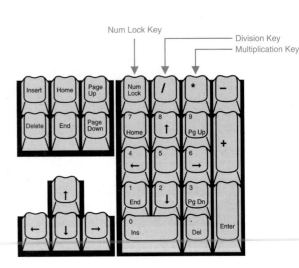

Standard
Keyboard Layout

Enhanced
Keyboard Layout

Illustration D2

Standard and enhanced keypads

The enhanced keypad has separate keys for the directional arrows, Insert, Home, Page Up, Page Down, Delete and End keys. This means that you can leave the Num Lock key on and use the numeric keypad for entering numbers. Usually a light is on near the numeric keypad when the Num Lock key is on.

Unlike calculators, there is usually no division key (÷) or multiplication key (×) on the numeric keypad of a desktop computer. Instead, you must use the forward slash key (/) for division and the asterisk key (∗) for multiplication. Also, note that the asterisk key on a desktop calculator is often used to get a <u>total</u>, not to multiply.

TEN-KEY TOUCH SYATEM

Striking the numbers 0 to 9 on a calculator or numeric keypad without looking at the keyboard is called the *touch system*. Using the touch system develops both speed and accuracy.

The 4, 5, and 6 keys are called the *home row*. If the right hand is used for the keyboard, the index finger is placed on the 4 key, the middle finger on the 5 key, and the ring finger on the 6 key. If the left hand is used, the ring finger is placed on the 4 key, the middle finger on the 5 key, and the index finger on the 6 key.

Place the fingers on the home row keys. Curve the fingers and keep the wrist straight. These keys may feel slightly concaved or the 5 key may have a raised dot. The differences in the home row keys allow the operator to recognize the home row by touch rather than by sight.

Maintain the position of the fingers on the home row. The finger used to strike the 4 key will also strike the 7 key and the 1 key. Stretch the finger up to reach the 7; then stretch the finger down to reach the 1 key. Visualize the position of these keys.

Again, place the fingers on the home row. Stretch the finger that strikes the 5 key up to reach the 8 key, then down to reach the 2 key. Likewise, stretch the finger that strikes the 6 key up to strike the 9 and down to strike the 3 key. This same finger will stretch down below the 3 key to hit the decimal point.

If the right hand is used, the thumb will be used to strike the 0 and 00 keys and the little finger to strike the addition key. If the left hand is used, the little finger will be used to strike the 0 and 00 keys and the thumb to strike the addition key.

HANDHELD CALCULATORS

Handheld calculators are slightly different from desktop calculators, not only in their size and features but also in their operation. Therefore, the touch system is usually not used on handheld calculators. Refer to your operator's manual for instructions for your calculator.

PERFORMING MATHEMATICAL OPERATIONS

Desktop Calculators

The basic operations of addition, subtraction, multiplication, and division are used frequently on a calculator.

Addition

Each number to be added is called an *addend*. The answer to an addition problem is called the *sum*.

Addition is performed by entering an addend and striking the addition key (+). All numbers are entered on a calculator in the exact order they are given. To enter the number 4,455.65, strike the 4, 4, 5, 5, decimal, 6, and 5 keys in that order, and then strike the addition key. Commas are not entered. Continue in this manner until all addends have been entered. To obtain the sum, strike the total key on the calculator.

Subtraction

The top number or first number of a subtraction problem is called the *minuend*. The number to be subtracted from the minuend is called the *subtrahend*. The answer to a subtraction problem is called the *difference*.

Subtraction is performed by first entering the minuend and striking the addition key (+). The subtrahend is then entered, followed by the minus key (–), followed by the total key.

Multiplication

The number to be multiplied is called the *multiplicand*. The number of times the multiplicand will be multiplied is called the *multiplier*. The answer to a multiplication problem is called the *product*.

Multiplication is performed by entering the multiplicand and striking the multiplication key (x). The multiplier is then entered, followed by the equals key (=). The calculator will automatically multiply and give the product.

Division

The number to be divided is called the *dividend*. The number the dividend will be divided by is called the *divisor*. The answer to a division problem is called the *quotient*.

Division is performed by entering the dividend and striking the division key (÷). The divisor is then entered, followed by the equals key (=). The calculator will automatically divide and give the quotient.

Correcting Errors

If an error is made while using a calculator, several methods of correction may be used. If an incorrect number has been entered and the addition key or equals key has not yet been struck, strike the clear entry (CE) key one time. This key will clear only the last number that was entered. However, if the clear entry key is depressed more than one time, the entire problem will be cleared on some calculators. If an incorrect number has been entered and the addition key has been struck, strike the minus key one time only. This will automatically subtract the last number added, thus removing it from the total.

 PERFORMING MATHEMATICAL OPERATIONS

Computers and Handheld Calculators

On a computer keypad or a handheld calculator, addition is performed in much the same way as on a desktop calculator. However, after the + key is depressed, the display usually shows the accumulated total. Therefore, the total key is not found. Some computer programs will not calculate the total until Enter is pressed.

Subtraction is performed differently on many computer keypads handheld calculators. The minuend is usually entered, followed by the minus (–) key. Then the subtrahend is entered. Pressing either the + key the = key will display the difference. Some computer programs will not calculate the difference until Enter is pressed.

Multiplication and division are performed the same way on a computer keypad and handheld calculator as on a desktop calculator. Keep in mind that computers use the * for multiplication and / for division.

SAFETY CONCERNS

Whenever electrical equipment such as a calculator or computer is being operated in a classroom or office, several safety rules apply. These rules protect the operator of the equipment, other persons in the environment, and the equipment itself.

1. Do not unplug equipment by pulling on the electrical cord. Instead, grasp the plug at the outlet and remove it.
2. Do not stretch electrical cords across an aisle where someone might trip over them.
3. Avoid food and beverages near the equipment where a spill might result in an electrical short.
4. Do not attempt to remove the cover of a calculator, computer, or keyboard for any reason while the power is turned on.
5. Do not attempt to repair equipment while it is plugged in.
6. Always turn the power off or unplug equipment when finished using it.

CALCULATION DRILLS

Instructions for desktop calculators: Complete each drill using the touch method. Set the decimal selector as shown in each drill. Compare the answer on the calculator to the answer in the book. If the two are the same, go on to the next problem. It is not necessary to enter 00 in the cents column if the decimal selector is set at 0-off. However, digits other than zeros in the cents column must be entered preceded by a decimal point.

Instructions for computer keypads: Complete each drill using the touch method. There is no decimal selector on computer keypads. Set the number of decimal places as directed in the instructions for the computer program. In spreadsheets, for example, use the formatting options to set the number of decimal places. When the drill requires you to set the decimal selector to off, leave the computer application in its default format. Compare the answer on the computer monitor to the answer in the book. If the two are the same, go on to the next problem. It is not necessary to enter 00 in the cents column. However, digits other than zeros in the cents column must be entered preceded by a decimal point.

Decimal Selector—2

4.00	444.00
5.00	555.00
6.00	666.00
5.00	455.00
4.00	466.00
5.00	544.00
6.00	566.00
5.00	655.00
4.00	644.00
5.00	654.00
49.00	5,649.00

DRILL	D-2	Performing addition using the 0, 1, 4, and 7 keys

Decimal Selector—2

4.00	444.00
7.00	777.00
4.00	111.00
1.00	741.00
4.00	740.00
7.00	101.00
4.00	140.00
1.00	701.00
4.00	700.00
7.00	407.00
43.00	4,862.00

DRILL	D-3	Performing addition using the 2, 5, and 8 keys

Decimal Selector—2

5.00	588.00
8.00	522.00
5.00	888.00
2.00	222.00
5.00	258.00
8.00	852.00
5.00	225.00
2.00	885.00
5.00	882.00
8.00	228.00
53.00	5,550.00

DRILL D-4 Performing addition using the 3, 6, 9, and decimal point keys

Decimal Selector—2

6.00	666.66
9.00	999.99
6.00	333.33
3.00	666.99
6.36	999.66
3.36	333.66
9.36	696.36
9.63	369.63
6.33	336.69
9.93	963.36
68.97	6,366.33

DRILL D-5 Performing subtraction using all number keys

Decimal Selector—off

456.73	789.01	741.00
− 123.21	− 456.00	− 258.10
333.52	333.01	482.90

DRILL D-6 Performing multiplication using all number keys

Decimal Selector—off

654.05	975.01	487.10
× 12.66	× 27.19	× 30.21
8,280.273	26,510.5219	14,715.291

DRILL D-7 Performing division using all number keys

Decimal Selector—off

$$900.56 \div 450.28 = \quad 2.$$
$$500.25 \div 100.05 = \quad 5.$$
$$135.66 \div \quad 6.65 = 20.4$$
$$269.155 \div 105.55 = \quad 2.550023685*$$
$$985.66 \div \quad 22.66 = 43.49779346*$$

*Number of decimal places may vary due to machine capacity.

Appendix E

APPLIED MATH PREVIEW ANSWERS

Job 1
1. 215
2. 6,754
3. 230.714
4. $1,204.64
5. $7,591.87

Job 2
1. 438
2. 9.58
3. 1,504.558
4. $63,206.06

Job 3
1. 1,508
2. 66,950
3. 10,000
4. $48
5. $376.20
6. $587
7. $4,900
8. $3.60
9. $0.71
10. $61.70

Job 4
1. 7
2. 124
3. $6.00
4. $7.80
5. $68.00
6. $3.14
7. $24.00
8. $6.05
9. $4.00
10. $126.00

Job 5
1. 0.30
2. 0.15
3. 0.50
4. 0.75
5. 0.25
6. 0.43
7. 0.06
8. 0.13
9. 0.79
10. 0.98
11. 0.80

12. 0.20
13. 0.10
14. 0.62
15. 0.18
16. 0.05
17. 0.02
18. 0.01
19. 0.045
20. 0.0751

Job 6
1. 90%
2. 25%
3. 50%
4. 75%
5. 36%
6. 27%
7. 3%
8. 10%
9. 6%
10. 1%
11. 7%
12. 40%
13. 15%
14. 18%
15. 99%
16. 5%
17. 3.5%
18. 9%
19. 9.5%
20. 7.51%

Job 7
1. $2,925.85
2. $6,791.13
3. $1,124.80
4. $23.25
5. 95.4%
6. 0.548

Job 8
1. $549.20
2. $443.30
3. $384.83
4. $1,714.63
5. $23.80, $121.23, $1,324.99, $1,621.94, $3,091.96

Job 9
1. $516.65
2. $253.69
3. $1,207.73
4. $899.33
5. $419.54, $517.63, $1,069.33, $870.90, $2,877.40

Job 10
1. $21,593.05
2. $40,871.40
3. $25,510.91
4. $15,865.11
5. $30,957.64, $7,081.79, $65,801.04, $103,840.47

Job 11
1. $324.00
2. $1,001.24
3. ($192.63)
4. ($493.27)

Job 12
1. $31,200.00
2. $23,400.00
3. $19,500.00
4. $22,289.80
5. $24,500.84
6. $3,000.00
7. $1,313.00
8. $1,545.00
9. $1,188.24
10. $1,877.01

Job 13
1. $0.09
2. $0.18
3. $4.50
4. $0.09
5. $18.00

Job 14
1. $37.87
2. $364.19
3. $142.43
4. $542.76
5. $687.36
6. $243.36
7. $610.31
8. $456.53

9. $269.35

Job 15

1. $900.00
2. $810.00
3. $262.77
4. $450.00
5. $1,350.00
6. $186.50
7. $851.96
8. $44.39
9. $765.58
10. $1,142.42

Job 16

1. $4,998.27
2a. 58
   b. 170
   c. 214
   d. 248
   e. 236
   f. 228, 184, 182, 332, 926

Job 17

1. $40.42
2. $13.24
3. $15.41
4. $23.87
5. $7.31

Job 18

1. $18.21
2. $13.47
3. $13.85
4. $25.85
5. $150.04
6. $11.02
7. $49.65

Job 19

1. $200.00
2. $110.00
3. $90.00
4. $87.00
5. $24.00
6. $4.25
7. $17.40
8. $8.85
9. $6.37

Job 20

1. $2,565.24
2. $1,931.67
3. $1,253.12
4. $4,779.79
5. $2,015.28

Job 21

1. $1,600.00
2. $2,100.00
3. $103.00
4. $181.00
5. $3,180.00
6. $650.00
7. $64.50
8. $9.81

Job 22

1. $4,820.00
2. $343.05
3. $1.61
4. $180.11
5. $4,090.08

Job 23

1. $8,657.77
2. $1,809.12
   $2,036.04
3. $876.10
   $1,227.70
4. $4,303.52
   $6,248.91

Job 24

1. $8,517.64
   $6,371.14
2. $9,810.10
   $2,598.24
3. $1,521.63
   $4,415.99
4. $749.97
   $2,031.51

Job 25

1. $621.12
   $529.72
   $503.19
2. $287.53
   $178.10
   $802.40
3. $1,999.95
   $1,915.63
   $1,652.29
4. $3,871.48
   $3,886.77
   $2,911.52

Job 26

1. $1,151.67
2. $499.70
3. $1,152.69
4. $4,129.07

Job 27

1. $691.57
2. $2,594.07
3. $442.81; $362.81
4. $2,065.78; $1,945.78

Job 28

1. $801.70
   $576.84
   $564.69
2. $752.69
   $674.27
   $981.01
3. $77.02
   $889.27
   $432.83

Job 29

1. $3,958.56
   $3,275.44

$3,217.07
2. $4,719.07
   $3,416.16
   $4,056.16
3. $3,522.65
   $4,401.06
   $3,747.79

Job 30

1. $503.81
   $506.90
   $375.27
   $426.59
2. $2,634.69
   $2,846.52
   $2,839.52
   $2,486.68
3. $605.22
   $598.82
   $838.56
   $845.64

Job 31

1. $145.08
2. $106.05
3. $52.25
4. $41.84
5. $35.03
6. $28.06

Job 32

1. $100.88
2. $118.79
3. $95.24
4. $88.68
5. $57.12
6. $131.21

Job 33

1. $74.35
2. $97.24
3. $121.07
4. $5.82
5. $21.05
6. $52.60

Job 34

1. $138.44
2. $84.33
3. $106.35
4. $165.43

Job 35

1. $24.92
2. $6.03
3. $5.88
4. $62.40
5. $9.45
6. $4.68
7. $2.99
8. $93.01
9. $39.36
10. $5.10
11. $148.97
12. $6.68

Job 36
1. $4.92
2. $8.48
3. $75.20
4. $18.57
5. $13.95
6. $77.48
7. $2.86
8. $34.71

Job 37
1. $7.70
2. $12.59
3. $12.75
4. $14.18
5. $13.61
6. $7.82
7. $19.60
8. $6.00

Job 38
1. $10.02
2. $10.02
3. $57.04
4. $28.52
5. $6.97
6. $7.97
7. $79.66
8. $12.16

Job 39
1. $3.50
2. $27.20
3. $15.06
4. $11.09
5. $9.18
6. $91.84
7. $40.96
8. $1.80

Job 40
1. $1,355.70
2. $1,311.78
3. $5,333.00
4. $2,331.82
5. $5,804.04
6. $10,659.36

Job 41
1. $1,154.67
2. $743.31
3a. $2,087.00
3b. $1,361.11
4a. $3,188.04
4b. $2,882.29

Job 42
1. 95
2. 65
3. 40
4. 160
5. 190
6. 40
7. 40
8. 44
9. 116

10. 133

Job 43
1. $165.00
2. $4,227.90
3. $32.00
4. $674.00
5. $22,490.00
6. $8,370.00
7. $378.00
8. $2,040.00
9. $820.00
10. $2,756.00
11. $1,738.00
12. $425.00

Job 44
1. $7.54
2. $3.77
3. $2.63
4. $6.93
5. $2.42
6. $32.13
7. $40.55
8. $14.91
9. $26.51
10. $21.10

Job 45
1. June 18
2. May 5
3. June 10
4. April 4
5. November 17
6. October 22
7. January 9
8. July 11
9. June 9
10. October 2

Job 46
1. March 19
2. February 28
3. February 9
4. May 10
5. July 6
6. November 23
7. December 18
8. December 31
9. August 13
10. October 9

Job 47
1.
$$= \$100.00$$
$$= 105.00$$
$$= 176.40$$
$$= 94.80$$
$$= 97.00$$
$$\$354.80 + \$218.40 = \$573.20$$
2.
$$= \$ 22.00$$
$$= 63.00$$
$$= 18.00$$
$$= 160.00$$
$$= 20.00$$
$$\$533.00 - \$250.00 = \$283.00$$

Job 48
1.
$$= \$ 82.00$$
$$= 64.00$$
$$= 37.60$$
$$= 59.70$$
$$= 127.75$$
$$\$234.80 + \$136.25 = \$371.05$$
2.
$$= \$ 50.00$$
$$= 45.00$$
$$= 22.40$$
$$= 48.25$$
$$= 10.60$$
$$\$391.15 - \$214.90 = \$176.25$$

Job 49
1. 97
2. 370
3. 3,297
4. 1,173

Job 50
1. 1,027; 231
2. 214; 107
3. 19,551; 2,382
4. 5,610; 1,735

Job 51
1. 167
2. 79
3. 223
4. 629
5. 689
6. 481
7. 978
8. 1,189

Job 52
1. $4,115.75
2. $1,553.25
3. $26,955.50
4. $41,808.00
5. $12,358.15
6. $27,325.80
7. $263,852.10
8. $11,536.80

Job 53
1. $1,699.44
2. $77,138.05
3. $143.10
4. $1,705.95
5. $144,846.63
6. $135,240.00
7. $21,321.00
8. $4,873.78

Job 54
1. $51.60
2. $269.90
3. $752.00
4. $2,831.00
5. $5,140.00
6. $102.00
7. $210.00
8. $328.00
9. $525.00

10. $720.00

Job 55
1. $47,902.10
2. $41,726.38
3. $270.16
4. $1,380.60
5. $9,361.65
6. $448.50
7. $928.63
8. $50.08

Job 56
1. 395
2. 791
3. 5,216
4. 3,029

Job 57
1. August 3
2. May 30
3. April 16
4. June 8
5. August 22
6. July 28
7. December 3
8. December 14

Job 58
1. 369
2. 4,815
3. $416.87
4. $0.00

Job 59
1. $2,131.46; $1,086.34; $4,862.52
2. $6,175.96; $6,971.14; $3,799.02
3. $997.05; $284.28; $6,381.16

Job 60
1. $4,682.55; $1,483.50; $4,655.68
2. $3,592.17; $3,488.37; $911.11
3. $552.87; $512.92; $493.09

Job 61
1. $8,803.91
2. $5,813.31
3. $21,668.90
4. $17,749.62

Job 62
1. $12,628.81
2. $5,341.37
3. $2,073.39
4. $5,782.49

Job 63
1. Bottom row: $95.00, $106.29, $57.89, $181.52, $440.70
   Right column: $33.38, $61.93, $88.65, $48.70, $208.04, $440.70
2. Bottom row: 194, 257, 178, 298, 927
   Right column: 215, 173, 161, 173, 205, 197

Job 64
1. $17,139.84

2. $23,984.78
3. $20,577.59
4. $18,749.46

Job 65
1. $16,488.47
2. $11,185.70
3. $8,537.70
4. $4,810.98

Job 66
1. Bottom row: $118.98, $94.47, $170.59, $256.61, $640.65
   Right column: $115.90, $103.98, $160.34, $146.10, $114.33, $640.65
2. Bottom row: 280, 234, 290, 247, 247, 1,051
   Right column: 152, 102, 229, 270, 298, 1,051

Job 67
1. $16,914.00
2. $22,965.36
3. $10,078.06
4. $20,743.25

Job 68
1. $12,945.95
2. $14,737.95
3. $1,465.20
4. $2,889.22
5. $16,860.86
6. $1,561.10

Job 69
1. $8,000.00
2. $6,800.00
3. $3,328.00
4. $3,152.00
5. $6,176.00
6. $4,800.00
7. $4,376.00
8. $1,347.20

Job 70
1. $6,888.98
2. $181,724.38
3. $12,145.92
4. $51,030.50
5. $914.58
6. $24,337.27
7. $45,970.99
8. $20,108.49

Job 71
1. $20,000.00
2. $30,000.00
3. $61,500.00
4. $20,850.20
5. $68,961.00
6. $40,930.42

Job 72
1. $12,362.80
2. $104,663.08
3. $8,580.77
4. $2,026.29

5. $1,614.26
6. $20,322.75

Job 73
1. 25 $\frac{1}{2}$
2. 26
3. 34 $\frac{1}{4}$
4. 58
5. 41 $\frac{1}{2}$

Job 74
1. 36 $\frac{1}{2}$
2. 33 $\frac{1}{2}$
3. 30
4. $326.25
5. $474.30

Job 75
1. 31 $\frac{3}{4}$
2. 44 $\frac{3}{4}$
3. 38 $\frac{1}{2}$
4. $363.75
5. $454.02

Job 76
1. 38 $\frac{1}{2}$
2. 37 $\frac{3}{4}$
3. 40 $\frac{3}{4}$
4. $15.00
5. $13.05
6. $21.525
7. $18.96
8. $18.825
9. $13.275

Job 77
1. 40 $\frac{1}{2}$
2. $14.85
3. $11.10
4. $18.405
5. $19.89
6. $17.22
7. $16.425

Job 78
1. $720.00
2. $1,305.00
3. $2,288.50
4. $1,151.56
5. $3,486.48
6. $4,609.56
7. $991.24
8. $2,166.93
9. $1,056.64
10. $861.49

Job 79
1. $100.00
2. $112.50
3. $107.90
4. $96.00
5. $52.21
6. $488.00
7. $752.00
8. $1,608.54
9. $47.00

10. $19.83

Job 80

1. $26.16
2. $27.58
3. $37.10
4. $46.56
5. $24.56
6. $33.99

Job 81

1. $47.17
2. $38.16
3. $40.66
4. $45.02

Job 82

1. $604.73
2. $364.36
3. $72.74
4. $104.60

Job 83

1. 43
2. $12,203.08

3. $8,275.72
4. $15.45
5. $18.24
6. $22.61
7. $35.04
8. $30.31
9. $41.02

Job 84

1. $3,547.92
2.

$$= 211$$
$$= 190$$
$$= 120$$
$$= 200$$
$$= 585$$

407 442 253 204 = 1,306

Job 85

1. $185,946.00
2.

$$= 252$$
$$= 224$$
$$= 104$$
$$= 437$$
$$= 554$$

534 233 469 335 = 1,571

Job 86

1. $128,006.48
2.

$$= 227$$
$$= 214$$
$$= 896$$
$$= 2,062$$
$$= 2,273$$

599 1,726 1,667 1,680 = 5,672

Appendix A

1. $28,026.83
2. $13,598.11
3. $844.21
4. $1,366.26
5. $16,290.79
6. $27,394.24

Glossary

The page number on which the key term is defined is listed following the definition.

A

ABA number A number assigned to banks. 188

account balance Total debits minus total credits. 316

accounting equation Assets equal liabilities plus capital. 561

accounts payable ledger A group of creditor accounts. 450

accounts receivable account A customer account. 316

accounts receivable clerk An employee who keeps records for charge customers. 316

accounts receivable ledger A group of customer accounts. 348

adjusted gross income Amount remaining after subtracting adjustments from gross income. 677

adjustmens to gross income Amounts subtracted from gross income. 677

allowance A reduction in price given for damaged merchandise or to correct an overcharge. 372

alphabetically By the alphabet. 24

amount due Principal plus interest owed on the due date of a promissory note. 130

amount financed Installment price less down payment; amount borrowed. 122

amount tendered The amount of cash given to the cashier by the customer. 150

annual Yearly. 104

annual percentage rate The annual finance charge shown as a rate or percentage. 123

assets Things owned with money value. 561

ATM access card A card that allows you to use an ATM to make deposits, withdraw cash, or transfer money (see, also, automated teller machine). 223

audit To verify or check for accuracy and completeness. 553

authorization number Means customer's credit is good. 302

authorize To approve. 108

automated teller machine (ATM) A machine that allows 24-hour banking. 223

B

backordered Out of stock temporarily. 429

badge A special employee card that is read by a badge reader. 587

badge reader A machine that reads employee badges and records the time. 587

balance The amount of stock on hand. 390

balance due When total tax due is greater than estimated tax paid. 553

balance sheet A form that shows that assets equal liabilities plus capital. 561

bank credit cards Credit cards issued by banks. 299

bank deposit Money placed in a bank account. 173

bank reconciliation statement A statement that brings the checkbook and bank statement balances into agreement. 228

bank statement A detailed record from the bank of a checking account. 227

bank statement balance The money remaining in a checking account according to the bank's records. 227

bill A sales slip. 294

billing clerks Employees who spend most of their time preparing customer statements. 330

biweekly Every two weeks. 640

blank endorsement An endorsement consisting of the payee's signature only. 213

budget A plan for receiving and spending money. 60

budget variance report A form that compares budgeted amounts with actual amounts. 89

C

C One hundred. 283

cancelled checks Checks that have been paid by the bank. 215

capital The worth of a business. 556

capital statement A form that shows changes in capital over a period of time. 556

cash box A box in which cash is kept. 142

cash budget A report showing the estimated cash flow of a business. 81

cash count report A form used to find the amount of cash on hand. 163

cash discount Small discount given for early payment. 436

cash flow How money is received and spent over time. 81

cash overage More cash on hand than there should be; when actual currency is more than the balance in the petty cash book. 164

cash payments journal A record of cash payments; a record of expenses paid. 465

cash price The amount an item costs if bought for cash. 121

cash receipts journal A record of all cash received. 360

cash register A machine used to handle money. 148

cash register receipt A written record of transactions printed by a cash register. 148

cash shortage When there is less cash in the register at the end of the day than there should be; when actual currency is less than the balance in the petty cash book. 164

cashier A person who receives and pays out money. 140

cashier's check A check that is guaranteed by the bank. 224

cell On a spreadsheet, where a row and column meet. 46

central processing unit The computer system part that processes the data. 23

chaining Continuous calculation without clearing. 399

change fund An amount given to a cashier at the beginning of the day for making change. 162

characters A computer word for numbers and letters. 41

charge account A form of credit offered by stores. 105

charge sales Sales made on credit. 299

check A written order by the depositor to his or her bank to pay a company or person. 191

check protector A machine used to write checks. 196

check register A book for recording checks and deposits when stubs are not used. 206

check stub The part of a check that is kept by the depositor. 191

checkbook A book of checks. 191

checkbook balance The money left in a checking account according to the depositor's records. 227

check-cashing privilege card Allows you to cash checks at a store. 155

chronological By date. 113

chronologically By date. 24

classification The name for a group of similar items. 254

classified Grouped together. 68

classify To place in groups. 274

clearinghouse A central place where banks exchange checks. 213

clerk Person who keeps records as a major part of his or her daily work. 445

commission pay A pay plan based on how much an employee sells. 593

commissions A pay plan based on how much is sold. 614

computer printout A document prepared by a computer. 5

computer program Instructions the computer follows to process the data. 23

computer software A set of programs that perform related tasks. 46

computer system Input and output devices, and a central processing unit. 23

credit When you buy now and pay later; a decrease in a customer account; the column used to record a payment or a return in a customer account. 104; 316

credit application Provides information about your ability to pay your debts. 105

credit card Identifies the person buying on credit. 105

credit card sales slip A sales slip used with bank credit cards. 302

credit card statement A form showing the transactions and balances for a credit card account. 112

credit card verification terminal A device that automatically checks credit cards. 303

credit memo A form that shows that a charge customer has returned merchandise and owes less money; a form used by the seller to show that the balance of an account has been reduced because of a return or an allowance. 323

credit slip A form used to return goods bought with a bank credit card. 306

creditor A source of credit; lender. 105

creditors People or businesses to whom money is owed. 450

crossfooting Adding a row of figures across a business form. 63

currency Bills and coins. 250

cursor A flashing marker on a display screen. 40

customer statement A monthly report listing all transactions in a customer account during the month. 330

cycle billing Billing groups of customers at different times during the month. 330

D

data Information. 8

database A group of files. 38

data entry clerk A worker who enters data into a computer system. 8

data processing Doing something to data to make it more useful. 17

date of note The day a note is signed. 128

debit The column used to record a charge sale in a customer account. 316

debit card A card, similar in appearance to a credit card, that automatically deducts funds from the owner's checking account. 154

debit memo A form used by the buyer to notify a creditor of a return or an allowance. 480

deductions Amounts subtracted from wages. 630

delivery receipt Form which describes contents of a shipment. 428

denomination The value of a coin or bill. 162

deposit slip A form that lists the money deposited in a bank account. 175

detailed audit tape A record of all cash register transactions. 161

discontinued No longer sold by a vendor. 429

division of labor Dividing a job up. 96

documents Letters, bills, and business papers. 30

double-entry system A system in which each transaction has at least one debit and one credit. 498

double ruling A set of lines used to show that the math on a form has been completed. 10

down payment The part of the installment price paid at the time an item is bought. 122

drawee The bank that pays the check. 192

drawer The person who writes the check. 192

drawing Money taken out of the business by the owner. 515

due date The date a note must be paid; the date by which an invoice should be paid. 128; 345

duplicate An exact copy. 142

E

electronic funds transfer The use of a computer to transfer money from one party to another. 223

electronically By computer. 4

embossed Printed in raised characters. 112

employee earnings record A record of an employee's earnings and deductions. 651

endorsement A signature or stamp on the back of a check transferring ownership. 212

enter To record information on a form or into a computer. 4

entry-level jobs Jobs in which first-time workers are placed. 55

estimate A careful guess. 552

estimated tax Estimated amount of income tax and self-employment tax paid to the IRS during the year. 552

estimating Making a careful guess. 60

exemptions Deductions based on number of dependents claimed. 678

expenses Costs of operating a business. 515

expiration date The last day on which a credit card can be used. 302

extend an amount To record an amount again in a second column. 62

extended Entered again in a second column. 62

extension Quantity times unit price. 284

F

Federal income tax Federal government's tax on income. 674

Federal Insurance Contributions Act (FICA) Law passed by Congress to cover the cost of the social security program. 630

FICA tax Tax collected to pay for social security. 630

field A group of letters and numbers. 38

file A group of records. 38

file Send in your return to the IRS. 675

finance charge The difference between the cash and installment prices of an item. 121

financial statements Summaries of the results of a business. 546

fixed payments Cash payments that are the same from period to period. 81

flextime A plan that allows employees to vary the time they arrive and leave work. 625

footing The total of the money column written in small figures. 10

forged signature A name falsely signed by someone else. 187

Form 1099-INT Report of interest earned on savings. 676

formula Math steps performed by a spreadsheet program. 49

four-column ledger account A general ledger account with two balance columns. 502

full endorsement An endorsement that names the person to whom a check is transferred. 218

FWT Federal withholding tax. 653

G

general columns Columns in a journal used for many items. 517

general ledger A group of accounts other than customer or creditor accounts. 502

good credit risks People likely to pay their debts. 106

graduated commission When the rate of commission increases as the amount of sales increases. 614

graduated piecework pay A pay plan that increases the amount paid as the number of units of work completed increase. 620

grand total A total of other totals. 143

gross Twelve dozen or 144. 283

gross pay Total wages. 594

guides Used to help find records in a file. 24

H

hourly pay A wage plan that pays workers for each hour they work. 593

I

imprinter A device for recording a credit card sale; a machine that transfers data from a credit card to a sales slip. 112

in rack Where you place your time card when you start work. 584

income Money received from the sale of merchandise or services. 496

income statement A form that shows income, expenses, and net income or net loss. 546

income tax A tax on net income earned. 552

income tax return Shows how income taxes were calculated. 675

indexing Arranging the parts of a name so that it can be filed. 33

individual checking account A checking account used by only one person. 186

input The first step in the data processing cycle. 17

input device Used to put data into a computer. 23

installment contract A form that describes the time, place, and amounts for an installment purchase. 121

installment plan A form of credit in which you pay for an item in monthly payments. 121

installment price The down payment plus the total of all monthly payments. 123

insufficient funds When there is not enough money in the checking account to pay a check. 199

interest Money paid for the use of money. 128

Internal Revenue Service Collects federal income tax. 674

issue To send out; to give out or ship out. 192; 390

itemized deductions List of expenses you subtract from adjusted gross income. 678

J

joint account An account for two people. 107

joint checking account A checking account used by two or more people. 186

journalize To record in a journal. 357

K

key To enter data using a keyboard. 40

L

leading edge The right side of a check. 214
legible Clear and easy to read. 194
liabilities Amounts owed to creditors. 561
loan clerk A bank clerk who handles bank loans. 133
logging on Identifying yourself as an authorized user of a computer. 392
loose bills and coins Bills and coins that do not fill their wrappers. 175

M

M One thousand. 283
magnetic media Kinds of storage, such as disks, diskettes, and tape. 38
manually By hand. 4
maximum The highest amount of stock. 390
memorandum column A type of column used to help you remember information. 503
menu A list of choices or options on a display screen; a list of computer programs. 40
menu bar A bar on a computer screen that contains the names of other menus. 393
merchandise Goods that a business is selling. 5
merchandising business A business that sells a product. 496
MICR Magnetic Ink Character Recognition. 11
minimum The least amount of stock. 390
money column Column on a form used for recording amounts of money. 9

N

negative cash flow When cash payments are greater than cash receipts. 84
negotiable Transferable to another party. 212
net decrease in capital When withdrawals are greater than net income. 558
net income When income is greater than expenses. 546
net increase in capital When net income is greater than withdrawals. 558
net loss When expenses are greater than income. 546
net pay Gross pay less deductions, or take-home pay. 631

normal balance The side of an account where the balance is usually found. 535
numerically By number. 24

O

OCR Optical Character Recognition. 12
open order An order not yet received. 406
open order report Lists filled and unfilled purchase requisitions. 406
optical mark recognition Allows pencil marks to be read by special machines. 13
option A choice from a menu. 393
out rack Where you place your time card when you leave work. 584
output The third step in the data processing cycle. 18
output device Used to get data out of a computer. 23
outstanding checks Checks issued by the drawer but not yet paid by the bank. 230
outstanding deposit A deposit not shown on the bank statement. 233
over More than ordered. 429
overcharge A price on the invoice is more than it should be. 372
overcharged When you are charged more than you should be. 114
overtime Time worked beyond 40 hours in a week. 601
overtime rate of pay The rate of pay for any hours beyond 40 hours in a week. 601

P

packing slip A form that describes the contents of a shipment. 428
passwords Secret words that let you use a computer. 392
payee The person or business who receives the check and is paid. 192
payments Amounts spent. 60
payments on account Partial payments of the amount due. 318
payroll register A record of wages earned by a group of workers. 597
pegboard A special writing board that allows you to prepare the payroll check, employee earnings record card, and payroll register in one writing. 667

periodic inventory Actual count of stock on hand. 391

perpetual inventory system Running balance is kept for each item of stock. 390

personal computer A microcomputer. 68

personalized deposit slip A deposit slip on which the depositor's name and address are preprinted. 188

personalized identification number (PIN) A secret number that allows you to use an automated teller machine. 223

petty Small. 250

petty cash book A form used to record and classify petty cash receipts and payments. 260

petty cash box A storage box for petty cash. 250

petty cash clerk A person who keeps records of petty cash. 250

petty cash fund Currency set aside for making small cash payments. 250

petty cash record Form used to record and classify petty cash payments. 254

petty cash voucher A record of payment from the petty cash fund. 250

piecerate The rate paid for each piece. 619

piecework pay A wage plan that pays workers for each piece of work completed. 593

PIN Personalized identification number used with an ATM. 223

policies Rules or procedures. 155

POS terminal A computer terminal used to record sales. 280

position A job. 4

positive cash flow When cash receipts are greater than cash payments. 83

post To transfer data from one record to another. 355

postdate To record a future date on a document. 194

posting references Abbreviations, such as S1, that show where entries were posted from. 356

prenumbered Numbered in advance. 422

previous balance The balance of an account at the end of the last month. 332

price quotation record A record of vendors, information, and prices relating to one item. 416

principal The amount borrowed on a loan. 128

printer The output device in a computer system. 23

processing The second step in the data processing cycle. 18

promissory note A written promise to pay. 127

prompts Questions or commands on a display screen. 281

proof of cash A form on which you compare how much cash you are supposed to have with what you actually have in the drawer. 163

punching in Having the time you arrive at work printed on your time card. 584

punching out Having the time printed on your time card when you leave work. 584

purchase invoice What the buyer calls the bill from the vendor. 436

purchase on account Buying merchandise on credit. 450

purchase order A form used to order merchandise. 422

purchase order clerk Assists the purchasing agent. 416

purchase requisition Tells the purchasing agent to place an order. 403

purchases journal A record of purchases on account. 457

purchases returns and allowances journal A record of all credit memos received. 480

purchasing agent The buyer for a business. 403

Q

quarter A three-month period; $\frac{1}{4}$-year or 13 weeks. 80; 651

R

rate of commission The commission percentage. 614

ream About 500 sheets of paper. 283

receipt A form issued for cash received. 141

receipts Amounts of money received. 60

receiving clerk Receives goods and compares with goods ordered. 427

receiving report A form that shows goods ordered and received. 427

reconciled Brought into agreement. 228

record Form on which information is recorded. 4

record clerks Workers trained to store and retrieve data. 30

record keeping jobs Jobs in which workers spend most of their time handling records. 6

refund Money given back to a customer for returned merchandise; when estimated tax paid is greater than total tax due. 155; 553

regular time The first 40 hours worked in a week. 601

regular time rate of pay The rate of pay for the first 40 hours worked in a week. 601

reorder level The point at which stock reaches minimum. 424

replenish the fund Add an amount to the petty cash fund to bring it back to its original balance. 266

restrictive endorsement An endorsement that limits the use of a check. 216

retailers Store owners who sell directly to consumers. 288

retrieve To find a document. 30

revenue Another word for income. 548

run To activate a program on a computer system. 47

running balance The balance found after each entry is made. 316

S

salary A fixed amount of pay. 613

salary plus commission A fixed amount of pay plus the amount of commission. 614

sales invoice A bill; what the vendor calls the bill issued to the buyer. 342

sales journal A record of all charge sales. 354

sales order A form on which a customer's request for merchandise is first recorded. 342

sales returns and allowances journal A journal in which you record credit memos. 372

sales slip A written record of a sale. 111

sales slip register A mechanical device used to record sales. 280

sales tax Percent of selling price collected by retailers for governments. 288

savings account A bank account that earns interest. 220

schedule of accounts payable A list of creditors with the amounts owed to them. 452

schedule of accounts receivable A list of customers who owe money. 350

scrolling Moving up or down on a computer screen. 74

self-employment tax Social security tax for self-employed people. 551

semimonthly Twice a month. 640

service business A business in which a service for a customer is performed. 496

service charge A fee charged for bank services. 221

short Less than ordered. 429

signature card A form used to indicate to the bank which signature to accept on signed checks. 187

slide Entering an amount a column or more off, such as 50 for 5,000. 535

Social Security Act Law that allows qualified persons to receive monthly payments from the federal government. 630

social security number An account number in the social security system. 631

sort To file in some order. 24

source documents Forms from which you get data to enter into the computer. 17

special column A column in a petty cash book for a specific expense; a column in a journal used for only one type of item. 262; 517

specialization of labor A system in which employees are responsible for a limited range of work. 338

split deposit When part of a check is deposited and part is returned in cash. 217

spreadsheet A computer program that lets you create and enter data into forms. 74

spreadsheet software A program that takes the place of paper pad and calculator. 46

standard deduction Fixed amount you can deduct. 678

stock Merchandise. 388

stock record A record of each item of stock. 388

stock record clerk A person who keeps track of stock amounts. 389

stop-payment order A form instructing a bank not to pay a check. 224

store To file a document. 30

straight commission Total sales multiplied by the rate of commission. 614

straight piecework pay A pay plan that pays the same amount for each unit of work. 619

stub The part of the receipt or check that stays in the book. 142

subsequent After or following. 123

subtotal A total on which other calculations will be made. 150

surname Last name. 33

T

take-home pay Net pay. 635

tally sheet A checklist of money to be deposited. 175

taxable income Amount on which you pay federal income taxes. 677

template A spreadsheet that contains the headings, labels, and formulas that will not change. 46

terms The length of time the customer has to pay a bill, such as 10 days. 344

third-party checks Checks from people other than customers. 156

three-column account An account that has debit, credit, and balance columns. 316

tickler file A chronological file of important dates. 26

time card A record of the hours worked by one employee. 584

time clock A machine that records worker times in and out on time cards. 584

time of note The amount of time for which money is borrowed on a note. 128

trailing edge The left side of a check. 213

transaction Something that happens in a business and that is recorded. 112

transposition error A reversal of digits in a number, such as 45 for 54. 19

traveler's checks A safe form of cash to use when taking a trip. 224

trial balance A form used to prove that debits equal credits in the ledger. 532

triplicate Three copies. 302

U

unauthorized charges Transactions not approved. 114

undercharged When you have been charged less than you should be. 114

unit price The price of each item. 283

universal product code (UPC) A special bar code read by electronic cash registers. 151

UPC See universal product code. 13

update To replace old data with new data. 40

V

variable payments Cash payments that change from period to period. 81

variance A difference. 91

vendor A seller; if the sale is on account, the vendor is also a creditor. 42

verify To check for accuracy. 18

void Unusable. 195

vouch To guarantee that something is correct. 438

voucher The part of the check that shows the purpose of the check and a description of the payment. 201

voucher check A check with a special stub attached. 201

W

W-2 form A statement of a worker's wages, FICA, and withholding taxes prepared once each year by the employer. 658

W-4 form A form that shows how many withholding allowances a worker claims. 641

wage and tax statement W-2 form. 658

wand A scanner that reads bar codes on tags. 281

warning bulletin A list of lost or stolen card numbers. 302

weekly pay A wage plan in which workers are paid for a fixed number of hours per week. 593

wholesaler A business that sells in large quantities to retailers. 342

withdrawal To take money out of an account; cash or other items of value taken for the owner's use. 221; 556

withdrawal slip A bank form used to withdraw money from an account. 222

withholding allowances Deductions claimed for the support of another person. 640

withholding tax An income tax deducted from a worker's wages each payday. 640

work sheet A form used to summarize information for financial statements. 568

Index

Photo and Illustration Credits

Chapter 1 2, 8, 16, 19, 21, 22, 24, 27, 32, 37, 40, 45, 46 © 1999 PhotoDisc

Chapter 2 58, 60, 68, 79, 89, 90 © 1999 PhotoDisc

Chapter 3 102, 103, 106, 113, 121, 122, 128 © 1999 PhotoDisc

Chapter 4 138, 141, 150, 155, 161, 162, 167, 168, 173, 174 © 1999 PhotoDisc

Chapter 5 184, 187, 192, 200, 207, 210, 213, 215, 217, 221, 228, 233, 234, 239 © 1999 PhotoDisc

Chapter 6 248, 249, 251, 255, 260, 261, 267, 268, 269 © 1999 PhotoDisc

Chapter 7 278 © 1999 PhotoDisc; 279 (top left) © EyeWire; 279 (bottom), 282, 284, 286, 288, 289, 294, 295, 300, 301, 307, 312 © 1999 PhotoDisc

Chapter 8 314, 315, 317, 325, 331 © 1999 PhotoDisc

Chapter 9 340, 341 (left) © 1999 PhotoDisc; 341 (right) © EyeWire; 343, 349, 356, 361, 364, 366, 368, 373, 381, 382, 383 © 1999 PhotoDisc

Chapter 10 386 © 1999 PhotoDisc; 387 © EyeWire; 389, 391, 397, 403, 404, 406, 409, 410, 412 © 1999 PhotoDisc

Chapter 11 414, 417, 423, 427, 431, 437, 440, 441, 445, 446 © 1999 PhotoDisc

Chapter 12 448, 452, 459, 467, 474, 483, 486, 488 © 1999 PhotoDisc

Chapter 13 494 © 1999 PhotoDisc; 495 © EyeWire; 495, 497, 503, 509, 515, 517, 520, 526, 532, 533 © 1999 PhotoDisc

Chapter 14 544 © 1999 PhotoDisc; 545 © EyeWire; 547, 548, 552, 556, 557, 562, 568, 573 © 1999 PhotoDisc

Chapter 15 582, 587, 593, 597, 602, 607, 615, 620, 626 © 1999 PhotoDisc

Chapter 16 628, 629, 631, 635, 641, 646, 651, 659, 666 © 1999 PhotoDisc

Appendix C 702, 703, 705, 706: Netscape Communicator browser windows © 2000 Netscape Communications Corporation. Used with permission. Netscape Communications has not authorized, sponsored, endorsed, or approved this publication and is not responsible for its content.